T0178699

Textual Information Access

Textual Information Access

Statistical Models

Edited by
Eric Gaussier
François Yvon

First published 2012 in Great Britain and the United States by ISTE Ltd and John Wiley & Sons, Inc.

ISTE Ltd
27-37 St George's Road
London SW19 4EU
UK

www.iste.co.uk

John Wiley & Sons, Inc.
111 River Street
Hoboken, NJ 07030
USA

www.wiley.com

© ISTE Ltd 2012

Library of Congress Cataloging-in-Publication Data

Textual information access : statistical models / edited by Eric Gaussier, François Yvon.
p. cm.
Includes bibliographical references and index.
 ISBN 978-1-84821-322-7
 1. Text processing (Computer science)--Statistical methods. 2. Automatic indexing. 3. Discourse analysis--Data processing. I. Gaussier, Eric. II. Yvon, François.
 QA76.9.T48T56 2011
 005.52--dc23

2011041292

British Library Cataloguing-in-Publication Data
A CIP record for this book is available from the British Library
ISBN: 978-1-84821-322-7

Printed and bound in Great Britain by CPI Group (UK) Ltd., Croydon, Surrey CR0 4YY

Table of Contents

Chapter 6. Conditional Random Fields for Information Extraction 179
Isabelle TELLIER and Marc TOMMASI

PART 3: MULTILINGUALISM 221

Chapter 7. Statistical Methods for Machine Translation 223
Alexandre ALLAUZEN and François YVON

Introduction

The information society in which we live produces a constantly changing flow of diverse types of data which needs be processed quickly and efficiently, be it for professional or leisure purposes. Our capacity to evolve in this society depends more and more on our capacity to find the information that is most suitable for our needs, on our capacity to filter this information so as to extract the main topics, snippets, tendencies and opinions, but also on our capacity to visualize, summarize and translate this information. These various processes raise two important issues: on the one hand, the development of complex mathematical models which fully take into account the data to be processed, and, on the other hand, the development of efficient algorithms associated with these models and capable of processing large quantities of data and of providing practical solutions to the above problems.

In order to meet these requirements, several scientific communities have turned to probabilistic models and statistical methods which allow both richness in modeling and robustness in processing large quantities of data. Such models and methods can furthermore adapt to the evolution of data sources. Scientific communities involved in text processing have not stayed away from this movement, and methods and tools for natural language processing or information retrieval are largely based today on complex statistical models which have been developed over several years.

Students, engineers or researchers exposed to the area of textual information access are faced with an abundant literature which exploits different statistical models, sometimes difficult to apprehend and not always presented in detail. The main objective of this book is to precisely present, in the most explicit way, the statistical models

---

Introduction written by Eric GAUSSIER and François YVON.

used to access textual information. The problems we address are linked to traditional applications of information access:

– information extraction and information retrieval;

– text classification and text clustering;

– comprehension aid via automatic summarization, machine translation and visualization tools;

– opinion detection.

Beyond these applications, which have all been the subject of specifically dedicated work, be it in information retrieval, data mining, machine learning or natural language processing, we have tried here to focus on the main statistical and probabilistic models underlying them so as to propose a homogeneous and synthetic view of the fundamental methods of the tools used for textual information access. Such a summary seems all the more desirable as the different communities concerned converge, as we will see throughout the various chapters of this book, on numerous points. These points relate to the numeric representations derived from textual data as well as to the development of models for large data sets and to the reliance on standard benchmarks and evaluation campaigns for evaluation purposes. The scope of the models presented here actually goes beyond text-based applications, and readers are likely to re-use in other domains, such as image/video processing or recommendation systems, what they will learn in this book.

That said, we have wished to maintain a strong relationship between models and their main applications. For this reason, each chapter presents, for one or several problems, an associated group of models and algorithms (for learning and/or interference). The links between applications on the one hand and models on the other hand are explained and illustrated, as much as possible, on real collections.

For the sake of readability, the contributions to this work are organized into 4 parts. Part 1 concerns *Information Retrieval* and comprises two chapters. The first one, entitled "Probabilistic Models for Information Retrieval", written by S. Clinchant and E. Gaussier, presents an overview of probabilistic models used for information retrieval, from the binary independence model to the more recent models founded on the concepts of information theory. The mathematical grounds and hypotheses on which these models rely are described in detail and the chapter concludes by comparing the performance of these models. The second chapter, entitled "Learnable Ranking Models for Automatic Text Summarization and Information Retrieval", written by M.-R. Amini, D. Buffoni, P. Gallinari, T.V. Truong, and N. Usunier, presents learning models for ranking functions, which have recently gained attention from several research communities, since (a) they allow a complete modeling of certain information access problems, and (b) yield very good performance in several practical settings. These models are presented here in relation to their application to automatic text summarization and information retrieval.

Part 2 of this work classification and partitioning, concerns text classification and clustering, and comprises four chapters. The first one, entitled "Logistic Regression and Text Classification", written by S. Aseervatham, E. Gaussier, A. Antoniadis, M. Burlet, and Y. Denneulin, concerns a family of models among which the simplest and most popular is the logistic regression model. After a review of generalized linear models and the IRLS algorithm, the logistic regression model (under both its binomial and multinomial forms) is presented in detail along with associated regularization methods (ridge, LASSO, and selected ridge). This model is illustrated through a document classification task involving a large number of categories. The second chapter, entitled "Kernel Methods for Textual Information Access", is written by J.-M. Renders. It presents different kernels which have been proposed for text processing. After a review of the fundamentals of kernel methods and of the contexts in which kernels are used (logistic regression, large margin separators, principal component analysis), this chapter describes the kernels associated with different representations of texts: kernels for bags of words, for chains (of characters or words), for trees, for graphs, or for probability distributions. The following chapter, entitled "Topic-based Generative Models for Text Information Access" is a contribution by J.-C. Chappelier. It describes topic models, focusing on PLSI (*Probabilistic Latent Semantic Indexing*) and LDA (*Latent Dirichlet Allocation*), which constitute the basis of most of the topic models used today. Topic models aim at automatically discovering topics underlying (hence the term *latent*) a document collection, and are used in applications such as clustering, classification and information extraction. This chapter provides several illustrations of the topics discovered by these models along with a detailed description of two (generic) methods to estimate the parameters of these models: through variational approximation and through Gibbs sampling. The last chapter of this part, entitled "Conditional Random Fields for Information Extraction", written by I. Tellier and M. Tommasi, gives a detailed description of a particular graphic model, conditional random fields. This model was recently introduced in machine learning and natural language processing in order to account for the complex dependencies between elements of a sequence, or more generally of between subparts of structured representations. Conditional random fields generalize hidden Markov models which have been (and still are) largely exploited to label word sequences. The targeted application here is information extraction and named entity recognition, but these models can also be applied for information retrieval in structured documents such as XML documents.

Part 3 of this work concerns *Multilinguilism*. The reader will find a single but substantial chapter dedicated to "Statistical Methods for Machine Translation" written by A. Allauzen and F. Yvon. The main probabilistic models used in machine translation systems are described in detail, as are the different modules comprised in a statistical translation system. The authors also discuss the evaluation of translation systems as well as recent research paths.

Finally, the last part of this work is dedicated to *Emerging applications*, and comprises two chapters. The first one, entitled "Information Mining: Methods and Interfaces for Accessing Complex Information", is written by J. Mothe, K. Englmeier and F. Murtagh. It introduces numerous tools for information visualization, for buildings maps from data sets along different aspects, and for analyzing the variability of different results (e.g. for data fusion or to analyze the dependencies between different evaluation measures such as those used in information retrieval). The second chapter entitled "Opinion Detection as a Topic Classification Problem" is a contribution written by J.-M. Torres-Moreno, M. El-Bèze, P. Bellot, and F. Béchet. It describes in detail the task of detecting opinions in text documents. After a review of the problems encountered in this task, and the associated evaluation campaigns, the authors present several systems developed by different teams. The performance of most systems on standard data sets is also supplied. Finally, the authors investigate opinion detection on audio streams, thus widening the scope of this book.

In addition to these contributions, which aim at presenting in detail the main statistical models used to access textual information, the reader will find in the Appendix a general introduction to probability for text mining, written by F. Yvon. This Appendix presents in detail the probabilistic models used for the statistical analysis of texts, the objective being to give a theoretical foundation to the probabilistic models presented throughout this book.

As one can see, this book contains rich and varied contributions. Even if the models considered are sometimes sophisticated, we have tried (a) to present them with a constant concern for precision, and (b) to illustrate them within the framework of standard information access applications. The appendix should, we hope, allow readers not familiar with probability reasoning to acquire the necessary foundations required for understanding the different chapters. We also hope this book will be a valuable reference to researchers and engineers who wish to review the different statistical models and methods used in textual information access, as well as to Masters and engineering school students who want to study further specific models in this domain.

To conclude, we want to thank the contributors to this book for having followed us in this enterprise and for having dedicated a huge amount of work, with no guarantee of profit, for presenting their research work as clearly as possible and for relating it to the work conducted in connected areas. We are convinced all this effort and work was worth it, and that the result will benefit many.

Notations

Wherever possible, we have tried to use the following notations throughout the entire book. In some chapters, additional and/or alternative notations have sometimes been chosen to adhere to the conventions of a specific sub-domain. These alternative notations will be introduced when needed at the begining of the corresponding chapter(s).

V	a set, often a set of words (a *vocabulary*)
$\|V\|$	cardinality of the set V
$A \cup B$	the union of A and B
$A \cap B$	the intersection of A and B
$A \times B$	the Cartesian product of A and B: $\{(a, b), a \in A, b \in B\}$
x	a m-dimensional vector
x^T	the transpose of vector x
$\|x\|_2$	the L^2 norm of vector x: $\|x\|_2 = \sqrt{\sum_i x_i^2}$
$\|x\|_1$	the L^1 norm of vector x: $\|x\|_1 = \sum_i \|x_i\|$
$x_{[1:T]}$	a sequence $x_{[1:T]} = x_1 \ldots x_t \ldots x_T$
$x_{[1:T]}$	a sequence of m dimensionsional vectors
A	a matrix
A^T	the transpose of the matrix A
X	a random variable
$\mathcal{X}$	the sample space of X
$P(X = x), P(x)$	the probability that X takes the value x
$P(X = x\|Y = y), P(x\|y)$	the conditional probability of $X = x$ given that $Y = y$
X	a m-dimensional random vector
$X_{[1:T]}$	a sequence of random variables $X_{[1:T]} = X_1 \ldots X_t \ldots X_T$
$\mathcal{C}$	a group of i.i.d observations $\mathcal{C} = \{x^{(1)} \ldots x^{(n)}\}$
$\mathcal{L}(\mathcal{C}; \theta)$	the likelihood of a corpus for the model parameterized by θ
$\ell(\mathcal{C}; \theta)$	the logarithm of the likelihood function (the log-likelihood): $\ell(\mathcal{C}; \theta) = \log(\mathcal{L}(\mathcal{C}; \theta))$
$F(e)$	the frequency of event e

Table 1. *Notations*

PART 1

Information Retrieval

Chapter 1

Probabilistic Models for Information Retrieval

In this chapter, we wish to present the main probabilistic models for information retrieval. We recall that an information retrieval system is characterized by three components which are as follows:

1) a module for indexing queries;

2) a module for indexing documents;

3) a module for matching documents and queries.

Here, we are not interested in the indexing modules, which are the subjects of development elsewhere (see for example [SAV 10]). We are interested only in the matching module. In addition, among all the information retrieval models, we will concentrate only on the probabilistic models, as they are considered to be the strongest performers in information retrieval and have been the subject of a large number of developments over recent years.

1.1. Introduction

Information Retrieval (IR) organizes collections of documents and responds to user queries by supplying a list of documents which are deemed relevant for the user's requirements. In contrast to databases, (a) information retrieval systems process non-structured information, such as the contents of text documents, and (b) they fit well within a probabilistic framework, which is generally based on the following assumption:

Chapter written by Stéphane CLINCHANT and Eric GAUSSIER.

Assumption 1. *The words and their frequency in a single document or a collection of documents can be considered as random variables. Thus, it is possible to observe the frequency of a word in a corpus and to study it as a random phenomenon. In addition, it is possible to imagine a document or query as the result of a random process.*

Initial IR models considered words as predicates of first order logic. From this point of view, a document is considered to be relevant if it implies, in the logical sense, the query. Later, vector space models represented documents in vector spaces the axes of which correspond to different indexing terms. Thus, the similarity between a document and a query can be calculated by the angle between the two associated vectors in the vector space. Beyond the Boolean and vector representation, the probabilistic representation provides a paradigm that is very rich in models. For example, it is possible to use different probability laws for modeling the frequency of words.

In all these models, a pre-processing stage is necessary to achieve a useful representation of the documents. This pre-processing consists of filtering the words that are used frequently (empty words), then normalizing the surface form of the words (removing conjugations and plurals) and then finally counting, for each term, the number of occurrences in a document. Consider for example the following document (extracted from "The Crow and the Fox", by Jean de la Fontaine):

> *"Mr Crow, perched on a tree,*
> *Holding a cheese in his beak.*
> *Mr Fox, enticed by the smell,*
> *This is what he said:*
> *Well, hello, Mr Crow*
> *How lovely you are! How handsome you seem!"*

The filtering of empty words leads to the removal of words such as "a" and "the", etc. Afterward, the word occurrences are counted: the term *Crow* occurs twice in this document, whereas the term *cheese* appears once. We can thus represent a document by a vector, the coordinates of which correspond to the number of occurrences of a particular term, and a collection of documents by a group of such vectors, in matrix form.

In all the models, we shall see that the number of occurrences of different words are considered to be statistically independent. Thus, we can suppose that the random variable corresponding to the number of occurrences of *cheese* is independent of that of the random variable for *Crow*. We define the random variable associated with the word w as X_w. A document is a multi-varied random variable noted X^d. The definitions used in this chapter are summarized in Table 1.1. These definitions represent those that are more commonly (and more recently) used in information retrieval. We will often refer to a probability law for predicting the number of occurrences as a *frequency law*.

Notation	Description
$RSV(q, d)$	Retrieval status value: score of document d for query q
q_w	Number of occurrences of a term w in the query q
x_w^d	Number of occurrences of a term w in the document d
N	Number of documents in the collection
M	Number of indexing terms
F_w	Average frequency of w: $F_w = \sum_d x_w^d / N$
N_w	Document frequency of w: $N_w = \sum_d I(x_w^d > 0)$
z_w	$z_w = F_w$ or $z_w = N_w$
l_d	Document length d
l_c	Length of collection
m	Average length of document
X_w	Random variable associated with the word w
X^d	Multivariate random variable associated with the document d

Table 1.1. *Notations*

Historically, we can classify the probabilistic models for information retrieval under three main categories:

1) **Probability ranking principle**

These models assume that for a query there exists both a class of relevant documents and a class of non-relevant documents. This idea leads to ordering the documents according to the probability of relevance of the document $P(R_q = 1|X^d)$. This principle will be presented in section 1.3. Different frequency laws on the frequency classes of documents thus generate different models. The major model in this family is *BM25* or *Okapi*. We shall see this model in section 1.3.2.

2) **Language models (LM)**

The idea at the heart of language models is to estimate the probability $P(q|d)$: the probability that the query is generated from a document. Language models are the models that are best known and most widely used nowadays. These models are the subject of section 1.4.

3) **Informational approaches**

These approaches aim to quantify the importance of a term in a document in relation to its behavior in the collection. Thus, the weight of a term in a document can be measured by using a Shannon information function. The models in these approaches have very good performance in diverse evaluation campaigns, but, as they have been introduced recently, they are less widespread. These models will be presented in section 1.5.

There exists a complete literature dedicated to the modeling of word frequency in a collection of documents. One of the first attempts relied on Poisson's law for modeling the number of occurrences of a word in a document. A mixture of two Poisson laws was then used with success in information retrieval. This mixture was later generalized to a negative binomial distribution, that is an infinite mixture of Poisson laws, or was replaced by geometric distributions. A mixture of multinomial distributions to represent a document corpus was then introduced by Nigam [NIG 99]. This model was generalized either by probabilistic latent semantic analysis (PLSA) [HOF 99], or by latent Dirichlet analysis (LDA) [BLE 03]. Finally, stochastic processes like the Dirichlet possess have also been used to model a text corpus[1].

Because of the role it played in the development of probabilistic information retrieval models, we will return later to the 2-Poisson model. Before this, we first present a certain number of properties that information retrieval models should satisfy.

1.1.1. *Heuristic retrieval constraints*

Following Fang *et al.* [FAN 04], who proposed formal definitions of heuristic retrieval constraints which can be used to assess the validity of an IR model, we introduce here analytical conditions a retrieval function should satisfy to be valid. We consider here retrieval functions, denoted *RSV*, of the form:

$$RSV(q,d) = \sum_{w \in q} a(x_w^q) h(x_w^d, l_d, z_w, \omega)$$

where ω is a set of parameters and where h, the form of which depends on the IR model considered, is assumed to be of class C^2 and defined over $\mathbb{R}^{+*} \times \mathbb{R}^{+*} \times \mathbb{R}^{+*} \times \Omega$, where Ω represents the domain of the parameters in ω and a is often the identity function[2]. Language models [ZHA 04], Okapi [ROB 94] and Divergence from Randomness [AMA 02] models as well as vector space models [SAL 83] all fit within the above form.

A certain number of hypotheses, experimentally validated, sustain the development of IR models. In particular, it is important that documents with more occurrences of query terms get higher scores than documents with less occurrences. However, the increase in the retrieval score should be smaller for larger term frequencies, inasmuch as the difference between say 110 and 111 is not as important as the one between 1 and 2 (the number of occurrences has doubled in the second case, whereas the increase is relatively marginal in the first case). In addition, longer documents, when compared to shorter ones with exactly the same number of occurrences of query terms, should be penalized as they are likely to cover additional topics than the ones present in the

---

1 We refer the reader to Chapter 5 of the current volume for a detailed presentation of these models.

2 A function of class C^2 is a function for which second derivatives exist and are continuous.

query. Lastly, it is important, when evaluating the retrieval score of a document, to weigh down terms occurring in many documents, i.e. which have a high document/collection frequency, as these terms have a lower discrimination power. Fang *et al.* [FAN 04] proposed formal criteria to account for these phenomena. We recall here the four main criteria and provide an analytical version of them which leads to conditions on h which can be easily tested (the names of the different criteria are directly borrowed from Fang *et al.* [FAN 04]).

Criterion 1 - TFC1: Let $q = w$ be a query with only word w. Suppose that $l_{d1} = l_{d2}$. If $x_w^{d1} > x_w^{d2}$, then $RSV(d1, q) > RSV(d2, q)$ (Fang *et al.*).

This criterion can be reformulated as:

Condition 1 [Term Frequency]: $\forall (l, z, \omega)$, $n \in \mathbb{N}^*$, $h(n, l, z, \omega)$ is increasing in n, that is:

$$\forall (l, z, \omega), \quad \frac{\partial h(x, l, z, \omega)}{\partial x} > 0$$

Criterion 2 - TFC2: Let $q = w$ be a query with only word w. Suppose that $l_{d1} = l_{d2} = l_{d3}$ and $x_w^{d1} > 0$. If $x_w^{d2} - x_w^{d1} = 1$ and $x_w^{d3} - x_w^{d2} = 1$, then $RSV(d2, q) - RSV(d1, q) > RSV(d3, q) - RSV(d2, q)$ (Fang *et al.*).

This criterion can be reformulated as:

Condition 2 [Concavity]: $\forall (l, z, \omega)$, $n \in \mathbb{N}^*$, $h(n + 1, l, z, \omega) - h(n, l, z, \omega)$ is decreasing with n, that is:

$$\forall (l, z, \omega), \frac{\partial^2 h(x, l, z, \omega)}{\partial x^2} < 0$$

Criterion 3 - LNC1: Let $q = w$ be a query and $d1$, $d2$ two documents. If, for a word $w' \notin q$, $x_{w'}^{d2} = x_{w'}^{d1} + 1$ but for another query word w, $x_w^{d2} = x_w^{d1}$, then $RSV(d1, q) \geq RSV(d2, q)$ (Fang *et al.*).

This criterion can be reformulated as:

Condition 3 [Document Length Normalization]: $\forall (x, z, \omega)$, $l \in \mathbb{N}^*$, $h(x, l, z, \omega)$ is decreasing with l, that is:

$$\forall (x, z, \omega), \frac{\partial h(x, l, z, \omega)}{\partial l} < 0$$

Criterion 4 - TDC: Let q be a query and $w1$, $w2$ two words. Suppose that $l_{d1} = l_{d2}$, $x_{w1}^{d1} + x_{w2}^{d1} = x_{w2}^{d1} + x_{w2}^{d2}$. If $idf(w1) \geq idf(w2)$ and $x_{w1}^{d1} \geq x_{w1}^{d2}$, then $RSV(d1,q) \geq RSV(d2,q)$ (Fang *et al.*).

$idf(w)$ denotes the inverse document frequency of word w. A special case of TDC corresponds to the case where $w1$ occurs only in document $d1$ and $w2$ only in $d2$. In such a case, the constraints can be written as:

speTDC: Let q be a query and $w1$, $w2$ two words. Suppose that $l_{d1} = l_{d2}$, $x_{w1}^{d1} = x_{w2}^{d2}$, $x_{w1}^{d2} = x_{w2}^{d1} = 0$. If $idf(w1) \geq idf(w2)$, then $RSV(d1,q) \geq RSV(d2,q)$.

This last criterion can be reformulated as:

Condition 4 [IDF]:

$$speTDC \forall (x, l, \omega), \frac{\partial h(x, l, z, \omega)}{\partial z} < 0$$

Conditions 1, 3 and 4 directly state that h should be increasing with the term frequency, and decreasing with the document length and the document/collection frequency (IDF effect). Conditions 1 and 2 state that h should be an increasing, concave function of the term frequency, the concavity ensuring that the increase in the retrieval score will be smaller for larger term frequencies. All these conditions are termed *form conditions* in [CLI 10a].

1.2. 2-Poisson models

Here, we wish to present an indexing model known as the 2-Poisson model [HAR 75], which was introduced in the 1970s and had an important influence on many information retrieval models. It is based on the idea that a good descriptor for a document is a word which is quite frequent within the document but relatively rare within the collection. Thus, it would both describe the document relatively well and would isolate it from the other documents in the collection. Many words appear with a relatively low frequency in many documents, and appear with a high frequency, or more densely, in a selected group of documents. The latter group is called an "elite" (denoted as E) group because it is supposed to contain the documents which generally possess the word in question. The idea is then to model the elite group through a Poisson law with parameter λ_E, and the non-elite group by another Poisson law with parameter λ_G, with $\lambda_E > \lambda_G$. The 2-Poisson model is thus a mixture of two Poisson laws:

$$P(X_w = x_w | \alpha, \lambda_E, \lambda_G) = \alpha \frac{e^{-\lambda_E} \lambda_E^{x_w}}{x_w!} + (1 - \alpha) \frac{e^{-\lambda_G} \lambda_G^{x_w}}{x_w!}$$

We can thus calculate the probability that a document belongs to an "elite" group by:

$$P(d \in E | X_w = x_w) = \frac{P(X = x_w, d \in E)}{P(X_w = x_w)} = \frac{\alpha \frac{e^{-\lambda_E} \lambda_E^{x_w}}{x_w!}}{\alpha \frac{e^{-\lambda_E} \lambda_E^{x_w}}{x_w!} + (1 - \alpha) \frac{e^{-\lambda_G} \lambda_G^{x_w}}{x_w!}}$$

It is this quantity that Harter uses to sort the words likely to be the indexing terms of a document. However, this model has three parameters for each word, the estimation of which is cumbersome. Harter proposes an estimation method which often presents degenerate cases as there is sometimes not enough data to separate the two Poisson distributions. Figure 1.1 shows two 2-Poisson mixtures: the non-elite component is represented by an average Poisson law (3) and the elite component by an average Poisson law (10). These two mixtures are different as the mixing parameters differ for each Poisson law.

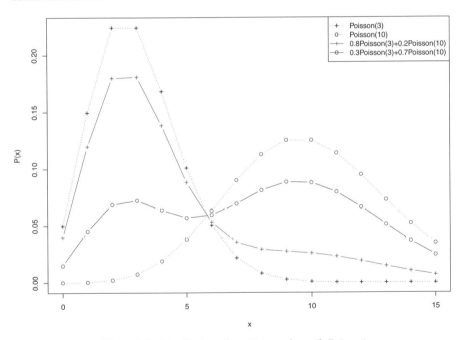

Figure 1.1. *Distribution of two Poisson laws (2-Poisson)*

With the aim of modeling frequencies, the 2-Poisson mixture model has been extended to the cases of *n* Poisson distributions by [MAR 92]. Church and Gale also studied the negative binomial distribution [CHU 95], which is an infinite mixture of Poisson distributions. In particular, they showed that the negative binomial distribution fit the data better than a finite mixture of Poisson distributions. Following this, Clinchant and Gaussier proposed the Beta negative binomial distribution, which dispenses with one of the model parameters [CLI 08]. To summarize, even if the assumptions of the 2-Poisson model are slightly naive (other models fit the data more favorably), this model has had significant influence on the development of information retrieval models. It is at the heart of Okapi models (section 1.3.2) and has in part inspired the information-based models.

1.3. Probability ranking principle (PRP)

The models that are based on the probability ranking principle [ROB 97] are all based on the following assumption:

Assumption 2. *The relevance of a document in relation to a query can be encoded by a random variable. The advantage of this formulation is that it allows us to address some deficiencies in the concept in relevance, namely that relevance is difficult to define and especially partially observable.*

The above assumption leads to document sorting, for a given query, according to the probability $P(R_q = 1|X^d)$, where R_q represents the random variable of relevance (for a given query q) and a document representation X^d. In general, X^d is a word vector in which the x_w^d component represents the number of occurrences or the presence/absence of word w in document d. Robertson [ROB 77] attributes this principle to W.S. Cooper and presents it in the following form:

The probability ranking principle (PRP) *"If a reference retrieval system's response to each request is a ranking of the documents in the collection in order of decreasing probability of relevance to the user who submitted the request, where the probabilities are estimated as accurately as possible on the basis of whatever data have been made available to the system for this purpose, the overall effectiveness of the system to its user will be the best that is obtainable on the basis of those data".*

Figure 1.2 illustrates the probability ranking principle. This principle is based on Bayes decision law. Indeed, the probability of making a bad decision can be written as:

$$P(error|X^d) = \begin{cases} P(R_q = 1|X^d) & \text{if one chooses } R_q = 0 \\ P(R_q = 0|X^d) & \text{if one chooses } R_q = 1 \end{cases}$$

Thus, in order to minimize the error, one should choose the class (relevant, $R_q = 1$, or not relevant, $R_q = 0$) with the highest probability.

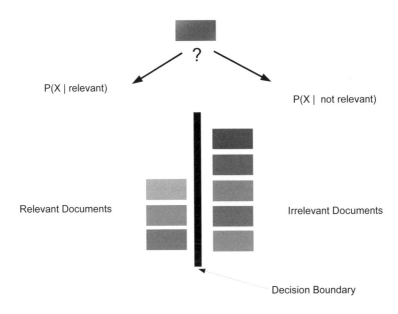

Figure 1.2. *Probability ranking principle: a probability law models the documents for each of the relevant and non-relevant classes; for a new document, the probabilities of the two classes are calculated in order to decide to which class the document belongs*

A few remarks are required for the PRP presented in the above manner. Firstly, the average error is not the only function that can be minimized. It is possible to imagine different costs associated with each error type. Following that, the assumption of independence of the documents is of course debatable (as one can find duplicated documents, or documents covering the same topics). However, without this assumption, the majority of the probabilistic models would become intractable. Finally, this principle assumes that the probabilities $P(R_q|X^d)$ can be computed with a certain degree of accuracy. This assumption is quite problematic. In general, relevant documents are unknown. Therefore, there is no direct method to calculate these probabilities. In practice, they can be calculated via an iterative method, which involves the user annotating the documents retrieved during a search session. This annotation is then used to refine the relevance estimation of the terms. A new search can then be made, with a new round of annotation, and so on and so forth till the user is satisfied with the results obtained.

Because it is a general principle, the PRP can take different forms. The form given below is one of the most commonly used.

1.3.1. *Reformulation*

Assuming, in the absence of prior knowledge, that $P(R_q = 1) = P(R_q = 0)$, the above discussion concerning the Bayesian decision rule shows that, in the PRP, the following quantity can be used to rank documents:

$$RSV(q, d) = \log \left(\frac{P(X^d = x | R_q = 1)}{P(X^d = x | R_q = 0)} \right) \qquad [1.1]$$

where *RSV(q, d)* *(Retrieval Status Value)* designates the score given to document *d* for query *q* (see Table 1.1). An additional assumption is however necessary to simplify this formula. This assumption ascertains that terms in documents are independent of one another given the relevance class ($R_q = 1$ or $R_q = 0$). The probabilities $P(X^d | R_q)$ can thus be written as a product of probabilities over the terms common to both the query and the document, as is done in the binary independence model, which we are presenting now.

1.3.1.1. *Binary independence model*

The *Binary Independence Retrieval (BIR)* model assumes that the weights of the terms in the documents and queries are binary: ($X^d = (1010 \cdots 010 \cdots)$). Each word is characterized by a binary variable A_w, which indicates the presence or absence of a word. Variables A_w are considered independent of one another conditioned on R_q. Let us note as $a_w = P(A_w = 1 | R_q = 1)$ the probability that word w appears in a relevant document and $b = P(A_w = 1 | R_q = 0)$ the probability that it appears in a non-relevant document. We have:

$$\begin{cases} P(X^d = (x_1^d, \ldots, x_M^d) | R_q = 1) = \prod_w a_w^{x_w^d} a_w^{(1-x_w^d)} \\ P(X^d = (x_1^d, \ldots, x_M^d) | R_q = 0) = \prod_w b_w^{x_w^d} b_w^{(1-x_w^d)} \end{cases}$$

where x_w^d in this context denotes the presence ($x_w^d = 1$) or absence ($x_w^d = 0$) of word w in document d. In other words, the documents are modeled by independent Bernoulli laws. Substituting the above values in equation [1.1] leads to the following formula:

$$RSV(q, d) = \sum_{w \in q \cap d} \log \left(\frac{a_w}{1 - a_w} \frac{1 - b_w}{b_w} \right) \qquad [1.2]$$

The estimation of probabilities a_w and b_w is, as mentioned above, performed through an iterative procedure:

1) Initialization: typically, $a_w^0 = 0.5$ and $b_w^0 = \frac{N_w}{N}$, corresponding to the fact that (a) we generally do not have any prior knowledge on a_w, so that setting it to 0.5 seems reasonable, and (b) for any given query, the vast majority of documents in the collection are not relevant; thus, setting b_w to $\frac{N_w}{N}$ (i.e. assuming that all documents are not relevant) provides a first, good approximation of its actual value.

2) Retrieve documents using equation [1.2] and the current values of a_w and b_w;

3) Update the parameters (aw_w and b_w) from the results found (possibly with the help of the user). For example, if N^p denotes the number of documents deemed relevant in the list of retrieved documents and if N_w^p is the number of these documents containing w, then, a possible update is:

$$a_w = \frac{N_w^p}{N^p}, \; b_w = \frac{N_w - N_w^p}{N - N^p}$$

The foundations of the BIR model are clear and theoretically sound, aiming at directly modeling the probability of relevance of a document for a given query. In addition, the iterative process used to re-estimate the parameters naturally introduces a search session in which users' preferences and requirements can be integrated and refined depending on the documents retrieved. However, this model is sensitive to the initial values chosen for the parameters, and relies on a binary representation of words in the documents which limits its possibilities (and performance).

1.3.2. BM25

The BM25 model [ROB 94], proposed by Robertson and Walker, corrects some of the problems associated with the BIR model. The BM25 model assumes that word frequencies are distributed according to a mixture of two Poisson distributions. However, it is assumed that in the relevant group ($R_q = 1$) the Poisson distribution representing the elite group has a stronger influence than in the non-relevant class. These assumptions are represented more formally below:

$$X_d - x|R = 1 \sim 2 \text{ Poisson}(\alpha, \lambda_E, \lambda_G)$$

$$X_d = x|R_q = 0 \sim 2\text{-Poisson}(\beta, \lambda_E, \lambda_G)$$

with $\alpha > \beta$ and $\lambda_E > \lambda_G$. From this assumption, using the development we have seen previsouly for the 2-Poisson mixture, equation [1.1] takes the form:

$$RSV(q, d) = \sum_{w \in q} \log \underbrace{\left(\frac{\alpha \frac{e^{-\lambda_E} \lambda_E^{x_w^d}}{x_w^d!} + (1 - \alpha) \frac{e^{-\lambda_G} \lambda_G^{x_w^d}}{x_w^d!}}{\beta \frac{e^{-\lambda_E} \lambda_E^{x_w^d}}{x_w^d!} + (1 - \beta) \frac{e^{-\lambda_G} \lambda_G^{x_w^d}}{x_w^d!}} \frac{\beta e^{-\lambda_E} + (1 - \beta) e^{-\lambda_G}}{\alpha e^{-\lambda_E} + (1 - \alpha) e^{-\lambda_G}} \right)}_{h(x_w^d)}$$

This model suffers from the same problems as the 2-Poisson model, namely the difficulty of estimating its parameters. Let us study the properties of the weight function $h(x)$. Knowing that $\alpha > \beta$, one can show that this function increases with x. In addition, the limit of h when x tends to infinity exists and takes the following value:

$$\lim_{x \to +\infty} h(x) = \log \left(\frac{\alpha \ (\beta e^{-\lambda_E + \lambda_G} + 1 - \beta)}{\beta \ (\alpha e^{-\lambda_E + \lambda_G} + 1 - \alpha)} \right) \approx \log \left(\frac{\alpha}{\beta} \frac{1 - \beta}{1 - \alpha} \right)$$

The approximation of this limit, which assumes $\lambda_E > \lambda_G$, has a form similar to the BIR model. In order to simplify the RSV given above, the idea of Robertson and Walker [ROB 94] is to find a function which has similar properties to those of the h function, and a simpler form. They first introduced a function of the form $r(x) = \frac{x}{x+K}$, which increases and tends to 1 when x tends to infinity, and then multiplied this function by the weight given in the BIR model, leading to:

$$h^*(x_w^d) = \frac{x_w^d}{x_w^d + K} \log \left(\frac{a_w}{1 - a_w} \frac{1 - b_w}{b_w} \right)$$

a_w and b_w can again be estimated iteratively. Finally, they introduced two modifications to the above formula which make the model obtained compliant with the heuristic constraint we reviewed in section 1.1.1:

1) Renormalization of frequencies in the documents: the function $r(x)$ above is replaced by:

$$r * (x_w^d) = \frac{(k_1 + 1)x_w^d}{k_1((1 - b) + b\frac{l_d}{m}) + x_w^d}$$

where l_d is the length of document d and m is the average length of the documents in the collection. k_1 is fixed at 1.2 by default and b at 0.75.

2) Renormalization of the frequencies in the query: the following formula is used to renormalize q_w

$$\frac{(k_3 + 1)q_w}{k_3 + q_w}$$

By default, $k_3 = 1,000$, even if values such as 8 or 7 are chosen on certain collections.

Finally, if we use for a_w and b_w the initial values mentioned in the iterative estimation procedure we discussed before (i.e. $a_w^0 = 0.5$ and $b_w^0 = \frac{N_w}{N}$), the BM25 model is written as:

$$RSV(q, d) = \sum_{w \in q} \frac{(k_3 + 1)q_w}{k_3 + q_w} \frac{(k_1 + 1)x_w^d}{k_1((1 - b) + b\frac{l_d}{m}) + x_w^d} \log \left(\frac{N - N_w + 0.5}{N_w + 0.5} \right)$$

As can be seen, the model obtained is quite complex and comprises three parameters $(k1, k2, k3)$ which can be optimized on a particular dataset. This model appeared in 1995 and was very successful in evaluation campaigns such as TREC. It is still considered as a reference model and performs well in a large number of situations.

The presentation of the BM25 model concludes the part on models developed under the probability ranking principle. We now review another important family of probabilistic models for information retrieval, namely the language models.

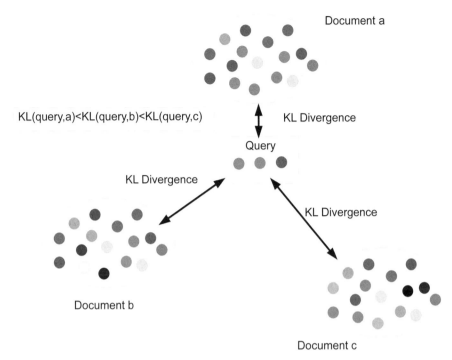

Figure 1.3. *Documents are seen as multivariate random variables distributed according to multinomial distributions. The KL-divergence serves as a distance between queries and documents. Document a has a lower KL-divergence compared to other documents because it contains more query terms*

1.4. Language models

DEFINITION 1.1. – *A language model is a probability distribution on a set of words.*

The fundamental idea of the language model approach to information retrieval is to rank documents by their probability to generate query q, $P(q|d)$. In this sense, the most relevant documents are the documents that are most likely to have generated the query. The analogy with the vector model is very simple. Instead of representing a document by a vector, it is represented by a probability distribution, and instead of computing the cosine similarity between queries and documents, "distances" between probability distributions are used. Figure 1.3 illustrates the language model approach to information retrieval using KL-divergence (see section 1.4.2) as the distance between probability distributions. Ponte and Croft [PON 98] were the first ones to propose this type of approach in information retrieval, an approach which has since been extended in several directions. [ZHA 01b] provides an interesting and detailed presentation of the basic model and its extensions.

In the basic model, the multinomial distribution is chosen to represent documents. For each document d, there thus exists a vector $\theta^d = (\theta^d_{w_1}, \cdots, \theta^d_{w_M})^T$ such that[3]:

$$\begin{cases} X^d \sim & \text{Multinomial}(\theta^d, l_d), \; \sum_w \theta^d_w = 1 \\ P(X^d)|\theta^d, l_d) = \frac{l_d!}{\prod_{w \in d} x^d_w!} \prod_{w \in d} (\theta^d_w)^{x^d_w} \end{cases}$$

As one can note, it is assumed that for each document d, there is a probabilistic model, namely a multinomial distribution parameterized by θ^d_w, which can explain the generation of d. Parameters θ^d_w must be estimated for each word and document, and one usually resorts to maximum likelihood to do so. This leads to:

$$\hat{\theta}^d_w = \frac{x^d_w}{\sum_w x^d_w} = \frac{x^d_w}{l_d}$$

In order to rank documents with respect to a given query, one computes the likelihood that the query was generated according to the document model, again under the assumption that the underlying distribution is multinomial. This gives:

$$P(q|\theta^d, l_q) = \prod_{w \in q} P(q_w|\theta^d) = \frac{l_q!}{\prod_{w \in q} q_w!} \prod_{w \in q} (\theta^d_w)^{q_w}$$

The retrieval status value is directly the log-likelihood of this generation process:

$$RSV(q,d) = \log(P(q|\theta^d, l_q)) = \sum_{w \in q} q_w \log(\theta^d_w) + \log \frac{l_q!}{\prod_{w \in q} q_w!} \qquad [1.3]$$

The above formulation is known as the *query likelihood model*.

The direct application (as above) of the maximum likelihood principle to estimate the parameters in θ^d however poses problems: if a word in the query does not appear in the document then it is given a score of zero. The fact that we have not seen a word does not mean that it is not associated with the document (e.g. it could be a synonym of a word used in the document). In addition, equation [1.3] is undefined in the case of a zero score. Only the documents containing all the words in the query receive a finite score according to this formula, which is not satisfactory (the majority of documents relevant for a query contain only some of the query words). To avoid these problems, one has to resort to smoothing methods.

1.4.1. *Smoothing methods*

The most common smoothing methods are the so-called Jelinek-Mercer and Dirichlet smoothing[4].

---

3 We use the symbol ^{T} to denote transposition.
4 Other smoothing methods are presented in [ZHA 01b].

1.4.1.1. *Jelinek-Mercer smoothing*

The idea here is to consider an additional language model associated with the document collection. The entire collection, denoted $\mathcal{C}$, is thus modeled by a multinomial distribution, the parameters of which will be denoted $\beta = (\beta_{w_1}, \ldots, \beta_{w_M})^T$. As before, the maximum likelihood estimators for β_w take the simple form:

$$\beta_w = \frac{\sum_d x_w^d}{\sum_d l_d} \qquad [1.4]$$

The language model for document d is then obtained through a linear interpolation between the parameters $\hat{\theta}_w^d$ and β_w:

$$\theta_w^d = \alpha \hat{\theta}_w^d + (1 - \alpha)\beta_w \qquad [1.5]$$

α is here the smoothing paprameter, which, when relevance judgements are available, can be learned so as to optimize a desired evaluation metric (precision at 10 documents or *MAP – Mean Average Precision*). In the absence of relevance judgements, default values can be used.

The document score for a query can be broken down into two parts: the first part concerns the words appearing in both the document and the query and the second part concerns the words appearing only in the query. This latter part will be "explained" through the language model of the corpus (i.e. β). This leads to the following re-writing of the retrieval status value:

$$\begin{aligned}
RSV(q, d) &= \sum_{w \in q} q_w \log(\theta_w^d) \\
&= \sum_{w \in q \cap d} q_w \log(\theta_w^d) + \sum_{w \in q \setminus d} q_w \log(\theta_w^d) \\
&= \sum_{w \in q \cap d} q_w \log(\alpha \hat{\theta}_w^d + (1 - \alpha)\beta_w) + \sum_{w \in q \setminus d} q_w \log((1 - \alpha)\beta_w) \\
&= \sum_{w \in q \cap d} q_w \log\left(\frac{\alpha \hat{\theta}_w^d + (1 - \alpha)\beta_w}{(1 - \alpha)\beta_w}\right) + \underbrace{\sum_{w \in q} q_w \log((1 - \alpha)\beta_w)}_{g(\alpha, q)}
\end{aligned}$$

where $g(\alpha, q)$ depends only on the query and in practice can be omitted as it has no impact on the ranking of documents. In this form, the $\frac{\alpha}{(1-\alpha)}$ factor rules the trade-off between the document and the collection language models. It corresponds to the smoothing intensity.

1.4.1.2. *Dirichlet smoothing*

The second smoothing method is reminiscent of Bayesian methods, and makes use of the Dirichlet distribution as the *prior* distribution for the parameters θ_d:

$$\theta^d | \beta, \mu \sim Dirichlet(\mu\beta)$$

where β is a vector $(\beta = (\beta_{w_1}, \dots, \beta_{w_M})^T)$ the coordinates of which are given by equation [1.4], and μ is a parameter controlling the "strength" given to the prior. As the Dirichlet and multinomial distributions are conjugated, the posterior distribution of θ_d takes the form:

$$\theta^d | d, \beta, \mu \sim Dirichlet(\mu\beta + x^d)$$

where x^d is the document vector: $(x_{w_1}^d, \dots, x_{w_M}^d)^T$. Finally, it is the average value of this distribution which is chosen as the document language model:

$$\theta_w^d = E[\theta_d | d, \beta, \mu] = \frac{x_w^d + \mu\beta_w}{l_d + \mu} \qquad [1.6]$$

As one can note, the larger μ, the less x_w^d influences the final value of θ_w^d.

As before, we can also break down the ranking function into two parts:

$$RSV(q, d) = \sum_{w \in q \cap d} q_w \log\left(\frac{x_w^d + \mu\beta_w}{l_d + \mu}\right) + \sum_{w \in q \backslash d} q_w \log\left(\frac{\mu\beta_w}{l_d + \mu}\right)$$

$$= \sum_{w \in q \cap d} q_w \log\left(\frac{x_w^d + \mu\beta_w}{\mu\beta_w}\right) + \sum_{w \in q} q_w \log\left(\frac{\mu\beta_w}{l_d + \mu}\right)$$

$$= \sum_{w \in q \cap d} q_w \log\left(1 + \frac{x_w^d}{\mu\beta_w}\right) + l_q \log\frac{\mu}{l_d + \mu} + g(0, q)$$

where the function g is defined as before. The factor $\frac{l_d}{\mu}$ controls the trade-off with the prior distribution. As before, μ can be optimized or set to pre-defined values. [ZHA 01b] furthermore proposes to choose μ so as to maximize the "likelihood minus 1". This criterion eliminates the need for relevance judgments and gives good results in practice.

The smoothing methods seen above penalize terms frequent in the collection, as β_w is high for such terms. They ensure that condition 4 of section 1.1.1 (related to the IDF effect) is verified. Furthermore, in the case of Dirichlet smoothing, the smoothing parameter also ensures that condition 3 (reagrding document legnth normalization) is verified. Smoothing is thus a key element of language models.

1.4.2. *The Kullback-Leibler model*

The basic language model, given by equation [1.3], involves the computation of the likelihood of the query for each document. This model can be expanded by considering the query as a sample of a random variable q (see [ZHA 06]). In this case, pseudo-relevance feedback and query enrichment mechanisms become more natural and have a better foundation (see [ZHA 08] for a discussion on this matter). If we consider, as for each document and the collection, that a query is also a sample of a random multinomial variable $(q|\theta^q, l_q \sim Multinomial(\theta_q, l_q))$, queries and documents can be compared by a "probability distance", such as the Kullback-Leibler divergence:

$$RSV(q, d) = -KL(\theta^q, \theta^d)$$

$$= -\sum_{w \in q} P(w|\theta^q) \log \frac{P(w|\theta^q)}{P(w|\theta^d)}$$

$$= \sum_{w \in q} P(w|\theta^q) \log P(w|\theta^d) - \sum_{w \in q} P(w|\theta^q) \log P(w|\theta^q)$$

$$= \sum_{w \in q} \theta_w^q \log \theta_w^d - \sum_{w \in q} \theta_w^q \log \theta_w^q$$

$$\overset{\text{rank}}{=} \sum_{w \in q} \theta_w^q \log \theta_w^d$$

where θ_w^d is given either by equation [1.5] or [1.6]. Estimating the parameters θ^q through maximum likelihood leads to:

$$\theta_w^q = \frac{q_w}{\sum_w q_w} = \frac{q_w}{l_q}$$

With this setting, the KL model becomes equivalent in rank, an equivalence denoted by $\overset{}{=}_{\text{rank}}$, to the likelihood model defined by equation [1.3].

Thus, the KL model can be considered as a generalization of the likelihood model. Considering the query as a distribution of words, and no longer as a sample from a document model, we can elegantly account for query enrichment and pseudo-relevance feedback mechanisms. An interpolation scheme is generally used to combine the initial query and another language model θ^E derived from the query enrichment or the pseudo-relevance feedback model:

$$\theta_{\text{final}}^q = \alpha \theta^q + (1 - \alpha) \theta^E$$

where θ_{final}^q denotes the query obtained after enrichment or feedback. The value of α is chosen experimentally and very often depends on the collection.

We now turn our attention to another model of this family, namely the noisy channel model.

1.4.3. *Noisy channel model*

The study detailed in [BER 99] builds on statistical machine translation and the noisy channel model to propose a document model richer than the unigram model. The process of formulating an information need is considered here as a translation process. Thus, for each word v, a probability distribution is defined on the vocabulary set, $P(w|v)$, which represents the probability that the word v is "translated" by w. The document language model can thus be re-written in the following format:

$$P(w|d) = \sum_v P(w|v)P_{lm}(v|d)$$

where $P_{lm}(v|d)$ represents the "standard" document language model as previously defined. Query and documents are compared either by the query likelihood model or the Kullback-Leibler model.

This statistical translation-based approach has had a significant impact on the use of language models. In effect, this model proposes an elegant solution for changing one language to another in the case of multilingual information retrieval. It can also be used to enrich documents in a monolingual framework. Indeed, $P(w|v)$ can be used in this case to model the semantic relationship between the two words v and w, an approach which can be considered as an adaptation of the generalized vector model [WON 85] in the language model framework. Having said that, the question of the estimation of translation probabilities still remains. A bilingual probability lexicon can be directly used in a multilingual framework. In a monolingual framework, several studies have investigated the use of measures based on mutual information or vector similarities [CLI 06, WEI 07, KAR 10], to derive probabilities between words.

1.4.4. *Some remarks*

The query likelihood model, with either Jelinek-Mercer or Dirichlet smoothing, and its extension through KL-divergence or the noisy channel model, are interesting information retrieval models as they are easy to adapt to different frameworks as multilingual information retrieval or pseudo-relevance feedback. Furthermore, several projects have recently explored the coupling of language and topic models, resulting in better smoothing and a better representation of the underlying information retrieval processes. Language models had considerable success in the early 2000s, and have been the subject of a large number of developments. They currently constitute one of the best performing models for ad hoc information retrieval.

We now turn to another important family of probabilistic information retrieval models, based on the notion of information.

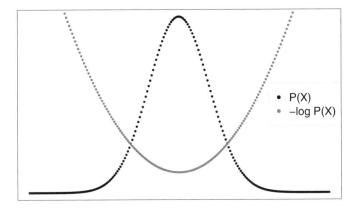

Figure 1.4. *Probability distribution and information*

1.5. Informational approaches

Informational approaches are reminiscent of the work by Harter [HAR 75] in which the indexing of a word in a document depends on its frequency relative to its overall distribution in the collection. Consider for example that a word follows, in a collection of documents, the distribution given in Figure 1.4[5], where the x axis represents the word frequency (normalized number of occurrences) and the y axis represents the probability of observing this frequency in a document of the collection. The mode of the distribution corresponds to the most observed frequency within the collection. If the word is observed in a document with the mode frequency, then this observation is standard, and even expected given the distribution of the word. The information brought by this observation is therefore low. However, if the word has a small frequency in a document, then its behavior in the document differs from its average behavior in the collection and thus from what is expected. The information brought by the observation of the word in the docuemnt is this time high, and the word is a good descriptor of the document.

Let us assume that the distribution of X_w in the collection is given by a probability function P with one parameter λ_w. In other words, the $P(X_w|\lambda_w)$ distribution summarizes the behavior of w in the collection. The amount of information brought by a word in a document can be directly measured through the self-information used in Shannon entropy[6] and defined by $-\log P(X_w = x|\lambda_w)$ (a representation of the self-information is given by the gray curve, in Figure 1.4).

---

5 It is of course only an illustrative example as this distribution is not appropriate to model the behavior of a word.

6 The use of the self-information to continuous distributions requires the discretization of the domain considered, which can be done in different ways.

We present in this section two families of models which fit within the general framework we have just described. The first family, introduced in the early 2000s, corresponds to models known as *DFR* (for *Divergence From Randomness*). This family is important from both a historical and practical point of view. However, this family raises a certain number of theoretical problems, to which the second family, introduced in 2010 under the name *information models*, provides solutions.

1.5.1. *DFR models*

The DFR model family, which was proposed by Amati and van Rijsbergen [AMA 02], relies on the information content of the words in a document, a quantity which is then corrected by the risk of accepting each term as a document descriptor (*first normalization principle*). The renormalization of the frequencies in relation to the length of a document is the *second normalization principle*. In DFR, the information content $Inf_1(t_w^d)$ of a term is initially calculated according to a first probability distribution: $Inf_1(t_w^d) = -\log Prob_1(t_w^d)$. The first normalization principle introduces a second probability distribution, leading to a complete model which combines these two information types.

This family can be summarized by the following three steps:

1) Normalize the occurrences of the words to account for the variation in document length;

2) Choose a first probability distribution $Prob_1$ which serves to measure the information content of a term in a document;

3) Choose a second "pseudo-probability" $Prob_2$ which renormalizes the information content of a term[7].

The resulting models thus have the following form:

$$RSV(q,d) = \sum_{w \in q \cap d} q_w(1 - \text{Prob}_2(t_w^d)) \overbrace{(-\log(Prob_1(X_w = t_w^d)))}^{\text{Inf}_1(t_w^d)}$$

We now explain in more detail the above steps.

1.5.1.1. *Frequency normalization*

The normalization of the number of occurrences is performed, in the DFR family, through one of the following two formulas:

---

7 Contrary to what the term suggests, $Prob_2$ does not always define a valid probability distribution. This is why we use the term *pseudo-probability* here.

$$t_w^d = x_w^d c \frac{m}{l_d} \text{ or } x_w^d \log\left(1 + c\frac{m}{l_d}\right) \tag{1.7}$$

where m is the average document length and c is a parameter which is set for each collection.

1.5.1.2. Inf_1 model

Two main distributions are used for $Prob_1$: the geometric and Poisson distributions. The geometric model assumes that the occurrences of a term follows a geometric law, the parameter of which is given by the average frequency of the word in the collection: $\lambda_w = \frac{F_w}{N}$. The Poisson model assumes that the occurrences of a term follows a Poisson law the parameter of which is, as before, equal to the average frequency of the word within the collection: $\lambda_w = \frac{F_w}{N}$. We thus have:

$$Inf_1(t_w^d) = \log_2(1 + \lambda_w) + t_w^d \log_2\left(\frac{1 + \lambda_w}{\lambda_w}\right) \quad \text{(geometric)}$$

$$Inf_1(t_w^d) = \log_2\left(\frac{e^{-\lambda_w}\lambda_w^{t_w^d}}{t_w^d!}\right) \approx t_w^d \log_2\left(\frac{t_w^d}{\lambda_w}\right) + \left(\lambda_w + \frac{1}{12t_w^d} - t_w^d\right)\log_2(e)$$

$$+ 0.5\log_2(2\pi t_w^d) \quad \text{(Poisson)}$$

where the last approximation is based on Stirling's formula.

1.5.1.3. $Prob_2$ model

The study presented in [AMA 02] provides two ways to define the model $Prob_2$, based on either Laplace succession law or a binomial ratio. In each case, the probability of an additional occurence of a word in a document is computed and used for $Prob_2 1$. For Laplace succession law, a Bernoulli distribution is used to model this additional occurrence, the parameter of this distribution being: $\frac{t_w^d}{t_w^d+1}$. $Prob_2$ is then defined as:

$$Prob_2(t_w^d) = \frac{t_w^d}{t_w^d + 1}$$

In the case of the binomial ratio, the assumption is made that the occurrences of term w in the N_w documents in which it appears follow a binomial law with parameter $\frac{1}{N_w}$. The probability of observing x_w^d occurrences of word w in document d is thus given by:

$$P(X_w = x_w^d | N_w, F_w) = \binom{x_w^d}{F_w}\left(\frac{1}{N_w}\right)^{x_w^d}\left(\frac{N_w - 1}{N_w}\right)^{F_w - x_w^d}$$

As for the Laplace law, it is the change in number of occurrences from t to $t + 1$ which is selected to define $Prob_2$ in the DFR model. The probability variation, while considered an additional occurrence for a term, is calculated in the following manner for the binomial law:

$$\frac{P(X_w = x_w^d | N_w, F_w) - P(X_w = x_w^d + 1 | N_w, F_w + 1)}{P(X_w = x_w^d | N_w, F_w)} = 1 - \frac{F_w + 1}{N_w(x_w^d + 1)}$$

This process leads, by using the normalized frequencies t_w^d, to the following form:

$$Prob_2(t_w^d) = 1 - \frac{F_w + 1}{N_w(t_w^d + 1)}$$

1.5.1.4. Combination of Inf₁ and Prob₂ models

The DFR models are obtained from a choice of the first probability $Prob_1$ and the normalization function $Prob_2$. The majority of these models use the second frequency normalization given in equation [1.7]. For example, the Geometric-Laplace model with the second normalization (named GL2 in the literature) corresponds to:

$$RSV(q, d) = \sum_{w \in q \cap d} q_w \frac{\log_2(1 + \lambda_w) + x_w^d \log(1 + c\frac{m}{l_d})\log_2(\frac{1 + \lambda_w}{\lambda_w})}{x_w^d \log(1 + c\frac{m}{l_d}) + 1}$$

Similarly, the Poisson-Laplace model with the second normalization (written PL2) corresponds to:

$$RSV(q, d) = \sum_{w \in q \cap d} \frac{q_w}{t_w^d + 1} \left(t_w^d \log_2\left(\frac{t_w^d}{\lambda_w}\right) + \left(\lambda_w + \frac{1}{12t_w^d} - t_w^d\right)\log_2(e) \right.$$

$$\left. + \sum_{w \in q \cap d} 0.5\log_2(2\pi t_w^d) \right)$$

One can find in [AMA 02] different models obtained by combining the above elements (as PB2, GB2, I(n)B2, I(F)L2). In practice, these models behave similarly and rougly yield the same level of performance. One can note however that the models PL2 and I(n)L2 are among the most frequently chosen DFR models. All these models rely on a single unknown parameter c, used for frequency normalization and based on the average length of a document. This parameter can either be learned from existing annotated collections, or set according to past experience (the TERRIER information retrieval tool, for example, provides default values for this parameter).

1.5.1.5. *Critiques*

A major drawback of DFR models lies in the use of discrete distributions with continuous elements (normalized frequencies), which is not valid from a theoretical point of view. Furthermore, the justification of the principle combining Inf_1 with $Prob_2$ proposed in [AMA 02] is somewhat remote and concerns can be raised regarding the usefulness of this combination. We now present a family of models that corrects these problems.

1.5.2. *Information-based models*

As mentioned above, several projects in IR and text collection modeling are linked to the idea of information brought by a term in a document: the more the behavior of a word in a document differs from its average behavior in the collection, the more this word is significant for the document in question. Information models fully exploit this idea and are based on the following score function:

$$RSV(q,d) = \sum_{w \in q \cap d} -x_w^q \log Prob(X_w \geq t_w^d | \lambda_w) \qquad [1.8]$$

which amounts to compute the *average information* that a document brings to a query (as one can note, it is similar in its form to the Inf_1 part of DFR models). We refer to this family of models as "information models". Relating this family with the IR conditions discussed in section 1.1.1, one can note:

– $Prob(X \geq t_w^d | \lambda_w)$ is, by definition, a function that decreases with t_w^d. As standard term frequency normalization formulas are such that t_w^d is a function that increases with x_w^d and decreases with the length of the document l_d, conditions 1 and 3 are verified.

– For information models, condition 2 takes the form:

$$\frac{\partial^2 \log(Prob(X \geq t_w^d | \lambda_w))}{\partial (x_w^d)^2} > 0 \qquad [1.9]$$

Thus, as long as the probability distribution used satisfies equation [1.9], condition 2 will also be satisfied.

[CLI 10b] relates equation [1.9] to burstiness, a phenomenon usually observed in texts. In particular, they show that the probability distributions satisfying equation 1.9 are bursty, and thus "explain" the burstiness phenomenon observed in texts. This relation is however beyond the scope of this chapter.

We now turn to two instances of this model, based on distributions that satisfy equation [1.9]. In both cases, the parameter λ_w can be either set to $\frac{F_w}{N}$ or $\frac{N_w}{N}$. Other values are of course possible but the previous choices (a) are intuitive (average word frequency in the collection) and (b) render condition 4 satisfied (see [CLI 10b] for more details).

1.5.2.1. *Two instances*

Two information models are detailed here, one using a log-logistic law and the other a Smoothed Power Law.

We use here the log-logistic distribution with the parameter fixed at 1:

$$P_{LL}(X < x; \lambda, \beta = 1) = \frac{x}{x + \lambda}$$

The associated information model is defined by:

$$(LGD) \begin{cases} t_w^d &= x_w^d \log(1 + c\frac{m}{l_d}) \\ \lambda_w &= \frac{N_w}{N} \\ RSV(q,d) &= \sum_{w \in q \cap d} q_w (\log(\lambda_w + t_w^d) - \log(\lambda_w)) \end{cases}$$

The above model satisfies both IR conditions 2 and 4 (as we have seen before, it also satisfies conditions 1 and 3). The satisfication of condition 2 goes through the verificaiton of equation [1.9]. For condition 4, the derivation is purely technical and skipped here. The motivation for relying on a log-logistic distribution resorts to previous work on text modeling. Following Church and Gale [CHU 95] and Airoldi [AIR 04], Clinchant and Gaussier [CLI 08] studied the negative binomial distribution in the context of text modeling. They then assumed a uniform Beta prior distribution over one of the parameters, leading to a distribution they refer to as the Beta negative binomial distribution, or BNB for short. One problem with the BNB distribution is that it is a discrete distribution and cannot be used for modeling t_w^d. However, the log-logistic distribution, with its β parameter set to 1, is a continuous counterpart of the BNB distribution since $P_{LL}(x \leq X < x + 1;) = P_{BNB}(x)$.

Let us now consider the probability law defined, for $x > 0$, by:

$$f(x; \lambda) = \frac{-\log \lambda}{1 - \lambda} \frac{\lambda^{\frac{x}{x+1}}}{(x + 1)^2} (0 < \lambda < 1)$$

$$P(X > x|\lambda) = \int_x^\infty f(x; \lambda) = \frac{\lambda^{\frac{x}{x+1}} - \lambda}{1 - \lambda}$$

where f represents the probability density. From this law, one obtains the following information mdodel, called SPL (*Smoothed Power Law*) model:

$$(SPL) \begin{cases} t_w^d &= x_w^d \log(1 + c\frac{m}{l_d}) \\ \lambda_w &= \frac{N_w}{N} \\ RSV(q,d) &= \sum_{w \in q \cap d} -x_w^q \log(\frac{\lambda_w^{\frac{t_w^d}{t_w^d+1}} - \lambda_w}{1 - \lambda_w}) \end{cases}$$

Here again, one can show that both IR conditions 2 and 4 are satisfied, so that the above model is compliant with all the IR conditions.

Information models have recently been extended to the pseudo-relevance feedback (PRF) and cross-language information retrieval (CLIR) settings, and seem to outperform other models in these settings. These models will thus likely be the subject of further developments in the coming years.

1.6. Experimental comparison

We want here to illustrate (a) the general behavior of several models presented before and (b) the fact that many of these models produce relatively similar results in standard information retrieval tasks. To do so, we make use of the results reported in [CLI 10b]. Standard IR collections from two evaluation campaigns are used in this evaluation: TREC (trec.nist.gov) and CLEF (www.clef-campaign.org). Table 1.6 gives the number of documents (N), number of unique terms (M), average document length and number of test queries for the collections retained: ROBUST (TREC), TREC3, CLEF03 AdHoc Task, GIRT (CLEF Domain Specific Task, from the year 2004 to 2006).

	N	M	Avg DL	# Queries
ROBUST	490 779	992 462	289	250
TREC-3	741 856	668 648	438	50
CLEF03	166 754	80 000	247	60
GIRT	151 319	179 283	109	75

Table 1.2. *Characteristics of the different collections*

The parameters of the different IR models are optimized on a part of the collection reserved for training, the other part being used for testing. The results reported are averaged over 10 train/test splits. The performance is evaluated through Mean Average Precision (MAP) and precision at 10^8. As the study presented in [CLI 10b] focuses on information models, the model LGD is alternatively compared to other models. The fact that the train/test splits differ in each comparison explains why the results for LGD are not always the same. Table 1.3 gives the results of this comparison. We have chosen here the models JM (language model with Jelinek-Mercer smoothing), DIR (language model with Dirichlet smoothing), BM25, the model PL2 from the DFR family and the model LGD from the information family. As one can note, the results for the different models are relatively on par.

Before concluding this chapter, we briefly review three available information retrieval platforms which allow one to index document collections and which implement most of the retrieval models we have reviewed.

---

8 See [SAV 10] for a general presentation of information retrieval evaluation measures.

MAP	ROB-d	ROB-t	GIR	T3-t	CL-d	CL-t	MAP	ROB-d	ROB-t	GIR	T3-t	CL-t	CL-d
JM	26.0	20.7	40.7	22.5	49.2	36.5	DIR	27.1	25.1	41.1	**25.6**	36.2	48.5
LGD	**27.2**	**22.5**	**43.1**	**25.9**	**50.0**	**37.5**	LGD	**27.4**	25.0	**42.1**	24.8	**36.8**	**49.7**

P10	ROB-d	ROB-t	GIR	T3-t	CL-d	CL-t	P10	ROB-d	ROB-t	GIR	T3-t	CL-t	CLF-d
JM	43.8	35.5	67.5	40.7	33.0	26.2	DIR	45.6	43.3	68.6	54.0	28.4	33.8
LGD	**46.0**	**38.9**	**69.4**	**52.4**	**33.6**	**26.6**	LGD	**46.2**	43.5	**69.0**	**54.3**	28.6	34.5

MAP	ROB-d	ROB-t	GIR	T3-t	CL-t	CL-d	MAP	ROB-d	ROB-t	GIR	T3-t	CL-t	CL-d
BM25	26.8	22.4	39.8	25.4	34.9	46.8	PL2	26.2	24.8	40.6	**24.9**	36.0	47.2
LGD	**28.2**	**23.5**	**41.4**	**26.1**	34.8	48.0	LGD	**27.3**	24.7	40.5	24.0	36.2	47.5

P10	ROB-d	ROB-t	GIR	T3-t	CL-t	CL-d	P10	ROB-d	ROB-t	GIR	T3-t	CL-t	CL-d
BM25	45.9	42.6	62.6	50.6	28.5	33.7	PL2	46.4	**44.1**	**68.2**	55.0	28.7	33.1
LGD	46.5	**44.3**	**66.6**	**53.8**	28.7	34.4	LGD	46.6	43.2	66.7	53.9	28.5	33.7

Table 1.3. *Comparison of the models after 10 splits; bold indicates significant difference*

1.7. Tools for information retrieval

Lemur The Lemur project[9] proposes several tools for the statistical analysis of texts and information retrieval (among others, an efficient construction of an inverted index for a collection of documents). Lemur has played an important role in the development of language models. Indeed, many variants of the language modeling approach were developed with this platform, which facilitated its diffusion into the scientific community. Lemur is mainly developed using C++.

Terrier Terrier[10] supplies a similar service to Lemur with indexing tools and information retrieval models. Its distinctive characteristic is an important emphasis on DFR models. The LGD model of the information family is also available. Terrier is encoded in JAVA.

Lucene Lucene[11] is an open source project based on Apache, encoded in Java. Lucene also contains a large number of standard models, and allows for easy development of new applications.

1.8. Conclusion

We have reviewed in this chapter the main probabilistic information retrieval models. These models rely on different assumptions and fit within slightly different

---

9 www.lemurproject.org.

10 terrier.org.

11 urllucene.apache.org/java/docs/index.htm.

theoretical frameworks. They are also based on different probability distributions. The following equations provide a synthetic view of the form of the main models reviewed here.

Model	
BM25	$\begin{cases} \text{Parameter } k_1, k_3, b \\ t_w^d = \dfrac{(k_1+1)x_w^d}{k_1((1-b)+b\frac{l_d}{m})+x_w^d} \\ RSV(q,d) = \sum_{w \in q \cap d} \dfrac{(k_3+1)q_w}{k_3+q_w} t_w^d \log(\frac{N-N_w+0.5}{N_w+0.5}) \end{cases}$
Dirichlet	$\begin{cases} \text{Parameter } \mu \\ \beta_w = F_w/l_c \\ RSV(q,d) = l_q \log \frac{\mu}{l_d+\mu} + \sum_{w \in q \cap d} q_w \log(1+\frac{x_w^d}{\mu\beta_w}) \end{cases}$
PL2	$\begin{cases} \text{Parameter } c \\ \lambda_w = F_w/N \\ t_w^d = x_w^d \log(1+c\frac{m}{l_d}) \\ RSV(q,d) = \sum_{w \in q \cap d} q_w(\dfrac{t_w^d \log_2(\frac{t_w^d}{\lambda_w})}{t_w^d+1} + \dfrac{\log_2(e)(\lambda_w-t_w^d)}{t_w^d+1} + \dfrac{0.5\log_2(2\pi t_w^d)}{t_w^d+1}) \end{cases}$
LGD	$\begin{cases} \text{Parameter } c \\ \lambda_w = N_w/N \\ t_w^d = x_w^d \log(1+c\frac{m}{l_d}) \\ RSV(q,d) = \sum_{w \in q \cap d} q_w \log \frac{\lambda_w+t_w^d}{\lambda_w} \end{cases}$

All the models considered in this chapter comply with the heuristic constraints of information retrieval, introduced in section 1.1.1, and provide, for some of them, the best current results in the ad hoc information retrieval task. In addition to its performance, the strengths of a model also lie on the validity of its assumptions, comprehension, and expansion ability. Some of the models presented were developed in the nineties, while others are more recent and have not yet been thoroughly studied. Additional studies and improvements thus still lie ahead of us.

1.9. Bibliography

[AMA 02] AMATI G., RIJSBERGEN C.J.V., "Probabilistic models of information retrieval based on measuring the divergence from randomness", *ACM Transactions on Information and System*, vol. 20, no. 4, p. 357-389, ACM, 2002.

[AMA 03] AMATI G., CARPINETO C., ROMANO G., BORDONI F.U., Fondazione ugo bordoni at TREC 2003: robust and web track, 2003.

[AIR 04] AIROLDI E.M., COHEN W.W., FIENBERG S.E., Statistical Models for Frequent Terms in Text, CMU-CLAD Technical Report, 2004.

[BER 99] BERGER A., LAFFERTY J., "Information retrieval as statistical translation", in *Proceedings of the 1999 ACM SIGIR Conference on Research and Development in Information Retrieval*, 1999.

[BLE 03] BLEI D.M., NG A.Y., JORDAN M.I., "Latent dirichlet allocation", *Journal of Machine Learning Research*, vol. 3, p. 993-1022, 2003.

[CHU 95] CHURCH K.W., GALE W.A., "Poisson mixtures", *Natural Language Engineering*, vol. 1, p. 163-190, 1995.

[CHU 00] CHURCH K.W., "Empirical estimates of adaptation: the chance of two noriegas is closer to p/2 than p2", in *Proceedings of the 18th Conference on Computational Linguistics*, Association for Computational Linguistics, Morristown, New Jersey, USA, p. 180-186, 2000.

[CLI 06] CLINCHANT S., GOUTTE C., GAUSSIER E., "Lexical entailment for information retrieval", in *Lecture Notes in Computer Science*, Springer, p. 217-228, 2006.

[CLI 08] CLINCHANT S., GAUSSIER E., "The BNB distribution for text modeling", in MACDONALD C., OUNIS I., PLACHOURAS V., RUTHVEN I., WHITE R.W. (eds), *ECIR*, vol. 4956 of *Lecture Notes in Computer Science*, Springer, p. 150-161, 2008.

[CLI 10a] CLINCHANT S., GAUSSIER E., "Retrieval constraints and word frequency distributions: a log-logistic model for IR", *Information Retrieval*, vol. 4, no. 1, 2010.

[CLI 10b] CLINCHANT S., GAUSSIER E., "Information-based models for ad hoc IR", in *SIGIR '10: Proceeding of the 33rd International ACM SIGIR Conference on Research and Development in Information Retrieval*, ACM, New Jersey, New York, USA, p. 234-241, 2010.

[FAN 04] FANG H., TAO T., ZHAI C., "A formal study of information retrieval heuristics", in *SIGIR '04: Proceedings of the 27th Annual International ACM SIGIR Conference on Research and Development in Information Retrieval*, 2004.

[FEL 68] FELLER W., *An Introduction to Probability Theory and Its Applications*, vol. I, Wiley, New York, 1968.

[HAR 75] HARTER S.P., "A probabilistic approach to automatic keyword indexing", *Journal of the American Society for Information Science*, vol. 26, 1975.

[HOF 99] HOFMANN T., "Probabilistic latent semantic indexing", in *SIGIR '99: Proceedings of the 22nd International ACM SIGIR Conference on Research and Development in Information Retrieval*, ACM, p. 50-57, 1999.

[JEO 03] JEON J., LAVRENKO V., MANMATHA R., "Automatic image annotation and retrieval using cross-media relevance models", *Proceeding of the ACM SIGIR Conference on Research and Development in Information Retrieval*, p. 119-126, 2003.

[KAR 10] KARIMZADEHGAN M., ZHAI C., "Estimation of statistical translation models based on mutual information for ad hoc information retrieval", in *SIGIR '10: Proceeding of the 33rd International ACM SIGIR Conference on Research and Development in Information Retrieval*, ACM, New York, USA, p. 323-330, 2010.

[KAT 96] KATZ S.M., "Distribution of content words and phrases in text and language modeling", *Natural Language Engineering*, vol. 2, no. 1, p. 15-59, Cambridge University Press, 1996.

[LAV 01] LAVRENKO V., CROFT W.B., "Relevance based language models", in *SIGIR '01: Proceedings of the 24th Annual International ACM SIGIR Conference on Research and Development in Information Retrieval*, ACM, New York, USA, p. 120-127, 2001.

[LAV 02] LAVRENKO V., CHOQUETTE M., CROFT W.B., "Cross-lingual relevance models", in *SIGIR '02: Proceedings of the 25th Annual International ACM SIGIR Conference on Research and Development in Information Retrieval*, ACM, New York, USA, p. 175-182, 2002.

[MAR 92] MARGULIS E.L., "N-Poisson document modeling", in *SIGIR '92: Proceedings of the 15th Annual International ACM SIGIR Conference on Research and Development in Information Retrieval*, ACM, New York, USA, p. 177-189, 1992.

[NIG 99] NIGAM K., MCCALLUM A.K., THRUN S., MITCHELL T., "Text classification from labeled and unlabeled documents using EM", *Machine Learning*, p. 103-134, 1999.

[PON 98] PONTE J.M., CROFT W.B., "A language modeling approach to information retrieval", in *SIGIR*, ACM, p. 275-281, 1998.

[ROB 77] ROBERTSON S., "The probability ranking principle in IR", *Journal of Documentation*, vol. 33, 1977.

[ROB 94] ROBERTSON S.E., WALKER S., "Some simple effective approximations to the 2-Poisson model for probabilistic weighted retrieval", in *SIGIR '94: Proceedings of the 17th Annual International ACM SIGIR Conference on Research and Development in Information Retrieval*, Springer-Verlag New York, Inc., New York, USA, p. 232-241, 1994.

[ROB 97] ROBERTSON S.E., *The Probability Ranking Principle in IR*, Morgan Kaufmann Publishers Inc., San Francisco, CA, USA, p. 281-286, 1997.

[SAL 83] SALTON G., MCGILL M.J., *Introduction to Modern Information Retrieval*, McGraw-Hill, Inc., New York, USA, 1983.

[SAV 10] SAVOY J., GAUSSIER E., "Information retrieval", in INDURKHYA N., DAMERAU F.J. (eds), *Handbook of Natural Language Processing*, 2nd Edition, Chapman & Hall/CRC, 2010.

[WEI 07] WEI X., CROFT W.B., "Modeling term associations for ad-hoc retrieval performance within language modeling framework", in *ECIR '07: Proceedings of the 29th European Conference on IR Research*, Springer-Verlag, Berlin, Heidelberg, p. 52-63, 2007.

[WON 85] WONG S.K.M., ZIARKO W., WONG P.C.N., "Generalized vector spaces model in information retrieval", in *SIGIR '85: Proceedings of the 8th Annual International ACM SIGIR Conference on Research and Development in Information Retrieval*, ACM, New York, USA, p. 18-25, 1985.

[ZHA 01a] ZHAI C., LAFFERTY J., "Model-based feedback in the language modeling approach to information retrieval", in *CIKM '01: Proceedings of the 10th International Conference on Information and Knowledge Management*, ACM, New York, USA, p. 403-410, 2001.

[ZHA 01b] ZHAI C., LAFFERTY J., "A study of smoothing methods for language models applied to ad hoc information retrieval", in *Proceedings of the 24th Annual International ACM SIGIR Conference on Research and Development in Information Retrieval*, ACM, New York, USA, p. 334-342, 2001.

[ZHA 04] ZHAI C., LAFFERTY J., "A study of smoothing methods for language models applied to information retrieval", *ACM Transactions on Information Systems*, vol. 22, no. 2, p. 179-214, 2004.

[ZHA 06] ZHAI C., LAFFERTY J., "A risk minimization framework for information retrieval", *Information Processing Management*, vol. 42, no. 1, p. 31-55, Pergamon Press, Inc., 2006.

[ZHA 08] ZHAI C., *Statistical Language Models for Information Retrieval*, Morgan & Claypool, Princeton, New Jersey, 2008.

Chapter 2

Learnable Ranking Models for Automatic Text Summarization and Information Retrieval

2.1. Introduction

Until recently, the two main problems studied in Machine Learning (ML) were classification and regression. In these cases, the goal is to learn a prediction function, which will induce, for each entry, a value in accordance with a desired output. The problem of ranking, in which the aim is to learn an ordering of observations, has lately gained much attention in ML. A ranking function considers several entries, compares them, and returns them in the form of an ordered list. The predicted order must agree with a preferred ordering specific to the problem being treated. In the literature, there are two types of ranking problems:

– Ranking of alternatives which concerns the problem where the elements from a given collection (named alternatives) must be ranked with respect to an entry example. A typical example is automatic summarization of texts in this case, an entry example represents a document and the alternatives correspond to sentences of the document). Another example is that of information retrieval, where the documents of a given collection must be ranked in response to a user's query (the entry is a query, and alternatives are documents of the collection). For this type of problem, we assume that the entry samples are independently and identically distributed (i.i.d.) and the aim is to return, for each sample, a ranked list of alternatives where the relevant alternatives in relation to the given entry are ranked before the non-relevant ones;

Chapter written by Massih-Réza AMINI, David BUFFONI, Patrick GALLINARI, Tuong Vinh TRUONG, and Nicolas USUNIER.

– Ranking of instances concerns the ordering of a set of entry samples. These samples are also assumed to be i.i.d., but now they must be ordered among themselves. This framework formalizes, for example, the application of such document routing, where a user is seeking information in a controlled manner, and the system has a certain number of relevant and non-relevant documents in relation to the demand. The aim is to sort the new entering documents and to insert them in the list of existing documents, so that the relevant documents are ranked above the non-relevant documents.

In general, the ranking of alternatives corresponds to the cases where different queries are sent to the system (*dynamic* query), but the collection of documents is fixed (*static* collection). The ranking of instances, however, treats the case where the query is fixed (*static* query), and the collection of documents varies with time (*dynamic* collection). From the learning point of view, the major differences between these two ranking frameworks focus on the entities that have to be ranked. In the case of instance ranking, entities are entry samples, whereas in the case of ranking of alternatives, it is alternatives that have to be ranked with respect to each entry.

In this chapter, these two formalisms will be presented. The important ideas which led to the development of these two frameworks are introduced first. However, a detailed description of these methods will be avoided: only the framework and the resolution principles will be discussed. Secondly, we will present the tasks of automatic summarization and information retrieval, which are the two symbolic applications that led to the development of these models.

2.1.1. *Ranking of instances*

This formulation is part of a *reduction* principle [USU 07], which resolves a complicated task (ranking) using simpler and better controlled tasks (classification).

2.1.1.1. *Formalism*

Through an analogy with the classification framework, we assume that the observations to rank among themselves with respect to their desired labels, and using a real-valued function, are generated according to an unknown distribution $\mathcal{D}$. We note $\mathcal{X}$ as the vectorial space in which observations are described and $\mathcal{Y} \subset \mathbb{R}$ represents the output space.

Thus, for a set $\mathcal{S} = \{x_i, y_i\}_{i=1}^n$ of sampled labeled instances i.i.d. following $\mathcal{D}$, we will consider an order $\succ$ on the labels $\mathcal{Y}$, these labels expressing a preferential relationship over the observations. Let us take two labeled instances (x_i, y_i) and (x_j, y_j), $y_i \succ y_j$ signifying that x_i must be ranked above x_j.

2.1.1.1.1. Score function

Learning consists of finding a function $h: \mathcal{X} \to \mathbb{R}$ which enables us to correctly assign a higher score to a preferred observation over a less preferred one. At the end, the real-valued scores assigned by h, induces an ordering over the set of samples. Figure 2.1 illustrates this case.

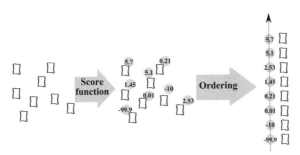

Figure 2.1. *Ranking with a score function*

2.1.1.1.2. Error function

The learning of score function h is generally carried out by minimizing a ranking loss. For a given set of instances, this error enables us to compare the order induced by the score function and the desired order[1]. It, therefore, measures the degree to which the first order differs from the second. As mentioned above, in ranking, the result of the score function is only used to compare the instances between one another. The absolute value of the score is meaningless. The ranking error functions, therefore, consider a set of scores alone and not the individual scores.

In this chapter, it will be considered that error functions on $\mathcal{S}$, a set of n entries, can be written as:

$$L_o: \mathbb{R}^n \times \mathbb{R}^n \to \mathbb{R}^+$$

In other words, the error function measures the agreement between, on the one hand, the order induced by the scores assigned returned by the learned function, and on the other hand, the desired scores, also known as the relevance judgments.

Here, the error functions used in ranking will be discussed in more detail, beginning with a particular instance ranking formalism: the classification of critical pairs.

---

1 In other words, the order induced by the label values.

2.1.1.2. Classification of critical pairs

Ideally, the researched score function allows us to rank correctly the instances of $\mathcal{X}$:

$$\forall (x_i, y_i), (x_j, y_j) \in (\mathcal{X} \times \mathcal{Y})^2, \quad y_i \succ y_j \Rightarrow h(x_i) > h(x_j)$$

In this case, the error can be defined on each critical pair (x_i, x_j) such that $y_i \succ y_j$. A generalization ranking error, which measures the proportion of critical pairs for which the order predicted by h is not the desired order [COH 97]:

$$L(h) = \mathbb{E}_{(x_i, y_i) \sim \mathcal{D}, (x_j, y_j) \sim \mathcal{D}}[[h(x_i) \leq h(x_j)]]$$

where $[[P]]$ is equal to 1, if the predicate P is true and 0, if not.

An empirical ranking loss, L_{cp}, which is an unbiased estimator of $L(h)$, $L(h) = \mathbb{E}_{(X,Y) \sim \mathcal{D}^n} \{ L_{cp}(h(X), Y) \}$ can be defined as:

$$L_{cp}(h(X), Y) = \frac{1}{\sum_{i,j}[[y_i \succ y_j]]} \sum_{i,j: y_i \succ y_j} [[h(x_i) \leq h(x_j)]]$$

with $h(X) = (h(x_1), \ldots, h(x_n))$ and $Y = (y_1, \ldots, y_n)$.

Note that this error has an interesting relationship with the binary classification. By considering a critical pair (x_i, x_j), a binary relationship can be defined with sign $(h(x_i) - h(x_j))$. This relationship can be interpreted as an entry pair classifier and the error L_{cp} can be viewed as the classification error of critical pairs[2] made by the binary relationship.

Finally, in the learning set framework, it must be noted that the test set and the samples have the same format in classification or regression (according to the nature of the space $\mathcal{Y}$). The difference comes from the definition of the generalization error, which takes into account the relative scores between the two observations, and not the relationship between the predicted value and the desired value.

2.1.1.3. Application with a linear model

Linear function class will now be discussed. These functions are generally sufficient for treating information retrieval problems. The score function is defined as $h(x) = w^T x$ with w being a weight of dimension d. The properties of the scalar product allow us to write the error on a critical pair by:

$$[[h(x_i) \leq h(x_j)]] = [[w^T x_i \leq w^T x_j]]$$
$$= [[w^T (x_i - x_j) \leq 0]]$$
$$= [[h(x_i - x_j) \leq 0]]$$

---

2 By labeling the critical pairs with 1.

In this format, the resemblance to the classification error is evident. In this case, the pair is also represented by the representation difference: $x_i - x_j$ and the ranking interpreted as the ordering of the *classification of critical pairs* can be resolved in two stages:

1) forming the set of critical pairs $T(\mathcal{S}) = \{(x_i - x_j, 1)|x_i, x_j \in \mathcal{S}, \ y_i \succ y_j\}$;

2) learning a classification function on the set obtained $T(\mathcal{S})$.

It can be noted here that the classification of critical pairs differs from classical classification on two major points. Firstly, the instance pairs are not independent. An instance can, in fact, intervene in several critical pairs. On the other hand, the new learning basis is solely composed of positive examples.

This approach has the advantage to adapt any classification algorithm to ranking. The use of a convex upper bound of the indicator function $t \mapsto [[t \leq 0]]$ allows us to define optimizable ranking losses. The reader can refer to Table 2.1 and Figure 2.2 to find a non-exhaustive list of the main convex upper bounds associated with a critical pair (x_i, x_j).

Name	Functions
exponential	$\exp\left(w^T(x_j - x_i)\right)$
logistic regression	$\log\left(1 + exp(w^T(x_j - x_i))\right)$
hinge	$\max\left(1 + w^T(x_j - x_i), 0\right)$

Table 2.1. *Examples of loss functions adapted for ranking*

However, in binary classification terms, the classification of critical pairs violates the i.i.d. assumption of $T(\mathcal{S})$ [USU 05b] learning samples.

The theoretical justification of this method is thus questioned. Generalization bounds on the learning error have thus been proposed, initially in a restricted case: bipartite ranking where output labels take only two values [AGA 05a, AGA 05b, AGA 05c, USU 05a]. Recent work has involved a more general case [USU 05b, USU 07]. Finally, the work conducted by [BAL 08, AIL 08] in a similar framework but easily adapted for score function learning must be noted. Thus, these works have validated the use of classification algorithms for the classification of critical pairs.

2.1.1.3.1. Learning and interference complexities

A naive approach for the classification of critical pairs consists of first critical pairs and then applying a classification method. From an algorithmic point of view, the formation of critical is costly. In general, there can be $O(n^2)$, where n is the numbers of instances to rank. This limitation is not convenient to learn a binary classifier. In some cases, the complexity can be greatly reduced by avoiding the explicit formation

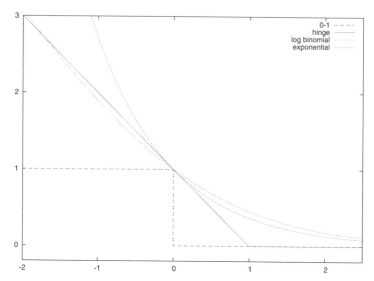

Figure 2.2. *Examples of convex upper bound functions adding to the indicator function on the y axis, function h, and the associated error ranking L(h)*

of all critical pairs. For example, let us cite in the bipartite framework (see section 2.1.1.6), the RANKBOOST algorithm [FRE 03].

Once the ranking function is learned, it can be used to rank any set. The inference can be summarized as: (1) estimate the scores for each instance and (2), order examples with respect to the output of the scoring function. By noting the number of instances to rank m, the first stage requires $O(m.d)$ calculations and the second is performed with an efficient sorting algorithm such as QUICKSORT [HOA 62], which has an average complexity of $O(m.\log(m))$. The total complexity is thus:

$$inference\ complexity\ =\ O(d.m + m\log(m))$$

2.1.1.4. *Ranking induced by the output of a classifier*

In the case of bipartite ranking (section 2.1.1.6), the instances to rank have binary relevance judgments: some of them are *relevant*, and others are *non-relevant*. It is thus possible to learn a binary classifier which discriminates the relevant instances from the non-relevant ones. These instance classifiers are generally real functions $h: \mathcal{X} \rightarrow \mathbb{R}$ whose sign is used to classify the examples. Thus, in this particular case, it is possible to use the scores given by an instance classifier to rank the examples.

Figure 2.3 shows a toy model which illustrates the difference between the two error types: h_1 and h_2 are two score functions which give different scores for seven instances (three relevant and four non-relevant). In terms of classification, they are wrong with respect to the class of a single instance, which implies that the same classification error is present for both functions. However, contrary to h_2, h_1 gives a higher score to a non-relevant instance than to relevant instances. Thus, the two functions induce identical classification errors but different ranking errors.

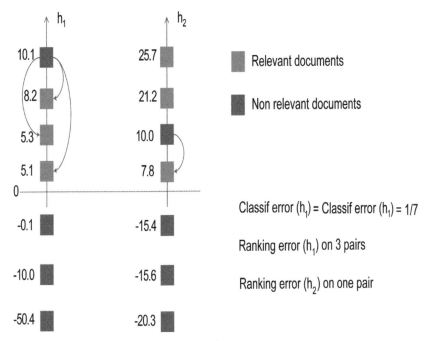

Figure 2.3. *Toy samples illustrating the difference between the classification error and the ranking error*

The example thus illustrates the weak correlation between the classification error and ranking error. From a theoretical point of view, the work of [COR 03] highlights these differences while the preference judgments are binary. The authors consider a given set of instances as well as all the possible orders for this set with a fixed classification error. They thus show that the average of the ranking error is an increasing function with respect to the classification error. This illustrates the overall link between these two errors. However, it also shows that the variance can be important for unstable bases. Thus, an identical ranking error can lead to very different classification errors.

We can also note the work of [CAR 04, CAR 08], which empirically shows the difference between the errors based on prediction (classification, regression) and those that measure the agreement between a predicted order and a desired order. The results are based on a performance analysis of thousands of models learnt on several different bases.

However, it must be noted that these conclusions are based on a comparison of error functions and not on model performance. Thus, in certain cases, the method ADABOOST and its analog in ranking, RANKBOOST, return identical solutions [RUD 05]. Furthermore, the results in [CAR 04] show that algorithms of the SVM type obtain good performances for ranking tasks. The analysis presented in [CAR 08] shows that the adaptations of linear SVM for ranking obtain significantly better results than for linear SVM used to minimize the classification error for medium-sized bases.

2.1.1.5. *Other criteria*

In information filtering research, there exists a range of performance measures for the evaluation of systems. There are, for example, ranking measures which focus on the instances placed at the top of the list. These measures are generally used in search engines. For Internet applications, the users also have a tendency to look at the first given link.

The optimization of these methods is hard but has recently been the subject of many works. The first is those of [MET 05], but the results seem to be unrealistic. The work of [JOA 05] and [TEO 07] must be examined to find new learning approaches for the direct optimization of these methods.

2.1.1.6. *Special cases: bipartite ranking*

Bipartite ranking is a special case since the preference judgments are binary, in other words $\mathcal{Y} = \{-1, 1\}$. The learning base is similar to that used in classification. We recall that the two tasks are fundamentally different in their objectives. In this case, the ranking can be summarized by ranking the positive instances above the negatives instances, which reintroduces a partial order in these samples.

Bipartite ranking thus represents the most simple form of instance ranking. But, it allows the treatment of existing applications such as information routing [IYE 00]. Its similarity with the classification has generated interest from people and has been the subject of a number of theoretical studies [AGA 05a, AGA 05b, AGA 05c, USU 05a, USU 05b].

2.1.1.6.1. Area under the ROC curve and ranking

The ROC (Receiver Operating Characteristic) curve [FAW 03] was introduced for the first time in the signal analysis of radars. It is now often used in statistical learning for model selection.

This curve allows the visualization of the evolution rate of the false-relevant instances in relation to the rates of the true relevant instances. For a score function $h(x)$, the relevance of an example can be estimated by comparing its score to a threshold b. The classifier obtained thus has the form $f(x) = \text{sign}\,(h(x) + b)$. For a given sample:

$$TP = \frac{\text{well classified relevant instances}}{\text{total relevant instances}}$$

$$FP = \frac{\text{Bad classified unrelevant instances}}{\text{total non-relevant instances}}$$

The curve is obtained by varying threshold b. Figure 2.4 illustrates two ROC curves: the dashed curve represents a random decision and the solid line is an example of a curve obtained by a deterministic score function.

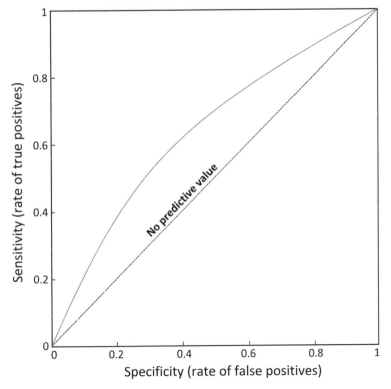

Figure 2.4. *ROC curve example*

A common method for summarizing this information is to estimate the area under the ROC curve, known as AUC. It can be shown that its value ranges from 0 to 1 and that for a random score function (green curve), its value is 0.5. A realistic score function should therefore have an AUC above 0.5.

From a statistical point of view, the AUC has an important property: it is equivalent to the probability that a score function ranks a randomly chosen relevant instance above a randomly chosen negative instance. This is equivalent to the Wilcoxon test on the ranks. In terms of learning a ranking function for the bipartite case, it is important to note that the classification error of critical pairs is equal to $1 - AUC$. The minimization of the error on crucial pairs is therefore equivalent to the optimization of the area under the ROC curve.

The aim of ranking instances is to rank entries, i.i.d. sampled, given to the system. However, the problem of learning a ranking function can be posed, where for each entry, a fixed set of elements must be ordered. This formalism, known as ranking of alternatives will be developed in the following section.

2.1.2. *Ranking of alternatives*

2.1.2.1. *Formalism*

The ranking of alternatives (also called label ranking in [HAR 02, DEK 03, AIO 04]) refers to a ranking formalism in which the entries are no longer the elements to rank. The set to rank is another predefined set, the alternatives. For each entry, order must be inferred on a subset of the alternatives.

Formally, $\mathcal{X}$ is the entry set and $\mathcal{A}$ is the set of alternatives. $x \in \mathcal{X}$ is associated with a subset of valid labels $A_x \subset A$. m_x is the number of labels in $\mathcal{A}$, the subset of A one has to order for the entry x. This set also has a $\succ_x$ order, which can be expressed as before by the following labels: $l_x = \{y_1, \ldots, y_{m_x}\}$. y_i expresses the degree of relevance of the ith label.

It is assumed that the learner has n samples with their subset of A as well as their associated tags. Theoretically, it should be the order on the the corresponding set of alternatives, but it is considered that this order is induced by the value of the tags. This training set is denoted $\mathcal{S}$. The examples are supposed to be generated in a i.i.d. fashion according to a fixed and unknown distribution on $\cup_{x \in \mathcal{X}} \{x\} \times \mathcal{Y}_x$. The main objective of the ranking of alternatives is to learn a function which, for a given sample, must find the desired order of the set of alternatives associated with it.

2.1.2.2. *Linear model for ranking of alternatives*

In this section, a linear model for the ranking of alternatives will be presented, introduced in [AIO 08] which enables the generalization of previous works in this area [HAR 02, DEK 03, AIO 04, SIN 06]. This model enables the learning of a function $h: \mathcal{X} \times \mathcal{A} \to \mathbb{R}$ which gives a score to each alternative label for a given sample. This function is very similar to the score function seen for instance ranking (see section 2.1.1.1). Ideally, it should verify the following property:

$$\forall x \in \mathcal{X}, \ \forall (a, y), (a', y') \in (A_x \times \mathcal{Y}_x)^2, \quad y \succ_x y' \Leftrightarrow h(x, a) > h(x', a')$$

2.1.2.2.1. Joint representation

In label ranking, it is rare to have, on the one hand, a representation of entry samples and on the other hand, a representation of the alternatives. The state of the art is to consider a joint representation of an entry and an alternative written as $\Psi \colon \mathcal{X} \times \mathcal{A} \to \mathbb{R}^d$, with $d \in \mathbb{N}$. The sample and the alternative can then be represented by a feature vector.

This representation is linked to the application discussed naturally. For example, in the case of document research, one usually takes as feature representation various measures of similarity between the query and the document (cosine similarity, Dice or Jacard coefficients, etc.). The Microsoft® Letor datasets (described in section 2.3) use such a representation. In this case, Ψ is written as:

$$\Psi(x, a) = [s_1(x, a), s_2(x, a), \dots, s_d(x, a)]^T$$

with s_i, a measure of similarity.

2.1.2.2.2. Learning and error functions

From the statistical learning point of view, this representation is interesting as functions can be defined by taking the joint representation as input. In the linear case, the research models are in the following format:

$$h(x, a) = w^T \psi(x, a)$$

For a fixed entry x, this function gives a score to each alternative. As for instance ranking, the scores will induce an order on $\mathcal{A}$. The learning aims to minimize an error function which measures the inadequacy between the order returned by h and the desired order. In section 2.1.1.3, several errors (or performance measures) used for quantifying this difference have been considered. They can be used again by taking the average of the available entries. L is a ranking error function of a given set. The empirical error for the ranking of alternatives, on the training set $\mathcal{S}$ of size n, is defined by:

$$R_{OA}(h, \mathcal{S}) = \frac{1}{n} \sum_{(x, l_x) \in \mathcal{S}} L\left(\{h(x, a)\}_{a \in \mathcal{A}_x}, l_x \right)$$

For example, the pair classification error can be written as:

$$R_{OA}(h, \mathcal{S}) = \frac{1}{n} \sum_{(x, l_x) \in \mathcal{S}} \left[\frac{1}{\sum_{y_x, y'_x \in l_x} [y_x > y'_x]} \sum_{y_x, y'_x \in l_x : y_x > y'_x} [h(x, y_x) \leq h(x, y'_x)] \right]$$

The generalization error is defined as before:

$$R(h) = \mathbb{E}\left[\{L(h(x, a)\}_{a \in \mathcal{A}_x}, l_x) \right] \tag{2.1}$$

2.1.2.2.3. Classification of critical pairs

With a joint representation, critical pairs can be formed and the classification of these pairs can be performed to learn the score function. It should be noted here that there is a major theoretical difference between instance ranking and ranking of alternatives. In effect, the basic *initial* learning elements of label ranking are not i.i.d. An alterntaive can intervene in several joint representations $\psi(x, a)$ and $\psi(x', a)$. In practice, the i.i.d. assumption is rarely verified and is seen here as invalid. The works of [USU 05b, USU 07] gives theoretical guarantees for datasets formed from the elements which are dependent on each other.

2.1.2.2.4. Algorithmic complexity

This approach can be extremely costly. In effect, computational complexity is the same as in instance ranking, but a large number of critical pairs may be generated.

2.1.3. *Relation to existing frameworks*

In this section, ordinal regression and the learning of preference relationships will be introduced. These two formalisms also make it possible to treat ranking but from different angles.

2.1.3.1. *Ordinal regression*

In the literature, a very similar framework to that of instance ranking is encountered: ordinal regression. In both cases, the data are labeled instances. The labels take values in a $\mathcal{Y}$ space on which there exists an overall order. Without loss of generality, let, $\mathcal{Y} = \{1, \ldots, K\}$. The objective of ordinal regression is to predict the label but in the case of an error, the predicted label must be the closest[3] possible to the true label. For example, for a label with a value of 5, it is preferable to predict 4 instead of 3.

Figure 2.5. *Ranking in the ordinal regression framework*

---

3 An overall order in effect enables the definition of a distance between the labels by the difference between the label ranks.

Ordinal regression can thus be seen as a multiclass classification with an overall order on the labels. A common approach is to learn a real-valued function as well as $K - 1$ thresholds $\theta_1, \ldots, \theta_{K-1}$ in order to determine the label. This involves the partition of the set of reals and associating a label with each partition. The prediction is thus done in two stages: a score $h(x)$ is assigned to an instance x and is then given the label associated with the partition in which the score is found.

Several classification algorithms have been expanded in this area. For example, the perceptron [CRA 01], the SVM [CHU 05b, CHU 07, SHA 02] or the Gaussian processes [CHU 05a].

When there are more than two classes, ordinal regression can thus indirectly rank the instances. It thus constitutes an alternative approach to the approach using critical pairs. However, in the binary case, ordinal regression is equivalent to the classification, whereas the approach using the critical pairs enables AUC optimization.

2.1.3.2. *Preference relationship learning*

For now, only the case where the order can be induced according to the labels has been considered. This framework enables the easy and simple expression of an order. Its similarity with classification and ranking gives it a certain advantage.

However, it does not enable the representation of a relationship which is not necessarily transitive. To do this, works have considered a binary relationship which simply indicates that one entry (or label) is preferred to another. This relationship also induces an order on the set of instances. In practice, it expresses itself over a preference graph. It is an oriented graph. A (x, x') edge means that x is preferred to x'. The training set is composed of examples and a preference graph.

The approach using the crucial pairs is thus adapted for learning. However, this approach necessitates the formation of a graph, which is more costly than simply giving the labels.

2.2. Application to automatic text summarization

In this section, we will present the application of ranking models for automatic text summarization and information retrieval. Automatic summarization consists of extracting relevant parts of a document in relation to a given subject or an underlying theme. This approach can, for example, help users to navigate and better select the documents which can interest them.

2.2.1. *Presentation of the application*

The classical systems of information retrieval return to the user an ordered list of the most relevant documents in relation to a given query. However, these documents may not be relevant and their inspection can be time-consuming. Presenting the user with document summaries may facilitate the research in the retrieved list. A summary can also help the user to categorize the documents or to answer questions.

Summaries similar to those made by a human (manual summary) are, however, difficult to carry out without prior knowledge of the content of the text [MAN 01]. There are too many writing styles, syntax structures, and so on to construct a generic summary system. An ideal system for summarization comprises the relevant information retrieved by the user and is reconstituted in a comprehensible and coherent manner, which is difficult to do without a natural language process.

To get around this problem, summarization systems extract text passages and present to the user a summary linking the passages. There are two ways to automatically summarize texts:

– the generic summary which summarizes the content in relation to the main idea of the text;

– a summary in relation to a query which summarizes the text according to the user's query.

The majority of text summarization techniques are focused on summarizing via text entity extraction. These entities may be groups of words, phrases, or sections. The summaries are thus generated by linking the base entities selected from the original document. Thus, the automatic summary is done by extraction of text entities by ranking those which convey the general ideas (those which are the most likely to be part of the summary) at the top of the list. Figure 2.6 shows the original text of Abraham Lincoln's Gettysburg Address and Figures 2.7 and 2.8 provide an example of a summary using 25% and 15% of the initial phrases in the document (examples taken from [MAN 01]).

2.2.1.1. *Summary format*

Other than the distinction between abstraction and extraction, the summaries can be of a different nature according to the objective of the application. Does the summary serve to give a simple indication of the content? Or is it a condensation of the information within the document? These questions allow us to identify the two summary types: *indicative* and *informative* summaries.

Indicative summaries allow the user to determine whether he needs to read the source material in more detail. This is, for example, the role of a film synopsis, which gives enough information to make the reader refer to it. At the other end of the spectrum, informative summaries provide a set of important information. Briefly, it is a representative but condensed version of the original text. *Abstracts* given at the beginning of scientific documents are informative summaries.

In the literature, a third type of summary has been added to the previous two: the *critical* summary. It includes advice, judgment, or commentary from the summary

Four score and seven years ago our fathers brought forth on this continent a new nation, conceived in liberty and dedicated to the proposition that all men are created equally. Now we are engaged in a great civil war, testing whether that nation or any nation so conceived and so dedicated can long endure. We are met on a great battlefield of that war. We have come to dedicate a portion of that field as a final resting-place for those who here gave their lives that nation might live. It is altogether fitting and proper that we should do this. But, in a larger sense, we cannot dedicate, we cannot consecrate, and we cannot hallow this ground. The brave men, living and dead who struggled here have consecrated it far above our poor power to add and detract. The world will little note nor long remember what we say here, but it can never forget what they did here. It is for us the living rather to be dedicated here to the unfinished work which they who fought here have thus far so nobly advanced. It is rather for us to be here dedicated to the great task remaining before us – that from these honored dead we take increased devotion to that cause for which they gave the last full method of devotion – that we here highly resolve that these dead shall not have died in vain, that this nation under God shall have a new birth of freedom, and that government of the people, by the people, for the people shall not perish from the earth.

Figure 2.6. *The Gettysburg Address, transcription of the speech by A. Lincoln, 19th November 1863*

Four score and seven years ago our fathers brought forth upon this continent a new nation, conceived in liberty, and dedicated to the proposition that all men are created equal. Now we are engaged in a great civil war, testing whether that nation, or any nation so conceived and so dedicated, can long endure. The brave men, living and dead, who struggled here, have consecrated it far above our poor to add or detract.

Figure 2.7. *Example of an automatic summary of the Gettysburg Address using 25% of the text*

Four score and seven years ago our fathers brought forth on this continent a new nation, conceived in liberty, and dedicated to the proposition that all men are created equal. Now we are engaged great civil war, testing nation, nation conceived dedicated, long endure. We are met great battlefield war.

Figure 2.8. *Example of an automatic summary of the Gettysburg Address using 15% of the text*

writer. An example is provided in Figure 2.9. Film reviews or the views of the committee members for the acceptance of scientific documents are other examples of this.

> The Gettysburg address, though short, is one of the greatest American speeches. Its ending words are especially powerful – "that government of the people, by the people, for the people, will not perish from the earth".

Figure 2.9. *Example of a critical summary of the Gettysburg Address*

2.2.2. *Automatic summary and learning*

In practice, the extraction focuses on several heuristics which can be grouped in seven large classes [GOL 99]. For example, if a passage contains words in the title then it is likely to be part of the summary. Also for example, it is considered that if a passage contains key words such as *in summary*, *in conclusion* or on the contrary words such as *for example*, *perhaps* and so on that passage is also likely to be in the summary. In practice, each heuristic translates through a score: the higher it is, the more the heuristic gives importance to the passage so it can be in the summary.

The aim is to be able to combine[4] them together to obtain a good selection criteria. The early works manually searched for the best way to do this [GOL 99]. Thereafter, learning was used to automate the procedure. In this case, the system provides a set of documents as well as their summaries. Each passage is represented by a vector (by using for example the heuristic scores or an altogether different characteristic) and forms a learning-based sample. Its label simply indicates if the passage is part of the summary or not. The classical approach is to then learn a classifier by estimating the probability of it belonging to the summary [KUP 95, AMI 01]. The results of a classifier is then used to select the passages to be used for the summary.

Summarizing a new document thus consists of finding the vectorial representation of each passage, estimating their probability of belonging to the summary, and ranking them according to the criteria. Finally, the document is then summarized by a factor k corresponding to the proportion of relevant passages. In the literature, k is defined as the compression rate.

The use of a classifier for the automatic summarization is justified by the fact that a zero classification error implies a correct order of the phrases. In effect, the scores allocated to the relevant phrases by the classifier are all larger than the constant c (c corresponds to the opposite of the classifier bias). The non-relevant phrase scores are smaller than c.

---

4 The works are generally interested in linear combinations.

In practice, the classification error is never zero. In this case, a badly classed non-relevant phrase is considered. Its score s is thus greater than the previous constant c. But it is unknown if a well-classed relevant phrase has a score smaller than s and how many relevant phrases are in the same situation. The classification error does not provide enough information to predict the order, induced by the classifier score, of the phrases of an identical document. Optimizing the classification error therefore does not optimize the relevant phrase ranks in relation to the non-relevant phrases of an identical document.

Recently, works of [AMI 05, AMI 07] were interested in learning a direct score function in the label ranking framework, where the entries represent the documents and the labels represent the different passages. These works showed evidence of the advantages of ranking in relation to classification for this task.

2.3. Application to information retrieval

In this section we will discuss the application of learning to rank to information retrieval, more specifically, search engine applications on a corpus of textual documents. The problem of document search is the archetype of a task of ranking alternatives from a query entered by the user; a ranked list of documents is presented to the user. Because of the economic importance of search engines, this application has become an specific subdomain of machine learning.

In the following section, the problem of document scoring according to a user query will be presented. The associated learning task will be discussed, as well as its specificities in relation to the general framework described in section 2.1. Then, the benefit of learning the ranking function for search engines will be shown on experiments carried out on the Letor corpus [LIU 07].

2.3.1. *Application presentation*

The problem of document search is well known: from a user query (for example, a group of keywords), the system sends a ranked list of documents issued from a predefined corpus. The presentation order of the documents must reflect their relevance with respect to the information need expressed by the query.

The order of appearance of the documents is a crucial point for the search engine, since a user is interested only in the first documents returned for his query. According to the general principle of document retrieval (see for example [BAE 99]), this order is given by a matching function which gives a score for each document according to the query. The resulting problem is to define a score function which positions the relevant documents of the query at the beginning of the results list.

To answer this problem, the information retrieval community has developed a certain number of heuristic functions, whose principles can be fitted into three categories:

– The similarity heuristic between the key words of the query and the words appearing in the document: it aims to give higher scores to the documents which contain words from the query, while accounting for the importance of a word for the research, and eventually, the document size. It is in this category that the most common matching functions are to be found (query, document), such as *tf.idf*, Okapi BM25, or even language models. The reader can refer to [BAE 99] or [MAN 08] for a more detailed description on heuristics.

– The heuristics using the document structure or meta information: they refine the previous heuristics by restricting certain particularly informative parts of the document in the search, such as the title. The INEX initiative (*Initiative for the Evaluation of XML Retrieval*[5]) aims to intensively study this type of heuristic in information retrieval for XML corpora. These heuristics are very useful for the Web, where the HTML tags enable the supply of relevant meta information, such as the document title.

– The heuristics using the corpus structure, for example, the hypertext links between documents. The PageRank [PAG 98] and HITS [KLE 99] algorithms are some of the most common examples. These methods use the principle that the values (for the search) of a Web page are linked to the number of entry links (in other words, the number of hypertext links, on other Web pages, which link to the original Web page) and output links.

These heuristic matching functions are therefore numerous (for example, the recent versions of the Letor corpus [LIU 07] have 65 different heuristics) and complement each other: each of the three categories is based on the information which is not used by the other categories. Therefore, it is natural that we want to combine them in order to use all of the available information. The traditional approach for search engines is to establish an overall matching function, by manually applying an importance to each heuristic. However, with the number of increasing criteria to account for, this approach has become difficult to apply. It is for this reason that the information retrieval community has begun to interest itself in ranking function learning techniques.

2.3.2. *Search engines and learning*

We describe now the learning of the overall matching function of a search engine in the framework of the ranking of alternatives described in section 2.1.2.2. The overall score function can be written as $h(x, a)$, where instance x is the user query, and alternative a corresponds to a document (according to the defined framework, the

---

5 http://www.inex.otago.ac.nz/

task is to rank a set of documents according to the user query). Learning the score function requires learning a linear model, in other words $h(x, a) = w^T \Psi(x, a)$, where w is the weight vector, and:

$$\Psi(x, a) = [s_1(x, a), s_2(x, a), \ldots, s_d(x, a)]^T$$

where each $s_i(x, a)$ is the score given by the ith heuristic function, among which some are described in the previous section.

The application to search engines brings a certain number of specific problems. In the following sections, the two most important will be described: the building of a training set, and the selection of the cost function optimized by the learning algorithms.

2.3.2.1. *Constitution of a learning base*

A training set is comprised of a set S, containing n entries, with their sets of alternatives and associated relevance judgments. In our case, this means that for each query x, there is a set m_x of documents A_x, with their associated relevance judgments $l_x = (y_1, \ldots, y_{m_x})$.

The definition of this training set poses two difficulties in information retrieval. On the one hand, it is impossible to learn to rank the set of documents of the entire collection (which contain thousands and thousands of pages, as on the Web). The set of valid alternatives A_x must therefore be defined for each query x, in such a way as to reduce as far as possible the number of documents considered during the learning while conserving the high recall rates. The second difficulty is to obtain the relevance judgments. In fact, the number of documents m_x preselected for query x is typically in the order of a thousand (see for example, the *benchmark* Letor). It is illusory to label several thousand documents by queries: even a "small" learning base containing hundreds of queries would require hundreds of thousands of human judgments. It is therefore necessary to have methods that use fewer human judgments per query, while conserving the feasibility of the optimized error methods.

Important biases can appear when the training set is made in an incorrect manner. In [MIN 08], the authors show that the first public version of *benchmark* Letor [LIU 07] suffered from an inherent bias at the selection stage of the document set A_x, which made the training set inadequate for real usage. A pressured experimental study was then conducted in [ASL 09], bringing to light that *pooling*[6] techniques used to create evaluation bases of TREC conference search engines permit the creation of feasible learning bases, both to select the set of documents to rank (in other words the label set A_x for query x) and to gather the relevance judgments.

---

6 Pooling is a technique which enables the building of a varied set of documents from many different models.

The creation of a learning base goes through a selection of heuristics to combine. This problem will not be dealt with here, as it relies on the selection of learning characteristics, which is not within the scope of this chapter. The reader can, however, refer to [LIU 07, GEN 07] for a view of the relevant heuristic choices according to the document collection on which the research is conducted (e.g. the Web or an encyclopedia).

2.3.2.2. *Favoring the top of the list of documents returned*

Learning ranking functions for information retrieval has another fundamental particularity: although thousands of documents per query must be ranked, only the first few documents returned by the search engine will actually be seen by the user. It is for this reason that search engines generally evaluate themselves with the average precision or *(Normalized) Discounted Cumulated Gain* ((N)DCG) (see section 2.1.1.5), which gives great importance to the first elements that are returned (e.g. the first 10) and does not depend on the total number of non-relevant documents in the ordered list.

These evaluation measures contrast with the area under the ROC (AUC) curve, which is equal to the proportion of non-relevant documents with a better rank than a relevant document taken at random. Thus, on a list of 1,000 documents, containing only two relevant documents, the AUC will be the same in both of the following cases: (1) one of the relevant documents is in the first position and the other is in the last position; (2) the two relevant documents are in the middle of the ordered list (in 500th position). For a search engine, the first list is definitely better than the second: in the first case, the user can access one of the relevant documents, whereas in the second list, the user would have access to none of the relevant documents, as he will not look that far down in the results list.

AUC is thus not an evaluation measure adapted for information retrieval. However, the learning principle based on pair classification which is strongly linked to the AUC criteria (see section 2.1.1.6) may not perform well. Recently, several authors have proposed making ranking algorithms more appropriate to search engine problems than algorithms based on pair classification such as RANKBOOST or RANKSVM. The existing approaches can be devised into three categories:

– In the first category, the algorithms optimize error functions which are differentiable approximations of IR evaluation measures. For example, in [COS 06], the authors proposed to approximate the (N)DCG in a regression framework.

– In the second category, the algorithms optimize a convex upper bound of these same evaluation methods. The work described in [LE 07, XU 08, YUE 07] uses the structural SVM formulation of [TSO 05] to optimize a convex upper bound of the average precision or the NDCG. The authors of [XU 07] proposed an alternative formulation in the form of a boosting algorithm.

– In the last category, the algorithms do not directly optimize IR evaluation methods, which are extremely sensitive to small parameter changes. The authors thus define surrogate costs which are not directly linked to an existing method, but maintain their main properties while being the most easy to optimize. In this domain, the studies of [CAO 07, XIA 08, BUR 06, USU 09] can be cited, which generally have the best practical performance.

2.3.3. *Experimental results*

The research on learning ranking functions in IR was greatly facilitated by the introduction of the Letor 3.0 corpus[7] [LIU 07], which offers a benchmark dataset on which we can compare different algorithms. In Table 2.2, the results of different learning methods, on several corpora, are shown. The results for the six corpora from TREC competitions in 2003–2004, named TD03, TD04 (*topic distillation* task), HP03, HP04 (*homepage finding* task), and NP03, NP04 (*named page finding* task) are presented. Each corpus has between 50 and 150 queries. For each query, 1,000 documents are sampled. For each document and each query, there are 65 heuristics to combine. The results given are the test errors, according to the mean average precision[8], obtained by using the experimental protocol by [LIU 07].

The results of the algorithms REGRESSION, RANKSVM [JOA 02], SVM^{map} [YUE 07] and LISTNET [CAO 07] have been reproduced from the *benchmark* Letor Website. The OWARANK values were reproduced from [USU 09]. It can be noted that all the algorithms learn linear functions. These algorithms have been chosen as representatives for their category: RANKSVM uses an approach based on pair classification, SVM^{map} is an algorithm from the second category, optimizing a convex upper bound on average precision. LISTNET and OWARANK are part of the third category, optimizing a substitution function. To illustrate the benefit of learning ranking functions, the results of two *baselines* are given: REGRESSION, learns a linear combination of heuristics by doing a linear regression on the relevance judgments, and BM25, which is the most powerful of the heuristics involved in the combination.

The results show a very significant difference between the performance of ranking learning algorithms and the BM25 heuristic or the regression models. The last one is, on average, slightly better than BM25, but is still poor on two of the six corpora. This shows that the existing regression framework is not adapted to the learning of ranking functions. Among the ranking algorithms, the best results are, averaged over the six given sets, obtained from the algorithms of the third category LISTNET and OWARANK.

---

7 Letor version 3.0, published in 2008, does not suffer from the selection bias of documents in [MIN 08].

8 The average macro-precision is the average, on the different queries, of the average precision (see section 2.1.1.5).

	TD03	TD04	HP03	HP04	NP03	NP04
BM25	0.134	0.150	0.567	0.498	0.578	0.514
REGRESSION	0.241	0.208	0.497	0.526	0.564	0.514
RANKSVM	0.263	0.224	0.741	0.668	**0.696**	0.659
SVM^{map}	0.245	0.205	0.742	0.718	0.687	0.662
LISTNET	0.275	0.223	**0.766**	0.690	0.690	0.672
OWARANK	**0.290**	**0.229**	0.757	**0.726**	0.685	**0.683**

Table 2.2. *Test performance of different algorithms on the six Letor bases. The average macro-precision is the method used. BM25 is an IR heuristic (learning free), REGRESSION uses learning, but not within the ranking framework. RANKSVM is a ranking algorithm which favors the precision of the first elements returned*

2.4. Conclusion

Ranking function learning emerged in the early 2000s, strongly pushed by the diverse problems of retrieval or access to information. This new framework extends binary classification, and linear score functions can be learnt by slightly modifying the existing classification algorithms. The new techniques developed can achieve performances which were up to now unattainable, for example in automatic summarization or documentary research.

Ranking research is, for now, mostly focused on the supervised learning framework. However, new directions in research are beginning to emerge, with very promising results. For example, new methods have studied limiting the size of labeled data required without degrading performance. Thus, new works have appeared in the semi-supervised learning framework [DUH 08, AMI 08, TRU 09], where one tries to use this information in instances where the labels are not available, or as part of active learning [AMI 06], where the algorithm itself selects the examples that it is necessary to label.

2.5. Bibliography

[AGA 05a] AGARWAL S., GRAEPEL T., HERBRICH R., HAR-PELED S., ROTH D., "Generalization bounds for the area under the ROC curve", *Journal of Machine Learning Research*, vol. 6, p. 393-425, 2005.

[AGA 05b] AGARWAL S., NIYOGI P., "Stability and generalization of bipartite ranking algorithms", *Proceedings of the Eighteenth Annual Conference on Computational Learning Theory (COLT)*, Bertinoro, Italy, June 27-30, p. 32-47, 2005.

[AGA 05c] AGARWAL S., ROTH D., "Learnability of bipartite ranking functions", *Proceedings of the Annual ACM Workshop on Computational Learning Theory (COLT)*, Bertinoro, Italy, June 27-30, p. 16-31, 2005.

[AIL 08] AILON N., MOHRI M., "An efficient reduction of ranking to classification", *21st Annual Conference on Learning Theory - COLT 2008*, Helsinki, Finland, July 9-12, p. 87-98, 2008.

[AIO 04] AIOLLI F., SPERDUTI A., "Learning preferences for multiclass problems", *Advances in Neural Information Processing Systems 17 - NIPS 2004*, Vancouver, Canada, MIT Press, 2004.

[AIO 08] AIOLLI F., SPERDUTI A., "Supervised learning as preference optimization: recent applications", in *Proceedings of the ECML/PKDD-Workshop on Preference Learning*, 2008.

[AMI 01] AMINI M.R., Apprentissage automatique et recherche de l'information: application à l'extraction d'information de surface et au résumé de texte, PhD thesis, Pierre and Marie Curie University, LIP6, July 2001.

[AMI 05] AMINI M.R., USUNIER N., GALLINARI P., "Automatic text summarization based on word-clusters and ranking algorithms", in *Proceedings of the 27th European Conference on Information Retrieval - ECIR 2005*, Spain, Springer, p.142-156, 2005.

[AMI 06] AMINI M.R., USUNIER N., LAVIOLETTE F., LACASSE A., GALLINARI P., "A selective sampling strategy for label ranking", in *Proceedings of the European Conference on Machine Learning - ECML 2006, Berlin, Germany*, p. 18-29, 2006.

[AMI 07] AMINI M.R., TOMBROS A., USUNIER N., LALMAS M., "Learning-based summarisation of XML documents", *Information Retrieval*, vol. 10, no. 3, p. 233-255, 2007.

[AMI 08] AMINI M.R., TRUONG T.V., GOUTTE C., "A boosting algorithm for learning bipartite ranking functions with partially labeled data", in *Proceedings of the 31st Annual International ACM SIGIR Conference on Research and Development in Information Retrieval - SIGIR 2008*, Singapore, ACM, p. 99-107, 2008.

[ASL 09] ASLAM J.A., KANOULAS E., PAVLU V., SAVEV S., YILMAZ E., "Document selection methodologies for efficient and effective learning-to-rank", in *SIGIR '09: Proceedings of the 32nd International ACM SIGIR Conference on Research and Development in Information Retrieval*, ACM, New York, USA, p. 468-475, 2009.

[AUE 05] AUER P., MEIR R. (eds), *Learning Theory, Proceedings of 18th Annual Conference on Learning Theory*, COLT 2005, Bertinoro, Italy, 27-30 June, 2005, vol. 3559 of *Lecture Notes in Computer Science*, Springer, 2005.

[BAE 99] BAEZA-YATES R., RIBEIRO-NETO B., *Modern Information Retrieval*, Addison Wesley, May 1999.

[BAL 08] BALCAN M.F., BANSAL N., BEYGELZIMER A., COPPERSMITH D., LANGFORD J., SORKIN G.B., "Robust reductions from ranking to classification", *Machine Learning*, vol. 72, no. 1-2, p. 139-153, 2008.

[BUR 06] BURGES C.J.C., RAGNO R., LE Q.V., "Learning to rank with nonsmooth cost functions", in *Advances in Neural Information Processing Systems 19 - NIPS 2006*, Vancouver, Canada, p. 193-200, 2006.

[CAO 07] CAO Z., QIN T., LIU T.Y., TSAI M.F., LI H., "Learning to rank: from pairwise approach to listwise approach", in *Proceedings of the 24th International Conference on Machine Learning - ICML 2007*, p. 129-136, 2007.

[CAR 04] CARUANA R., NICULESCU-MIZIL A., "Data mining in metric space: an empirical analysis of supervised learning performance criteria", *Proceedings of the Tenth ACM SIGKDD International Conference on Knowledge Discovery and Data Mining - KDD 2007*, New York, USA, p. 69-78, 2004.

[CAR 08] CARUANA R., KARAMPATZIAKIS N., YESSENALINA A., "An empirical evaluation of supervised learning in high dimensions", *Proceedings of the 25th International Conference on Machine Learning - ICML 2008*, p. 96-103, 2008.

[CHU 05a] CHU W., GHAHRAMANI Z., "Gaussian processes for ordinal regression", *Journal of Machine Learning Research*, vol. 6, p. 1019-1041, MIT Press, 2005.

[CHU 05b] CHU W., KEERTHI S.S., "New approaches to support vector ordinal regression", *Proceedings of the 22nd International Conference on Machine learning - ICML 2005*, p. 145-152, 2005.

[CHU 07] CHU W., KEERTHI S.S., "Support vector ordinal regression", *Neural Computation*, vol. 19, no. 3, p. 792-815, 2007.

[COH 97] COHEN W.W., SCHAPIRE R.E., SINGER Y., "Learning to order things", *Advances in Neural Information Processing Systems 10 - NIPS 1997*, Vancouver, Canada, 1997.

[COR 03] CORTES C., MOHRI M., "AUC optimization *versus* error rate minimization", in *Advances in Neural Information Processing Systems 16 - NIPS 2003*, Vancouver, Canada Press, 2003.

[COS 06] COSSOCK D., ZHANG T., "Subset ranking using regression", *19th Annual Conference on Learning Theory - COLT 2006*, p. 605-619, 2006.

[CRA 01] CRAMMER K., SINGER Y., "Pranking with ranking", *Advances in Neural Information Processing Systems 14 - NIPS 2001*, Vancouver, Canada, p. 641-647, 2001.

[DEK 03] DEKEL O., MANNING C.D., SINGER Y., "Log-linear models for label ranking", in *Advances in Neural Information Processing Systems 16 - NIPS 2003*, Vancouver, Canada, 2003.

[DUH 08] DUH K., KIRCHHOFF K., "Learning to rank with partially labeled data", in *Proceedings of the 31st Annual International ACM SIGIR Conference on Research and Development in Information Retrieval - SIGIR 2008*, Singapore, p. 251-258, 2008.

[FAW 03] FAWCETT T., ROC graphs: notes and practical considerations for researchers, Report, HP Laboratories, 2003.

[FRE 03] FREUND Y., IYER R., SCHAPIRE R.E., SINGER Y., "An efficient boosting algorithm for combining preferences", *Journal of Machine Learning Research*, vol. 4, p. 933-969, MIT Press, 2003.

[GEN 07] GENG X., LIU T.Y., QIN T., LI H., "Feature selection for ranking", in *SIGIR '07: Proceedings of the 30th Annual International ACM SIGIR Conference on Research and Development in Information Retrieval*, ACM, New York, USA, p. 407-414, 2007.

[GOL 99] GOLDSTEIN J., KANTROWITZ M., MITTAL V.O., CARBONELL J.G., "Summarizing text documents: sentence selection and evaluation metrics", in *Proceedings of the 22nd Annual International ACM SIGIR Conference on Research and Development in Information Retrieval*, ACM, p. 121-128, 1999.

[HAR 02] HAR-PELED S., ROTH D., ZIMAK D., Constraint classification: a new approach to multiclass classification and ranking, Report, University of Illinois at Urbana-Champaign, Champaign, IL, USA, 2002.

[HOA 62] HOARE C.A.R., "Quicksort", *The Computer Journal*, vol. 5, no. 1, p. 10-16, 1962.

[IYE 00] IYER R.D., LEWIS D.D., SCHAPIRE R.E., SINGER Y., SINGHAL A., "Boosting for document routing", in *Proceedings of the Ninth International Conference on Information and Knowledge Management CIKM 2000*, ACM, p. 70-77, 2000.

[JOA 02] JOACHIMS T., "Optimizing search engines using clickthrough data", in *Proceedings of the 5th ACM SIGKDD International Conference on Knowledge Discovery and Data Mining - KDD 2002*, New York, USA, p. 133-142, 2002.

[JOA 05] JOACHIMS T., "A support vector method for multivariate performance measures", in *Proceedings of the 22nd International Conference on Machine Learning - ICML 2005*, p. 377-384, 2005.

[KLE 99] KLEINBERG J.M., "Authoritative sources in a hyperlinked environment", *The Journal of the Association for Computing Machinery*, vol. 46, no. 5, p. 604-632, ACM, 1999.

[KUP 95] KUPIEC J., PEDERSEN J.O., CHEN F., "A trainable document summarizer", in *Proceedings of the 18th Annual International ACM SIGIR Conference on Research and Development in Information Retrieval*, p. 68-73, 1995.

[LE 07] LE Q., SMOLA A., Direct optimization of ranking measures, ArXiv, April 2007.

[LIU 07] LIU T.Y., XU J., QIN T., XIONG W., LI H., "LETOR: benchmark dataset for research on learning to rank for information retrieval", in *LR4IR 2007, in conjunction with SIGIR 2007*, 2007.

[MAN 01] MANI I., *Automatic Summarization (Natural Language Processing, 3 (Paper))*, John Benjamins Publishing Co., June 2001.

[MAN 08] MANNING C.D., RAGHAVAN P., SCHTZE H., *Introduction to Information Retrieval*, Cambridge University Press, New York, USA, 2008.

[MET 05] METZLER D.A., CROFT W.B., MCCALLUM A., Direct maximization of rank-based metrics for information retrieval, Report, CIIR, 2005.

[MIN 08] MINKA T., ROBERTSON S., "Selection bias in the LETOR datasets", in *LR4IR 2008, in conjunction with SIGIR 2008*, 2008.

[PAG 98] PAGE L., BRIN S., MOTWANI R., WINOGRAD T., The pagerank citation ranking: bringing order to the web, Technical Report, Stanford InfoLab, 1999.

[PAI 93] PAICE C.D., JONES P.A., "The identification of important concepts in highly structured technical papers", in *Proceedings of the 16th Annual International ACM SIGIR Conference on Research and Development in Information Retrieval - SIGIR 1993*, p. 69-78, 1993.

[RAE 05] RAEDT L.D., WROBEL S. (eds), *Machine Learning, Proceedings of the 22nd International Conference (ICML 2005), Bonn, Allemagne, 7-11 August, 2005*, vol. 119 of *ACM International Conference Proceeding Series*, ACM, 2005.

[RUD 05] RUDIN C., CORTES C., MOHRI M., SCHAPIRE R.E., "Margin-based ranking meets boosting in the middle", in *18th Annual Conference on Learning Theory - COLT 2005*, p. 63-78, 2005.

[SHA 02] SHASHUA A., LEVIN A., "Ranking with large margin principle: two approaches", in *Advances in Neural Information Processing Systems 15 - NIPS 2002*, Vancouver, Canada, p. 937-944, 2002.

[SIN 06] SINGER Y., BENNETT P., PARRADO-HERNÁNDEZ E., "Efficient learning of label ranking by soft projections onto polyhedra", *Journal of Machine Learning Research*, 2006.

[TEO 07] TEO C.H., SMOLA A.J., VISHWANATHAN S.V.N., LE Q.V., "A scalable modular convex solver for regularized risk minimization", in *Proceedings of the Tenth ACM SIGKDD International Conference on Knowledge Discovery and Data Mining – KDD 2007*, New York, USA, p. 727-736, 2007.

[THR 04] THRUN S., SAUL L.K., SCHÖLKOPF B. (eds), *Advances in Neural Information Processing Systems 16 [Neural Information Processing Systems, NIPS 2003*, 8-13 December, 2003, Vancouver and Whistler, British Columbia, Canada, MIT Press, 2004.

[TRU 09] TRUONG N.T.V., Apprentissage de fonctions d'ordonnancement avec peu d'exemples étiquetés: une application au routage d'information, au résumé de textes et au filtrage collaboratif, PhD thesis, Pierre and Marie Curie University - Paris VI, 2009.

[TSO 05] TSOCHANTARIDIS I., JOACHIMS T., HOFMANN T., ALTUN Y., "Large margin methods for structured and interdependent output variables", *Journal of Machine Learning Research*, vol. 6, p. 1453-1484, MIT Press, 2005.

[USU 05a] USUNIER N., AMINI M.R., GALLINARI P., "A data–dependent generalisation error bound for the AUC", in *ICML '05 workshop on ROC Analysis in Machine Learning*, 2005.

[USU 05b] USUNIER N., TRUONG V., AMINI M.-R., GALLINARI P., "Ranking with unlabeled data: a first study", in *NIPS '05 Workshop on Learning to Rank (NIPS '05-LR)*, Whistler, Canada, p. 4, December 2005.

[USU 07] USUNIER N., Apprentissage de fonctions d'ordonnancement: une étude théorique de la réduction à la classification et deux applications à la Recherche d'Information, PhD thesis, Pierre and Marie Curie University - Paris VI, 2007.

[USU 09] USUNIER N., BUFFONI D., GALLINARI P., "Ranking with ordered weighted pairwise classification", in *ICML '09: Proceedings of the 26th Annual International Conference on Machine Learning*, New York, USA, ACM, p. 1057-1064, 2009.

[XIA 08] XIA F., LIU T.Y., WANG J., ZHANG W., LI H., "Listwise approach to learning to rank: theory and algorithm", in *Proceedings of the 25th International Conference on Machine Learning - ICML 2008*, p. 1192-1199, 2008.

[XU 07] XU J., LI H., "AdaRank: a boosting algorithm for information retrieval", in *Proceedings of the 30th Annual International ACM SIGIR Conference on Research and Development in Information Retrieval - SIGIR 2007*, p. 391-398, 2007.

[XU 08] XU J., LIU T.Y., LU M., LI H., MA W.Y., "Directly optimizing evaluation measures in learning to rank", in *Proceedings of the 31th Annual International ACM SIGIR Conference on Research and Development in Information Retrieval - SIGIR 2008*, p. 107-114, 2008.

[YUE 07] YUE Y., FINLEY T., RADLINSKI F., JOACHIMS T., "A support vector method for optimizing average precision", in *Proceedings of the 30th Annual International ACM SIGIR Conference on Research and Development in Information Retrieval - SIGIR 2007*, p. 271-278, 2007.

PART 2

Classification and Clustering

Chapter 3

Logistic Regression and Text Classification

3.1. Introduction

Machine learning has been the focus of many studies in recent years. Given an unknown source generating data of which only one sample is available, learning is the induction process aiming at modeling the source from the avilable sample. The model can then be used to generate new data and reason about it. This setting occurs in many situations. For example, the information about a client, the source, is often only partially available through a questionnaire; the behavior of a system is observed through a set of physical measurements captured by sensors. The generating source is sometimes modeled by an expert the more complex the source, the more difficult and error-prone the modeling task. Machine learning is in this case an elegant solution which automatizes the work of the expert with the capacity to process large volumes of data.

Supervised learning is a branch of machine learning which is characterized by the fact that the data generated by the source is comprised of so-called independent data x and dependent data y which is correlated with the independent data and constitutes the "annotation", hence the name "supervised". Both independent and dependent data are observed in the available sample. In many cases, the independent data x takes on real values and can be represented as a vector. This particular setting is often referred to as statistical learning and is one of the most active branches of machine learning

Chapter written by Sujeevan ASEERVATHAM, Eric GAUSSIER, Anestis ANTONIADIS, Michel BURLET and Yves DENNEULIN.

because of the fact that it is based on solid statistical theories [VAP 95] and that its field of application includes decision-making. The problem of decision-making consists of taking a decision that is characterized by the dependent data as a function of an observation (independent data). This problem requires only a partial model of the source, in order to know the generation of the decision as a function of the observation.

One of the most well-known problems of textual information access is text classification, where documents x have to be assigned one or more categories y. This problem can be addressed through supervised learning by representing the documents in a numerical vector form. The studies presented in [JOA 98, JOA 02] have shown that supervised learning for text classification by large margin separators, and more particularly Support Vector Machines (SVM) [VAP 95] with a simple vector, representation can provide excellent performances. These studies have largely directed research in text classification toward SVMs. However, logistic regression, which fits in the generalized linear models framework, has begun to interest researchers, particularly in the area of large scale text classification when the number of categories, documents and features is large. Indeed, the works of [ZHA 01] and recently of [GEN 07] have demonstrated that the use of logistic regression associated with a LASSO penalty [TIB 94, EFR 04] provides models with good performance and is applicable to large volumes of data.

The objective of this chapter is to present generalized linear models (GLM) and logistic regression. Generalized linear models, which provide "strong" supervised learning tools, were introduced for the first time in [NEL 72] and discussed in [HAS 90, MCC 89, DOB 02]. Different types of model selection which can be associated with generalized linear models in order to improve their performance will be discussed, before illustrating the behavior of logistic regression on the task of text classification.

The rest of the chapter is organized in the following manner: section 3.2 provides the general statistical framework in which generalized linear models are defined. Parameter estimation of these models is given in section 3.3. The logistic regression model is presented in section 3.4. Section 3.5 introduces the notion of model selection by presenting the main methods used with generalized linear models. Section 3.6 illustrates an application of logistic regression for text classification; this section supplies, among other things, experimental results on well known collections. Section 3.7 concludes this chapter.

3.2. Generalized linear model

The generalized linear model seeks to explain the conditional expectation of a random variable (or a vector of random variables) Y with a function of the linear combination of the values observed in the random vector X. In the following, a simple definition of the exponential family is given which then serves to characterize the generalized linear model and the logistic regression models that are used for text classification, or more generally for the classification of text elements such as sections, sentences, or groups of words.

DEFINITION 3.1. – *An exponential family with simple parameters[1] is a set of probability distributions the density of which takes the following form:*

$$f(y; \theta) = B(y) \exp(C(\theta)T(y) - A(\theta)) \qquad [3.1]$$

with B, C, T, and A functions specific to the distribution. When $T(y) = y$, the exponential probability density function $f(y; \theta)$ is said to be on canonical form[2].

The majority of commonly used distributions can be written in a canonical exponential form, and even in a more restricted form, known as *natural (exponential) form*, which can be characterized by the fact that $C(\theta) = \theta$. The natural form is thus written as:

$$f(y; \theta) = B(y) \exp(y\theta - A(\theta))$$

Probability density functions in the exponential family with a natural form have three important properties:

1) $\frac{\partial}{\partial \theta} \int_y f(y; \theta) dy = \int_y \frac{\partial}{\partial \theta} f(y; \theta) dy = 0$
2) $\mathbb{E}(Y; \theta) = A'(\theta)$
3) $\text{Var}(Y; \theta) = A''(\theta)$

with A' (respectively, A'') the first (respectively, second) derivative with respect to θ.

Proof. Property 1 can be deduced from the fact that a probability density verifies $\int_y f(y; \theta) dy = 1$. Property 2 is obtained as follows:

$$\frac{\partial}{\partial \theta} f(y; \theta) = [y - A'(\theta)] f(y; \theta)$$

$$\Rightarrow \int \frac{\partial}{\partial \theta} f(y; \theta) dy = \int [y - A'(\theta)] f(y; \theta) dy$$

$$= \mathbb{E}(Y; \theta) - A'(\theta) = 0$$

Property 3 is proven in the same way by considering $\frac{\partial^2}{\partial \theta} f(y; \theta)$. $\quad\square$

---

1 The extension to the case where θ is a vector is direct and is not presented here. We refer interested readers to [DOB 02].

2 The definition of the canonical form of an exponential probability density function varies from one author to another. We use here the definition from [DOB 02].

We can now introduce generalized linear models, which are characterized by the following three elements:

1) a dependent random variable Y associated with a distribution function $f(y; \theta)$ which belongs to the exponential family;

2) a linear predictor of the form: $\eta = \beta^T x$;

3) a link function g such that $\mathbb{E}(Y|X) = \mu = g^{-1}(\eta) = g^{-1}(\beta^T x)$.

The linear predictor η captures, in a linear combination, the information contained in the independent variables, information which is integrated into the model through the link function g which relates the linear predictor to the expectation of the conditional distribution. The use of different link functions leads to different models, the simplest one, associated with linear regression, being founded on the identity function. The choice of the link function is generally dictated by the values the conditional expectation can take. If this expectation takes its values in the interval of $[0; 1]$, for example, then a link function with values within this interval should be chosen.

In practice, one observes values of the variables X and Y from which β can be estimated, so as to be able to compute the conditional expectation of Y for new values of X. X and Y thus play a central role for the determination of β. In the case of the natural exponential family, there exists a canonical link function g such that $\theta = \eta = g(\mu)$ (g thus corresponds to $(A')^{-1}$). The canonical link function ensures that $X^T Y$ is a sufficient statistic for β, in other words no other statistics derived from the observed sample will bring additional information on the values of β, a property which directly derives from the Fisher-Neyman factorization theorem (see [SCH 95], p. 89). Indeed, in this case: $f(y; x, \theta) = B(y) \exp(x^T y \beta - A(x^T \beta))$. The second term of the right-hand side of the equation depends on y only through $x^T y$, and is thus a sufficient statistic for β (we recall here that the x vector is known, and the random variable is y). The approach which estimates β from values taken by X and Y from a sample thus takes all its meaning. The currently used Gaussian (or linear), Poisson, and logistic regressions fit within this framework. Table 3.1 presents a summary of the main generalized linear models.

In this chapter, we assume that the probability distributions under study can be written under a natural exponential form, even if certain results may expand to the canonical exponential form. We thus have the following characteristics for these distributions, which will be exploited in the remainder of this chapter:

1) $f(y; \theta) = B(y) \exp(y\theta - A(\theta))$

2) $\theta = \beta^T x$

3) $\mathbb{E}(Y|X) = g^{-1}(\theta) = A'(\theta)$

4) $\mathrm{Var}(Y|X) = A''(\theta)$

Name	Distribution	Link	Model
Linear regression	normal	$g(\mu) = \mu$	$\mathbb{E}(Y\|X) = \beta\boldsymbol{x}$
Poisson regression	Poisson	$g(\mu) = \log(\mu)$	$\mathbb{E}(Y\|X) = \exp(\beta\boldsymbol{x})$
Logistic regression	binomial/multinomial	$g(\mu) = \log(\frac{\mu}{1-\mu})$	$\mathbb{E}(Y\|X) = \frac{1}{1+\exp(-\beta\boldsymbol{x})}$

Table 3.1. *The three principle generalized linear models*

3.3. Parameter estimation

For an exponential probability density distribution, the parameter vector β of the model is determined by maximizing the likelihood of the model on a learning sample $\{(x^{(1)}, y^{(1)}), \ldots, (x^{(n)}, y^{(n)})\}$. This likelihood is given by:

$$h_\beta = \prod_{i=1}^{n} f(y^{(i)}; \theta^{(i)})$$

The logarithmic function strictly increasing, maximizing the likelihood is equivalent to maximizing the "log-likelihood" which is defined as:

$$l(h_\beta) = \sum_{i=1}^{n} y^{(i)}\theta^{(i)} - A(\theta^{(i)}) + \log(B(y^{(i)})) \qquad [3.2]$$

Maximizing $l(h_\beta)$ is equivalent to minimizing $-l(h_\beta)$, and the problem amounts to determining a minimum, in general local, of this function. There are several methods to determine the local minimum of a function. For historical reasons, we first present here the IRLS method, before mentioning other ones which can be used to accelerate the estimation of β. In IRLS, the local minimum β^* is obtained by using an iterative Newton-Raphson type approach in an Iteratively Reweighted Least Square method [DOB 02], the idea being to estimate a first solution for $\beta^{(t)}$ and to improve this solution in its neighborhood. For this, the method uses a first order Taylor expansion in the neighborhood of $\nabla l(h_{\beta^{(t)}})$:

$$\nabla l(h_{\beta^{(t+1)}}) \approx \nabla l(h_{\beta^{(t)}}) + (\beta^{(t+1)} - \beta^{(t)})H(\beta^{(t)}) \qquad [3.3]$$

where $H(\beta^{(t)})$ represents the Hessian of $l(h_{\beta^{(t)}})$. One then looks for $\beta^{(t+1)}$ local minimum of $l(h)_\beta$, i.e. which satisfies $\nabla l(h_{\beta^{(t+1)}}) = 0$. The update rule to approach the local minimum β^* is thus[3]:

$$\beta^{(t+1)} = \beta^{(t)} - H(\beta^{(t)})^{-1}\nabla l(h_{\beta^{(t)}}) \qquad [3.4]$$

---

[3] The opposite of the Hessian $-H(\beta^{(t)})$ can be replaced by the Fisher information matrix: $I(\beta^{(t)}) = -\mathbb{E}(H(\beta^{(t)}))$. One then obtains Fisher's update method [DOB 02].

For each coordinate β_j of β, the partial derivative of $l(h_\beta)$ with respect to β_j is:

$$\frac{\partial l(h_\beta)}{\partial \beta_j} = \frac{\partial}{\partial \theta^{(i)}} \left(\sum_{i=1}^{n} y^{(i)} \theta^{(i)} - A(\theta^{(i)}) \right) \frac{\partial \theta^{(i)}}{\partial \beta_j}$$

$$= \sum_{i=1}^{n} (y^{(i)} - g^{-1}(\beta^T x^{(i)})) x_j^{(i)}$$

[3.5]

The Hessian of $l(h_\beta)$ is then given by:

$$H_{j,k}(\beta) = \frac{\partial}{\partial \beta_k} \frac{\partial l(h_\beta)}{\partial \beta_j} = -\sum_{i=1}^{n} x_j^{(i)} x_k^{(i)} (g^{-1})'(\beta^T x^{(i)})$$

By defining the diagonal matrix $W_{n \times n}$ such that:

$$W_{ii} = (g^{-1})'(\beta^T x^{(i)})$$

[3.6]

the following matrix notation is obtained:

$$H(\beta) = -XWX^T$$

where each column i of X, $1 \leq i \leq n$, corresponds to an observation vector $x^{(i)}$. Furthermore, setting:

$$z_i = \frac{(y^{(i)} - g^{-1}(\beta^T x^{(i)}))}{W_{ii}}$$

[3.7]

the gradient of equation [3.5] becomes, in matrix notation:

$$\nabla l(h_\beta) = XWz$$

This enables rewriting the parameter vector β from equation [3.4] at iteration $(t+1)$ as:

$$\beta^{(t+1)} = \beta^{(t)} + (XW^{(t)}X^T)^{-1}XW^{(t)}z^{(t)}$$

$$= (XW^{(t)}X^T)^{-1}[(XW^{(t)}X^T)\beta^{(t)} + XW^{(t)}z^{(t)}]$$

$$= (XW^{(t)}X^T)^{-1}(XW^{(t)})[X^T\beta^{(t)} + z^{(t)}]$$

$$= (XW^{(t)}X^T)^{-1}XW^{(t)}z^{*(t)}$$

[3.8]

where $z^{*(t)} = X^T\beta^{(t)} + z^{(t)}$.

Equation [3.8] is the solution to a weighted least square problem with a weight matrix W, hence the name IRLS given to this method. The different steps of IRLS are described in Algorithm 3.1. The algorithm stops when the vector β converges or when a sufficient number of iterations has been performed. Convergence here can be defined by using the notion of statistical deviance. The deviance is defined as the difference of the log-likelihoods of the current model and that of an ideal saturated model, the latter being a complete model for which each observation is associated with a parameter which allows a maximum likelihood such that $\mathbb{E}(Y^{(i)}|X) = y^{(i)}$. Thus, for the family of exponential distributions, the deviance is defined by:

$$D(y, \hat{\theta}) = -2 \left(\log \prod_{i=1}^{n} f(y^{(i)}|x^{(i)}; \hat{\theta}^{(i)}) - \log \prod_{i=1}^{n} f(y^{(i)}|x^{(i)}; \widetilde{\theta}^{(i)}) \right)$$

$$= -2 \sum_{i=1}^{n} \left[y^{(i)}(\hat{\theta}^{(i)} - \widetilde{\theta}^{(i)}) - (A(\hat{\theta}^{(i)}) - A(\widetilde{\theta}^{(i)})) \right]$$

[3.9]

with $\hat{\theta}$ and $\widetilde{\theta}$ being the parameters of the current model and ideal saturated models, respectively. Furthermore, $\widetilde{\theta}^{(i)} = g(y^{(i)})$, where g is the link function of the model.

Algorithm 3.1. IRLS algorithm

---

    iter $\leftarrow$ 0;
    devOld $\leftarrow$ 0;
    devNew $\leftarrow$ 1;
    Initialize β with random variables;
    for *(ABS(devNew $-$ devOld) $> \epsilon$ **and** iter $<$ iterMax)* **do**
        Update the weighting matrix W with equation [3.6];
        Calculate z with equation [3.7];
        $z^* \leftarrow X^T\beta + z$;
        Update β with equation [3.8];
        devOld $\leftarrow$ devNew;
        $\widehat{\theta} \leftarrow \beta^T X$;
        devNew $\leftarrow$ D($y, \widehat{\theta}$) (equation [3.9]);
        iter $\leftarrow$ iter + 1;
    end

The IRLS method enables the efficient induction of a solution β from a learning sample in a few iterations. However, the calculation that uses the matrices can very rapidly become expensive in memory terms and calculation time when the number of dimensions and/or the number of individuals ($x^{(i)}$) are high. To address this problem, several methods have been proposed [ZHA 01, MIN 03, FRI 08, GEN 07], including the Cyclic Coordinate Descent method. This method updates the β vector in an iterative way, following [3.4]. During each iteration, a cycle is made on each coordinate of β, each β_j being optimized with the help of equation [3.4] while keeping the other coordinates constant.

$$\beta_j^{(t+1)} = \beta_j^{(t)} - \left(\frac{\partial^2 l(h_{\beta^{(t)}})}{\partial \beta_j^2}\right)^{-1} \frac{\partial l(h_{\beta^{(t)}})}{\partial \beta_j} \tag{3.10}$$

It is worth noting that neither IRLS nor the cyclic coordinate descent method guarantee convergence. Indeed, to guarantee convergence, the update step induced by the relationship between the gradient and the Hessian in equations [3.4] and [3.10] must be controlled in order to satisfy Wolfe conditions [NOC 99]. This can be done by using a *line search* method or the Newton confidence region method [SHI 05].

3.4. Logistic regression

An interesting special case of generalized linear models is obtained when the dependent variable Y takes only two values 0 and 1. Thus:

$$\mathbb{E}(Y|X) = P(Y = 1|X)$$

This model can therefore be directly used to predict the category (0 or 1) of an example in a binary categorization framework (and by extension in a multi-class framework).

When the conditional law of Y can only have two values, it is natural to assume that it follows a Bernoulli law with parameter μ, $Ber(\mu)$ (this law is equivalent to a binomial law $Bin(1, \mu)$, which explains that the standard logistic regression is often presented as being associated with the binomial distribution). It is easy to see that the Bernoulli law belongs to the exponential family. Indeed:

$$Ber(y; \mu) = \mu^y(1 - \mu)^{1-y} = \exp\left[y \log\left(\frac{\mu}{1 - \mu}\right) + \log(1 - \mu)\right]$$

By setting $\theta = \log(\frac{\mu}{1-\mu})$, one obtains:

$$f(y; \theta) = \exp\left[y\theta - \overbrace{\log(1 + \exp(\theta))}^{A(\theta)}\right] \tag{3.11}$$

This last form corresponds to a natural exponential form. The associated canonical link function is defined by:

$$\theta = g(\mu) = \log\left(\frac{\mu}{1 - \mu}\right); \; \mu = g^{-1}(\eta) = \frac{1}{1 + \exp(-\eta)}$$

The model finally obtained is defined as follows:

$$\mathbb{E}(Y|X) = P(Y = 1|X) = \frac{1}{1 + \exp(-\beta^T x)}$$

Many authors consider that Y can take on values -1 and $+1$ (instead of 0 and 1). In this case, $P(Y = y|X)$ can be written in the following simplified form:

$$P(Y = y|X) = \frac{1}{1 + \exp(-y\beta^T x)}$$

The log-likelihood is then defined by:

$$l(h_\beta) = \sum_{i=1}^{n} -\ln(1 + \exp(-y^{(i)}\beta^T x^{(i)}))$$

Once the parameter vector β has been learned, this model can be used directly to create a binary categorization. In addition, the same model can equally be used (and is in practice) for multiclass problems by using a *1-against-all* approach, for example. An extension of this model based on the multinomial distribution has however been proposed, and it is this extension we want to review now.

3.4.1. *Multinomial logistic regression*

A categorization problem often involves several categories. In this case, instead of considering that the conditional law of the random variable Y is binomial, a multinomial law, $Mult(1, \mu_1, \ldots, \mu_C)$, can be used. The realizations y of Y are now vectors with C coordinates, of which only one is non-null and is equal to 1. With these assumptions, we have:

$$P(Y = y; \mu) = f_M(y; \mu) = \prod_{i=1}^{C} \mu_i^{y_i}$$

subject to the constraint: $\sum_{i=1}^{C} \mu_i = 1$.

By defining $\mu_C = 1 - \sum_{i=1}^{C-1} \mu_i$, one has:

$$P(Y = y; \mu) = \mu_C^{(1 - \sum_{j=1}^{C-1} y_j)} \prod_{i=1}^{C-1} \mu_i^{y_i}$$

Writing this equation in an exponential form, one obtains:

$$f_M(y; \mu) = \exp\left[\sum_{i=1}^{C-1} y_i \log(\mu_i) + (1 - \sum_{j=1}^{C-1} y_j)\log(\mu_C) \right]$$

$$= \exp\left[\sum_{i=1}^{C-1} y_i \log(\frac{\mu_i}{\mu_C}) + \log(\mu_C) \right]$$

which shows that this distribution belongs to the exponential family and admits a natural form (the definition of the exponential family previously given must be extended here in order to account for the fact that random vectors are now being manipulated, but this extension is direct). We furthermore have:

$$\forall i, \ 1 \leq i \leq C, \ \mathbb{E}(Y_i = 1|X) = \mu_i = P(Y_i = 1|X) = g^{-1}(\eta_i) = g^{-1}(\theta_i)$$

The link function g, now defined with $\mathbb{R}^C$ and with values in $\mathbb{R}^C$, has the following form:

$$\begin{cases} g(\ldots, \mu_i, \ldots) = (\ldots, \log \frac{\mu_i}{\mu_C}, \ldots)^T \\ g^{-1}(\ldots, \eta_i, \ldots) = (\ldots, \frac{\exp(\eta_i)}{1 + \sum_{j=1}^{C-1} \exp(\eta_j)}, \ldots)^T \end{cases} \quad [3.12]$$

which finally leads to the following multinomial logistic regression:

$$\begin{cases} \mathbb{E}(Y_i|X) = \frac{\exp(\beta_i \cdot x)}{1 + \sum_{j=1}^{C-1} \exp(\beta_j \cdot x)} & \text{for } 1 \leq i \leq C - 1 \\ \mathbb{E}(Y_C|X) = \frac{1}{1 + \sum_{j=1}^{C-1} \exp(\beta_j \cdot x)} \end{cases} \quad [3.13]$$

The optimal solution β_j^* can be obtained by the IRLS method or the other methods previously mentioned. In practice, in text classification, there does not seem to be much difference between the two versions of the logistic regression, and many authors rely on the standard binomial form.

3.5. Model selection

The problem with the maximization of the log-likelihood $l(h_\beta)$ (equation [3.2]), used to learn the vector parameter β, is sometimes ill-posed. A well-posed problem is characterized by three properties: 1) existence of a solution, 2) uniqueness, and 3) stability of this solution. The problem of optimizing generalized linear models violates two of these propoerties:

1) the function $-l(h_\beta)$ is not strictly convex; the property concerning the uniqueness of the solution is therefore not guaranteed;

2) the calculation of the inverse of the Hessian (equations [3.4] and [3.7]) leads to an instability of the solutions which can be important in the presence of strongly correlated variables (the determinant of the matrix to be inversed being close to 0).

These problems can be corrected by resorting to model selection methods. We present, in what follows, two selection methods commonly used with the logistic regression (Ridge and LASSO regressions), before introducing another method which combines them.

3.5.1. *Ridge regularization*

Ridge regularization[4] leads to an optimization problem well adapted for logistic regression [HOE 70, TIK 77, CES 92]. This method introduces a strictly convex regularization term $\lambda\|\beta\|^2$, with a positive real hyperparameter λ which defines the importance of the penalization. Ridge regularization therefore maximizes the log-likelihood while minimizing the regularization term. The new problem is written as:

$$\beta^* = \underset{\beta}{\text{argmin}} \; -l(h_\beta) + \lambda\|\beta\|_2^2 \qquad [3.14]$$

The function $-l(h_\beta) + \lambda\|\beta\|_2^2$ is strictly convex as soon as the function A of the underlying density is convex[5]. From a probabilistic point of view, the Ridge regularization amounts to considering that the parameter vector β follows a normal law $\mathcal{N}(\mathbf{0}, \frac{1}{2\lambda})$ $(\forall i, j \neq i, \text{cov}(\beta_i, \beta_j) = 0)$. The minimization problem above corresponds to the maximization of the likelihood:

$$h_\beta = \left[\prod_{i=1}^{n} f(y^{(i)}|x^{(i)}; \theta^{(i)})\right] P(\beta; \lambda)$$

$$= \left[\prod_{i=1}^{n} f(y^{(i)}|x^{(i)}; \theta^{(i)})\right] - \left(\frac{2\lambda}{2\pi}\right)^{\frac{d}{2}} \exp(-\lambda\|\beta\|_2^2)$$

d being the dimension of β. The maximization of the logarithm of this likelihood (or minimization of the opposite of its logarithm) yields equation [3.14]. As mentioned above, this new optimization problem is strictly convex, which guarantees the uniqueness of the solution. Furthermore, the Hessians of equations [3.4] and [3.7] integrate new terms, $2\lambda I$ and $-2\lambda I$, respectively. The instability of the solution can thus be controlled by giving a sufficiently large value to λ.

3.5.2. *LASSO regularization*

Even if the Ridge regularization leads to a well-posed problem, it has the enormous disadvantage of having a dense solution β, meaning that the solution vector has very few nil coordinates. The use of such a solution, particularly in high dimensions, can lead to a large computation time. In order to obtain a *sparse* solution, in other words having numerous nil coordinates, the LASSO regularization (*Least Absolute Shrinkage*

---

4 Also known as Ridge penalization.

5 This function is given in equation [3.11]. Its convexity, as a function of β, can be directly verified from the Hessian matrix. It is not done here for space reasons, and we refer interested readers to the references already given.

and Selection Operator) was proposed [TIB 94, EFR 04]. It differs from the Ridge regularization through the use of the norm L_1. The new problem becomes:

$$\beta^* = \underset{\beta}{\text{argmin}} -l(h_\beta) + \lambda\|\beta\|_1 \tag{3.15}$$

As for the Ridge regularization, a probability interpretation is possible based on Laplace law, $\text{Lap}(\mathbf{0}, \frac{1}{\lambda})$:

$$P(\beta; \lambda) = \left(\frac{\lambda}{2}\right)^m \exp(-\lambda\|\beta\|_1) \tag{3.16}$$

The LASSO regularization not only controls the norm β by attributing a probability that is more important for β in the $\mathbf{0}$ neighborhood, just as with Ridge regularization, but also by performing a selection of variables resulting in a sparse solution [TIB 94]. Indeed, the Laplace distribution gives a high probability to the coordinates of β being equal to zero. Figure 3.1 illustrates the behavior of the Gaussian and Laplace distributions.

However, the LASSO regularization does not lead to a strictly convex problem, and consequently, does not guarantee the uniqueness of the solution. In fact, the strict convexity of the regularized problem depends on the strict convexity of the regularization used. As the Lasso regularization is not strictly convex, the regularized problem is not strictly convex either.

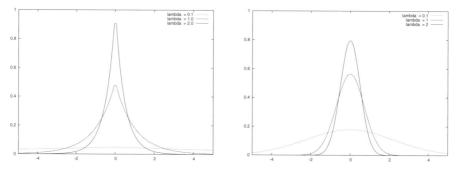

Figure 3.1. *a) Laplace distribution $lap(\mathbf{0}, \frac{1}{\lambda})$ and b) Normal distribution $\mathcal{N}(\mathbf{0}, \frac{1}{2\lambda})$*

3.5.3. *Selected Ridge regularization*

The use of LASSO regularization is well adapted to high dimensional problems as, its solution being sparse, it will lead to a reasonable execution time (contrary to the Ridge). However, the performance (in terms of accuracy) of the LASSO solution is not as good as that of the Ridge solution in two cases [TIB 94, EFR 04, ZOU 05]:

1) when the number of dimensions m is greater than the number n of observations x_i (see the experimental section at the end of this chapter);

2) when the attributes are strongly correlated; in this case the LASSO selects only one attribute among the group of correlated attributes.

In the majority of large-scale problems, the number of dimensions is often higher than the number of available observations, as in text classification for example. Furthermore, in text problems, the attributes are strongly correlated. Thus, in such cases, the Ridge regression will provide more accurate results, at the price however of a longer computation time. To solve this problem, the *Selected Ridge* method was proposed in [ASE 09, ASE 11]. The objective of this method is to make a selection of variables on the Ridge solution by using the LASSO regularization, while guaranteeing the sparse LASSO solution will stay in the neighborhood of the Ridge solution. The method was proposed in [ASE 09, ASE 11] for large-scale categorization problems addressed with the logistic regression. It can, therefore, be generalized to generalized linear models. *The Selected Ridge* method starts by solving the Ridge problem formalized by equation [3.14], the Ridge solution being noted β^*. One then looks for a solution $\hat{\beta}$ verifying the following two properties:

1) $\hat{\beta}$ must reside in the neighborhood of β^*;

2) $\hat{\beta}$ must be a sparse solution.

The first property is ensured by using a second order Taylor expansion of the objective function $l_R(h_\beta)$ of equation [3.14]:

$$l_R(h_\beta) = -l(h_\beta) + \lambda\|\beta\|_2^2 \qquad [3.17]$$

This expansion leads to:

$$l_R(h_\beta) \simeq l_R(h_{\beta^*}) + (\beta - \beta^*)^T \nabla l_R(h_{\beta^*}) + \frac{1}{2}(\beta - \beta^*)^T H_{l_R}(h_{\beta^*})(\beta - \beta^*) \quad [3.18]$$

with $\nabla l_R(h_{\beta^*})$ and $H_{l_R}(h_{\beta^*})$ being the gradient and the Hessian of $l_R(h_\beta)$ at point β^*, respectively. It is important to note that as β^* is a solution to the minimization problem of equation [3.17], $\nabla l_R(h_{\beta^*})$ is null. Thus, the solutions are obtained by minimizing the third term of equation [3.18]. To account for the constraint imposed by the second property cited above, a LASSO regularization term is added. Consequently, the solution of the *Selected Ridge* is given by:

$$\hat{\beta} = \underset{\beta}{\operatorname{argmin}}(\beta - \beta^*)^T H_{l_R}(h_{\beta^*})(\beta - \beta^*) + \alpha\|\beta\|_1 \qquad [3.19]$$

where α is a hyperparameter which controls the degree of "sparsity" of the solution $\hat{\beta}$. In order to limit the number of hyperparameters, the authors proposed, in [ASE 09, ASE 11], to automatically fix α with the following formula:

$$\alpha = \sqrt{\frac{2\log(m)}{m}} \qquad [3.20]$$

m being the dimension of $\hat{\beta}$. Furthermore, inasmuch as the traditional "bag of words" representation used for texts relies on the assumption of independence between words, it is natural to use only the diagonal of the Hessian in equation [3.19], which simplifies the calculations. The solution in this case for each $\hat{\beta}_i$ is:

$$\hat{\beta}_i = \begin{cases} \beta_i^* - \dfrac{\alpha}{2H_{l_{R_{ii}}}(h_{\beta^*})} & \text{if } \beta_i^* > \dfrac{\alpha}{2H_{l_{R_{ii}}}(h_{\beta^*})} \\ \beta_i^* + \dfrac{\alpha}{2H_{l_{R_{ii}}}(h_{\beta^*})} & \text{if } \beta_i^* < -\dfrac{\alpha}{2H_{l_{R_{ii}}}(h_{\beta^*})} \\ 0 & \text{if not} \end{cases} \qquad [3.21]$$

for all $H_{l_{R_{ii}}}(h_{\beta^*}) \neq 0$ ($\hat{\beta}_i = 0$ in the opposite case).

Fisher information provides an interesting interpretation of the previous development. The empirical Fisher information matrix $\hat{I}(\beta^*)$ is such that: $H_i(\beta^*) = \hat{I}_{i,i}(\beta^*) + 2\lambda$. Inasmuch as Fisher information summarizes the quantity of information provided by the data on the estimation of β, equation [3.21] amounts to setting to 0 the coordinates of β which have low values and for which the data brings little information. This result is interesting since it shows that it is not sufficient to cancel all the low values of the Ridge solution to obtain a good sparse solution. If a value is low but strongly corroborated by the data ($\hat{I}_{i,i}(\beta^*)$ high), it should be kept.

3.6. Logistic regression applied to text classification

3.6.1. Problem statement

Text classification is the problem of assigning one or more labels representing one or more categories to a text document [SEB 99, SEB 02]. More formally, the problem amounts to building a function $f: \mathcal{X} \rightarrow \mathcal{Y}$ which can assign a label $y_i \in \mathcal{Y}$ to a document $x_i \in \mathcal{X}$. To do so, a hypothesis space, where the appropriate function should be selected, is first chosen. If, for example, the family of functions $f_{\vec{\alpha}}$ with parameters $\vec{\alpha}$ is chosen, then the hypothesis space is defined by $\mathcal{F} = \{f_{\vec{\alpha}}: \vec{\alpha} \in \mathcal{A}\}$, namely the space of all the possible functions for different values of $\vec{\alpha}$. The solution function $f_{\vec{\alpha}^*} \in \mathcal{F}$, characterized by $\vec{\alpha}^*$, is searched for in this hypothesis space. Text classification is a supervised learning task aiming at selecting the best function (in other words learning the optimal parameter vector $\vec{\alpha}^*$) on a training sample, through an induction criterion. A training sample consists of a set of text documents together with their category, generally manually assigned. The most commonly used induction criteria are the minimization of the empirical risk, equivalent in several cases to the maximization of the likelihood (generally regularized), and the minimization of the structural risk [VAP 95]. In text classification, categories can usually be represented by a finite set of integers. Thus, in the framework of generalized linear models, the most reasonable assumption is to consider that the random variable associated with categories follows a binomial or multinomial distribution. The generalized linear model that is the most adapted to text classification is thus the logistic regression with the maximum likelihood induction criterion. Recent studies have shown that the logistic regression applied to text classification gives comparable, or even better, results to the ones obtained by other methods such large margin separators [JOA 98, ZHA 01, GEN 07, ASE 09].

3.6.2. *Data pre-processing*

The use of logistic regression requires text documents to be pre-processed to obtain a vector representation. Pre-processing has a considerable impact on the performance of the method. Consequently, special attention must be paid to it [ASE 08]. Figure 3.2 shows the main steps of standard pre-processing methods for texts. The first step represents the document in a vector form. The representation commonly used is the vector space model [SAL 75]. This representation is also known as the "bag of words" representation. It relies on the use of words in a dictionary which induces a vector space in which each dimension corresponds to a word in the dictionary. This dictionary is often constructed from terms appearing in the training corpus. In this model, a text document is segmented into words and is represented by a vector x, where each x_i coordinate represents the number of occurrences of term i from the dictionary in the text document considered. This representation leads to sparse vectors with large dimensions. Indeed, the number of dimensions of the space is equal to the size of the dictionary, which is often large for natural language documents. The "sparsity" of the vectors is due to the fact that a document contains a small number of words.

The second pre-processing step consists in filtering out all the words that are considered to be noise for classification purposes. In natural language, under the vector space model, elements such as punctuation signs and empty words such as auxiliaries and connective words can be eliminated as they do not bring any valuable information to the categorization task. Furthermore, numeric symbols are often eliminated. In addition, statistical methods such as information gain can be used to eliminate less relevant terms [YAN 97, SEB 99, SEB 02]. Such methods quantify the degree of correlation between a term and the categories, the terms with little correlation being finally filtered out.

The third and last step consists in weighting terms according to their discrimination power [ASE 09]. The most widely used weighting method in the context of text classification is undoubtedly TF-IDF (*Term Frequency - Inverse Document Frequency*) [JON 72, JOA 97]. Given a text collection $\mathcal{C}$, the TF-IDF weight of a term t_i in a document d is given by the following equation:

$$\text{TF-IDF}(t_i, d, \mathcal{C}) = \text{tf}(t_i, d) \log \left(\frac{|\{d'|d' \in \mathcal{C}\}|}{|\{d'|t_i \in d', d' \in \mathcal{C}\}|} \right) \qquad [3.22]$$

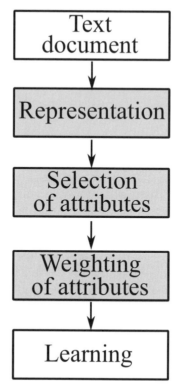

Figure 3.2. *The different pre-treatment stages of a document for learning*

where $\text{tf}(t_i, d)$ is the occurrence frequency of term t_i in d. $\|$ represents the cardinal of the set. The TF-IDF is made of two terms, where each term makes a modeling assumption. The first term, TF, expresses the assumption that a term which appears several times is better adapted for describing the content of a document than a term that appears only few times in the document. The second term, IDF, assumes that a term which appears in numerous documents of the collection provides less discriminating information than a term appearing in fewer documents. In addition to this weighting, the document vectors can also be normalized by their norm.

3.6.3. *Experimental results*

Logistic regression has been evaluated on a set of three "classical" corpora and one large corpus introduced more recently for the evaluation of large-scale category systems [KOS 10]. The first three corpora are Reuters-21578, Ohsumed, and 20-NewsGroups [HER 94, JOA 98, JOA 02]. All these corpora have been studied in depth in the text classification literature. The last corpus is a subset of documents extracted from the

DMOZ Website[6]. This DMOZ corpus was collected in order to evaluate how systems behave when the number of categories, features, and documents was increased. The characteristics of the corpora are indicated in Table 3.2.

Name	#app. obs. (n)	#test obs.	#attributes (m)	#categories	Cas
Reuters-21578	7770	3019	6760	90	$\frac{m}{n} \approx 1$
Ohsumed	6286	7643	20520	23	$\frac{m}{n} \approx 3$
20-NewsGroups	12492	6246	51666	20	$\frac{m}{n} \approx 4$
DMOZ	20249	7257	133348	3503	$\frac{m}{n} \approx 6$

Table 3.2. *The corpora used for the experiments. The number of observations (n) for the training and test sets, as well as the dimension of the space (m) are indicated*

All the data sets have been pre-processed following the steps indicated in the previous section and detailed in [JOA 02]:

1) segmentation of each document into a list of words using non-Latin characters as separators;

2) cleaning phase in which all non-Latin characters, numeric symbols, and punctuation symbols are removed;

3) stop-word removal;

4) stemming: each term in the list is reduced to its stem by using the Porter *stemming* algorithm [POR 80];

5) weighting with TF-IDF;

6) normalization of the document vector.

For collections in which a document may be assigned to more than one category, we used, for simplicity reasons, the binomial logistic regression with the "1-vs-the-rest" strategy, instead of the multinomial logistic regression. To assign a document to a unique category in monolabel problems, the decision function max was used:

$$\underset{c}{\mathrm{argmax}}\, P(y_i = +1|\beta_c, x_i) \qquad [3.23]$$

In the case of multilabel problems, all the c verifying: $P(y_i = +1|\beta_c, x_i) \geq 0.5$ are assigned to document x_i.

In our experiments, we use the F_1 score [RIJ 79] to evaluate the performance of classifiers. For a binary classification problem with a positive and a negative class, it is defined as:

$$F_1 = \frac{2 \times \mathrm{TP}}{2 \times \mathrm{TP} + \mathrm{FP} + \mathrm{FN}} \qquad [3.24]$$

6 http://www.dmoz.org.

where TP represents the number of well-classified positive documents (true positives), FP is the number of negative documents assigned to the positive class (false positives), and FN is the number of positive documents assigned to the negative class (false negatives). For corpora with more than two categories, micro-F_1 and macro-F_1 are used. Micro-F_1 is defined as:

$$\text{micro-}F_1 = \frac{2 \times \sum_{c=1}^{C} \text{TP}_c}{\sum_{c=1}^{C} 2 \times \text{TP}_c + \text{FP}_c + \text{FN}_c} \qquad [3.25]$$

with C the number of categories, TP_c the number of true positives for category c, FP_c and FN_c being similarly defined. Macro-F_1 is the average arithmetic of F_{1_c} for each category c:

$$\text{macro-}F_1 = \frac{1}{C} \sum_{c=1}^{C} F_{1_c} \qquad [3.26]$$

The micro-F_1 gives an identical weight to each document, thereby favoring the categories that contain numerous documents, whereas the macro-F_1 gives an identical weight to each category, without accounting for the category size. The "sparsity" degree is also calculated for each model. "Sparsity" is defined as:

$$1 - \frac{m_{\text{avg}}}{m} \qquad [3.27]$$

where m is the space dimension (the number of features in the corpus) and m_{avg} is the average number of features used by the model. Thus, a model using all the features of the corpus will have a degree of "sparsity" equal to 0.

Furthermore, it is important to note that the regularization hyperparameter was fixed, for each algorithm, through cross-validation, except for the DMOZ corpus, for which the hyperparameter was optimized on a validation set comprising 7,256 documents. For the *Selected Ridge* method the α hyperparameter from equation [3.19] was automatically set with equation [3.20].

To solve the optimization problems of the Ridge and LASSO logistic regression, the algorithm described in [GEN 07] was used. This algorithm is more efficient than the IRLS method with text data, as the document vectors are sparse, i.e. most of their coordinates are null. The training and prediction time reported in the result tables are indicative. Since the computation has been distributed over a network of computers, the time given is the sum of the computation time on each node of the network and the time used by the system (network time, task management, etc.).

3.6.3.1. *Experiment on Reuters-21587*

Reuters-21587 is a collection of news articles in which each document has been manually assigned to one or several categories according to its topic. For this collection, a subset of documents known as "ModApte" was used and is composed of a training and test set. The results of this experiment are reported in Table 3.3. The LASSO and Ridge models roughly achieve the same level of performance. However, the Ridge solution is dense, whereas the LASSO one uses only 0.0043% of the original features. The feature selection method used on the Ridge model (*Selected Ridge* regression method) achieves the same performance as the Ridge in terms of micro-$F1$, but with only 5% of the features of the Ridge.

Algorithm	Micro-F_1	Macro-F_1	Sparsity	App. time (sec)	Prediction time (sec)
LASSO	0.8711	0.5167	0.9957	164.07	0.44
Ridge	0.8690	0.5099	0.0	257.96	13.20
Selected Ridge	0.8645	0.4563	0.9447	180.24	1.55

Table 3.3. *Results of the categorization on the Reuters-21587 base (ModApte)*

3.6.3.2. *Ohsumed experiment*

The Ohsumed corpus [HER 94] is a subset of the MEDLINE database which contains bibliographic data from the field of medicine. Each document is a reference from a medical article published in a medical review. Following the experiments reported in [JOA 98, JOA 02], only the first 20,000 references, with a summary published in 1991, have been retained. This set has been split into a training set composed of 10,000 documents and a test set composed of the other 10,000 documents. Only the "summary" part of the documents is used for the categorization task. After pre-processing, the training set is reduced to 6,286 unique documents and the test set to 7,643 documents. Each document belongs to one or more cardio-vascular categories. As reported in Table 3.4, the LASSO method works well with this base. Indeed, it not only provides the best performance in terms of micro- and macro-F_1, but does so with very few features. The *Selected Ridge* method slightly increases the performance, in terms of micro-F_1, of the Ridge method while eliminating 88% of its features.

3.6.3.3. *20-Newsgroups experiment*

20-Newsgroups is a collection of emails extracted from Usenet discussion groups. Each email is assigned to a unique category according to the subject of the discussion. The 20-Newsgroups experiment, the results of which are shown in Table 3.5, clearly shows that the Ridge regularization is better than the LASSO method here. For this corpus, the variable selection done by LASSO is too aggressive and eliminates interesting attributes. However, the *Selected Ridge* method achieves micro- and macro-F_1 values comparable to those obtained by the Ridge method while using only 10% of the features of the Ridge. The feature selection done by this method is thus more accurate.

Algorithm	Micro-F_1	Macro-F_1	Sparsity	App. time (sec)	Prediction time (sec)
LASSO	0.6533	0.6053	0.9800	81.16	1.83
Ridge	0.6387	0.5897	0.0	144.06	31.20
Selected Ridge	0.6409	0.5802	0.8827	107.08	5.32

Table 3.4. *Results of the categorization on Ohsumed*

Algorithm	Micro-F_1	Macro-F_1	Sparsity	App. time (sec)	Prediction time (sec)
LASSO	0.8663	0.8644	0.9861	384.16	1.72
Ridge	0.9038	0.9018	0.0	157.96	71.25
Selected Ridge	0.8966	0.8939	0.9050	136.01	7.51

Table 3.5. *Results of the categorization on 20-Newsgroups*

3.6.3.4. *DMOZ experiments*

In order to evaluate the behavior of the different methods in a large-scale categorization framework, 34,762 HTML documents (Web pages) were collected from the DMOZ Website (www.dmoz.org). DMOZ (*Mozilla Directory*) is an open source project the objective of which is to classify all Web pages into categories. For the collected corpus, the number of categories was limited to 3,503 and the corpus was divided into three parts: a training set composed of 20,249 documents, a validation set composed of 7,256 documents, and a test set with 7,257 documents. The validation set is used to optimize the hyperparameters. During the pre-processing phase, HTML tags were removed to conserve only the text and the standard pre-processing steps described above were then applied. As expected in case where the number of features is way larger than the number of documents, the Ridge method is clearly better than the LASSO one, as indicated by Table 3.6. However, the Ridge solution is dense which makes it inappropriate for categorization in large-scale category systems (a time consuming process). Both the LASSO and *Selected Ridge* methods produce a sparse solution with a "sparsity" of 99%. The *Selected Ridge* method is better than the LASSO method in terms of micro-F_1, but has a macro-F_1 with a slightly lower performance than that obtained by LASSO.

Algorithm	Micro-F_1	Macro-F_1	Sparsity	App. time (sec)	Prediction time (sec)
LASSO	0.2936	0.1661	0.9999	9805.78	41.51
Ridge	0.3434	0.2020	0.0	13299.40	31084.90
Selected Ridge	0.3124	0.1586	0.9993	10996.80	42.52

Table 3.6. *Results of the categorization on DMOZ*

Regularization (α)	Micro-F_1	Macro-F_1	Sparsity	App. time (sec)	Prediction time (sec)
1	0.1188	0.0353	0.9999	11103.9	8.33
0.1	0.2604	0.1209	0.9999	11065.8	32.81
0.05	0.2835	0.1343	0.9998	11325.1	39.82
0.03	0.2953	0.1436	0.9997	11013.4	39.34
0.02	0.3040	0.1524	0.9996	11164.6	49.07
0.0133	**0.3124**	**0.1586**	**0.9993**	**10996.8**	**42.52**
0.01	0.3156	0.1604	0.9992	10965.5	52.97
10^{-7}	0.3434	0.1949	0.5423	11090.2	8858.31
0	0.3434	0.2020	0.0	13299.40	31084.90

Table 3.7. *The performance of the Selected Ridge method on DMOZ as a function of the penalty value α of equation [3.19]. The results corresponding to the optimal value given by equation [3.20] are written in bold*

Table 3.7 shows the performance of the *Selected Ridge* method as a function of the values of α, the penalty hyperparameter L_1 in equation [3.19]. The results show that the standard value given by equation [3.20] (in bold in the table) is a good penalty value in terms of trade-off between the micro-F_1 performance and the degree of "sparsity". It is also interesting to note that with α fixed to 10^{-7}, *Selected Ridge* obtains practically the same results as those obtained by the Ridge method, which are otherwise the best in terms of micro- and macro-F_1, while using only half of the features and being four times faster.

3.7. Conclusion

In this chapter, generalized linear models have been presented which relate, via a link function, the expectation of a variable to predict to a linear combination of the observed data. These models are based on the assumption that the variable to predict follows an exponential distribution law. Thus, each model differentiates itself from the others through the distribution adopted, and therefore the link function stemming from it. Furthermore, the variable to predict can be of different nature, numerical with a real value, categorical, or even binary. The choice of the exponential distribution and the link function thus depends on the problem addressed.

We also presented logistic regression in the context of text classification. The experiments reported here on standard text collections show that regularized logistic regression provides a good level of performance, and yields a true probability of classification. This probability can be used in later processings or for interpretation purposes. Furthermore, by using regularization methods which perform some form of variable selection, such as LASSO or *Selected Ridge*, the logistic regression models obtained are sparse models, which require little computation time and can thus be applied in large-scale category settings.

3.8. Bibliography

[ASE 08] ASEERVATHAM S., *Apprentissage à base de Noyaux Sémantiques pour le Traitement de Données Textuelles*, Edilivre - Collection Universitaire, Paris, France, 2008.

[ASE 09] ASEERVATHAM S., ANTONIADIS A., GAUSSIER E., BURLET M., DENNEULIN Y., A model selection method to improve the ridge logistic regression for large-scale text categorization, Report, LIG, University Joseph Fourier, Grenoble, 2009.

[ASE 11] ASEERVATHAM S., ANTONIADIS A., GAUSSIER E., BURLET M., DENNEULIN Y., "A sparse version of the ridge logistic regression for large-scale text categorization", *Pattern Recognition Letters*, vol. 32, p. 101-106, 2011.

[CES 92] LE CESSIE S., VAN HOUWELINGEN J.C., "Ridge estimators in logistic regression", *Applied Statistics*, vol. 41, no. 1, p. 191-201, 1992.

[DOB 02] DOBSON A.J., *An Introduction to Generalized Linear Models*, 2nd ed., Chapman & Hall/CRC, Boca Raton, 2002.

[EFR 04] EFRON B., HASTIE T., JOHNSTONE L., TIBSHIRANI R., "Least angle regression", *Annals of Statistics*, vol. 32, p. 407-499, 2004.

[FRI 08] FRIEDMAN J., HASTIE T., TIBSHIRANI R., Regularization paths for generalized linear models via coordinate escent, Report, Department of Statistics, Stanford University, 2008.

[GEN 07] GENKIN A., LEWIS D.D., MADIGAN D., "Large-scale bayesian logistic regression for text categorization", *Technometrics*, vol. 49, no. 14, p. 291-304, August 2007.

[HAS 90] HASTIE T.J., TIBSHIRANI R.J., *Generalized Additive Models*, Chapman & Hall, London, United Kingdom, 1990.

[HER 94] HERSH W., BUCKLEY C., LEONE T.J., HICKAM D., "OHSUMED: an interactive retrieval evaluation and new large test collection for research", in *SIGIR '94: Proceedings of the 17th Annual International ACM SIGIR Conference on Research and Development in Information Retrieval*, Springer-Verlag, New York, Inc., New York, USA, p. 192-201, 1994.

[HOE 70] HOERL A.E., KENNARD R.W., "Ridge regression: biased estimation for non-orthogonal problems", *Technometrics*, vol. 12, p. 55-67, 1970.

[JOA 97] JOACHIMS T., "A probabilistic analysis of the Rocchio algorithm with TFIDF for text categorization", in *ICML '97: Proceedings of the Fourteenth International Conference on Machine Learning*, Morgan Kaufmann Publishers Inc., San Francisco, CA, USA, p. 143-151, 1997.

[JOA 98] JOACHIMS T., "Text categorization with support vector machines: learning with many relevant features", in *Proceedings of the ECML-98, 10th European Conference on Machine Learning*, Springer Verlag, Heidelberg, DE, p. 137-142, 1998.

[JOA 02] JOACHIMS T., *Learning to Classify Text Using Support Vector Machines: Methods, Theory and Algorithms*, Kluwer Academic Publishers, Norwell, MA, USA, 2002.

[JON 72] JONES K.S., "A statistical interpretation of term specificity and its application in retrieval", *Journal of Documentation*, vol. 28, p. 11-21, 1972.

[KOS 10] KOSMOPOULOS A., GAUSSIER E., PALIOURAS G., ASEERVATHAM S., "The ECIR 2010 large scale hierarchical classification workshop", *SIGIR Forum*, vol. 44, no. 1, p. 23-32, 2010.

[MCC 89] MCCULLAGH P., NELDER J.A., *Generalized Linear Models*, Chapman & Hall, London, UK, 1989.

[MIN 03] MINKA T.P., A Comparison of Numerical Optimizers for Logistic Regression, Report, Department of Statistics, Carnegie Mellon University, 2003.

[NEL 72] NELDER J.A., WEDDERBURN R.W.M., "Generalized linear models", *Journal of the Royal Statistical Society, Series A, General*, vol. 135, p. 370-384, 1972.

[NOC 99] NOCEDAL J., WRIGHT S.J., *Numerical Optimization*, Springer Verlag, New York, USA, 1999.

[POR 80] PORTER M.F., "An algorithm for suffix stripping", *Program*, vol. 14, no. 3, p. 130-137, July 1980.

[RIJ 79] VAN RIJSBERGEN C.J., *Information Retrieval*, Butterworths, London, UK, vol. 2, 1979.

[SAL 75] SALTON G., WONG A., YANG C.S., "A vector space model for automatic indexing", *Communications of the ACM*, vol. 18, no. 11, p. 613-620, ACM Press, 1975.

[SCH 95] SCHERVISH M.J., *Theory of Statistics*, Springer-Verlag, New York, USA, 1995.

[SEB 99] SEBASTIANI F., "A tutorial on automated text categorisation", in *Proceedings of the 1st Argentinian Symposium on Artificial Intelligence (ASAI '99)*, Buenos Aires, AR, p. 7-35, 1999.

[SEB 02] SEBASTIANI F., "Machine learning in automated text categorization", *ACM Computing Surveys*, vol. 34, no. 1, p. 1-47, 2002.

[SHI 05] SHI Z.J., ZHANG X.S., "From line search method to trust region method", *Lecture Notes in Operations Research*, vol. 5, p. 156-170, 2005.

[TIB 94] TIBSHIRANI R., "Regression shrinkage and selection via the Lasso", *Journal of the Royal Statistical Society, Series B*, vol. 58, p. 267-288, 1994.

[TIK 77] TIKHONOV A.N., ARSENIN V.Y., *Solution of Ill-Posed Problems*, V.H. Winston Sons, Washington D.C., 1977.

[VAP 95] VAPNIK V.N., *The Nature of Statistical Learning Theory*, Springer-Verlag, New York, Inc., 1995.

[YAN 97] YANG Y., PEDERSEN J.O., "A comparative study on feature selection in text categorization", in FISHER D.H. (ed.), *Proceedings of ICML-97, 14th International Conference on Machine Learning*, Morgan Kaufmann Publishers, Nashville, San Francisco, p. 412-420, 1997.

[ZHA 01] ZHANG T., OLES F.J., "Text categorization based on regularized linear classification methods", *Information Retrieval*, vol. 4, p. 5-31, 2001.

[ZOU 05] ZOU H., HASTIE T., "Regularization and variable selection via the elastic net", *Journal of the Royal Statistical Society, Series B*, vol. 67, no. 2, p. 301-320, 2005.

Chapter 4

Kernel Methods for Textual Information Access

4.1. Kernel methods: context and intuitions

It is striking to note that, in the communities using statistical modeling and machine learning, in the past 50 years there has been a pendulum motion between approaches using rigor and simplicity on the one hand, and more experimental approaches on the other, which aim at investigating other areas and at exceeding the limitations of a too rigid framework, in particular the framework of linear models. In the last 20 years, things have gone from using more or less heuristic methods, with a huge flexibility but sometimes badly handled (in particular, in the structure and number of parameters of the underlying models), to much more "controlled", statistically and mathematically principled methods, where the flexibility and quality of the generalization of the models are controlled as far as possible. A flagrant example of a very popular method during this period is the artificial neural network [PER 03], whose modeling power seemed to be almost unlimited and, it must be admitted, gave rise to numerous abuses and excesses, through lack of theoretical foundations or, more simply, through an inability on the part of the modeler to introduce effective means to control the generalization capacities of such systems and to avoid "overfitting".

Motivated in part by these excesses and the disillusionment resulting from them, new theories (of which [VAP 98] is a leading paper) have emerged to respond to the problems raised by these methods: the kernel methods are part of these new theories. In fact, the idea that under-pins the kernel methods is exactly to try to profit both from the

Chapter written by Jean-Michel RENDERS.

rigor and simplicity of linear methods and from a structure which takes into account the complex and nonlinear relationships in the data to be used; to profit from the two visions and to reconcile them, the task will simply be divided into two:

– on the one hand, a vehicle with special properties, called kernel, will be designed. It is suitable for capturing nonlinearities and subtle relationships in the data;

– on the other hand, a general, often linear, "solver" will be designed, to use these kernels (the support vector machine is a typical example of this: it will be seen afterward why this type of solver complements the kernel concept).

More precisely, a kernel $k(x, y)$ is a symmetric function with two arguments x and y (x and y are two objects which belong to some initial set; this set is not necessarily a vector space), which determines a generalized similarity measure, with particular mathematical properties which guarantee that the general solver, to which it will be coupled to resolve the task, will normally work well (convergence of algorithms, solution uniqueness, etc.).

Let us emphasize at the outset that, in view of the statistical learning approach, the kernel methods have lost some of their panache in recent years. The glory period was from 2000 to 2005, with a peak in 2003/2004. It can be seen that journal and conference articles in the domain are mentioning kernel approaches less and less; it can also be noted that many bibliographic references in this chapter are from this period. It could be said that, as with all mastered techniques, from now on forms it an integral part in the state of the art. This is true, but incomplete. As it can be seen, kernel methods have (at least) a complexity that is quadratic in the number of instances intervening in the learning problem. However, the trend is now to be able to deal with problems involving a huge number of instances (typically millions of objects) and the kernel methods can no longer scale up to this size. One must rely on approximations (e.g. see [BOT 07]) in order to treat these large-scale problems. A recent more drastic approach – which is, in some sense, reminiscent of the neural network approach – consists of applying stochastic methods (e.g. a stochastic gradient optimization method) with a complexity linear in the number of instances, even if in theory they converge more slowly (for a given number of instances); see [BOT 05, BOT 08] for an excellent introduction to these approaches.

Using similarity measures to solve textual information access (TIA) tasks is not counter intuitive, far from it: many algorithms in this application field rely on exploiting the similarity which exists between a query and text elements from an indexed database (information retrieval), or between the elements of a set of textual objects to regroup them (clustering), or between a new text entity to be categorized and some training examples (classification), and so on. Being even more precise on the type of similarity measure, many classical resolution algorithms of TIA tasks in fact use the inner product between the representative vectors of textual objects. The particular cases of Rocchio algorithms (used in information retrieval with relevance feedback, as well as in document classification), logistic regression (classification problems), principal component analysis (dimension reduction) and, of course, support vector machines will be discussed in the rest of this chapter. In fact, all these algorithms can be put in a form with only the inner products intervening between text entities, in certain cases moving to the dual form (where the parameters of the models to be identifed are expressed as an linear combination of input examples). Defining a kernel as an inner product in a space where all initial objects are (virtually) projected and only the inner products intervene in the basic algorithms, constitutes another fundamental point of kernel methods: one can profit from the "kernel trick" idea, as will be seen in the following, that, in many cases, inner products in very complex spaces (with a potentially infinite number of dimensions) can be computed without explicitly doing the computation (sum of products for each dimension), but by using derivations very efficient in computing time. This enables, among other things, the capture of nonlinear effects and subtle dependencies (by using an inner product, therefore a kernel, in a space whose axes represent the nonlinearities and multiple order dependencies between the components of the input objects), all the while keeping a standard universal solver.

We have just mentioned the passage to the dual form in many TIA algorithms, to make the input objects appear only in the inner product form between one another, and thus only in terms of kernels. To understand the intuition, it is important to familiarize oneself with a very important theorem for kernel methods, one which is even fundamental. This theorem, known as "representer theorem" (all the theoretical detail in papers such as [SCH 02, SHA 04]) stipulates that:

– when wishing to find a function $f(x)$ of input objects x, in the infinite space of the functions which can be generated from a kernel $k(x, y)$ by taking different values for y, more precisely by considering the linear (even infinite) combinations of the base functions in the form $k(x, y_i)$ (where y_i designates a fixed but totally arbitrary object of the input space);

– when it is otherwise required that this function optimizes the sum between an arbitrary cost function which expresses the quality of $f(x)$ to explain the observations related to n particular input objects (known as training objects and denoted by x_i), possibly including labels, and a monotonically increasing function of the norm of f (which is known as the regularization term, to avoid the function f being too flexible and "sticking" to the data);

– then this optimal function is in the following form: $\sum_{i=1}^{n} \alpha_i k(x, x_i)$, in other words, a linear combination of the kernels[1] centered on the n input objects only.

---

1 By convention, it is said that the kernel function with two variables $k(x, y)$ with the second argument y fixed to a value x_i is a function with a single variable x centered on x_i. There is no proper centering to speak of. It is really an inheritance of the kernel functions used in statistics to approach a probability distribution in a non-parametric way from a sample of observations.

All the interest in this theorem is to show that from an infinite space of kernel functions $k(x, x_i)$ centered on any possible point in the domain of k, the function which will respond to the task can be expressed as a finite combination of n kernel functions $k(x, x_i)$ centered on the n training objects. In a similar manner, as k is a inner product in a space (even virtual) indexed by axes $\phi(x)$, in other words, $k(x, x_i) = \phi(x_i)^T \phi(x)$, it can be seen that $f(x)$ has the following linear form:

$$f(x) = \sum_{i}^{n} \alpha_i \phi(x_i)^T \phi(x) = w^T \phi(x) \tag{4.1}$$

where T, used as a superscript, indicates the transposition and $w = \sum_{i}^{n} \alpha_i \phi(x_i)$. This as if by magic, comes back to a perfect justification for the use of a linear model! Going from the standard linear formulation with w weighting (and $\phi(x)$) to another linear formula with the new parameters α_i (and the kernels $k(x, x_i)$) is known as the passage to the dual form. It allows us to switch from one problem with unknown w with m dimensions (number of components of vector $\phi(x)$, possibly infinite) to another problem with the unknown α_i and n dimensions (number of input objects). Owing to this framework, "we can have our cake and eat it": the benefits of linear algorithms (with regularization, in other words, control of their complexity) and accounting for nonlinearities and complex interactions via an adequate choice of kernel functions.

After this brief and quite simplified introduction, the subject will be more formally approached.

4.2. General principles of kernel methods

We present here a partial and biased summary of the theoretical aspects linked to kernel methods. In this summary, the aspects selected are those which, linked together, can provide the reader with an intuitive understanding of the concepts behind kernel functions, as well as the application aspects which have a certain use when considering TIA problems. Certain theoretical details have been deliberately omitted or simplified, since they were outside the limited domain (at least in size) of this work. However, there exists a relatively rich bibliography of books and articles which address these theoretical aspects in a very rigorous and systematic fashion. The reader should refer to the following references for additional information on the theoretical aspects of kernel methods: [CRI 00, HOF 08, SCH 02, SHA 04].

The fundamentals of kernel methods rely on a simple idea: finding an adequate representation in a transformed input (vector) space, so the resolution of a task is simpler, typically done by a linear algorithm whose implementation easiness, convergence proofs, and robustness have been demonstrated for a long time. Figure 4.1 illustrates this idea: from a space which can be un-structured or non-vectorial (therefore, a simple set of objects), a transformation ϕ enables the projection of the objects toward

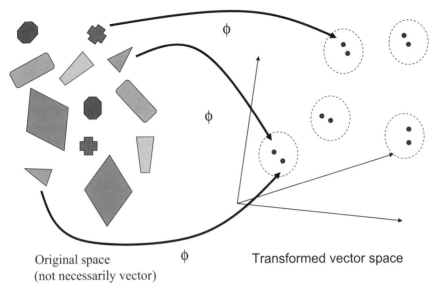

Original space   φ   Transformed vector space
(not necessarily vector)

Figure 4.1. *Kernel method strategies: transformation toward a vector space*
where the task resolution is simpler

a vector space where two objects of the same semantic category[2] find themselves very
close.

The kernel represents the similarity between two objects (document, term, etc.) in
the transformed vector space. More precisely, the kernel is defined as the inner product –
a similarity measure with particular properties – in the new space, taking care to leave
the projection in the new space completely implicit. In other words, it is rare that a
true inner product will be computed in the transformed space; it will be seen that there
are very often efficient formulas which allows to avoid computing the inner product
explicitly.

All the elegance of the kernel methods also exploits the fact that many
TIA algorithms (classification, ranking, dimension reduction, information retrieval
algorithms, etc.) can be put in a form making only the input variables appear in inner
products; in other words, all the useful information from the input data rests on inner
products (therefore kernels) between text object pairs, with a very wide choice of vector
space representing these objects.

---

2 The definition of a semantic category is deliberately vague: it entirely depends on the task in
hand.

Formally, a kernel $k(x, y)$ between two text objects x and y is a similarity measure defined from an (often implicit) transformation $\boldsymbol{\phi}$ of the original space toward a transformed vector space, such that:

$$k(x, y) = \boldsymbol{\phi}(x) \bullet \boldsymbol{\phi}(y) \qquad [4.2]$$

where the symbol $\bullet$ is the inner product between two vectors (which corresponds to the vector operation $\boldsymbol{\phi}(x)^T \boldsymbol{\phi}(y)$, T being the transposition operator). This similarity measure, and therefore the transformation $\boldsymbol{\phi}$, are designed by following the general principles:

– to include invariance properties and all the other types of *a priori* knowledge of the same kind;

– to ensure that the structure in the transformed space is simpler to resolve the task (for example, when a linear model is sufficient);

– more generally, to adopt or constrain the class of functions/models from which a solution is obtained, even if this space has an infinite dimension, all the while ensuring computing time efficiency when determining the kernel values $k(x, y)$.

Regarding the latter point, let us recall the representer theorem: the function class in which we are looking for the one optimizing a cost function mixing the approximation quality of the n training objects and a regularization term (penalizing the complexity and the potential of overfitting) is that generated, *in fine*, by the linear combinations of kernel functions centered on the n input objects.

The benefits obtained generally come from the (nonlinear) expansion of many ranking, classification, density estimation, regression, dimension reduction, etc. TIA algorithms, by replacing the $(x \bullet y)$ inner products with the more general kernels $k(x, y) = \boldsymbol{\phi}(x) \bullet \boldsymbol{\phi}(y)$ in these algorithms. This is the case of very standard methods such as: linear discriminant analysis, logistic regression, perceptron, self-organizing maps, principal component analysis, independent component analysis, non-negative matrix factorization, etc. even if it has to pass through a "dual" formulation algorithm to make the desirable inner products. It should also be noted that many algorithms based just on the distances between text objects can also be extended to their "kernel" version by replacing all distance $d(x, y)$ by $k(x, x) + k(y, y) - 2k(x, y)$ (formula obtained by considering the distance as the squared norm of the difference between the two vectors in the transformed vector space).

For a function with any two variables $k(x, y)$, the question of knowing when this function defines a valid kernel can be put. It is known that, by definition, a function $k(x, y)$ is a valid kernel if there can be found a transformation $\boldsymbol{\phi}(x)$ toward a vector space where k can be expressed as: $k(x, y) = \boldsymbol{\phi}(x) \bullet \boldsymbol{\phi}(y)$. A useful theorem gives an equivalent condition to verify the "validity" of a kernel: $k(x, y)$ is a function that defines a valid kernel, if k is symmetric and positive-definite. We can recall that a $k(x, y)$ function is positive-definite if and only if:

$$\int_{x,y} k(x, y).f(x).f(y).dx.dy \geq 0 \quad \forall f \in L_2 \tag{4.3}$$

In a similar manner, if matrix K is considered where the (i,j) entry is $k(x_i, x_j)$ for all the posssible pairs of elements x_i, x_j of the input space, this matrix, known as the Gram matrix, must be positive-definite and symmetric. We recall that matrix K $(n \times n)$ is positive-definite if and only if:

$$\alpha^T K \alpha \geq 0 \quad \forall \alpha \in \Re^n \tag{4.4}$$

An equivalent condition is that all the eigenvalues of K are positive. It should be noted that the Gram matrix represents by itself all the useful information of the algorithm input data.

The following section is a little more abstract and theoretical. It aims to make the reader understand the representer theorem more profoundly (very simply explained in the introductory section), all the while remaining at a very intuitive and therefore simple theoretical level detail. The reader will find all the necessary details in [SCH 02, SHA 04]. Let us consider a symmetric kernel $k(x, y)$ positive-definite and the space of the monovariable functions $f(x)$ that can be generated from $k(x, y)$ by fixing the variable y to any point x_i of the initial space: $f(x) = \sum_i \alpha_i k(x, x_i)$ (the sum can be infinite, but must converge). Imagine two functions in this space: $f(x) = \sum_i \alpha_i k(x, x_i)$ and $g(x) = \sum_j \beta_j k(x, x_j)$ (the x_i do not necessarily coincide with the x_j of our initial space); the inner products between two functions f and g are thus defined by:

$$<f, g> = \sum_i \sum_j \alpha_i \beta_j k(x_i, x_j) \tag{4.5}$$

Symbols "<·>" are used to define a inner product between two functions, to distinguish it from the usual inner product between two vectors (denoted by •).

In particular, the squared norm of f, written as $\|f\|^2$, is defined by $<f, f>$ and is therefore:

$$\|f\|^2 = \sum_i \sum_j \alpha_i \alpha_j k(x_i, x_j) \tag{4.6}$$

or in matrix notation, by using the Gram matrix:

$$\|f\|^2 = \alpha^T K \alpha \tag{4.7}$$

If the kernel $k(x, y)$ is a valid kernel, this inner product definition is valid: it has all the properties required for a inner product (application to the real numbers, bilinear, symmetric, positive, and defined). The function space generated, with this inner product definition, is a Hilbert space; this space is written as $\mathcal{H}$ and the associated norm as $\|f\|^2_{\mathcal{H}}$. Moreover, the kernel function $k(x, y)$ has a remarkable property: it reproduces itself automatically through a inner product. In effect, $< k(\cdot, x), k(\cdot, y) > = k(x, y)$, by noting through $k(\cdot, x)$ the monovariable function in the argument "$\cdot$" centered on x.

Let us suppose that a TIA task needs to be resolved by formulating it through the search, in the $\mathcal{H}$ space, for the function which minimizes the following functional:

$$Q(x_1, y_1, f(x_1), x_2, y_2, f(x_2), \ldots, x_n, y_n, f(x_n)) + R(\|f\|^2_{\mathcal{H}}) \qquad [4.8]$$

where Q is a *loss function* materializing the approximation quality of model $f(x)$ on the n training objects $(x_1, x_2, \ldots, x_n)$, accompanied (in the case of supervised task) by their possible label $(y_1, y_2, \ldots, y_n)$; and R is an monotonically increasing function. As will be seen in section 4.4, many TIA algorithms can be put in this form: this is the case not only with logistic regression (if a quadratic regularization term is adjoined), and support vector machines, but also with principal component analysis.

The fundamental theorem of kernel methods (representer theorem) proclaims that the optimal function f^* admits a representation of the following form:

$$f^* = \sum_{i=1}^{n} \alpha_i k(x_i, x) \qquad [4.9]$$

In other words, f^* is a linear combination with only n kernel functions, namely those centered on the n training objects. Regularizing by using a $\|f\|^2_{\mathcal{H}}$ type criteria is important, as other types of regularization (based on the norm L_1 for example) do not enjoy the same property.

After this slightly theoretical interlude, let us return to the more concrete question of kernel choice. A relatively simple method of constructing the kernels is to combine the basic kernels (or kernels which are more or less relevant for the task) by using one or more of the rules below; these rules preserve the validity of the kernel; in other words, the resulting kernel is symmetric positive-definite, if the base kernels are. Let $k_1(x, y)$ and $k_2(x, y)$ be the two valid base kernels; the following kernels are also valid (see [SHA 04] for a justification on the validity of these kernels):

$$k(x, y) = a k_1(x, y) + b k_2(x, y) \quad a, b > 0 \qquad [4.10]$$

$$k(x, y) = k_1(x, y) k_2(x, y) \qquad [4.11]$$

$$k(x, y) = f(x)f(y) \quad \text{where Image}(f) = \Re \tag{4.12}$$

$$k(x, y) = k_1(\psi(x), \psi(y)) \tag{4.13}$$

$$k(x, y) = x^T P y \quad \text{with } P \text{ symmetric positive-definite} \tag{4.14}$$

$$k(x, y) = \frac{k_1(x, y)}{\sqrt{k_1(x, x)k_1(y, y)}} \tag{4.15}$$

The last combination mode, which generalizes the computation of a cosine in a vector space, is known as *kernel normalization*.

Some of the most widely-used kernel functions shall now be examined. Let us assume that the initial input variables are vectors belonging to $\Re^n$. The first example is the polynomial kernel with degree d, defined by: $k(x, y) = (x \bullet y)^d$. This kernel is valid, as it is symmetric and positive-definite (product d times of the same base kernel and application of rule [4.11]). It is easy enough to show that this kernel corresponds to the inner product in a (implicit) space which contains all the monomials with degree d: for example, if x is a vector in a space with three dimensions with components (u, v, w), for $d = 2$, the transformed space is the one that has for axes[3] monomials $u^2, v^2, w^2, uv, vw, uw$ (if x is the *bag-of-words* representation of a text object, uv would correspond to the uv bigram frequency without taking word order into account). It is as if all the d-grams (non-contiguous, unordered) of the text objects were taken as new input variables, in other words, all the possible combinations of d words simultaneously present in the object, without the need to make them explicit. The use of a kernel, which does not demand the explicit building of the d-grams, therefore presents a considerable advantage: for example, for $n = 250$ (vocabulary size) and $d = 5$ (polynomial degree), the dimension of the transformed space is from 10^{10}! By using the kernel formulation $(k(x, y) = (x \bullet y)^d)$, the computation of the latter takes hardly any more time than the computation of the inner product in the initial space (with dimension n).

It can also easily be shown that the kernel $k(x, y) = (1 + x \bullet y)^d$ corresponds to a transformed vector space whose axes have all the monomials (in other words, the d-grams) from 0 to d degrees. It is a valid kernel as it is symmetric and positive-definite (product applied d times on the sum of the identity kernel $k(x, y) = 1$ and the base kernel; application of rules [4.10] and [4.11]). Yet again, the computation of this kernel is only slightly more complex than the inner product in the initial space, all the while offering an implicit representation in a much larger dimension.

Another kernel frequently used is the Gaussian kernel: (or the "radial basis function" type):

$$k(x, y) = \exp\left(-\frac{\|x - y\|^2}{\sigma^2}\right) \tag{4.16}$$

---

3 To be totally exact, axes uv, uw, and vw have a scale factor of $\sqrt{2}$.

This corresponds to a transformation toward a space with infinite dimensions: each input vector x is transformed into one function which is the Gaussian centered on x and of covariance matrix $\sigma^2 I$, where I is the identity matrix (through shortening, it can be considered that the function is a vector with infinite dimensions, if the input space has an infinite number of possible points). It is a valid kernel as it is symmetric and positive-definite $(k(x,y) = \exp(2x \bullet y).\exp(-\frac{\|x\|^2}{\sigma^2}).\exp(-\frac{\|y\|^2}{\sigma^2})$; the first kernel factor is valid through the application of rules [4.10] and [4.11] on the development of a Taylor series expansion of the exponential function; the product of the second and third factors is a valid kernel through the application of rule [4.12]).

Figure 4.2 illustrates how classification problems – two nested clusters and a double spiral respectively – which are difficult to resolve in the original space (no linear separator), become linearly separable, after an appropriate kernel choice. In the first case, an ellipse (in a quadratic form) can serve as a separator in the original space; in the transformed space corresponding to a polynomial kernel of degree 2, this ellipse simply becomes a hyperplane. In the second case (Gaussian kernel), the transformed space has an infinite number of dimensions and is therefore difficult to represent, but the kernel choice makes it so that in this (implicit) space, the projected points from the blue category find themselves regrouped and separable from the projected points of the red category.

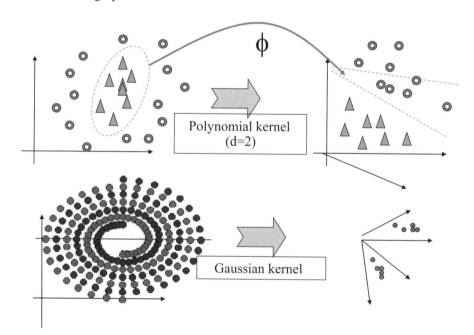

Figure 4.2. *Illustration of two particular kernels and their effects for a classification task in sets nonlinearly separable in the original space*

4.3. General problems with kernel choices (kernel engineering)

There are no absolute rules for choosing a good kernel, adapted to a particular problem. The design of the kernel can rely on the desired characteristics in the transformed vector space (for example, invariance properties); kernels can also be designed from combinations of other base kernels, by using some of the combination rules mentioned above. A relevant kernel can also be determined from the data itself (to account for the local topology of the input data) and/or from their label in the classification problem framework: this shall be seen in more detail in the following chapter.

Certain considerations prevail when choosing a kernel. First of all, it is interesting to introduce a maximum amount of *prior* information in the kernel; an example of this strategy will be given further with the semantic smoothing kernels, which use linguistic resources such as thesauri. Then, even if experimentally it can be concluded that there is a certain strength in the precise choice of a kernel (or its parameters, as for the Gaussian kernel), the dosage must be controlled between the two poles: the search for a more efficient structure for the resolution of the task (e.g. in view of a linear separability), which requires an "explosion" of the original space and, secondly, the preservation of the information structure, which requires that the "explosion" is not too strong. This can be intuitively understood by considering only the family of Gaussian kernels with standard deviation (σ) as the only parameter: if σ is very small, the problem will certainly be separable, but all the structure information will have been lost (there will be a kernel with a quasi-diagonal Gram matrix, where all the points are orthogonal with each other), so that the learned solution cannot generalize; if σ is too big, the classes will never be able to be separated; therefore there is a trade-off to find.

Let us examine the present case where the kernel choice is decided by observing the data. For example, the input space topology can be captured, in particular the fact that the representative points of the data find themselves regrouped into one or more clusters. In the same fashion as the Mahalanobis distance makes it possible to weight the distances differently following the axes of a cluster of points modeled by an ellipsoid (the axis with the largest variance has a lower weighting), it is possible to design kernels which generalize this concept: these are the kernels constructed from generative models (Fisher kernels and marginalized conditional independence kernels), which shall be discussed in a later section for the case of textual data.

Figure 4.3 illustrates this idea. The standard kernels (inner product (a), normalized or cosine inner product (b), Gaussian kernel (c)), are, in some way, isotropic. Kernel (d) constructed from a generative model (mix of bi-dimensional Gaussians in occurrence) favors certain directions locally and reflects the topography in clusters of the input space well; belonging to the same cluster gives the kernel a value close to 1, whereas belonging to different clusters will result in a kernel value close to 0, independently of the original Euclidean distance.

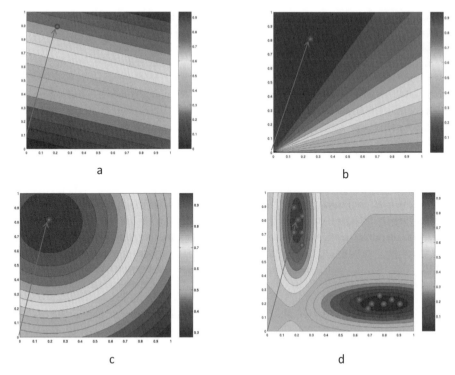

Figure 4.3. *Iso-similarity level in relation to* $y = (0.2; 0.8)$*; in other words, the kernel values* $k(x, y)$ *when* y *is a constant: (a) inner product kernel; (b) cosine kernel; (c) Gaussian kernel; (d) kernel adapted to data, generalizing the concept of Mahalanobis distance (marginalized conditional independence kernel)*

Finally, all outside information constraining certain points to *semantically* belong to the same classes or to the same clusters can be used to find a transformation such that, in the transformed space, these constraints are respected. In this situation, the ideal kernel is such that $k(x_i, x_j)$ is +1 if x_i and x_j belong to the same class, and is -1 if x_i and x_j belong to different classes. In particular, for a classification (or categorization) task, if the label information is known for certain points, a so-called kernel "alignment" strategy can be adopted [CRI 01]: this works by decomposing the Gram matrix of a base kernel (giving the kernel value for all pairs of points for which the label is known) into its eigenvalues/eigenvectors; these eigenvectors are conserved, but the eigenvalues are modified by considering them as parameters to be optimized to maximize the alignment of the kernel with an ideal kernel. The alignment criteria are often chosen as the Fröbenius norm between the reconstructed Gram matrix and the ideal Gram matrix composed of +1 and -1 values.

As demonstrated above, it can be seen that certain kernels correspond to transformed spaces with very large dimensions, even infinite dimensions. For certain tasks (clustering, classification, etc.), this number of dimensions can become problematic in relation to the number of available observations (for example, the number of labeled examples for a categorization task). It is much more a statistical complexity problem (generalization capacities), than a computation or memory problem (since the kernel is generally designed to avoid an explicit computation in the transformed space). This implies that, in the decoupling between the kernel (as the only interface to the data) and the general learning algorithm, it is the latter that should often take charge of the resolution of the statistical complexity problem: this is what is known as regularization, which typically takes the form of an extra term in the cost function to be optimized to resolve the learning problem, as seen in the formulation of the representer theorem via equation [4.8]. This regularization term penalizes solutions that are too complex, typically via the norm of the coefficients introduced in the model. Historically, kernel methods have been associated with methods such as support vector machines[4], as the latter addressed the regularization problem (or complexity control) at the root, with very solid theoretical foundations. It should be noted, however, that many classical learning algorithms (linear regression, logistic regression, etc.) can be expanded by introducing this regularization factor as well, the only differences being the formulation of the cost function to express the model errors in relation to the training data (the so-called "logit" function for logistic regression, the hinge-loss function for the support vector machines, etc.). Before entering the heart of the subject with the design of kernels for textual entities (the body of this chapter), a few standard TIA algorithms in their kernel version will be illustrated, by giving an intuition of their dual formulation (making only the Gram matrix of the input data intervene), through the application of the representer theorem.

4.4. Kernel versions of standard algorithms: examples of solvers

Here, three particular instances of general solvers in their kernel version will be considered, often used to resolve TIA tasks. It is done here without going into too much theoretical detail and by only giving the outline or intuition of the underlying algorithms. It concerns logistic regression, support vector machines, and the principal component analysis, respectively, all revisited in their kernel version. Any reader interested in further details and theoretical proofs should refer to [ZHU 05] for logistic regression, to [CRI 00, JOA 02, SCH 02] for support vector machines, and to [MIK 99, SCH 02, SHA 04] for principal component analysis with kernels.

---

4 In this case, it can be shown that the "margin" concept is directly connected to the inverse of the norm of the hyperplane separator coefficients; therefore there is no fundamental difference with regularization terms on the norm of the model coefficients.

The following is a slightly trivial matter. It is the kernel version of the Rocchio algorithm used for both the relevance feedback mechanism in information retrieval, as well as a classifier for documents. One is given, as input data, n objects (denoted as x_i) with their relevance label ($y_i = +1$, if the object is labelled positive; -1 if the object is labelled negative). The Rocchio algorithm considers that the relevance score of a new object x is given, in its standard vector form, by the difference of the inner products with the centroid of the positive examples and the centroid of the negative examples:

$$f(x) = x^T \left(\frac{1}{n_+} \sum_{i:y_i=+1} x_i \right) - x^T \left(\frac{1}{n_-} \sum_{j:y_j=-1} x_j \right) \qquad [4.17]$$

where n_+ and n_- are the number of positive and negative examples, respectively. The resulting prediction is obtained simply from the sign of $f(x)$.

In the kernel version, a new representation $\phi(x_i)$ of the text objects is considered and, by using the kernel definition $k(x, x_i) = \phi(x)^T \phi(x_i)$, the kernel version of the Rocchio formula becomes:

$$f(x) = \frac{1}{n_+} \sum_{i:y_i=+1} k(x, x_i) - \frac{1}{n_-} \sum_{j:y_j=-1} k(x, x_j) \qquad [4.18]$$

Trivially, this algorithm has no need for an explicit representation of $\phi(x_i)$, but only for the kernel values with all the positive and negative examples. It will be seen in the following sections that classifiers like logistic regression and support vector machines have the same form as equation [4.18], but with another choice of coefficients (instead of $\frac{1}{n_+}$ and $\frac{1}{n_-}$).

4.4.1. Kernel logistic regression[5]

Let us assume a training set characterized by n labelled objects (x_i, y_i) is available. The objects x_i are not necessarily vectorial, but they can be associated, implicitly or explicitly, with a representation in a transformed (vector) space denoted $\phi(x_i)$. Labels y_i are binary and, conventionally, take the value of 0 or 1. Logistic regression consists of finding a linear function $f(x) = w^T \phi(x)$ which minimizes a criteria mixing the quality of the prediction on the learning set and a regularization term:

$$C = - \sum_{i=1}^{n} [y_i f(x_i) - \log(1 + \exp(f(x_i)))] + \lambda \|f\|_{\mathcal{H}}^2 \qquad [4.19]$$

---

5 See Chapter 3 for a description of standard logistic regression.

where λ is a positive real number. This criterion is nothing more than equation [4.8] for a particular choice of the loss function Q. This function Q is represented in Figure 4.4 (solid line).

We note that this loss function can easily be derived (by simple algebraic manipulations) from the log-likelihood of the training data by considering the following model as a hypothesis:

$$p(y = 1|x) = \frac{\exp(\boldsymbol{w}^T \boldsymbol{\phi}(x))}{1 + \exp(\boldsymbol{w}^T \boldsymbol{\phi}(x))} \qquad [4.20]$$

with a Gaussian prior on the coefficients w.

Since the conditions to apply the representer theorem are verified, $f(x) = \sum_i \alpha_i k(x, x_i)$ can be written, or in an equivalent manner:

$$w = \sum_i \alpha_i \boldsymbol{\phi}(x_i) \qquad [4.21]$$

By reinserting equation [4.21] into equation [4.19], the problem comes back to finding the n parameters α_i which minimize the criteria:

$$C = -\boldsymbol{y}^T \boldsymbol{K}\boldsymbol{\alpha} + \mathbf{1}^T \log(1 + \exp(\boldsymbol{K}\boldsymbol{\alpha})) + \lambda \boldsymbol{\alpha}^T \boldsymbol{K}\boldsymbol{\alpha} \qquad [4.22]$$

where y is the label vector (n components), $\mathbf{1}$ is the column vector formed from n 1, K is the Gram matrix of the training instances ($k(x_i, x_j)$) and α is the column vector of α_i (n components). By definition, $k(x_i, x_j) = \boldsymbol{\phi}(x_i) \bullet \boldsymbol{\phi}(x_j)$. Resolving the optimization which is convex in coefficients α_i but unfortunately not quadratic (due to the exponential term of the cost function), must be done. Nevertheless, it is easy to derive the analytical form of the gradient of this function and to use a Newton-Raphson (or quasi-Newton) method to converge toward the unique optimal solution of this problem. Overall, the algorithm has a complexity of $O(n^3)$. Being able to use any kernel $k(x_i, x_j)$ and using only the Gram matrix of the training objects obviously makes this version of logistic regression very flexible. The choice of the regularization constant λ relies on a delicate problem and depends, in particular, on kernel choice; typically, a cross validation-type approach is used to guide the choice of this constant.

4.4.2. *Support vector machines*

It is easy to introduce the support vector machine as a variant of the previous classifier, by simply changing the Q which measures the quality of the prediction on the learning set. More precisely, by conventionally adopting labels y_i with values of -1 or 1 (not 0 and 1), the support vector machine relies on the identification of

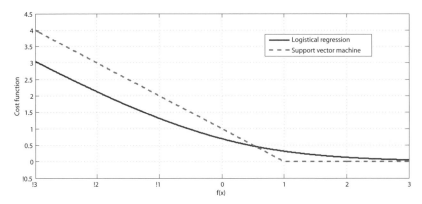

Figure 4.4. *Cost function (limited to its Q component measuring the prediction quality) corresponding to an example with label y = +1 of function f(x). The solid line corresponds to the cost function of a logistic regression, whereas the dashed line corresponds to the support vector machine*

linear function $f(x) = \mathbf{w}^T \boldsymbol{\phi}(x)$, which minimizes a criterion mixing the quality of the prediction on the learning set and a regularization term:

$$C = \sum_{i=1}^{n} \max(0, 1 - y_i f(x_i)) + \lambda \|f\|_{\mathcal{H}}^2 \qquad [4.23]$$

where λ is a positive real number. This criterion is nothing more than equation [4.8] for a particular choice of the loss function Q. This function Q is represented in Figure 4.4 (with a dotted line).

Being in the application conditions of the representer theorem, the function can be written as $f(x) = \sum_i \alpha_i k(x, x_i)$ or, in an equivalent fashion, equation [4.21]. After some manipulations aiming to transform function $\max(0, 1 - y_i f(x_i))$ (somewhat problematic for the differentiation of the equation) into a constraint of the problem, and by putting $\beta_i = \alpha_i . y_i = \alpha_i / y_i$, the problem comes back to finding the n parameters α_i (or, β_i) which minimize the criterion:

$$L = \boldsymbol{\alpha}^T K \boldsymbol{\alpha} - \frac{1}{2} \mathbf{1}^T \boldsymbol{\beta} \qquad [4.24]$$

under the constraints that $\boldsymbol{\beta}^T \mathbf{y} = 0$ and that $\beta_i \in [0, \frac{1}{2\lambda}] \; \forall i; \boldsymbol{\beta}$ denotes the column vector of β_i (n components). It is a quadratic optimization problem, with linear constraints, for which there already exists well-established resolution algorithms (hence all the interest in support vector machines as compared to kernel logistic regression for example).

Several things must be noted in relation to the resolution of the quadratic problem. First of all, it only makes the kernels intervene between training objects (for the classifier learning phase) or in between a new object to be classified and the training objects (for the so-called test phase). Entire flexibility of kernel choice is available, including in a transformed space with potentially infinite dimensions. But this was also the case with the kernel version of the logistics version. What is more remarkable with support vector machines is that the particular choice of the cost function has a "truncation" effect on the training instances: the majority of the coefficients α_i are zero! In other words, the classifier $f(x)$ is a function of a small set of training objects (via the kernel); the training objects which contribute to the classifier definition are known as "support vectors", hence the name support vector machines. We note that the kernel version of logistic regression does not benefit from this sparsity property.

From a practical point of view, to avoid complexity in $O(n^3)$ which would preclude the algorithm to process a very large number of instances (typically over 10,000), it is common to use the approaches resolving the quadratic program through successive iterations on a subset of instances which are "active" candidates to be support vectors. See [SCH 02] in particular for the implementation details of these algorithms.

Finally, let us note that this manner of introducing support vector machines is not usual. Here, they have been introduced and demonstrated to be an application of the representer theorem. There exists another maybe more direct, manner, which has otherwise no need of the representer theorem and which aims to maximize the margin (in other words, the distance of a hyperplane separator in relation to the positive and negative examples closest to the hyperplane), all the while treating nonlinearly separable cases. Besides, the given references [CRI 00, JOA 02, SCH 02] introduce the support vector machines in these geometric terms exactly. This formulation gives rise to a quadratic problem (moreover, it is easily proven that maximizing the margin comes back to minimizing the Euclidean norm of the coefficient vector w_i), with constraints which materialize the more or less intuitive definition of margin. By introducing Lagrangian parameters corresponding to these constraints to form the Lagrangian equations of the system, it can be shown that this leads exactly to the formulation [4.24] with the same constraints, and that the coefficients β_i (and therefore α_i) can be interpreted as Lagrangian parameters of the original constrained margin maximization problem.

4.4.3. *Principal component analysis*

This time, there is a set of non-labeled objects, x_i $(i = 1, \ldots, n)$; let us recall, these objects are not necessarily vectors, but they can be associated, implicitly or explicitly, with a representation in transformed (vector) space written as $\phi(x_i)$. It is assumed that one is restricted to a single principal component, for clarity in the explanation. Principal component analysis on this set consists of finding a linear projection $f(x) = w^T \phi(x)$

which minimizes the opposite of the variance (in other words, which keeps as much information as possible), increased by a regularization term:

$$C = -\sum_{i=1}^{n}[w^T \phi(x_i).\phi(x_i)^T w] + \lambda \|f\|_{\mathcal{H}}^2 \qquad [4.25]$$

by assuming that the data ($\phi(x_i)$) is centered or, mathematically, that for each component j, $\sum_i \phi_j(x_i) = 0$.

We note that the last term is nothing more than $\lambda \|w\|^2$ and can also be interpreted as the Lagrangian term corresponding to constraint[6] $\|w\|^2 = 1$. These are once again the application conditions of the representer theorem, so w can be replaced by its expression in equation [4.21]. This gives a new optimization criterion:

$$C = -\alpha^T K^2 \alpha + \lambda \alpha^T K \alpha \qquad [4.26]$$

The optimum condition is obtained by imposing that the gradient of the cost function is equal to 0, therefore giving:

$$K^2 \alpha = \lambda K \alpha \qquad [4.27]$$

As K is positive-definite, this condition is equivalent to:

$$K\alpha = \lambda \alpha \qquad [4.28]$$

It can be seen that kernel principal component analysis consists of extracting the dominant eigenvector α (in other words, the one corresponding to the largest eigenvalue) of the Gram matrix K. The projection coefficients are obtained simply through relation [4.21]. It can also be seen that constant λ (or, with the alternative interpretation, the Lagrangian parameter associated with the constraint on the norm of the vector of coefficients w) must be equal to the dominant eigenvalue. Evidently, if a set of k orthonormal vectors are sought to represent a projection in a new space with dimension k which conserves a variance maximum, the k eigenvectors corresponding the k largest eigenvalues must be extracted. This algorithm expands the standard principal component analysis by giving all the flexibility of the kernels (nonlinearity and space representation with potentially infinite dimensions), all the while requiring only the Gram matrix of the initial instances as input data.

4.4.4. Other methods

Dimension reduction methods other than principal component analysis (PCA) have been expanded in their kernel version. Thus, independent component analysis (which

---

6 If there was no regularization term, the problem would be ill-posed as infinite coefficients would be needed to maximize the variance.

aims for the superposition of independent factors rather than orthogonal factors to explain a matrix of data) has a kernel variant that can also be found in [BAC 02]. The non-negative factorization methods of data matrices (generalizing principal component analysis by imposing supplementary positivity constraints) have their own kernel version [LEE 09]. There also exists expansions of canonical correlation analysis, where the aim is to explain parallel matrices of matched observations, following the same principle as the PCA kernel version [VIN 02].

It is worth noting that algorithms as popular as *K-means* for clustering tasks have their kernel version. However, these are mostly spectral clustering techniques which exploit most efficiently and naturally the notion of kernels, as they apply themselves directly to the Gram matrix of objects to be regrouped. See the excellent review article [FIL 08] for a panorama of actual clustering techniques based on kernels.

Finally, it is also worth noting the most recent developments around structured output prediction, where the task consists of predicting a label y which is no longer a simple binary variable, but a more complex structure such as a sequence, a tree, or a graph. These applications are particularly interesting for natural language processing and TIA tasks, since tasks such as extraction of entities, extraction of facts and relations, machine translation, and the segmentation of text can be considered in terms of the prediction of structured outputs. The fundamental principle guiding the application of kernel methods for the resolution of this type of task consists of completing the input space (which is denoted by $\phi(x_i)$ up to now) by the possible (structured) outputs: components $\phi(x_i, y_j)$ are worked on and we are looking for a *ranking* function $f(x, y) = w^T \phi(x, y)$ which orders all the possible outputs such that the true output (the structured label) appears in first place. The prediction problem is thus transformed into a problem of ranking all types of possible structured outputs. The benefit is to be able to consider characteristics $\phi(x, y)$ bearing on both the input and output variables, via the kernel design $k[(x_i, y_u), (x_j, y_v)]$ capable of capturing complex dependencies (potentially nonlinear) between the input and output variables. The reader can refer to [TSO 05, JOA 06] for further details.

4.5. Kernels for text entities

After addressing, in a general manner, the problem of kernel choice, textual data will now be focused on. There are numerous ways of considering and representing a text entity. This very much depends on the particular TIA task. A non-exhaustive list of representation modes are proposed here, going from less to more structured:

– bag-of-words representation (the word order has no importance; only the number of occurrences of the word in the entity is counted);

– representation in a concept vector (the concepts are a more compact and semantic representation of the entity with, ideally, resolution of polysemy and synonymy problems; the concepts can correspond to given thesauri, such as Wordnet, or can be automatically extracted from a collection using dimension reduction methods which conserve the maximum amount of information);

– string of characters representation (here, the sequential aspect is important);

– string of words or concepts representation (corresponds to the first two representation modes, but accounts for the order of the text);

– tree set representation (typically resulting from an analysis of the syntactic dependecies).

To complete this distinction of structures, a transverse dimension is added:

– representation as a realization from a probability distribution (generative models of text entities).

To each of these modes corresponds different kernels:

1) for the bag-of-words, the classical vector space kernels (inner product, cosine, polynomial kernel, Gaussian kernel);

2) for the concept vector, the generalized vector space models, the kernel version of principal component analysis (or of latent semantic analysis, etc.);

3) for the character strings, string kernels;

4) for the word string, "word sequence" kernels;

5) for the tree sets, tree kernels;

6) for the realization of probability distributions, Fisher kernels and the marginalized conditional independence kernels.

Type 1 and 2 kernels aim to encode prior information to make the similarity measures between text objects more robust and more semantic. Kernels 3, 4, and 5 exploit the structure information and belong to the family of convolution kernels [COL 01, HAU 99]: the text is seen as a structure of data defined in a recursive fashion and the kernel, in the same way, is recursively constructed from "atomic" or local kernels. Finally, the type 6 kernels adopt a strategy which has already been spoken about: which bases itself on the data and their distribution to capture the "topology" of the problem and to encode it in the kernel. All these text-specific kernels will now be examined in more detail.

4.5.1. "Bag-of-words" kernels

The "bag-of-words" kernels rely on a vector space representation of a text object (written as d to recall the documentary aspect), indexed by the elements (known as terms) of a given vocabulary: element i of this vector is the number of occurrences of the term w_i in the object. The nature of term w_i is generally the result of a series of standard linguistic processes on the original sequence of words of the text entity (typically: tokenization, lemmatization or stemming, stopword removal; if necessary, the term can be of a more complex linguistic nature, such as a nominal group (set of lemmas), a named entity with its type, a collocation, etc.). It is common to proceed to a linear transformation in the term space by adopting a *td-idf* type weighting scheme where element i of the text object vector d contains the number of occurrences of term w_i in d multiplied by $\log(\frac{Ndoc}{n_i})$ with *Ndoc*, the number of documents in the collection and n_i, the number of documents in the collection which contain the term w_i. To compute a kernel $k(d_1, d_2)$, the inner product of the two vectors $(k(d_1, d_2) = d_1 \bullet d_2 = d_1^T d_2)$ is typically used; alternatively, one can use its normalized (cosine) version $\tilde{k}(d_1, d_2) = \frac{k(d_1, d_2)}{\sqrt{k(d_1, d_1)k(d_2, d_2)}}$, or its polynomial version $(k_p(d_1, d_2) = (1 + d_1 \bullet d_2)^p)$. The algorithmic complexity of the kernel will be in $O(|d_1| + |d_2|)$ by using the "sparse" version of the inner product computation ($|d_i|$ denoted as the number of different terms in document d_i).

As already underlined, the use of a p degree polynomial kernel makes it possible to take into account efficiently and implicitly for all the n-grams (n has values of 1 to p, or p only), but without accounting for the order of the words (*the girl kicked the dog* is not distinguished from *the dog kicked the girl*), nor their contiguity. If the order of the words and the contiguous n-gram restrictions are important, these n-grams must be explicitly indexed or we must return to the kernel for sequences, which is described in the following section.

An obvious expansion is to use a term-to-term similarity matrix (Q), which must be positive-definite, and expand the kernel in the following fashion: $k(d_1, d_2) = d_1^T Q d_2$. The following section adopts this approach exactly and gives several proposals for the choice of matrix Q.

The reader can refer to [LEO 02] for a more in-depth analysis of this type of representation. Application examples of this type of TIA kernel are described in [DRU 99] (spam filtering), [ISO 02] (entity recognition) and [JOA 01] (Web page categorization).

4.5.2. *Semantic kernels*

The semantic kernels [KAN 02] aim to expand the basic kernels for "bags of words" by accounting for the relationships between terms (in other words, accounting for the fact that the vector representation components are always more or less correlated: this is the nature of the human language). These kernels will therefore implement a sort of semantic smoothing which will enable, among other things, the treatment of synonymous relations and, more generally, projection of the data toward a space with a reduced dimension, known as concept or latent space, more robust and more efficient to resolve the TIA task.

The basic idea is to use a kernel with the following form: $k(d_1, d_2) = d_1^T Q d_2$, where Q is positive-definite (so that k is a valid kernel, through the application of rule

[4.14]). If Q ($m \times m$, where m is the number of terms in the indexation vocabulary) is positive-definite, it can be broken down into $Q = PP^T$, where P has the dimension $m \times k$. All this is done as if document d ($m \times 1$ vector) is projected into a new space (with a dimension of k) by the linear projection operator P^T, the new representation of the document being $P^T d$. Owing to the presence of Q, the kernel between two text objects can be non-zero even if they have no common terms.

Let us denote through D ($m \times n$) the term-document matrix of the reference collection (e.g. the training collection for the task). A first choice for Q is to adopt the co-occurrence term–term matrix (DD^T), which is symmetric positive-definite: this is known as the generalized vector model. Any object d is therefore projected toward $D^T d$.

It is always very practical to consider that all TIA tasks have need of the data in only two compact interface forms: the (static) Gram matrix K ($n \times n$) taking the similarities for all object pairs of the reference collection or the training collection and a (dynamic) vector t ($n \times 1$ vector) containing the similarities between a new test object o (or a new query) and all objects of the reference collection or the training collection. With the simple vector space model, $K = D^T D$ and $t = D^T o$. The kernel of the generalized vector model corresponds to a new Gram matrix $\tilde{K} = K^2$ (valid as it is a product of a valid kernel itself; see equation [4.11]) and a new vector-kernel test $\tilde{t} = Kt$. These values are therefore very simple to compute, once the base kernel K is determined; noting that K does not necessarily have to correspond to the "inner product" kernel: it can be the polynomial or Gaussian kernel (through the principle of kernel composition). It is, therefore, very simple to take into account, in an implicit and efficient manner, the multigrams of the objects and the correlation between these multigrams (in the reference collection) in the kernels.

As a variant of this generalized vector space model, a narrower context (window of words or section, etc.) than the entire document can be used to compute the term-term co-occurrence matrix. A similarity measure between the terms other than a measure derived from the inner product can be used, as long as it gives rise to a similarity matrix between terms that are positive definite. Stopping only at K^2 is not necessary: the Gram matrix K^p can also be considered, or any linear combination of $K, K^2, \ldots, K^p$. It will be seen later that this corresponds to the diffusion kernel notion in a graph which will be the document-term bipartite graph (the importance of an edge between document-node d_i and term-node w_j corresponds to the importance of term w_j in document d_i). Another variant is using a thesaurus (such as Wordnet [FEL 98]) to compute the term-term similarity matrix Q: the similarity between two terms corresponds to the number of common ancestors (weighted and normalized) of their representative nodes in the hierarchical tree of the thesaurus [SIO 00]; it is easy to show that this similarity definition would give a positive-definite similarity matrix between terms.

Another family of semantic kernels, known as the latent semantic kernel [CRI 02], is based on the singular value decomposition (SVD) of the term–document matrix. The decomposition into singular values truncated to $k (\leq \min(m,n))$ dimensions of D is: $D \cong USV^T$ with U: $m \times k$, S diagonal matrix of the largest k singular values, V: $k \times n$. The U matrix serves as a projection matrix toward the latent concepts space: all d documents are represented (implicitly) by $U^T d$ in a space with k dimensions (typically $k \ll m,n$). With the previous notations, $Q = UU^T$, but U must not be used in order to respect the principle of using the kernels (K and t) as the only interfaces with respect to the input data. As the new kernel $\tilde{K} = D^T UU^T D \cong VSU^T UUU^T SV^T = VS^2 V^T$, as V is nothing more than the matrix formed from the k eigenvectors of $K = D^T D$ corresponding to the largest k eigenvalues and as S^2 corresponds to the diagonal of the matrix of the largest k eigenvalues of K, it can be seen that the new kernel can be computed according to the decomposition into eigenvector/eigenvalues of the base matrix K (recalling that, K can be a polynomial, cosine, Gaussian kernel etc.). $\tilde{K}$ is nothing more than the k rank approximation of the original matrix; it is a valid kernel as it is symmetric by construction and as, for the whole Gram matrix, the eigenvalues of the reduced matrix are necessarily positive as well. Moreover, the kernel-vector for the new test objects is obtained by equation $\tilde{t} = VV^T t$, without resorting to the explicit representation (vector space) of text objects. Of course, if $k = \min(m,n)$, $\tilde{K} = K$.

It can be shown that other types of matrix decomposition (like the decomposition into non-negative matrices [LEE 09] and the decomposition into independent components [BAC 02]) also admit a formulation that involves operations on base kernels only (Gram matrix K and kernel vector t): therefore they totally respect the kernel method philosophly. It should also be noted that the kernel combination rules permit the use of the kernel composition in the desired order: the k-rank approximation of the Gram matrix of the polynomial kernels can therefore be used (initially, it implicitly expands the data in the multigram space, then a projection in a reduced dimension space which conserves the maximum amount of information is searched for), but the k rank approximation of the "inner product" kernel can also first be taken and raised to power p. Roughly speaking, this would correspond respectively to a representation of concepts of multigrams and a representation of multigrams of concepts.

4.5.3. Diffusion kernels

Diffusion kernels [KON 02] are a special family of semantic smoothing kernels. It has been demonstrated that it is natural to take into account, in the kernel computation between two text entities, the correlations between terms materialized by a term–term similarity matrix (for Q, D, K). When choosing $Q = DD^T$, a new kernel is obtained $\tilde{K} = K^2$. However, this reasoning can be followed recursively: two documents are similar if they share many similar terms (with semantic smoothing) and, reciprocally, two terms are similar if they conjointly appear in many similar documents. This recursive reasoning leads to a kernel definition, known as the "Von Neumann diffusion kernel": $\tilde{K} = K.(I + \lambda K + \lambda^2 K^2 + \cdots) = K(I - \lambda K)^{-1}$, where λ is the semantic smoothing constant (if λ is 0, it is a simple "bag-of-words" kernel; if $\lambda > 0$, the correlations between the words are accounted for, but with a discounting factor). In order for this kernel to exist or, in other words, in order for the series defining the kernel to converge, λ must be less than the inverse of the spectral radius[7] of K. It is easy to show that, since this condition is verified, this diffusion kernel is symmetric positive-definite, as it is obtained through the sums and products of valid kernels (application of rules [4.10] and [4.11]). Other diffusion kernels that follow the same principle can be imagined: for example, the kernel $\tilde{K} = K \exp(\lambda K)$ (exponential diffusion kernel) is a valid kernel, with a much more rapid discounting than the Von Neumann diffusion kernel (the coefficients of the series are $1, \frac{\lambda^2}{2!}, \frac{\lambda^3}{3!}, \frac{\lambda^4}{4!}, \ldots$).

Diffusion kernels have an interpretation in terms of propagation in a bipartite graph: if we consider the weighted bipartite graph of documents and terms (the weight of the edge corresponds to the weight of the term-node in the document-node), matrix K represents the number of paths with a length of 2 between all document pairs (weighted by the path weight, the path weight being the product of the constitutive edge weights). The Von Neumann diffusion kernel considers all paths with a length of $2*p$ ($p = 1, 2, 3, 4 \ldots$) and generalizes matrix K by summing the contributions of paths with a length of $2*p$ by penalizing them with a discounting factor λ^p. It is easy to imagine other diffusion kernels by limiting oneself to paths with finite lengths and limited to $2*p$, for a given p. It is clear that, as long as it involves the linear combinations of integer powers of K, the resulting kernel is always a symmetric positive-definite kernel.

However, the diffusion kernels also have another interpretation in terms of a regularization or smoothing method of a function (for prediction, *ranking*, etc.) defined on the nodes of a graph [SMO 03]; the edges of the graph constrain, in a flexible manner, the values of this function to be consistent on the whole graph. An application consists of using this interpretation (and therefore of the diffusion kernel) to predict the labels of non-labeled nodes of a graph, by only using the proximity information encoded by the edges of the graph. This interpretation will naturally lead to the use of the Laplacian of the graph and, more precisely, the pseudo-inverse of the Laplacian (or the inverse of a regularized Laplacian) like the diffusion kernel.

For a wider view of diffusion kernels (and, more generally, kernels defined on the nodes of a graph), see [FOU 06] which makes a synthesis of the different members of this family and compare them for a collaborative filtering task.

---

7 The spectral ray of a matrix is the largest eigenvalue in absolute value.

4.5.4. *Sequence kernels*

The kernels which take into account the order of the text entities will now be addressed: these are the sequence kernels, members of the general family of convolution kernels. We can recall that convolution kernels [HAU 99] consider that the text entity is a recursive structure of data and will, as a consequence, adopt a recursive step in the similarity computation, from (local) atomic similarity measures. A text entity is generally a sequence of symbols defined on a certain alphabet (possible values of symbols). Depending on the task, the symbol can consist of characters (letters), words, terms (normalized words, or collocations or groups of words), or concepts (after projection in a semantic space). Sequence kernels all aim to count the number of subsequences in common with the two text objects, but the manner of counting them can be very diverse as will be seen. It can be limited to subsequences with a given length (or limited to a maximum length), forbid or permit the "gaps" in the subsequences (in other words, impose a contiguity constraint or not), and so on. In the following text, the term "string" will be used when imposing the contiguity of symbols and the term "subsequence" when not imposing this constraint.

4.5.4.1. *"p-spectrum" kernels*

For the "p-spectrum" kernels [LES 02], a text is represented in the (implicit) space indexed by all the possible (contiguous) sub-strings of symbols with length p. Component u of text S in this vector space is the number of occurrences of the sub-string u (of length p) in S. The "p-spectrum" kernel is the inner product in this space; it is therefore valid by definition. For example, for $p = 2$, the text "A D V K" will have as non-zero elements of the corresponding vector: AD, DV, and VK; the text "B D V E K" is represented by BD, DV, VE, and EK, and the "p-spectrum" kernel between these two texts is 1 (only the DV is in common). A naive implementation of this kernel would consist of listing all the (contiguous) p-grams of the two objects (S and T) and comparing them, which gives a $O(p.|S|.|T|)$ algorithm (where $|S|$ is the length of the sequence S). There exists better implementation methods, based on classical string matching algorithms, using a "prefix tree" representation; these implementation methods normally have a complexity of $O(p.(|S| + |T|))$.

4.5.4.2. *"All subsequence" kernels*

For "all subsequence" kernels [LES 03, LES 03], a text is represented in a (implicit) space indexed by all the possible (not necessarily contiguous) subsequences, of all possible lengths. Component u of a text S in this vector space is the number of occurrences of the subsequence u in S, even in a non-contiguous form. The "all subsequence" kernel is the inner product in this space; it is a valid by definition. The empty string (length of 0) is defined by ϵ. For the kernel considered, the text "A D V" will have as non-zero elements of the corresponding (implicit) vector: ϵ, A, D, V, AD, AV, DV, ADV; text "A V D" is represented by ϵ, A, V, D, AD, AV, VD, AVD, and the "all subsequence" kernel between these two texts is 6 (the common elements are ϵ, A, V, D, AD, AV). An explicit of the inner product in this space becomes rapidly unfeasible. A recursive implementation must be adopted (a little reminiscent of the dynamic programming algorithms). This is based on the following reasoning: if symbol a is added to string S, the number of common subsequences between Sa and string T is given by:

$$k(Sa, T) = k(S, T) + \sum_{j:T_j=a} k(S, T_{[1:j-1]}) \qquad [4.29]$$

where T_j designates the jth symbol of string T and $T_{[1:j-1]}$ designates the sub-string made of the first $(j-1)$ characters of T. By introducing the initial conditions and the notation $k'(Sa, T) = \sum_{j:T_j=a} k(S, T_{[1:j-1]})$, the complete recurrence equations are as follows:

$$k(S, \epsilon) = 1 \qquad [4.30]$$

$$k'(S, \epsilon) = 0 \qquad [4.31]$$

$$k(Sa, T) = k(S, T) + k'(Sa, T) \qquad [4.32]$$

$$k'(Sa, Tb) = k'(Sa, T) + k(S, T)\delta_{ab} \qquad [4.33]$$

where δ_{ab} is 1 if a is identical to b and 0 in any other case. It is important to note that the roles of S and T are interchangeable in the above equations and that the kernel is obviously symmetric. Typically, the recurrence equations for the computation of a complete kernel between S and T are applied in the following manner: $k'(S_1, T_1), k'(S_1, T_{[1:2]}), k'(S_1, T_{[1:3]}), \ldots, k'(S_1, T), k(S_1, T_1), k(S_1, T_{[1:2]}), k(S_1, T_{[1:3]}), \ldots, k(S_1, T), k'(S_{[1:2]}, T_1), k'(S_{[1:2]}, T_{[1:2]}), \ldots, k(S, T)$. This recursive algorithm has a $O(|S|.|T|)$ complexity. However, there exists a more efficient version $O(|S| + |T|)$ [VIS 02].

4.5.4.3. *"Fixed-length subsequence" kernels*

For "fixed-length subsequence" kernels [CAN 03, LES 04], a text is represented in a (implicit) space indexed by all the possible (not necessarily contiguous) subsequences of length p. The component u of text S in this vector space is the number of occurrences of the subsequence u in S, even in a non-contiguous form. The "fixed-length subsequence" kernel is the inner product in this space; it is valid by definition. An explicit computation of the inner product in this space rapidly becomes unfeasible and once again a recursive implementation must be used. This gives rise to recurrence equations a little more complicated than the previous kernel (but from exactly the same vein):

$$k_0(S, \epsilon) = 1 \qquad [4.34]$$

$$k_p(S, \epsilon) = 0 \quad \forall p > 0 \qquad [4.35]$$

$$k'_p(S, \epsilon) = 0 \quad \forall p \tag{4.36}$$

$$k_p(Sa, T) = k_p(S, T) + k'_p(Sa, T) \tag{4.37}$$

$$k'_p(Sa, Tb) = k'_{p-1}(Sa, T) + k_{p-1}(S, T).\delta_{ab} \tag{4.38}$$

This recursive algorithm has a $O(p|S||T|)$ complexity, but it should be noted that by computing the kernel for length p, we have at the same time, as intermediary results, all the kernels for the lengths shorter than p. It is, therefore, very easy to compute a more general kernel, linear combination of the kernels for lengths varying from 1 to p: $\tilde{k}(S, T) = \sum_1^p \lambda_i k_i(S, T)$. As for the previous kernel, there is a more efficient version of complexity in $O(p(|S| + |T|))$ [VIS 02].

The "gaps" in the common subsequences can also be penalized, by now considering that the component u of text S in this vector space is the number of subsequences u in S multiplied by a penalization factor $\lambda^{|u|}$, the real length of u (written $|u|$) in S including both the matched symbols and gaps. Thus, the value of the "A B C" component in the string S = "A E B V U C K" is λ^6. The recursive algorithm for computing this kernel is derived from the non-penalizing version, by introducing an auxiliary quantity $\bar{k}(S, T)$ [CAN 03]:

$$k_0(S, \epsilon) = 1 \tag{4.39}$$

$$k_p(S, \epsilon) = 0 \quad \forall p > 0 \tag{4.40}$$

$$k'_p(S, \epsilon) = 0 \quad \forall p \tag{4.41}$$

$$\bar{k}_0(S, T) = 1 \tag{4.42}$$

$$\bar{k}_p(S, T) = 0 \quad \forall p : \min(|S|, |T|) < p \tag{4.43}$$

$$k_p(Sa, T) = k_p(S, T) + \sum_{j:T_j - u} \lambda^2 \bar{k}_{p-1}(S, T_{[1:j-1]}) \tag{4.44}$$

$$\bar{k}_p(Sa, T) = \lambda \bar{k}_p(S, T) + k'_p(Sa, T) \tag{4.45}$$

$$k'_p(Sa, Tb) = k'_{p-1}(Sa, T).\lambda + \bar{k}_{p-1}(S, T).\delta_{ab}.\lambda^2 \tag{4.46}$$

To use these equations, the quantities k' and $\bar{k}$ are computed alternately; once these quantities are computed, the final kernel value k is deduced. This new kernel is obviously valid as it always corresponds to a inner product in the subsequence space.

When the chosen symbols are the indexation terms (the same as those used in the "bag-of-words" approach), it is evident that, for $p = 1$, one comes back to the classical vector space model, a model that does not take into account the order. For $p > 1$ and $\lambda = 1$, there is a kernel which resembles the polynomial kernel on the "bag-of-words", but this time taking into account the order of the terms. There are many variants for the term sequence kernels, which exploit *prior* information on the type of terms manipulated. Among the most relevant variants [CAN 03], let us cite those which use a penalization factor λ depending on the term or class of term; the term class can be the frequency class of the term (to obtain an IDF effect), belonging to a list of empty words, or its grammatical function (name, verb, adjective, etc.); the penalization factor can also be different depending on the fact that, in the effective length of the subsequence u, the contributions of the gaps and matched symbols are distinguished. In general, two values λ can be associated with each symbol s: $\lambda_{s,match}$ and $\lambda_{s,gap}$; the recursive algorithm of the kernel computation becomes:

$$k_p(Sa, T) = k_p(S, T) + \sum_{j:T_j=a} \lambda_{a,match}^2 \overline{k}_{p-1}(S, T_{[1:j-1]}) \qquad [4.47]$$

$$\overline{k}_p(Sa, T) = \lambda_{a,gap} \overline{k}_p(S, T) + k_p'(Sa, T) \qquad [4.48]$$

$$k_p'(Sa, Tb) = k_{p-1}'(Sa, T).\lambda_{v,gap} + \overline{k}_{p-1}(S, T).\delta_{ab}.\lambda_{v,match}^2 \qquad [4.49]$$

This can be taken further by considering that, locally, the symbols are dependent and that the matching between symbols can be flexible rather than strict; in other words, a symbol u can be matched to symbol v with force $f_{u,v}$ ($f_{u,u} = 1$). In this case the recursive algorithm of the kernel computation is written as:

$$k_p(Sa, T) = k_p(S, T) + \sum_{j=1}^{|T|} \lambda^2.f_{a,T_j} \overline{k}_{p-1}(S, T_{[1:j-1]}) \qquad [4.50]$$

$$\overline{k}_p(Sa, T) = \lambda \overline{k}_p(S, T) + k_p'(Sa, T) \qquad [4.51]$$

$$k_p'(Sa, Tb) = k_{p-1}'(Sa, T).\lambda + \overline{k}_{p-1}(S, T).f_{a,b}.\lambda^2 \qquad [4.52]$$

This kernel, which corresponds to a combination of the type in rule [4.14], is therefore valid only if the matrix of $f_{u,v}$ is itself symmetric and positive-definite. As in this case the symbols are language terms, the benefit of this last variant is to group the semantic similarities (like synonymy) at the heart of sequence kernels.

4.5.5. *Tree kernels*

It is common to consider a text object in the form of one or many trees. An obvious example is a document in XML format where all the structure information (titles, sections, paragraphs, etc.) can be put in the form of a tree, each tree node having a label (the structure type) and textual content. Another example is the result of syntactic disambiguation analysis, where a phrase is "peeled" in the form of a dependence tree. Figure 4.5 gives a possible syntactic analysis tree corresponding to the "John loves Mary" textual object.

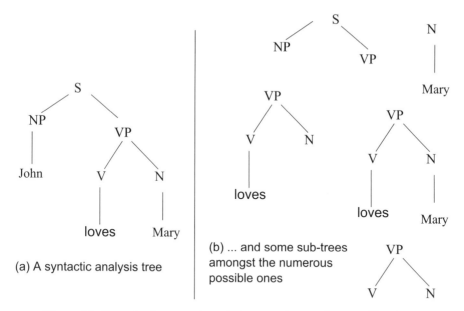

Figure 4.5. *Example of a syntactic analysis tree and some of its possible sub-trees*

Tree kernels also belong to the convolution kernel family: the structure is implicitly "dismantled" into its reccurrent constitutive parts and the kernel proceeds by starting with "atomic" similarities (in other words, locals defined on base elements of the structure) to recursively reconstruct the overall similarity between the two trees. As for the sequence kernels, the tree kernels count the number of common sub-trees, but there are many ways to count them. [COL 01, GÄR 03, GÄR 04] should be consulted for an in-depth view of the subject.

A (valid) sub-tree is defined as being any part of a tree which groups more than one node, with the restriction that, if a "child" from a node is included in the sub-tree, all its "brothers" are as well (in other words, partial production at node level is not permitted). On the right-hand side of Figure 4.5, some examples are given of valid sub-trees from the left tree.

An indirect manner of defining a tree kernel is to represent the tree in the form of a sequence delimited by special characters and to employ one of the sequence kernels described in the previous section but by limiting the possible subsequences. For instance, the tree from Figure 4.5 can be encoded in the following format: [S [NP [JOHN]] [VP [V [loves]] [N [MARY]]]], by using the characters [and] to designate the descendence of a node (in a nested fashion). The subsequences are limited so they correspond to an admissible sub-tree by limiting the subsequences to beginning with "[" and ending with "]", with an equal number of open brackets and closed brackets.

More directly, for the two trees T_1 and T_2, a tree kernel will compare the production (in other words the direct children) of all the possible node pairs (n_1, n_2), with $n_1 \in T_1$ and $n_2 \in T_2$: if the production is identical, the number of common sub-trees taking root in n_1 and n_2 is computed recursively, by considering the number of common sub-trees taking root in the common children. Formally, by designating through $k_{co-rooted}(n_1, n_2)$ the number of common sub-trees taking root in both n_1 and n_2:

$$k(T_1, T_2) = \sum_{n_1 \in T_1} \sum_{n_2 \in T_2} k_{co-rooted}(n_1, n_2)$$

The following recursive equations are used to compute $k_{co-rooted}(n_1, n_2)$, following in the spirit of convolution kernels:

– $k_{co-rooted}(n_1, n_2) = 0$, if n_1 or n_2 is a terminal node;

– $k_{co-rooted}(n_1, n_2) = 0$, if n_1 or n_2 have a different production or, if the nodes are labeled, with different labels;

– in the other cases, $k_{co-rooted}(n_1, n_2) = \prod_{child\ i}(1 + k_{co-rooted}(child(n_1, i), child(n_2, i)))$,

where the $child(n, i)$ function returns the i-th child of node n. This algorithm has a $O(|T_1|.|T_2|)$ complexity, where $|T|$ is the number of nodes in tree T. It corresponds to the inner product in the space indexed by all the possible sub-trees (with roots) and is therefore a valid kernel.

This kernel, which totally accounts for all the common sub-trees, can prove to be too "diagonal" in many cases: in other words, the similarity of a tree with other trees is very badly distributed and very quickly falls to zero. Experimentally speaking, it is better to use variants limiting the sub-trees to a given depth or variants which penalize all the very large sub-trees. More concretely, the first of these strategies (limiting the depth of sub-trees with value p) gives a recursive algorithm:

$$k_p(T_1, T_2) = \sum_{n_1 \in T_1} \sum_{n_2 \in T_2} k_{co-rooted}(n_1, n_2, p)$$

where $k_{co-rooted}(n_1, n_2, p)$ is given by:

– $k_{co-rooted}(n_1, n_2, 1) = 1$ if n_1 and n_2 have the same production;

– in other cases, $k_{co-rooted}(n_1, n_2, p) = \prod_{child\ i}(1 + k_{co-rooted}(child(n_1, i), child(n_2, i), p - 1))$,

whose complexity is $O(p.|T_1|.|T_2|)$. The kernel is valid as it represents the inner product in the space indexed by the sub-trees with a depth smaller than or equal to p. The second strategy which implicitly weights each component of the sub-tree space by a factor of $\lambda^{size(sub-trees)}$, gives rise to a recursive kernel:

$$k(T_1, T_2) = \sum_{n_1 \in T_1} \sum_{n_2 \in T_2} k_{co-rooted}(n_1, n_2)$$

where:

– $k_{co-rooted}(n_1, n_2) = 0$, if n_1 or n_2 is a terminal node;

– $k_{co-rooted}(n_1, n_2) = 0$, if n_1 or n_2 have a different production or, if the nodes are labeled with different labels;

– in the other cases, $k_{co-rooted}(n_1, n_2) = \prod_{child \ i} \lambda^2(1 + k_{co-rooted}(child(n_1, i), child(n_2, i)))$.

The variants around the kernels are almost infinite, but are always treated in the same manner. For example, if there are labeled nodes but partial productions are permitted in the implicit space of the sub-trees (in other words, one or many children of a node are accepted, without the other brothers being present), the algorithm which determines the corresponding kernel can be written as:

$$k(T_1, T_2) = \sum_{n_1 \in T_1} \sum_{n_2 \in T_2} k_{co-rooted}(n_1, n_2)$$

where:

– $k_{co-rooted}(n_1, n_2) = 0$, if n_1 or n_2 have no children;

– $k_{co-rooted}(n_1, n_2) = 0$, if n_1 or n_2 have different labels;

– in other cases, $k_{co-rooted}(n_1, n_2) = \prod_{x,y \in common\ child}(2 + k_{co-rooted}(x, y)) - 1$.

This kernel is valid since it corresponds to the inner product in the space indexed by the partial production sub-trees (with labeled nodes). [COL 01] gives the derivation stages of this recursive formulation.

We conclude with an example of a very particular tree, which corresponds to a sequence of pairs, each pair being a couple (state, associated term). This kind of representation is, for instance, the result of a morpho-syntactic analysis: the states are the grammatical functions associated with the sequence of constitutive terms of the sentence. Figure 4.6 illustrates this concept. It is considered that the possible sub-sequences (or sub-trees) to index the sequence are all contiguous sub-sequences formed by two or more states with or without their associated terms. The right-hand side of Figure 4.6 gives some valid subsequences corresponding to the left sequence.

This sequence can be seen as a tree whose root is the initial state of the sequence. Each "state" type node s has two descendants: a successor state (designated by $next(s)$, equivalent to $child(s, 1)$ with the previous notations) and an associated term (designated by $word(s)$, equivalent to $child(s, 2)$ with the previous notations); a label written as $label(s)$ is associated with this node s.

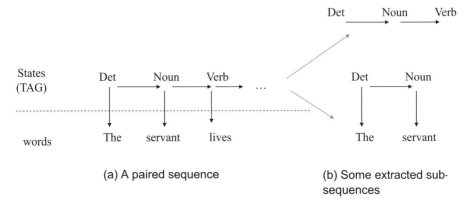

(a) A paired sequence

(b) Some extracted sub-sequences

Figure 4.6. *Pair sequence example (state, term)*

A "term" type node is always terminal (i.e. a leaf). For this particular tree, the recursive kernel can be computed, by following the same principles as the base tree kernels:

$$k(T_1, T_2) = \sum_{n_1 \in states(T_1)} \sum_{n_2 \in states(T_2)} k_{co-rooted}(n_1, n_2)$$

with:

- $k_{co-rooted}(n_1, n_2) = (1 + x) * (1 + y + k_{co-rooted}(next(n_1), next(n_2)))$ if $label(n_1) = label(n_2)$ and $label(next(n_1)) = label(next(n_2))$, with $x = \delta(word(n_1), word(n_2))$ and $y = \delta(word(next(n_1)), word(next(n_2)))$;

- $k_{co-rooted}(n_1, n_2) = 0$ if not.

[COL 01] provides the details of the stages enabling the recursive kernel to be obtained.

4.5.6. *Graph kernels*

The general case of the directed graph will now be explored in more detail. The graphs are labeled both on the nodes and the edges, with the possibility of a cycle. This corresponds to a quite abstract representation of the document, in the forms of a network (graph) of concepts for example, linked to each other through definite relations in the text itself. This can also be a graph of named entities (like people, organizations, etc.), the edges representing the type of relation which links the two entities (the type is itself deduced from the syntactic analysis of the sentences and, in particular, the verbs linking the two entities). Defining a general kernel on this type of object is not easy; it is known for example that determining if two graphs are isomorphic is an NP-complete problem. This implies that the design of a ideal kernel for graphs is not reasonable in practice. It is necessary to fall back on approximations such as counting sub-trees included in the graph, or the number of common (labeled) paths that can be followed in the two graphs. All the material to deepen the understanding of these graph kernels, as well as certain theoretical justifications, can be found in [GÄR 03, GÄR 04, SUZ 03a, SUZ 03b].

If it is decided to use the approximation of the number of common paths as a basis, the implicit space of the graph representation is indexed by all the possible paths, with lengths 1, 2, ..., p (possibly infinite). Thus, for a simple graph (with unlabeled edges) such as in Figure 4.7, the non-zero components in this space are: A (2x), B, C, AB, AC, BA, CA, ABA, and ACA. These components are weighted, as usual, by the $\lambda^{\text{path length}}$, in order to accord less importance to very long paths (and thus avoid a kernel that is too "sharp" or diagonal). An explicit inner product in this space becomes unfeasible very quickly. Luckily, there exists a useful theorem to compute more efficiently the kernel of the number of common paths. This theorem stipulates that the common paths of two graphs G_1 and G_2 are the paths of graph $G_1 \times G_2$, which is known as the direct product of the two graphs. The direct product of the two graphs is, by definition, a new graph:

– whose nodes correspond to all the respective node pairs of G_1 and G_2 which have the same label;

– whose edges correspond to all respective edge pairs of G_1 and G_2 which have at the same time the same label (if edges are labelled) and end nodes (head and tail) with the same label.

Examples of direct products of simple graphs (with unlabeled edges) are given in Figure 4.8.

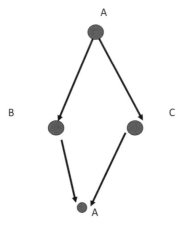

Figure 4.7. *Simple graph example*

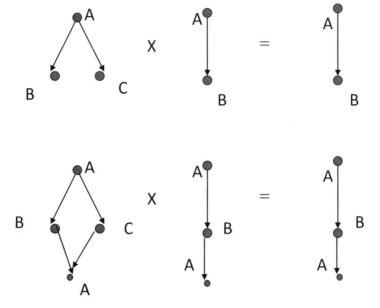

Figure 4.8. *Example of the direct product of two graphs*

The kernel $k(G_1, G_2) = \sum_g \lambda^{length(g)}$, where the sum carries on all the possible paths g in the graph of the direct product $G = G_1 \times G_2$, is a valid kernel (as it corresponds well to a inner product, by virtue of the previous theorem). As in the case of diffusion kernels, the paths g are obtained by the power series of the adjacency matrix of G and the kernel has an analytical form involving $(I - \lambda G)^{-1}$ (G being the adjacency matrix of the direct product graph), provided that λ is less than the inverse of the spectral radius of G. The complexity of the kernel computation is $O(|V_1|.|V_2|.|D(V_1)|.|D(V_2)|)$ where $|V_i|$ designates the number of nodes of graph G_i and $|D(V_i)|$ designates the average degree (number of outgoing edges) of the nodes of graph G_i. There are more efficient $O(|V_1| + |V_2|)$ implementations instead of $O(|V_1|.|V_2|)$ [HID 09].

There exists a variant of this kernel [SUZ 03b, TAK 03] which does not use the direct product of the graphs and which is based on a "lazy random walk" formulation (see the famous PageRank algorithm [BRI 98]). This variant is almost equivalent to the previous one and has the same complexity. The kernel sums up the probabilities of the common paths taken by coupled random walkers (on G_1 and G_2, respectively), knowing that at each stage, the (lazy) walkers can decide to stop at the current node (absorbing node) with a probability of $(1 - \lambda)$. This gives the following kernel: $k(G_1, G_2) = \sum_{n \in G_1} \sum_{n \in G_2} k_{co-rooted}(n_1, n_2)$, where $k_{co-rooted}(n_1, n_2)$ is the sum of the probabilities of the common paths starting at n_1 and n_2, respectively. The function that sends 1, if the label of object x is identical to the label of object y, and 0 otherwise is designated by $I(x, y)$ (here, an object can be an edge or a node). The set of edges coming from node n and the head node of the edge e of tail n are designated by $A(n)$ and $next(n, e)$, respectively. It is easy to see that the kernel can be defined in a recursive manner through a system of equations:

$$k_{co-rooted}(n_1, n_2) = I(n_1, n_2). \left\{ (1 - \lambda) \right.$$

$$\left. + \lambda \left(\sum_{e_1, e_2} \frac{I(e_1, e_2)}{|A(n_1)|.|A(n_2)|} . k_{co-rooted}(next(n_1, e_1), next(n_2, e_2)) \right) \right\}$$

[4.53]

where, in the sum of the second line, $e_1 \in A(n_1)$ and $e_2 \in A(n_2)$. However, contrary to what happens for the sequences or the trees, this equation system cannot be simply resolved by the propagation of the initial conditions: the same variables $k_{co-rooted}(n_1, n_2)$ appear to the left and to the right of the equals sign. In effect, in matrix form, the system is written as: $k = (1 - \lambda)k_0 + \lambda Gk$, where k is the vector of all the $k_{co-rooted}(n_1, n_2)$ (with a size of $|V_1|.|V_2|$) and G is a matrix (with a size of $|V_1|.|V_2|$ x $|V_1|.|V_2|$) which directly deduces itself from the adjacency matrices G_1 and G_2 (it is evidently linked to the adjacency of the direct product of the two graphs). The final kernel is the sum of the components of vector k and, in practice, the resolution of the linear system is done iteratively, using the equation above.

To finish this section, let us mention other kernels for text entities which are based on other representation modes of textual information:

– when the textual information is represented in the form of automatons or transducers, certain authors [COR 04] have developed kernels which compute a similarity measure between two automatons (or two transducers) in an efficient manner (through a transducer): these are known as "rational" kernels;

– when the textual information is represented in the form of a set of dependency relationships (n-ary relationships), such as those obtained as a result of an analysis of syntactic dependencies, certain kernels [CUM 03, ZEL 03] have been designed to measure a similarity between such sets of relationships.

4.5.7. Kernels derived from generative models

The objective of kernels derived from generative models[8] is to help and capture the topology of the problem (a cluster structure with varied shapes for example) and to encode it in the kernels in order to facilitate the TIA task. It is also an elegant and natural manner to resolve semi-supervised learning tasks which mix labeled and unlabeled input data. It will also be seen that some of the kernels already discussed

8 These models are addressed in detail in Chapter 5.

in previous sections (such as "bag-of-words" and sequence kernels) are "simplistic" particular instances of generative models. The latter thus introduce a very interesting flexibility source. The three families of kernels derived from generative models will now be introduced: these are the marginalized conditional independence kernels, marginalized latent variable kernels, and the Fisher kernels. It is assumed in the following that the structure of the generative model is fixed and that this model makes latent variables (written z) appear, explaining the observations (written x) via a parameter vector (written $\boldsymbol{\theta}$). It will be assumed that the latent variables have discrete values to simplify the notations (even if nothing precludes the use of continuous latent variables; the sums will thus be replaced by integrals). The reader can refer to [JAA 98, KAS 03, KAS 04, TSU 02] for a more detailed view of these techniques.

4.5.7.1. *Marginalized conditional independence kernels*

Let us assume that parameters $\boldsymbol{\theta}$ of the generative model are fixed. The generative model thus permits the association of any object x with a vector in a new space whose components are $p(x|z).\sqrt{p(z)}$ (the dimension of the transformed space is therefore determined by the number of discrete values that the variable z can take). The marginalized conditional independence kernel [KAS 03] corresponds to the joint probability between two objects x_1 and x_2, with a conditional independence assumption with respect to the latent variable:

$$k(x_1, x_2) = p(x_1, x_2) = \sum_{z_i} p(x_1|z_i)p(x_2|z_i)p(z_i) \qquad [4.54]$$

This kernel is symmetric, positive-definite, since it corresponds to the inner product in the new transformed space.

Let us consider a generative "PLSA" (Probabilistic Latent Semantic Analysis) model, such as described in Chapter 5 and [HOF 99]. In this model, the probability of observing the co-occurrence (d, w) of word w in document d is $p(d, w) = \sum_z p(z)p(d|z)p(w|z)$. Here, the latent concepts (or aspects) are designated by the variable z. The application of a conditional independence kernel on this model gives the following kernel:

$$p(d_1, d_2) = \sum_z p(d_1|z)p(d_2|z)p(z) = \kappa \sum_z \frac{p(z|d_1)p(z|d_2)}{p(z)} \qquad [4.55]$$

by using the Bayesian theorem and by assuming a uniform distribution for $p(d)$ (constant $\kappa = p(d)^2$).

Figure 4.5, part (d), illustrates the result of such a kernel for a generative model which is a mixture of multidimensional Gaussians ($p(x) = \sum_z p(z)\mathcal{N}(x|\mu_z, A_z)$) with $\mathcal{N}$ a Gaussian distribution, μ_z the center of the zth Gaussian and A_z, the inverse of its variance–covariance matrix).

Another interesting example consists of considering, as an generative model, a hidden Markov model to explain a string of terms. Let us denote as $s = (s_1, s_2, \ldots, s_n)$ the observed string and as $z = (z_1, z_2, \ldots, z_n)$ the chain of hidden states (z_i can take Z discrete values). $p(s|z) = \prod_{i=1}^{n} p(s_i|z_i)$ is obtained. The conditional independence kernel for two term strings (s and t) gives:

$$p(s, t) = \sum_{z} \prod_{i=1}^{n} p(s_i|z_i)p(t_i|z_i)p(z_i|z_{i-1}) \qquad [4.56]$$

(the sum concerning all the possible paths z), which can be computed in an efficient manner by using a variant of the dynamic programming algorithm (see *forward* algorithms and *forward–backward* algorithms for the inference in the hidden Markov models introduced in Appendix A, section A.5). The complexity is therefore $O(nH^2)$.

4.5.7.2. Marginalized latent variable kernels

The strategy adopted by this type of kernel differs from the previous strategies by considering dual vision (in the Bayesian theorem sense): the *posterior* probabilities $p(z|x)$ will be focused on rather than direct probabilities $p(x|z)$. It is assumed in a first stage (before marginalizing) that, for two objects, not only the observed variables (x_1 and x_2) are known but also the latent variables (z_1 and z_2); further it is assumed that a joint kernel is imposed on the pairs (observed variable, latent variable), written as $k_j((x_1, z_1), (x_2, z_2))$. It should be noted that this approach is more flexible than the previous approach which implicitly assumes $k_j((x_1, z_1), (x_2, z_2)) = 0$ if $z_1 \neq z_2$. The marginalized latent variable kernel is obtained by marginalizing (in other words, averaging) the core kernel k_j:

$$k(x_1, x_2) = \sum_{z_1, z_2} p(z_1|x_1)p(z_2|x_2)k_j((x_1, z_1), (x_2, z_2)) \qquad [4.57]$$

In this equation, the *posterior* probabilities $p(z|x)$ are obtained through the Bayes theorem from the generative model. The benefit of such a kernel, among other things, is the ability to weight an identical term x differently following its hidden context z (the context can be, for example, the title, the development or the conclusion, without this structure information being explicit). The kernel thus constructed is valid if the joint kernel k_j is, itself, valid; in effect, k is therefore symmetric and is obtained through a combination of the type in rule [4.14].

In the case of the "PLSA" generative model, trivially this gives:

$$k(d_1, d_2) = \sum_{z_1, z_2} p(z_1|d_1)p(z_2|d_2)k_z((d_1, z_1), (d_2, z_2)) \qquad [4.58]$$

In the Gaussian mixing example ($p(x) = \sum_z p(z)\mathcal{N}(x|\mu_z, A_z)$ with μ_z the center of the zth Gaussian and A_z the inverse of its variance–covariance matrix), it is natural to choose $k_j((x_1, z_1), (x_2, z_2)) = x_1^T A_z x_2$ if $z_1 = z_2 = z$, and 0 if not. This corresponds to a local Mahalanobis similarity. The marginalized kernel will thus be:

$$k(x_1, x_2) = \frac{\sum_z p(x_1|z)p(x_2|z)p^2(z)x_1^T A_z x_2}{p(x_1)p(x_2)} \qquad [4.59]$$

4.5.7.3. Fisher kernels

Let us write the generative model in the format $\log(p(x|\theta_0))$ where θ_0 is typically identified by a maximum likelihood method. Each object x is represented by the gradient of this function (with respect to the parameter vector) at point x: all objects are therefore vectors in a space with as many dimensions as there are parameters: $\nabla_\theta \log(p(x|\theta))|_{\theta=\theta_0}$. Intuitively, an object is characterized by the manner it "stretches" the model (or more exactly the log-likelihood of the model) so that the latter fits better to the new object. Two objects shall be considered as similar if they stretch (or deform) the model in the same manner, in the same directions, since their individual influence is considered in the construction of the model. The Fisher kernel [JAA 98, SAU 02, SHA 04, SIO 02] is defined as a generalized inner product in this space (with the Fisher information matrix inside the inner product):

$$k(x_1, x_2|\theta_0) = (\nabla_\theta \log(p(x_1|\theta))|_{\theta=\theta_0})^T I_F^{-1}(\theta_0)(\nabla_\theta \log(p(x_2|\theta))|_{\theta=\theta_0})) \qquad [4.60]$$

where the Fisher information matrix $(I_F(\theta_0))$ is:

$$I_F(\theta_0) = E_x[(\nabla_\theta \log(p(x|\theta))|_{\theta=\theta_0}))(\nabla_\theta \log(p(x|\theta))|_{\theta=\theta_0})^T)] \qquad [4.61]$$

This positive-definite matrix guarantees that the Fisher kernel is itself positive-definite. In practice, it is approximated by the empirical covariance matrix of the gradients (in other words, computed on the observations and not the general distribution of x) or, more often, approximated by the identity matrix.

Let us consider a first example: the language models which constitute a generative model of term w_n from its predecessors: the values of $p(w_n|w_{n-k}, \ldots, w_{n-1})$ are the parameters. The log-likelihood of text $(w_1, w_2, \ldots, w_n)$ is given by: $\sum_{j=1}^{n-k} \log p(w_{j+k}|w_j \ldots w_{j+k-1})$. The gradient of the log-likelihood of this text with respect to parameter $p(v|U)$, where U is a string of length k, is nothing more than the number of occurrences of string Uv, divided by the probability $p(v|U)$; this means that, when two strings are compared by this kernel, the number of common strings is indeed computed (here Uv for example), but by weighting them through the inverse of $p(v|U)$. More weight is given to infrequent $U \to v$ transitions, which seems to be a good idea for comparing two texts (generalization of the tf-idf concept for sequences). It should be noted that the standard "p-spectrum" kernels do not perform this weighting and will be as if the probability $p(v|U)$ is uniform over all v.

As a second example, the PLSA generative model will be considered. The parameters (θ) are $p(z), p(d|z)$ and $p(w|z)$. By deriving the log-likelihood of a set of co-occurrence observations $\sum_{w,d} \log p(w, d|\boldsymbol{\theta})$ and by computing the inner products, after certain algebraic manipulations the first approximation is obtained (see [NYF 06] for a simpler version and Chapter 5 for more details):

$$k(d_1, d_2) = \sum_z \frac{p(z|d_1)p(z|d_2)}{p(z)}$$

$$+ \sum_w \tilde{tf}(w, d_1)\tilde{tf}(w, d_2) \sum_z \frac{p(z|d_1, w).p(z|d_2, w)}{p(w|z)}$$

where $\tilde{tf}(w, d)$ is the number of occurrences of w in d, normalized (divided) by the total length of document d. The first term, identical to that given to the marginalized conditional independence kernel for "PLSA", measures to which extent the two documents d_1 and d_2 share the same latent concepts: in particular, this allows the synonymy to be accounted for. The second term generalizes the classical inner product of the "bag of words" representation, but weighting words (w) by the degree with which these words, in their context (materialized by (w, d_1) and (w, d_2)), actually belong to the same concepts: it is a manner of accounting for the polysemy since the same word, in two different contexts d_1 and d_2, will activate different concepts (the distribution of $p(z|w, d_1)$ can be totally different from $p(z|w, d_2)$).

4.6. Summary

In this chapter, the use of kernel methods for textual information access (TIA) tasks has been addressed. As remarked in the previous chapters, many of these tasks are based on notions of similarity between text entities; for instance, a principle of information retrieval is to compute a well-defined similarity between the user query and each document in a targeted collection, in order to determine a relevance score and an optimal presentation order; what is more, numerous non-supervised learning methods are based on the systematic exploitation of the similarity matrix between all document pairs; supervised categorization methods also rely on similarity measures between new documents to be classified and training documents. Formalizing the numerous TIA algorithms around the notion of similarities between text entities is the first key element of kernel methods. It has been demonstrated that kernel functions are nothing more than similarity measures with particular properties (in particular, those being positive-definite, which guarantees the convergence of certain algorithms).

The second key element of these kernel methods relies on the idea of separating a particular learning task (for example clustering, classification, and prediction) into two distinct stages: first, finding the best representation space of the input data in order to resolve the task with the most chance of success with generic and well-behaved methods (typically those based on linear assumptions, such as the discriminant Fisher analysis, linear regression, etc.). The search for a transformation of the original input variable space toward another space where the task will be easier to resolve is known as kernel engineering, and in this chapter, it has been demonstrated that specific kernels can be designed for textual data, according to the task to resolve.

Finally, the third key point of kernel methods consists of formulating generic task resolution algorithms (independent of the type of input data) in a manner so as to not directly manipulate the objects in their transformed representation (it has been demonstrated that the representation can have, in certain cases, an extremely high number of dimensions, even infinite). Rather, the algorithms are only re-expressed in terms of inner product of the objects in the transformed space, these inner products being the kernels, all the while assuring that these inner products can be computed in an implicit and efficient manner: this is another facet in the art of kernel engineering.

4.7. Bibliography

[BAC 02] BACH F.R., JORDAN M.I., "Kernel independent component analysis", *Journal of Machine Learning Research*, vol. 3, 2002.

[BOT 05] BOTTOU L., LECUN Y., "On-line learning for very large datasets", *Applied Stochastic Models in Business and Industry*, vol. 21, no. 2, p. 137-151, 2005.

[BOT 07] BOTTOU L., CHAPELLE O., DECOST D., WESTON J. (eds), *Large-Scale Kernel Machines*, Neural information processing series, MIT Press, 2007.

[BOT 08] BOTTOU L., BOUSQUET O., "Learning using large datasets", in *Mining Massive DataSets for Security*, NATO ASI Workshop Series, IOS Press, 2008.

[BRI 98] BRIN S., PAGE L., "The anatomy of a large-scale hypertextual web search engine", *Computer Networks and ISDN Systems*, vol. 30, no. 1-7, p. 107-117, 1998.

[CAN 03] CANCEDDA N., GAUSSIER E., GOUTTE C., RENDERS J.-M., "Word-sequence kernels", *Journal of Machine Learning Research*, vol. 3, p. 1059-1082, 2003.

[COL 01] COLLINS M., DUFFY N., "Convolution kernels for natural language", in *Advances in Neural Information Processing Systems 14*, MIT Press, p. 625-632, 2001.

[COR 04] CORTES C., HAFFNER P., MOHRI M., "Rational kernels: theory and algorithms", *Journal of Machine Learning Research*, vol. 5, p. 1035-1062, 2004.

[CRI 00] CRISTIANINI N., TAYLOR J.S., *An Introduction to Support Vector Machines*, Cambridge University Press, 2000.

[CRI 01] CRISTIANINI N., SHAWE-TAYLOR J., ELISSEEFF A., KANDOLA J.S., "On kernel-target alignment", in *Advances in Neural Information Processing Systems 14*, MIT Press, p. 367-373, 2001.

[CRI 02] CRISTIANINI N., SHAWE-TAYLOR J., LODHI H., "Latent semantic kernels", *Journal of Intelligent Information Systems*, vol. 18, no. 2-3, p. 127-152, 2002.

[CUM 03] CUMBY C.M., ROTH D., "On kernel methods for relational learning", in *Proceedings of the ICML Conference (ICML 2003)*, p. 107-114, 2003.

[DRU 99] DRUCKER H., VAPNIK V., WU D., "Support vector machines for spam categorization", *IEEE Transactions on Neural Networks*, vol. 10, no. 5, p. 1048-1054, 1999.

[FEL 98] FELLBAUM C., *WordNet: An Electronic Lexical Database*, MIT Press, 1998.

[FIL 08] FILIPPONE M., CAMASTRA F., MASULLI F. ROVETTA S., "A survey of kernel and spectral methods for clustering", *Pattern Recognition*, vol. 41, no. 1, p. 176-190, 2008.

[FOU 06] FOUSS F., YEN L., PIROTTE A., SAERENS M., "An experimental investigation of graph kernels on a collaborative recommendation task", in *Proceedings of ICDM 2006*, 2006.

[GÄR 03] GÄRTNER T., "A survey of kernels for structured data", *SIGKDD Explorations*, vol. 5, no. 1, p. 49-58, 2003.

[GÄR 04] GÄRTNER T., LLOYD J.W., FLACH P.A., "Kernels and distances for structured data", *Machine Learning*, vol. 57, no. 3, 2004.

[HAU 99] HAUSSLER D., Convolution Kernels on Discrete Structure, Report no. UCSC-CRL-99-10, University of California at Santa Cruz, 1999.

[HID 09] HIDO S., KASHIMA H., "A linear-time graph kernel", in *ICDM 2009, The Ninth IEEE International Conference on Data Mining*, 2009.

[HOF 99] HOFMANN T., "Probabilistic latent semantic indexing", in *Proceedings of 22th Annual International ACM SIGIR Conference on Research and Development in Information Retrieval*, Berkeley, California, p. 50-57, 1999.

[HOF 08] HOFMANN T., SCHÖLKOPF B., SMOLA A.J., "Kernel methods in machine learning", *Annals of Statistics*, vol. 36, no. 3, 2008.

[ISO 02] ISOZAKI H., KAZAWA H., "Efficient support vector classifiers for named entity recognition", in *Proceeedings of the COLING Conference*, 2002.

[JAA 98] JAAKKOLA T.S., HAUSSLER D., "Exploiting generative models in discriminative classifiers", in *Advances in Neural Information Processing Systems*, vol. 11, 1998.

[JOA 01] JOACHIMS T., CRISTIANINI N., SHAWE-TAYLOR J., "Composite kernels for hypertext categorisation", in *Proceedings of the ICML Conference*, p. 250-257, 2001.

[JOA 02] JOACHIMS T., *Learning to Classify Text Using Support Vector Machines: Methods, Theory, and Algorithms*, Kluwer Academic Publishers, 2002.

[JOA 06] JOACHIMS T., "Structured output prediction with support vector machines", *Structural, Syntactic, and Statistical Pattern Recognition*, p. 1-7, 2006.

[KAN 02] KANDOLA J.S., SHAWE-TAYLOR J., CRISTIANINI N., "Learning semantic similarity", in *Proceedings of NIPS 2002*, 2002.

[KAS 03] KASHIMA H., TSUDA K., INOKUCHI A., "Marginalized kernels between labeled graphs", in *Proceedings of ICML 2003*, 2003.

[KAS 04] KASHIMA H., TSUBOI Y., "Kernel-based discriminative learning algorithms for labeling sequences, trees, and graphs", in *Proceedings of ICML 2004*, 2004.

[KON 02] KONDOR R.I., LAFFERTY J.D., "Diffusion kernels on graphs and other discrete input spaces", in *Proceedings of ICML 2002*, 2002.

[LEE 09] LEE H., CICHOCKI A., CHOI S., "Kernel nonnegative matrix factorization for spectral EEG feature extraction", *Neurocomputing*, vol. 72, no. 13-15, p. 3182-3190, 2009.

[LEO 02] LEOPOLD E., KINDERMANN J., "Text categorization with support vector machines. How to represent texts in input space?", *Machine Learning*, vol. 46, no. 1-3, p. 423-444, 2002.

[LES 02] LESLIE C.S., ESKIN E., NOBLE W.S., "The spectrum kernel: a string kernel for SVM protein classification", in *Pacific Symposium on Biocomputing*, 2002.

[LES 04] LESLIE C.S., ESKIN E., COHEN A., WESTON J., NOBLE W.S., "Mismatch string kernels for discriminative protein classification", *Bioinformatics*, vol. 20, no. 4, 2004.

[LES 03] LESLIE KUANG, "Fast kernels for inexact string matching", in *COLT: Proceedings of the Workshop on Computational Learning Theory*, 2003.

[MIK 99] MIKA S., SCHÖLKOPF B., SMOLA A.J., MÜLLER K.-R., SCHOLZ M., RÄTSCH G., "Kernel PCA and de-noising in feature spaces", in KEARNS M.S., SOLLA S.A., COHN D.A. (eds), *Advances in Neural Information Processing Systems 11*, 1999.

[NYF 06] NYFFENEGGER M., CHAPPELIER J.-C., GAUSSIER É., "Revisiting fisher kernels for document similarities", in *Proceedings of the ECML 2006 Conference*, 2006.

[PER 03] PERSONNAZ L., RIVALS I., *Réseaux de neurones formels pour la modélisation, la commande et la classification*, CNRS Editions, 2003.

[SAU 02] SAUNDERS C., SHAWE-TAYLOR J., VINOKOUROV A., "String kernels, fisher kernels and finite state automata", in *Proceeding of NIPS 2002*, 2002.

[SCH 02] SCHOELKOPF B., SMOLA A.J., *Learning with Kernels*, The MIT Press, Cambridge, MA, 2002.

[SHA 04] SHAWE-TAYLOR J., CRISTIANINI N., *Kernel Methods for Pattern Analysis*, Cambridge University Press, 2004.

[SIO 00] SIOLAS G., D'ALCHE BUC F., "Support vector machines based on a semantic kernel for text categorization", in *Proceedings of IJCNN-00, 11th International Joint Conference on Neural Networks*, 2000.

[SIO 02] SIOLAS G., D'ALCHÉ BUC F., "Mixtures of probabilistic PCAs and fisher kernels for word and document modeling", *Lecture Notes in Computer Science*, vol. 2415, p. 769-780, 2002.

[SMO 03] SMOLA KONDOR, "Kernels and regularization on graphs", in *COLT: Proceedings of the Workshop on Computational Learning Theory*, 2003.

[SUZ 03a] SUZUKI J., HIRAO T., SASAKI Y., MAEDA E., "Hierarchical directed acyclic graph kernel: methods for structured natural language data", in *Proceedings of the ACL 2003 Conference*, 2003.

[SUZ 03b] SUZUKI J., SASAKI Y., MAEDA E., "Kernels for structured natural language data", in *Proceedings of NIPS 2003*, 2003.

[TAK 03] TAKIMOTO E., WARMUTH M.K., "Path kernels and multiplicative updates", *Journal of Machine Learning Research*, vol. 4, p. 773-818, 2003.

[TSO 05] TSOCHANTARIDIS I., JOACHIMS T., HOFMANN T., ALTUN Y., "Large margin methods for structured and interdependent output variables", *Journal of Machine Learning Research*, vol. 6, p. 1453-1484, 2005.

[TSU 02] TSUDA K., KAWANABE M., RÄTSCH G., SONNENBURG S., MÜLLER K.-R., "A new discriminative kernel from probabilistic models", *Neural Computation*, vol. 14, no. 10, p. 2397-2414, October 2002.

[VAP 98] VAPNIK V., *Statistical Learning Theory*, Wiley, 1998.

[VIN 02] VINOKOUROV A., SHAWE-TAYLOR J., CRISTIANINI N., "Inferring a semantic representation of text via cross-language correlation analysis", in *Proceedings of NIPS 2002*, 2002.

[VIS 02] VISHWANATHAN S.V.N., SMOLA A.J., "Fast kernels for string and tree matching", in *Proceedings of NIPS 2002*, 2002.

[ZEL 03] ZELENKO D., AONE C., RICHARDELLA A., "Kernel methods for relation extraction", *Journal of Machine Learning Research*, vol. 3, p. 1083-1106, 2003.

[ZHU 05] ZHU J., HASTIE T., "Kernel logistic regression and the import vector machine", *Journal of Computational and Graphical Statistics*, vol. 14, no. 1, p. 185-205, 2005.

Chapter 5

Topic-based Generative Models for Text Information Access

5.1. Introduction

In this chapter, *generative* models of text documents are presented. They can either be used to classify texts (in *a priori* known classes/labels) or to cluster them (into groups, not known *a priori*). As presented in Appendix A, the only difference between classification/categorization and clustering comes from the data available for learning. In the case of classification, (document, class) couples are considered – this is called *supervised learning*, whereas in the case of clustering, only single documents are considered – this is called *unsupervised learning*. Semi-supervised learning also exists, where only a sub-part of the learning data is associated with a class [CHA 06b, ZHU 09]. From here in, the generic term "categorization" will be used for all of these situations.

Numerous generative models exist for text categorization [SEB 02, ZHO 05], but here we focus on the most successful of the most recent models (last decade): the Topic Models, also known as "latent semantic-based models", or "discrete principal component analysis" [BUN 06, STE 07, BLE 09].

5.1.1. *Generative versus discriminative models*

Generative and discriminative models (see Chapters 4 and 6) share the same framework, which can be described in general terms by two random variables X and Y, one of which (X) is observed, and the other (Y) is assumed or hidden, latent. These

Chapter written by Jean-Cédric CHAPPELIER.

models differ, however, in their objective: generative models supply an overall model of X *and* Y, whereas discriminative models focus on the possible values of Y for known values of X.

In mathematical terms, generative models model the joint probability distribution $P(x, y)$ (and therefore also the conditional distribution $P(x|y)$, where the *generative* aspect of x for known y is emphasized; as well as the distribution $P(x)$, allowing us to address unsupervised or semi-supervised learning [CHA 06b, ZHU 09]). On the other hand, discriminative models "only" model the conditional distribution $P(y|x)$, without making any further assumption about X itself[1].

Let us consider a concrete illustration with the automatic filtering of "spam" (undesirable emails, see also Appendix A). In such a case, the variable Y (scalar) represents the category/label ("desirable" or "undesirable"), whereas variable X represents the email itself.

Assuming simplified assumptions, a generative model aims at modeling the production of spam (in other words $P(x|$"undesirable"$)$) and of normal emails (in other words $P(x|$"desirable"$)$), as well as their proportions (in other words, $P($"desirable"$)$ and $P($"undesirable"$) = 1 - P($"desirable"$)$).

A discriminative model, however, aims at modeling the probability that a given email is spam or not (in other words $P($"undesirable"$|x)$), and does not make any further assumption about the way desirable or undesirable emails are generated.

Generative models, therefore, have the advantage of being able to be used to simulate (generate) new occurrences of all the variables of the model (in other words, both X and Y), whereas discriminative models "only" enable us to sample hidden variables (Y) for known values of the observed variables (X).

A contrario, during the learning process, generative models try to create a general model based on the observations, whereas the discriminative models "simply" model the observations, and make, in this sense, fewer assumptions.

If there are no good reasons for proposing a generative model of the data (little knowledge of the end mechanisms which underpin them), and if the only aim is to predict the hidden variables while knowing the observed variables, then using a generative model would certainly require more assumptions than necessary. In such a case, it would thus be preferable to choose a discriminative model, which will probably lead to better results.

---

1 The initial aim of discriminative models is not necessarily to model these *a posteriori* probabilities $P(y|x)$, but rather to find an association between the observed variables X and the variables Y to predict. The *a posteriori* estimation of probabilities is often only a consequence.

If, however, the proposed generative model is adequate, i.e. if the observed data do indeed come from such a model or a similar one, its learning through maximum likelihood on the data will be correct enough and the model could then be used either as a generator (of new data), or as a good predictor of the hidden variables for new observed variables.

Generative models are furthermore easy to interpret and correspond to natural intuitions in data. They can therefore be employed to express miscellaneous observations in an intuitive manner in terms of (conditional) probability distributions.

5.1.2. *Text models*

In the case of text documents, the aim of generative models is to find compact descriptions which can efficiently manipulate (categorize, cluster, search, etc.[2]) large quantities of documents. These descriptions aim at preserving the essential statistical dependencies that are necessary for the success of the targeted tasks.

In this framework, the observed variable X represents a document, often modeled as a term stochastic process[3]; and the hidden variable Y represents the category/label to be associated, as well as all the other unobserved parts of the assumed document model.

Although it is more intuitive to see a document as a sequence of terms, most models represent the documents as a "bags of words", in other words as sets of (term, count) pairs, where "count" represents the number of times the term is used in the corresponding document (see section A.2.2 of Appendix A).

Passing from one model to another ("sequence"/"bag of words") is trivial, but should be underlined in a first presentation, in order to disambiguate the frequently loose terminology used in the literature of the domain:

– for a sequence, the probability space is the space of all sequences of given length N; its cardinal is $|V|^N$, where V is the set of terms;

– for a "bag of words", the probability space is the space of all the integer $|V|$-tuples with sum N (given); its cardinal is $C_{N+|V|-1}^{|V|-1}$.

---

2 This domain also includes document retrieval and *text-mining* as particular sub-cases. Here a "document" generically designates a unit of processing, which can in practice correspond to entities smaller than "true" documents, such as queries (document retrieval) or sections (*text-mining*, information extraction).

3 Here "term" implies "indexation term", corresponding in reality to either words, stems, lemmas, or any other sophisticated feature considered as pertinent in the document pre-processing phase.

Table 5.1 summarizes the characteristics of these two models. Note that the two probabilistic models only apply to the set of documents with the same length[4], and only differ by the factor $\frac{N!}{\prod_w \text{tf}(w,d)!}$, where $\text{tf}(w, d)$ stands for the number of occurrences of term w in document d. This factor results from the transformation of one representation to another by assuming the invariance through the permutation of the sequence.

	"sequence"	"bag of words"
document:	terms sequences	"bag of words"
example:	cat ate mouse black cat	(cat, 2) (ate,1) (black,1) (mouse,1)
probability space:	V^N	$[\![1, N]\!]^{|V|}$ (summing up to N: simplex)
cardinal of this space:	$|V|^N$	$C_{|V|+N-1}^{|V|-1}$
parameters:	μ of size $|V|$ and of sum 1, representing $P(w)$	μ (same conditions) and N
probability of a document:	$\prod_{w \in V} \mu_w^{\text{tf}(w,d)}$	$\dfrac{N!}{\prod_{w \in V} \text{tf}(w, d)!} \prod_{w \in V} \mu_w^{\text{tf}(w,d)}$
usual notation:	Discrete(μ), but also sometimes loosely written as Multinomial(μ) by analogy with Multinomial($\mu, 1$)	Multinomial(μ, N) or simply Multinomial(μ)

Table 5.1. *Compared characteristics of "sequence" and "bag of words" models*

All the models considered later in this chapter use the "bag of words" representation; in other words, the order of the terms in a document can be ignored (for the considered task); the only information taken into account is the number of times a term appears in a document.

This assumption of ignoring the order of the terms in the representation of documents seems too simplistic from a linguistic point of view. However, it is justified, not only by the fact that, in practice, it leads to efficient and relatively high performance methods for the tasks considered, but also by the fact that the terms, in other words the features selected for representing the documents, are not necessarily limited to the surface forms in the linguistic sense. A linguistic pre-processing could increase

---

4 The probabilities of two documents of different lengths shall thus not be directly compared, unless the (implicit) assumption is made that all document lengths are all equally probable.

the interchangeable aspect of the features that are finally selected for indexing the documents.

As underlined by Blei *et al.* [BLE 03b], we also note that the notion of interchangeable random variables is not equivalent to the more usual assumption of independent identically distributed variables ("i.i.d."): interchangeable random variables are only *conditionally* independent and identically distributed. The assumptions which underline the "bag of words" model are therefore weaker than those of an i.i.d. model.

5.1.3. *Estimation, prediction and smoothing*

Application of generative probabilistic models to documents categorization confronts two typical problems in practice:

1) finding "good" values for all the parameters on which the model depends; "good" often signifying "which explains best a given set of documents" (the learning corpus $\mathcal{C}$);

2) processing new documents of which nothing but their contents (the terms) is yet known (as opposed to documents already known, contained in $\mathcal{C}$).

These two problems of inference are quite different: the first is known as "learning", "training" or "parameter *estimation*". The second is known as "reconstruction", "projection" or "*prediction*".

Let x be the new document to consider. The prediction problem requires the computation of $P(x|\mathcal{C})$. From a Bayesian point of view:

$$P(x|\mathcal{C}) = \int P(x|\mu) P(\mu|\mathcal{C}) \, d\mu$$

where μ is a general representation of the model parameters. Very often this integral is simply estimated in a point by.

$$P(x|\mathcal{C}) \simeq P(x|\widehat{\mu}_{\mathcal{C}})$$

where $\widehat{\mu}_{\mathcal{C}}$ is an estimation of μ on the corpus $\mathcal{C}$, for example the "maximum likelihood" estimate: $\widehat{\mu}_{\mathcal{C}} = \text{argmax}_{\mu} P(\mathcal{C}|\mu)$. The prediction problem becomes difficult when the computation of $P(x|\mu)$ requires the marginalization of hidden variables ($P(x|\mu) = \int P(x,y|\mu)dy$), too numerous or too difficult to estimate. This latter point is discussed in depth for a particular case in section 5.3.2.6.

The estimation problem addresses the following question: given a corpus $\mathcal{C}$ of documents, what values of the model parameters are best to explain the creation of this corpus? The estimation problem involves maximizing $P(\mu|\mathcal{C})$, or even explicitly computing it. The first case leads to punctual estimates, either "maximum *a posteriori*" or "maximum likelihood", whereas the second case is known as "Bayesian estimation".

Maximum likelihood estimation often leads the learned model to assign a zero probability to the terms that are absent from the learning corpus. Processing an entirely new document, not seen in the learning corpus, has, in practice, a strong chance of containing terms that were absent from the learning corpus. These terms will therefore, at best, be ignored by the models resulting from such an estimation and, at worst, be cancelers of the likelihood for such documents; which, in practice, is catastrophic.

Classical practical estimations of generative models therefore include "smoothing" of the model learned, so that a strictly zero probability to the unobserved terms is no longer imposed. Diverse smoothing techniques exist [ZHA 04], most of which can be related to a "maximum *a posteriori*" estimation for a well chosen *a priori* distribution over the model parameters.

Several usual smoothing techniques are justified only for simple models, but not for more complex models, such as those addressed in this chapter. In fact, they do not correspond to a "maximum *a posteriori*" estimation anymore. It is therefore desirable for such models, instead of using maximum likelihood estimation and some arbitrary smoothing, to directly introduce the non-observed events via *a priori* distributions over the model parameters (Bayesian approach) and perform estimation through "maximum *a posteriori*". This role, equivalent to smoothing, is controlled by "meta-parameters" (or "hyper-parameters").

5.1.4. *Terminology and notations*

Before giving an in-depth presentation of the topic models, let us conclude this introduction by a summary of the specific notations used in this chapter.

A corpus $\mathcal{C}$ can be seen in two ways: either as a set of documents or as a set of occurrences of terms. Let $|\mathcal{C}|$ denote the number of documents in the corpus, whereas $\|\mathcal{C}\|$ designates the number of occurrences of terms in the corpus.

The notion of "document model" or "theoretical document", (ideal) modeling of a document, is written as d, and the notion of "concrete document", which represents a real document, is written as $\widehat{d}$ where necessary, and more simply d when there is no ambiguity and when we want to underline its relationship with a particular document model. Concrete documents can also be written as w when we are only interested in their content (list of terms), and do not want to underline its relationship with a specific model.

In the same spirit, the following notations must be emphasized: $\sum_{w \in V}$ and $\sum_{w \in d}$ represent summations over term *values*, as opposed to $\sum_{w \in \widehat{d}}$ or $\sum_{w \in w}$, which represent summations over term *occurrences*. Both are linked by the following relation:

$$\sum_{w \in \widehat{d}} f(w) = \sum_{w \in V} \mathrm{tf}(w, \widehat{d}) f(w).$$

We also note $\widehat{P}(w|d)$ for the "empirical probability" of w in the document $\widehat{d}$, in other words $\widehat{P}(w|d) = \mathrm{tf}(w, \widehat{d})/|\widehat{d}|$.

Concerning probability laws, "Discrete(μ)" denotes the discrete law with parameter μ. When it is necessary to explicitly represent the underlying random variable, for example X, we write "Discrete($x|\mu$)" to mean "$X \simeq$ Discrete(μ)". A similar notation is used for multinomial and Dirichlet laws: Multinomial(μ) and Dirichlet(μ).

To conclude on the mathematical notation side, $\delta_{i,j}$ represents the Kronecker symbol ($\delta_{i,j} = 1$ if $i = j$ and 0 if not), and the tensors (third order in this chapter) are noted by an underline: $\underline{\Phi}$; $\Phi(k)$ is then a matrix, of term $\varphi_{ij}(k)$.

5.2. Topic-based models

5.2.1. Fundamental principles

The multinomial model (presented in section A.2.3 of Appendix A) represents in the same way all the documents considered. This can be useful for general considerations on the language or the overall corpus, but cannot differentiate between sub-sets such as categories or documents.

The very similar mixture of multinomials model (a.k.a. "Naive Bayesian model") [LEW 98, MCC 98, NIG 00], models the documents through the *a priori* choice of one theme, unique for the whole document, followed by the succession of the term choices for this theme (see section A.3 of the Appendix A).

The Topic Models are generative models which represent the documents as *mixtures* of "topics"; a topic being nothing more than a probability distribution over the vocabulary.

The essential contribution of these models comes from their ability to represent the documents, not simply as collections of terms, but as a much less numerous collections of topics, from which the document terms were chosen.

These models assume that the essential semantic information contained in the documents necessary for their categorization can be obtained from the term-document co-occurrence matrix. The reduction of underlying dimensions of this matrix is an essential part of the representation mechanism[5]. Furthermore, the topic representation

---

5 Topic models can be seen as a discrete variant of both principal component analysis and independent component analysis [BUN 02, BUN 06].

of documents allows us, through the processing of the co-occurrences, to take polysemy (same term corresponding to different topics) and synonymy (different terms corresponding to the same topic) into account.

The common fundamental generative mechanism of the topic models is to imagine a document as the result, for each of the document terms, of the choice of a topic followed by the choice of a term corresponding to this topic.

This idea (topic modeling) comes directly from the "bag of words" nature retained for representing the documents. In fact, the Finetti theorem [FIN 31], as well as its generalization in a non-binary case [HEW 55], shows that all collections of interchangeable random variables (in other words, invariants through circular permutations, assumptions precisely made in the "bag of words" model) can be represented as a mixture (generally of infinite size) of conditional distributions. In the case of text documents, it is precisely these conditional distributions which are known as "topics".

5.2.2. *Illustration*

Before going into the mathematical details, let us start with a concrete illustration of the topic models. This example comes from a real case resulting from the application of one of the models described later in the chapter (LDA, section 5.3.2) to a corpus of 7,486 news from the Associated Press agency collected in 1989[6].

Here are the 15 most probable terms from 4 topics (among 100) of this model:

CHURCH	UNIVERSITY	OIL	FARM
CATHOLIC	AMERICAN	PRODUCTION	LAND
RELIGIOUS	PROFESSOR	MILLION	FARMERS
SUNDAY	RESEARCH	PRICES	SCALE
GOD	YEARS	OPEC	AGRICULTURE
POPE	INSTITUTE	PETROLEUM	DAMAGE
REV	COLLEGE	BARRELS	QUAKE
SERVICE	SCIENCE	CRUDE	ACRES
JOHN	ACADEMY	GAS	EARTHQUAKE
PEOPLE	YORK	MARKET	WILDLIFE
PAUL	GREAT	ENERGY	DEPARTMENT
VATICAN	SOCIETY	DAY	AGRICULTURAL
CHURCHES	FOUNDATION	PRODUCERS	RICHTER
PART	DIRECTOR	COUNTRIES	ANIMAL
ST	DEAN	INDUSTRY	AREA

---

6 Documents AP890101-0001 to AP890131-0311 of the "TREC–AP 89" corpus [HAR 95]. This excerpt contains 1,517,844 occurrences of 52,425 terms, filtered and lemmatized. The longest document has 728 term occurrences and the average size of a document is 201 term occurrences.

Some of terms are of course ambiguous (polysemic), for example *play* which appears in the 15 most frequent terms of the following two topics:

Topic 64	Topic 97
GAME	FILM
TEAM	MOVIE
WORLD	**PLAY**
WON	ACTOR
YEAR	DIRECTOR
BOWL	THEATER
PLAYED	FILMS
SUPER	WEEKS
YEARS	MAN
DOWNTOWN	MOVIES
FOOTBALL	SCREEN
FIELD	BROADWAY
OFFICE	ACTRESS
PLAYING	MISS
GAMES	CHARACTER

Here there are two typical documents for the usage of topics 64 and 97 (in subscript, a probabilistic estimation of the topic corresponding to each term in this context. The ignored terms, filtered during the pre-processing, are in gray):

Document AP890113–0056:

[...] In Israel$_{81}$, it was estimated$_7$ that more than 2 million$_{64}$ of the 4.2 million$_{64}$ people$_{13}$ followed the game$_{64}$ in the first live$_{81}$ broadcast$_{35}$ from Moscow$_{50}$. Maccabi$_{64}$ held$_{74}$ a 71–51 lead$_{41}$ with 12 minutes$_{29}$ to $\boxed{\text{play}_{64}}$ but the Soviet$_{50}$ team$_{64}$ stormed$_{15}$ back$_1$ to within 93–89 on the $\boxed{\text{play}_{64}}$ of guard$_{65}$ Vladimir$_{50}$ Gorin$_{64}$ and forward$_{50}$ Sergei$_{50}$ Tarakanov$_{64}$, [...]

Document AP890127–0153:

The London$_{72}$ premiere$_{35}$ of David$_{35}$ Mamet$_{97}$'s "Speed$_{97}$-the-Plow$_{97}$" received$_{58}$ mixed$_{97}$ reviews$_{97}$ for the $\boxed{\text{play}_{97}}$ itself and for the actress$_{97}$ in the role$_{97}$ created$_{97}$ by Madonna$_{97}$. The acerbic$_{97}$ comedy$_{97}$, which ended$_{20}$ its hit$_{97}$ Broadway$_{97}$ run$_{97}$ New Year$_{20}$'s Eve$_{27}$, opened$_{97}$ in London$_{31}$ on Wednesday$_{60}$ at the National$_{24}$ Theatre$_7$, [...]

Their probability distributions over the topics are given in Figure 5.1. It can be seen that the topic model illustrated here considers document AP890113–0056 to be

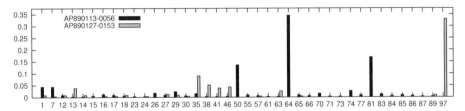

Figure 5.1. *Probabilistic distribution over the topics (of non-zero probability) for two documents taken as an example in the text*

essentially composed of topics 64, 81, and 50, whereas document AP890127–0153 is essentially composed of topics 97, 35, 38, 46, and 41.

5.2.3. *General framework*

The general framework of the topic models [BUN 02, BUN 04, BUN 06, HEI 09a] consists of two ingredients: on the one hand, the modeling $P(z|d)$ of a discrete choice of topics for a given document, and on the other hand the modeling $P(w|z)$ of the choice, also discrete, of terms for a given topic.

Formally, the probability of each term w in a document model d is:

$$P(w|d) = \sum_{z \in Z} P(z|d)\ P(w|z)$$

where Z is the set of topics used by the model, $P(z|d)$ is the modeling choice of the topic z for the document model d, and $P(w|z, d)$, by assumption equal to $P(w|z)$, models the choice of a term w for the z topic (in the document model d).

For example, if the model of document d is represented by a general parameter θ_d, the probability of a real document $\widehat{d}$ considered as the implementation of the model d is obtained by marginalizing on θ_d:

$$P(\widehat{d}) = \int \prod_{w \in \widehat{d}} \overbrace{\sum_{z \in Z} P(z|\theta_d)\ P(w|z)}^{P(w|\theta_d)}\ \mathrm{d}\,P(\theta_d)$$

This general framework can be summarized with the aid of the graphical model[7] given in Figure 5.2. A summary of the most common models in view of these two components is presented in Table 5.2. The mixture of multinomials (MM) is presented in section A.2.3 of Appendix A, PLSI in section 5.3.1 of this chapter, LDA in section 5.3.2, and DCM and DCM–LDA in sections 5.4.2 and 5.4.3, respectively. The other models are simply mentioned as extensions in section 5.3.3.2 and in the conclusion.

To these two fundamental ingredients should another one, often unemphasized, be added: the way to compute the (thematic/semantic) similarity between two documents. This later point is addressed in section 5.5.

---

7 A "graphical model" is a compact visual representation of a probabilistic model which highlights the dependencies between the different parameters and components of this model [JEN 01, BIS 06, KOL 09]. See also Chapter 6.

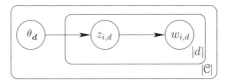

Figure 5.2. *General graphical representation of topic models: the circles represent random variables and the rectangles represent random process. For each of the $\mathcal{C}$ documents in the corpus, for each of the $|d|$ occurrences of terms $w_{i,d}$ in such a document, a topic $z_{i,d}$ is first drawn according to a distribution parametrized by θ_d. Term $w_{i,d}$ is then drawn according to a distribution parametrized by $z_{i,d}$. Real examples are illustrated in Figure 5.5*

	$P(\theta_d)$	$P(w|z)$ multinomial	$P(w|z)$ Pólya	$P(w|z)$ Poisson
$\delta_{\theta_d\,\widehat{\theta}}$ (in other words a fixed parameter *a priori*, the same for all documents)		MM (section A.2.3 of Appendix A)	DCM (section 5.4.2)	
$\delta_{\theta_d\,\widehat{\theta}_d}$ (in other words, one parameter for each d, fixed *a priori*)		PLSI (section 5.3.1)		NMF [LEE 99]
Dirichlet		LDA (section 5.3.2)	DCM–LDA (section 5.4.3)	
logistic		CT [BLE 05, BLE 07]		
gamma				GaP [CAN 04]

Table 5.2. *Compared characteristics of several generative document models. θ_d is the vector which parametrizes $P(z|d)$*

5.2.4. *Geometric interpretation*

The topic probabilistic models have a quite intuitive geometric interpretation: a real document $\widehat{d}$, represented in the form of a "bag of words", corresponds to a point in the term-simplex (of dimension $|V| - 1$), the coordinates of which are $\widehat{P}(w|d)$ (for all $w \in V$). Moreover, a topic (which is a probability distribution over V) is also a point in this simplex: the set of topics therefore define a sub-simplex with dimension $|Z| - 1$ in the term-simplex, the topic-simplex.

Finally, a theoretical document (in other words a generator following the model), expressed as a linear combination of topics, is a point situated in the topic-simplex.

When the number of topics is much smaller than the number of terms, the topic-simplex constitutes only a small part of the term-simplex and the projection of a concrete document on this topic-simplex therefore allows a "dimension reduction" which hopefully characterizes the (semantic) content of the document.

To graphically illustrate this geometric interpretation, let us consider a trivial example with four terms and three topics (see Figure 5.3). Suppose that the vocabulary is reduced to $V = \{$charcoal, chocolate, cake, black$\}$ and the three topics are $z_1 = (0, 0.75, 0, 0.25)$ (for example, talking only about "chocolate", one third of the time about "black chocolate" and the other two thirds about "chocolate" on its own), $z_2 = (0, 0.5, 0.5, 0)$ (for example, only "chocolate cake" is occurring) and $z_3 = (0.1, 0, 0, 0.9)$ ("black" is often occurring, but sometimes also "charcoal").

In this 4D-space, the term-simplex is therefore the 3D tetrahedral represented in light gray in Figure 5.3, and the topic-simplex is the triangle defined by z_1, z_2, and z_3.

In a topic model, a theoretical document is characterized by the proportion of topics; for example $(\frac{1}{3}, \frac{2}{3}, 0)$, which corresponds to the point $d_0 = (0, \frac{7}{12}, \frac{1}{3}, \frac{1}{12})$ of the term-simplex and can lead to the document $\{$(chocolate, 7), (cake, 4), (black, 1)$\}$. This point also lies in the topic-simplex.

Imagine the real document $\widehat{d_1} = \{$(chocolate, 3), (cake, 2), (black, 1)$\}$. It corresponds to the point $(0, \frac{1}{2}, \frac{1}{3}, \frac{1}{6})$ of the term-simplex. This point is not necessarily in the topic-simplex (the model is not exact or the documents are "noisy").

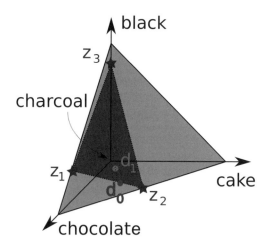

Figure 5.3. *A geometric interpretation of the topic models: the topic-simplex (triangle z_1, z_2, z_3) is a sub-simplex of the term-simplex (tetrahedral in clear gray, (charcoal, chocolate, cake, black)). d_0 is a document model, a point in the topic-simplex. d_1 corresponds to a real document, seen as a distribution over the terms, in other words a point in the term-simplex*

To deepen this geometric illustration: the multinomial model (see section A.2.3 of Appendix A) would be reduced to only one point in the term-simplex (and all the documents are considered as a noisy sample of this point); and the mixture of multinomials model assumes that each real document is a sample of one of the points corresponding to the corners of the topic-simplex.

More complex models associate a document with a point in the topic-simplex, or propose even further a probabilistic model for the position of such points (in other words, a probability distribution over the topic-simplex). This aspect is re-addressed in section 5.3.2.2.

5.2.5. *Application to text categorization*

There exist many applications of the topic models[8], which are used for text categorization in several different manners, the principles of which are summarized here. These models can be used either in a direct generative manner, or in a discriminative framework. Furthermore, they can be applied to either supervised (classification) or unsupervised (clustering) problems. A major part of topic models take place in the unsupervised framework, either for corpus analysis or for the prediction of documents. These models produce a "soft clustering" through the $P(z|d)$ probability distributions over the topics they provide for each document [BAN 05]. They can thus be used to regroup semantically similar documents, hopefully close in the topic-simplex (see section 5.5.2). The $P(z|d)$ vectors are used as a dimension reduction for the representation of d. In other words, each document is represented by its affine coordinates in the topic-simplex instead of its coordinates in the the the term-simplex [HOF 99, GRI 04, STE 07, BLE 07]. In this framework (generative and unsupervised), another similarity measure between the documents can also be used, based on the probability of producing one document knowing the parameters of another document [AZZ 04, WEI 06] (see section 5.5.1).

Moreover, topic models can be adapted to the prediction of classes/labels in supervised applications, still relying on the generative framework. The introduction of the classes is done in different ways:

– by constructing a topic model for each class, and maximizing the prediction $P(w|Class)$ [BLE 03b];

– by introducing the class as an extra variable in the general model [BUN 04, BUN 06, BLE 08, LAC 09];

---

8 Consider for instance the proceedings of two recent workshops dedicated to this subject in two very reputable conferences in automatic statistical learning: the "Workshop on Applications for Topic Models: Text and Beyond" at *NIPS 2009*, and the "Workshop on Topic Models: Structure, Applications, Evaluation, and Extensions" at *ICML 2010*.

– by adding a metric between the topics and the desired classes [MEI 07, HEI 05];

– by conditioning by the class, the topics of a document: $P(z|d, \text{Class})$ instead of $P(z|d)$ [RAM 09];

– or by other ad-hoc techniques [BLE 03c, FLA 05, MCC 06].

Finally, the topic models, although intrinsically generative, can also be used in the discriminative framework: either by using Fisher kernels as proposed by Jaakkola and Haussler [JAA 99] (see section 5.5.3); or by using the $P(z|d)$ vector as a dimension reduction of the d representation (*feature extractor*) and applying a usual discriminating algorithm (SVM for example, see Chapter 4) on this representation [BLE 03b].

Whatever the approach used, the representation of new documents w (not seen during the estimation from a corpus $\mathcal{C}$) is necessary; whether through their probability $P(w|\mathcal{C})$ or through their topic distribution, $P(z|w, \mathcal{C})$. This is done by re-estimating the corresponding parameters [BLE 03b, BUN 04, GRI 04, HEI 09b, MIS 08, WAL 09, BUN 09].

The main well-known difficulty comes from $P(w|\mathcal{C})$, since the marginalization on z of the joint distribution $P(w, z|\mathcal{C})$ operates on a space that is too large to be directly computed or even estimated in a simple and viable manner (in a reasonable time). Different techniques have therefore been developed to efficiently estimate $P(w|\mathcal{C})$ for example, by the evaluation of $P(w|\widehat{z})$ for a single (well chosen) estimate $\widehat{z}$ of z [BUN 04, GRI 04][9], or more sophisticated techniques based on different sampling methods [WAL 09, BUN 09]. These techniques are discussed in-depth for LDA in section 5.3.2.6.

5.3. Topic models

Section 5.2.3 emphasized that the core of topic generative models has three constituents: topic generation models, $P(z|d)$, term generation models $P(w|z)$, and the thematic similarity measures between documents.

This section presents the main topic generation models, which are often used in combination with multinomials as term (counts) generation models. Section 5.4, addresses the alternatives to the multinomial for the generation of terms. Finally, similarity measures are addressed in section 5.5.

---

9 The *harmonic* mean corresponds in this case to the *importance sampling* estimator [ROB 99] with minimal variance; but it is biased [WAL 09, BUN 09].

5.3.1. *Probabilistic Latent Semantic Indexing*

5.3.1.1. *Model*

"Probabilistic Latent Semantic Indexing" (PLSI) [HOF 99, HOF 00, HOF 01] was a founding model of the topic-based probabilistic generative approach for text categorization and information retrieval. It led to diverse expansions and applications on text [COH 00, VIN 02, GAU 02, STE 04, JIN 04, MEI 06], sound [AHR 05], and graphical [MON 04, QUE 05, BOS 06, MON 07, LIE 07] data.

PLSI models the corpus documents as successive samples of random (document index, term) couples: iteratively, a topic $z \in Z$ is first drawn, according to a probability $P(z)$ following a Discrete(τ) law, then a term w, and a document index d (in other words a number between 1 and $|\mathcal{C}|$) are drawn according to $P(w|z)$ and $P(d|z)$ probabilities following Discrete(φ_z) and Discrete(χ_z) laws, respectively. In PLSI, w and d are assumed to be independent for a known z, in other words:

$$P(w, d|z) = P(w|z)\ P(d|z)$$

The probability of a (d, w) pair is therefore:

$$P(d, w) = \sum_{z \in Z} \tau_z\ \varphi_{zw}\ \chi_{zd}$$

and the probability of a real document $\widehat{d}$ (with index d in the corpus) is:

$$P(\widehat{d}) = \prod_{w \subset \widehat{d}} P(d, w).$$

The corpus is thus seen as a set of occurrences of pairs (d, w), regrouped by d to form real documents, and for each of which an (unknown) topic z was drawn.

The graphical model for PLSI is given in Figure 5.4. Its parameters are $\mu = (\tau_z, \varphi_{zw}, \chi_{zd})$, for all z, w, and d of the model. Other equivalent parametrization are possible, but this one is the most often used. The equivalent parametrization clarifying the link with the other models presented in this chapter is as follows:

$$P(d, w) = \nu_d \sum_{z \in Z} \theta_{dz}\ \varphi_{zw}$$

where ν_d parameters $P(d)$ and θ_{dz}, $P(z|d)$. Of course, the following relationships hold: $\nu_d = \sum_z \tau_z\ \chi_{zd}$ and $\theta_{dz} = \tau_z\ \chi_{zd} / \nu_d$.

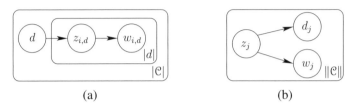

Figure 5.4. *Equivalent graphical representations of the PLSI model. Presentation (a) is similar to the one given in Figures 5.2, and 5.5. Presentation (b) accentuates the usual parametrization of this model*

For a learning corpus $\mathcal{C}$, these parameters are estimated by a "tempered" variant (annealing) of the *Expectation-Maximization* algorithm (EM, see section A.3.2 of Appendix A) [HOF 99, HOF 01]:

E-step:
$$P(z|w,d) = \frac{\tau_z \, (\chi_{zd} \, \varphi_{zw})^{1/t}}{\sum_{z' \in Z} \tau_{z'} \, (\chi_{z'd} \, \varphi_{z'w})^{1/t}}$$

M-step:
$$\tau_z = \frac{\sum_{d \in \mathcal{C}} \sum_{w \in d} \text{tf}(w,d) \, P(z|w,d)}{\|\mathcal{C}\|}$$

$$\varphi_{zw} = \frac{\sum_{d \in \mathcal{C}} \text{tf}(w,d) \, P(z|w,d)}{\|\mathcal{C}\| \, \tau_z}, \qquad \chi_{zd} = \frac{\sum_{w \in d} \text{tf}(w,d) \, P(z|w,d)}{\|\mathcal{C}\| \, \tau_z}$$

where the "temperature" parameter t used in the E-step is necessary for limiting overfitting of this model. This parameter linearly increases from 1 to an optimal value empirically estimated on the validation set.

Notice that, apart from the temperature parameter, the above formulas can simply be expressed according to the Bayesian formula and the maximum likelihood estimator $P(w,d)$, $\widehat{P}(w,d) = \text{tf}(w,d)/\|\mathcal{C}\|$:

E-step:
$$P(z|w,d) = \frac{P(z) \, P(d,w|z)}{P(d,w)} = \frac{P(z) \, P(d|z) \, P(w|z)}{\sum_{z'} P(z') \, P(d|z') \, P(w|z')}$$

M-step:
$$P(z) = \sum_d \sum_w P(d,w) \, P(z|w,d) \simeq \widehat{P}(z) = \sum_{d \in \mathcal{C}} \sum_{w \in d} \widehat{P}(d,w) \, P(z|w,d)$$

$$P(w|z) = \frac{\sum_d P(d, w) P(z|w, d)}{P(z)} \simeq \frac{\sum_{d \in \mathcal{C}} \widehat{P}(d, w) P(z|w, d)}{\widehat{P}(z)}$$

$$P(d|z) = \frac{\sum_w P(d, w) P(z|w, d)}{P(z)} \simeq \frac{\sum_{w \in d} \widehat{P}(d, w) P(z|w, d)}{\widehat{P}(z)}$$

5.3.1.2. Illustration

Let us illustrate the PLSI model on a concrete case resulting from its application with 64 topics to a corpus of 425 *Times* magazine articles from 1963, corresponding to 114,850 occurrences of 13,367 terms.

Here are the 10 most probable terms of 6 topics chosen at random (among the 64, where the first illustrated is the most probable topic):

GOVERN	PAKISTAN	PARK	SPI	FORC	SOVIET
DIEM	KASHMIR	SOUTH	AGENT	NATO	MOSCOW
BUDDHIST	KASSEM	KOREA	TRAIN	NUCLEAR	KHRUSHCHEV
VIET	INDIA	CIVILIAN	SOVIET	EUROP	CHINES
GENERAL	INDIAN	JUNTA	GEHLEN	BRITAIN	RED
SOUTH	PAKISTANI	POLIT	RUSSIAN	ALLI	COMMUNIST
NAM	AREF	KIM	SECRET	NATION	RUSSIAN
SAIGON	TALK	GENERAL	BRITISH	FRANC	PEKE
PRESID	NEHRU	INDONESIA	OFFICI	EUROPEAN	RUSSIA
FORC	NEGOTI	POWER	INTELLIG	BRITISH	PARTI

The beginning of the most probable document for the second topic given above is (after pre-processing):

```
kashmir talking at last the british raj , which once controlled
india 's northwest frontier province of kashmir , exacted a
token annual tribute of two kashmiri shawls and three
handkerchiefs from the maharajah . never since has the price of
peace been as small . in the years after independence in 1947
split the indian subcontinent into the sovereign states [...]
```

and its distribution over the 64 topics (in other words its θ_d parameter) is:

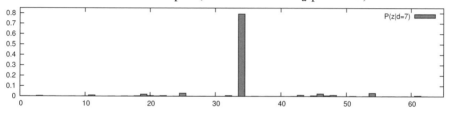

where topic 34 (peak) is the one previously illustrated in the second column above.

5.3.1.3. *Limitations*

When it was introduced, PLSI performed very well on several corpora of modest size, up to several million occurrences. This contributed to its popularity. However, PLSI remains incomplete in the sense that it explicitly depends on the variables d, in other words on document identifiers, for which it provides no models. In PLSI, each known document is represented by its list of topics weights (θ_{dz} parameters), but there is not even a single model (and even less a generative one) for these weight lists.

This downside leads to several problems [POP 01, BLE 03b, WEL 08]:

1) the number of parameters in PLSI increases linearly with the size of the learning corpus, which is a serious practical limitation, leading to over-fitting;

2) there are no clear theoretical methods for applying parameters to new documents (and therefore using them), in other words for working outside of the learning corpus: the "*folding-in*" method originally proposed [HOF 99], being nothing more than a theoretically problematic practical palliative [WEL 08].

For these reasons Blei, Ng, and Jordan proposed another model: Latent Dirichlet Allocation (LDA), a Bayesian extension of PLSI.

5.3.2. *Latent Dirichlet Allocation*

The main problem with PLSI is that it is requires us to know the θ_{dz} parameters, representing $P(z|d)$, probability over topics for a given document. It is therefore impossible to correctly account for new documents, for which these parameters are unknown. The analysis through "Latent Dirichlet Allocation" (LDA) [BLE 03b] compensates for this problem by proposing a general model for θ_{dz} (instead of limiting it to a particular document d). The idea is to include an *a priori* distribution over the parameters controlling the choices of topics, i.e. a probability distribution on the θ_{dz} themselves.

LDA therefore solves the two fundamental problems of PLSI (over-fitting and incapacity to properly modeled documents outside of corpus learning) by considering the mixture of topics introduced by the documents as a hidden random variable (with $|Z|$ dimensions) instead of an enormous set of ad-hoc parameters specifically linked to the learning corpus (the θ_{dz}). Doing so, LDA is able to generalize to new documents that are not found in the learning corpus.

Furthermore, LDA can also be considered as an extension of the mixture of multinomials model (see Appendix A) for which the constraint of having a single topic per document is relaxed to having a topic for each term. Other diverse intermediary models with different criteria between the terms and document can then be thought up, for example associating a topic per section. This amounts to applying the mixture of multinomials model to shorter "documents", for instance the sections of a document. From this point of view LDA constitutes an extreme, associating one topic with every smallest unit, i.e. the terms.

5.3.2.1. *Model*

LDA is a topic model such as the one presented in section 5.2, where the topics are drawn according to a Dirichlet distribution and the terms for a given topic according to a discrete distribution, smoothed by a meta-model that follows another Dirichlet distribution.

This model corresponds to the generator scheme given in Table 5.3 and graphically represented in Figure 5.5. Its complete likelihood is:

$$P(w, z, \theta, \Phi | \alpha, \beta) = \text{Dirichlet}(\theta | \alpha) \, \text{Dirichlet}(\Phi | \beta) \prod_{i=1}^{|w|} \theta_{z_i} \, \varphi_{z_i w_i} \qquad [5.1]$$

where z represents the set of topic assignments to each term occurrence (in other words, to each w component) and Φ is the matrix of φ_z.

    – choose meta-parameters: (a vocabulary V,) a number of topics $|Z|$, a vector α of $|Z|$ strictly positive real numbers and a vector β of $|V|$ strictly positive numbers;

    – for each topic z, draw the φ_z parameters according to a Dirichlet(β) distribution;

    – for each document:

       - draw a document size $|d|$ (e.g. according to a Poisson law ζ, with $\zeta \simeq \text{Gamma}(\sum_z \alpha_z, 1)$),

       - draw a θ_d distribution over the topics according to Dirichlet(α);

       - for each term occurrence (i from 1 to $|d|$):

       (1) draw a topic $z_{i,d}$ according to Discrete(θ_d);

       (2) draw a term $w_{i,d}$ according to Discrete($\varphi_{z_{i,d}}$).

An alternative for the last loop consists of directly simulating word counts of the "bag of words" model by:

    - for the terms w in the vocabulary V, draw the count vector tf(w, d) according to Multinomial($\sum_z \theta_{dz} \, \varphi_z, |d|$).

Table 5.3. *Generative model of a set of documents following LDA*

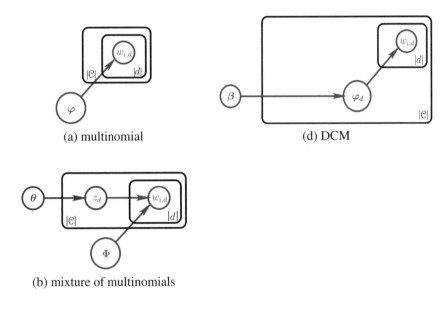

(a) multinomial   (d) DCM

(b) mixture of multinomials

(c) LDA   (e) DCM–LDA

Figure 5.5. *Graphical illustration of the LDA model (c) in comparison to other generative models presented in Appendix A and in this chapter*

The log-likelihood given a corpus $\mathcal{C}$ is therefore:

$$\ell(\mathcal{C}; \boldsymbol{\alpha}, \boldsymbol{\beta}) = \sum_{d \in \mathcal{C}} \log \iint P(\boldsymbol{\theta}|\boldsymbol{\alpha}) \, P(\boldsymbol{\Phi}|\boldsymbol{\beta}) \prod_{i=1}^{|d|} \sum_{z \in Z} \theta_z \, \varphi_{zw_{id}} \, d\boldsymbol{\theta} \, d\boldsymbol{\Phi}$$

$$= \sum_{d \in \mathcal{C}} \log \iint P(\boldsymbol{\theta}|\boldsymbol{\alpha}) \, P(\boldsymbol{\Phi}|\boldsymbol{\beta}) \prod_{w \in V} \left(\sum_{z \in Z} \theta_z \, \varphi_{zw} \right)^{\text{tf}(w, d)} d\boldsymbol{\theta} \, d\boldsymbol{\Phi}$$

where we can see in the second equation the second formulation of the model given in Table 5.3.

An illustration of this model was provided in section 5.2.2, for the following parameters: $|V| = 52, 425$, $|Z| = 100$, $\alpha = 0.5$, and $\beta = 0.01$.

The choice of the terms according to a discrete law is quite common and usual; what is really new in LDA is the choice of topics:

1) not once for all, for a given document (like in mixture of multinomials model), but for each new term occurrence (as in PLSI), therefore offering a larger thematic richness to the documents;

2) this choice of topic itself follows a parametrized *a priori* distribution. The choice of a Dirichlet distribution sounds here appropriate from a theoretical point of view: the Dirichlet distribution is a conjugate prior for the multinomial distribution, the resulting distribution being thus also a Dirichlet distribution, thereby making computations much easier[10].

A $|Z|$-dimensional Dirichlet distribution parametrized by α (a $|Z|$-sized vector, the components of which are all strictly positive) is a distribution over the simplex with dimension $|Z| - 1$ such that:

$$P(\boldsymbol{\theta}|\boldsymbol{\alpha}) = \Gamma(S) \prod_{i=1}^{|Z|} \frac{\theta_i^{\alpha_i - 1}}{\Gamma(\alpha_i)}$$

where Γ represents the "gamma function" and $S = |\alpha|_1 = \sum_{i=1}^{|Z|} \alpha_i$.

The components of α represent the relative importance of each component of θ, the average point being $\bar{\theta} = \frac{1}{S}\alpha$. Their sum S (inversely) influences the variance around this average point[11], as illustrated in Figures 5.6 and 5.7. When one of the α_i approaches 1, the corresponding component approaches 0. For α_i smaller than 1, the distribution tends to "sharply increase" (in other words, to discretize) to the maximum α_i values (see Figures 5.6 and 5.7). When α_i is larger than 1 the mode (in other words the most probable point) is given by:

$$\check{\theta} = \frac{1}{S - |Z|}(S\bar{\theta} - 1) = \frac{1}{|\alpha - 1|_1}(\alpha - 1)$$

---

10 In addition, the Dirichlet distribution is in the exponential family. It therefore has sufficient statistics that remain of finite dimensions (Pitman-Koopman-Darmois theorem). This is an advantage for its estimation. Furthermore, the conjugate distributions in the exponential family have a geometric interpretation [AGA 10].

11 $\mathbf{Var}(\theta) = (\mathbf{diag}(\bar{\theta}) - \bar{\theta}\bar{\theta}^T)/(S + 1)$.

5.3.2.2. *Geometric interpretation of LDA*

To illustrate the difference between LDA and PLSI, let us consider the geometric framework presented in section 5.2.4.

Through its parameters, PLSI positions the different documents of the learning corpus as so many points in the topic-simplex; but nothing is known beyond these points (no generalization to the documents outside the learning corpus).

LDA, however, represents each document (known or unknown) as a (Dirichlet) probability *distribution* over the topic-simplex.

The underlying Dirichlet distributions of the LDA model have a smoothing effect on topic and term distributions. As mentioned in the previous section, in Figures 5.6 and 5.7, when the norm of these parameters is large, the variation over the possible distributions is quite low, whereas when these parameters are smaller, the possible distributions are widely varied. This smoothing effect is reduced by decreasing the α and β values. This leads to a more strict association of the topics to the documents (α) and of the terms to the topics (β), as the Θ and Φ matrices become more sparse.

When Φ is sparse (this is controlled by β), the model assigns fewer terms to each topic, which in turn influences the number of topics that the model can find in the corpus. This relates to the similarity between the terms of a given topic: with "sparse"

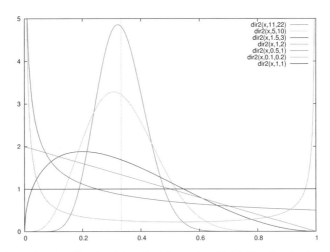

Figure 5.6. *Several probability densities of unidimensional Dirichlet distributions ("beta law") corresponding to different parameters α: $(11, 22)$, $(5, 10)$, $(\frac{3}{2}, 3)$, $(1, 2)$, $(\frac{1}{2}, 1)$, $(\frac{1}{10}, \frac{1}{5})$, and $(1, 1)$. Note how the $S = \alpha_1 + \alpha_2$ parameter (inversely) influences the concentration of the probability density and how, when the components are lower than 1, the distribution tends to "sharply increase" at the edges*

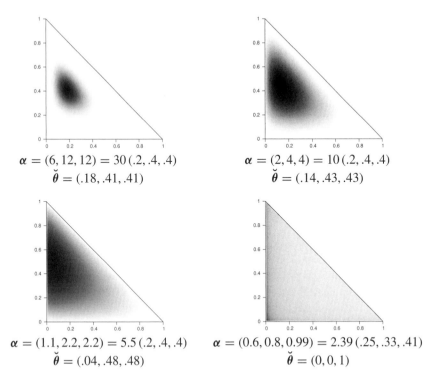

Figure 5.7. *Several Dirichlet probability densities on the 2-simplex (triangle) corresponding to different α parameters. Darker zones indicate higher values. Note how the $S = \alpha_1 + \alpha_2 + \alpha_3$ parameter (inversely) influences the concentration of the probability density. It should also be noticed how when one of the α components approaches 1 the corresponding density tends to 0 and when the components are smaller than 1 the distribution "sharply increases" (on (0,0) in the bottom right figure, in other words concentrates on $\theta - (0,0,1)$)*

topics, the higher the number of topics, the better the model will be able to describe the corpus (due to the fact that in this case the model avoids associating several topics to the same term). The number $|Z|$ of topics must therefore be chosen in relation to the meta-parameters.

The sparseness of Θ (controlled by α) indicates that the model tries to associate a small number of topics with each document.

α is, therefore, an indicator of how much the documents can differ in the choice of topics and β is an indicator of the size of the terms sets which frequently co-occur, in other words by how much the topics can differ in the choice of their terms.

The values of α, β, and $|Z|$ thus enable us to modulate the LDA model behavior. In an empirical manner, Griffiths and Steyvers proposed for example $\alpha \simeq 50/|Z|$

and $\beta \simeq 0.01$ with symmetrical Dirichlet distributions (in other words $\boldsymbol{\alpha} = \alpha \mathbf{1}$ and $\boldsymbol{\beta} = \beta \mathbf{1}$) [GRI 02, STE 07]. This symmetrical aspect, that is usually used, implies in theory a reduction of the variation in the usage of topics. This effect can however be controlled by the α value, as previously discussed. It nevertheless seems to be preferable not to use symmetrical distributions and to estimate the $\boldsymbol{\alpha}, \boldsymbol{\beta}$ values instead of fixing them *a priori* [HEI 09b, DOY 09, ASU 09, WAL 10]. This point is re-addressed in section 5.3.2.5.

The number $|Z|$ of topics is another meta-parameter of the model, which also influences its application: too few topics in relation to the target (corpus) thematic complexity, generates very unspecific and ultimately too similar topics, whereas a large $|Z|$ leads to relatively arbitrary and hardly interpretable topics, too specific to the peculiarities of the learning corpus (fortuitous co-occurrences between terms).

Deciding the most appropriate number of topics is often done through "cross validation". This consists of minimizing, in this parameter $|Z|$, the perplexity of the model on a validation corpus (complementing the learning corpus and very clearly distinct from the evaluation corpus!) [BLE 03b, GRI 04, ROS 04]. Another possibility for estimating this number is to use non-parametric Bayesian methods [TEH 06].

Let us now present the usual inference algorithms (see section 5.1.3) for LDA: first the inference of hidden variables, then the estimation of meta-parameters, and eventually the prediction for new documents.

5.3.2.3. *Variational inference*

For LDA, the problem of hidden variable inference requires the computation of $P(z, \boldsymbol{\theta}, \boldsymbol{\Phi}|w, \boldsymbol{\alpha}, \boldsymbol{\beta})$, or even $P(z|w, \boldsymbol{\alpha}, \boldsymbol{\beta})$ directly, when this is possible and when only topic inference is desired.

Unfortunately, the probability distribution over these hidden parameters ($\boldsymbol{\theta}$, $\boldsymbol{\Phi}$, and z) knowing the observables (documents) and meta-parameters ($\boldsymbol{\alpha}$ and $\boldsymbol{\beta}$),

$$P(z, \boldsymbol{\theta}, \boldsymbol{\Phi}|w, \boldsymbol{\alpha}, \boldsymbol{\beta}) = \frac{P(w, z, \boldsymbol{\theta}, \boldsymbol{\Phi}|\boldsymbol{\alpha}, \boldsymbol{\beta})}{P(w|\boldsymbol{\alpha}, \boldsymbol{\beta})},$$

cannot be computed in practice due to the normalization

$$P(w|\boldsymbol{\alpha}, \boldsymbol{\beta}) = \iint \sum_z P(w, z, \boldsymbol{\theta}, \boldsymbol{\Phi}|\boldsymbol{\alpha}, \boldsymbol{\beta}) \, d\boldsymbol{\theta} \, d\boldsymbol{\Phi}$$

which does not factorize and includes $|Z|^{|w|}$ terms [DIC 83, GRI 04][12].

---

12 This is equally true of the marginalized version $P(z|w, \boldsymbol{\alpha}, \boldsymbol{\beta})$.

The solution, therefore, consists of using approximated inference algorithms, such that Expectation Propagation [MIN 02], not presented here[13], mean-field variational methods [JOR 99, BUN 02, BLE 03b], which are now detailed, or Gibbs sampling [GRI 02][14] detailed in the next section and which seemed for a long time to lead to better practical results than variational methods [GRI 04, BUN 04]; but competitive improvements of the latter have recently been developed [TEH 07, ASU 09].

The basic idea of "convex variational methods" is to use the Jensen inequality to find a computationally tractable lower bound approximation of $P(z, \theta, \Phi|w, \alpha, \beta)$; and to maximize this approximation. The closest possible approximation is searched through the "*variation*" of additional parameters (the "variational parameters") of a parametrized family chosen *a priori* [JOR 99]. The process occurs in two steps: first search for the best approximation through the computation of variational parameters; and then maximize, in the original parameter, this approximation.

In the precise case of LDA, the difficulty of computing the normalization coefficient $P(w|\alpha, \beta)$ comes from the coupling between θ and Φ (via the $\theta_z\varphi_{zw}$ term, see equation [5.1]). The family of considered approximations aims at removing this dependency between the parts of model by introducing:

$$a(z, \Theta, \Phi; H, \Xi, \Lambda)$$
$$= \prod_{z \in Z} \text{Dirichlet}(\varphi_z|\lambda_z) \prod_{d \in \mathcal{C}} \text{Dirichlet}(\theta_d|\eta_d) \cdot \text{Multinomial}(z^{(d)}|\Xi_d)$$

as an approximation of $P(z, \Theta, \Phi|\mathcal{C}, \alpha, \beta)$, where Θ is the matrix of θ_d for all the corpus documents $\mathcal{C}$; H, Ξ, Λ are the variational parameters, and $z^{(d)}$ is the part of z corresponding to document d.

Notice that Ξ_d and η_d depend on the document: η_d being a means to represent document d in the topic-simplex (approximation of θ_d).

The best approximation is then found by minimizing (numerically, through a "fixed point" method) the Kullback–Leibler divergence between $a(z, \Theta, \Phi; H, \Xi, \Lambda)$ and $P(z, \Theta, \Phi|\mathcal{C}, \alpha, \beta)$. This leads, for each document d of corpus $\mathcal{C}$, to the following iterative (in t) formula (for all z of Z and all i between 1 and $|d|$):

---

13 Even though this algorithm seems to lead to better results than the two presented approaches, it requires much more memory than these: its spatial complexity is $\mathcal{O}(|Z| \cdot \|\mathcal{C}\|)$, where those of the algorithms presented is that of $\mathcal{O}(|Z| \cdot (|V| + \mathcal{C}))$. This limitation is prohibitive for its application to large size corpora ($\|\mathcal{C}\| \gg \max(|V|, \|\mathcal{C}\|)$).

14 Pritchard, Stephens, and Donnelly [PRI 00] have applied the same algorithm to a model very similar to LDA but in the genetic domain.

$$\xi_{d,i,z}^{(t+1)} \propto \varphi_{zw_i} \exp\left(\Psi(\eta_{dz}^{(t)})\right) \quad \text{and} \quad \eta_{dz}^{(t+1)} = \alpha_z + \sum_{i=1}^{|d|} \xi_{d,i,z}^{(t+1)}$$

where Ψ is the "Di gamma" function, which is the derivative of the logarithm of the gamma function.

Λ is independent of d and is iteratively (in t) estimated by (for all $z \in Z, w \in V$):

$$\lambda_{zw}^{(t+1)} = \beta_w + \sum_{d \in \mathcal{C}} \sum_{i \in I(d,w)} \xi_{d,i,z}^{(t+1)}$$

where $I(d,w)$ represents the set of positions (indexes) where term w is found in document d.

Note that more sophisticated versions marginalizing variables θ_d and φ_z have been developed (*collapsed variational Bayes* [TEH 07]), which lead to better results [ASU 09].

5.3.2.4. *Gibbs sampling inference*

The previously mentioned inference method requires us to explain the dependencies on Θ and Φ. Instead of estimating these parameters (φ_{zw} and θ_{dz}), Griffiths and Steyvers directly estimate the *a posteriori* distribution $P(z|\mathcal{C}, \alpha, \beta)$ by marginalizing on these parameters, therefore enabling a model estimation only in terms of topic assignments z for each term w of the corpus [GRI 02]. In a second step, θ and Φ can, if necessary, be estimated from the empirical evaluation of the conditional distribution $P(z|\mathcal{C}, \alpha, \beta)$.

The problem with the direct estimation of the distribution $P(z|\mathcal{C}, \alpha, \beta)$ is that it has very large dimensions. Specifically:

$$P(z|\mathcal{C} = w, \alpha, \beta) = \frac{\prod_i P(w_i, z_i | \alpha, \beta)}{\prod_i \sum_z P(w_i, z_i = z | \alpha, \beta)},$$

the difficulty in the evaluation of which emerges from the sum in the denominator, which includes $|Z|^{\|\mathcal{C}\|}$ terms.

Gibbs sampling, and more generally Markov Chain Monte Carlo methods (MCMC), aims at simulating high-dimensional probability distributions in terms of the stationary states of Markov chains.

One advantage of such approaches is that it is not necessary to explicitly represent the model parameters, as they can be totally marginalized. In the example that we are currently concerned with, it is not necessary to explicit the Θ and Φ parameters since they can be interpreted as statistics related to topic–term associations, the states of the simulated Markov chain. This approach consisting of marginalizing internal parameters of the model is known as the Rao-Blackwell approach [ROB 99]. The models can, therefore, be expressed more simply in terms of the assignments of a topic to each term occurrence; the hidden part to be reconstructed are the z_i assignments of the topics to each of the corpus terms.

Gibbs sampling consists of looking in turn at each occurrence of a term from the learning corpus and estimating the probability $P(z_i|w_i, \alpha, \beta)$ such that topic z_i corresponds to the considered term occurrence w_i, taking into account the assignment of topics made till now for all the other corpus term occurrences. From this estimation, a new topic is allocated to the term considered; then the procedure is repeated on the next term occurrence. A typical run of the algorithm is illustrated in Figure 5.8.

Specifically, Gibbs sampling includes three phases: the initialization (a topic is assigned at random to each occurrence of a term in the corpus), the "*burn-in*" (calibration), and the exploitation (or sampling itself). The "burn-in" phase is necessary for the exploitation phase not to be too much dependent on the initial conditions. Determining how long the "burn-in" phase has to be is one of the difficulties of Gibbs sampling.

To derive the sampling algorithm in the case of LDA, the following formula is used [GRI 02, GRI 04, STE 07, HEI 09b]:

$$P(z_i|w, z_{(-i)}, \alpha, \beta) = \frac{P(w, z|\alpha, \beta)}{P(w, z_{(-i)}|\alpha, \beta)} \propto P(w_i|w_{(-i)}, z, \beta)\, P(z_i|z_{(-i)}, \alpha)$$

where $w_{(-i)}$ is the set of (occurrences of) terms w without that in position i and $z_{(-i)}$ is an assignment of topics to each of these (occurrences of) terms. At each step, a topic z is drawn at random according to this distribution, which is then re-estimated:

$$P(z_i = z|C, z_{(-i)}, \alpha, \beta) \propto \frac{N_{(-i)}(w_i, z) + \beta_{w_i}}{\sum_{w \in V}\left[N_{(-i)}(w, z) + \beta_w\right]} \frac{M_{(-i)}(d(w_i), z) + \alpha_z}{\sum_{z \in Z}\left[M_{(-i)}(d(w_i), z) + \alpha_z\right]}$$

where $N_{(-i)}(w, z)$ corresponds to the number of times topic z is assigned to term w in the $z_{(-i)}$ assignment, $M_{(-i)}(d, z)$ corresponds to the number of times topic z is assigned to any one of the document terms d, without counting the occurrence i currently under consideration, and $d(w_i)$ represents the document containing the ith term of the corpus.

The previous equation clearly denotes the parameters that influence the assignment of a topic to a given term:

– the first part of the equation (about $N_{(-i)}$) is an estimator of the probability of term w_i in topic z, $P(w_i|z)$;

– the second part (about $M_{(-i)}$) represents an estimator of the probability of topic z, but only estimated from the view of document $d(w_i)$ for the current assignment.

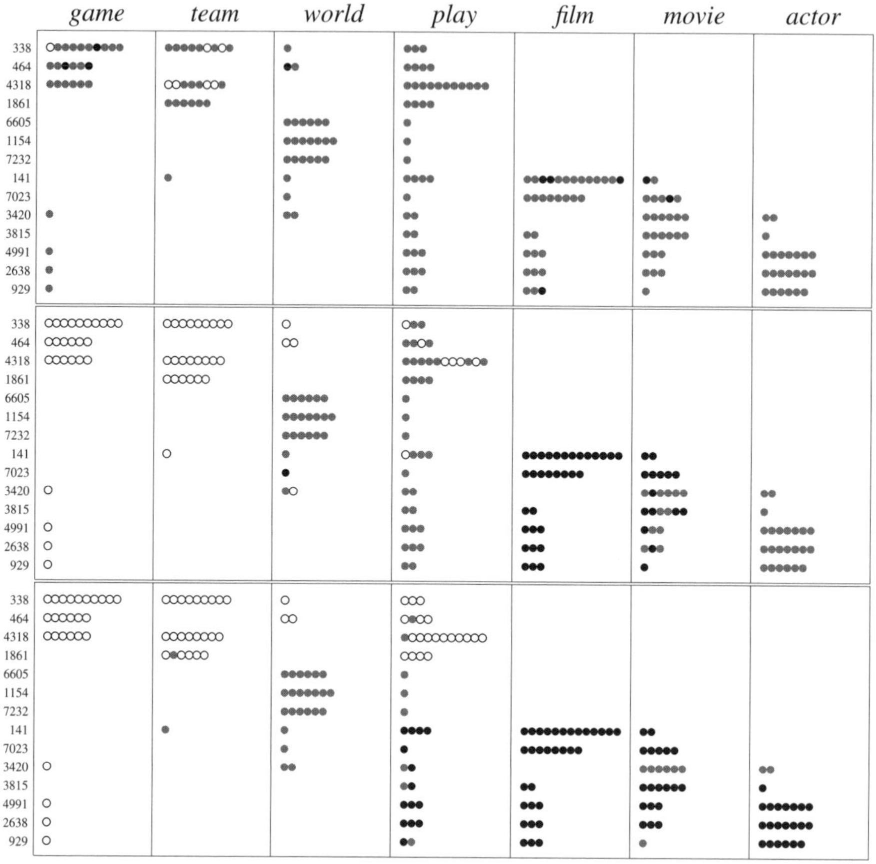

	game	team	world	play	film	movie	actor

(Illustration of Gibbs sampling — documents as rows: 338, 464, 4318, 1861, 6605, 1154, 7232, 141, 7023, 3420, 3815, 4991, 2638, 929 — in three groups of rows corresponding to 10, 100, and 1000 iterations; each cell plots the topic assignments as white, black, and gray circles.)

Figure 5.8. *Illustration of the Gibbs sampling algorithm. For 7 terms (columns) of 14 documents extracted from TREC-AP (rows), the chosen topic is plotted for each corresponding term occurrence in the corresponding document after 10, 100, and 1000 iterations of the algorithms (group of rows). For simplification, a white circle ○ represents the assignment of topic 64 from the example in section 5.2.2, a black circle ● represents topic 97 and a gray circle • represents the assignment of whatever other topic (at each occurrence of the same term). It can clearly be seen how the terms and the topics are organizing over the iterations*

If, at the corpus level, several occurrences of a same term are assigned to the same topic z, this increases the first estimator and therefore the probability of (again) assigning another occurrence of this term to topic z. Furthermore, if topic z was assigned to several terms of the same document, this increases the second estimator and therefore the probability of (again) assigning to topic z all occurrences of any term of this document.

The Gibbs sampling algorithm enables us only to estimate the assignment of a topic to an occurrence of a given term in a given document. However, several applications require estimators for Φ and Θ. This can be achieved with the help of the following formulas:

$$\varphi_{zw} = \frac{N(w, z) + \beta_w}{|\boldsymbol{\beta}|_1 + \sum_{w' \in V} N(w', z)} \quad \text{and} \quad \theta_{dz} = \frac{M(d, z) + \alpha_z}{|d| + |\boldsymbol{\alpha}|_1}$$

where $N(w, z)$ represents the number of times, in the whole corpus, term w is assigned to topic z, and $M(d, z)$ is the number of times topic z is assigned to any of the terms of document d. We can see in these formulas, maximum *a posteriori* estimators of $P(w|z)$ and $P(z|d)$ respectively, estimated from a corpus where all the occurrences of a term would be labeled (by a topic).

From a practical point of view, notice that the partial counts in the sampling algorithm can be computed very simply through successive updates of the total counts:

$$N_{(-i)}(w, z) = N(w, z) - \delta_{z, z_i}, \quad M_{(-i)}(d, z) = M(d, z) - \delta_{z, z(w_i)} \delta_{d, d(w_i)}$$

To summarize, Algorithm 5.1 precisely details the estimation of the LDA model through Gibbs sampling.

5.3.2.5. *Estimation of the meta-parameters*

Several approaches have been developed to estimate the α and β meta-parameters, either by deterministic (variational methods, section 5.3.2.3) or by non-deterministic (Gibbs sampling, see section 5.3.2.4) estimation methods. These approaches aim at maximizing the likelihood $\ell(\mathcal{C};\alpha,\beta)$ given the learning corpus or some validation corpus.

This maximization can simply be performed by multiple evaluations on diverse validation corpora once the other parameters have been learned (*grid search* [ASU 09]), or can be integrated in the learning algorithm itself.

In variational inference methods, the variational approximation is optimized (in α and β) over the whole learning corpus:

1) find Λ and, for each document d of the corpus, Ξ_d, and η_d as indicated in section 5.3.2.3;

2) maximize (in α and β) the resulting variational approximation $a(z, \Theta, \Phi; H, \Xi, \Lambda)$. This is done through Newton–Raphson numerical approximation [BUN 02, BLE 03b].

For the Gibbs sampling method, α and β are estimated using a fixed point algorithm as proposed by Minka [MIN 00, HEI 09b]:

$$\alpha_z^{(t+1)} = \alpha_z^{(t)} \frac{\left(\sum_{d \in \mathcal{C}} \Psi(M(d, z) + \alpha_z^{(t)})\right) - |\mathcal{C}| \Psi(\alpha_z^{(t)})}{\left(\sum_{d \in \mathcal{C}} \Psi(|d| + |\boldsymbol{\alpha}|_1)\right) - |\mathcal{C}| \Psi(|\boldsymbol{\alpha}|_1)}$$

Algorithm 5.1. Estimation of the LDA model by Gibbs sampling.

Inputs: $\mathcal{C}$, α, β, $|Z|$

Initialization:

  for all the v *of V and* z *of Z (or of 1:$|Z|$),* **do** n[v][z] $\leftarrow 0$

  for all the z *of Z,* **do** nt[z] $\leftarrow 0$

  for all the d *of* $\mathcal{C}$ *and* z *of Z,* **do** m[d][z] $\leftarrow 0$

  for all the d *of* $\mathcal{C}$, **do**

    for all the w, *(occurrence of) word of d,* **do**

      draw z according to Discrete($\frac{1}{|Z|}$ **1**)

      update:

        topic[d][w] $\leftarrow$ z

        increment m[d][z], n[w][z] and nt[z]

    end

  end

Then, *until necessary* (first "burn-in" phase, then exploitation phase, as long as samples are required):

  for all the d *of* $\mathcal{C}$ **do**

    for all the w *of d* **do**

      suppression of the current topic assignment:

        z $\leftarrow$ topic[d][w]

        decrease m[d][z], n[w][z] and nt[z]

      re-sampling: draw z according to

$$P(z_i = z|z_{(-i)}, \mathcal{C}, \alpha, \beta) \propto \frac{(n[w][z]+\beta_w)\,(m[d][z]+\alpha_z)}{|\beta|_1 + n[z]}$$

      update:

        topic[d][w] $\leftarrow$ z

        increment m[d][z], n[w][z] and nt[z]

    end

  end

Estimate (best, if possible, averaged over several samples, adequately spaced away from one another) $\varphi_{zw} = \frac{n[w][z]+\beta_w}{|\beta|_1 + n[z]}$ and $\theta_{dz} = \frac{m[d][z]+\alpha_z}{|d|+|\alpha|_1}$

return Φ, Θ *and topic[d][w] for all the occurrences [d][w] of the corpus* $\mathcal{C}$.

(and similar in β). This method can be refined, either by averaging over several steps of the Gibbs sampling [WAL 06], or by introducing some smoothing, in a Bayesian manner by considering α and β themselves as random variables following an *a priori* Dirichlet [WAL 10] or Gamma [ASU 09] distribution.

5.3.2.6. *Prediction*

Let us recall section 5.2.5: the main difficulty with topic models is the computation of the likelihood $P(w|\mathcal{C})$ for a new document w, outside of the learning corpus, once the estimation of the model parameters has been conducted.

In the case of LDA, this amounts to computing $P(w|\alpha, \Phi)$, where α and Φ are estimated on the $\mathcal{C}$, and both z and θ are marginalized. The problem specifically comes from the marginalization of z: there is no known analytical form and its exhaustive computation requires the evaluation of $|Z|^{|w|}$ terms. Several techniques exist for estimating it, the best of which include "left to right sequential sampling" methods, which is unbiased but has a time-complexity that is quadratic in the size of the document, and "mean-field approximation importance sampling", which is slightly biased but has a linear time-complexity [BUN 09].

Important sampling [ROB 99] consists of evaluating values of the kind of $\mathbb{E}(f(X))$ through Monte Carlo simulations, by replacing the true underlying distribution $P(X)$, often unknown or too complex, with a well-chosen approximation $Q(X)$, easier to compute and leading to a good approximation (low bias and low variance). The evaluation is performed by:

$$\mathbb{E}(f(X)) \simeq \frac{1}{N} \sum_{n=1}^{N} f(x_n) \frac{P(x_n)}{Q(x_n)}$$

for N Monte Carlo samples x_n of X according to $Q(X)$ (instead of $P(X)$).

In our case, the aim is to evaluate:

$$P(w|\alpha, \Phi) = \mathbb{E}_z(P(w|z, \alpha, \Phi))$$

by simulating the unknown assignments of topics z_i to word w_i in the considered document. Estimation through importance sampling therefore becomes (for N Monte Carlo samples of assignment z):

$$\mathbb{E}_z(P(w|z, \alpha, \Phi)) \simeq \frac{1}{N} \sum_{n=1}^{N} \frac{P(w, z_n|\alpha, \Phi)}{Q(z_n|\alpha, \Phi)}$$

In the approach proposed by Buntine [BUN 09], the $Q(z|\alpha, \Phi)$ distribution is itself constructed iteratively by a mean field approximation of the theoretical optimum; leading to the following formulation:

$$Q(z|\alpha, \Phi) = \prod_{i=1}^{|z|} Q_i(z_i|\alpha, \Phi)$$

with:

$$Q_i(z|\alpha, \Phi) \propto \varphi_{zw_i} \left(\alpha_z + \sum_{j \neq i} Q_j(z|\alpha, \Phi) \right)$$

initialized as:

$$Q_i(z|\alpha, \Phi) \propto \varphi_{zw_i} \alpha_z$$

The other approach, unbiased but more computationally demanding, consists of breaking down $P(w|\alpha, \Phi)$ "from left to right":

$$P(w|\alpha, \Phi) = \prod_{i=1}^{|w|} P(w_i|w_1^{i-1}, \alpha, \Phi)$$

(where $w_1^{i-1} = w_1, \ldots, w_{i-1}$) and to estimate each term $P(w_i|w_1^{i-1}, \alpha, \Phi) = \mathbb{E}_{z_1^{i-1}}(P(w_i|w_1^{i-1}, z_1^{i-1}, \alpha, \Phi))$ independently by:

$$P(w_i|w_1^{i-1}, \alpha, \Phi) \simeq \frac{1}{N} \sum_{n=1}^{N} P(w_i|w_1^{i-1}, z_1^{i-1}, \alpha, \Phi)$$

over N Monte Carlo sequential samples z_1^{i-1} according to $P(z_1^{i-1}|w_1^{i-1}, \alpha, \Phi)$, and where:

$$P(w_i|w_1^{i-1}, z_1^{i-1}, \alpha, \Phi) = \sum_{z_i \in Z} \varphi_{z_i w_i} P(z_i|z_1^{i-1}, \alpha)$$

5.3.3. Conclusion

5.3.3.1. Link between PLSI and LDA

Section 5.3.1 shows that the main disadvantage of the PLSI model is not having a generative model for the variable d that represents the documents. This lack leads to theoretical and practical difficulties in the computation of the probabilities for unknown documents (not included in the learning corpus). This drawback can however be bypassed by noting, as done in [BUN 02] and [GIR 03], that PLSI is a simpler version of LDA.

In fact, PLSI appears to be an LDA model for which a uniform *a priori* distribution was chosen, in other words a Dirichlet distribution with a α parameter with all components equal to 1[15].

---

15 More precisely, with a uniform *a priori* probability (Dirichlet(1)) and without β smoothing on Φ, LDA is a complete Bayesian estimator of the same model as that for which PLSI is a maximum likelihood estimator (or a maximum *a posteriori* estimator, both being equal in this case).

5.3.3.2. *Other topic models*

There are several extensions of the general generative topic model presented in section 5.2, described by Buntine as *Discrete Principal Component Analysis* [BUN 02, BUN 06] and of which LDA is the most commonly known instance: e.g. changing of the *a priori* distribution over the topics in order to better capture their hierarchical correlations (*Correlated Topics Model*) [BLE 05, BLE 07][16], hierarchical versions allowing for better organization of the topics [BUN 04, BLE 04, HEI 09a, BLE 10], generalizing to graphs with any dependencies (*Pachinko Allocation*) [LI 06], separating the features into different categories, each with its own model [BUN 04, AZZ 04, NAL 08] or processing term sequences (correlations) using *n*-grams [WAL 06] or HMM's [GRI 05, TEH 06].

A large survey of topic methods, and in particular of their estimation methods, was published by Buntine [BUN 02, BUN 04, BUN 06, BUN 09]. He derived the LDA variational estimation algorithm from a more general theoretical framework (exponential families), and including some adaptations on the normalizations, showed how it corresponds to *Non-negative Matrix Factorization* (NMF) [LEE 99] and PLSI[17].

By introducing a model of the document length, he also showed an analogy with the independent components analysis (ICA) [HYV 01]. Finally, he underlined how the Gamma Poisson (GaP) model [CAN 04] is also part of the topic model framework[18]. Table 5.2 shows a summary of these different models.

5.4. Term models

5.4.1. *Limitations of the multinomial*

Independently of the modeling of the underlying topics of a document, another line of text document modeling involves the production of the terms themselves (or more precisely of their counts, in the "bag of words" models). The fundamental model usually used for this is the multinomial. However, the multinomial only very roughly models the term distributions empirically observed [CHU 95, KAT 96, BAA 01, REN 03, MAD 05, CLI 08]. In particular, it does not correctly represent the empirically observed phenomenon of "burstiness", repetition of terms already used: when a term has appeared once in a document, its probability of appearing again is increased

---

16 "Correlated Topics" are an extension of LDA in which the *a priori* distribution over the topics no longer is a Dirichlet distribution, but another distribution in the exponential family: the logistic-normal distribution.

17 The analogy between these two models was also noticed in [GAU 05].

18 Notice that independent Gamma random variables follow, conditionally to their sum, a Dirichlet law, and independent Poisson random variables follow, conditionally to their sum, a multinomial.

(as opposed to a term that would have the same probability at the beginning, but was then not used).

The multinomial is able to represent the burstiness effect only for the most frequent terms, but not at all for the rarest: making their probability of being seen k times exponentially decreasing with k is a very bad approximation for such terms. These terms badly approximated by the multinomial typically represent 95–99% of the vocabulary and typically 30% of the corpus, and are furthermore often the most discriminant ones.

Other models for the generation of terms have therefore been proposed. The remainder of this section focuses on "Dirichlet compound multinomial" (DCM) models [MAD 05]. Other choices are also possible, such as the Poisson law (GaP model [CAN 04]), although its usage for modeling term counts is questionable [KAT 96], the "Negative Binomial" law [CHU 95] or the "β-Negative Binomial" (BNB) [CLI 08].

5.4.2. Dirichlet compound multinomial

The DCM (*Dirichlet Compound Multinomial*) model [MAD 05] aims at being an alternative to the multinomial that takes the burstiness effect into account. The idea is to replace the multinomial with a Pólya distribution. The Pólya distribution is in fact the *a posteriori* distribution of a multinomial having an *a priori* Dirichlet distribution over its parameters[19].

The usual presentation is thus made through an *a priori* Dirichlet distribution over the multinomials generating the term counts. The description of this model is given in Table 5.4 and its graphical illustration in Figure 5.5.

In this framework, the probability of a document d becomes:

$$P(d|\beta) = \int_\phi P(d|\varphi)\,P(\varphi|\beta)\,d\varphi = \int_\varphi \text{Multinomial}(d|\varphi)\,\text{Dirichlet}(\varphi|\beta)\,d\varphi$$

$$= \frac{|d|!}{\prod_{w \in V} \text{tf}(w, d)!} \frac{\Gamma(S)}{\Gamma(S + |d|)} \prod_{w \in V} \frac{\Gamma(\beta_w + \text{tf}(w, d))}{\Gamma(\beta_w)}$$

$$= \text{Pólya}(d|\beta)$$

with $S = |\beta|_1 = \sum_i \beta_i$. A consequence of the Dirichlet distribution properties (see Figures 5.6 and 5.7) is that the larger S, the more the Pólya law tends toward a multinomial.

---

19 This distribution comes from the modeling of a "Pólya urn", where the urn contains N colored balls (with K possible colors). Each time a ball is drawn, not only is it placed back in the urn, but another additional ball of the same color is also introduced. Therefore the most probable colors become even more probable, illustrating the burstiness effect well.

> – draw a φ topic according to Dirichlet($\boldsymbol{\beta}$)
> – for each term occurrence (i from 1 to $|d|$):
>   - draw a term w_i according to Discrete(φ).

Table 5.4. *Generative model of a document according to DCM [MAD 05]*

Regarding the parameter estimation, there is unfortunately no exact formula for the maximum likelihood. A method similar to EM is thus applied, thereby giving rise to the following re-estimation formula:

$$\beta_w^{(t+1)} = \beta_w^{(t)} \frac{\left(\sum_{d\in\mathcal{C}} \Psi(\text{tf}(w, d) + \beta_w^{(t)})\right) - |\mathcal{C}| \Psi(\beta_w^{(t)})}{\left(\sum_{d\in\mathcal{C}} \Psi(\text{tf}(w, d) + |\boldsymbol{\beta}^{(t)}|_1)\right) - |\mathcal{C}| \Psi(|\boldsymbol{\beta}^{(t)}|_1)}$$

In practice, this estimation is moreover *a posteriori* smoothed by a small additive constant (in other words, a hundredth of the smallest of the β_i is added to all of them). From a Bayesian point of view, it would be preferable to introduce an *a priori* distribution over the values of $\boldsymbol{\beta}$ itself, a Dirichlet [WAL 10] or Gamma [ASU 09] distribution for example.

The DCM model performs just as well as the best sophistications on the multinomials [MAD 05], but the framework is here more clearly established, if not theoretically justified.

5.4.3. *DCM–LDA*

A quite natural idea therefore consists of replacing the term generation module of LDA (multinomials) with a module that takes burstiness into account, e.g. DCM. This was proposed in [DOY 09]. The description of this model is given in Table 5.5 and its graphical illustration in Figure 5.5.

The difference rests in the fact that in LDA, the multinomial distribution of the terms of each topic depends on the whole corpus, whereas in DCM this distribution is specific to each document: in LDA, $\boldsymbol{\Phi}$ is a matrix of size $|Z| \times |V|$ representing the (conditional) probabilities of the terms by topic; whereas in DCM–LDA, $\underline{\boldsymbol{\Phi}}$ becomes a third order tensor of size $|Z| \times |V| \times |\mathcal{C}|$ representing the conditional of these terms by topic *for each document*. Thus, $\underline{\boldsymbol{\Phi}}$ cannot be used as the general representation of the model vocabulary (since it depends on each document). This role is performed by the matrix $\boldsymbol{B}$ of the $\boldsymbol{\beta}_z$, whereas in LDA vector $\boldsymbol{\beta}$ has only a minor role and the general representation of the vocabulary is carried out by $\boldsymbol{\Phi}$.

In addition, in DCM–LDA, the components of $\boldsymbol{B}$ are not constrained to sum up to 1 (as opposed to those of $\boldsymbol{\Phi}$ in LDA), which offers to this model $|Z|$ more degrees of freedom, enabling it to capture the "burstiness" effect of the per-topic term

> – draw a topic distribution θ_d according to Dirichlet(α);
> – for each topic z, draw the $\varphi_z(d)$ parameters according to a Dirichlet(β_z) distribution;
> – for each term occurrence (i from 1 to $|d|$):
> - draw a topic z_i according to Discrete(θ_d),
> - draw a term w_i according to Discrete($\varphi_{z_i}(d)$).

Table 5.5. *Generative model of a document according to DCM–LDA [DOY 09]*

distributions [ELK 06]. The smaller the sum of a β_z component, the more "bursty" the model can be. On the other hand, the larger it becomes, the closer to a multinomial the distribution becomes.

Regarding inference, the hidden z parameters, Θ and $\underline{\Phi}$ must be predicted and the α and B meta-parameters must also be estimated, as in the case of LDA. The difference, however, comes from $\underline{\Phi}$, which becomes a document-dependent parameter. Still, Gibbs sampling can be used in DCM–LDA to infer the parameters in a way similar to LDA [DOY 09].

The DCM–LDA model was evaluated on a corpus of 5,21,000, occurrences of 6,871 words in 390 documents using a non-Bayesian ad-hoc estimation of the likelihood for the test documents, the "empirical likelihood" [LI 06][20]. It was shown to be better than a LDA model with "standard" α and β parameters (symmetrical $\alpha = 50/|Z|$ and $\beta = 0.01$ [GRI 02, STE 07]) or with symmetrical ad-hoc parameters in relation to the DCM–LDA learning. Unfortunately, the comparison with a state-of-the-art LDA model with unsymmetrical Dirichlet distributions (in other words α instead of $\alpha\mathbf{1}$, and the same for β) has not been done.

5.5. Similarity measures between documents

In this section, the third aspect of the generative topic models is addressed: the different measures used to evaluate the thematic similarity between documents. These metrics between documents are ultimately at the core of clustering algorithms, and to a lesser extent to those of classification or information retrieval[21].

For topic models, three approaches exist for the construction of similarities between documents: (1) from "language models" (see Chapter 1), in which the probability of producing a given document from the model of another is used, (2) considering the topic-simplex (dimension reduction), or (3) using Fisher kernels.

---

20 The methods presented in section 5.3.2.6 would be more adequate.

21 For the latter two applications, other more direct means than the thematic similarity between documents can be used.

5.5.1. *Language models*

In the framework of information retrieval, the approaches based on "language modeling" (see Chapter 1, section 1.4) [PON 98, ZHA 08, ZHA 09] use as a similarity measure between the documents, the conditional probability of a document q (recently observed) knowing another document d (already known, present in the corpus) [AZZ 04, WEI 06]:

$$P(q|d) = \prod_{w \in \widehat{q}} P(w|d) = \prod_{w \in \widehat{q}} \sum_{z \in Z} P(w|z) P(z|d)$$

or in an equivalent manner the Kullback–Leibler divergence between the empirical distribution for document q and the distribution modeled by document d [ZHA 01, LAF 01, CHA 09a]:

$$S_{KL}(q, d) = \sum_{w \in V} \widehat{P}(w|q) \log \frac{\widehat{P}(w|q)}{P(w|d)}$$

This point of view is developed further in section 1.4 of Chapter 1.

5.5.2. *Similarity between topic distributions*

Another idea is simply to consider that two documents are thematically similar as their probability distributions over the topics are similar; in other words, that their points are close in the topic-simplex. Typically, the Kullback–Leibler divergence between the $P(z|d)$ is used:

$$S_{KL\text{-topic}}(d, q) = \sum_{z \in Z} P(z|d) \log \frac{P(z|d)}{P(z|q)}$$

or a symmetrized version of this (Jensen–Shannon or half-sum) [LIN 91], as for example:

$$S_{\text{topic}}(d, q) = \frac{1}{2} \Big(S_{KL\text{-topic}}(d, q) + S_{KL\text{-topic}}(q, d) \Big)$$

For example, in the case of LDA the $P(z|d)$ correspond to the vector θ_d and:

$$S_{\text{topic}}(d, q) = \frac{1}{2} \sum_{z \in Z} \left(\theta_{dz} \log \frac{\theta_{dz}}{\theta_{qz}} + \theta_{qz} \log \frac{\theta_{qz}}{\theta_{dz}} \right) = \frac{1}{2} \sum_{z \in Z} (\theta_{dz} - \theta_{qz}) \log \frac{\theta_{dz}}{\theta_{qz}}$$

If the toy example from section 5.2.4 and Figure 5.3 is reconsidered, the similarity measure between document $\widehat{d_1} = \{(\text{chocolate}, 3), (\text{cake}, 2), (\text{black}, 1)\}$, for which $\theta_{d_1} \simeq (0.22, 0.67, 0.11)$ could for example have been estimated, and a document

$\widehat{d_2} = \{(\text{carbon}, 2), (\text{black}, 8)\}$, for which $\theta_{d_2} \simeq (0.06, 0.04, 0.90)$ could have been estimated, would be $(0.22 - 0.06) \log(22/6) + (0.67 - 0.04) \log(67/4) + (0.11 - 0.90) \log(11/90) \simeq 5.3$ bit[22]. Its distance from the document $\widehat{d_3} = \{(\text{chocolate}, 4), (\text{cake}, 2)\}$, for which $\theta_{d_3} \simeq (0.19, 0.80, 0.01)$ could have been estimated, would be 0.4 bit.

5.5.3. Fisher kernels

The "natural" metric [AMA 98] between instances of generative models is the "Fisher kernel", popularized by Jaakkola and Haussler [JAA 99]. This notion, coming from the "geometry of the information" [AMA 00], directly follows the metric between probabilistic models (in the space of possible models): for a $P(X|\mu)$ family of stochastic models parametrized by μ, the Fisher kernel supplies a similarity measure between instances: for two instances X_1 and X_2 of this family at the μ point, it is defined by:

$$K(X_1, X_2) = U_{X_1}(\mu)^T \; G(\mu)^{-1} \; U_{X_2}(\mu)$$

where $U_X(\mu)$ is the gradient of the log-likelihood parameters of the model: $U_X(\mu) = \nabla_\mu \log P(X|\mu)$, and $G(\mu)$ is the Fisher information matrix, in other words the variance of $U_X(\mu)$: $G(\mu) = \mathbb{E}(U_X(\mu) \; U_X(\mu)^T)$, which, for "regular enough" probability distributions such as those used in this chapter, is also the Hessian of the entropy: $G(\mu) = \partial^2 H(X|\mu)/\partial\mu^2$.

These Fisher kernels can therefore be used as a similarity measure between documents, which are seen as instances of a topic model. It has been used on PLSI [HOF 00, NYF 06, CHA 09b], DCM [ELK 05], and LDA [CHA 06a, SUN 08]. Here, their applications to the PLSI model are illustrated.

As presented in section 5.3.1, PLSI is a topic model which models the corpus as an i.i.d. sample of (document index, term) pairs.

The Fisher kernel between two instances X_1^n and Y_1^m of an i.i.d. process is the sum of the Fisher kernels between each of the individual random variables X_i and Y_j, divided by the number of variables in each of the instances [CHA 09b]:

$$K(X_1^n, Y_1^m) = \frac{1}{nm} \sum_{i=1}^{n} \sum_{j=1}^{m} K(X_i, Y_j)$$

---

22 The logarithm was here taken in base 2 (units: bit). Furthermore, in practice, from the *a priori* distributions over the parameters, the estimations of θ_d have no zero coordinates (smoothing effect). The half-sum of the Kullback-Leibler is in fact rigorously defined only for "same support" distributions, in other words, if the probability of a topic z is zero for one, it shall be zero for the other.

In the case of PLSI, $X_i = (d, w)$ and $Y_i = (q, w')$ (for two document models d and q, and two terms w and w'). It can be shown [CHA 09b] that, accepting the approximation of the Fisher information matrix $G(\boldsymbol{\mu})$ by its diagonal components:

$$G(\boldsymbol{\mu})_{(ii)} \approx \sum_{d \in \mathcal{C}} \left(U_d(\boldsymbol{\mu})_{(i)} \right)^2,$$

the above expression becomes:

$$K^{\text{PLSI}}(d, q) = \frac{1}{|d|\,|q|} \sum_{w \in d} \sum_{w' \in q} \text{tf}(w, d) \cdot \text{tf}(w', q) \cdot \frac{P(d|z)}{P(d, w)} \frac{P(q|z)}{P(q, w)}$$

$$\cdot \sum_z \left[\frac{\varphi_{zw}\, \varphi_{zw'}}{g(z)} + \frac{\delta_{w,w'}}{h(w, z)} \right]$$

where:

$$g(z) = \sum_{d \in \mathcal{C}} \sum_{w \in d} \text{tf}(w, d) \left(\frac{\varphi_{zw}\, P(d|z)}{P(d, w)} \right)^2$$

$$h(w, z) = \sum_{d \in \mathcal{C}} \text{tf}(w, d) \left(\frac{P(d|z)}{P(d, w)} \right)^2$$

are the terms corresponding to the diagonal of $G(\boldsymbol{\mu})$.

This form is not very useful in practice since it is too costly to compute (complexity in $\mathcal{O}(|d||q|)$). It requires further approximations in order to be more efficient. For this, two experimentally reasonable assumptions are introduced: $P(d) \simeq |d|/\|\mathcal{C}\|$, and following the first development proposed by Hofmann [HOF 00]:

$$\sum_{w \in V} \frac{\widehat{P}(w|d)}{P(w|d)} \varphi_{zw} \simeq 1$$

With these approximations, the following formula is obtained [CHA 09b]:

$$K^{\text{DFIM-H}}(d, q) = \sum_{z \in Z} \frac{\theta_{dz}\, \theta_{qz}}{\tau_z} g_2(z)^{-1} + \sum_{w \in V} \frac{\widehat{P}(w|d)\, \widehat{P}(w|q)}{P(d, w)\, P(q, w)} \sum_{z \in Z} \chi_{zd}\, \chi_{zq}\, h_2(w, z)^{-1}$$

with:

$$g_2(z) = \frac{1}{\tau_z} \sum_{d \in \mathcal{C}} \theta_{dz}^2 \quad \text{and} \quad h_2(w, z) = \sum_{d \in \mathcal{C}} \left(\frac{\widehat{P}(w|d)}{P(d, w)} \chi_{zd} \right)^2$$

To make the link with the original formulation proposed by Hofmann [HOF 00], the contributions of the Fisher information matrix $G(\mu)$ have to be neglected[23], which eliminates the $g_2(z)^{-1}$ term and replaces $h_2(w, z)^{-1}$ with $\tau_z^2 \, \varphi_{zw}$ in the above expression [CHA 09b, CHA 09c].

At the experimental level, Hofmann showed that, for the PLSI model, Fisher kernels were the best of the classical methods [HOF 00]. We confirmed [NYF 06] and extend [CHA 09b] these results, on the one hand by underlining the importance of the normalization role performed by the Fisher information matrix, and on the other hand by observing that the language model similarity measures can be on par with the Fisher kernels only when the number of topics is large.

5.6. Conclusion

In the large amount of generative models available for categorization and useful for text documents, a general framework focusing on the principles regrouping the most recent models dedicated to discrete data analysis, "topic models" or "discrete principal component analysis" [BUN 02] has been presented. We have illustrated this general framework on a specific and representative case, LDA, and also on its original variant, PLSI, pioneers in the text domain that have opened the door for numerous applications and many other richer models.

Relatively simple from the probabilistic point of view, the topic models are an important building block, very useful for analyzing corpora with discrete features (terms, in the text domain), either for proposing a completely explicit model or for creating representations in spaces with lower dimensions than those of the observed features ("dimension reduction").

The main advantage of the generative models is their intuitive descriptive power which makes them easier to modularize, expand, and integrate into larger, more complex models. The models presented here can for instance be extended to observable pairs [BLE 03a, AZZ 04, MCC 07, NAL 08] or term sequences [GRI 05, WAL 06] or hierarchic models [BUN 04, BLE 04, HEI 09a, BLE 10].

An overview of the major software implementations of topic models is provided in the Appendix of this chapter (section 5.7). In practice, these models remain relatively costly to use (time and memory), but implementations that limit memory consumption [GOM 08] or that are distributed [NEW 09, ASU 11] exist.

---

23 Hofmann assimilates $G(\mu)$ to the identity matrix by a re-parametrization only justified in the case of multinomials (but also holds in the exponential family). However, PLSI is neither multinomial, nor in the exponential family, and $G(\mu)$ can be significantly different from the identity matrix in this case.

5.7. Appendix: topic model software

	Name	Language	Principal original/author	First/last version	Model implemented
[1]	DCA (0.202) (former MPCA of the Helsinki Institute for IT)	C	Wray Buntine, NICTA and Australian National University	2004-2009	DCA (incl. LDA Gibbs)
[2]	Mallet (2.0.7)	Java	Andrew McCallum, University of Massachusetts	2002-2011	LDA Gibbs
[3]	R-lda (1.3.1)	R + C	Jonathan Chang, Princeton University	2009-2011	LDA Gibbs
[4]	Latent Dirichlet Allocation in LingPipe	Java	Bob Carpenter, Alias-i Inc. (New-York)	2003-2010	LDA Gibbs
[5]	Stanford Topic Modeling Toolbox (0.4.0)	Scala	Daniel Ramage and Evan Rosen, Stanford University	2011	LDA Gibbs
[6]	Matlab Topic Modeling Toolbox (1.4)	Matlab (+ C++)	Mark Steyvers and Tom Griffiths, University of California	2004-2011	LDA Gibbs
[7]	lda-j	Java	Georg Heinrich	2005	LDA Gibbs
[8]	GibbsLDA++ /JGibbLDA (0.2)	C++ or Java	Xuan-Hieu Phan, University of Tohoku (Japan)	2007-2008	LDA Gibbs
[9]	npbayes	C and Matlab	Yee Whye Teh, University College London	2004	HDP (incl. LDA VB)
[10]	LDA-C	C	David M. Blei, Princeton University	2002-2006	LDA VB
[11]	lda	C or Matlab	Daichi Mochihashi, NTT (Japan)	2004	LDA VB

Websites:

[1] *http://nicta.com.au/people/buntinew/discrete_component_analysis*

[2] *http://mallet.cs.umass.edu*

[3] *http://cran.r-project.org/web/packages/lda/*

[4] *http://alias-i.com/lingpipe/*

[5] *http://nlp.stanford.edu/software/tmt/*

[6] *http://psiexp.ss.uci.edu/research/programs_data/toolbox.htm*

[7] *http://www.arbylon.net/resources.html*

[8] *http://gibbslda.sourceforge.net/*

[9] *http://www.gatsby.ucl.ac.uk/ ywteh/research/software.html*

[10] *http://www.cs.princeton.edu/ blei/lda-c/index.html*

[11] *http://chasen.org/ daiti-m/dist/lda/*

5.8. Bibliography

[AGA 10] AGARWAL A., DAUMÉ H., "A geometric view of conjugate priors", *Machine Learning*, vol. 81, no. 1, p. 99-113, Springer, 2010.

[AHR 05] AHRENDT P., GOUTTE C., LARSEN J., "Co-occurrence models in music genre classification", in *IEEE International Workshop on Machine Learning for Signal Processing*, 2005.

[AMA 98] AMARI S.I., "Natural gradient works efficiently in learning", *Neural Computation*, vol. 10, p. 251-276, 1998.

[AMA 00] AMARI S.I., NAGAOKA H., *Methods of Information Geometry*, vol. 191 of *Translations of Mathematical Monographs*, American Mathematical Society, 2000.

[ASU 09] ASUNCION A., WELLING M., SMYTH P., TEH Y.W., "On smoothing and inference for topic models", in *Proceedings of 25th Conference on Uncertainty in Artificial Intelligence (UAI '09)*, p. 27-34, 2009.

[ASU 11] ASUNCION A.U., SMYTH P., WELLING M., "Asynchronous distributed estimation of topic models for document analysis", *Statistical Methodology*, vol. 8, no. 1, p. 3-17, Elsevier, January 2011.

[AZZ 04] AZZOPARDI L., GIROLAMI M., VAN RIJSBERGEN C., "Topic based language models for ad hoc information retrieval", in *Proceedings of the International Joint Conference in Neural Networks*, 2004.

[BAA 01] BAAYEN R.H., *Word Frequency Distributions*, Kluwer Academic Publishers, 2001.

[BAN 05] BANERJEE A., MERUGU S., DHILLON I.S., GHOSH J., "Clustering with Bregman divergences", *Journal of Machine Learning Research*, vol. 6, p. 1705-1749, 2005.

[BIS 06] BISHOP C.M., "Graphical model", *Pattern Recognition and Machine Learning*, p. 359-422, Springer, 2006.

[BLE 03a] BLEI D.M., JORDAN M.I., "Modeling annotated data", in *Proceedings of 26th Annual International ACM SIGIR Conference on Research and Development in Information Retrieval*, p. 127-134, 2003.

[BLE 03b] BLEI D.M., NG A.Y., JORDAN M.I., "Latent Dirichlet Allocation", *Journal of Machine Learning Research*, vol. 3, p. 993-1022, January 2003.

[BLE 03c] BLEI D.M., JORDAN M.I., "Modeling annotated data", in *Proceedings of 26th Annual International ACM SIGIR Conference on Research and Development in Informaion Retrieval (SIGIR '03)*, ACM, p. 127-134, 2003.

[BLE 04] BLEI D.M, GRIFFITHS T., JORDAN M.I., TENENBAUM J.B., "Hierarchical topic models and the nested Chinese restaurant process", in *Proceedings of NIPS 16*, 2004.

[BLE 05] BLEI D.M., LAFFERTY J.D., "Correlated topic models", *Advances in Neural Information Processing Systems 18*, p. 147-154, 2005.

[BLE 07] BLEI D.M., LAFFERTY J.D., "A correlated topic model of science", *Annals of Applied Statistics*, vol. 1, no. 1, p. 17-35, 2007.

[BLE 08] BLEI D.M., MCAULIFFE J.D., "Supervised topic models", in PLATT J., KOLLER D., SINGER Y., ROWEIS S. (eds), *Advances in Neural Information Processing Systems 20 (NIPS '07)*, MIT Press, p. 121-128, 2008.

[BLE 09] BLEI D.M., LAFFERTY J.D., "Topic models", in SRIVASTAVA A., SAHAMI M. (eds), *Text Mining: Theory and Applications*, 2009.

[BLE 10] BLEI D., GRIFFITHS T., JORDAN M., "The nested Chinese restaurant process and Bayesian nonparametric inference of topic hierarchies", *Journal of the Association for Computing Machinery*, vol. 57, no. 2, p. 1-30, 2010.

[BOS 06] BOSCH A., ZISSERMAN A., MUNOZ X., "Scene classification via pLSA", in *Proceedings of the European Conference on Computer Vision*, 2006.

[BUN 02] BUNTINE W., "Variational extensions to EM and multinomial PCA", in *Proceedings of ECML '02*, vol. 2430 of *LNAI*, p. 23 34, 2002.

[BUN 04] BUNTINE W., JAKULIN A., "Applying discrete PCA in data analysis", in *Proceedings of 20th Conference on Uncertainty in Artificial Intelligence*, p. 47-52, 2004.

[BUN 06] BUNTINE W., JAKULIN A., "Discrete component analysis", in *Proceedings of SLSFS '05*, vol. 3940 of *LNCS*, p. 1-33, 2006.

[BUN 09] BUNTINE W., "Estimating likelihoods for topic models", in *Proceedings of ACML '09*, vol. 5828 of *LNAI*, p. 51-64, 2009.

[CAN 04] CANNY J., "GaP: a factor model for discrete data", in *Proceedings of the 27th Annual International ACM SIGIR Conference on Research and Development in Information Retrieval (SIGIR '04)*, 2004.

[CHA 06a] CHANDALIA G., BEAL M., "Using Fisher kernels from topic models for dimensionality reduction", in *Proceedings of NIPS 2006 Workshop on Novel Applications of Dimensionality Reduction*, 2006.

[CHA 06b] CHAPELLE O., ZIEN A., SCHÖLKOPF B. (eds), *Semi-Supervised Learning*, MIT Press, 2006.

[CHA 09a] CHAPPELIER J.C., ECKARD E., "An ad hoc information retrieval perspective on PLSI through language model identification", in AZZOPARDI L., *et al.* (eds), *Advances in Information Retrieval Theory (Proceedings of ICTIR '09)*, vol. 5766 of *Lecture Notes in Computer Science*, Springer-Verlag, p. 346-349, 2009.

[CHA 09b] CHAPPELIER J.C., ECKARD E., "PLSI: The true Fisher kernel and beyond - IID processes, information matrix and model identification in PLSI", in BUNTINE W., *et al.* (eds), *Machine Learning and Knowledge Discovery in Databases (Proceedings ECML-PKDD '09)*, vol. 5781 of *Lecture Notes in Computer Science*, Springer-Verlag, p. 195-210, 2009.

[CHA 09c] CHAPPELIER J.C., ECKARD E., "Utilisation de PLSI en recherche documentaire", in *Actes 16ème Conférence sur le Traitement Automatique des Langues Naturelles (TALN 09)*, ATALA, 2009.

[CHU 95] CHURCH K.W., GALE W.A., "Poisson mixtures", *Natural Language Engineering*, vol. 1, p. 163-190, 1995.

[CLI 08] CLINCHANT S., GAUSSIER E., "The beta-negative binomial for text modeling", in *Advances in Information Retrieval (Proceedings of 30th European Conference on Information Retrieval)*, vol. 4956 of *Lecture Notes in Computer Science*, Springer, p. 150-161, 2008.

[COH 00] COHN D., CHANG H., "Probabilistically identifying authoritative documents", in *Proceedings of 17th International Conference on Machine Learning (ICML '00)*, p. 167-174, 2000.

[DIC 83] DICKEY J., "Multiple hypergeometric functions: probabilistic interpretations and statistical uses", *Journal of the American Statistical Association*, vol. 78, p. 628-637, 1983.

[DOY 09] DOYLE G., ELKAN C., "Accounting for burstiness in topic models", in *Proceedings of the 26th Annual International Conference on Machine Learning (ICML '09)*, p. 281-288, 2009.

[ELK 05] ELKAN C., "Deriving TF-IDF as a Fisher kernel", in CONSENS M., NAVARRO G. (eds), *Proceedings of String Processing and Information Retrieval (SPIRE '05)*, vol. 3772 of *Lecture Notes in Computer Science*, Chapter 33, p. 295-300, Springer, 2005.

[ELK 06] ELKAN C., "Clustering documents with an exponential-family approximation of the Dirichlet compound multinomial distribution", in *Proceedings of the 23rd International Conference on Machine Learning (ICML '06)*, p. 289-296, 2006.

[FIN 31] DE FINETTI B., "Funzione caratteristica di un fenomeno aleatorio", *Atti della R. Academia Nazionale dei Lincei, Serie 6: Memorie, Classe di Scienze Fisiche, Mathematice e Naturale*, vol. 4, p. 251-299, 1931.

[FLA 05] FLAHERTY P., GIAEVER G., KUMM J., JORDAN M.I., ARKIN A.P., "A latent variable model for chemogenomic profiling", *Bioinformatics*, vol. 21, no. 15, p. 3286-3293, Oxford University Press, August 2005.

[GAU 02] GAUSSIER E., GOUTTE C., POPAT K., CHEN F., "A hierarchical model for clustering and categorising documents", in *Proceedings of 24th BCS-IRSG European Collaboration on IR Research*, p. 229-247, 2002.

[GAU 05] GAUSSIER E., GOUTTE C., "Relation between PLSA and NMF and implications", in *Proceedings of 28th Annual International ACM SIGIR Conference on Research and Development in Information Retrieval*, p. 601-602, 2005.

[GIR 03] GIROLAMI M., KABÁN A., "On an equivalence between PLSI and LDA", in *Proceedings of 26th Annual International ACM SIGIR Conference on Research and Development in Information Retrieval*, p. 433-434, 2003.

[GOM 08] GOMES R., WELLING M., PERONA P., "Memory bounded inference in topic models", in MCCALLUM A., ROWEIS S. (eds), *Proceedings 25th International Conference on Machine Learning (ICML '08)*, Omnipress, p. 344-351, 2008.

[GRI 02] GRIFFITHS T.L., STEYVERS M., "A probabilistic approach to semantic representation", in *Proceedings of the 24th Annual Conference of the Cognitive Science Society*, 2002.

[GRI 04] GRIFFITHS T., STEYVERS M., "Finding scientific topics", *Proceedings of the National Academy of Sciences*, vol. 101 (suppl. 1), p. 5228-5235, 2004.

[GRI 05] GRIFFITHS T.L., STEYVERS M., BLEI D.M.I., TENENBAUM J.B., "Integrating topics and syntax", in *Proceedings of Advances in Neural Information Processing Systems 17*, 2005.

[HAR 95] HARMAN D., "Overview of the fourth text retrieval conference (TREC-4)", in *Proceedings of the 4th Text Retrieval Conference*, p. 1-23, 1995.

[HEI 05] HEINRICH G., KINDERMANN J., LAUTH C., PAAß G., SANCHEZ-MONZON J., "Investigating word correlation at different scopes - a latent topic approach", in *Workshop Learning and Extending Lexical Ontologies at 22nd International Conference on Machine Learning*, 2005.

[HEI 09a] HEINRICH G., "A generic approach to topic models", in BUNTINE W., *et al.* (eds), *Machine Learning and Knowledge Discovery in Databases (Proceedings ECML-PKDD '09)*, vol. 5781 of *Lecture Notes in Computer Science*, Springer-Verlag, p. 517-532, 2009.

[HEI 09b] HEINRICH G., Parameter Estimation for Text Analysis (v. 2.9), Report, Fraunhofer Institute for Computer Graphics Research, Darmstadt, Germany, 2009.

[HEW 55] HEWITT E., SAVAGE L., "Symmetric measures on Cartesian products", *Transactions of the American Mathematical Society*, vol. 80, no. 2, p. 470-501, 1955.

[HOF 99] HOFMANN T., "Probabilistic latent semantic indexing", in *Proceedings of 22nd Annual International ACM SIGIR Conference on Research and Development in Information Retrieval*, Berkeley, California, p. 50-57, 1999.

[HOF 00] HOFMANN T., "Learning the similarity of documents: an information-geometric approach to document retrieval and categorization", in *Advances in Neural Information Processing Systems*, vol. 12, p. 914-920, 2000.

[HOF 01] HOFMANN T., "Unsupervised learning by probabilistic latent semantic analysis", *Machine Learning*, vol. 42, no. 1, p. 177-196, 2001.

[HYV 01] HYVÄRINEN A., KARHUNEN J., OJA E., *Independent Component Analysis*, John Wiley & Sons, 2001.

[JAA 99] JAAKKOLA T., HAUSSLER D., "Exploiting generative models in discriminative classifiers", in *Advances in Neural Information Processing Systems*, vol. 11, MIT Press, p. 487-493, 1999.

[JEN 01] JENSEN F.V., *Bayesian Networks and Decision Graphs*, Springer, 2001.

[JIN 04] JIN X., ZHOU Y., MOBASHER B., "Web usage mining based on probabilistic latent semantic analysis", in *Proceedings of 10th International Conference on Knowledge Discovery and Data Mining*, p. 197-205, 2004.

[JOR 99] JORDAN M., GHAHRAMANI Y., JAAKKOLA T., SAUL L., "Introduction to variational methods for graphical models", *Machine Learning*, vol. 37, p. 183-233, 1999.

[KAT 96] KATZ S.M., "Distribution of content words and phrases in text and language modelling", *Natural Language Engineering*, vol. 2, p. 15-59, 1996.

[KOL 09] KOLLER D., FRIEDMAN N., *Probabilistic Graphical Models: Principles and Techniques*, MIT Press, 2009.

[LAC 09] LACOSTE-JULIEN S., SHA F., JORDAN M., "DiscLDA: discriminative learning for dimensionality reduction and classification", in KOLLER D., SCHUURMANS D., BENGIO Y., BOTTOU L. (eds), *Advances in Neural Information Processing Systems 21 (NIPS '08)*, p. 897-904, 2009.

[LAF 01] LAFFERTY J., ZHAI C., "Document language models, query models, and risk minimization for information retrieval", in *Proceedings of 24th Annual International ACM SIGIR Conference on Research and Development in Information Retrieval (SIGIR '01)*, p. 111-119, 2001.

[LEE 99] LEE D.D., SEUNG H.S., "Algorithms for non-negative matrix factorization", *Nature*, vol. 401, p. 788-791, 1999.

[LEW 98] LEWIS D., "Naive (bayes) at forty: the independence assumption in information retrieval", in *Proceedings of 10th European Conference on Machine Learning (ECML '98)*, vol. 1398 of *Lecture Notes in Computer Science*, Springer, p. 4-15, 1998.

[LI 06] LI W., MCCALLUM A., "Pachinko allocation: DAG-structured mixture models of topic correlations", in *Proceedings of 23rd International Conference on Machine Learning (ICML '06)*, p. 577-584, 2006.

[LIE 07] LIENHART R., SLANEY M., "PLSA on large-scale image databases", in *Proceedings of the 2007 International Conference on Acoustics, Speech and Signal Processing, IEEE*, (ICASSP 2007), vol. 4, p. 1217-1220, 2007.

[LIN 91] LIN J., "Divergence measures based on Shannon entropy", *IEEE Transactions on Information Theory*, vol. 37, no. 14, p. 145-151, 1991.

[MAD 05] MADSEN R.E., KAUCHAK D., ELKAN C., "Modeling word burstiness using the Dirichlet distribution", in *Proceedings of the 22nd International Conference on Machine Learning (ICML '05)*, p. 545-552, 2005.

[MCC 98] MCCALLUM A., NIGAM K., "A comparison of event models for naive bayes text classification", in *Proceedings of AAAI-98 Workshop on Learning for Text Categorization*, p. 137-142, 1998.

[MCC 06] McCallum A., Pal C., Druck G., Wang X., "Multi-conditional learning: generative/discriminative training for clustering and classification", in *Proceedings of AAAI '06*, 2006.

[MCC 07] McCallum A., Wang X., Corrada-Emmanuel A., "Topic and role discovery in social networks with experiments on enron and academic email", *Journal of Artificial Intelligence Research*, vol. 30, no. 1, p. 249-272, AI Access Foundation, 2007.

[MEI 06] Mei Q., Zhai C., "A mixture model for contextual text mining", in *Proceedings of 12th International Conference on Knowledge Discovery and Data Mining*, p. 649-655, 2006.

[MEI 07] Meilă M., "Comparing clusterings-an information based distance", *Journal of Multivariate Analysis*, vol. 98, no. 5, p. 873-895, 2007.

[MIN 00] Minka T., "Estimating a Dirichlet distribution", available on the Internet (revision 2009), 2000.

[MIN 02] Minka T., Lafferty J., "Expectation-propagation for the generative aspect model", in *Proceedings of the 18th Conference on Uncertainty in Artificial Intelligence*, p. 352-359, 2002.

[MIS 08] Misra H., Cappé O., Yvon F., "Using LDA to detect semantically incoherent documents", in *Proceedings 12th Conference Computational Natural Language Learning (CONLL '08)*, p. 41-48, 2008.

[MON 04] Monay F., Gatica-Perez D., "PLSA-based image auto-annotation: constraining the latent space", in *Proceedings of ACM International Conference on Multimedia (ACM MM)*, 2004.

[MON 07] Monay F., Gatica-Perez D., "Modeling semantic aspects for cross-media image indexing", *IEEE Transactions on Pattern Analysis and Machine Intelligence*, vol. 29, 2007.

[NAL 08] Nallapati R., Ahmed A., Xing E.P., Cohen W.W., "Joint latent topic models for text and citations", in *Proceedings of KDD '08*, 2008.

[NEW 09] Newman D., Asuncion A.U., Smyth P., Welling M., "Distributed algorithms for topic models", *Journal of Machine Learning Research*, vol. 10, p. 1801-1828, 2009.

[NIG 00] Nigam K., McCallum A.K., Thrun S., Mitchell T., "Text classification from labeled and unlabeled documents using EM", *Machine Learning*, vol. 39, p. 103-134, 2000.

[NYF 06] Nyffenegger M., Chappelier J.C., Gaussier E., "Revisiting Fisher kernels for document similarities", in *Proceedings of 17th European Conference on Machine Learning*, p. 727-734, 2006.

[PON 98] Ponte J.M., Croft W.B., "A language modeling approach to information retrieval", in *21st SIGIR Conference on Research and Development in Information Retrieval*, p. 275-281, 1998.

[POP 01] Popescul A., Ungar L.H., Pennock D.M., Lawrence S., "Probabilistic models for unified collaborative and content-based recommendation in sparse-data environments", in *Proceedings of the 17th Conference in Uncertainty in Artificial Intelligence*, p. 437-444, 2001.

[PRI 00] PRITCHARD J.K., STEPHENS M., DONNELLY P., "Inference of population structure unsing multilocus genotype data", *Genetics*, vol. 155, p. 945-959, 2000.

[QUE 05] QUELHAS P., MONAY F., ODOBEZ J.M., GATICA-PEREZ D., TUYTELAARS T., GOOL L.V., "Modeling scenes with local descriptors and latent aspects", in *Proceedings of ICCV 2005*, vol. 1, p. 883-890, 2005.

[RAM 09] RAMAGE D., HALL D., NALLAPATI R., MANNING C.D., "Labeled LDA: a supervised topic model for credit attribution in multi-labeled corpora", in *Proceedings of 2009 Conference on Empirical Methods in Natural Language Processing (EMNLP '09)*, Association for Computational Linguistics, p. 248-256, 2009.

[REN 03] RENNIE J.D.M., SHIH L., TEEVAN J., KARGER D.R., "Tackling the poor assumption of naive bayes text classifiers", in *Proceedings of ICML '03*, p. 616-623, 2003.

[ROB 99] ROBERT C.P., CASELLA G., *Monte Carlo Statistical Methods*, Springer-Verlag, 1999.

[ROS 04] ROSEN-ZVI M., GRIFFITHS T., STEYVERS M., SMYTH P., "The author-topic model for authors and documents", in *Proceedings of the 20th Conference on Uncertainty in Artificial Intelligence (UAI '04)*, p. 487-494, 2004.

[SEB 02] SEBASTIANI F., "Machine learning in automated text categorization", *ACM Computing Surveys*, vol. 34, no. 1, p. 1-47, 2002.

[STE 04] STEYVERS M., SMYTH P., ROSEN-ZVI M., GRIFFITHS T., "Probabilistic author-topic models for information discovery", in *Proceedings of 10th International Conference on Knowledge Discovery and Data Mining*, p. 306-315, 2004.

[STE 07] STEYVERS M., GRIFFITHS T., "Probabilistic topic models", in LANDAUER T., MCNAMARA D., DENNIS S., KINTSCH W. (eds), *Handbook of Latent Semantic Analysis*, Chapter 21, p. 427-448, Laurence Erlbaum, 2007.

[SUN 08] SUN Q., LI R., LUO D., WU X., "Text segmentation with LDA-based Fisher kernel", in *Proceedings of 46th Annual Meeting of the ACL on Human Language Technologies (HLT '08)*, ACL, p. 269-272, 2008.

[TEH 06] TEH Y.W., JORDAN M.I., BEAL M.J., BLEI D.M., "Hierarchical dirichlet processes", *Journal of the American Statistical Association*, vol. 101, no. 476, p. 1566-1581, 2006.

[TEH 07] TEH Y.W., NEWMAN D., WELLING M., "A collapsed variational bayesian inference algorithm for latent Dirichlet allocation", in *Advances in Neural Information Processing Systems 19 (NIPS '06)*, p. 1353-1360, 2007.

[VIN 02] VINOKOUROV A., GIROLAMI M., "A probabilistic framework for the hierarchic organisation and classification of document collections", *Journal of Intelligent Information Systems*, vol. 18, no. 2-3, p. 153-172, 2002.

[WAL 06] WALLACH H., "Topic modeling: beyond bag-of-words", in *Proceedings of 23rd International Conference on Machine Learning (ICML '06)*, p. 977-984, 2006.

[WAL 09] WALLACH H.M., MURRAY I., SALAKHUTDINOV R., MIMNO D., "Evaluation methods for topic models", in *Proceedings of 26th Annual International Conference on Machine Learning (ICML '09)*, ACM, p. 1105-1112, 2009.

[WAL 10] WALLACH H., MIMNO D., MCCALLUM A., "Rethinking LDA: why priors matter", in BENGIO Y., SCHUURMANS D., LAFFERTY J., WILLIAMS C.K.I., CULOTTA A. (eds), *Advances in Neural Information Processing Systems 22 (NIPS '09)*, p. 1973-1981, 2010.

[WEI 06] WEI X., CROFT W.B., "LDA-based document models for ad-hoc retrieval", in *Proceedings of the 29th Annual International ACM SIGIR Conference on Research and Development in Information Retrieval (SIGIR '06)*, p. 178-185, 2006.

[WEL 08] WELLING M., CHEMUDUGUNTA C., SUTTER N., "Deterministic latent variable models and their pitfalls", in *Proceedings of SIAM Conference on Data Mining (SDM '08)*, 2008.

[ZHA 01] ZHAI C., LAFFERTY J., "Model-based feedback in the language modeling approach to information retrieval", in *Proceedings of 10th International Conference on Information and Knowledge Management (CIKM)*, p. 403-410, 2001.

[ZHA 04] ZHAI C., LAFFERTY J., "A study of smoothing methods for language models applied to information retrieval", *ACM Transactions on Information Systems*, vol. 22, no. 2, p. 179-214, 2004.

[ZHA 08] ZHAI C., "Statistical language models for information retrieval a critical review", *Foundations and Trends in Information Retrieval*, vol. 2, no. 3, p. 137-213, 2008.

[ZHA 09] ZHAI C., *Statistical Language Models for Information Retrieval*, Synthesis Lectures on Human Language Technologies, Morgan & Claypool, 2009.

[ZHO 05] ZHONG S., GHOSH J., "Generative model-based document clustering: a comparative study", *Knowledge and Information Systems*, vol. 8, no. 3, p. 374-384, Springer-Verlag, 2005.

[ZHU 09] ZHU X., GOLDBERG A., *Introduction to Semi-Supervised Learning*, Morgan & Claypool, 2009.

Chapter 6

Conditional Random Fields for Information Extraction

6.1. Introduction

In Natural Language Processing, the final ideal goal of allowing computers to *understand* all texts has, little by little, made way for more modest and pragmatic goals, which can be expressed as *specific tasks*. Information extraction is typically one of these tasks. It aims to identify factual information elements within a document, able to fill the fields of a predefined form. In a way, it aims to fill the gap between the way humans apprehend information, where the understanding of natural languages plays a large part, and the way computers do, in the form of typed data ordered in structured files or in databases. In a review article on the subject, McCallum discusses an information *distillation* process [MCC 05].

To achieve such a task, several methods have been used. As it is more and more the case for most other natural language engineering tasks, approaches based on statistical models are currently the most efficient. But this is true only when we correctly reformulate the task as an annotation or labeling problem. The best statistical models capable of learning data annotation are conditional random fields (CRFs).

This chapter is thus an opportunity to present the task of information extraction and the statistical labeling models able to handle it. The first two sections concentrate on the task, by discussing its issues and the specific problems posed. The following four sections focus on statistical models which give rise to definitions of conditional

Chapter written by Isabelle TELLIER and Marc TOMMASI.

random fields. They constitute a theoretical and practical introduction to annotation models in general, and to CRF in particular, which are increasingly used in many other contexts than information extraction.

6.2. Information extraction

In this section, the problem of information extraction will be presented and the approaches attempting to solve it without calling upon machine learning techniques will be discussed.

6.2.1. *The task*

Information extraction, in terms of a specific language engineering task, emerged at the end of the 1980s and has become increasingly significant with the development of the Internet and digital documents. Its aim is to automatically extract, from *text or semi-structured documents, factual information* ready to fill the fields of a form.

This task first garnered interest during the MUC (*Message Understanding Conferences*) conference series which were held between 1987 and 1998 under the direction of DARPA[1]. These conferences made available to the participants a corpus of texts as well as a list of fields to fill in. The participants had to supply a program that was capable of automatically filling in the fields from any text of the kind of those in the corpus. The programs were ranked based on their performance. For example (extracted from MUC-4 in 1992), from the dispatch of a press agency:

> *"San Salvador, 19 April 1989 (ACAN-EFE) – [text] The President of San Salvador Alfredo Cristani has condemned the terrorist attack on Minister of justice Robert Garcia Alavo and has blamed the murder on the Farabundo Martí National Liberation Front. (...)"*

the following factual information will be extracted:

Date of the incident	19 April 1989
Location of the incident	El Salvador: San Salvador (City)
Author	Farabundo Martí National Liberation Front
Victim	Roberto Garcia Alavo

1 Defense Advanced Research Projects Agency.

Press agency texts were, therefore, among the first initially targeted by the information extraction task. However, many other applications have since appeared, such as transforming small ads or special purpose emails (e.g. announcing seminars or conferences) in standardized forms, automatically inserting into a database the pieces of information concerning individuals that are known only by their Internet page or their curriculum vitae, and indexing scientific articles to build bibliographic databases (such as CiteSeer[2]) and so on [MCC 05].

These examples illustrate that information extraction has a very strong connection with the recognition and the typing of named entities, these words or groups of words which are absent in usual dictionaries, which identify either proper names (of people, places, and organizations, etc.) or measurable quantities (dates, numerical or monetary values, etc.) and which convey a large part of the informational content of certain texts, such as journalistic. The fields to be filled in during an information extraction task are often of this kind. But recognizing the named entities in a text is not enough, as the role played by each of them in the related event must also be found to correctly fill in the fields of the form. Notably, this requires the recognition of their relationships, which are often expressed by the predicates of the text. Spotting named entities is, therefore, not the only problem to resolve: the texts to process can also contain ellipses, pronominal references, or other types of anaphora that need to be solved to complete the task. All these problems will not be addressed in this chapter: extracting and typing named entities, through the best current methods from machine learning, is what we will focus on.

In the 2000s, information extraction extended to emerging or growing new types of data: HTML pages and XML documents. These objects are often referred to as *semi-structured documents*. Their specificity is that they allow several different readings. As a matter of fact, they can be considered as strings, and in this case fundamentally do not differ from other texts, except for the presence of an additional vocabulary made of markups. However, these documents can also be seen as describing a tree structure. In this case, new notions such as *node* notions or even, for example, *next sibling node of the same father* become relevant. The programs charged with extracting factual information of such documents are, in general, interested in accounting for this structure. It is, however, not as rigid and well typed as those of databases, hence the *semi-structured* term to describe them.

The term *wrapper* is sometimes used to designate an information extraction program which relies on structural elements to identify certain information. It is, therefore, generally employed in the context of semi-structured documents, but not exclusively.

---

2 http://liinwww.ira.uka.de/bibliography/Misc/CiteSeer.

6.2.2. *Variants*

To characterize the different possible instances of an information extraction problem, it is possible to classify them according to the input and output of the associated programs.

The input is specified both by the representation of the considered documents, and by the valency of the values to extract. The documents can always be considered as sequences of items, either of linguistic nature (words or multiword units) or of structural nature (separators, markups). Semi-structured documents can otherwise be represented by a tree. The valency of the values to be extracted can be defined as the relationship between the units which make up the documents and those expected on the form. Must the fields be filled by a unique item, a portion of an item or a sequence of (consecutive) items? In the initial example, all the fields receive a sequence of words as a value. This choice is usual for "raw" texts, that is unstructured texts. In this case, the *segmentation* of documents seems to be a fundamental preliminary phase, which is assumed to be already accomplished in the following. When the documents are represented by XML trees, the information to extract can be found in the leaves. Even here, they can correspond to a leaf portion, an entire leaf of a sequence of "consecutive" leaves. A new segmentation problem arises here, similar to the previous one but at a different level of granularity.

The output expected by an information extraction program can also take several formats. In the most simple case, also said to be unary, the data to be extracted are of a single and same type. The form to be filled in is composed of a single field. When it consists of n fields, the problem is said to be n-valued. But this is not all. The multiplicity of expected responses must also be specified, that is the link between a document and the number of response instances it contains. If, for example, the problem is to recognize all the individuals, referenced by their name, cited in a text or on a HTML page, this is a multiple unary case (a single field with numerous instances). The example cited above is from a single n-ary problem (several fields filled in once per document). Certain situations are hybrid: the number of authors in a book can be different from one book to another. . .

6.2.3. *Evaluations*

To evaluate the quality of an information extraction system, the measures used are the same as for the information retrieval task, namely: the recall, the precision, and the F-measure. The specificities of information extraction, and its variations discussed in the previous section, make these measures much more problematic and subject to further discussions. The human inter-annotation agreement is in fact often less strong than in other contexts and the recognition of "partially correct" or semantically equivalent values with reference extractions are particularly delicate. To get an idea of the debates, which cannot be detailed here, one can read for example [SIT 04, LAV 04].

6.2.4. *Approaches not based on machine learning*

Before machine learning techniques became the most frequently used, the information extraction task was processed by the *manual conception of specialized resources*. Typically, for the extraction of named entities in texts, the necessary resources are the following:

– specialized dictionaries (lists of proper names);

– extraction patterns, in general in the form of sequences of automata or of cascading transducers, such as in recursive transition networks. In addition to selecting patterns, the transducers add annotations to the texts, to help the transducers applied after them to achieve their task.

This is, for example, how the Faustus system worked [HOB 97], one of the most famous participants of the MUC campaigns.

When extracting information from HTML pages or XML documents, the patterns generally take the form of queries written in XQUERY or XSLT. However, the manual writing of these extractors is often complicated, difficult to maintain and verify. To avoid having to write grep, sed, and awk-based programs, various assisted conception softwares exist to help the design of patterns: Unitex[3] and Nooj[4] are tools for multilingual linguistic engineering which integrate transducer editors and are often used to write extractors operating on raw texts, whereas XWrap[5] or Lixto[6] assist in writing wrappers for semi-structured documents. A platform for text and document management such as Gate[7] is also capable of integrating extraction programs of different types.

When they are carefully written, the patterns provide good results in terms or precision, and are much poorer in recall. In fact, it is difficult to predict all the possible ways to express certain information. However, in all cases, the writing is a long and fastidious task, which requires precise technical and/or linguistic skills. The maintenance of pattern-based systems is also problematic as their number increases. By applying the "manual" development strategy, a specialized extractor on a very specific type of corpus is the best that can be expected, to be entirely reviewed as soon as the format, specialty language, or domain changes.

---

3 http://www-igm.univ-mlv.fr/ unitex.

4 http://www.nooj4nlp.net/pages/nooj.html.

5 http://www.cc.gatech.edu/projects/disl/XWRAP.

6 http://www.lixto.com/lixto_visual_developer.

7 http://gate.ac.uk.

6.3. Machine learning for information extraction

As long as new challenges and new applications emerged, it became more and more obvious that developing patterns to create information extraction programs by hand was not a perennial solution. The best alternative solution came from supervised machine learning. In this section, all the techniques coming from this approach will be discussed, before focusing on the reformulation of the information extraction problem which allows for the introduction of conditional random fields.

6.3.1. *Usage and limitations*

The use of supervised machine learning was encouraged by the last MUC conferences, which proposed data from several different domains and in different languages, accompanied by examples of extraction results, without leaving sufficient time to the participants to enable them to develop the specific extractors manually. The majority of the systems having participated in the last of these conferences, in 1998, thus already used, at one stage or another in their development, a machine learning phase.

The benefit acquired is a better flexibility: the same machine learning program can be applied to data with different (language, style, genre, structure, etc.) properties, and supply an adapted extractor each time. In return, these programs require a sufficient set of *labeled examples* to be applied. These data take the form of input data (raw texts or semi-structured documents) associated with the corresponding filled in forms. The collection and processing of these examples can also be time-consuming and fastidious, but in general demands less technical skill than the direct writing of an extractor.

The various national (ESTER, DEFT, etc.) or international (TREC, CoNLL, ACE, etc.) challenges which have taken the place of MUC conferences all implicitly assume that the participants use techniques of this kind. They supply labeled data several weeks before publishing the real data on which the competition rests. The time just allows the process of automatic learning to take place, but is never enough to build a competitive extractor by hand.

But machine learning is not an easy path to follow, and new problems arise. In fact, there are few directly applicable supervised machine learning algorithms: most of them are conceived to perform a classification or an annotation task. The information extraction task must often be reformulated so that the problem becomes one of these more general tasks. Such reformulation examples will be seen further in this chapter. Once this first step is accomplished, other difficulties appear. As a matter of fact, the available learning data are only *positive examples*, in other words correctly extracted data. The majority of machine learning programs also need *negative examples*. In certain cases, depending on the variants (see section 6.2.2), the supplied data enable the introduction of negative examples. For example when the multiplicity of the expected response is unique then all responses other than the correct one are negative examples. However, in this case, an imbalance set of examples may deteriorate the efficiency of the algorithm.

Finally, as always when considering the intervention of automatic learning in a language engineering task, the problem of accounting for external knowledge or linguistic resources arises. How can we take advantage of carefully hand-built patterns? How can we reinvest them in a program which is designed only to learn from examples? We will see that CRFs suggest some interesting answers to these questions.

6.3.2. *Some applicable machine learning methods*

Numerous supervised machine learning methods have been employed to address the information extraction task [SAR 08]. Certain methods fit only to a certain type of input data (text or semi-structured), whereas others can be applied to any. Here, only certain methods will be discussed, before developing those which rely on conditional random fields.

First of all, since most of the extractors written by hand take the form of patterns, it is natural to try and infer directly such patterns from the available examples. Historically, symbolic machine learning strategies inspired by this statement have been tried; the pioneering Rapier system can be cited first, which came from Inductive Logical Programing (ILP) [CAL 03]. Grammatical inference, which refers to the automatic learning of representations of languages (such as regular expressions, automata and formal grammars of various classes) is another possible symbolic approach. When applied to texts, it gave few convincing results (see however, [FRE 97, FRE 00a]). However, it appeared to be efficient for learning tree wrappers [KOS 06, CAR 07]. Patterns can also be introduced from the analysis and generalization of sequences, using *suffix tree* algorithms [RAV 02] or using methods inspired by sequential data mining [CHA 09].

However, the most common approach, as it is applicable to all types of input data, consists in reformulating the problem as a kind of *supervised classification*, for which numerous systems and algorithms (neural networks, decision trees, Bayesian classifiers, SVM, etc.) already exist. For texts, the idea could be to class each item of a sequence as "to be extracted" or not. It has been seen however that extracted data often corresponds to a *sequence of items*. It, therefore, seems to be more efficient to class the *separators* between the items, according to whether they correspond to the "start" of a piece of data to extract, to the "end" of such data or if they are "neutral", in other words situated in a non-relevant zone for the extraction. It is this approach which is used in BWI [FRE 00b]. It is also possible to try to class the *separator couples* according to whether they outline or not a sequence of text items to extract, as in the Elie system

[FIN 04]. These strategies have been generalized for information extraction in trees in [MAR 07].

6.3.3. *Annotating to extract*

For the remainder of this chapter, our chosen approach involves focusing on another different reformulation of the information extraction task, into an *annotation* problem. In such a problem, the initial data is composed of several items, each of which must be associated with a *label* belonging to a new finite vocabulary. In a way, the approach discussed at the end of the previous section is a particular case of annotation, in which the items considered are the separators. In this section we will suppose that the items are of linguistic nature (words or multiword units), but they can also be of structural nature (separators, labels). The fundamental difference between this task and classification is that, in the context of an annotation, it is relevant to take into account the *relationships between labels* to assign them correctly. An annotation is, therefore, not a series of independent classifications: it is the set of all the labels associated with the items which is the learning target, and not each of them independently. This is what the statistical models developed further will allow.

Numerous linguistic engineering tasks are annotation tasks: this is of course the case of morpho-syntactic labeling, where the purpose is to associate each linguistic item of a text with a category among "common name", "verb", "adjective", and so on with possible additional morphological information such as the genre, number, conjugation, and so on. It is in fact obvious that, in this case, the label to associate with a particular word strongly depends on the labels associated with the neighboring words in the same sentence.

To reformulate an information extraction task into an annotation task, a set of labels must be defined. They are built in two parts: the first part is an identifier of the field to be filled in and the second part is an additional letter generally chosen among the letters BCEO (B for *Begin*, C for *Continue*, E for *End*, and O for *Other*) or BIO (I for *Inside*) [SAR 08]. A simple label couple IO (*In/Out*) does not enable us to distinguish between a sequence of items which constitutes a single value for a field to fill in (e.g. a single entity such as "19 April 1989" or "Olympic Games") and a sequence of distinct values for the same field (e.g. a list of distinct proper names).

In the following example, which describes an event, the label starting with P is relative to a location (*Place*) and those starting with E (Event) refer to the nature of the event:

London	will	host	the	next	Olympic	Games
PB		O	O	O	EB	EI

From such a labeling, it is easy to fill in a form about the described event. Information extraction from semi-structured documents can, in general, also be described as an annotation task, where the items coincide this time with the nodes of the tree to label.

6.4. Introduction to conditional random fields

Conditional random fields (CRF) constitute a family of statistical models which enable data label learning[8]. They have common traits with numerous formalisms defining joint or conditional distributions. They also borrow from models based on logistic regression and on the principle of maximum entropy [BER 96], often used for natural language processing, the definition of a set of parameters associated with feature functions. With Bayesian networks or hidden Markov models, they share a graph that relates variables and most of the algorithmic solutions to inference problems. For these reasons, conditional random fields can be introduced by both points of view: from the maximum entropy angle and from the hidden Markov model angle. In this section, the maximum entropy models will be focused on, but the link with hidden Markov models will also be established in section 6.6.

6.4.1. *Formalization of a labelling problem*

For this introduction, the previous example about the Olympic Games in London will be re-addressed. The modeling of the problem consists of considering that a sentence of six words is the realization $x = (x_1, \ldots, x_6)$ of a field of six random variables $X = (X_1, \ldots, X_6)$. These variables X_i are said to be *observation* variables. The labeling is the realization $y = (y_1, \ldots, y_6)$ of random variables $Y = (Y_1, \ldots, Y_6)$:

x:	London	will	host	the	next	Olympic	Games
y:	PB		O	O	O	EB	EI

Once the x variables are observed, the probabilistic approach of the problem relies on the definition of the conditional probability:

$$P(Y = y | X = x) \tag{6.1}$$

It is usually assumed that P belongs to a given distribution class, which is often parametric. This class will condition on the algorithms for solving the two main problems: on the one hand, the determination of the labels to associate with a new

---

8 Annotation or labeling is interchangeably used to designate the operation which consists of associating a label with each piece of data.

observed sequence of words, and on the other hand, the identification of P from the labeled examples (in other words, the training of the model for the identification of its parameters). The difficulty of these problems also depends on the class P belongs to of course.

PROBLEM **Pr1.**– Inference. *Given P and x, find the realization y which maximizes the conditional probability* $P(Y = y | X = x)$.

PROBLEM **Pr2.**– Learning or training. *Given a finite sample S of "associated annotation observation" couples of the form* $\{(x^1, y^1), \ldots, (x^m, y^m)\}$ *with unknown P, identify the parameters of P.*

6.4.2. *Maximum entropy model approach*

Taking into account the domain knowledge in a statistical model is often achieved by the definition of a finite set of feature functions. They are most of the time functions providing a value among $\{0, 1\}$, such as the following one, defined on a pair of arguments: an item and a label:

$$f(v, u) = \begin{cases} 1 \text{ if } u \text{ has a capital letter and } v \neq \text{``O''} \\ otherwise \text{ if} \end{cases}$$

For data pairs (x, y) which are sequences, this function can apply to any position i. In the example of section 6.4.1, it gives a result 1 for positions $i = 1$, $i = 5$, and $i = 6$, and is 0 everywhere else. It is also 0 in the first position of a sentence which does not begin with a named entity. The application of such a feature function to a sequence consists of, in fact, performing such calls to each position in this sequence and combining the results. In certain cases, the useful knowledge for labeling an item relies on its neighbors in the sequence. The feature functions are therefore a little more complex, as the following one, applying on a couple (u, u') of consecutive items and a label v associated with the first one:

$$f(v, u, u') = \begin{cases} 1 \text{ if not } u = \text{``Olympic''} \ u' = \text{``Games''} \text{ and } v \text{``EB''} \\ otherwise \text{ if not} \end{cases} \quad [6.2]$$

The definition of the statistical model is fundamentally based on the maximum entropy principle: it is the distribution $\hat{P}$ which contains as less information as possible, and imposes the fewest assumptions on the data (therefore, here, limiting itself to the knowledge carried by the feature functions), which must be chosen:

$$\hat{P}(Y \mid X) = \underset{P}{\text{argmax}} \ H_P(Y \mid X) = \underset{P}{\text{argmax}} - P(Y|X) \log P(Y|X) \quad [6.3]$$

With this assumption, the **Pr2** problem can be reformulated as an optimization problem under the constraint that the distribution[9] $\hat{P}$. Each feature introduces a constraint in the optimization problem. The expression of its solution therefore goes through the introduction of Lagrange multipliers θ_k^i, the coefficients associated with each feature function f_k^i. The definition of the model, parameterized by the θ_k^i, for each Y_i results in a characteristic format [KLI 07, BER 96] of the maximum entropy models:

$$P(Y_i = y_i | X = x) = \frac{1}{Z(x)} \exp\left(\sum_k \theta_k^i f_k^i(y_i, x) \right) \qquad [6.4]$$

where $Z(x) = \sum_{y \in \mathcal{Y}} \exp\left(\sum_k \theta_k^i f_k^i(y, x) \right)$ is a normalization coefficient. Basically, each coefficient θ_k^i characterizes the "importance" of the associated function f_k^i. A similar form is found for the conditional random fields.

Problem **Pr1** can therefore be easily resolved. Furthermore, it is unnecessary to calculate $Z(x)$ to find the best y_i and the algorithmic complexity of this approach stays simple: for each variable Y_i and for each possible value y_i in its domain $\mathcal{Y}_i$, it is in fact easy to calculate $\sum_k \theta_k^i f_k^i(y_i, x)$. If we consider that the value of each function f_k can be calculated in a constant time[10], the algorithm is linear in the number of variables, the number of feature functions, and the cardinality of $\mathcal{Y}_i$.

In this case, problem **Pr2** can also be resolved without too many difficulties. Given a sample of labeled data S, finding the best parameters, that is, those which maximize the entropy, corresponds to finding the solution to the corresponding likelihood maximization problem [NIG 99, PIE 97]. The model described in equation [6.4] being an exponential product of feature functions weighted by the parameters θ_k, the likelihood is convex and it is therefore possible to find this unique maximum, for example using a descending gradient algorithm.

Tying parameters. The model proposed till now relies on a field of six random variables, each associated with sentence labels of six observed words. How can we predict in this case the labels of sentences of seven words or more? In equation [6.4], each variable Y_i of Y has its own set of feature functions and parameters. A solution consists in imposing a set of feature functions *common to all variables Y, no matter their position*. The functions are no longer indexed by the position, but the position becomes one of their arguments and the parameters θ are assumed to be the same for all the variables:

---

9 Each value is between 0 and 1 and their sum is 1.

10 This is an assumption kept for the remaining of the entire chapter.

$$P(Y_i = y_i | X = x) = \frac{1}{Z(x)} \exp\left(\sum_k \theta_k f_k(y_i, x, i)\right)$$ [6.5]

Here a finite set $f_1, \ldots, f_K$ of functions is considered, identically applied for all variables Y_i.

6.4.3. Hidden Markov model approach

An important criticism is often argued against the maximum entropy model approach: it does not take into account the data structure, their sequential organization for example. The dependencies between consecutive labels are not currently integrated into the model. In this sense, it is more a *classification* model than an *annotation* model. Hidden Markov models[11] are a second possible classical approach for processing the problem of sequence labeling, which begins to correct this default.

In a hidden Markov model, it is the joint probability $P(X, Y)$ which is represented. Using the definition of conditional probability and with the help of the decomposition rule, the conditional probability of a sequence of six variables Y_i is written:

$$P(Y|X) = \frac{P(X, Y)}{P(X)}$$ [6.6]

$$= \frac{1}{P(X)} P(Y_1) P(X_1 | Y_1)$$

$$\prod_{i=2}^{6} P(X_i | Y_i, X_{i-1}, Y_{i-1} \ldots, X_1, Y_1) P(Y_i | X_{i-1}, Y_{i-1} \ldots, X_1, Y_1)$$ [6.7]

As this formula shows, looking for the value $\hat{y}$ which maximizes $P(Y|X)$ becomes impossible to compute in practice with the length of the sequence and the cardinality of $\mathcal{Y}$. In hidden Markov models, a set of conditional independence hypotheses is added to limit this computational complexity. It is assumed that (i) each X_i only depends on the corresponding Y_i and that (ii) each Y_i is independent of any other Y_j conditionally to Y_{i-1}. A simplified expression is therefore obtained:

$$P(Y|X) = \frac{1}{P(X)} P(Y_1) P(X_1 | Y_1) \prod_{i=2}^{6} P(X_i | Y_i) P(Y_i | Y_{i-1})$$ [6.8]

In this case, the parameterization thus consists of determining the set of probabilities $P(X_i | Y_i)$ and $P(Y_i | Y_{i-1})$ and the input probability $P(Y_1)$.

---

11 See their definition in the Appendix.

The addition of these hypotheses allows for the solutions of the two problems **Pr1** and **Pr2** to be computed in polynomial time, by a dynamic programming algorithm based on the factorization of equation [6.8] (for more details, refer to the Appendix which presents hidden Markov models). This technique is also used in the case of conditional random fields.

However, hidden Markov models are not exempt from criticism either. The first criticism rests on the assumptions associated with the variables X which are finally observed. The model forbids the expression of *dependencies between words*, although their realization is observable. It is therefore impossible to condition the labeling of a word by the presence of other words in the sentence, even though they are known. The second criticism focuses on the fact that hidden Markov models implement a more difficult task than the one initially targeted: they produce a *data generation* model (using the computation of $P(X, Y)$) and by consequence a model of the observed data too, whereas the annotation task does not require it. It will be seen that conditional random fields are a way to answer these two criticisms.

Hidden Markov models, conditional random fields, and even maximum entropy models presented here all belong to the class of *graphical models*, so called not because they can be given a graphical representation, but because the relations between their underlying variables form a graph. Graphical models will be briefly discussed in the following section.

6.4.4. *Graphical models*

In a graphical model, the random variables of the annotation problem become the nodes of a graph, and the absence of edge between two nodes means a conditional independence relationship between the corresponding variables, given the other variables of the graph. Without any particular assumption, all the variables are dependent on one another and the graph is complete: for each pair of nodes, there is an edge that links them. Under the hypotheses of hidden Markov models (section 6.4.3) the graph obtained is the one of Figure 6.1. It is a directed graph which displays the *generative* nature of the model: the labels (Y) in fact "generate" the words (X).

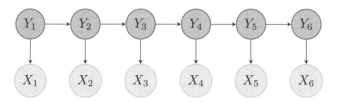

Figure 6.1. *Graph of hidden Markov chain models*

The conditional independence relations underlying the model are in fact used to rewrite equation [6.6]. For hidden Markov models, it has been seen that it can be rewritten in equation [6.8]: the probability $P(X, Y)$ is therefore a product of conditional probabilities of which each of the factors makes explicit the dependence of a variable with respect to its antecedent (or father) in the graph.

Under the assumptions of maximum entropy models (section 6.4.2), the graph is even simpler as all the variables Y are conditionally independent of all the variables X, which gives the graph of Figure 6.2. For readability, the node X represents the clique (in other words, a totally connected subgraph) of all the variables X, and the edge between an Y_i and X constructs a complete clique between all these nodes. The graph, this time, is not directed since the dependencies in this case are expressed by functions in which y_i and all the x elements play a symmetrical role, for each value of i (see for an example, equation [6.2]).

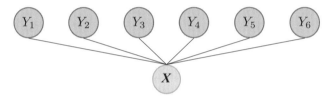

Figure 6.2. *Graph of the maximum entropy model. Here, the node X represents a clique that contains all the variables of X*

In the case of non-directed graphs, the probability of the field of variables does not take the form of a product of probabilities, as in the case in directed models, but takes the form of a product of arbitrary positive functions on the set $\mathcal{C}$ of the cliques of the graph:

$$P(Y = y, X = x) = \frac{1}{Z} \prod_{c \in \mathcal{C}} \Psi_c(y_c, x_c) \qquad [6.9]$$

Here, Z is always a normalization factor and x_c and y_c refer to realizations of the variable fields X_c and Y_c of the clique c. For this maximum entropy model, the expressions of equations [6.4] and [6.9] can be compared. The first is written for a single variable Y_i. Notice that distinct Y_i are in different cliques: Distinct Y_i being independent of one another conditionally to X, $P(Y|X)$ is in fact a product according to the graph cliques. Furthermore, in equation [6.9], if the X values are observed then the normalization factor Z depends on these values when evaluating the conditional probability $P(Y|X)$. Finally, let us also note that the potential functions are only specific to the maximum entropy model, where they take the form of an exponential of a linear combination of feature functions.

Integrating these two formalisms, and soon that of conditional random fields, into the graphical model framework enables a uniform presentation of the algorithms which solve the **Pr1** and **Pr2** problems. When computing the marginal probabilities such as $P(Y_1 = y_1|X = x) = \sum_{y_2,\dots,y_6} P(Y = y|X = x)$, the conditional independence relationships allow the sum to be simplified, resulting in an efficient calculation. For example, in the case of hidden Markov models, the sums are "pushed" as far as possible in the product, giving the following expression:

$$P(Y_1 = y_1|X = x) = \frac{1}{P(X)} P(Y_1) P(X_1|Y_1) \left(\sum_{y_2} P(X_2|Y_2) \right.$$

$$\left. P(Y_2|Y_1) \left(\sum_{y_3} P(X_3|Y_3) P(Y_3|Y_2) \dots \left(\sum_{y_6} P(X_6|Y_6) P(Y_6|Y_5) \right) \right) \right)$$

This rewriting allows an optimization of the computation through dynamic programmic techniques. In fact, the most embedded factor in the loops identified by the sums, namely $\sum_{y_6} P(X_6|Y_6) P(Y_6|Y_5)$, can be memorized as it does not depend on other intermediate index loop variables smaller than five. By repeating this memorization to each intermediate factor, and in such a way that constant access to the memorized factors is possible, the complexity falls to a second degree polynomial.

It is the graph underlying the definition of probabilities which makes this factorization possible. This property is essential for efficiently computing marginal probabilities. We note also that the definition of the conditional independence graph concerning the variables X is not useful when representing $P(Y|X)$, since the realizations of X are observed. In the following, only graphs on the output variables Y will be considered. This will mean that all the variables of the field X are implicitly linked to all those of the field Y.

6.5. Conditional random fields

6.5.1. *Definition*

Let us define two sets of random variables, or random fields: X, representing the inputs or observables and Y, representing the outputs or annotations. Let G be a non-directed graph whose set of nodes is the set of random variables Y and let $\mathcal{C}$ be the set of cliques of the graph G. The variable fields of a clique c are called X_c and Y_c and their outputs are x_c and y_c. The conditional random fields are distributions $P(Y|X)$ that factorize according to G:

$$P(Y = y|X = x) = \frac{1}{Z(x)} \prod_{c \in \mathcal{C}} \Psi_c(y_c, x) \qquad [6.10]$$

$$\text{with } Z(\mathbf{x}) = \sum_{\mathbf{y},\, y_i \in \mathcal{Y}} \prod_{c \in \mathcal{C}} \Psi_c(\mathbf{y}_c, \mathbf{x}) \qquad [6.11]$$

In conditional random fields, as in maximum entropy models, the linguistic knowledge is expressed by the feature functions and the maximum entropy principle is applied. In addition, the parameters are linked so that each potential function Ψ_c can be written as:

$$\Psi_c(\mathbf{y}_c, \mathbf{x}) = \exp \left(\sum_k \theta_k f_k(\mathbf{y}_c, \mathbf{x}, c) \right) \qquad [6.12]$$

The parameters are $\Theta = (\theta_k)_k$. As already done for equation [6.5], tying the parameters leads to defining feature functions having the clique (or an index that identifies it) as an argument[12]. As a consequence, the inference and training of a conditional random field are not limited to data (that is to say, fields of variables) with identical size and structure.

Conditional random fields bring solutions to the problems posed by the models presented in the previous sections. As a matter of fact:

– they are adapted to *structured data*, composed of non-independent items, such as for example, the words of a sentence or the nodes of a tree. Each item in such a structure is associated both with an observed random variable for its content and an output random variable for its label. The graph enables the expression of non-trivial conditional independence relationships between the labels. Thanks to this expressivity, CRF models overtake the maximum entropy models of section 6.4.2 which perform independent classifications and not a real overall annotation;

– conditional random fields directly model a conditional probability. How the labels are associated with the data is the only target and it is not necessary to describe how these data are generated. This removes, in particular, the strong limitations of hidden Markov models: the labeling of an element of the data can, while remaining efficiently computable (provided the dependencies between outputs are not too complex), depend on an arbitrary subset (or on the total set) of the observed data.

In the following section, we will study how and under which limitations it is possible to efficiently resolve both the inference and training problems (see page 188) for conditional random fields. All the complexity of the inference problem is already found in the computation of $Z(\mathbf{x})$. The summation on all the possible values of $\mathbf{y}$ in fact leads to a combinatorial explosion: if n is the size (in number of variables) of the

---

12 In [SUT 06], the authors speak of *features templates*.

random field Y, then there are $|\mathcal{Y}|^n$ possible different labelings. How this computation can nonetheless be effectively performed, will be studied.

6.5.2. Factorization and graphical models

Let us consider a graph G which is represented in Figure 6.3, on the left. Only the node Y_4 assures the connection between the two "parts" of G. If this node is taken away, then the graph G separates into two disjointed sub-graphs: $G_{1,2,3}$ and $G_{5,6}$. This separability expresses a conditional independence of all the variables of $G_{1,2,3}$ with respect to the variables of $G_{5,6}$ (and vice versa)[13]. The separability property can concern a single node, as in this example, or a set of nodes. In this example, there are four maximal cliques[14]: the two sub-graphs $G_{1,2,3}$ and $G_{5,6}$ and the two cliques with two elements $G_{3,4} = \{Y_3, Y_4\}$ and $G_{4,5} = \{Y_4, Y_5\}$. The normalization coefficient Z can be written, as done in the case of hidden Markov models, by "pushing" the sums as far as possible under the products:

$$\sum_{\boldsymbol{y},\, y_i \in \mathcal{Y}} \prod_{c \in \mathcal{C}} \Psi_c(\boldsymbol{y}_c, \boldsymbol{x}) = \sum_{(y_1, y_2, y_3) \in \mathcal{Y}^3} \Psi_{G_{1,2,3}}(y_1, y_2, y_3, \boldsymbol{x})$$

$$\left(\sum_{y_4 \in \mathcal{Y}} \Psi_{G_{3,4}}(y_3, y_4, \boldsymbol{x}) \left(\sum_{y_5 \in \mathcal{Y}} \Psi_{G_{4,5}}(y_4, y_5, \boldsymbol{x}) \right. \right.$$

$$\left. \left. \left(\sum_{y_6 \in \mathcal{Y}} \Psi_{G_{5,6}}(y_5, y_6, \boldsymbol{x}) \right) \right) \right)$$

This factorization also rests on the order of the variables according to which the sums are pushed on the product: this is known as *variable elimination order*[15]. In the previous computation, the Y_1 to Y_6 order has been followed. Starting with Y_4 for example, would not enable the maximum exploitation of the evidenced separation. Thanks to this factorization, the complexity decreases from $|\mathcal{Y}|^6$ to $|\mathcal{Y}|^3$, where 3 is the size of the largest clique of G^{16} (and corresponds to the enumeration of all the possible triplet values for the Y_1, Y_2, and Y_3 variables).

---

13 The Hammersley–Clifford theorem [HAM 71] establishes the fact that separability in the graph, factorization according to the cliques of the graph and conditional independence are three equivalent properties which enable the definition of the same class of distributions.

14 The cliques included in these maximal cliques do not take part of the factorization which follows and their contribution to the probability can be easily integrated in the one of the maximal cliques.

15 This approach is known for the case of graphical models or Bayesian networks under the name of variables elimination algorithm [SHA 90].

16 The general principle of the algorithm is not given here. It is described on page 193 in the case of hidden Markov models and consists in conserving the computations already done.

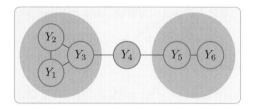 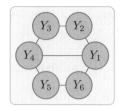

Figure 6.3. *Conditional and separability independences*

In the case of more complex graphs, as well as for the calculation of any marginal probability, the factorization and choice of the order of elimination of the variables seem to be less obvious. For example, for the case of Figure 6.3 (on the right), it is necessary to remove at least two nodes to be able to cut the graph into two disjointed sub-graphs. According to the choice of these two nodes, it is possible to obtain different factorizations, which will give rise to different complexities for the computation of Z.

A uniform approach to evaluate Z or any marginal probability relies on the construction of a *junction tree* and on the application of the *message passing* dynamic programming algorithm, presented in the following sections. The conditional independence graphs taking the form of a chain or of a tree have the properties that enable the direct application of this dynamic programming algorithm. The general message passing algorithm is a generalization of those which apply to hidden Markov models (*forward-backward*) or PCFG[17] (*inside-outside*, α-β).

6.5.3. *Junction tree*

A junction tree J for a graph G is a graph whose nodes are clique unions obtained from G and satisfying the following conditions:

– it is a tree, therefore there always exists only a single path between any two nodes of J;

– all cliques of G are contained in the nodes of J;

– for any couple of nodes A and B of J, if a variable Y_i belongs to A and to B at the same time, then it also belongs to all nodes of J that are found on the path between A and B.

The junction tree of a given graph is not unique. The tree reduced to a single node including all the cliques of the graph is, for example, always a junction tree, even if it is not very useful for factorizing calculations. Figure 6.4 gives two examples of junction trees for two same graphs.

---

17 Probabilistic context-free grammars, see for example [MAN 99].

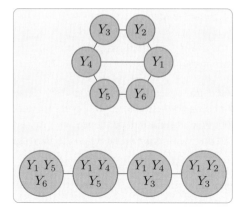 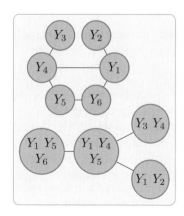

Figure 6.4. *Examples of two graphs (above) and one of their junction trees (below)*

The construction algorithm of a junction tree of a graph, quite classical in graph theory, is presented in [COW 99]. It relies on the determination of the order of elimination of variables which enables the triangulation[18] of the graph G. With the cliques created as such, a weighted graph of cliques is built, from which a recovery tree maximizing the weights is selected. The best tree is the one where the largest clique has the smallest cardinality, but the problem of identifying this tree is NP-hard[19]. Luckily, for certain graph classes, it is possible to build an optimal junction tree efficiently.

In a junction tree, by construction, to each node j corresponds a set of cliques S_j of the original tree, identified by the triangulation process. j is therefore associated with a new potential function Ψ'_j which represents the product of all the S_j potential functions. Through this association, several original factors Ψ are repeated in different Ψ'. The definition of Ψ' must therefore be adapted in order to avoid this duplication of factors. For example, for the graph of Figure 6.4 (on the right) there are the following potential functions: $\Psi_{3,4}(y_3, y_4)$, $\Psi_{4,5}(y_4, y_5)$, $\Psi_{5,6}(y_5, y_6)$, $\Psi_{6,1}(y_6, y_1)$, $\Psi_{1,2}(y_1, y_2)$, and $\Psi_{1,4}(y_1, y_4)$. By taking into account its junction tree, the following is proposed:

$$Z \times P(Y|X) = \Psi'_A(y_1, y_5, y_6)\Psi'_B(y_1, y_4, y_5)\Psi'_C(y_3, y_4)\Psi'_D(y_1, y_2) \qquad [6.13]$$

with:

$$\Psi'_A = \Psi_{5,6}\Psi_{6,1} \qquad\qquad \Psi'_B = \Psi_{1,4}\Psi_{4,5}$$
$$\Psi'_C = \Psi_{3,4} \qquad\qquad\qquad \Psi'_D = \Psi_{1,2}$$

---

18 In other words, elimination of the cycles whose length is longer than or equal to 4.

19 The factorization according to this order corresponds to a graph triangulation choice and the algorithm is equivalent to the computation of the tree width of the graph.

This way, a factorization of P on a set of cliques which corresponds to the cliques of its junction tree is displayed. This tree factorization (the factors and junction tree decomposition) is the structure from which the evaluation of all marginal probabilities P can be efficiently computed by dynamic programming.

What is essential is that the tree obtained preserves the good properties of the probabilistic decomposition as well as that of being a junction tree, whatever root node is chosen. In fact, due to this structure we obtain a certain independence with respect to the elimination order of the variables. This note will make sense when the message passing algorithm is explained.

Finally, note that when the original graph underlying P is a chain or a tree, the tree factorization is immediate.

6.5.4. Inference in CRFs

Once given a junction tree and the potential functions attached to its nodes, the message passing algorithm can be applied. Let us come back to definition [6.13] of the probability associated with the graph of Figure 6.4 (on the right). To compute the marginal probability in the first node A, for a given value of (y_1, y_5, y_6), the following sum is obtained:

$$\Psi'_A(y_1, y_5, y_6) \sum_{y_2, y_3, y_4} \Psi'_B(y_1, y_4, y_5) \Psi'_C(y_3, y_4) \Psi'_D(y_1, y_2)$$

that is factorized according to the tree:

$$\Psi'_A(y_1, y_5, y_6) \sum_{y_4} \Psi'_B(y_1, y_4, y_5) \sum_{y_3} \Psi'_C(y_3, y_4) \sum_{y_2} \Psi'_D(y_1, y_2)$$

The same process the one described on page 193 is found here, which enables the efficient computation of the marginal probability by dynamic programming. To be more explicit, the $m_{D \to B}(y_1) = \sum_{y_2} \Psi'_D(y_1, y_2)$ and $m_{C \to B}(y_4) = \sum_{y_3} \Psi'_C(y_3, y_4)$ factors, which will be memorized, can be displayed in such a way that:

$$\Psi'_A(y_1, y_5, y_6) \sum_{y_4} \Psi'_B(y_1, y_4, y_5) m_{C \to B}(y_4) m_{D \to B}(y_1)$$

The $m_{C \to B}(y_4)$ factor (and similarly for $m_{D \to B}(y_1)$) can be interpreted as a *message* passed from the node C to the node B (and from the node D to the node B, respectively). The message, parametered by a value of y_4, characterizes in the form of a function dependent on y_4 the computation achieved at the node B. Similarly, the computation achieved at the node B can be seen as a message sent to the node A with parameters (y_1, y_5):

$$m_{B \to A}(y_1, y_5) = \sum_{y_4} \Psi'_B(y_1, y_4, y_5) m_{C \to B}(y_4) m_{D \to B}(y_1) \qquad [6.14]$$

As a result, $P(Y_1 = y_1, Y_5 = y_5, Y_6 = y_6|X)$ is proportional to $\Psi'_A(y_1, y_5, y_6)$ $m_{B\to A}(y_1, y_5)$. What has been gained from this new formulation? Nothing for the moment, if no other marginal probability computation is performed. By applying exactly the same approach for the other marginal probabilities, it can be observed that the exchanged messages are identical, or that the senders and receivers are simply reversed. Figure 6.5 shows the exchanged messages in different cases, and the node which computes the marginal probability is put at the root. To obtain an efficient computation, the messages in both directions must be computed once for all. For this, a simple "round-trip" is sufficient.

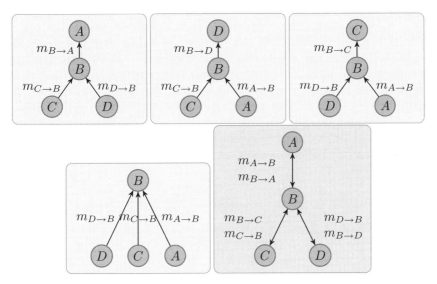

Figure 6.5. *Messages exchanged for the computation of marginal probabilities (the last figure shows that a simple to and fro enables the computation of all the messages and therefore of all the marginal probabilities)*

The similarity between this algorithm and the one applied for hidden Markov models can be noted. To perform this computation, the significant property used is the distributivity of the multiplication in relation to the addition. As the multiplication is equally distributive in relation to the "maximum" operation (when only manipulating positive numbers), the "sum-product" version of the computation shown here also extends to the "max-product" version which allows for the most probable labeling to be obtained.

6.5.5. *Inference algorithms*

To summarize, a general inference algorithm can now be given. Let us take a junction tree $\mathcal{T}$ associated with the graph on the output random variable Y of a conditional random field. For each node v of $\mathcal{T}$, we note $N(v)$ the set of the neighboring nodes of v. The variables in the node v are noted Y_v and their realization is y_v. The potential functions associated with each node v of $\mathcal{T}$ are written as $\Psi'(y_v)$. Finally, for any two nodes v and v', $Y_{v'} \setminus Y_v$ represents the set of variables of v' which are not in v and their realizations are written as $y_{v'} \setminus y_v$. Furthermore, $Y_{v'} \cap Y_v$ is the set of variables common to $Y_{v'}$ and Y_v.

The algorithm first computes all the messages between all the nodes of $\mathcal{T}$ in two steps: one "come" and one "go". This consists of collecting the messages coming from leaves and resending the messages toward the leaves. This recursion can start in any node of $\mathcal{T}$ the choice of which is implemented by the *RootChoice* function. The values of the messages are memorized in the structures noted $m_{v \to v'}$ and indexed by the variables $y_{v'} \cap y_v$. If, for example, $y_{v'} \cap y_v$ contains two variables Y_j and Y_k, then $m_{v \to v'}$ is a function with two arguments: it is therefore stored in a matrix with the values of Y_j in the rows and the values of Y_k in the columns, where each cell contains the value of the $m_{v \to v'}$ message for the values of the corresponding variables. For convenience, we note $m_{v \to v'}[y_{v'} \cap y_v]$ this value.

Function *Comego($\mathcal{T}$)*:
   $r \leftarrow RootChoice(\mathcal{T})$
   For all $v \in N(r)$
      $Come(r, v)$
   For all $v \in N(r)$
      $Go(r, v)$

Function *Come(v, v')*:
   For all $v'' \in N(v') \setminus \{v\}$
      $Come(v', v'')$
   $SendMessage(v', v)$

Function *Go(v, v')*:
   $SendMessage(v, v')$
   For all $v'' \in N(v') \setminus \{v\}$
      $Go(v', v'')$

Function *SendMessage(v', v)*:
   For all $y_{v'} \cap y_v$
$$m_{v' \to v}[y_{v'} \cap y_v] = \sum\nolimits_{y_{v'} \setminus y_v} \Psi'_{v'}(y_{v'}) \prod\nolimits_{v'' \in N(v') \setminus \{v\}} m_{v'' \to v'}[y_{v''} \cap y_{v'}]$$

Any marginal probability of the node v, for a given realization $\mathbf{y}_v$, is proportional to an expression which relies on only one potential function applying on $\mathbf{y}_v$ and on several messages:

$$P(\mathbf{Y} = \mathbf{y} \mid \mathbf{Y}_v = \mathbf{y}_v) \propto \Psi'_v(\mathbf{y}_v) \prod_{v' \in N(v)} m_{v' \to v}[\mathbf{y}_{v'} \cap \mathbf{y}_v]$$

6.5.6. Training CRFs

The problem of training a conditional random field consists of determining the parameters Θ of the model from labeled examples (see problem **Pr2** on page 188). As for maximum entropy models (see section 6.4.2), the classical way of resolving it relies on the principle of maximum likelihood, applied here to conditional distributions.

Let us consider a finite set of labeled data composed of couples providing a realization of X and Y:

$$S = \{(\mathbf{x}^1, \mathbf{y}^1), \dots, (\mathbf{x}^m, \mathbf{y}^m)\}$$

The examples of S are *i.i.d.* [20] and the $\mathbf{y}^i$'s are linked to the $\mathbf{x}^i$'s according to a fixed but unknown probability that we want to represent by a conditional random field whose structure (i.e. the graph and feature functions) is known. Also remember that the assumption of tying parameters (see section 6.4.2) of the conditional random field allows for fields of various size and structure in S (whose elements are not necessarily of the same size), even if the properties of the underlying graph apply identically to each variable Y_j.

In a conditional random field with parameters Θ, it is most often chosen to optimize a loss function which corresponds to the log-likelihood, written as:

$$\ell(S; \Theta) = \sum_{i=1}^{m} \log P(\mathbf{y}^i | \mathbf{x}^i; \Theta)$$

$$= \sum_{i=1}^{m} \sum_{c \in C} \sum_{k} \theta_k f_k(\mathbf{y}^i_c, \mathbf{x}^i, c) - \sum_{i=1}^{m} \log Z(\mathbf{x}^i)$$

The number of feature functions being often substantial, the number of parameters θ weighting these functions is too, and there is a significant risk of *over fitting*. To avoid this problem, a regularization term is very often added to the log-likelihood. For this, several possible solutions have been tested [PEN 04]. Often, too large values of parameters are penalized by introducting a term of the from: $\sum_k \frac{\theta_k^2}{2\sigma^2}$. Other approaches

---

20 It must be noted that the variables in the $(\mathbf{x}^i, \mathbf{y}^i)$ fields are not *i.i.d.*

based on the regularization ℓ_1 are also possible and have the advantage of adding parsimony [SUT 06, SOK 09, LAV 10].

The choice of the parameterization in the form of an exponential model guarantees there exists a global optimum which is unique. However, searching for this optimum cannot be resolved analytically, and the solution must therefore be approached through optimization techniques. The development of the log-likelihood gives a difference between two terms, one coming from the normalization coefficient Z. The derivatives with respect to each θ_k of this expression turn into a familiar computation of the maximum likelihood models for the families of exponential models [KLI 07, BER 96]. In fact, an interpretation in the following format appears:

$$\frac{\partial \ell(S; \Theta)}{\partial \theta_k} = \tilde{E}(f_k) - E(f_k)$$

where $\tilde{E}(f_k)$ represents the expectation of the feature function f_k according to the empirical distribution observed in the sample S, and $E(f_k)$ is the expectation in the model of parameters Θ. The expression is canceled out at the maximum likelihood and the computation therefore turns to evaluating both functions $\tilde{E}(f_k)$ and $E(f_k)$. The first one is simple to evaluate as it only counts how many times each feature function is realized in the sample. For the second one, the calculation is generally impractical as all the possible values of every variable y must be considered. The same factorization problem as for the inference problem occurs and the same solution applies. Thus, finally, the algorithm to be developed and the complexity of the training problem are directly linked to inference algorithms.

In their foundational article on conditional random fields, Lafferty *et al.* propose a training strategy based on the work of [PIE 97]. It is an adaptation to conditional random fields of the *Improved Iterative Scaling* (IIS) algorithm, which uses a Newton optimization technique. Unfortunately, the convergence is slow and a large number of iterations is required for it to occur. Using the results discussed in [MAL 02], Wallach [WAL 02] showed that the conjugated gradient methods, BFGS and L-BFGS, converge much more rapidly than IIS. These strategies are therefore more often chosen in the majority of conditional random fields implementations.

However, other solutions have also been considered for training. In [COL 02, ROA 04], an approximation of the log-likelihood gradient is computed by a technique similar to perceptrons. At each stage, an example is presented and the gap between the weight of each observed feature and the one predicted by the model is computed. An average of these gaps then corrects every θ_k. The functional approximation of the gradient is also addressed in [DIE 04]. The authors proposed a representation of the potential functions by weighted sums of regression trees. These trees are built the way the CART algorithm does, with the help of the feature functions. The algorithm can not only be seen as a generation of (combinations of) such feature functions, but also as an alternative training strategy, not based on the maximum likelihood. In fact, it is more a minimization criteria of a quadratic error that is applied in this case. In the same spirit, other works propose other criteria for the optimization problem. In the framework of structured output prediction, an adapted loss function can be considered. This is the case in [KAK 02], where the criteria used are based on the maximization of the likelihood of marginal probabilities (pseudo-likelihood). This way, predictions that incorrectly label only a few nodes are not too penalized. In numerous other works [TAS 04, COL 08], a max margin criterion is applied. A loss function is chosen, generally of a Hamming type, and an optimization formulation according to this loss is defined. Using a reformulation in a dual space, the marginal probabilities are exhibited. As in many works on structure prediction [TSO 05], the method suffers from scalability but the same separability and independance properties can be used in the dual space, and a complexity in a much lower number of variables can be obtained (for example, in $n * |\mathcal{Y}|^2$ for linear conditional random fields). Finally, methods borrowed from support vector machines (SVM, exponential gradient) have also been proposed to resolve the optimization problem in this dual space (see Chapter 4).

However, the training problem remains a difficult one, for which numerous variants can be considered, depending on the environment. For example, the domain knowledge is sometimes very wide and requires that several thousand or sometimes several million feature functions are considered. The selection of relevant features is therefore primordial. Several authors have underlined the difficulties of *a priori* feature selection. However, a dynamic approach seems to be possible [MCC 03b]. The same purpose can also be achieved using a ℓ_1 regularization approach: in [SOK 09], the authors show that for equal performances, the number of feature functions can be enormously reduced. It remains that an acceptable estimation of these models with numerous parameters require a large set of labeled examples. The availability of such examples is very rarely assured whereas numerous non-labeled examples are often easily accessible. The development of semi-supervised methods therefore seems to be natural. Unfortunately, this approach is even more complex in the case of discriminative models such as conditional random fields, than in the case of generative models. However, several authors have addressed this question [ZHU 03, LI 05, ALT 05, JIA 06]. Recently, Sokolovaka *et al.* [SOK 08] demonstrated conditions under which the input of unlabeled data can become relevant.

6.6. Conditional random fields and their applications

In this final section, we come back to the practical applications of CRFs to linguistic engineering. The most simple case, linear conditional random fields, are introduced, as they have given rise to the greatest number of implementations and experiments. In particular, their links with hidden Markov models will be shown and the domains in which they are used will be discussed. The more complex instances are also addressed and this chapter concludes by a panorama of software libraries, available on the Internet, which implement conditional random fields.

Figure 6.6. *Graph of a linear conditional random field*

6.6.1. *Linear conditional random fields*

Conditional random fields were introduced by Lafferty *et al.* [LAF 01] for the segmentation and annotation of *sequences*, whether of strings or of words. In this case, the structure of the conditional independence graph which is generally chosen is also sequential. These kinds of CRFs are known as *linear* conditional random fields, they are characterized by a natural and total order between the random variables of each field and by the independence of each annotation variable with the others conditioned to its immediate successor and predecessor. For the example of page 187 with its six words, the graph between the annotation variables is shown in Figure 6.6.

It is important to understand well what the structure of the graph associated with the conditional random field implies. For example, domain knowledge which would state that *the annotation of any word is more likely to be "EI" if the annotation of the first word is "EB"*, would be translated by a feature function and a dependence between each variable Y_i and Y_1. By choosing a graph such as the one in Figure 6.6, the use of such a feature becomes forbidden. Only the feature functions linking the value of the annotation of a word to the annotation of the following word (or the previous one since the graph is undirected) are enabled. We note, however, that knowledge concerning a long distance property in the observation remains possible, such as for example *the annotation of any word is more likely to be "EI" if the first word of the sentence is "London"*. Remember that, implicitly, all the random variables of the field X are linked to all the random variables of the random field Y. To make the limitation more explicit, the function arguments are designated by y_{i-1} and y_i, and the instantiation of the general model of linear CRF of size n gives the following formula:

$$P(Y = y | X = x) = \frac{1}{Z(x)} \exp \left(\sum_{i=2}^{n} \sum_{k=1}^{K} \theta_k f_k(y_{i-1}, y_i, x, i) \right)$$

with:

$$Z(x) = \sum_{y} \exp \left(\sum_{i=2}^{n} \sum_{k=1}^{K} \theta_k f_k(y_{i-1}, y_i, x, i) \right)$$

In the case of linear conditional random fields, the maximal cliques of the graph are of a size 2 (each couple of consecutive variables makes such a clique) and the optimal junction tree, here a chain, is obviously obtained without difficulty. For the inference problem, the message passing algorithm in this case is identical to the backward-forward algorithm (see Appendix A) used in hidden Markov models. The messages[21] going from the start of the chain towards the variable i coincide with the usual $\alpha_{y,i}$ and those going from the end of the chain towards the variable i with the usual $\beta_{y,i}$:

$$\alpha_{y,i} = \sum_{y'} \alpha_{y',i-1} \exp \sum_k \theta_k f_k(y', y, x, i)$$

$$\beta_{y,i} = \sum_{y'} \beta_{y',i+1} \exp \sum_k \theta_k f_k(y, y', x, i)$$

These new variables correspond to the non-normalized marginal probability of a partial labeling of the chain where the label Y_i has the value y. Their definition is totally similar, but adapted to the special case of a chain, to those of the messages defined in equation [6.14]. By adding the definitions of the extremities of the chain $\alpha_{y,1}$ and $\beta_{y,n}$ which define the basic cases of the recurrence of the computation of $\alpha_{y,i}$ and $\beta_{y,i}$, the marginal probabilities of each variable are obtained:

$$P(Y_i = y | X = x) = \alpha_{y,i} \beta_{y,i} / Z(x)$$

$$Z(x) = \alpha_{y,n} = \beta_{y,1}$$

The complexity of the inference problem in this case is in the order of $n|\mathcal{Y}|^2$.

In the case of linear conditional random fields, it can be seen that the computation algorithms are similar to those used for hidden Markov models. Going even further, it can be very simply verified that every probability model defined by a HMM can also be defined by a linear conditional random field.

6.6.2. *Links between linear CRFs and hidden Markov models*

To show that the probabilistic distributions modeled by linear CRFs include those described by hidden Markov models, the simplest thing to do is to consider the one presented in this book in Appendix A, Figure A.2. The main thing to do is to transform the structure of this hidden Markov model into feature functions for a conditional random field. For this, three types of feature function are required:

– feature functions which characterize the *initial states*: for each state u of the hidden Markov model which is an initial state ($u \in \{1, 2, 3\}$ in this example), the following feature function is defined:

$$f_{k_1, u}(y_i, x, i) = \begin{cases} 1 \text{ if } i = 1 \text{ and } y_1 = u, \\ 0 \text{ elsewhere} \end{cases}$$

---

21 Messages can be written as $m_{i-1 \to i}(y)$ and $m_{i+1 \to i}(y)$, respectively.

– feature functions which characterize the *transitions between states*: for each pair of states (u, u') in the hidden Markov model (in the example, $(u, u') \in \{1, 2, 3\}^2$), the following feature function is defined:

$$f_{k_2,u,u'}(y_{i-1}, y_i, X, i) = \begin{cases} 1 \text{ if } i > 1 \text{ and } y_{i-1} = u \text{ and } y_i = u' \\ 0 \text{ elsewhere} \end{cases}$$

– feature functions which characterize the *emission of an output by a given state*: for each state u of the hidden Markov model ($u \in \{1, 2, 3\}$ in this example) capable of emitting an observation v ($v \in \{1, 2, 3\}$ in this example), the following feature function is defined:

$$f_{k_3,u,v}(y_i, x, i) = \begin{cases} 1 \text{ if } y_i = u \text{ and } x_i = v \\ 0 \text{ elsewhere} \end{cases}$$

Going back to equation [6.10]:

$$P(Y = y | X = x) = \frac{1}{Z(x)} \prod_{c \in C} \exp \left(\sum_k \theta_k f_k(y_c, x, c) \right)$$

Let us instantiate this formula to the example of the hidden Markov model of Appendix A, where $y = 2312$ and $x = 1211$. The cliques c to be considered on the annotation variables Y_i for this calculation are as follows:

– the "unary" cliques composed of a unique variable $Y_i = u$: on each of these cliques, the only non-zero feature functions are as follows:
  - for the variable of Y_1, the one defined for the value $u = 2$: the function $f_{k_1,2}$,
  - for each variable Y_i, initial or not, only the ones defined for the value u when $X_i = v$: the feature function $f_{k_3,u,v}$;

– the "binary" cliques composed of two consecutive variables Y_{i-1} and Y_i, with the respective values of u and u': the only feature functions which do not get canceled out on each of the cliques are those defined as $f_{k_2,u,u'}$.

On each clique c (with the exception of the clique Y_1), a single feature function takes the value 1 whereas all the others are canceled out: the value of each sum on k thus leads to the parameter θ_k associated with this unique non-zero feature function. The following simplified formula is thus obtained:

$$P(Y = 2312 | X = 1211) = \frac{R}{Z(1211)}$$

with:

$$R = \exp(\theta_{k_1,2} + \theta_{k_3,2,1}) \exp \theta_{k_3,3,2} \exp \theta_{k_3,1,1} \exp \theta_{k_3,2,1} \exp \theta_{k_2,2,3} \exp \theta_{k_2,3,1} \exp \theta_{k_2,1,2}$$

For each index value k, let us call $\lambda_k = \exp \theta_k$. After reordering to make the parameters whose first index is k_3 appear at the end, the following is obtained:

$$R = \lambda_{k_1,2} \times \lambda_{k_2,2,3} \times \lambda_{k_2,3,1} \times \lambda_{k_2,1,2} \times \lambda_{k_3,2,1} \times \lambda_{k_3,3,2} \times \lambda_{k_3,1,1} \times \lambda_{k_3,2,1}$$

Now, the only thing required to interpret the parameters λ_k is to compare this computation with the one of page:

– $\lambda_{k_1,2}$ coincides with the probability that 2 is an initial state, in other words the probability that the feature function $f_{k_1,2}$ is satisfied;

– each $\lambda_{k_2,u,u'}$ coincides with the probability of going from state u to state u', in other words the probability of satisfying the feature function $f_{k_2,u,u}$;

– each $\lambda_{k_3,u,v}$ coincides with the probability that the state u expresses v, in other words the probability of satisfying the feature function $f_{k_3,u,v}$.

For the simulation to be complete, it must also be noted that the computation performed in the hidden Markov model was only a joint probability. To obtain the corresponding conditional probability, the following must in fact be calculated:

$$P(Y = 2312 | X = 1211) = \frac{P(X = 1211, Y = 2312)}{P(X = 1211)}$$

For reasons similar to those previously discussed, it can easily be established that the computation of $P(X = 1211)$ in the hidden Markov model is similar to $Z(1211)$ in the conditional random field. Note also that if the structure of the hidden Markov model was not a complete graph, to assure the parallelism of the computations, we would have to define the feature functions corresponding to missing connections between states and to associate them with a parameter $\theta = \lim_{x \to 0^+} \ln x = -\infty$.

Thanks to this computation, it can be seen that given a hidden Markov model, it is very easy to build a set of feature functions as well as the set of associated parameters θ_k which define exactly the same probabilistic distribution for all data (x, y). This computation even shines an interesting light on the nature of the objects appearing in the definition of conditional random fields:

– the notion of feature function translates knowledge of diverse origins, because they express both the *label structure* (the connectivity between the states of the hidden Markov model) and *the relationships between the label and data* (the emissions of the hidden Markov model). But the feature functions for the above simulation are restricted with respect to the overall expressivity authorized in a conditional random field. The possibility, in a CRF, of defining feature functions which test properties of the input data *no matter their position in the sequence* brings an additional degree of freedom, not enabled in hidden Markov models. It is the reason why, when the feature functions are well chosen, conditional random fields generally outperform other models;

– the parameters θ_k which weight the feature functions are not probabilities: these are real numbers. In the particular case of this example, they can be expressed as

$\theta_k = \ln \lambda_k$ where the λ_k are themselves probabilities, therefore between 0 and 1. So, here, the θ_k will all be negative. But this situation it is not at all compulsary. Furthermore, the particular case of the weights worthing ∞ is not significant either. In practice, their value varies from -10 to $+10$ and the larger they are in absolute value, the most significant are the feature functions they are associated with. They measure the *discriminant power* of these feature functions. This power is not necessarily correlated with their satisfaction probability, this is why it is not recommended to proceed to an *a priori* selection of the feature functions based on the number of times they are satisfied.

6.6.3. *Interests and applications of CRFs*

The main advantage of linear conditional random fields with respect to hidden Markov models, which they generalize in some way as illustrated in the previous section, is that they enable to integrate knowledge of various natures into the definition of their feature functions. The relative importance of these feature functions for the overall labeling will be determined during the learning phase of the parameters θ_k which weight them. Several experimentations tend to show that the model is all the more efficient as it is based on a large number of feature functions. It is, therefore, interesting to examine the different possible sources of information for these functions.

The feature functions the linguist can consider in priority are those which translate explicit knowledge. If it is considered, for example, that starting with a capital letter is a significant clue for identifying the words which are part of a named entity, a feature function which exactly expresses this property can be defined (see the first feature function defined in section 6.4.2). Furthermore, if a list of words or multiword units likely to fill in a specific field of an extraction form is available, it is also simple to transform it into feature functions. For example, let L_1 be a list of the first words of location names, and L_2 a list of the remaining parts of the same location names (e.g. for "Rio de Janeiro", "Rio" belongs to L_1 whereas "de" and "Janeiro" belong L_2). As these names are likely to fill in the "location" field (label P for "place") of a database, the following feature functions can be defined:

$$f_k(y_i, \mathbf{x}, i) = \begin{cases} 1 \text{ if } x_i \in L_1 \text{ (respectively } L_2) \text{ and } y_i = \text{"PB" (respectively "PI")} \\ 0 \text{ otherwise} \end{cases}$$

Hand-written regular expressions able to characterize sequences of words occurring before or after an extraction zone can also easily be integrated into the definition of feature functions, like in the following generic example where R is any regular expression:

$$f_{k'}(y_i, \mathbf{x}, i) = \begin{cases} 1 \text{ if } x_1 \ldots x_i \text{ satisfies } R \text{ and } y_i = \text{"PB"} \\ 0 \text{ otherwise} \end{cases}$$

It can, therefore, be seen that the knowledge integrated into an information extraction system conceived without taking advantage of any machine learning approach (see section 6.2.4) can nevertheless also be taken into account by the feature functions of a conditional random field. However, this knowledge is necessarily limited, and it is recommended to add more. In general, the vast majority of the feature functions used by a CRF are produced from the available labeled examples in the learning set, using parametered patterns. A pattern, in this context, is a partially specified function which can be instantiated by browsing the examples. Imagine, for example, a pattern of the form:

$$f_{k''}(y_{i-1}, y_i, \boldsymbol{x}, i) = \begin{cases} 1 \text{ if } x_{i-1} =? \text{ and } x_i =? \text{ and } x_{i+1} =? \text{ and } y_{i-1} =? \text{ and } y_i =? \\ 0 \text{ otherwise} \end{cases}$$

For each pair of data $(\boldsymbol{x}, \boldsymbol{y})$ in the learning set and for each position i such that $1 < i < n$ in the sequence (assumed to be of size n), the question marks in the pattern can be replaced by the values encountered in the example $(\boldsymbol{x}, \boldsymbol{y})$. A labeled sentence of n words therefore gives rise to $n - 2$ distinct feature functions. A pattern must of course respect the limitations of feature functions: it can impose conditions on any value of the sequence $\boldsymbol{x}$, but only on the values of the sequence $\boldsymbol{y}$ which are inside the clique identified by i. All the software libraries which implement conditional random fields (see section 6.6.5) offer the possibility of writing such patterns.

McCallum and Li were the first to use linear conditional random fields to identify various types of named entities, by mixing feature functions issued from the learning data with others translating knowledge collected on the Internet, in the form of lists of proper names [MCC 03a]. Other authors have adopted the same approach, mostly for the identification of biological named entities (genes, proteins, illnesses, etc.) and their relationships in medical texts, which is one of the most studied applications of information extraction [MCD 05, BUN 08].

Conditional random fields also allow to easily combine several successive models, by integrating the results obtained by the first models inside the feature functions of the following one. In [JOU 06, GIL 08], several combination propositions following this method are considered. When a first annotation, even a simplified and imperfect one, is obtained, it can become part of the observation of the following annotation process, and therefore be taken into account in the definition of its feature functions, even if they concern words far away from one another in the sentence. This strategy has several advantages. It enables the simulation of long distance dependencies between the annotation variables. It also enables the progressive introduction of several knowledge levels, translated into several sets of feature functions. Such an approach can naturally be adopted when the labels can themselves be decomposed into sub-labels either hierarchically organized or independently learnable. Generally, there is a computational advantage in achieving several (sequential or parallel) learnings, since each one is simpler than the learning of the more complex labels directely. These approaches have been developed for different applicative domains [ZID 10, TEL 10, BUN 08]. In [COH 05b], the set of labels is coded into binary digits and each binary labeler is learned independently. Classical code correcting strategies are then applied. The algorithmic complexity of the inference directly depends on the number of distinct possible labels: reducing this number by considering simpler sub-labels can therefore bring a significant gain in computation time.

Finally, note that linear conditional random fields applied on texts are of course not only useful for information extraction. All problems which can be expressed as a sequence labeling problem can be efficiently processed by a linear conditional random field. Sha and Pereira have, for example, proposed to label the words of a text with "B", "I", and "O" to identify the boundaries of its non-recursive nominal phrases, therefore cheaply producing a shallow parser *shallow parser* [SHA 03]. *Chunks, clause,* or sentence boundaries [LIU 05] can be recognized this way. *Parts of speech* (POS) labeling, or more general morpho-syntactic labeling, is the other important task where conditional random fields immediately excelled [LAF 01]. More recently, the task of bilingual sentence alignment, achieved by annotating each sentence with the word positions of the other one, has also been successfully addressed with linear CRFs. This task is an indispensable preliminary to all statistical-based machine translation systems [BLU 06, ALL 09] (see Chapter 7). Finally, annotation models also allow the labeling of portions of documents according to semantic criteria, for example to identify advertising messages in web pages [SPE 10]. In this case, the items to be labeled are sentences, or even larger portions of texts.

6.6.4. *Beyond linear CRFs*

In the theory of conditional random fields, nothing constrains the graphs to be linear chains. Numerous works have tried to overcome this limitation by considering more complex graphs, allowing to take into account richer domain knowledge. This change is essentially a complexity problem, both for the inference and the training algorithms. Remember that the complexity of the inference is in $n|\mathcal{Y}|^k$, where n is the number of variables (in other words the size of the data), and k is the size of the largest clique in the junction tree.

For named entities recognition, and more generally for domains where the annotation codes an overall processing of the sentence, the model of linear conditional random fields is not always complex enough. For example, in this kind of model it is not possible to avoid global incoherent labelings, such as a label indicating the middle of an entity (I for *Inside*) without its beginning (B for *Begin*) being identified somewhere before on its left. This type of control can only be achieved under a Markovian assumption if it is assumed that the dependencies between the labels are separated at most by a certain *a priori* determined number of items. However, the larger the bound, the larger the graph clique, and therefore the more complex the computation. To avoid intractability, a possible solution is provided by semi-Markovian random fields [SAR 04]. In this model, segments of texts, i.e. sequences of consecutive words, are the labeled items. The words in the same segment receive the same label and the dependence conditions are defined between the segments. In *skip-chain* CRFs the annotations of identical words depend on one another, which produces graphs whose triangulation leads to cliques of sizes greater than 10 or 20. The DCRFs (dynamic conditional random fields) [SUT 04] propose another possible extension to the basic initial model, by making the assumption of a hidden layer of labels, simultaneously learned with the final one.

For labeling more complex data, such as images or semi-structured documents, the domain knowledge also integrates long distance dependencies. In the case of images, the underlying graphs are often 2D or 3D allowing to connect the label of a pixel (or of a set of pixels) to those of its direct neighbors [KUM 03, HE 04]. To extract information from HTML pages or semi-structured documents, it is still possible to treat these data as linear texts [PIN 03]. But the natural underlying structure in this case is a tree whose nodes coincide with the tags, not with the words. If the only dependencies taken into account between the annotation variables coincides with the tree branches, then the size of the maximal cliques in the graph stays bounded by two and each path from the root to a leaf can be seen as a linear graph. The labeling of a tree is therefore not fundamentally more complex than that of a chain [COH 05a]. However, if the labeling of a node is also supposed to depend on the labeling of its previous and next siblings in the tree, then the graph structure becomes more complex: maximal cliques of size 3 appear. Figure 6.7 shows two possible graphs associated with the same tree. Various experiments have shown that a richer structure brings a gain for the labeling of HTML pages or tree banks [JOU 06, GIL 08, MOR 09]. In [GIL 08], it is also proved that all the probabilistic distributions which can be expressed by the *runs* of a probabilistic tree automaton operating on binary trees can be simulated by a conditional random field whose conditional independence graph has the structure of Figure 6.7 (on the right). This result generalizes the one discussed in section 6.6.2.

When the structure of the graph is too complex to enable an exact inference, approximative methods can be employed. In fact, approximative inference algorithms on graphs with cycles exist. In this case, the initial graph is not triangulated, and variational methods [WAI 08] are applied. For example, in the *loopy belief propagation* algorithm, the message passing algorithm is used but with a slight modification: the messages are updated at each iteration by ignoring the cycles. Although it does not generally benefit from any convergence guarantee, the approach works very well in practice.

6.6.5. *Existing libraries*

To finish this state-of-the-art, it remains to enumerate the implementations of CRFs freely available on the web, so that anybody can check their efficiency. The majority of these software libraries are restricted to linear conditional random fields, with the exception of XCRF, conceived for the annotation of XML trees. The formats of

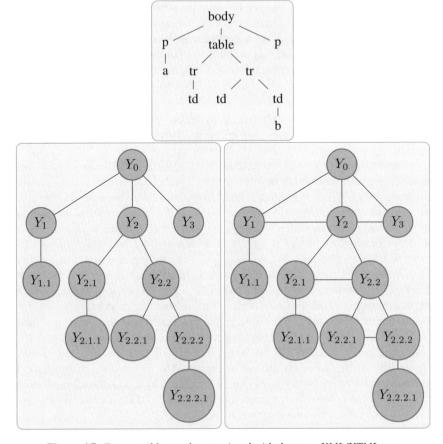

Figure 6.7. *Two possible graphs associated with the same XML/HTML tree*

expected data as well as the way to specify the feature functions strongly depend on the implementation.

Libraries which implement conditional random fields. Here is a list of freely available and most often used implementations, as well as their main properties:

- *general libraries which include conditional random fields among other tools*:
    - MALLET[22], Java library specialized in the statistical processing of texts,
    - MINOR THIRD[23], set of Java classes for manipulating texts;
- *libraries specifically designed for CRFs*:

---

22 http://mallet.cs.umass.edu.

23 http://sourceforge.net/apps/trac/minorthird/wiki.

- CRF library in Java by Sarawagi[24] which also includes an implementation of semi-Markovian CRFS,

- CRF++[25], an efficient C++ implementation of CRFs and POCKET CRF[26], a modified version of the same software,

- Wapiti[27], an optimized version for large CRF performing feature selection during the learning phase: it is the most efficient currently available implementation of linear CRFs [LAV 10],

- CARAFE[28], an OCaml implementation,

- FLEXCRFS[29], another C++ version which also includes a parallelized version known as PCRFS,

- CRFSUITE[30], a C++ implementation,

- CRF tool boxes for Matlab[31];

– *beyond linear CRFs*:

- XCRF[32], an implementation of conditional random fields for XML trees able to manage rich dependencies (Figure 6.7-right).

In addition to these available implementations, some of which already going beyond the strict perimeter of CRFs, one can add FACTORIE[33], the project on which McCallum works, which aims to implement more general statistical inferences on more complex graph structures.

Finally, let us mention some softwares issued from training a CRF on labeled data, therefore adapted to a precise and specialized task for a particular language; by default this language is English but other languages are sometimes available.

Specialized software for an applicative task:

– a chunker[34] and a part of speech (POS)[35] labeler both trained with the Penn Treebank with FLEXCRFS, at the University of Tohoku (Japan);

---

24 http://crf.sourceforge.net.

25 http://crfpp.sourceforge.net.

26 http://sourceforge.net/projects/pocket-crf-1.

27 http://wapiti.limsi.fr.

28 http://sourceforge.net/projects/carafe.

29 http://flexcrfs.sourceforge.net.

30 http://www.chokkan.org/software/crfsuite.

31 http://www.cs.ubc.ca/ murphyk/Software/CRF/crf.html or http://www.computervisiononline. com/software/conditional-random-field-crf-toolbox-matlab

32 http://treecrf.gforge.inria.fr.

33 http://code.google.com/p/factorie.

34 http://crfchunker.sourceforge.net.

35 http://crftagger.sourceforge.net.

– a named entities labeler from Stanford[36], trained thanks to a corpus integrating data from various challenges (CoNLL, MUC-6, MUC-7 and ACE), and available under the GPL license;

– a tool for analyzing the structure of a document and identifing the references and the citations it contains[37], under the LGPL license and also available in an on-line demonstration interface;

– in the domain of bio-informatics, one can cite ABNER[38], a recognizer of biomedical named entities (names of genes, proteins, cell types, etc.) and CONRAD[39], a predictor of genes in a DAN.

– Finally, for French, LIA_NE[40], a named entites labeler trained from the ESTER challenge data (transcriptions of radio broadcasts) is now available, as well as a multiword units segmenter and POS tagger, lgtagger[41], trained form the French Treebank.

6.7. Conclusion

In this chapter, both a generic task (information extraction) and a family of statistical models (conditional random fields) able to process it as efficiently as possible have been presented. The path was long between the definition of the task and the description of its best current solution. It required several stages of diverse natures: reformulation of the task as an annotation problem, definition of random variable fields modeling the domain, choice of a graph structure on these variables and of a probabilistic model for expressing the conditional probability that links them, and most significantly choice of feature functions describing the domain knowledge taken into account. For a common user, this work is the essential required contribution, since efficient software libraries already exist to solve the inference and learning problems (except for exotic graph structures).

Conditional random fields are attractive because they are able to take into account explicit domain knowledge expressed as feature functions, and to integrate them into a gobal model. We have seen that resources manually produced for processing an information extraction task can easily be reinterpreted as feature functions of a CRF. In hidden Markov models, part of this knowledge lies in the structure of the model itself, which in fact aims to *generate* the data it processes. It must also be added that

---

36 http://nlp.stanford.edu/software/CRF-NER.shtml.
37 http://wing.comp.nus.edu.sg/parsCit.
38 http://pages.cs.wisc.edu/ bsettles/abner.
39 http://www.broadinstitute.org/annotation/conrad.
40 http://pageperso.lif.univ-mrs.fr/ frederic.bechet/download.html.
41 http://igm.univ-mlv.fr/ mconstan/research/software.

the model learned by a conditional random field is, at least partly, understandable. The weights θ_k associated with the feature functions in fact characterize their relative importance: a high absolute value weight indicates a discriminative feature, that is a positive or negative piece of information, useful for solving the task. By associating local symbolic knowledge and overall statistical weighting, conditional random fields combine the advantages of both families of models, which have competed against one another for a long time. It also combines readability and robustness.

Conditional random fields have already demonstrated their efficiency on a large number of problems, they now naturally belong to the classical "toolbox" of every computational linguist.

6.8. Bibliography

[ALL 09] ALLAUZEN A., WISNIEWSKI G., "Modèles discriminants pour l'alignement mot-à-mot", *Traitement Automatique des Langues*, vol. 50, no. 3, p. 173-203, 2009, Special issue, Apprentissage automatique pour le TAL.

[ALT 05] ALTUN Y., MCALLESTER D.A., BELKIN M., "Margin semi-supervised learning for structured variables", in *Advances in Neural Information Processing Systems 18 (NIPS)*, 2005.

[BER 96] BERGER A.L., PIETRA S.D., PIETRA V.J.D., "A maximum entropy approach to natural language processing", *Computational Linguistics*, vol. 22, no. 1, p. 39-71, 1996.

[BLU 06] BLUNSOM P., COHN T., "Discriminative word alignment with conditional random fields", in *Proceedings of the 21st International Conference on Computational Linguistics and 44th Annual Meeting of the Association for Computational Linguistics*, Sydney, Australia, p. 65-72, July 2006.

[BUN 08] BUNDSCHUS M., DEJORI M., STETTER M., TRESP V., KRIEGEL H.-P., "Identifying gene and proteins mentions in text using conditional random fields", *BMC Bioinformatics*, vol. 207, no. 9, 2008.

[CAL 03] CALIFF M.E., MOONEY R., "Bottom-up relational learning of pattern matching rules for information extraction", *Journal of Machine Learning Research*, vol. 4, p. 177-210, 2003.

[CAR 07] CARME J., GILLERON R., LEMAY A., NIEHREN J., "Interactive learning of node selecting tree transducers", *Machine Learning*, vol. 66, no. 1, p. 33-67, January 2007.

[CHA 09] CHARNOIS T., PLANTVIT M., RIGOTTI C. CRÉMILLEUX B., "Fouille de séquence pour le TAL", *Traitement Automatique des Langues*, vol. 50, no. 3, p. 59-87, 2009, Special issue, Apprentissage automatique pour le TAL.

[COH 05a] COHN T., BLUNSOM P., "Semantic role labelling with tree conditional random fields", in *CoNLL '05: Proceedings of The Ninth Conference on Natural Language Learning*, 2005.

[COH 05b] COHN T., SMITH A., OSBORNE M., "Scaling conditional random fields using error-correcting codes", in *43rd Annual Meeting of the ACL*, 2005.

[COL 02] COLLINS M., "Discriminative training methods for hidden markov models: theory and experiments with perceptron algorithms", in *Proceedings of the Conference on Empirical Methods in Natural Language Processing (EMNLP)*, p. 1-8, 2002.

[COL 08] COLLINS M., GLOBERSON A., KOO T., CARRERAS X., BARTLETT P., "Exponentiated gradient algorithms for conditional random fields and max-margin Markov networks", *Journal of Machine Learning Research*, vol. 9, p. 1775-1822, August 2008.

[COW 99] COWELL R., DAWID A., LAURITZEN S., SPIEGELHALTER D., *Probabilistic Networks and Expert Systems*, Information Science and Statistics, Springer-Verlag, 1999.

[DIE 04] DIETTERICH T.G., ASHENFELTER A., BULATOV Y., "Training conditional random fields via gradient tree boosting", in *Proceedings of the Twenty-first International Conference (ICML 2004)*, vol. 69 of *ACM International Conference Proceeding Series*, ACM, 2004.

[FIN 04] FINN A., KUSHMERICK N., "Multi-level boundary classification for information extraction", in *Proceedings of the European Conference on Machine Learning*, Pisa, 2004, p. 111-122, 2004.

[FRE 97] FREITAG D., "Machine Learning for information extraction in informal domains using grammaical inference to improve precision in information extraction", in *ICML Workshop on Automata Induction, Grammatical Inference and Language Acquisition*, 1997.

[FRE 00a] FREITAG D., "Machine learning for information extraction in informal domains", *Machine Learning*, vol. 39, no. 2/3, p. 169-202, 2000.

[FRE 00b] FREITAG D., KUSHMERICK N., "Boosted wrapper induction", in *AAAI/IAAI*, p. 577-583, 2000.

[GIL 08] GILLERON R., JOUSSE F., TOMMASI M. TELLIER I., Conditional random fields for XML applications, Research Report no. RR-6738, INRIA, 2008.

[HAM 71] HAMMERSLEY J.M., CLIFFORD P., "Markov fields on finite graphs and lattices", 1971.

[HE 04] HE X., ZEMEL R., CARREIRA-PERPIÑÁN M.Á., "Multiscale conditional random fields for image labelling", in *Proceedings of CVPR 2004*, 2004.

[HOB 97] HOBBS J., APPELT D., BEAR J., ISRAEL D., KAMEYAMA M., STICKEL M., TYSON M., "FASTUS: a cascaded finite-state transducer for extracting information in natural-language text", ROCHE E., SCHABES E. (eds), *Finite State Language Processing*, MIT Press, p. 383-406, 1997.

[JIA 06] JIAO F., WANG S., LEE C.-H., GREINER R., SCHUURMANS D., "Semi-supervised conditional random fields for improved sequence segmentation and labeling", in *Proceedings of the 21st International Conference on Computational Linguistics and 44th Annual Meeting of the Association for Computational Linguistics*, 2006.

[JOU 06] JOUSSE F., GILLERON R., TELLIER I., TOMMASI M., "Conditional random fields for XML trees", in *ECML Workshop on Mining and Learning in Graphs*, 2006.

[KAK 02] KAKADE S., TEH Y.W., ROWEIS S.T., "An alternate objective function for Markovian fields", in *Proceedings of the Nineteenth International Conference (ICML 2002)*, Morgan Kaufmann, p. 275-282, 2002.

[KLI 07] KLINGER R., TOMANEK K., Classical probabilistic models and conditional random fields, Report no. TR07-2-013, Department of Computer Science, Dortmund University of Technology, December 2007.

[KOS 06] KOSALA R., BLOCKEEL H., BRUYNOOGHE M., DEN BUSSCHE J.V., "Information extraction from structured documents using-testable tree automaton inference", *Data & Knowledge Engineering*, vol. 58, no. 2, p. 129-158, 2006.

[KUM 03] KUMAR S., HEBERT M., "Discriminative fields for modeling spatial dependencies in natural images", in *Proceedings of NIPS 03*, 2003.

[LAF 01] LAFFERTY J.D., MCCALLUM A., PEREIRA F.C.N., "Conditional random fields: probabilistic models for segmenting and labeling sequence data", in *Proceedings of the Eighteenth International Conference on Machine Learning (ICML)*, p. 282-289, 2001.

[LAV 04] LAVELLI A., CALIFF M.-E., CIRAVEGNA F., FREITAG D., GIULIANO C., KUSHMERICK N., ROMANO L., "IE evaluation: criticisms and recommendations", in *Proceedings of Workshop Adaptive Text Extraction and Mining, American National Conference on Artificial Intelligence*, 2004.

[LAV 10] LAVERGNE T., CAPPÉ O., YVON F., "Practical very large scale CRFs", in *Proceedings the 48th Annual Meeting of the Association for Computational Linguistics (ACL)*, Association for Computational Linguistics, p. 504-513, July 2010.

[LI 05] LI W., MCCALLUM A., "Semi-supervised sequence modeling with syntactic topic models", in *Proceedings, The Twentieth National Conference on Artificial Intelligence and the Seventeenth Innovative Applications of Artificial Intelligence Conference*, AAAI Press / MIT Press, p. 813-818, 2005.

[LIU 05] LIU Y., STOLCKE A., SHRIBERG E., HARPER M., "Using conditional random fields for sentence boundary detection in speech", in *43rd Annual Meeting of the ACL*, p. 451-458, 2005.

[MAL 02] MALOUF R., "A comparison of algorithms for maximum entropy parameter estimation", in *Proceedings of the Sixth Conference on Natural Language Learning (CoNLL-2002)*, p. 49-55, 2002.

[MAN 99] MANNING C., SCHÜTZE H., *Foundations of Statistical Natural Language Processing*, MIT Press, Cambridge, 1999.

[MAR 07] MARTY P., Induction d'extraction n-aire pour les documents semi-structurés, PhD thesis, Charles de Gaulle University, Lille 3, 2007.

[MCC 03a] MCCALLUM A., LI W., "Early results for named entity recognition with conditional random fields", in *Proceedings of CoNLL 2003*, 2003.

[MCC 03b] MCCALLUM A., "Efficiently inducing features of conditional random fields", in *Proceedings of the 19th Conference in Uncertainty in Artificial Intelligence*, Morgan Kaufmann, p. 403-410, 2003.

[MCC 05] MCCALLUM A., "Information extraction: distilling structured data from unstructured text", *ACM Queue*, vol. 3, no. 9, 2005.

[MCD 05] MCDONALD R., PEREIRA F., "Identifying gene and proteins mentions in text using conditional random fields", *BMC Bioinformatics*, vol. 6, suppl. 1, no. 6, 2005.

[MOR 09] MOREAU E., TELLIER I., BALVET A., LAURENCE G., ROZENKNOP A., POIBEAU T., "Annotation fonctionnelle de corpus arborés avec des champs aléatoires conditionnels", in *Actes de TALN 09*, 2009.

[NIG 99] NIGAM K., LAFFERTY J. MCCALLUM A., "Using maximum entropy for text classification", in *Proceedings of the IJCAI-99 Workshop on Machine Learning for Information Filtering*, 1999.

[PEN 04] PENG F., MCCALLUM A., "Accurate information extraction from research papers using conditional random fields", in *HLT-NAACL*, 2004.

[PIE 97] PIETRA S.D., PIETRA V.D., LAFFERTY J., "Inducing features of random fields", *IEEE Transactions on Pattern Analysis and Machine Intelligence*, vol. 19, no. 4, p. 380-393, 1997.

[PIN 03] PINTO D., MCCALLUM A., LEE X., CROFT W., "Table extraction using conditional random fields", in *SIGIR '03: Proceedings of the 26th ACM SIGIR*, 2003.

[POI 03] POIBEAU T., *Extraction automatique d'information*, Hermès, Paris, 2003.

[RAV 02] RAVICHANDRAN D., HOVY E., "Learning surface text patterns for a question answering system", in *Proceedings of the ACL conference*, 2002.

[ROA 04] ROARK B., SARACLAR M., COLLINS M., JOHNSON M., "Discriminative language modeling with conditional random fields and the perceptron algorithm", in *ACL*, p. 47-54, 2004.

[SAR 04] SARAWAGI S., COHEN W.W., "Semi-Markov conditional random fields for information extraction", in *Proceedings of NIPS*, p. 1185-1192, 2004.

[SAR 08] SARAWAGI S., "Information extraction", *Foundations and Trends in Databases*, vol. 1, no. 3, 2008.

[SHA 90] SHACHTER R.D., D'AMBROSIO B., FAVERO B.D., "Symbolic probabilistic inference in belief networks", in *AAAI*, p. 126-131, 1990.

[SHA 03] SHA F., PEREIRA F., "Shallow parsing with conditional random fields", in *Proceedings of HLT-NAACL*, 2003.

[SIT 04] SITTER A.D., CALDERS T., DAELEMANS W., *A Formal Framework for Evaluation of Information Extraction*, 2004.

[SOK 08] SOKOLOVSKA N., CAPPÉ O., YVON F., "The asymptotics of semi-supervised learning in discriminative probabilistic models", in *Proceedings of the Twenty-Fifth International Conference (ICML 2008)*, vol. 307, ACM, p. 984-991, 2008.

[SOK 09] SOKOLOVSKA N., CAPPÉ O., YVON F., "Sélection de caractéristiques pour les champs aléatoires conditionnels par pénalisation l1", *Traitement Automatique des langues*, vol. 50, no. 3, p. 139-171, 2009, Special issue, Apprentissage automatique pour le TAL.

[SPE 10] SPENGLER A., GALLINARI P., "Document structure meets page layout: loopy random fields for web news content extraction", in *DocEng '10: Proceedings of the 10th ACM Symposium on Document engineering*, ACM, New York, USA, p. 151-160, 2010.

[SUT 04] SUTTON C., ROHANIMANESH K., MCCALLUM A., "Dynamic conditional random fields: factorized probabilistic models for labeling and segmenting sequence data", in *Proceedings of the Twenty-First International Conference on Machine Learning (ICML)*, p. 783-790, 2004.

[SUT 06] SUTTON C., MCCALLUM A., "An introduction to conditional random fields for relational learning", GETOOR L., TASKAR B. (EDS), *Introduction to Statistical Relational Learning,* MIT Press, 2006.

[TAS 04] TASKAR B., Learning structured prediction models: a large margin Approach, PhD thesis, Stanford University, 2004.

[TEL 10] TELLIER I., ESHKOL I., TAALAB S., PROST P., "POS-tagging for oral texts with CRF and category decomposition", *Research in Computing Science*, vol. 46, p. 79-90, 2010.

[TSO 05] TSOCHANTARIDIS I., JOACHIMS T., HOFMANN T., ALTUN Y., "Large margin methods for structured and interdependent output variables", *Journal of Machine Learning Research*, vol. 6, p. 1453-1484, 2005.

[WAI 08] WAINWRIGHT M.J., JORDAN M.I., "Graphical models, exponential families, and variational inference", *Foundations and Trends in Machine Learning*, vol. 1, no. 1-2, p. 1-305, 2008.

[WAL 02] WALLACH H., Efficient training of conditional random fields, Master's thesis, University of Edinburgh, 2002.

[ZHU 03] ZHU X., GHAHRAMANI Z., LAFFERTY J.D., "Semi-supervised learning using Gaussian fields and harmonic functions", in *Proceedings of the Twentieth International Conference (ICML 2003)*, AAAI Press, p. 912-919, 2003.

[ZID 10] ZIDOUNI A., GLOTIN H., QUAFAFOU M., "Semantic annotation of transcribed audio broadcast news using contextual features in graphical discriminative models", in *Proceedings of CICLing 2010*, vol. 6008 of *LNCS*, Springer, p. 279-290, 2010.

PART 3

Multilingualism

Chapter 7

Statistical Methods for Machine Translation

7.1. Introduction

7.1.1. *Machine translation in the age of the Internet*

Machine Translation (MT) is a long established research area, which has, over the years, fostered the development of many technologies now widely accessible both to professional translators and the general public. Research on machine translation can be traced back to the early 1950s and was initially strongly influenced by the American mathematician Warren Weaver. Weaver compared a foreign language with a (secret) code to be deciphered, at a time when computers had already proven useful for breaking such codes. The history of the development of machine translation technology has not been linear and has given rise to many hopes and delusions (see, for instance, the writings of John Hutchins on the history of MT (e.g. [HUT 92, HUT 01, HUT 03]). The slow pace of the progresses of MT systems and the poor quality of automatic translations have often been mocked. Nonetheless, improvements have been steady and genuine and the actual situation of the domain, before the great "statistical shift", can be roughly described as follows.

Several professional MT systems were on the market, delivering automatic translations for multinational industries and multilingual institutions such as the European Union and the Canadian government. These systems, an example of which is the software produced by Systran, relied primarily on manually developed translation rules, integrating fine-grained linguistic resources for specific domains. Another successful case was the METEO system [CHE 78], translating weather forecasts from

Chapter written by Alexandre ALLAUZEN and François YVON.

English into French, often cited as a typical MT system for constrained domains. Research in *rule-based translation* was thus progressing at a steady pace, capitalizing on the developments of automatic analysis and text generation tools.

Technological developments were also targeting professional translators, in the form of integrated translation environments offering Computer Aided Translation (CAT) tools such as *translation memories*, bilingual dictionaries and terminology management tools[1]. Translation memories are particularly helpful for translating repetitive texts and can also help make the translation of terms more consistent. Extending the usability of translation memories was also the subject of much research and development, following the original propositions made in [NAG 04], in the framework of *example-based machine translation* (see e.g. [CAR 03] for recent developments of this research paradigm).

However, very little MT was aimed at the general public, except for restricted application domains, such as mobile translation aids for tourists or travelers.

The accelerated globalization of economic exchanges, population migrations, and the advent of a universal medium, the Internet, have, in less than a decade, greatly changed this picture. On the Internet, much useful information is only available in foreign language(s); many potential "friends", customers, readers, "followers" etc. are only to be met across language barriers. The highly uneven distribution of languages on the Internet is another strong incentive for publishing and communicating in languages other than one's mother tongue, so as to attract a larger audience.

In this context, Machine translation (MT) appears to be a key technology, as it responds to Internet users' growing demand for instant access to information published in foreign languages, or for carrying out electronic exchanges with foreigners (via e-mail, in chatrooms, on social networks, recommendation sites, and on commercial platforms such as eBay). These translations have to be produced on the spot and for free, all the more so as the source texts may themselves be of poor quality: this is, for instance, the case of tweets, SMS, e-mails, comments on forums, or have a short lifespan (news articles, etc). Correctness is then less of an issue and approximations are accepted, for lack of better alternatives: as such, these usages create a new demand, that cannot be served by professional translators.[2] In many situations, such professional services would even be difficult to find: just in Europe, there are no less than 23 official languages which are used to publish and disseminate information, with a potential of 506 language pairs.

---

1 See, for instance, products distributed by Trados www.trados.com.

2 It is estimated that the online translation services offered by software editors (Systran (www.systran.com), Microsoft (www.microsofttranslator.com/)) or by the main search engines (Google (translate.google.com/), Yahoo (fr.babelfish.yahoo.com/)), have to process millions of translation queries everyday.

To satisfy this demand, machine translation systems have made dramatic progress, particularly due to the maturing of a new generation of translation methods. These methods are based on statistical learning techniques and exploit large corpora of parallel bilingual texts (up to tens of millions of sentences) and achieve an average quality sufficient for many uses [LOP 08a, KOE 10]. The success of MT is epitomized by the popularity of online translation Web sites, bringing translation to all Web users and handling daily amounts of translation requests that are incomparably larger than what professional translators could handle. MT has thus turned into a virtuous circle in which the needs of a growing base of users, who are more aware of the qualities and shortcomings of automatic translations, stimulates the efforts to improve technology and develop new features. This is evidenced by the proliferation of applications of these technologies: multilingual/crosslingual navigation, translation embedded in mobile devices, speech translation, computer assisted translation, new language learning environments, etc.

It is lucky, but not entirely fortuitous, that the exponential increase in the number of online digital documents which resulted from the expansion of the Internet has provided part of the solution to this problem. The development of electronic corpora, advances in statistical language processing techniques [MAN 99], including machine translation, have enabled the advent of a new family of machine translation technologies, based on the statistical analysis of large corpora of electronic documents. The pioneering work of the IBM group [BRO 90], in the early 1990s, provided strong foundations for a new way to do machine translation, which, after a rapid maturation, has been found to be the most adapted and most efficient answer to these new demands. First, the use of statistical methods guarantees a certain robustness against ill-formed inputs which abound in numerous sub-genres of electronic documents. Second, the use of probabilistic modeling tools provides MT developers with a sound mathematical framework for dealing with the ambiguities that often make translations difficult. Finally, resorting to statistical tools[3] is the most efficient means to take advantage, in the context of MT, of these immense corpora available on the Internet.

In summary, machine translation techniques, especially statistical machine translation techniques, give instant access to any document, written in (almost) any language[4]. As such, they contribute in transforming our abilities to access and to process information in a multilingual environment like the Internet. It was therefore quite natural to devote, in a book dedicated to probabilistic methods for information access, a large part to these methods.

---

3 It is fair to say that other approaches to machine translation are still being explored and developed, often successfully: expert rule-based MT or example-based MT remain useful in many application areas, and can be viewed as complementary to the entirely statistical approaches presented in this chapter.

4 If one restricts it to languages that are massively represented on the Internet.

7.1.2. *Organization of the chapter*

Section 7.2 is a simplified presentation of the first generation of statistical machine translation models:*word-based models*. This presentation aims to introduce the main components of statistical machine translation systems in a simplified framework, and to help figure out the motivations which have led to the elaboration of state-of-the-art models, *phrase-based models*. We also take the opportunity to introduce a certain number of notations and concepts that will be used throughout the rest of the chapter.

The "internals" of these systems will be detailed in the following sections, by first addressing questions related to the design and estimation of *translation models* in section 7.3: conceptually, these models are similar to large bilingual dictionaries recording correspondences between groups of source and target words. We first introduce *word alignment models* (sections 7.3.1 and 7.3.2), which are usually a starting point for building and estimating *phrase translation models*. (section 7.3.3).

Reordering models are the subject of section 7.4, where we discuss issues of word order differences between the source and target languages. The main principles underlying these models will first be demonstrated, before addressing problems related to their estimation.

Equipped with a better comprehension of those statistical models, we then explain how these models are used to compute translations of new source sentences. This problem and some possible solutions are presented in section 7.5. Finally, in section 7.6, we discuss issues related to the evaluation of statistical translation systems. This question does not have a single answer, and depending on the use of these evaluations, several scenarios can be entertained. As we will see, making these evaluations less subjective and less costly, through the use of quantitative metrics, is an important concern for scientists and system developers willing to evaluate incremental improvements.

Two brief sections close the chapter. In the first (section 7.7), we review some of the limitations of the standard model and briefly address several recent extensions and prospects; the second (section 7.8) gives a series of pointers to resources (software and data) available on the Internet. We encourage readers to download these resources, to build their own translation systems and experiment with them.

Note finally there are several good reviews and textbooks on statistical machine translation that the reader may wish to refer to: [LOP 08a] is a very nice overview of the domain, while the recent textbook by Ph. Koehn [KOE 10] is an exhaustive reference regarding SMT in general, and phrase-based systems in particular. [TIE 11] focuses more on alignment, notably on sentence alignments, which are out of the scope of this chapter; yet, it also provides a very complete overview of word and phrase alignment techniques.

7.1.3. *Terminological remarks*

The recent literature on machine translation, and particularly on statistical machine translation, is sometimes obscured by the improper use of terms whose meaning seemed to be firmly established either in computer science or in linguistics. It is therefore probably useful to give some indication of the choices made in this chapter. The *source language* (*target language* respectively) is used to refer to the language to be translated from (respectively into). An (historical) reason for the possible ambiguity of these terms is related to the use of the *noisy channel model* (see section 7.2.1): in this approach, translating from language *A* to language *B* requires a translation model mapping *B* into *A*.

A more difficult problem is posed by the term *phrase*, often used to refer to the family of phrase-based models studied in this chapter. To insist on the non-linguistic character of the basic translation units used in these models, we use the term of "segment" to refer to a monolingual translation unit and "bisegment" to denote a matched pair of "segments" made of a source and a target unit. This is also the choice made in the recent survey [TIE 11]. We will nonetheless continue to use the term "phrase-based" models to refer to these models.

The term *alignment* is also problematic: in computer science, notably in pattern recognition, this term denotes a relationship between two sequences of symbols which preserves the relative order of each sequence. As will be seen in Section 7.3.1, in machine translation, this term has a more general sense of a relationship between the source and target sequences, irrespective of possible reorderings within these sequences. We have decided to adhere to this broader sense, which does not seem too confusing in practice, and is well accepted within the community.

7.2. Probabilistic machine translation: an overview

In this section, we present a brief overview of probabilistic machine translation, focusing on the *word-based models*, considered as the state of the art till the early 2000s. In doing so, our main objective is not to give a technical understanding of these complex models (see section 7.3.1) but rather to outline their main modeling hypotheses. After presenting the underlying principles of the standard model in section 7.2.1, we discuss in section 7.2.2 a certain number of linguistic issues that these models have to address and which have ultimately caused their replacement by "phrase-based models". These models will be introduced in section 7.2.3.

Before starting, let us underline that all the translation models presented in this chapter are very limited in their behavior. In particular, they can only translate individual sentences considered in isolation; and most often will produce one single output sentence for each input sentence. They are therefore totally blind to discourse level issues, and even less capable of reproducing in the target language subtle nuances related to style or register, which often constitute the most difficult aspects of human translation. Modeling discourse phenomena is the subject of active research (some of which will be discussed in section 7.7); yet, for the remainder of the presentation, these aspects will be entirely ignored.

7.2.1. *Statistical machine translation: the standard model*

Let us first introduce some notations used throughout the chapter. A sentence in the source language is written as f and contains J words $f_1 \ldots f_J$; a sentence in the target language is written as $e = e_1 \ldots e_I$[5]. Viewed as a probabilistic decision problem, translation consists in solving the following problem:

$$e^* = \underset{e}{\operatorname{argmax}} P(e|f) \qquad\qquad [7.1]$$

This simple formulation hides two very difficult challenges: a *modeling* challenge, consisting of defining, for each possible source sentence, a conditional distribution over the set of all possible target sentences; a *search* challenge, consisting of finding the most likely output among the set of target sentences. Historically, these problems have been addressed by reformulating [7.1] through the application of Bayes' rule in the following way:

$$e^* = \underset{e}{\operatorname{argmax}} P(e, f) = \underset{e}{\operatorname{argmax}} P(e) P(f|e) \qquad\qquad [7.2]$$

This model is known in the literature as the *noisy channel model*, as it decomposes the generation of a pair (e, f) into two stages: first the choice of a sentence e, according to a prior probability $P(e)$; then its transmission along a noisy channel whose distortions are modeled by $P(f|e)$, finally yielding f. The rationale given by [BRO 93b] for "inverting" equation [7.1] is as follows. The sentence f to be translated is assumed to be grammatically well-formed and the generation of a well-formed translation e is also desired. The probabilistic model involved in [7.1] must be such that for any source sentence f, it concentrates its probability mass on those target sentences that are both well-formed and plausible translations of f. By considering $P(f|e) P(e)$ instead of $P(e|f)$, a difficult problem is broken down into two simpler ones. On the one hand, the development of a *translation model* ensuring that $P(f|e)$ is high, for any target sentence paired with f, be it grammatical or not. This model is estimated on *parallel bilingual corpora*, associating source sentences with their translations[6]. On the other hand, the development of a probabilistic language model for target sentences will

---

5 These notations are historical: in [BRO 90], translation is from French (f) to English (e). Since then, this notation has denoted any foreign language.

6 Section 7.8 gives information regarding the availability of such resources.

give the term P(**e**). This language model must concentrate its probability mass on grammatical sentences and can therefore be estimated on monolingual corpora. Under these hypotheses, an overview of the development of a statistical translation system is represented in Figure 7.1.

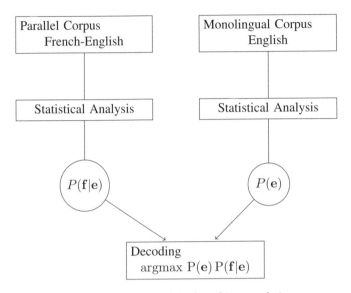

Figure 7.1. *Overview of a statistical machine translation system*

The decomposition of the joint probability in equation [7.2] separates the modeling problem into two sub-problems that can be addressed independently. In particular, there exists a rich literature on probabilistic language models, which are used in many applications of Natural Language Processing (see e.g. [MAN 99] or [JEL 97]) and Information Retrieval (see Chapter 1 of this book). Even if this problem is far from being solved in a satisfactory manner, proven techniques and tools are widely available, and can be readily plugged into statistical machine translation systems. Furthermore, as these models are built independently from the translation task, they can be estimated on the very large *monolingual corpora* that are nowadays available. In this chapter, it is assumed that these models decompose the probability of a target sentence $\mathbf{e} = e_1 \ldots e_I$ using a first order Markov assumption[7] as follows:

$$P(\mathbf{e}) = P(e_1) \prod_{i=2}^{I} P(e_i | e_{i-1}) \tag{7.3}$$

---

7 In practice, it is common to use higher order dependencies.

More details regarding the estimation of language models are given in the Appendix, notably in section A.4. We now turn to a first discussion of translation models and study the difficulties posed by the term $P(f|\mathbf{e})$, in the context of word-based translation models.

7.2.2. *Word-based models and their limitations*

An initial simplistic approach for modeling the translation process assumes that it can be performed on a word per word basis. The conditional model $P(f|\mathbf{e})$ is thus written as:

$$P(f|\mathbf{e}) = \prod_{i=1}^{I} P(f_i|e_i) \qquad\qquad [7.4]$$

7.2.2.1. *Lexical ambiguities*

A first well-known problem in translation is the non-determinism of bilingual word associations, where a source word can map onto more than one possible target words. This situation can be caused by homography or polysemy on the source side, and by synonymy on the target side. The first situation is illustrated by the French word "avocat", which can translate into *lawyer* or *avocado* in English; or by "mousse" in French, which can denote a *young sailor* or *foam*. The second situation is again illustrated by "mousse", which, in a botanical context, translates into *moss*, while its metaphorical sense translates into *foam*. This problem is well documented in the literature and does not need more explanation here. It is however noteworthy to examine how the choice of one or the other translation is performed in the framework of equation [7.4]. Let us assume that *lawyer* or *avocado* are the two possible translations of "avocat", and that both translations are equally likely, meaning that the two terms $P(\text{avocat}|lawyer)$ and $P(\text{avocat}|avocado)$ are comparable. The decision to select one or the other will therefore be performed based on their compatibility with the surrounding target words, as measured by the target language model. This may seem somewhat paradoxical, since the choice of the right translation only indirectly takes the source context into account, a point which is considered again in section 7.7.1.

We note that cases of non-deterministic translations exist even in the absence of ambiguity in the source language: *river* can be translated into French as "fleuve" or "rivière", depending on whether it flows into the sea or into another river; this distinction is not present in English, making the translation of the word *river* ambiguous. When inflected forms (e.g. conjugated verbs) are the translation units, this non-determinism is often amplified. This can be because of accidental homographs such as the French "souris", which corresponds to several forms of the verb sourire (*to smile*) (in the present and past tense) and also to the singular and plural form of the noun

f	cet avocat est mon défenseur
e$_1$ P(f|e$_1$)	*this lawyer is my defender* P(cet|*this*) × P(avocat|*lawyer*) × P(est|*is*) × P(mon|*my*) × P(défenseur|*defender*)
e$_2$ P(f|e$_2$)	*this avocado is my defender* P(cet|*this*) × P(avocat|*avocado*) × P(est|*is*) × P(mon|*my*) × P(défenseur|*defender*)

When the conditional probabilities of f given **e**$_1$ or **e**$_2$ are in the same ballpark, the choice of one or the other hypothesis only depends on the relative values of P(**e**$_1$) and P(**e**$_2$).

Table 7.1. *A difficult lexical choice*

(*mouse/mice*), which can denote both the animal and the computer device[8]. A more substantial cause of ambiguity stems from the fact that the source and target languages do not always mark the same distinctions. Some languages, for example, distinguish three genders for nouns (masculine, neutral, feminine), where others only distinguish two; the situation is similar (more complex, however) for verbs: where English only has at most five different forms for each verb, other languages have dozens (French and more generally the romance languages) or even thousands (e.g. Georgian). The fewer distinctions the source language has, the greater the importance of the target language model will be for selecting the right translation.

The model defined by equation [7.4] breaks down the probability of the association between f and **e** as into product of word associations, therefore implicitly relying on the assumption of *compositionality* of the translations[9]. This hypothesis is also very naive and it is well known that the sense (and therefore often the translation) of numerous word groups cannot be directly deduced from the sense of their components. There exists a variety of situations ranging from the completely frozen idiomatic expressions, such as "casser sa pipe" in French (English *kick the bucket*), to technical terms whose sense is no longer entirely compositional. The previous model however computes the probabiliy of the correct translation as P(*kick*\|casser) × P(*the*\|sa) × P(*bucket*\|pipe) which is much smaller than the probability of a literal transition such as *break his pipe* would be. This is because the probability of the literal transition only involves very likely factors such as P(*break*\|casser) and P(*pipe*\|pipe).

7.2.2.2. A word for a word

A second major issue with the model defined in equation [7.4] is that it assumes that a source sentence and its translation have the same number of words and only

8 Note that this ambiguity is preserved in English.

9 In the model, random variables corresponding to the translation of each word are independent.

gives a non-zero probability to such pairs of sentences. This hypothesis is of course highly simplistic. A first big problem is that the notion of 'word' differs, sometimes considerably, from one language to another. For instance, while some languages express complex meanings through syntactic combinations of isolated units (this is typically the case for French and English), others (in particular *agglutinative* languages such as Finnish, Hungarian or most Turkish languages) resort to combinations of smaller meaningful units taking the form of prefixes or suffixes. Such complex forms are illustrated by the example in Figure 7.2.

Form	Decomposition	Gloss
görüntülenebilir	görüntüle+n+ebil+ir	visualize + passive + to be able to + be *this can be visualized*
sakarlıklarından	sakar+lık+ları+ndan	clumsy + ness + their + due to *due to their clumsiness*

Figure 7.2. *Complex forms in Turkish*

Similar processes are also at play, for instance in German, where it is possible to build compound words by concatenating simpler units[10]: for instance, from *Flashe* (*bottle*), *Wasser* (water), *Mineral* (mineral), is formed *die Wasserflasche* (*bottle of water*), *die Mineralwasserflasche* (*bottle of mineral water*).

Even in the case where the target and source languages are close, as is the case for French and English, the situations in which a French word translates into several English words, or the opposite, are numerous. Compounding processes in these two languages lead to many situations where an English word corresponds to several French words: *laptop*-"ordinateur portable", *widescreen*-"grand écran", and so on. Translations between verb groups provide many examples of the opposite situation. In particular, while English uses particles to mark nuances of a verb sense, French will typically use different words. This is illustrated by cases such as: *switch on/off* for "allumer/éteindre"; *break out/up/down* for "s'évader", "s'achever", "briser", respectively and so on. While French uses a particular conjugation to express the conditional mood, English uses modal verbs, giving rise to pairings such as *(I) would come*-"je viendrais" and so on. It should be noted that, to make matters worse, the English words translating one single French word are not necessarily adjacent: this is, for example, the case with particles such as *She said she would never take her husband back again*, where the two parts of the verb group *take ... back* are separated here by the direct object of the verb.

An obvious conclusion is that translation cannot be faithfully modeled on a one word for one word basis, and that word-based translation models should be extended

---

10 The reality is slightly more complex since letters can be inserted at the junction of words.

to account for these phenomena. A possible extension is to design a model in which associations between segments of variable size occur as the result of a two-step process: for each target word e_i, the number of corresponding source words n_i is first chosen; each of these n_i copies of e_i is then translated, resulting in n_i source words. This generation process is reflected by the following decomposition of the conditional distribution:

$$P(f|e) = \prod_{i=1}^{I} P(n_i|e_i) \prod_{j=1}^{n_i} P(f_j|e_i) \qquad [7.5]$$

This model is a simplified version of the word-based translation models developed by IBM in the 1990s [BRO 90, BRO 93b][11]. By allowing target words to have no counterpart in the source sentence (which amounts to having $n_i = 0$) and by adding a fictitious "empty" word in e, other common situations are also taken into account. This is for instance the case of the deletion of the French indefinite article "des", which usually has no English counterpart or, conversely, the insertion of the English auxiliary *do* which has no French equivalent.

7.2.2.3. *Word order issues*

The third problem, and without doubt the most serious one, with the models sketched in previous sections, is the underlying assumption that the order of words is the same in the source and target sentences. This hypothesis is again linguistically naive, except for pairs of very close languages. The most common situation, by far, is the situation where word order differs in the target and source languages. Word order differences can be local to clauses or syntactic phrases; they can also span over larger chunks and encompass major syntactic changes at the sentence level.

On a macroscopic level, linguistic typology classifies languages into groups depending on the relative order of the subject (S), the object complement (O) and the main verb (V): languages like English, French and other romance languages are classified as SVO, since the canonical order in the sentence is subject-verb object; Japanese and Turkish are mainly SOV, classical Arabic is VSO, and so on. In addition, there are languages in which the order of constituents is not as strictly regulated and which are mainly order free (e.g. Latin). In these languages, syntactic roles of phrases are identified through a system of *case markers*, and do not rely so much on the relative word order. Modeling the translation between languages belonging to different families requires us to make provision for the syntactic reorderings that take place when going from one language to the other. As these reorderings apply to whole syntactic constituents, they can yield very important movements at the word level, oftern refered to as *long distance reorderings* in the literature.

---

11 These models, which are widely used today to train translation models, are presented in detail in section 7.3.

Syntactic divergences between languages also exist at a smaller level, that of the internal structure of syntactic phrases: for instance, French and English differ by the relative position of adjectives (and also to some extent adverbs) in relation to their head noun (respectively to the head verb). These phenomena are referred to as *local reordering*.

Modeling these divergences between languages in a probabilistic word-based model is quite challenging. The "historical" propositions made in [BRO 90], which have never been fundamentally improved, are based on a simplistic model that adds a third generation stage to the model described by equation [7.5]. This third step deals with the generation of the relative position of source words, making sure that close words in the target sentence preferably correspond to words that are also close in the source language.

7.2.3. Phrase-based models

To remedy to some deficiencies of word translation models, *phrased-based* models, initially described in [ZEN 02, KOE 03b, OCH 04], have progressively emerged as the most effective alternative. Contrary to word-based models, the translation units considered in these models are segments of variable length, and source sentences are translated segment by segment. This approach improves over the word-based approach in many ways:

– increasing the length of translation units has the effect of making many lexical ambiguities disappear. Let us consider the previous example of English to French translation, where we emphasized that in a word-based model, a verb form such as *think* can be projected onto almost all the forms of the French verb "penser" in the present tense. By contrast, the segment *we think* has only one possible translation. The same applies to adjectives, which are invariable in English, but must agree in genre and in number with the head noun in French: if *small* is ambiguous and can be translated by "petit", "petite" and so on in French, *small car* is no longer a problem and "petite voiture" is the only translation;

– matching multi-word units is a very simple way to account for cases where the number of words is not the same in the target and the source languages. It also becomes much easier to account for non-compositional translations of technical terms or idioms;

– finally, using variable-length units allows for an implicit modeling of local reordering. For instance, associating the English *natural language processing* with French "traitement des langues naturelles" dispenses to model reordering that takes place within the noun phrase.

From the point of view of implementing statistical systems, two important and difficult problems remain. The first concerns the modeling of associations between bisegments (these pairings define the *translation model*) and the estimation of these models from data. The second problem concerns the modeling of segment reordering in translation; the design and estimation of these reordering models are discussed in section 7.4. It will then be time to address a problem which has deliberately been left aside, that is the integration of these models with the target language model and the search for the solution of combinatorial problems such as [7.2].

7.3. Phrase-based models

In a statistical machine translation system, the *translation model* is the main knowledge source encoding relationships between words or group of words in the source and target languages. Its main role is to generate a set of translation hypotheses for any source sentence, and to associate a plausibility score with them. As explained above, the selection of the best translation within this set also involves a monolingual language model, whose role is to give preference to grammatically "correct" sentences.

The definition of a translation model depends on the choice of translation units: for each unit in the source language, this model supplies possible translations in the target language with associated scores. While the first statistical machine translation systems translated their input on a per word[12] basis, the units used in today's state-of-the-art systems are *segments*, that is variable-length sequences of words. The association between a source segment and a possible translation in the target language defines a *bisegment*. It is possible that a segment admits several alternative translations, resulting in several bisegments sharing the same source segment. A phrase-based translation model encodes this information about bisegments and their associated scores. In this section, we describe how such models can be automatically trained from parallel bilingual corpora.

Figure 7.3 presents an overview of the training of a translation model from a parallel bilingual corpus, as described in [ZEN 02, KOE 03b]. The example chosen is the French/English language pair. In this figure, only one pair of sentences has been represented; in practice, parallel corpora contain between tens of thousands and several million pairs of sentences (see Section 7.8).

Starting with a bilingual corpus, the objective is to extract and evaluate a set of bisegments. This task is not trivial and the construction of sub-sentential alignments from parallel sentences requires knowledge of the translation units which make up these sentences. Unfortunately, this knowledge is not available, since the training step aims at identifying those units. Part of the difficulty stems from the fact that the objective is in fact twofold: to spot the relevant translation units in source and target (*segmentation*) and to relate segments which are mutual translations (*alignment*).

---

12 The notion of the word must be understood as a mere string of characters.

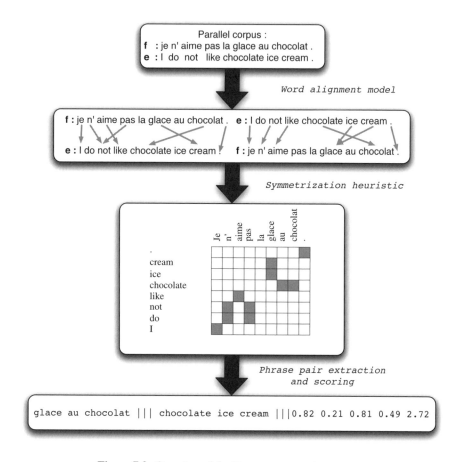

Figure 7.3. *Overview of the bisegment extraction process*

In order to simplify the problem, the usual approach is to start with a fixed and well defined segmentation into single words. The first step of the process then consists of building word-based associations for each sentence pair, using word alignment models. This alignment step, presented in section 7.3.1, relies on a series of heuristics and simplifying assumptions which restrict the alignments so that their computation is possible.

Once word alignments have been computed, it becomes possible to reconsider the segmentation into translation units (bisegments) and their evaluation. These issues are addressed in section 7.3.3. In the standard approach, building a translation model is thus a two-step process, in which the extraction and evaluation of bisegments is heuristically derived from word alignments. This approach is considered the most efficient empirically, and is widely used. Multiple variations have been proposed, aiming at simplifying a process that remains very heuristic and computationally very demanding (see e.g. [MAR 02, VEN 03, ZHA 03, VOG 05]).

7.3.1. *Building word alignments*

A parallel corpus is a made of sentence pairs which are mutual translations: the source sentence f is a sequence of J words $f = f_1, \ldots, f_j, \ldots, f_J$ and the target sentence $\mathbf{e}$ is a sequence of I words $\mathbf{e} = e_1, \ldots, e_i, \ldots e_I$. Word alignments between f and $\mathbf{e}$ relate words which are mutual translations. A first possible representation of an alignment between two sentences is a binary matrix $A = (a_{i,j})$, where each cell $a_{i,j}$ indicates whether word f_j is aligned with the word e_i, as in the example in Figure 7.4.

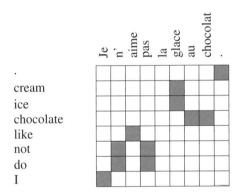

Figure 7.4. *Example of an alignment matrix between an English sentence and a French sentence. The non-zero cells in the matrix are represented by shaded squares. The set of links associated with this matrix is {(1,1), (2, 2), (2, 3), (3, 4), (4,2), (4,3), (6, 6), (6, 7), (7, 5), (8, 5), (9, 8)}*

Under the matrix representation of word alignments, there are $2^{I \times J}$ possible alignments, as many as the number of possible values for A. Rather than directly modeling these matrices, which yields untractable combinatorial problems, simpler representations are usually considered. An effective way to restrict the number of alignments is to only consider *applications* from $[0: I]$ into $[0: J]$, of which there are only I^J. Under this simplifying assumption, each word of one of the sentences is labeled with the position index of the corresponding word in the other sentence. The model is no longer symmetric.

Building such an alignment then amounts to finding the label sequence[13] $\mathbf{a} = a_1, \ldots, a_j, \ldots a_J$ associated with f, where, for a given sentence pair, each label a_j belongs to the set of positions in the target sentence: $a_j \in \mathcal{A} = 0, 1, \ldots, I$. a_j represents the index in $\mathbf{e}$ with which f_j is aligned: the word f_j is therefore aligned with the word e_{a_j}. When a word cannot be aligned, we use the conventional label $a_j = 0$. Licensing null alignments thus introduces an additional empty word $e_0 = \text{null}$ in the target sequence, which is then composed of $I + 1$ words.

Word alignment models were introduced in [BRO 90]. In this pioneering work, the word alignments represent hidden variables of the word-based translation process. In the following presentation of word alignments, aspects related to translation are deliberately left aside[14]. The insightful presentation of the most common alignment models given in [OCH 03b] will be our main source of inspiration. This presentation covers the IBM models of [BRO 90] as well as the hidden Markov model (*HMM*) proposed in [VOG 96] and several additional heuristic models.

Modeling alignment as a sequence labeling problem can be presented by decomposing the joint probability of a sequence of observations (the source sequence f) and of the associated label sequences $\mathbf{a}$ (alignments). This probability is conditioned here by the target phrase $\mathbf{e}$ which is assumed to be known and, which restricts the realisation space of the alignments. Equation [7.6] will be our starting point:

$$P(\mathbf{a}, f | \mathbf{e}) = P(\mathbf{a} | \mathbf{e}) \, P(f | \mathbf{a}, \mathbf{e}) \qquad [7.6]$$

This equation introduces two terms on the right hand side, corresponding respectively to the conditional probability of the label sequence, $P(\mathbf{a} | \mathbf{e})$, and that of the observation sequence given the labels $P(f | \mathbf{a}, \mathbf{e})$. The latter term is usually denoted as the *translation probability*, and the former the *distortion probability*.

Starting from [7.6], the authors of [BRO 90] study four generative models of increasing complexity denoted by the acronyms IBM1–IBM4. Each of these models corresponds to a set of simplifying hypotheses which make the model tractable.

7.3.1.1. *IBM model 1*

IBM model 1 is based on the following assumptions:

---

13 Under this restricted view, computing an alignment is a sequence labeling problem, which can be solved using the tools that are presented in Chapter 6.

14 The presentation of these models in a word-based translation framework would involve numerous details which are omitted here. It is, nowadays, accepted that word-based systems underperform the phrase-based systems, and are no longer used.

– each alignment link a_j is independent from the other alignments and is uniformly distributed, implying that:

$$P(\mathbf{a}|\mathbf{e}) = \prod_{j=1}^{J} P(a_j|\mathbf{e}) = \prod_{j=1}^{J} \frac{1}{I+1} = \frac{1}{(I+1)^J}$$

– given a_j, each source word f only depends on the target word e_{a_j} it aligns with:

$$P(f|\mathbf{a}, \mathbf{e}) = \prod_{j=1}^{J} P(f_j|\mathbf{a}, \mathbf{e}) = \prod_{j=1}^{J} P(f_j|e_{a_j})$$

Under these conditional independence assumptions, equation [7.6] can be simplified as follows:

$$P(\mathbf{a}, f|\mathbf{e}) = \prod_{j=1}^{J} P(a_j, f_j|e_{a_j}) = \frac{1}{(I+1)^J} \prod_{j=1}^{J} P(f_j|e_{a_j}) \qquad [7.7]$$

This model is only parameterized by the set of conditional distributions modeling the translation equivalents of each target word e; this model is therefore often described as a *lexical translation model*. The parameter vector $\boldsymbol{\theta}$ of the IBM1 model is therefore written as $\boldsymbol{\theta} = \{P(f|e), \forall(f, e) \in \mathcal{V}_f \times \mathcal{V}_e\}$. In practice, the vocabulary $\mathcal{V}_f$ (respectively $\mathcal{V}_e$) only contains the words that are seen in the source (respectively target) side of the parallel corpus.

Given the parameter $\boldsymbol{\theta}$, it is easy to infer the most probable alignment for any pair of sentences by applying the maximum *a posteriori* rule:

$$\mathbf{a}^* = \underset{\mathbf{a}}{\operatorname{argmax}} P(\mathbf{a}|f, \mathbf{e}) = \underset{\mathbf{a}}{\operatorname{argmax}} P(\mathbf{a}, f|\mathbf{e}) \qquad [7.8]$$

The search for the best alignment $\mathbf{a}^*$ is particularly efficient as the evaluation of each alignment link a_j is independent of the other alignments. The most probable sequence $\mathbf{a}^*$ is thus the one that maximizes the joint probability $P(\mathbf{a}, f|\mathbf{e})$. From equation [7.7], this joint probability is a product of terms in the internal [0: 1]. This product is maximum when each term is itself a maximum:

$$\forall j, a_j^* = \underset{a_j \in \mathcal{A}}{\operatorname{argmax}} P(f_j|e_{a_j}) \qquad [7.9]$$

Estimation can be straightforwardly performed in a supervised fashion, i.e. given a set of parallel sentences and their word alignments. Unfortunately, this type of data is rarely available in sufficient quantity. It is however possible to train the model in a unsupervised way from a sentence aligned bilingual corpus. In this setting, alignments correspond to hidden variables and parameter estimation has to resort to numerical procedures such as the *Expectation-Maximization* (EM) algorithm [DEM 77][15], so as to maximize the *log-likelihood* of the parameters on the learning corpus. The specific assumptions of the IBM1 model, in which each word is aligned independently from its context, make this optimization problem tractable. In addition, the authors of [BRO 93b] show that the *log-likelihood* is concave[16], which guarantees the convergence of the algorithm toward an overall optimum. Implementing the EM algorithm for the IBM model 1 proceeds as follows:

– *Initialization:* randomly or uniformly set initial values for $\boldsymbol{\theta}$;

– *Until convergence or for a predefined number of iterations*:

- *E-step:* knowing $\boldsymbol{\theta}$, the model is used to compute the posterior distribution of each alignment link:

$$P(a_j | f_j, \mathbf{e}) = \frac{P(a_j, f_j | \mathbf{e})}{P(f_j | \mathbf{e})} = \frac{P(f_j | e_{a_j})}{\sum_{j'=0}^{J} P(f_{j'} | e_{a_{j'}})} \qquad [7.10]$$

Knowing the posterior probabilities, the expectation of the number of occurrences of an alignment between f and e in the parallel corpus is computed by summing the posteriors over all sentence pairs $(\mathbf{f}, \mathbf{e})$:

$$F(f | e) = \sum_{(\mathbf{f}, \mathbf{e})} \left[P(a | f, \mathbf{e}) \left(\sum_{j=1}^{J} \delta(f, f_j) \right) \left(\sum_{i=0}^{I} \delta(e, e_i) \right) \right] \qquad [7.11]$$

In Equation [7.11], a denotes the alignment link between f and e, and $\delta(,)$ is the Kronecker function whose values is 1 if both arguments are equal, and 0 otherwise.

- *M-step:* Once these expectations have been computed, the parameters $\boldsymbol{\theta}$ are estimated as follows:

$$P(f | e) = \frac{F(f | e)}{\sum_{f' \in V_f} F(f' | e)} \qquad [7.12]$$

The IBM model 1 is a very simple alignment model, which only uses the cooccurence information between source and target words in parallel sentences to estimate the translation model according to equation [7.11]. Although rudimentary, this model obtains good results when very large amounts of data are available [BRA 07].

---

15 See Appendix A, in particular section A.3, for a detailed presentation of the EM algorithm applied to a simpler model.

16 But not strictly concave, which implies that the optimum is not necessarily unique [TOU 11].

7.3.1.2. *Computing alignments with hidden Markov models*

One obvious weakness of the IBM1 model is the hypothesis that all the alignment links a_j are equally likely: this is false especially for related languages, where the word order is globally (if not locally) preserved. For example with the French/English language pair, a source word at the beginning of a sentence is rarely aligned with a target word at the end of the sentence. To take this information into account, the IBM model 2 [BRO 90] introduces a dependency between the value of a_j and the absolute position j in the sentence, expressed by the term $P(a_j|j, J, I)$. This dependency is used to favor certain alignments over others.

This model misses another important point, though: the tendency of alignment to respect some kind of *monotonicity*. This means that if the source word a position $j - 1$ is aligned with the target word a_{j-1}, it is then highly likely that the source word at position j will be aligned with the target word $a_j = a_{j-1} + 1$, or at least, with a word nearby. In other words, it seems relevant to model the "jump" between two consecutive alignments based on the difference $| a_j - a_{j-1} |$. As an illustration, take the case of a sequence composed of a determiner followed by a noun: in such a situation, the alignment a_j of the noun is influenced by the alignment a_{j-1} of its preceding determiner. The monotonic character of alignments is better modeled with a first order hidden Markov model[17] (HMM), which introduces a dependence between the alignment links of two consecutive words a_{j-1} and a_j [VOG 96]. HMMs have thus superseded IBM model 2, which is hardly used today. The main assumptions of the model are modified as follows (to be compared to IBM1):

– each "label" a_j depends on the value of the previous label a_{j-1}. The probability of a label sequence is therefore written as[18]:

$$P(\mathbf{a}|\mathbf{e}) = \prod_{j=1}^{J} P(a_j|a_{j-1}, \mathbf{e})$$

– each word f_j in f only depends on a_j, or rather, on the target word in position a_j.

Under the hypothesis of first order Markovian dependencies, the joint probability of the source sequence and the associated label sequence is simplified as follows:

$$P(\mathbf{a}, f|\mathbf{e}) = \prod_{j=1}^{J} P(a_j|a_{j-1}, \mathbf{e})\, P(f_j|e_{a_j}) \qquad [7.13]$$

where, as for the IBM1 model, $P(f_j|e_{a_j})$ denotes the probability of translating word e_{a_j} by f_j. In order to parameterize the transition probabilities $P(a_j|a_{j-1}, \mathbf{e})$, the authors

---

17 See Appendix A, especially section A.4.

18 Assuming a conventional value for a_0.

of [VOG 96] make an additional assumption, stipulating that this transition probability only depends on the size of the jump between a_{j-1} and a_j:

$$P(a_j | a_{j-1}, \mathbf{e}) = \frac{s(a_j - a_{j-1})}{\sum_{a \in A} s(a - a_{j-1})} \qquad [7.14]$$

where $\{s(j - j')\}$ is a set of positive parameters. The set of parameters $\boldsymbol{\theta}$ of the model therefore comprises the same parameters as the IBM1 model, complemented with the parameters related to the transition probability. Knowing the model parameters $\boldsymbol{\theta}$, the most probable alignment for a given sentence pair is determined using equation [7.8]. The introduction of dependencies between two successive labels make the problem more complex than the equivalent problem for the IBM1 model. It can however be solved efficiently using the Viterbi algorithm[19].

Like for the IBM1 model, parameter estimation from unlabeled data can be performed using the EM algorithm. It involves the following steps:

– *Initialization:* randomly or uniformly set the initial values for $\boldsymbol{\theta}$.

– *Until convergence or for a predefined number of iterations*:

- *E-step:* the dependencies between labels make the computation of link posteriors more challenging, since it can no longer be done on a per word basis. Yet, using standard algorithms for HMMs such as the Forward-Backward algorithm, link posteriors $P(a_j | f, \mathbf{e})$ are readily derived. Likewise, it is also possible to compute jump posteriors $P(i, i' | f, \mathbf{e})$ where i and i' are the labels of two consecutive target words. Once these posterior probabilities are known, it is possible to compute the expectations of word association counts $F(f | e)$ and of jump counts $F(i | i')$ by summing up over all sentences and alignment links.

- *M-step:* the parameters $\boldsymbol{\theta}$ of the model are directly re-estimated by normalizing the expectations of the counts as in equation [7.12].

An important difference between the HMM model and the IBM1 model is that the *log-likelihood* is no longer concave and it presents numerous local extrema, removing any convergence guarantee toward a global maximum. In numerous application frameworks, this problem is not considered harmful as long as the initial values of the parameters are properly set. The most common choice consists of initializing the lexical association parameters $P(e | f)$ with values of a previously estimated IBM1 model.

7.3.1.3. *Modeling fertility, IBM model 3 and beyond*

When aligning a sequence f, each word f_j is linked to a unique target word e_{a_j}. This hypothesis is obviously limiting, since it often occurs that the same concept is expressed

---

19 See Appendix A, and especially section A.5.

by word groups of different lengths in the source and target languages. This problem is illustrated in Figure 7.5, which displays two extracts of parallel sentences. In the first example, the French compound "pommes de terre" is linked with a single English word *potatoes*. When aligning French words with positions in the English sentence, the alignment model can find a consistent solution for aligning the three source words *pomme*, *de* and *terre* with the same target word *potatoes*. However, depending on the training data, another solution can emerge which aligns "pomme" with *potatoes* and the two other source words with null.

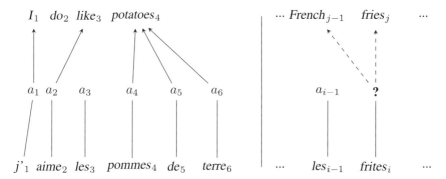

Figure 7.5. *Fertility, a problem for sequence labeling approaches*

A manner of guiding the alignment towards the "good" solution consists of introducing the notion of *fertility*: each target word is associated with a distribution $n(\phi|e)$ modeling the number of associated source words. This new distribution captures the tendency of certain target words to receive more (or less) than one single alignment link. For example, the probability distribution in Table 7.2 reflects the fact that *potatoes* prefers to align either with a single word or with three words.

ϕ	$n(\phi|\text{potatoes})$
0	0
1	0.42
2	0.1
3	0.48
4	0

Table 7.2. *Fertility distribution for the word potatoes*

Fertility can also model the preference of certain target words to remain unaligned. This is, for example, the case of an auxiliary verb such as *do* in the example of Figure 7.5. Such phenomena will simply be modeled by assigning a non-zero probability to the event corresponding to leaving *do* unaligned.

Another interesting case in this example is the source word "les", which must remain unaligned, that is, aligned with the null word. This phenomenon can be accounted for in the IBM1 and HMM models; it is however possible to refine the prediction of null alignments using the fertility model. Based on the intuition that, within a given sentence, the number of words aligned with null mainly depends on the sentence length, the authors of [BRO 90] propose to use a particular distribution for the fertility null $p(\phi_0)$ and that depends on the sentence length and of a parameter p_0 quantifying the prior probability of a null alignment.

To sum up, in the IBM model 3, the joint probability P($\mathbf{a}$, $f|\mathbf{e}$) includes two new terms with respect to model 2: the fertility of the null word (P(ϕ_0)) and, for each target word, its fertility is $n(\ |.)$ Finally, the authors of [BRO 90] also introduce the notion of *distortion*, which is used to model jumps.

Model 3 therefore corresponds to a better modeling of the interactions between the two languages, at the cost of an increased algorithmic complexity. This is because the model includes a much larger number of parameters than the IBM1 and HMM models, since it includes, for each target word, the corresponding fertility parameters[20]. Furthermore, due to the structure of dependencies between random variables, it is no longer possible to solve the inference problem [7.8] exactly; nor is it possible to compute the expectations needed to perform EM training.

In fact, in this new model, the search for an optimal alignment is a NP-hard problem [UDU 06], and can only be solved heuristically. Similarly, failing to compute the sums over all the possible alignments that are necessary for the link posteriors, learning algorithms have to resort to eg. sampling techniques to approximate the quantities required for the EM algorithm.

IBM models 4, 5, and 6 bring additional refinements to model 3 that we will briefly summarize here. Interested readers can refer to the following references [BRO 90, OCH 03b]. The IBM4 model improves the IBM3 model by introducing an enhanced distortion model which takes the relative positions of the word into account, and also includes first order Markovian dependencies. In addition, word classes are built into the source and target languages and are used to improve the lexical association probabilities. These classes can be computed in an unsupervised manner, from monolingual learning data [BRO 92]. The IBM5 model corrects a theoretical problem posed by the IBM3 and IBM4 models, which are said to be *deficient*. This is because a part of the probability mass is attributed to alignments which are impossible, due to fertility constraints. In fact, the sum over target words of fertility values cannot exceed the number of target words; yet, such configurations have a non zero probability. Finally, the IBM6 model

---

20 This represents $|\mathcal{V}_e| \times (F_{max})$ additional parameters, where F_{max} is the maximum value for the fertility.

is a combination of the IBM4 and HMM models introduced in [OCH 03b] to combine the advantages of both models. The increase in complexity incurred by these two latter models is usually not compensated by improvements of the resulting alignments, which explains why these models are rarely used in practice.

7.3.1.4. *Symmetrization*

The examples in Figure 7.5 illustrate some of the limitations of viewing alignment as a mere a sequence labeling problem. In the first example, three words must be aligned with a single word, which is only possible in one direction: when aligning English with French, rather than French with English, it becomes impossible to come up with a satisfactory solution. The same happens in the second example, where a single French word – "frites" is to be aligned with a pair of English words *French fries*. Here, the alignment of French with English is problematic, whereas the opposite direction poses no particular problem.

As it turns out, the two alignment directions provide complementary information, which can be merged into a unified representation using *symmetrization heuristics*. Using these heuristics, it is then possible to reconstruct symmetric alignments represented as a $J \times I$ boolean alignment matrix.

A first simple heuristic considers the *union* of all alignment links contained either in the source/target or in the target/source generative alignments. The resulting matrix may contain unsure links, which are only proposed in one alignment direction. A more conservative approach selects only links in the *intersection* of the two input alignments. In this case, the number of alignments obtained is much lower, and only contains reliable links which have been proposed in both alignment directions. Various additional heuristics are discussed in [OCH 03b, KOE 03b], aimed at completing the *intersection* alignments with some, but not all, links from the *union*.

7.3.2. **Word alignment models: a summary**

Word alignment models in statistical machine translation are used to compute two (one for each direction) asymmetrical alignments of parallel sentences, which are then heuristically symmetrized. An open source implementation of the generative models of section 7.3.1 is available in the Giza++ toolkit [OCH 03b].

Among the alignment models presented above, the IBM4 model seems to realize the best compromise between training time and alignment quality[21]. Training such models

---

21 To give an idea of the computational cost, aligning the French/English Hansard corpus in both directions takes approximately a day. This corpus contains over a million sentence pairs extracted from the proceedings of the Canadian Parliament.

cannot be done from scratch, and typically involves learning a cascade of models of increasing complexity, where simpler models are used to initialize the more complex ones: IBM1, then HMM, IBM3, IBM4 and so forth.

The performance of Giza++, from the point of view of the quality of the predicted alignments is not entirely satisfactory. Reducing word alignment errors is still the subject of much active research, even though better alignments do not necessary yield better translations [FRA 07]. For instance, some recent works explore the usage of discriminative models such as conditional random fields (CRFs, see Chapter 6) [BLU 06, NIE 08]. Discriminative models [MOO 05] are more expressive and enable us to combine multiple information sources to assess the validity of an alignment link. In particular, they can easily integrate linguistic features such as syntactic or morpho-syntactic analysis, or use surface similarities between source and target words. Training these models however requires *supervision* data, in the form of manually aligned sentence pairs. Such annotations are difficult and very costly to produce, and very few hand aligned corpora are available. This may explain why, despite their improved performance, discriminative models have not yet replaced the IBM alignment models.

7.3.3. *Extracting bisegments*

This section presents the last step of the translation model construction process outlined in Figure 7.3. This step aims to *extract* a set of bisegments from the symmetrized alignment matrix and to score them. As explained below, theses scores are based both on statistics accumulated on the parallel corpus and on parameter values computed by the word alignment models of section 7.3.1.

Let us first consider the alignment matrix represented in Figure 7.6. The objective of the extraction algorithm is to identify long bisegments, such as the one composed of the French noun group "la glace au chocolat" and its English counterpart *chocolate ice cream*. Long bisegment, which integrate a larger context, supply more reliable translations; furthermore, bisegments correspond to syntactic constituents are more likely to recombine more freely with neighboring groups than sequences of arbitrary words. Such long bisegments however are more rare than shorter ones, which implies that their associated statistics are less reliable. Moreover they are less likely to be used in future translation. Storing these translations thus presents a reduced benefit compared to storing shorter bisegments, such as the association of *glace* with *ice cream*. To achieve a good compromise between the reliability of a bisegment, and its potential reuse, the extraction heuristic must therefore extract segments of different lengths. [DEN 06] gives an insightful discussion regarding the merits of various extraction heuristics.

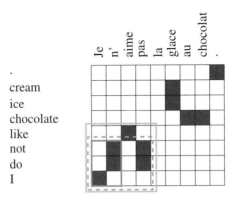

Figure 7.6. *Consistency of a bisegment in an alignment matrix. Only the green bisegment is consistent. The other two are not valid.*

7.3.3.1. *Consistent bisegments*

Recall that bisegments correspond to adjacent word groups in the source and target languages which are likely to correspond to mutual translations. To extract such groups, the standard approach relies on the notion of *consistency*, illustrated in Figure 7.6. Let us consider the bisegment (*I do not*, je n'). If this association is supported by several alignment links, it does however exclude the word *"pas"*, which is also aligned with *do not*. The translation of *I do not* can thus be regarded as being only partly covered by *je n'*. A more reliable association is obtained by extending the bisegment on the French side so as to include *"pas"*. As bisegments must be connected, this however requires us to also include *"aime"*, whose English counterpart is outside of the bisegment. The alignment must therefore be further extended, yielding the extraction of (*I do not like*, "Je n'aime pas").

Consistency can now be formally introduced as follows. Bisegment ($\overline{e}$, $\overline{f}$), occuring in an alignment matrix A is consistent if and only if:

$$\forall e_i \in \overline{e}, (e_i, f_j) \in A \Rightarrow f_j \in \overline{f} \tag{7.15}$$

$$\forall f_j \in \overline{f}, (e_i, f_j) \in A \Rightarrow e_i \in \overline{e} \tag{7.16}$$

$$\exists e_i \in \overline{e} \text{ et } \exists f_j \in \overline{f}, (e_i, f_j) \in A \tag{7.17}$$

The extraction algorithm formalizes these constraints. Consider again the example in Figure 7.6. The first two rules correctly exclude the bisegment (*I do not*, je n'aime pas), since the word aime is aligned with the word *like* which lay outside of this bisegment. However, these two rules leave a certain degree of flexibility for extending segments when unaligned words exist in A. An unaligned word corresponds to an empty column or row in the matrix: this is for example the case with "la" in Figure 7.6. The last rule restricts null alignments by imposing that all bisegments contain at least one alignment link. The unaligned words are thus absorbed into available bisegments, to the left and to the right. The following bisegments (and many others) are thus extracted: (*do not like*, n'aime pas la) and (*chocolate ice cream*, la glace au chocolat).

7.3.3.2. *bisegment extraction*

The extraction of all the bisegments from a sentence pair $(\mathbf{f}, \mathbf{e})$ is formalized by Algorithm 7.1. This algorithm considers all the possible segmentations of one sentence (for instance $\mathbf{e}$) and then explores the alignment matrix for each consistent counterpart of $\mathbf{e}$ in order to select the associated segment.

Algorithm 7.1. bisegment extraction algorithm using word aligned sentences

---

```
/* For a pair of sentences and the alignment matrix        */
Data: f, e, A
/* Set of bisegments                                       */
Result: BS
```

i_d, i_f // the start and end indices of the target segment;
```
/* Double loop over the segments of e                      */
```
for $i_f = 1 \ldots I$ **do**
  for $i_d = 1 \ldots i_f$ **do**
    $S_f = \{j | \exists i, \ i_d \leq i \leq i_f \ \text{and} \ A(i, j) = 1\}$;
    if consistency(S_f) **then**
      $j_d = \min(S_f)$// start index of the source segment;
      $j_f = \max(S_f)$ // end index of the source segment;
      $BS = BS \cup (\mathbf{e}_{i_d}^{i_f}, f_{j_d}^{j_f})$;
      while unaligned$(f_{j_f} + 1)$ **do**
        $j_f = j_f + 1$;
        $BS = BS \cup (\mathbf{e}_{i_d}^{i_f}, f_{j_d}^{j_f})$;
        $j' = j_d$;
        while unaligned$(f_{j'} - 1)$ **do**
          $j' = j' - 1$;
          $BS = BS \cup (\mathbf{e}_{i_d}^{i_f}, f_{j'}^{j_f})$;
        end
      end
    end
  end
end
end
```

---

The unaligned function returns **true** if there is no alignment link in the matrix $A$ for this source index. The consistency function simply checks the consistency of the
```

hypothetical bisegment. Finally, note that in practice, it is necessary to set a maximal length for the extracted bisegments in order to limit their number.

7.3.3.3. *Scoring bisegments*

The last step in the computation of the translation model consists of associating a confidence score with each extracted bisegments; this score will then be used when decoding (see section 7.5) and for guiding the translation algorithm so that the most probable bisegments are given preference over more rare associations, which are often artifacts introduced by alignment errors. In practice, each bisegment is weighted by several scores, which are combined during the search for the best translation. The most common confidence scores are briefly described below.

The question to be answered is the following: let $(\bar{e}, \bar{f})$ be a bisegment extracted from the parallel corpus, how adequate is it to translate $\bar{f}$ as $\bar{e}$? A simple approach to evaluate the quality of $(\bar{e}, \bar{f})$ consists of estimating on the parallel corpus the relative frequency of this association within all the occurrences of $\bar{e}$ or $\bar{f}$. The resulting values are estimations of the conditional translation probability, such as (a similar estimate is obtained for $\phi(\bar{f}|\bar{e})$):

$$\phi(\bar{e}|\bar{f}) = \frac{F(\bar{e}, \bar{f})}{\sum_{\bar{e}_k} F(\bar{e}_k, \bar{f})} \qquad [7.18]$$

where $F(\bar{e}, \bar{f})$ represents the number of times the bisegment $(\bar{e}, \bar{f})$ has been extracted. Estimations based on the relative frequencies are however overly optimistic, especially for rare bisegments. Consider the extreme case of bisegment comprised of two segments occurring only once. We would then have $\phi(\bar{f}|\bar{e}) = \phi(\bar{e}|\bar{f}) = 1$, even when the bisegment is only extracted because of an alignment error. To improve these estimates, a common solution is to take into account the quality of the individual word alignments which subsume the bisegment alignment: this is known as *lexical weighting* [KOE 03b]. To this end, the following scores are also computed:

$$lex(\bar{e}|\bar{f}, A) = \prod_{i=i_d}^{i_f} \frac{1}{F(j|A(i, j) = 1)} \sum_{j|A(i,j)=1} \frac{F(e_i, f_j)}{F(f_j)} \qquad [7.19]$$

where $F(e_i, f_j)$ and $F(f_j)$ respectively denote the number of times the word e_i is aligned with f_j in the parallel corpus and the frequency of word f_j; i_d and i_f are the indices in **e** of the start and end segment respectively. In addition, $F(j|A(i, j) = 1)$ corresponds to the number of active alignment links associated with f_j. From [7.19] a score can finally be deduced by taking the maximal value over all the alignments of $\bar{e}$ with $\bar{f}$. In practice, the two lexical weighting terms $lex(\bar{f}|\bar{e})$ and $lex(\bar{e}|\bar{f})$ are simultaneously used.

Other scoring functions have been proposed in the literature and can be used in conjunction with the previous scores. In fact, any numerical function evaluating a bisegment is a candidate confidence measure. For instance, boolean functions testing arbitrary syntactic properties of a bisegment $(\overline{f}, \overline{e})$, such as "Is $\overline{e}$ a target constituent?", "Is $\overline{f}$ a source constituent?", "Do $\overline{e}$ and $\overline{f}$ both contain a verb?", can also be used. The simplest such function is the constant function whose value is 1 for all the bisegments: its inclusion in the model is a way to make sure that the decoder will prefer to use few bisegments, and will therefore favor the longer ones. This additional score is called the *phrase penalty*.

In summary, each bisegment extracted from the parallel corpus is subject to various numerical evaluations. The most common scores are the translation probabilities $\phi(\overline{f}|\overline{e})$ and $\phi(\overline{e}|\overline{f})$, the two lexical weighting terms and the length penalty.

7.4. Modeling reorderings

As described in section 7.2.2.3, one of the main difficulties of machine translation is that different languages use different sentence construction patterns which entail differences in the relative positions of the constituents. As a consequence, the word or segment orders in the source and target sentences can be very different. As for the other differences between the source and target languages, it is thus necessary to (i) model these order differences and (ii) design scores that evaluate the plausibility of the possible target word arrangements based on the source words order. These models should be so designed as to make predictions regarding *non-local reorderings*, since the local ones are already largely captured in the segment models. Such models are all the more critical as the source and target languages strongly diverge with respect to their syntax: if translation from French into English can almost be achieved without reorderings, the same can not be said of the translation from German into English, *a fortiori* from Japanese or Korean into English (see [ALO 06, BIR 09] in which various quantitative measures of these divergences are proposed).

In this section, some common reordering models are presented: we first consider, in section 7.4.1, various ways to define the set of possible source reorderings, which restrict the search space of the decoder; we then discuss in section 7.4.1 how to evaluate the plausibility of those various reorderings.

7.4.1. *The space of possible reorderings*

The role of reordering models is better understood on a simple example. Let us assume that translation is word based and consider that the source sentence $f = a\ b\ c$ is to be translated. Let us further assume that each word has only one translation, α for a, β for b, and γ for c. Modeling the possible reorderings consists of (i) specifying which of the permutations of the set $\{\alpha \, \beta \, \gamma\}$ are plausible target sentences and (ii) to compute a score evaluating their plausibility.[22]

For the sake of this presentation, we will continue to assume simple word-based models; as discussed below, these models generalize straightforwardly to the segments-based approach. Any source sentence $f = f_1 \ldots f_J$ and its translation $e = e_1 \ldots e_I$ can then be represented as a sequence of word pairs: $(f_{j_1} : e_1) \ldots (f_{j_I} : e_I)$. For any index $t \in [1:I]$, the target word e_t is the translation of the source word f_{j_t}. A *monotone* translation is such that $\forall t \in [1:J]$, $j_t = t$, meaning that the relative word order is the same in source and target. These atomic associations between target and source can be represented in a more abstract manner in the form of a permutation π of the indices in $[1:I]$: $j_1 \, j_2 \ldots j_I$.

Most models presented below generate the possible permutations in the following iterative manner: at each stage $t \in [1 \ldots I]$, a new word e_t is added to the target sentence by selecting the word at index j_t; once translated, f_{j_t} is removed from the to-translate list and not considered in further steps. Within this general framework, the various reordering models express constraints and define scores based on the relative positions, in the source sentence, of words whose translations are adjacent in the target sentence. In defining these constraints, we note j_g the smallest index of an untranslated source word a step t, and j_d is the largest index of a translated word. The permutation generation process is illustrated in Figure 7.7, where words 1, 3, 4 and 8 of a 9 word sentence have already been translated. We thus have $j_g = 2$ and $j_d = 8$.

1	2	3	4	5	6	7	8	9
●	○	●	●	○	○	○	●	○

Figure 7.7. *The permutation generation process. Words that have already been translated are represented with* ●*, the remaining alternatives by* ○

7.4.1.1. *Local permutations*

The smallest deviation from the monotone setting consists in licensing only *local permutations*, that is permutations which only involve a limited number of adjacent source words. The constraint is parameterized by a value d which specifies the size of the corresponding neighborhoods. Let us illustrate this mechanism when $d = 1$: initially $(t = 1)$, only f_1 or f_2 can be translated. In the first hypothesis, we can then choose to continue with either f_2 or with f_3; in the second case, however, f_1 must be translated to complete the exchange between positions 1 and 2. This constraint is easy to implement using finite-state transducers [KUM 05]. It is noteworthy that, even under this very

---

22 For a three word sentence, it is possible to list and evaluate all the $3! = 6$ permutations; for longer sentences, this quickly becomes impossible.

strong constraint, the number of licit permutations of a sequence continue to increase rapidly with its length. For $d = 1$, it can be shown that the number of permutations of a sequence of J words is given by the nth term of the Fibonacci sequence, which increases with $(1 + \sqrt{5})^J$. The more liberal constraints that are described below allow for a much larger number of permutations.

7.4.1.2. "IBM" constraints

The so-called IBM constraints[23] restrict the generation process to select one among the d leftmost untranslated words, where d is a free parameter of the model. Consider, for instance, that $f = f_1 \ldots f_J$ is the source sentence, and take $d = 2$. The first target word is the translation of either f_1 or of f_2; if f_2 is chosen, the next step will chose between f_1 and f_3, if, on the other hand, f_1 is selected, the next step will consider f_2 or f_3, and so on. The development of these alternatives is represented in Figure 7.8.

1	2	3	4	5	6	7	8	9	10
$t = 4$									
●	○	●	●	○	●	○	○	★	★
$t = 5$									
●	●	●	●	○	●	○	○	○	★
$t = 6$									
●	●	●	●	○	●	●	○	○	○

Figure 7.8. *Development of the reordering alternatives in the IBM model with $d = 4$. The unattainable words are represented by ★. At $t = 4$, the possible choices are among words 2, 5, 7 and 8*

To further restrict these reorderings, it is possible to enforce additional constraints. For instance, the maximum distance between the index of a source word and its corresponding target index, or the total number of "gaps"[24] can, be limited.

The generation of the possible reorderings is computed by Algorithm 7.2.

---

23 See [LOP 09] or [TIL 03] regarding terminological issues.
24 This is the number of words which remain to be translated even though the immediate successors have already been translated. At stage 7 of Figure 7.8, there are such gaps, corresponding to words at index 2 and 5.

Algorithm 7.2. The "IBM" permutations

Data: d
$J_o = [1\!:\!d]$;
for $t \in [1\!:\!I]$ **do**
    $j_t \leftarrow \mathsf{Choose}(J_o)$
    if $(t + d \leq J)$ **then**
        $\mid$ $J_o \leftarrow J_o \setminus \{j_t\} \cup \{t + d\}$
    end
    else
        $\mid$ $J_o \leftarrow J_o \setminus \{j_t\}$
    end
end

These constraints are asymmetric and enforces stronger limitations on the last (rightmost) source words than on the first ones. In particular, when the source sentence contains more than d words, it is impossible to have the first target word translate the last source word, while the opposite is always possible. As noted by [KAN 05], the "inverse" IBM constraints, corresponding to a right-to-left processing of the source, will yield different reorderings that might also prove useful depending on the source and target languages under study.

7.4.1.3. *Distortion based reordering*

The simplest constraint in this family consists of restricting the span of licit movements, for instance, by imposing a maximum absolute value on the difference $\mid t - j_t \mid$. Such constraints are only meaningful when the source and target sentences have comparable lengths, so that the absolute positions can be compared. This limitation is easily overcome by working on *relative differences*, for instance enforcing the differences such as $\mid j_t + 1 - j_{t+1} \mid$, which measure the gap, in the source sentence, between two adjacent words in the target sentence, remains below a predefined threshold.

As noted in [LOP 09], this constraint ensures that the (source) discontinuities between untranslated words have a limited size. A stronger constraint makes the distance between j_g and j_t remain smaller than a predefined value. This constraint is used in the Moses system [KOE 07b].

7.4.1.4. *Hierarchical reordering*

A final useful reordering model is defined by *inversion transduction grammars*, which are a sub-class of context-free synchronous grammars introduced in [WU 97].

A context-free synchronous grammar[25] is a rewriting system defining parallel derivations of two languages, playing the role of source and target languages. Any rule of a grammar G is of the form $X \rightarrow \alpha_s; \alpha_t$, with α_s and α_t the respective source and target right-hand sides; a one-to-one mapping between the non-terminals in α_s and α_t is further assumed: matched non terminal have the same subscripts in the representation below. A synchronous grammar generates pairs of sentences, thus defining a relationship (or a transduction) between two languages. An inversion grammar is a synchronous context-free grammar generating permutations of a sentence. It is made up of just a single non-terminal X and two generic productions: $X \rightarrow X_1 X_2; X_1 X_2$ and $X \rightarrow X_1 X_2; X_2 X_1$. The production $X \rightarrow X_1 X_2; X_1 X_2$ splits a constituent X into two parts, which appear in the same order in the target and source; likewise, the production $X \rightarrow X_1 X_2; X_2 X_1$ specifies an inversion between the source and the target subparts (see Figure 7.9). The terminals of G are the words to be shuffled and G therefore contains a production $X \rightarrow w_i; w_i$ for each word.

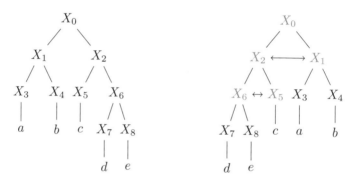

Figure 7.9. *A permutation of a b c d e in an inversion grammar. The left part represents the "source" derivation which reproduces the initial order; the right part represents the "target" derivation in which some indices have been shuffled. The correspondences between the non-terminals are expressed by identical indices in the two trees; the inversion between non-terminals are figured by arrows*

As noted in [WU 97], such a mechanism only generates a small fraction of the possible permutations of $[1: J]$: in particular, only 22 of the 24 permutations of $[1:4]$ are produced[26]. These grammars are further studied in [ZEN 03]; their linguistic relevance is also discussed in [KAN 05, WEL 06, HUA 09]. Due to their simplicity, these

---

25 The terminology is not totally fixed here: in compilation theory, it is known as a *Syntax Directed Transduction (or Translation) Scheme* in reference to the original work of [LEW 68, AHO 69].

26 It can be shown (see the references cited in [ZEN 03]) that the number of permutations of a J word sentence grows as $(3 + \sqrt{8})^J$.

reordering models are widely used both to construct alignments [SAE 09, HAG 09] and to define the search space of translation algorithms [EIS 06, ZHA 06].

7.4.1.5. *Reordering segments*

The constraints described in the previous sections generalize straightforwardly to segment models, assuming however that a joint segmentation of the source and target sentences is given. For each possible segmentation, the above defined constraints specify a set of possible reorderings; the set of all the licit reorderings of a source sentence is thus obtained by taking the union over the possible segmentations. Consider for instance the sequence a b c d: the segmentation [a b] [c d], associated with the inversion of two blocks, gives rise to the permutation c d a b; the segmentation [a] [b c d], associated with same transposition of segments, gives rise to the permutation b c d a, etc.

To conclude this section, let us emphasize that most reordering models have been conceived in the framework of word-based translation models, in which all the "movements" must be explicitly modeled. As explained in section 7.3, the advent of segment-based models dispenses with the modeling of local reorderings. For example, the extraction of a bisegment such as ("traduction automatique", *machine translation*) makes modeling the reordering of "traduction" and "automatique" useless. Reordering models should thus focus on the main syntactic restructuring, which typically give rise to long distance movements. The models described in this section (with the exception of the hierarchical model) are not well suited for this task and are only useful insofar as they define the search space of the translation process (see section 7.5). Their improvement is thus a major concern and remains the subject of active research.

For the rest of this chapter, a reordering will be defined with respect to (i) a joint segmentation of the target and the source (written σ) and (ii) a permutation (written π) expressing the order differences between the corresponding segments. These two pieces of information define an *alignment* between the target and source segments, which will be denoted $\mathbf{a} = (\sigma, \pi)$, to remain consistent with the notations introduced in section 7.3.1.

7.4.2. *Evaluating permutations*

Even when imposing strong limitations on the licit reorderings of a source sentence, their number increases exponentially with the sentence length. It is, therefore, necessary to score the reorderings and to integrate these valuations while searching for the best translation (see section 7.5 below).

Recall that in segment-based translation systems, each target language translation candidate is constructed by aggregating fragments $e_1 \ldots e_l$, which are such that there exists a permutation π of [1:l] and a set of fragments $\{f_1, \ldots, f_l\}$ satisfying:

$- \forall k \in [1{:}l], \pi(i_k) = k$ or, equivalently, $\pi^{-1}(k) = i_k$;

$- f_{i_1} f_{i_2} \ldots f_{i_l} = f$;

$- \forall k \in [1{:}l], (f_{i_k}{:}\mathbf{e}_k)$ is in the translation table.

Each source and target segment covers a certain span; in the following discussion, we denote $\mathbf{e}_i.g$ (respectively $\mathbf{e}_i.d$) the start (resp. end) index of the target span; similar notations are used for source spans. These notations are illustrated in Figure 7.10. In this figure, the English sentence is composed of the following segments $\mathbf{e}_1 = she$ $\mathbf{e}_2 = bravely$, $\mathbf{e}_3 = seized$ $that$, and so on; each of these segments is in correspondence with one of the source segments as expressed by π: thus $\pi(1) = 3$, denoting that $\mathbf{e}_1 = she$ is matched with $f_3 = \text{"}elle\text{"}$, $\pi(2) = 6$ since $bravely$ is the translation of "avec courage", and so on. The source segment f_2 ("menaces de mort") has as right and left boundaries $f_2.g = 4$ and $f_2.d = 6$, respectively corresponding to the fourth ("menaces") and sixth ("mort") word.

---

segmented source:
[en dépit de]₁ [menaces de mort]₂ [elle]₃ [a saisi sa]₄ [chance]₅ [avec courage]₆
reordered and segmented source:
[elle]₃ [avec courage]₆ [a saisi sa]₄ [chance]₅ [en dépit de]₁ [menaces de mort]₂
segmented target:
[she]₁ [bravely]₂ [seized that]₃ [opportunity]₄ [despite]₅ [threats to her life]₆

Figure 7.10. *A joint segmentation and the associated reordering*

7.4.2.1. *Modeling the target language*

One way to evaluate the plausibility of the permutations of a sequence is to use stochastic language models (see section 7.2.1 and Appendix A). Each translation hypothesis $e_1 \ldots e_J$ thus simply receives a probability score $P(e_1 \ldots e_J)$, that expresses the syntactic quality of the recombination of these different segments and therefore implicitly assesses the plausibility of their ordering.

As it turns out, n-gram language models, which are used in most statistical translation systems, only supply mediocre evaluations of possible reorderings. This was expected, given the restricted context that is captured by such models. The simple experiment reported in [ZAS 09] illustrates this fact. In this study, the authors generate random permutations of correct sentences and then try to use the scores produced by the statistical language model to recover the initial word order. One of their conclusions is that n-gram language models fail to reconstruct the correct order for most sentences, and that it is often possible to find reorderings that are better for these models than the non-permuted sentences.

7.4.2.2. *Distortion*

Another simple criterion consists of scoring each movement by a numerical factor which depends on the distance measured in the source sentence between two segments that are adjacent in the target language: this is known as *distortion*-based scoring. The valuation of the reordering induced by $\mathbf{a} = (\sigma, \pi)$ is therefore defined as the sum of the valuations associated with each concatenation between e_k and e_{k+1}. Assuming that scores simply correspond to the distance δ (in number of words) between the right boundary of f_{i_k} and the left boundary[27] of $f_{i_{k+1}}$, the following is obtained:

$$c((f_{i_k}:\mathbf{e}_k), (f_{i_{k+1}}:\mathbf{e}_{k+1})) = \mid f_{i_k}.d - f_{i_{k+1}}.g + 1 \mid$$

Considering again the example in Figure 7.10, the reordering cost associated with the two bisegments $(f_6, \mathbf{e}_2) = $ ("avec courage", *bravely*) and $(f_4, \mathbf{e}_3) = $ ("a saisi sa", *seized that*) is therefore $\mid 13 - 8 + 1 \mid = 6$.

The cost of a complete sequence consisting of l segments is then:

$$c(f, \mathbf{e}, \mathbf{a}) = \sum_{k=1}^{l-1} c((f_{i_k}:\mathbf{e}_k), (f_{i_{k+1}}:\mathbf{e}_{k+1})) \qquad [7.20]$$

Such valuations are used, for example in the Pharaoh [KOE 04] and Moses [KOE 07b] systems. They are of course very coarse, as they do not take into account any linguistic information regarding the reordered words and phrases. They are however very easy to compute, as they break down the total reordering cost as a sum of local valuations which involve only two adjacent bisegments, as in equation [7.20]. This property is very useful to design efficient decoding algorithms (see section 7.5.2).

7.4.2.3. *Lexical reordering*

Better reordering models for phrase-based systems have been proposed in [TIL 04] and extended in various ways in subsequent works. They also rely on the evaluation of the cost of each concatenation, where these local costs integrate additional knowledge regarding adjacent segments, such as the identity of the source or target segments, the corresponding sequence of part-of-speech labels, etc. In this general framework, a variety of models have been proposed. Most approaches start with a useful simplification, which consists in considering a small number of classes for distortion, so as to reduce the number of possible distortion values. Given a pair of adjacent target segments $\mathbf{e}_k$ and $\mathbf{e}_{k+1}$, the following configurations are generally distinguished:

– the two corresponding source segments are also adjacent in the source language and occur in the same order. Formally $\pi(k + 1) = \pi(k) + 1$: in this case, the concatenation has a *monotone orientation*. This orientation holds on the right of $\mathbf{e}_k$ and on the left of $\mathbf{e}_{k+1}$;

---

27 Other definitions of this distance can also be entertained, such as using the positions of the middle word.

– the two segments are also adjacent in the source language but their order is reversed with respect to the target. Formally $\pi(k+1) = \pi(k) - 1$), which corresponds to an *inverted or swap orientation*, it applies on the right for $\mathbf{e}_k$ and on the left for $\mathbf{e}_{k+1}$;

– the two segments are no longer adjacent in the source language but the order is preserved (formally $\pi(k+1) > \pi(k) + 1$);

– the two segments are no longer adjacent in the source language and, in addition, the order is inversed (formally $\pi(k+1) < \pi(k) - 1$).

All these situations are not necessarily distinguished: in the Moses system [KOE 07b], it is possible to single out the *monotone* orientation from the three other cases; or to consider a three-way partition between *monotone*, *swap*, and the other two situations (see also [TIL 04]). In the model described in [KUM 05], limitations on reorderings yield only *monotone* or *swap* patterns, etc.

Several proposals make the score c depend on the source and/or on the target segment. This is the case of the model proposed in [ALO 06], where c is a function of the distortion and of the source segment. In contrast, the approach of [KOE 07b] distinguishes only certain orientations (monotone, inversion, etc.) but makes c depend on the value of the orientation and of the bisegments involved in the concatenation.

In all these approaches, the score function c derives from a probabilistic model which expresses the conditional distribution of orientations given the involved bisegments. For example, in the approach implemented in [KOE 07b], the cost of a concatenation is broken down into two terms, one for the bisegment on the left (c_g) and one for the bisegment on the right (c_d) as follows:

$$c((f_{i_k}:\mathbf{e}_k), (f_{i_{k+1}}:\mathbf{e}_{k+1}), k) = c_g((f_{i_k}:\mathbf{e}_k), k) + c_d((f_{i_{k+1}}:\mathbf{e}_{k+1}), k) \qquad [7.21]$$

In this formulation, c_g is computed as $-\log(P(o_g|(f_{i_k}:\mathbf{e}_k)))$, where o_g is the relative orientation of the bisegment on the left with respect to the bisegment on the right (monotone, inverted, etc.); c_d has a similar form, and models the behavior of $(f_{i_{k+1}}:\mathbf{e}_{k+1})$ with respect to the previous bisegment. These conditional probabilities can be easily estimated from word aligned parallel corpora. When maximum likelihood estimates are used, they will simply take the form of count ratios.

No matter what the details of the computation of these concatenation costs, the resulting scoring function will remains additive. The overall cost of reordering of a translation hypothesis is indeed computed as a summation:

$$c(f, \mathbf{e}, \mathbf{a}) = \sum_{k=1}^{K-1} c((f_{i_k}:\mathbf{e}_k), (f_{i_{k+1}}:\mathbf{e}_{k+1}))$$

To conclude, it should be mentioned that it is possible to use other model families for constructing these evaluations, as is done by the authors of [ZEN 06], who use discriminatively trained exponential models (see Chapter 3), or by the authors of [XIO 06], who however resort to more complex hierarchical constraints.

7.5. Translation: a search problem

In previous sections, we have focused on the construction of statistical models from multilingual (translation and reordering models) or monolingual (language model) text resources. In this section, we explain how these models are used to produce new translations. Our first issue is the relevant combination of all these various models, where each model evaluates a specific aspect of the translation hypothesis. This question is discussed in section 7.5.1. We will next address theoretical issues related to the search of the best possible translation, before presenting several heuristic search techniques for solving this difficult problem. Two general approaches will be discussed: in section 7.5.4.1, we study *best first search* strategies, while *local search* techniques are the subject of section 7.5.4.2.

7.5.1. *Combining models*

7.5.1.1. *The problem*

Recall that in segment-based systems, the translation process consists in combining the following probabilistic decisions:

– segment the target sentence f into variable length $f_1 \ldots f_l$ segments;

– for each segment f_k, select a possible equivalent $\mathbf{e}_k$ in the target language;

– rearrange target segments $\mathbf{e}_1 \ldots \mathbf{e}_l$ so that the translation $\mathbf{e}$ is finally obtained, together with the corresponding word alignment $\mathbf{a}$.

These decisions are of course interdependent and in practice are not performed in any specific order, but rather simultaneously. To guide these decisions, several probabilistic scores are available, most notably:

– a translation model score, which evaluates the quality of an association between a source segment f and a target segment $\mathbf{e}$, and provides a cost $c_t(f, \mathbf{e}, \mathbf{a})$;

– a reordering model, which evaluates the plausibility of the reorderings induced by this alignment and delivers a cost $c_r(f, \mathbf{e}, \mathbf{a})$;

– a target language model, which evaluates the quality of the target sentence and thus introduces the cost $c_s(\mathbf{e})$ (generally $-\log(\Pr(\mathbf{e}))$).

The best translation is the one which achieves the best compromise between these various scoring functions. To obtain such a compromise, it is first necessary to quantify the contribution of each individual model to the global evaluation function. This "tuning" step is crucial, as the costs calculated by the different models are not directly comparable and do not necessarily have the same domain or the same dynamics. A simple way to combine these values is to form their linear combination and to score each translation hypothesis as follows:

$$c(f, \mathbf{e}, \mathbf{a}) = \lambda_t c_t(f, \mathbf{e}, \mathbf{a}) + \lambda_r c_r(f, \mathbf{e}, \mathbf{a}) + \lambda_s c_s(\mathbf{e}) \qquad [7.22]$$

Such additive cost functions are easily extended to account for additional models and scores, such as the length difference between the source and target sentences, scores evaluating the internal syntactic consistency of the source segments, supplementary translation or target language models, etc. A general formulation of the combined score function, known as the *log-linear model*[28], is thus as follows:

$$c(f, \mathbf{e}, \mathbf{a}) = \sum_{m=1}^{M} \lambda_m c_m(f, \mathbf{e}, \mathbf{a}), \qquad [7.23]$$

where $c_m()$ stands for the mth cost function and λ_m its associated parameter.

Under this view, the best translation of the source sentence f is the target sentence $\mathbf{e}$ which minimizes the total cost $c(f, \mathbf{e}, \mathbf{a})$; the search for this optimum defines the optimization program that the decoder must solve. Before studying this problem in details, we briefly consider the problem of properly setting the parameter vector $\lambda = \{\lambda_m, m = 1 \ldots M\}$.

7.5.1.2. *Minimum error rate training*

The computation of optimal values for λ is performed on a *development corpus* $\mathbf{D}$ associating a set of source sentences $\mathbf{F}$ and reference, hand-made, translations $\mathbf{E}$. It requires the definition of an adequate evaluation measure that will help quantify the evolution of the translation quality with respect to parameter values. Such evaluations need to be performed in an automatic fashion and are usually based on surface comparison of automatically generated translations with one (or more) reference translations (see section 7.6). For each value of λ, the system performance for the sentences in $\mathbf{D}$ is thus computed as some function $L(\lambda, \mathbf{D})$. The optimal parameters λ^* are then defined as:

$$\lambda^* = \underset{\lambda}{\mathrm{argmax}}\, L(\lambda, \mathbf{D}) \qquad [7.24]$$

This optimization program is far from trivial, as the relationship between the coefficients λ_m and the objective function in equation [7.24] is only indirect. Changing

---

28 The terminology is again misleading: if it is true that some costs are derived from log-probabilities (typically the language model cost), many other costs are just arbitrary numerical values, and the model defined by [7.22] is just a *linear* combination of several cost functions.

the paramaters will change the best translation output by the system, which, in turn, modifies the quality measure $L()$. Mathematically, this means that the objective function cannot be differentiated with respect to λ, which precludes the use of conventional numerical optimization techniques. When the parameters are few, it is possible to perform optimization by an exhaustive search; when (as is the case in practice) the number of coefficients is higher that some values (typically 10), more sophisticated optimization algorithms must be used.

The standard approach (*Minimum Error Rate Training*, often abbreviated as *MERT*) is presented in [OCH 03a, ZAI 09] and multiple variations and improvements are proposed in [CER 08, MOO 08, FOS 07, MAC 08]. This algorithm utilizes the fact that the objective function defined by Equation [7.24] is piecewise constant: small changes of the parameters typically leave the best translation hypotheses (hence the objective function) unchanged in large regions of the parameter space, while transitions to a new value correspond to changes in the best output hypothesis and yield discontinuities with respect to the parameters. This property makes it possible to compute *exactly* the optimum along any fixed direction, which allows the implementation of search techniques such as Powell's search algorithm [POW 64]. This method is far from perfect and yields very unstable parameter values, which are not very robust with respect to small changes in experimental conditions.

7.5.2. *The decoding problem*

The role of the decoding module is to construct a translation for any source sentence. In the statistical machine translation framework, the best translation hypothesis is the one with the highest model scores. Translating is thus a matter of searching, among the sentences which can be aligned with f, for the hypothesis $\mathbf{e}^*$ minimizing the cost function $c(f, \mathbf{e}, \mathbf{a})$ defined in equation [7.23]. To appreciate the difficulty of this problem, let us consider the set of translation hypotheses that need to be explored. This *search space* contains all the sentences that can be constructed by:

– segmenting f in all possible manners – there are 2^{J-1} such possible segmentations, where J is the length of f;

– translating each source segment f_k with a target segment $\mathbf{e}$ as licensed by the translation model;

– permuting the resulting set of sentences $\mathbf{e}_k$ in all possible ways – there are $l!$ permutations for a set of l segments.

The search space thus contains a number of translations equal to a sum, over an exponential number of segmentations, of a factorial number of permutations (assuming the number of translations can be upper bounded). Computing the best translation thus involves the resolution of a combinatorial optimization problem which cannot be effectively solved in an exact manner. A proof of the theoretical complexity of this problem is given in [KNI 99], which shows that, even with relatively simple assumptions, the search problem is NP-hard. This demonstration relies on the fact that the exploration of all possible reorderings formally makes this problem analogous[29] to the traveling salesman problem, which is a notoriously difficult combinatorial problem (also see, [ZAS 09]).

Two strategies to tackle this problem are presented in the following sections:

– the first imposes further restrictions on the search space and on the scoring function, thus enabling us to use *exact* resolution strategies;

– the alternative is to resort to *heuristic search techniques* and compute approximate solutions.

Before starting this discussion, a few additional notations must be introduced: in the following, h denotes an *incomplete translation hypothesis*, defined by:

– a cost vector, comprising one dimension for each model: $h.c_t$ is the cost of the translation model, $h.c_s$ is the cost of the language model, and so on. As for complete hypotheses, the overall cost of h is computed according to [7.23];

– a target sentence prefix, denoted $h.\mathbf{e}$, obtained by concatenating of $h.t$ segments $\mathbf{e}_1 \ldots \mathbf{e}_t$;

– a span, denoted $h.span$, which records the fragments of the source sentence f that have already been translated in h. Formally, $h.span$ is the union of t disjoint intervals of $[1{:}J]$.

7.5.3. *Exact search algorithms*

For phrase-based translation models, decoding can be performed exactly *when the set of possible reorderings is limited*. We first discuss the case where there is no reordering (monotone translation), which will help understand the notations, before discussing the more complex case of *local reorderings* (see section 7.4.1).

7.5.3.1. *Monotone translations*

Let us consider the toy translation model B represented in Table 7.3. When $b = B[i]$ is a bisegment, then $b.f$ (respectively, $b.\mathbf{e}$) denotes the source (respectively, target) segment of length $b.J$ (resp. $b.I$), $b.c_t$ is the translation model cost[30] (not represented in the table), $b.c_s$ is the "internal" language model cost, and $b.\mathbf{e}[i]$ is the ith word of the target segment.

---

29 In other words, there exists a polynomial reduction from one problem to the other.

30 The evaluations of bisegments are used as costs: the more likely a translation is, the smaller its cost. These costs correspond to the inverse of the log probabilities in [7.18] and [7.19].

b. f	b.e	b.I	b.J	b.e[1]	b.c_s
this	ce	1	1	ce	0
this	cet	1	1	cet	0
this	cette	1	1	cette	0
this small	ce petit	2	2	ce	$-\log(\text{P}(\text{petit}|\text{ce}))$
this small	cette petite	2	2	cette	$-\log(\text{P}(\text{petite}|\text{cette}))$
small	petit	1	1	petit	0
small	petite	1	1	petite	0
small	petits	1	1	petits	0
country	pays	1	1	pays	0
country	nation	1	1	nation	0
country	campagne	1	1	campagne	0

Table 7.3. *A simplified translation model*

The set of translation hypotheses is represented in the form of a labeled directed acyclic graph, or equivalently, in the form of an acyclic finite automaton (see Figure 7.11). This graph contains a vertex for each prefix of f and has an edge labeled by $B[i].f$ between vertices k and $k+1$ for all the bisegments such that $B[i].f = f[k:k+l-1]$[31]. In this case, the source words in $[k:k+l]$ are said to be *covered* by the corresponding bisegment.

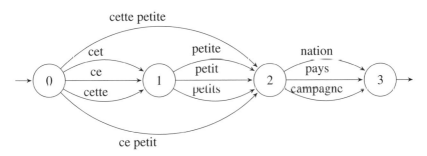

Figure 7.11. *The search space of a monotone translation, in the absence of a target language model . Costs are omitted. The source sentence is: this small country*

When all the model costs can be computed independently for each bisegment, and are simply summed to derive a global cost, they can easily be distributed on the edges

---

31 At this stage, it is standard practice to only consider a small set containing the best local translations, selected on the basis of the translation scores $B[i].c_t$.

of this graph. Thus, for example, the edges between vertices 0 and 2 covers the segment *this small* and carry a cost c which aggregates:

– the contribution of this bisegment to the total translation cost: $\lambda_t.B[3].c_t$;

– a fixed cost incurred by the addition of a supplementary segment, favoring hypotheses using long segments.

By proceeding in this manner, the total cost of a complete path between the starting node (0 in Figure 7.11) and the sink node 3, representing a particular set of segmentation and translation hypotheses, corresponds to the total model cost $c(f, \mathbf{e}, \mathbf{a})$. Finding the best translation in this graph can be done in polynomial time using standard shortest path algorithms; the decoding complexity is quadratic with respect to the length of the source sentence. The translation is produced from left to right, by concatenating translation hypotheses for prefixes of increasing lengths of f: the translation of the first word, then of the first two words and so on. Each index j in $[1:J]$ is thus associated with a set $\mathcal{H}_j$ of translation hypotheses, where each translation receives a partial score equal to the cumulated sum of costs up to the associated vertex. In the absence of other weights, only the best hypothesis in $\mathcal{H}_j$ needs to be considered and the others can be safely discarded. This is because any suboptimal partial hypothesis can only be developed into a complete suboptimal solution. Consider, for instance, the graph in Figure 7.11. The node 2 contains the following hypotheses {[ce][petit]; [ce][petite]; [ce][petits]; [ce petit]; [cette petite] . . .}: only the best of these can occur in a complete best path. This illustrates the application of a *recombination* principle among partial hypotheses, which guarantees the efficiency of the dynamic programming techniques used to solve shortest path problems.

Taking a target language model into account makes things slightly more complicated, as the syntactic cost c_s of each target segment now depends on its left context. Let us study how this cost is calculated, assuming, for the sake of simplicity, a bigram language model. For bisegments comprising more than two target words, the "internal" syntactic cost (see Table 7.3) corresponds to the inverse of the bigram log-likelihood of the segment: $B[i].c_s = -\sum_{t=2}^{T[x].I} \log (P(B[i].e[t]|B[i].e[t-1]))$. There is also an "external" cost, which corresponds to the bigram score of the word $B[i].e[1]$ *given the preceding word in the current hypothesis*. This means that such scores can no longer be used to weight arcs independently of the preceding arcs on the same path. An easy fix is to partition the hypotheses in $\mathcal{H}_j$ with respect to their last target word w, giving rise to subsets $\mathcal{H}_{j, w_1} \ldots \mathcal{H}_{j, w_n}$. Within each such subset, only the best hypothesis is kept and developed, by considering all the bisegments $B[i]$ covering the next untranslated word(s); the scores of resulting hypotheses will integrate, in addition to the translation model cost, a bigram cost $-\log P(B[i].e[1]|w)$. An implementation of this approach consists in expending the search graph so as to include one node for each prefix of f and for the last preceding target word, as in Figure 7.12. In this example, node (2c) corresponds to all the hypotheses translating *this small* and ending with "petite".

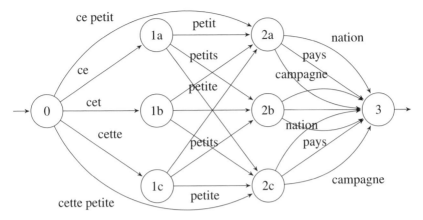

Figure 7.12. *The search space of monotone translation, with a bigram target language model . Some arcs are omitted. The source sentence is: this small country.*

This approach generalizes straightforwardly to higher order language models. Taking longer dependencies into account however badly affects the size of the search space, by increasing the number of hypotheses subsets that must be considered at each state. In fact, a separate set of hypotheses needs to be stored for each possible language model's history, a number which increases exponentially with the language model order (see section 7.2.3). When using "large" translation models[32] and high-order (3-gram or 4-gram) language models, handling the number of hypotheses to be considered becomes untractable, and pruning techniques must be used (see below), at the risk of no longer finding the optimal solution.

7.5.3.2. *Translating with local reorderings*

Now let us consider how this search strategy must be modified to take local reorderings into account. We consider here the simple case in which only adjacent source segments can be inverted in the target (see section 7.4.1). The only change of the search algorithm is to modify the definition of the underlying word graph (represented, in the monotone case, in Figure 7.11). This can be simulated by the following two-step process[33]:

1) compute the set of authorized permutations of the source as a weighted word graph G_r;

---

32 The Europarl corpus [KOE 05] currently contains approximately one and a half million parallel sentences for the French-English language pair; a translation model extracted from this data typically contains millions of bisegments.

33 This point of view is adopted to simplify the presentation: it is obviously possible to implement this idea by expending the dynamic search graph as needed while traversing it.

2) explore G_r in the same manner as before, making sure that:
    a) there exists a set of partial hypotheses for each vertex in G_r;
    b) the computation of the total cost includes the reordering model cost.

The first step is straightforward: it suffices to generate all the segmentations of f licensed by the phrase table, and, for each pair of adjacent segments, to consider the possibility that they might be swapped in the target language. Continuing with the sentence f = *this small nation* ..., the corresponding permutation graph is partially represented in Figure 7.13.

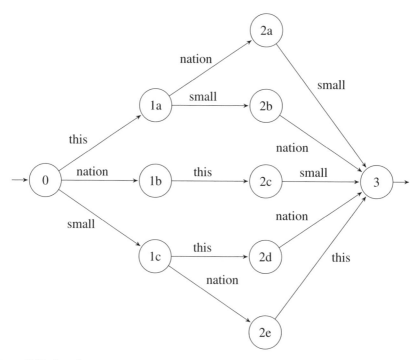

Figure 7.13. *Local source permutations of* this small nation. *Only a small subset of the actual permutations is represented*

The set of all possible translation candidates is obtained simply by replacing each arc in G_r labeled by the segment f with arcs labeled by possible translations of f. This graph can then be explored as before, associating sets of partial hypotheses with each vertex.

A generic implementation of the techniques described in this section rests on the formalism of finite-state transducers. Such implementations are presented in

[BAN 02, CAS 04] for word-based models, and in [KUM 03, KUM 06] for phrase-based models. The advantage is that this approach relies on well-known and efficient algorithms, for which efficient implementations exist and have been successfully used, for instance, for automatic speech recognition [MOH 02]. Many standard extensions of these techniques are also readily available, such as pruning parts of the search space (see below), generating lists of n-best hypotheses or word lattices[34], and so on.

7.5.4. *Heuristic search algorithms*

Exact search techniques are only possible at the cost of drastically restricting the reorderings that are explored during search. For many language pairs, local reorderings are too restrictive, and a much larger set of permutations needs to be explored by considering long distance reordering. This, in turn, implies that we have to abandon exact search techniques and to resort to heuristic search strategies. Four main approaches are discussed in the literature:

– the use of *best first* search techniques, which are mostly inspired by the A^* family of algorithms [PEA 84];

– the use of greedy *local search* techniques: in this framework, an initial translation hypothesis is incrementally improved by searching better translations in the neighborhood of the current solution;

– the use of monotone decoding techniques (see above), applied on much larger permutation sets: this strategy can be applied in the source (generation of permutations of the source followed by a monotone decoding step), or in the target language (generation of a monotone translation and exploration of the possible permutations of the translation hypotheses). This, for example, is the approach followed by [CRE 07]. The main difficulty here is the definition of a plausible set of permutations, as the search itself is performed according to the general principles described above;

– the transformation of the decoding problem into a known combinatorial problem which can then be solved using general purpose solvers; [GER 01] applies this technique by transforming the problem of translation with word models into a linear integer programming problem; more recently, [ZAS 09] uses a reduction into the traveling salesman problem.

In the remainder of this section, we detail possible implementations of the best-first and local search approaches.

7.5.4.1. *"Best first" search*

The general principle of "best first" search algorithms is to explore a subset of the possible reorderings while constructing partial translations of arbitrary parts of the

---

34 Formally, weighted automata representing a set of translation hypotheses.

source sentence. Each translation hypothesis h must therefore remember the portions $h.span$ of source sentence that have already been translated, so that the same fragment is not translated several times. Conceptually, the algorithm performs the following operations in an iterative manner, until exhaustion of the stock of partial translation hypotheses:

1) select a promising hypothesis h of cost $h.c$ in the stock of available hypotheses, h covering $h.span$;

2) choose an untranslated source segment not yet covered by h;

3) select a translation for this segment, giving rise to a new partial hypothesis h', which now covers a larger portion of the source sentence.

The efficiency of this approach depends on the selection of the next hypothesis to develop at a given step. At this stage, we need to compare the scores of translation hypotheses *covering different portions of the source sentence*. The most common approach is sketched in Algorithm 7.3, often referred to as "multistack" decoding[35]. In this implementation, partial hypotheses are grouped into subsets according to the length of the source span they cover. For a source sentence of length J, the algorithm thus maintains J priority queues. If two hypotheses belonging to the same queue are then more directly comparable, comparing partial costs is not always fair. In fact, hypotheses covering the *easy to translate* parts of the source will often have a smaller cost than hypotheses covering the *difficult* parts; so two hypotheses can only be compared if we can integrate the future cost incurred by the yet untranslated portions, or, at least, of a good approximation of this score. This approximation is denoted $h.g$ and includes an approximation of the future translation cost $h.g_t$, of the future language model cost $h.g_s$, and so on. Three additional elements are necessary to make a more formal presentation of the search algorithm:

– a *recombination* policy of the hypotheses sharing the same future, implemented below by the function AddRecombine;

– a *pruning* policy, which is needed to restrict the combinatorial explosion of partial hypotheses. Pruning is performed below by the function Pruning;

– *reordering constraints*, which are necessary to keep the number of hypotheses manageable. These constraints are integrated in the function Develop of Algorithm 7.3.

Using these functions, the multistack decoding algorithm for phrase-based translations [KOE 04, MOO 07] is formalized in Algorithm 7.3.

---

35 The terminology is once more a bit misleading here: the most obvious implementation of this strategy is to store hypotheses in priority queues, rather than in stacks.

Algorithm 7.3. Best first search

---

for $j \in [1{:}\,J]$ **do**
$\quad \mid \; \mathcal{H}_j \leftarrow \emptyset;$
end
$\mathcal{H}_0 \leftarrow \{h_0\};$
for $j \in [0{:}\,J-1]$ **do**
$\quad$ **for** $h \in \mathcal{H}_i$ **do**
$\qquad$ **for** $h' \in \mathtt{Develop}(h)$ **do**
$\qquad\quad k \leftarrow |h'.span|;$
$\qquad\quad \mathtt{AddRecombine}(h', \mathcal{H}_k);$
$\qquad\quad \mathtt{Prune}(\mathcal{H}_k);$
$\qquad$ **end**
$\quad$ **end**
end
$\mathbf{e}_c = \{\mathrm{argmin}_{h \in \mathcal{H}_J}\, h.c\}.\mathbf{e};$
return $(\mathbf{e}_c);$

7.5.4.1.1. Expending hypotheses

The function $\mathtt{Develop}$ develops a translation hypothesis h by adding a bisegment $b = (f, e)$ covering the (yet untranslated) segment $[j_1{:}\,j_2]$ in f. Specific constraints on the possible reorderings are used to restrict this choice (see section 7.4.1). The resulting hypothesis h' corresponds to a translation prefix $h'.\mathbf{e} = h.\mathbf{e}.e$ and covers $h'.span = h.span \cup [j_1 : j_2]$. Its actual cost is deduced from the score of h:

$$h'.c = h.c + \lambda_t c_t(f, e) + \lambda_r c_r(f, e, j_1, h) + \lambda_s(h.\mathbf{e}, e)$$

The *future cost* $h.g$ associated with h integrates several terms [MOO 07]:

– the first corresponds to the anticipated cost of the translation model, which can be approximated by taking the cost of the best possible translation for each non-covered portion of the source sentence;

– the second corresponds to an estimation of the language model cost, and is calculated from the internal syntactic costs of the segments used to produce the previous approximation;

– the third corresponds to an anticipated cost of reordering and is deduced, for example, from the particular form of the portion of the source yet to be covered.

The precision of the search depends on the quality of these approximations: for the A^* algorithm, it is necessary that they yield an overestimation of the actual cost.

7.5.4.1.2. Managing hypotheses

The hypothesis queue is managed by the function AddRecombine(h', $\mathcal{H}$), which performs two operations. The first consists of searching whether the queue already contains an *equivalent* hypothesis, in other words a hypothesis h'' (i) which covers the same part of the source sentence, and (ii) which shares with h' a common suffix of length equal to the language model order. If this is the case, the same hypotheses can be derived from h' and h'' with identical future scores, and only the best of the two needs to be kept. If there is no equivalent hypothesis, this function simply inserts h' into the queue.

7.5.4.1.3. Pruning

Pruning is required to ensure that the priority queues $\mathcal{H}_j$ do not grow too much, which would make their exploration too costly. There are two main pruning policies, which yield slightly different instantiations of the Prune function:

– one controls *the size of the search beam* and is known as *beam pruning*. It consists of conserving only the hypotheses whose cost (including the anticipated cost) is not too far from the cost of the best hypothesis h_b of $\mathcal{H}_|$: conversely, any hypothesis h in $\mathcal{H}_|$, such that $(h.c + h.g) > (1 + \alpha)(h_b.c + h_b.g)$, where α is a (positive) parameter which determines the size of the beam, is discarded;

– the other consists in setting a maximum size n for $\mathcal{H}_j$, and to keep only the n best values in each queue. This strategy is known as *histogram pruning*, and enables us to better control the memory footprint required to run the search algorithm.

7.5.4.2. *Greedy search and local exploration*

Local search algorithms implement a *greedy* exploration of the search space. Starting with an initial "cheap"[36] solution, the idea is to explore the neighborhood of this solution to find better hypotheses, i.e. hypotheses with lower costs. If one is found, the best current translation is updated and the search continues by exploring the resulting new neighborhood; if not, the search stops with a *locally optimal solution*, meaning that there may be better translations in the vicinity of this optimum. This idea is formalized by Algorithm 7.4.

One strength of this technique is that it only considers complete, rather than partial, translation hypotheses, which are therefore easier to compare and can be evaluated globally.

Local search strategies can be implemented in many ways, depending on the particular choices for (i) the computation of an initial solution and (ii) the definition of neighborhoods. The second point is particularly critical, since the compromise between

---

36 Obtained, for instance, by a monotone decoding.

Algorithm 7.4. Local search

$h_c \leftarrow$ SimpleTranslation(f);
$stop =$ false;
while $(stop =$ false$)$ **do**
  $h_v.\mathbf{e} = \{\}; h_v.c = +\infty;$
  for $(h \in$ Neighbors$(h_c))$ **do**
    if $(h.c < c_v)$ **then**
      $h_v \leftarrow h; c_v \leftarrow h.c;$
    end
  end
  if $(h.c < h_v.c)$ **then**
    $h_c \leftarrow h;$
  else
    $stop =$ true;
  end
end
return $(h_c.\mathbf{e})$;

the quality of the obtained approximation and the speed of the exploration depends on the definition of the neighborhood.

The approach proposed in [GER 01, GER 03], in the framework of word-based translation models, considers that the neighborhood of a candidate translation contains all the sentences that can be obtained by modifying the translation of one or two words, by inserting or removing a word, by merging two words or even by moving a group of words. [LAN 07] develops a similar approach in the framework of phrase-based translation models: the neighborhood of a translation is obtained by considering the possibility of moving a segment in the target language, changing the translation of one or two source segments, or of even modifying the underlying source segmentation. This study shows that local search can improve the solutions initially produced by the Pharaoh decoder [KOE 04] in almost 40% of the cases. The restrictive definition of the neighborhoods used in these works, in particular as far as reorderings are concerned, is obviously linked to the impossibility of searching all the possible permutations of the current translation hypothesis; [EIS 06], however, shows that it is possible, using dynamic programming techniques, to evaluate a neighborhood containing a combinatorial number of permutations (all the ITG permutations (introduced in section 7.4.1, page 254)) in polynomial time.

The main benefit of these approaches is in their conceptual simplicity, in particular with respect to tuning the compromise between the quality of the solution produced and the search complexity. It must be finally noted that these techniques can be easily improved by considering several different starting points for the search (*multiple restarts*), or by rejecting small local improvements that could cause the search to get trapped in poor local minima, or by carrying out the search in a non-deterministic fashion, etc.

7.5.5. *Decoding: a solved problem?*

Techniques used to combine multiple probabilistic models and compute translations for arbitrary input sentences have capitalized over years of development of heuristic search algorithms. These algorithms are ubiquitous in many subfields of artificial intelligence, pattern recognition (in particular, for automatic speech or hand-writing recognition), and machine learning. These techniques thus are nowadays relatively mature and deliver very good results, both in terms of processing time or in terms of search errors. Unsurprisingly, they do not seem to be the subject of much active research, with the exception of (i) the parameter tuning stage (see section 7.5.1), which remains computationally very demanding and is likely to produce unstable results and (ii) the definition of multi-pass search strategies, involving for instance the combination of several systems [ROS 07, HIL 08, MAT 08]. This is the general picture that can be drawn for phrase-based systems; other, more complex transduction models (relying, for instance, on synchronous grammars) are much more demanding, and improving the decoding time for these systems remains a important issue.

7.6. Evaluating machine translation

Recent progresses in human language technologies are often associated with the joint development of a scientific evaluation framework. This framework relies on the definitions of what the answer of the system ougth to be and of a metric for comparing systems proposals to this reference output. In most cases, the reference is generated by human annotators and can be considered as the only possible answer, while the metric is an automatic and objective mesure of the quality of the evaluated hypothesis.

For machine translation, both the reference and the metric depend on the application and its context[37] and this can yield to very different requirements. Therefore, in many respects, machine translation shares the same evaluation background as a lot of natural language processing tasks [GAL 95, KIN 96, CHA 08]. For instance, some usages may require us to assess the accuracy of machine translation systems with respect to the intrinsic quality of the produced translations. This, in turn, implies us to assess the quality of a translation, which can hardly be done without involving human judgment.

---

37 However, messing around with the results of online translation systems [ECO 07] cannot be considered as a scientific evaluation.

In other situations, other criteria will need to be taken into account: the computation time; the ability of the system to evolve, to adapt and learn from its errors; the easyness of integration with other softwares (for example, with a text editor or a web browser); or any combination of these criteria. The design of proper evaluation framework is also crucial for researchers and system developers, who need to find out the weaknesses of the systems and to measure the progress.

Thus, the evaluation of machine translation remains a challenging task and a very active research area, where both the subjective and automatic evaluations are used (see, for example, [CAL 10]). Summarizing all these researchs exceeds the scope of this chapter and we will only provide an overview of the most used methods and metrics.

7.6.1. *Subjective evaluations*

A *subjective evaluation* consists of asking one or more human anotators to judge a translation with respect to various subjective criteria. The most widely used criteria are intelligibility, fluency, fidelity, adequacy and informativity. Let us consider, for example, intelligibility: to evaluate this criterion judges would typically be asked to assess, on a numerical scale, how easy the translation is to understand. Note that bilingual judges are required to assess fidelity, since this criterion quantifies the degree of semantic equivalence between the source and target sentences. On the contrary, other criteria, such as fluency, only require us to look at the generated text and can be assessed by monolingual judges. This latter kind of judgments are thus easier to collect. Using this general framework, multiple evaluation protocols have been proposed, which differ according to:

– the translation units under consideration (a paragraph, a sentence or a fragment of sentence);

– the evaluated criteria;

– the numerical scales.

One drawback of using fixed numerical scales is the bias they introduce and the disagreements between annotators. Therefore, when several systems are to be evaluated on the same task, human evaluations may alternatively rely on comparisons and rank the outputs of different machine translation systems from best to worst. The resulting scores are *relative* and simply allow us to compare different systems or different variations of the same system. This is, for example, the approach adopted in recent evaluation campaigns [CAL 08, CAL 09b].

A third approach is to use *task-oriented evaluations*, where human annotators must complete a specific task with the help of a machine translation system [BLA 07], such as answering factual questions on the source document using only its translated texts, finding information online, or even translating a document by post-editing an automatic translation [SPE 11]. Translation quality is then based on the time needed to complete the task or on measures of fulfillment of the task.

The choice of an evaluation protocol for carrying out subjective evaluations ultimately depends on the goals that are pursued. Leaving aside methodological issues, related, for instance, to inter annotator agreement, subjective evaluations however remain very time consuming and costly to collect[38]. For these reasons, they are not well suited for the design phase of machine translation systems. This explains why part of the research effort is focussing on automatic ways to measure translation quality.

7.6.1.1. *Automatic evaluation*

The most common approach in automatic evaluation is a direct comparison of an automatic translation (the hypothesis) with one or several human translations (the reference(s)). The underlying assumption is that the closer the hypothesis is to the reference, the better its quality will be. Similar approaches have been used to evaluate many other natural language processing applications, such as automatic speech recognition. In comparison with subjective evaluations, human annotator are involved just once in the process, when the reference is generated; an arbitrary number of translations can then be automatically evaluated without any additional expense[39].

The key issue for these automatic evaluations is the design of the metric which is used to compare hypotheses and references. In automatic speech recognition, the standard metric is the WER (*Word Error Rate*), which is simply an average of the normalized sentence-level edit distance between hypothesis and reference[40]. While this metric can provide a similarity measurement between two arbitrary sentences, it does not seem appropriate for machine translation. While the definition of a unique reference is, in speech recognition, easy to achieve, this is not the usual case for machine translation. Given an input source, many correct translations are often possible, varying on specific lexical choices, or on the use of different syntactic constructions, changes

---

38 The fact that online translation systems are freely available and widely used makes the collection of subjective judgments on translations very cheap. This can be achieved by asking users to mark or rank the translations generated online. The authors of [CAL 09a] propose to take advantage of crowdsourcing environments as another cheap way to collect human judgements. The issue, here, is the lack of reliability and consistency of these evaluations, which make them difficult to use.

39 The cost of such evaluation does not depend on the number of systems to be compared, which makes a significant difference when organizing evaluation campaigns involving many participants.

40 The edit distance between two sequences measures the minimal amount of edit operations to transform one sequence into the other. In the standard definition, three edit operations are possible: insertion, deletion or substitution [WAG 74].

in word order, an so on: this means that a translation can be correct, and yet have a very poor WER with respect to a given reference. Conversely, small, localized changes, such as removing a negation, might dramatically change the meaning of correct translation, yet incur only a small WER.

Defining translation quality based on comparisons with human reference(s) thus requires us to come up with better metrics, capable, for instance, of accessing similarity of syntactic structure, or similarity of semantic content. Many propositions have been made in that direction, yielding metrics which remain far from perfect, but nonetheless provide the scientific community with useful evaluation tools. The most widely used is the *BLEU* score[41] originally proposed in [PAP 01].

7.6.2. *The BLEU metric*

Similar to the WER metric, the *BLEU* metric is based on the comparison between a hypothesis and one or several reference(s). Formally, $\mathbf{e}$ denotes a translation hypothesis and $\{\mathbf{e}_1, \ldots \mathbf{e}_l\}$ a set of l reference translations of a source sentence f. Let be $c_n(\mathbf{e})$ the number of n-grams occurring in $\mathbf{e}$ and $m_n(\mathbf{e})$ the number of n-grams $\mathbf{e}$ occurring both in $\mathbf{e}$ and *at least in one* reference. The *n-gram precision* $p_n(\mathbf{e})$ is then the ratio between $m_n(\mathbf{e})$ and $c_n(\mathbf{e})$[42]. The $BLEU_k$ score is defined as the *geometric* mean of the n-gram precisions, for n ranging between 1 and k, with two additional refinements:

– if, for a value of n, $c_n(\mathbf{e}) = 0$, then the geometric mean $\sqrt[k]{\prod_{n=1}^{k} p_n(\mathbf{e})}$ will be zero, yielding a zero *BLEU* score for the corresponding hypothesis $\mathbf{e}$, no matter the values of the lower order n-gram precisions. To avoid such situations, the n-gram precision is estimated on large sets (hundreds, even thousands) of hypotheses $\mathbf{E} = \{\mathbf{e}^{(1)} \ldots \mathbf{e}^N\}$ by:

$$p_n(\mathbf{E}) = \frac{\sum_{i=1}^{N} m_n(\mathbf{e}^{(i)})}{\sum_{i=1}^{N} c_n(\mathbf{e}^{(i)})}$$

A consequence is that *BLEU* is not suited for measuring the quality of isolated sentences, and is best used as a corpus-level metric.

– A simple way to obtain a high n-gram precision is to generate short hypotheses: with fewer words, there is less chance of making a mistake. It is therefore necessary to correct the average n-gram precision by a factor (BP, for *brevity penalty*, in equation [7.25]) which penalizes hypotheses that are too short, with respect to the

---

41 *BLEU* stands for *Bilingual Evaluation Understudy*.

42 In fact p_n is the *modified* n-gram precision: $\max(1, \frac{c_n}{m_n})$. Without this change, the precision may unduly reward a system producing a correct word or n-gram *several times*.

references. This factor is also averaged over a set of hypotheses[43]. For a hypothesis **e**, the corresponding penalty $BP(\mathbf{e})$ is defined as follows, where $\mathbf{e}_i$ denotes the "best" reference associated with **e**:

$$BP(\mathbf{e}) = \begin{cases} 1 \text{ if } |\mathbf{e}| > |\mathbf{e}_i| \\ \exp\left(1 - \frac{|\mathbf{e}_i|}{|\mathbf{e}|}\right) \text{ if not.} \end{cases}$$

In summary, the $BLEU$ score of the set of hypotheses **E** is given by[44]:

$$BLEU_k(\mathbf{E}) = BP \times \exp\left(\sum_{n=1}^{k} \frac{1}{k} \log(p_n(\mathbf{E}))\right) \qquad [7.25]$$

By construction, the $BLEU_k$ score is between 0 and 1, this last value being attained when the hypothesis is identical to a reference translation[45]. The computation of the $BLEU_4$ score is detailed in Figure 7.14, using one single sentence for the illustration.

f	I think the suggestion is worth looking into.
$\mathbf{e}_1$ $\mathbf{e}_2$	je pense que la suggestion vaut la peine que l' on s' y intéresse. à mon avis, la proposition est digne d' être prise en considération.
$\mathbf{e}$	je pense que la proposition est la peine de réfléchir.
$c_1(\mathbf{e})$ $c_2(\mathbf{e})$ $c_3(\mathbf{e})$ $c_4(\mathbf{e})$ BP $BLEU_4(\mathbf{e})$	9: je, pense, que, la, proposition, est, la, peine, . 6: je pense, pense que, que la, la proposition, proposition est, la peine 3: je pense que, pense que la, la proposition est 1: je pense que la $\exp(1 - 14/11) \approx 0.76$ $BP \times \exp\left(0.25 \times (\log(9/11) + \log(6/10) + \log(3/9) + \log(1/8))\right)$ ≈ 0.29

Figure 7.14. *Details of the BLEU score computation*

The $BLEU_k$ family of metrics introduces two innovations which compensate, to a certain extent, for the deficiencies of the WER mentioned earlier:

– This metric is able to take several references into account

---

43 When several references are available, there are different ways to estimate this factor by taking into account the longest, the shortest or the closest reference in terms of length.

44 In some variations of the $BLEU$ score, each each n-gram precision can be weighted differentially. However, in practice, the precisions are uniformly weighted.

45 When there is only one reference.

– For admissible word order variations, the $BLEU$ score is more tolerant than the WER and more accurate than metrics that only consider isolated word matching.

Moreover, this metric is extremely simple to compute and only involves straightforward comparisons between word sequences.

The $BLEU$ score only gives very raw estimates of the translation quality, delivering numerical values that are difficult to interpret. Its use by the scientific community is motivated by the observed statistical correlation between the $BLEU$ score at the corpus level and human judgments. It is therefore more or less accepted that (i) any improvement of $BLEU$ above a certain value would imply a significant improvement of the human judgments and that (ii) for a given corpus, the system with the best $BLEU$ score would also deliver the best translations as judged by human readers. The last international evaluations conducted in the framework of WMT[46] [CAL 08, CAL 09b] and NIST campaigns[47] conclude that these assertions are (almost) true, if sufficiently large evaluation corpora, containing several translation references, are used.

7.6.3. *Alternatives to $BLEU$*

The shortcomings of the $BLEU$ score are numerous and well documented: this metric is not able to evaluate the quality of isolated sentences; it is based only on statistics collected on a per sentence basis and therefore cannot evaluate the consistency of a translation at the text level; it relies only on word similarities between word surface forms and ignores the information carried by translated words; it favors statistical translation systems at the expense of other kinds of systems, in particular rule-based systems, and so on (see, for instance, [CAL 06, CHI 08a]).

New metrics have been recently introduced to achieve a better correlation with human judgment (see [CAL 09b]). These metrics rely, in particular, on the progress of the automatic processing of natural languages and on richer linguistic resources, which enable the implementation of fine-grained similarity measures. For instance, METEOR [BAN 05] uses lemmatization tools and semantic resources to detect synonymous words. This method does however require robust and efficient tools that are able to process machine translation outputs, which are sometimes far from being grammatically correct.

Another interesting proposition is the TER (*Translation Edit Rate*) family [SNO 06]. H-TER (for *Human* TER) quantifies the quality of a translation by the effort required by an expert to transform it into a correct translation. The post-edition cost

---

46 www.statmt.org/wmt10, http://www.statmt.org/wmt11, and so on.

47 www.itl.nist.gov/iad/mig/tests/mt.

measured by the H-TER is easier to interpret than $BLEU$. Moreover, H-TER is well suited for evaluation both at the sentence and corpus level. As long as one reference translation is available, a monolingual judge can carry on this post-editing at a much lower cost than the production of several references.

There is another good reason to prefer TER-like metrics. The comparison between a hypothesis and references implemented for instance in $BLEU$ only makes sense when the reference can be generated by the system: this implies, for instance, that the vocabulary of a translation system must contain all the words of the reference. Otherwise, the metric acts as a teacher punishing a student for not knowing a lesson which has not yet been taught. The H-TER metric, measuring the gap between the hypothesis and the *closest correct* translation, does not suffer such bias. In practice however, this human post-editing stage is skipped, and the TER metric is mostly used, replacing post-edited references with references constructed *a priori*.

Formally, TER is calculated as the minimal number of edit operations necessary to transform an automatic output to the closest reference translation; the authorized operations are the standard edit operations (substitution, deletion, word insertion), to which a new operation, consisting of moving a word or a group of words is added. By noting $\Delta(\mathbf{e}, \mathbf{e}_i)$ the minimum number of operations needed to transform $\mathbf{e}$ into $\mathbf{e}_i$, the TER score of $\mathbf{e}$ is expressed as:

$$TER(\mathbf{e}) = \min_{\mathbf{e}_1 \ldots \mathbf{e}_l} \frac{\Delta(\mathbf{e}, \mathbf{e}_i)}{|\mathbf{e}_i|} \qquad [7.26]$$

The computation of this illustrated in Figure 7.15.

Reference	*Saudi Arabia* denied *this week* information published in the *American New York times*
Hypothesis	*this week* *the Saudis* denied information published in the *New York times*
$\Delta(\mathbf{e}, \mathbf{e}') = 4$: move(*this week*), substitute(*Saudi, the*), substitute(*Arabia, Saudis*), delete(*American*)	

Figure 7.15. *Details of the TER score computation (according to [SNO 06])*

Computing the TER score however presents a major difficulty, since the evaluation of $\Delta(\mathbf{e}, \mathbf{e}_i)$ involves the resolution of a NP-hard optimization problem[48]: computing TER scores is thus algorithmically more costly than $BLEU$ scores, and, in practice,

---

48 The difficulty comes from the movement of blocks: when this operation is forbidden, the computation of the edit distance between two sequences is solved in a polynomial time and space through dynamic programming.

only approximations are ever obtained[49]. This metric remains widely used and several variations exist, which refine the definition of the edit operation costs by integrating linguistic knowledge (TERp [SNO 09]) so as, for instance, to reduce the cost of substituting synonyms or morphologically related words.

7.6.4. *Evaluating machine translation: an open problem*

In summary, most automatic evaluation metrics for machine translation rely on the availability of a set of reference translations with which the translation hypotheses will be compared. By nature, these metrics are not adapted to measure the overall quality of the translation of documents. In addition, the comparison functions used are most often very rough. Designing comparison scores between sentences which could take into account their semantic proximity, while being quick to calculate and robust to very ungrammatical inputs is a challenge which, despite active research, remains open.

The development of machine translation systems crucially depends on automatic scores such as $BLEU$ or TER, and they remain, for lack of better alternatives, widely used. In parallel, the use of evaluation protocols based on human judgments in addition to reference translations, provides an increasingly credible alternative for comparing systems and has been used in practice in several recent evaluation campaigns.

7.7. State-of-the-art and recent developments

In this section, some of the more recent developments in statistical translation are briefly discussed in order to highlight some limitations of the phrase-based translation models. One recurrent criticism which warrants many extensions presented below, is their lack of generalization, which needs to be compensated with more resources, more sophisticated models, and deeper linguistic analyses. The references mentioned below will serve as entry points into the very rich literature on the variations and extensions of the standard model.

Before getting started, note that we will not review here the recent works on alignment. On many aspects, alignment models have the same limitations as translation models, and there also exists a very active research aimed at improving these alignments. Refer to the recent [TIE 11] for an overview.

7.7.1. *Using source context*

Phrase-based models, similar to word-based models introduced in 7.2.2, do not take into account the context of source phrases for choosing their translation. In fact,

---

49 www.cs.umd.edu/~snover/tercom.

the scores associated with segments are computed once and for all during the learning stage (see section 7.3.3). When a source segment has several possible translations, they will be mainly disambiguated by the target language model (see the discussion in section 7.1). Intuitively, this situation is not very satisfactory: for an ambiguous word such as "voler" which can be translated as *to fly* or *to steal*, if source words such as "avion" (*plane*) or "voyage" (*travel*) are found in the context, then the translation *fly* should be reinforced and the translation of *steal* should be made less probable. Such inferences are made possible by the knowledge of the entire source sentence, sometimes of the entire source document. Use of the knowledge extracted from the neighbors of a segment to improve its translation is a well-known principle in example-based translation and has been implemented in many ways within the framework of probabilistic models. In the following discussion, we distinguish between the local or micro-context of a segment, which corresponds to a number of adjacent words, and the extended or macro-context, which may include other sentences from the same document, or from other, similar, documents.

7.7.1.1. *Using the micro-context*

The work of [CAR 05] proposes to address this problem by taking advantage of *word-sense disambiguation* techniques[50]: the preliminary experiences described in this work, however, show that disambiguating the sense of some isolated words before translating them gives no significant improvement. In [CAR 07], this work is extended to the disambiguation of all the segments: for each sentence to translate, word-sense disambiguation techniques are used to dynamically adapt the translation model to the current source phrase. This proposition is not far from that of [ITT 07], which proposes to define the probability of a bisegment $(f : \mathbf{e})$[51] with an exponential model by writing $P(\mathbf{e}|f) \propto \exp \theta^T F(f, \mathbf{e})$. The same idea is explored, with different means, in [STR 07, GIM 08] and several other papers.

The work of [BAN 07] pushes this approach one step further and studies the behavior of a translation system equipped with a richer translation model. This translation model is conceptually very simple: given the source sentence f, for each word e in the target vocabulary, a binary classifier decides the presence or the absence of this word in the translation. The authors propose to learn logistic regression models to define $P(e|f)$: the context taken into account includes the entire source sentence. A major difference with the previous context-based models is thus that *word alignments are no longer needed to estimate the model*. Translation of a new sentence f is performed as follows: the inclusion of all possible target words in the translation is first evaluated: the authors propose to keep all the words e such that $P(e|f)$ exceeds a threshold. Then, a target language model chooses the best permutation of the set of

---

50 Word-sense disambiguation (WSD for short) is understood in NLP as matching the occurrence of a lemma in its context and one of the possible sense in a finite inventory of possible senses.

51 In this model, the source segments do not contain a single word.

selected words. This approach has many weaknesses (translation is word-based, no reordering model is used) and does not compare favorably, in terms of its performance, with more standard approaches. Results obtained are, however, interesting and show an improvement in the lexical choices with respect to segment models.

To summarize, it seems that accounting for the micro-context to dynamically evaluate the segments can provide performance improvements, but these gains remain relatively modest in comparison to the computational cost needed to train and to use these models.

7.7.1.2. *Using the Macro-context*

Taking into account the macro-context has been comparatively less studied, perhaps because, as discussed above, most test protocols and corpora only consider the translation of isolated sentences. Several authors have, however, tried to take document-level information into account in order to improve the translation and/or the language models.

The problem is often formulated as an *adaptation* problem of a general translation model to a specific genre, register or topic. This problem is reminiscent of the well-known issue of adapting statistical language models for automatic speech recognition. There are numerous techniques for this (see e.g. [DEM 98, BEL 01]) which borrow both from the information retrieval toolbox and from standard statistical techniques, such as the dynamic construction of a learning corpus, the use of unsupervised document classification techniques, and of mixture or exponential models. These techniques can be directly used for adapting statistical language models in MT. Adapting the translation model is somewhat less direct, as this side of the problem presents both some simplifying (for instance, the entirety of the source documents to translate can be known beforehand) and complexifying (the collections that are modeled are parallel) aspects. The reader can refer to [FOS 07, BER 09, FOS 10] and to the references cited therein for a more complete presentation of this research area.

7.7.2. *Hierarchical models*

Phrase-based translation models make their decisions based on statistical analyses of large corpora of parallel texts. The uneven distribution of word occurrences in text corpora, aggravated by the imperfection of the alignment algorithms, cause most bisegments to occur with a very small frequency; furthermore, many good and useful phrases are not extracted at all.

A consequence of this state of affair is the relatively bad generalization capacity of these models, which require very large amounts of data to achieve reasonable results. The introduction of "hierarchical" segments by [CHI 05] is an attempt to overcome this limitation by licencing "gappy" segments, an idea already present in

[SIM 05]. The main idea of this generalization of phrase-based models consists of extracting synchronous context-free grammar rules (these grammars were presented in section 7.4.1) instead of bisegments from alignment matrices (see section 7.3.3.2).

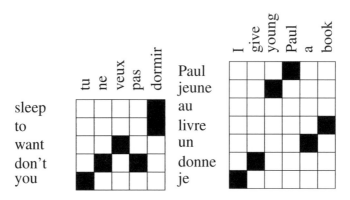

Figure 7.16. *Extraction of hierarchical segments*

Let us consider, for instance, the matrix reproduced in Figure 7.16. As the English *don't* aligns with two French words ("ne and pas") which surround "veux", extraction algorithm presented in section 7.3.3.2 can only identify two bisegments: (veux, *want*) and (ne veux pas, *don't want*). The "correct" linguistic generalization, consisting of detecting that negation in French is formed by encapsulating a verbal form between two negation adverbs, while the English uses an auxiliary, is thus missed. This means that the negation pattern learned for the pair (veux, *want*) will not generalize to other verbs. The proposal of [CHI 05] which was then reconsidered and refined in several subsequent works [ZOL 06, HUA 07, LOP 08b, IGL 09], consists of using synchronous context-free rules as the basic translation unit (see section 7.4.1). In the case of the previous example, the two rules $X \rightarrow$ veux; want and $X \rightarrow$ ne X pas; don't X would thus be extracted: in the latter, the sub-block (veux, *want*) is extracted and replaced by a variable X. In the example on the right of Figure 7.16, the extraction of hierarchical segments allows the extraction of rules such as $X \rightarrow$ donne X_1 à X_2 ; *give* $X_2 X_1$, which capture the inversion of the complements between the French "donne" and the English ditransitive *give*. This second example illustrates the benefit of hierarchical rules for modeling reorderings: the previous rule can be applied for swapping the complements of all occurrences of "donne", regardless of the number of words they contain.

This approach raises several issues: on the one hand, this procedure extracts many more rules than the algorithm described in section 7.3.3.1 would extract bisegments. This is because all the possible ways to extract *and to generalize* one or two sub-blocks must be considered. This means that numerous synchronous rules are extracted which are linguistically absurd or have no generalization capacity. This is the case for the following synchronous rule in which the determinant is generalized by a variable:

$X \rightarrow X$ livre au jeune Paul; young Paul X book

It therefore becomes necessary to design strategies for controlling the number of rules extracted, to filter the less probable ones and to finally associate probabilities with these different rules. Furthermore, the use of a synchronous grammar in translation implies that we need to replace the search algorithms presented in section 7.5 by parsing algorithms for context-free grammars. These algorithms not only have a worst complexity[52]; they also build the target sentence from bottom-to-top instead of left-to-right. This complicates the interaction with the language model during the decoding and requires the development of more elaborate search strategies [HUA 07].

7.7.3. *Translating with linguistic resources*

A great strength of statistical machine translation is that it can readily apply to almost any language pair, provided sufficient parallel data is available to train the model. This ability to adapt to diverse linguistic environments is also a consequence of their extreme linguistic naivety. In most cases, translation units correspond to strings of characters; segments are "flat" collections of adjacent word forms and do not have, contrary contrarily to what the terminology suggests, any syntactic relevance. From this point of view, these models comprise a regression with respect to traditional rule-based systems, where the transfer and generation rules typically rely on a lexical, morphological, and syntactic analysis of the source sentence, and likewise in the target language. This linguistic naivety is seen as a source of many translation errors and also a reason why MT systems deliver so many ungrammatical target sentences [VIL 06].

In many respects, the construction of a translation system suffers from this limitation and approaches are aiming to integrate more linguistic knowledge into the statistical translation models have been investigated for all the modeling steps presented in this chapter.

The most significant efforts have focused on the use of morphological and syntactic knowledge in the source and target language. Research on morphology-informed statistical machine translation has suffered from the relative morphological simplicity of the languages that often used as the source (especially Chinese) and as the target (English). On the other hand, works aimed at introducing more syntax have largely benefited from the availability of robust syntactic analysis tools (both dependency and constituent analyzers), which now exist for many languages.

---

52 The simplest of these algorithms, CYK [YOU 67], has a cubic complexity with respect to the length of the source phrase. To be able to work with non-normalized grammars, the generalization proposed in [CHA 98] is commonly used.

7.7.3.1. *Bilingual terminologies and dictionaries*

The most obvious idea for introducing linguistic knowledge consists of using bilingual dictionaries and terminologies, which contain valid associations between words and terms in the source and target languages. From a technical point of view, the use of such resources is straightforward. It suffices to include these resources during the alignment, resulting in a very positive effect on the parameters associated with rare words (see e.g. [BRO 93a, NIE 04]). For the construction of translation models, dictionary entries can be readily included in the segment table. The expected benefit of this strategy is obviously to reduce the number of words that are unknown to the system and which will cause systematic errors[53]. This strategy is not always a winner, as far as it can increase the ambiguity of the system, by inserting into translation models associations which do not exist in the training corpus and which are perhaps useless for the given application. Refer to [SCH 08] for example for a description of this approach and of the correlated performance improvements.

7.7.3.2. *Morphological analysis in MT*

Using non-analyzed word forms in statistical models raises three types of relatively distinct issues. The first problems derives from the fact that related morphological forms, for example conjugated forms of the same verb, or more generally inflected forms of the same lemma, are seen by the models as completely different entities. One consequence is that the statistical information collected on a morphological family cannot transmit to the other words of the same family. Knowing that *cat* is a translation of "chat" does not help to translate *cats* into "chats". This situation is particularly damaging for languages with rich inflected systems (Latin, German, Russian, etc.). The probability that the learning corpus covers (with enough representatives) all the forms of a lemma diminishes with the number of possible forms; the unknown forms are more numerous; the probabilities of the known forms are less well estimated. [NIE 04] proposes to remedy this problem by making the relationships between forms explicit, which will improve the generalization of the translation model. To this end, the authors propose to represent a form by a vector of features containing the form itself, its lemma and its morphological properties. The same kind of representation underpins the "factorized" models [KOE 07a]: in this approach, a complete statistical translations system is learned separately for *each of the component of the feature vector*. During the translation of an unknown sentence, translation proceeds through three stages: construction of the feature vectors, translation of each component and the *generation* of the target phrase from the target feature vectors.

A second problem stems from the divergence between the morphological systems in the target and source languages, in particular the divergences pertaining to the

---

53 The standard behavior is to copy unknown source words *verbatim* in the target sentence. This will often yield valid translations for proper names when the source and target languages use the sames script.

notion of a word. These situations are particularly problematic during the alignment stage, which involves the construction of correspondences in the two directions before symmetrization (see section 7.4.1), and which therefore, implicitly assumes that the source and target sentences are (more or less) of the same length. Depending on the translation direction, various hacks can be entertained. For instance, techniques can be used to segment complex forms into smaller units, which also has a positive effect on the model generalization capacities: see, for example [KOE 03a] for a work on the segmentation of German, [OFL 07] for a study of various segmentation strategies for translation from English to Turkish and [CHU 09] for a recent work aiming to learn the segmentation of complex forms in an automatic alignment context. The other option is obviously to construct word clusters in the language in which the sentences are the longest, see, for example, [NIE 04].

A third problem stems from the fact that languages differ in the way they use morphological marks (see section 7.2.2). This situation complicates the translation from languages which mark little distinction (e.g. English), into those which mark many (e.g. German), since most source forms can be translated into several target forms, requiring the implementation of new disambiguation strategies. Consider for instance the English form *think*, which can translate into French as "penser", "pense", "penses", "pensons", and so on. This problem is discussed in [UEF 03] which, for translating English to Spanish, constructs on the source side verbal complexes integrating certain clitic pronouns (the subject, reflex pronouns), modals and auxiliaries, in order to facilitate the alignment and translation. It is also possible to envisage this disambiguation in the form of a target post processing, as proposed by [MIN 07] and [GIS 08].

7.7.3.3. *Modeling syntactic congruences*

Attempts to use syntactic knowledge in translation share a common assumption: the existence of an isomorphism between the syntactic structures in the source and target languages. Under this hypothesis, the word-for-word associations are expected to be consistent with syntactic structures and are the reflex of associations between constituents. Such associations explain the tendency of words in the same source phrase to "move" as a group in the target language.

This hypothesis also predicts that the same dependency relationships should be found in the source and target sentences. Therefore, if *a* is a dependent of *b* in the source language, then the translation of *a* should be a dependent of the translation equivalent of *b*. The validity of such assumptions is explored in [FOX 02, HWA 02]. Even if they only partially account for the reality of translational equivalences, these assumptions can nonetheless be used at different stages of the development of a statistical translation system.

For instance, several authors have proposed improving the alignments by taking into account morpho-syntactic labels [TOU 02, NEY 04] or syntactic information such as boundaries of phrases or syntactic dependencies (e.g. [LIN 03, ZHA 04, CHE 06, MA 08]). The hypothesis of a syntactic isomorphism between source and target phrases seems, however, too strong and has lead to inconclusive performance improvements (see in particular the analysis of [WEL 06]). The studies reported in [KOE 03b, CHI 08b] aim to improve another stage of the translation model development, namely the extraction and evaluation of segments.

It is also quite natural to try to improve reordering models by integrating syntactic information, and the literature on this issue is abundant. For instance, the work described in [COL 05] shows that, using a small number of linguistically motivated transformations in a preprocessing (*preordering*) stage, it is possible to greatly reduce the divergences between the syntactic structures of German and English sentences, and therefore to simplify the alignment and translation task. It is also possible to learn reordering rules by observing the alignments of syntactic structures in the source and target language (see e.g. [XIA 04, CRE 08]). This idea is similar to the proposal in [CHE 08] to use syntactic constraints for limiting the search space of the translation.

It is finally possible to concentrate on the improvement of target language models, using, for example, stochastic context-free grammars or stochastic dependency grammar (e.g. [YAM 01, CHA 03, SHE 08, POS 08]). The question is more delicate that it might seem, because a target language model is mainly used to decide between (partial) translation hypotheses and to guide the search. In particular, it must be able to evaluate incomplete hypotheses. Stochastic grammars used as target language models are not always very good at that job; furthermore, they often fail to score properly the very ungrammatical sentences that are generated by MT system.

But the most active research seems to focus on the modeling of associations between units corresponding to syntactic constituents in at least one language. This requires us to define probabilistic models, together with their associated estimation and inference procedure, over more formal transduction mechanisms that go beyond rational transductions, so as to relate sub-trees, or sub-parts of dependency graphs. Numerous mechanisms have been proposed and studied in the recent literature, each corresponding to a particular translation mechanism (synchronous grammars, tree transductions, etc.). Early proposals along this line include [YAM 01, CHA 03], which present a translation model converting syntactic trees (in the target language) into word sequences (in the source language); in the "noisy channel" framework, this model is used to define the term $P(f|\mathbf{e})$ in equation [7.2].

Following [ALS 00], the work of [DIN 05] uses a stochastic transducer to relate dependency graphs in the source and target languages, an approach which requires us to analyze both "sides" of the bilingual corpora during learning. In contrast, the approach of [QUI 05] only requires a dependency analyzer in the *source language*. The main idea consists of constructing and estimating models manipulating units of the bilingual translation named *treelets*. These units are linguistically more motivated than segments as they are obtained by projecting source dependency graph on target sentences and by extracting fragments of the constructed graph. Recent works, such as [CAR 09, DEN 09], finally propose to use variants of synchronous tree adjoining grammar, a formalism introduced in [SHI 90]. In addition to these works, let us also mention several studies presenting more theoretical analyses of these various formal systems [EIS 03, MEL 04, SAT 05, GRA 04, KNI 08].

Like for hierarchical models, the use of these "syntax-based" models requires a syntactic analyzer in the target and/or source language. The additional computational effort has not yet been entirely rewarded by correlated improvements of the translation quality, in terms of the efforts engaged. Among the reasons that can explain this relative failure, let us mention that the language pairs which have been the most studied to date (Chinese: English, Arabic: English) are sufficiently close so that simple phrase-based models give results that are difficult to improve. Another reason is the noise introduced by the parsing errors: no analyzer is robust enough to analyze all source sentences without error; the situation is more problematic for the target side, since all the translation hypotheses would need to be analyzed, most of which are very often far from grammatical. It should finally be mentioned that the recent history of the domain has shown that there was much more to expect from an increase of the quantity of training data, which are easily handled by the simpler translation models, than from the design of more complex translation models.

7.8. Useful resources

Statistical machine translation is nowadays one of the most active research areas in computational linguistic. This is illustrated by the number of annual publications, as well as the number of participants to international evaluation campaigns. The main campaigns provide good opportunities to follow the main trends in the field:

– the recent series of international evaluations organized by the NIST (*National Institute of Standards and Technology*) started in 2002 and the last campaign (2009) focused on the translation of Arabic, Chinese, and Urdu into English (see www.itl.nist.gov/iad/mig/tests/mt/);

– the annual workshop on statistical machine translation (*WMT*) includes several shared tasks related to automatic machine translation, system combination and metrics (see www.statmt.org/wmt11);

– the evaluations organized as a shared task for the IWSLT (*International Workshop on Spoken Language Translation* series of workshop, see iwslt2011.org for the most recent edition).

The first two evaluations are focused on the translation of news texts, whereas IWSLT includes also manual and automatic transcriptions of speech. For *WMT*, most of the corpora are freely available on their Web site, whereas for the *NIST* and

IWSLT evaluations, the necessary resources are distributed by the *LDC (Linguistic Data Consortium)*[54] and the *National Institute of Information and Communication Technology* (in Japan), respectively. Note finally, that *IWLST* considers a more constrained task than the others and the associated corpora are significantly smaller. The publications associated with these evaluations will provide readers with a useful snapshot of today's scientific and technological concerns.

7.8.1. *Bibliographic data and online resources*

Most of publications on statistical machine translation are available online from one of the two following Web sites:

– www.mt-archive.info lists most of the articles on machine translation, with online access to those which are freely available in an electronic format;

– aclweb.org/anthology-new is a digital archive of research papers in Computational Linguistics. This Web site therefore covers a broad range of topics, including machine translation and related fields such as parsing and semantic studies.

7.8.2. *Parallel corpora*

In addition to the corpora available through evaluation campaigns (see the beginning of this section), the OPUS project (*open source parallel corpus*) [TIE 09] collects a large collection of parallel texts. The data can be browsed or downloaded from www.let.rug. nl/~tiedeman/OPUS/. These corpora have been produced by Web mining techniques and cover several fields such as official texts (the European Constitution), film subtitles, technical documents related to health or computer science, etc. Note finally that a small technical corpus for the meteorological domain, the RALI Météo corpus, can be downloaded from: www-rali.iro.umontreal.ca/Meteo/index.fr.html.

7.8.3. *Tools for statistical machine translation*

Moses is probably the most widely used *open-source* toolkit (www.statmt.org/moses/). It provides developers with all the necessary components to design vanilla phrase-based systems, and also includes more recent proposals such as hierarchical and factorized models. As an alternative, *cdec* is a mature software platform for research in development of translation models and algorithms (cdec-decoder.org). Finally, the Joshua system (www.cs.jhu.edu/ ccb/joshua/index.html) proposes a ready to use implementation of the hierarchical models presented in

---

54 www.ldc.upenn.edu.

section 7.7.2 and provides functionalities that are equivalent to the Jane hierarchical system (www-i6.informatik.rwth-aachen.de/jane/).

The development of statistical systems also requires tools for training and using word alignments models. The well known Giza++ (code.google.com/p/giza-pp/) implements the main generative alignment models (described in section 7.3.1); a more recent and parallel implementation also exists (geek.kyloo.net/software/doku.php/mgiza:overview), while some more recent innovations in unsupervised word alignment are proposed within the *Berkeley Aligner* package (code.google.com/p/berkeleyalignr/). However, to handle parallel corpora and word alignments, the reader may consider the Uplug tool box (sourceforge.net/projects/uplug/).

Finally, a machine translation system also requires us to estimate statistical language models as well as a programming interface to access probability distributions. The SRI-LM (www.speech.sri.com/projects/srilm/) and IRST-LM (sourceforge.net/projects/irstlm/) address both tasks, while the recent Ken-LM (kheafield.com/code/kenlm/) provides a fast and memory efficient access to large-scale language models.

7.8.3.1. *Evaluation of machine translation*

The automatic evaluation of machine translation can be performed in many ways. To get reliable and comparable numbers, it is necessary to use standard evaluation packages, which implement some of the metrics presented in section 7.6:

– The following script jaguar.ncsl.nist.gov/mt/resources/mteval-v13a.pl was released with the last NIST evaluation campaign and is used to compute $BLEU$ and NIST scores.

– The translation error rate (TER) and its variants (TERp) can be estimated with this package: www.cs.umd.edu/~snover/tercom/.

– The METEOR package (www-2.cs.cmu.edu/~alavie/METEOR/) contains the necessary tools to compute the METEOR score and its recent evolutions.

7.9. Conclusion

In this chapter, the main models and algorithms that are currently used in state-of-the-art statistical machine translation systems have been presented. Our study of translation models has shown the prevalence of word alignment models, which need to be computed in a preprocessing step. Once these word-to-word links have been predicted, extracting and scoring segment-to-segment associations becomes much simpler. Properly modeling translation requires us to model reordering phenomena: as discussed above, this task is quite challenging and the corresponding probabilistic models still fail to capture the subtlety of the underlying linguistic processes. We have then explained how these various models are used in heuristic search algorithms to *decode* input source sentences, thereby generating new translations, before finally discussing issues related to the evaluation of machine translation systems.

Despite their conceptual simplicity, the development of phrase-based systems remains very complex and computationally costly: millions of sentences must be processed, hundreds of millions of numerical parameters must be adjusted in order to finally derive, through optimization on test corpora, statistical decision rules integrating these multiple information sources. All these operations require hours, sometimes days of computations, and cannot be easily repeated when new data becomes available, or when new domains need to be considered. In addition to their lack of adaptability, these systems are also extremely dependent on the amount of available parallel data. For lack of such resources, one active area of research aims to compensate for this rarity by integrating more realistic linguistic models and/or by designing hybrid systems combining the strengths of rule-based and of data-intensive systems. Integration of linguistic models has been thus far been limited by the correlative increase in algorithmic or computational complexity, which is hardly justified by subsequent improvement in translation quality. For these reasons, it is anticipated that the current technology will continue to progress at a relatively slow pace.

Despite its imperfections, machine translation has nowadays achieved a level of quality that is sufficient for numerous uses. And even though artificial translators are unlikely to replace human translators *for the tasks that they currently do*, it is expected that machine translation technologies will continue to expand in the field of professional translations in the form of sophisticated computer-assisted translation environments.

Upon reaching a larger public, machine translation tools are bound to find new applications, and will help to shape the technological developments of tomorrow. For instance, the typical translation scenario, in which a document in a source language A, produced by a speaker/writer having no knowledge of language B, is translated by human translators and delivered to readers with no knowledge of A, is not the only possible one. There exists in fact a whole range of situations of "partial bilingualism" where writers (or readers) know some of the target (or source) language: take the case of travelers in a foreign country, of business partners in different part of the worlds, of migrants, of scientists, etc[55]. Such situations tend to multiply when considering historically related pairs of languages (e.g. romance language), where the understanding is facilitated by numerous shared roots and syntactic structures. In such contexts, multilingual writing/reading/listening modes can be designed in which machine translation devices would facilitate the production or reception of linguistic messages, depending on the specific needs and knowledge of the speaker or hearer.

---

[55] This chapter is yet another illustration of this state of affairs.

Machine Translation is a stimulating and vibrant area that is bound to stimulate much exciting research in the coming years. It is our hope that the basic models presented in this chapter will help readers understand, or, even better, play an active role in these extensions.

7.10. Acknowledgments

In writing this chapter, we have received much help and support from our colleagues at LIMSI/CNRS. We would especially like to thank G. Adda, J.M. Crego, H. Bonnaud-Maynard, and T. Lavergne, with a special mention to A. Max, G. Wisniewski and M. Apidianaki, who provided valuable remarks on initial versions of this chapter.

7.11. Bibliography

[AHO 69] AHO A. V., ULLMAN J., "Syntax Directed Translations and the Pushdown Assembler", *Journal of Computer and System Sciences*, vol. 3, p. 37–56, 1969.

[ALO 06] AL-ONAIZAN Y., PAPINENI K., "Distortion models for statistical machine translation", *Proceedings of the 21st International Conference on Computational Linguistics and 44th Annual Meeting of the Association for Computational Linguistics*, Sydney, Australia, p. 529–536, 2006.

[ALS 00] ALSHAWI H., DOUGLAS S., BANGALORE S., "Learning Dependency Translation Models as Collections of Finite-State Head Transducers", *Computational Linguistics*, vol. 26, num. 1, p. 45–60, 2000.

[BAN 02] BANGALORE S., RICCARDI G., "Stochastic Finite-State Models for Spoken Language Machine Translation", *Machine Translation*, vol. 17, p. 165–184, 2002.

[BAN 05] BANERJEE S., LAVIE A., "METEOR: an automatic metric for MT evaluation with improved correlation with human judgments", *Proceedings of the ACL Workshop on Intrinsic and Extrinsic Evaluation Measures for Machine Translation*, Ann Arbor, Michigan, p. 65–72, 2005.

[BAN 07] BANGALORE S., HAFFNER P., KANTHAK S., "Statistical Machine Translation through Global Lexical Selection and Sentence Reconstruction", *Proceedings of the 45th Annual Meeting of the Association of Computational Linguistics*, Prague, Czech Republic, p. 152–159, 2007.

[BEL 01] BELLAGARDA J. R., "An overview of statistical language model adaptation", *Proceedings of the ISCA Tutorial and Research Workshop (ITRW) on Adaptation Methods for Speech Recognition*, Sophia Antipolis, France, p. 165–174, 2001.

[BER 09] BERTOLDI N., FEDERICO M., "Domain Adaptation for Statistical Machine Translation with Monolingual Resources", *Proceedings of the Fourth Workshop on Statistical Machine Translation*, Athens, Greece, p. 182–189, 2009.

[BIR 09] BIRCH A., BLUNSOM P., OSBORNE M., "A quantitative analysis of reordering phenomena", *Proceedings of the Fourth Workshop on Statistical Machine Translation*, Athens, Greece, Association for Computational Linguistics, p. 197–205, 2009.

[BLA 07] BLANCHON H., BOITET C., "Pour l'évaluation externe des systèmes de TA par des méthodes fondées sur la tâche", *Traitement automatique des langues*, vol. 48, num. 1, p. 33–65, 2007.

[BLU 06] BLUNSOM P., COHN T., "Discriminative word alignment with conditional random fields", *Proceedings of the 21st International Conference on Computational Linguistics and 44th Annual Meeting of the Association for Computational Linguistics*, Sydney, Australia, p. 65–72, 2006.

[BRA 07] BRANTS T., POPAT A. C., XU P., OCH F. J., DEAN J., "Large language models in machine translation", *Proceedings of the 2007 Joint Conference on Empirical Methods in Natural Language Processing and Computational Natural Language Learning (EMNLP-CoNLL)*, p. 858–867, 2007.

[BRO 90] BROWN P. F., COCKE J., PIETRA S. D., PIETRA V. J. D., JELINEK F., LAFFERTY J. D., MERCER R. L., ROOSSIN P. S., "A statistical approach to machine translation", *Computational Linguistics*, vol. 16, num. 2, p. 79–85, 1990.

[BRO 92] BROWN P. F., DESOUZA P. V., MERCER R. L., PIETRA V. J. D., LAI J. C., "Class-based n-gram models of natural language", *Computational Linguistics*, vol. 18, num. 4, p. 467–479, MIT Press, 1992.

[BRO 93a] BROWN P. F., PIETRA S. A. D., PIETRA V. J. D., GOLDSMITH M. J., HAJIC J., MERCER R. L., MOHANTY S., "But Dictionaries Are Data Too", *Proceedings of the ARPA workshop on Human Language Technologies (HLT'93)*, Plainsboro, New Jersey, p. 202–206, 1993.

[BRO 93b] BROWN P. F., PIETRA S. A. D., PIETRA V. J. D., MERCER R. L., "The mathematics of statistical machine translation: parameter estimation", *Computational Linguistics*, vol. 19, num. 2, p. 263–311, 1993.

[CAL 06] CALLISON-BURCH C., OSBORNE M., KOEHN P., "Re-evaluating the role of BLEU in machine translation research", *Proceedings of European Chapter of the Association for Computational Linguistics (EACL)*, Genoa, Italy, p. 249–256, 2006.

[CAL 08] CALLISON-BURCH C., FORDYCE C., KOEHN P., MONZ C., SCHROEDER J., "Further meta-evaluation of machine translation", *Proceedings of the Third Workshop on Statistical Machine Translation*, Columbus, Ohio, p. 70–106, 2008.

[CAL 09a] CALLISON-BURCH C., "Fast, cheap, and creative: evaluating translation quality using Amazon's mechanical turk", *Proceedings of the 2009 Conference on Empirical Methods in Natural Language Processing*, Singapore, p. 286–295, 2009.

[CAL 09b] CALLISON-BURCH C., KOEHN P., MONZ C., SCHROEDER J., "Findings of the 2009 Workshop on Statistical Machine Translation", *Proceedings of the Fourth Workshop on Statistical Machine Translation*, Athens, Greece, p. 1–28, 2009.

[CAL 10] CALLISON-BURCH C., KOEHN P., MONZ C., PETERSON K., PRZYBOCKI M., ZAIDAN O., "Findings of the 2010 joint workshop on statistical machine translation and metrics for machine translation", *Proceedings of the Joint Fifth Workshop on Statistical Machine Translation and MetricsMATR*, Uppsala, Sweden, p. 17–53, 2010.

[CAR 03] CARL M., WAY A. (eds), *Recent Advances in Example-Based Machine Translation*, vol. 21 of *Text, Speech and Language Technology*, Springer, Verlag, 2003.

[CAR 05] CARPUAT M., WU D., "Word sense disambiguation vs. statistical machine translation", *Proceedings of the 43rd Annual Meeting of the Association for Computational Linguistics (ACL'05)*, Ann Arbor, Michigan, p. 387–394, 2005.

[CAR 07] CARPUAT M., WU D., "Improving statistical machine translation using word sense disambiguation", *Proceedings of the 2007 Joint Conference on Empirical Methods in Natural Language Processing and Computational Natural Language Learning (EMNLP-CoNLL)*, Prague, Czech Republic, p. 61–72, 2007.

[CAR 09] CARRERAS X., COLLINS M., "Non-projective parsing for statistical machine translation", *Proceedings of the 2009 Conference on Empirical Methods in Natural Language Processing*, Singapore, Association for Computational Linguistics, p. 200–209, August 2009.

[CAS 04] CASACUBERTA F., VIDAL E., "Machine translation with inferred stochastic finite-state transducers", *Computational Linguistics*, vol. 30, num. 3, p. 205–225, 2004.

[CER 08] CER D., JURAFSKY D., MANNING C. D., "Regularization and search for minimum error rate training", *Proceedings of the Third Workshop on Statistical Machine Translation*, Columbus, Ohio, p. 26–34, 2008.

[CHA 98] CHAPPELIER J.-C., RAJMAN M., "A generalized CYK algorithm for parsing stochastic CFG", *Proc. of 1st Workshop on Tabulation in Parsing and Deduction (TAPD'98)*, Paris (France), p. 133–137, April 1998.

[CHA 03] CHARNIAK E., KNIGHT K., YAMADA K., "Syntax-based language models for statistical machine translation", *Proceedings of the Machine Translation Summit IX*, New Orleans, USA, 2003.

[CHA 08] CHAUDIRON S., CHOUKRI K. (eds), *L'évaluation des technologies de traitement de la langue*, Hermès, 2008.

[CHE 78] CHEVALIER M., DANSEREAU J., POULIN G., TAUM-Météo: description du système, Report, Groupe TAUM, University of Montréal, Canada, 1978.

[CHE 06] CHERRY C., LIN D., "A Comparison of Syntactically Motivated Word Alignment Spaces", *Proceedings of EACL'06*, Genoa, Italy, p. 145–152, 2006.

[CHE 08] CHERRY C., "Cohesive Phrase-Based Decoding for Statistical Machine Translation", *Proceedings of ACL-08: HLT*, Columbus, Ohio, Association for Computational Linguistics, p. 72–80, June 2008.

[CHI 05] CHIANG D., "A Hierarchical Phrase-Based Model for Statistical Machine Translation", *Proceedings of the 43rd Annual Meeting of the Association for Computational Linguistics (ACL'05)*, Ann Arbor, Michigan, p. 263–270, 2005.

[CHI 08a] CHIANG D., DENEEFE S., CHAN Y. S., NG H. T., "Decomposability of translation metrics for improved evaluation and efficient algorithms", *Proceedings of the Conference on Empirical Methods in Natural Language Processing*, EMNLP '08, Stroudsburg, PA, USA, Association for Computational Linguistics, p. 610–619, 2008.

[CHI 08b] CHIANG D., MARTON Y., RESNIK P., "Online large-margin training of syntactic and structural translation features", *Proceedings of the 2008 Conference on Empirical Methods in Natural Language Processing*, Honolulu, Hawaii, p. 224–233, 2008.

[CHU 09] CHUNG T., GILDEA D., "Unsupervised tokenization for machine translation", *Proceedings of the 2009 Conference on Empirical Methods in Natural Language Processing*, Singapore, Association for Computational Linguistics, p. 718–726, August 2009.

[COL 05] COLLINS M., KOEHN P., KUCEROVA I., "Clause restructuring for statistical machine translation", *Proceedings of the 43rd Annual Meeting of the Association for Computational Linguistics (ACL'05)*, Ann Arbor, Michigan, USA, p. 531–540, 2005.

[CRE 07] CREGO J. M., NO J. B. M., "Improving SMT by coupling reordering and decoding", *Machine Translation*, vol. 20, num. 3, p. 199-215, 2007.

[CRE 08] CREGO J. M., HABASH N., "Using shallow syntax information to improve word alignment and reordering for SMT", *Proceedings of the Third Workshop on Statistical Machine Translation*, Columbus, Ohio, Association for Computational Linguistics, p. 53–61, June 2008.

[DEM 77] DEMPSTER A. P., LAIRD N. M., RUBIN D. B., "Maximum-likelihood from incomplete data via the EM algorithm", *Journal of the Royal Statistical Society*, vol. 39, num. 1, p. 1–38, 1977.

[DEM 98] DEMORI R., FEDERICO M., "Language model adaptation", PONTING K. (ed.), *Computational Models of Speech Pattern Processing*, Springer Verlag, p. 280–303, 1998.

[DEN 06] DENERO J., GILLICK D., ZHANG J., KLEIN D., "Why generative phrase models underperform surface heuristics", *Proceedings of the ACL workshop on Statistical Machine Translation*, New York City, NY, USA, p. 31–38, 2006.

[DEN 09] DENEEFE S., KNIGHT K., "Synchronous tree adjoining machine translation", *Proceedings of the 2009 Conference on Empirical Methods in Natural Language Processing*, Singapore, Association for Computational Linguistics, p. 727–736, August 2009.

[DIN 05] DING Y., PALMER M., "Machine translation using probabilistic synchronous dependency insertion grammars", *Proceedings of the 43rd Annual Meeting of the Association for Computational Linguistics (ACL'05)*, Ann Arbor, Michigan, USA, p. 541–548, 2005.

[ECO 07] ECO U., *Dire presque la même chose : Expériences de traduction*, Grasset, 2007.

[EIS 03] EISNER J., "Learning non-isomorphic tree mappings for machine translation", *Proceedings of the 41st Annual Meeting of the Association for Computational Linguistics (ACL), Companion Volume*, Sapporo, p. 205–208, 2003.

[EIS 06] EISNER J., TROMBLE R. W., "Local search with very large-scale neighborhoods for optimal permutations in machine translation", *Proceedings of the HLT-NAACL Workshop on Computationally Hard Problems and Joint Inference in Speech and Language Processing*, New York, USA, p. 57–75, June 2006.

[FOS 07] FOSTER G., KUHN R., "Mixture-model adaptation for SMT", *Proceedings of the Second Workshop on Statistical Machine Translation*, Prague, Czech Republic, p. 128–135, 2007.

[FOS 10] FOSTER G., GOUTTE C., KUHN R., "Discriminative instance weighting for domain adaptation in statistical machine translation", *Proceedings of the 2010 Conference on Empirical Methods in Natural Language Processing*, Cambridge, MA, USA, p. 451–459, October 2010.

[FOX 02] FOX H. J., "Phrasal cohesion and statistical machine translation", *EMNLP '02: Proceedings of the ACL-02 conference on Empirical methods in natural language processing*, Morristown, NJ, USA, Association for Computational Linguistics, p. 304–3111, 2002.

[FRA 07] FRASER A., MARCU D., "Measuring word alignment quality for statistical machine translation", *Computational Linguistics*, vol. 33, num. 3, p. 293–303, MIT Press, 2007.

[GAL 95] GALLIERS J. R., JONES K. S., *Evaluating Natural Language Processing Systems*, Lecture Notes in Artificial Intelligence, Springer, Berlin - Heidelberg - New York, 1995.

[GER 01] GERMANN U., JAHR M., KNIGHT K., MARCU D., YAMADA K., "Fast decoding and optimal decoding for machine translation", *Proceedings of the 39th Annual Meeting of the Association for Computational Linguistics (ACL'01)*, Toulouse, France, p. 228–235, 2001.

[GER 03] GERMANN U., "Greedy decoding for statistical machine translation in almost linear time", *Proceedings of the 2003 Conference of the North American Chapter of the Association for Computational Linguistics on Human Language Technology*, Edmonton, Canada, p. 1–8, 2003.

[GIM 08] GIMPEL K., SMITH N. A., "Rich source-side context for statistical machine translation", *Proceedings of the Third Workshop on Statistical Machine Translation*, Columbus, Ohio, USA, p. 9–17, June 2008.

[GIS 08] DE GISPERT A., MARIÑO J. B., "On the impact of morphology in English to Spanish statistical MT", *Speech Commununication*, vol. 50, num. 11-12, p. 1034–1046, Elsevier Science Publishers B. V., 2008.

[GRA 04] GRAEHL J., KNIGHT K., "Training tree transducers", SUSAN DUMAIS D. M., ROUKOS S. (eds), *HLT-NAACL 2004: Main Proceedings*, Boston, Massachusetts, USA, Association for Computational Linguistics, p. 105–112, May 2 - May 7 2004.

[HAG 09] HAGHIGHI A., BLITZER J., DENERO J., KLEIN D., "Better word alignments with supervised ITG models", *Proceedings of the Joint Conference of the 47th Annual Meeting of the ACL and the 4th International Joint Conference on Natural Language Processing of the AFNLP*, Suntec, Singapore, p. 923–931, 2009.

[HIL 08] HILDEBRAND A. S., VOGEL S., "Combination of machine translation systems via hypothesis selection from combined n-best lists", *Proceedings of the Eighth Conference of the Association for Machine Translation in the Americas*, Waikiki, Hawaii, p. 254–261, 2008.

[HUA 07] HUANG L., CHIANG D., "Forest rescoring: faster decoding with integrated language models", *Proceedings of the 45th Annual Meeting of the Association of Computational Linguistics*, Prague, Czech Republic, p. 144–151, 2007.

[HUA 09] HUANG L., ZHANG H., GILDEA D., KNIGHT K., "Binarization of synchronous context-free grammars", *Computational Linguistics*, vol. 35, num. 4, 2009.

[HUT 92] HUTCHINS W. J., SOMERS H. L., *An Introduction to Machine Translation*, Academic Press, 1992.

[HUT 01] HUTCHINS J., "Machine translation over fifty years", *Histoire, Epistémologie, Langage.*, vol. 23, num. 1, p. 3–31, 2001, special issue: Le traitement automatique des langues (edited by Jacqueline Léon).

[HUT 03] HUTCHINS J., "Has machine translation improved? Some historical comparisons", *Proceedings of the MT Summit IX: Proceedings of the Ninth Machine Translation Summit*, New Orleans, LO, USA, p. 181–188, 2003.

[HWA 02] HWA R., RESNIK P., WEINBERG A., KOLAK O., "Evaluating translational correspondence using annotation projection", *ACL '02: Proceedings of the 40th Annual Meeting on Association for Computational Linguistics*, Morristown, NJ, USA, Association for Computational Linguistics, p. 392–399, 2002.

[IGL 09] IGLESIAS G., DE GISPERT A., R. BANGA E., BYRNE W., "Hierarchical phrase-based translation with weighted finite state transducers", *Proceedings of Human Language Technologies: The 2009 Annual Conference of the North American Chapter of the Association for Computational Linguistics*, Boulder, Colorado, USA, Association for Computational Linguistics, p. 433–441, June 2009.

[ITT 07] ITTYCHERIAH A., ROUKOS S., "Direct translation model 2", *Human Language Technologies 2007: The Conference of the North American Chapter of the Association for Computational Linguistics; Proceedings of the Main Conference*, Rochester, New York, USA, p. 57–64, 2007.

[JEL 97] JELINEK F., *Statistical Methods for Speech Recognition*, The MIT Press, Cambridge, MA, USA, 1997.

[KAN 05] KANTHAK S., VILAR D., MATUSOV E., ZENS R., NEY H., "Novel Reordering Approaches in Phrase-Based Statistical Machine Translation", *Proceedings of the ACL Workshop on Building and Using Parallel Texts*, Ann Arbor, Michigan, USA, p. 167–174, 2005.

[KIN 96] KING M., "Evaluating natural language processing systems", *Communication of the ACM*, vol. 39, num. 1, p. 73–79, ACM, 1996.

[KNI 99] KNIGHT K., "Decoding complexity in word-replacement translation models", *Computational Linguistics*, vol. 25, num. 4, p. 607–615, 1999.

[KNI 08] KNIGHT K., "Capturing Practical Natural Language Transformations", *Machine Translation*, vol. 22, num. 2, p. 121–133, 2008.

[KOE 03a] KOEHN P., KNIGHT K., "Empirical methods for compound splitting", *EACL '03: Proceedings of the Tenth Conference on European Chapter of the Association for Computational Linguistics*, Morristown, NJ, USA, Association for Computational Linguistics, p. 187–193, 2003.

[KOE 03b] KOEHN P., OCH F. J., MARCU D., "Statistical phrase-based translation", *Proceedings of the Human Language Technology Conference of the North American Chapter of the Association for Computational Linguistic*, Edmondton, Canada, p. 127–133, 2003.

[KOE 04] KOEHN P., "Pharaoh: a beam search decoder for phrase-based statistical machine translation models", FREDERKING R. E., TAYLOR K. B. (eds), *Machine Translation: From Real Users to Research: Proceedings of the 6th Conference of the Association for Machine Translation in the Americas*, Lecture Notes in Computer Science 3265, Springer Verlag, p. 115–124, 2004.

[KOE 05] KOEHN P., "Europarl: a parallel corpus for statistical machine translation", *2nd Workshop on EBMT of MT-Summit X*, Phuket, Thailand, p. 79–86, 2005.

[KOE 07a] KOEHN P., HOANG H., "Factored translation models", *Proceedings of the 2007 Joint Conference on Empirical Methods in Natural Language Processing and Computational Natural Language Learning (EMNLP-CoNLL)*, p. 868–876, 2007.

[KOE 07b] KOEHN P., HOANG H., BIRCH A., CALLISON-BURCH C., FEDERICO M., BERTOLDI N., COWAN B., SHEN W., MORAN C., ZENS R., DYER C., BOJAR O., CONSTANTIN A., HERBST E., "Moses: open source toolkit for statistical machine translation", *Proc. Annual Meeting of the Association for Computational Linguistics (ACL)*, demonstration session, Prague, Czech Republic, 2007.

[KOE 10] KOEHN P., *Statistical Machine Translation*, Cambridge University Press, UK, 2010.

[KUM 03] KUMAR S., BYRNE W., "A weighted finite state transducer implementation of the alignment template model for statistical machine translation", *NAACL '03: Proceedings of the 2003 Conference of the North American Chapter of the Association for Computational Linguistics on Human Language Technology*, Morristown, NJ, USA, p. 63–70, 2003.

[KUM 05] KUMAR S., BYRNE W., "Local phrase reordering models for statistical machine translation", *Proceedings of Human Language Technology Conference and Conference on Empirical Methods in Natural Language Processing*, Vancouver, British Columbia, Canada, p. 161–168, 2005.

[KUM 06] KUMAR S., DENG Y., BYRNE W., "A weighted finite state transducer translation template model for statistical machine translation", *Natural Language Engineering*, vol. 12, num. 1, p. 35–75, 2006.

[LAN 07] LANGLAIS P., PATRY A., GOTTI F., "A greedy decoder for phrase-based statistical machine translation", *Proceedings of the 11th International Conference on Theoretical and Methodological Issues in Machine Translation (TMI'07)*, Skövde, Sweden, p. 104–113, 2007.

[LEW 68] LEWIS II P. M., STEARNS R. E., "Syntax-Directed Transduction", *Journal of the ACM*, vol. 15, num. 3, p. 465–488, 1968.

[LIN 03] LIN D., CHERRY C., "Word alignment with cohesion constraint", *NAACL '03: Proceedings of the 2003 Conference of the North American Chapter of the Association for Computational Linguistics on Human Language Technology*, Morristown, NJ, USA, Association for Computational Linguistics, p. 49–51, 2003.

[LOP 08a] LOPEZ A., "Statistical machine translation", *ACM Computing Surveys*, vol. 40, num. 3, p. 1–49, 2008.

[LOP 08b] LOPEZ A., "Tera-scale translation models via pattern matching", *Proceedings of the 22nd International Conference on Computational Linguistics (Coling 2008)*, Manchester, UK, p. 505–512, 2008.

[LOP 09] LOPEZ A., "Translation as weighted deduction", *Proceedings of the 12th Conference of the European Chapter of the ACL (EACL 2009)*, Athens, Greece, p. 532–540, March 2009.

[MA 08] MA Y., OZDOWSKA S., SUN Y., WAY A., "Improving word alignment using syntactic dependencies", *SSST '08: Proceedings of the Second Workshop on Syntax and Structure in Statistical Translation*, Morristown, NJ, USA, Association for Computational Linguistics, p. 69–77, 2008.

[MAC 08] MACHEREY W., OCH F., THAYER I., USZKOREIT J., "Lattice-based minimum error rate training for statistical machine translation", *Proceedings of the 2008 Conference on Empirical Methods in Natural Language Processing*, Honolulu, Hawaii, p. 725–734, 2008.

[MAN 99] MANNING C. D., SCHÜTZE H., *Foundations of Statistical Natural Language Processing*, The MIT Press, Cambridge, MA, USA, 1999.

[MAR 02] MARCU D., WONG D., "A phrase-based, joint probability model for statistical machine translation", *Proceedings of the 2002 Conference on Empirical Methods in Natural Language Processing*, p. 133–139, July 2002.

[MAT 08] MATUSOV E., LEUSCH G., BANCHS R. E., BERTOLDI N., DECHELOTTE D., FEDERICO M., KOLSS M., LEE Y.-S., MARIÑO J., PAULIK M., ROUKOS S., SCHWENK H., NEY H., "System combination for machine translation of spoken and written language", *IEEE Transactions on Audio, Speech and Language Processing*, vol. 16, num. 7, p. 1222-1237, 2008.

[MEL 04] MELAMED I. D., "Statistical machine translation by parsing", *ACL '04: Proceedings of the 42nd Annual Meeting on Association for Computational Linguistics*, Morristown, NJ, USA, Association for Computational Linguistics, p. 653, 2004.

[MIN 07] MINKOV E., TOUTANOVA K., SUZUKI H., "Generating complex morphology for machine translation", *Proceedings of the 45th Annual Meeting of the Association of Computational Linguistics*, Prague, Czech Republic, Association for Computational Linguistics, p. 128–135, June 2007.

[MOH 02] MOHRI M., PEREIRA F. C. N., RILEY M., "Weighted finite-state transducers in speech recognition", *Computer Speech and Language*, vol. 16, num. 1, p. 69–88, 2002.

[MOO 05] MOORE R. C., "A discriminative framework for bilingual word alignment", *Proceedings of Human Language Technology Conference and Conference on Empirical Methods in Natural Language Processing*, Vancouver, British Columbia, Canada, p. 81–88, 2005.

[MOO 07] MOORE R. C., QUIRK C., "Faster beam-search decoding for phrasal statistical machine translation", *Proceedings of the Machine Translation Summit XI*, Copenhagen, Denmark, p. 321–327, 2007.

[MOO 08] MOORE R. C., QUIRK C., "Random restarts in minimum error rate training for statistical machine translation", *Proceedings of the 22nd International Conference on Computational Linguistics (Coling 2008)*, Manchester, UK, p. 585–592, 2008.

[NAG 04] NAGAO M., "A framework of a mechanical translation between Japanese and English by analogy principle", ELITHORN A., BANERJI R. (eds), *Artificial and Human Intelligence*, Elsevier Science Publishers, 2004.

[NEY 04] NEY H., POPOVIC M., "Improving word alignment quality using morpho-syntactic information", *Proceedings of Coling 2004*, Geneva, Switzerland, COLING, p. 310–314, Aug 23–Aug 27 2004.

[NIE 04] NIEßEN S., NEY H., "Statistical machine translation with scarce resources using morpho-syntactic information", *Computational Linguistics*, vol. 30, num. 2, p. 181–204, MIT Press, 2004.

[NIE 08] NIEHUES J., VOGEL S., "Discriminative word alignment via alignment matrix modeling", *Proceedings of the Third Workshop on Statistical Machine Translation*, Columbus, Ohio, p. 18–25, 2008.

[OCH 03a] OCH F. J., "Minimum error rate training in statistical machine translation", *Proceedings of the 41st Annual Meeting of the Association for Computational Linguistics*, Sapporo, Japan, p. 160–167, 2003.

[OCH 03b] OCH F. J., NEY H., "A systematic comparison of various statistical alignment models", *Computational Linguistics*, vol. 29, num. 1, p. 19-51, 2003.

[OCH 04] OCH F. J., NEY H., "The alignment template approach to statistical machine translation", *Computational Linguistics*, vol. 30, num. 4, p. 417–449, MIT Press, 2004.

[OFL 07] OFLAZER K., EL-KAHLOUT I. D., "Exploring different representational units in English-to-Turkish statistical machine translation", *StatMT '07: Proceedings of the Second Workshop on Statistical Machine Translation*, Morristown, NJ, USA, Association for Computational Linguistics, p. 25–32, 2007.

[PAP 01] PAPINENI K., ROUKOS S., WARD T., ZHU W.-J., Bleu: a method for automatic evaluation of machine translation, Report num. RC22176 (W0109-022), IBM Research Division, Thomas J. Watson Research Center, 2001.

[PEA 84] PEARL J., *Heuristics: Intelligent Search Strategies for Computer Problem Solving*, Addison-Wesley, 1984.

[POS 08] POST M., GILDEA D., "Parsers as language models for statistical machine translation", *Proceedings of AMTA*, 2008.

[POW 64] POWELL M., "An efficient method for finding the minimum of a function of several variables without calculating derivatives", *Computer Journal*, vol. 7, p. 152–162, 1964.

[QUI 05] QUIRK C., MENEZES A., CHERRY C., "Dependency treelet translation: syntactically informed phrasal SMT", *ACL '05: Proceedings of the 43rd Annual Meeting on Association for Computational Linguistics*, Morristown, NJ, USA, Association for Computational Linguistics, p. 271–279, 2005.

[ROS 07] ROSTI A.-V., MATSOUKAS S., SCHWARTZ R., "Improved word-level system combination for machine translation", *Proceedings of the 45th Annual Meeting of the Association of Computational Linguistics*, Prague, Czech Republic, Association for Computational Linguistics, p. 312–319, 2007.

[SAE 09] SAERS M., WU D., "Improving phrase-based translation via word alignments from stochastic inversion transduction grammars", *Proceedings of the Third Workshop on Syntax and Structure in Statistical Translation (SSST-3) at NAACL HLT 2009*, Boulder, Colorado, Association for Computational Linguistics, p. 28–36, June 2009.

[SAT 05] SATTA G., PESERICO E., "Some computational complexity results for synchronous context-free grammars", *Proceedings of Human Language Technology Conference and Conference on Empirical Methods in Natural Language Processing*, Vancouver, British Columbia, Canada, Association for Computational Linguistics, p. 803–810, October 2005.

[SCH 08] SCHWENK H., FOUET J.-B., SENELLART J., "First steps towards a general purpose French/English statistical machine translation system", *StatMT'08: Proceedings of the Third Workshop on Statistical Machine Translation*, Morristown, NJ, USA, Association for Computational Linguistics, p. 119–122, 2008.

[SHE 08] SHEN L., XU J., WEISCHEDEL R., "A new string-to-dependency machine translation algorithm with a target dependency language model", *Proceedings of ACL-08: HLT*, Columbus, Ohio, p. 577–585, June 2008.

[SHI 90] SHIEBER S. M., SCHABES Y., "Synchronous tree-adjoining grammars", *Proceedings of the 13th Conference on Computational Linguistics*, Morristown, NJ, USA, p. 253–258, 1990.

[SIM 05] SIMARD M., CANCEDDA N., CAVESTRO B., DYMETMAN M., GAUSSIER E., GOUTTE C., YAMADA K., LANGLAIS P., MAUSER A., "Translating with Non-contiguous Phrases", *Proceedings of Human Language Technology Conference and Conference on Empirical Methods in Natural Language Processing*, Vancouver, British Columbia, Canada, p. 755–762, 2005.

[SNO 06] SNOVER M., DORR B., SCHWARTZ R., MICCIULLA L., MAKHOUL J., "A study of translation edit rate with targeted human annotation", *Proceedings of the Conference of the Association for Machine Translation in the America (AMTA)*, p. 223–231, 2006.

[SNO 09] SNOVER M., MADNANI N., DORR B., SCHWARTZ R., "Fluency, adequacy, or HTER? Exploring different human judgments with a tunable MT metric", *Proceedings of the Fourth Workshop on Statistical Machine Translation*, Athens, Greece, Association for Computational Linguistics, p. 259–268, March 2009.

[SPE 11] SPECIA L., "Exploiting objective annotations for measuring translation post-editing effort", FORCADA M. L., DEPRAETERE H., VANDEGHINSTE V. (eds), *Proceedings of the 15th conference of the European Association for Machine Translation (EAMT 2011)*, Leuven, Belgium, p. 73–80, 2011.

[STR 07] STROPPA N., VAN DEN BOSCH A., WAY A., "Exploiting source similarity for SMT using context-informed features", WAY A., GAWRONSKA B. (eds), *Proceedings of the 11th International Conference on Theoretical and Methodological Issues in Machine Translation (TMI'07)*, Skövde, Sweden, p. 231–240, 2007.

[TIE 09] TIEDEMANN J., "News from OPUS – a collection of multilingual parallel corpora with tools and interfaces", NICOLOV N., ANGELOVA G., MITKOV R. (eds), *Recent Advances in Natural Language Processing V*, vol. 309 of *Current Issues in Linguistic Theory*, Amsterdam & Philadelphia, John Benjamins, p. 227–248, 2009.

[TIE 11] TIEDEMANN J., *Bitext Alignment*, Num. 14, Synthesis Lectures on Human Language Technologies, GRAEME HIRST (ed), Morgan & Claypool Publishers, 2011.

[TIL 03] TILLMANN C., NEY H., "Word reordering and a dynamic programming beam search algorithm for statistical machine translation", *Computational Linguistics*, vol. 29, num. 1, p. 97–133, 2003.

[TIL 04] TILLMAN C., "A unigram orientation model for statistical machine translation", DUMAIS S., MARCU D., ROUKOS S. (eds), *HLT-NAACL 2004: Short Papers*, Boston, Massachusetts, USA, p. 101–104, 2004.

[TOU 02] TOUTANOVA K., ILHAN H. T., MANNING C. D., "Extensions to HMM-based statistical word alignment models", *EMNLP '02: Proceedings of the ACL-02 Conference on Empirical Methods in Natural Language Processing*, Morristown, NJ, USA, Association for Computational Linguistics, p. 87–94, 2002.

[TOU 11] TOUTANOVA K., GALLEY M., "Why initialization matters for IBM Model 1: multiple optima and non-strict convexity", *Proceedings of the 49th Annual Meeting of the Association for Computational Linguistics: Human Language Technologies*, Portland, Oregon, USA, Association for Computational Linguistics, p. 461–466, June 2011.

[UDU 06] UDUPA R., MAJI H. K., "Computational complexity of statistical machine translation", *Proceedings of the Meeting of the European Chapter of the Association for Computational Linguistics*, Trento, Italy, p. 25–32, 2006.

[UEF 03] UEFFING N., NEY H., "Using POS information for statistical machine translation into morphologically rich languages", *EACL '03: Proceedings of the Tenth Conference on European Chapter of the Association for Computational Linguistics*, Morristown, NJ, USA, Association for Computational Linguistics, p. 347–354, 2003.

[VEN 03] VENUGOPAL A., VOGEL S., WAIBEL A., "Effective phrase translation extraction from alignment models.", *ACL*, p. 319–326, 2003.

[VIL 06] VILAR D., XU J., LUIS FERNANDO D., NEY H., "Error analysis of statistical machine translation output", *Proceedings of the Fifth International Conference on Language Resources and Evaluation (LREC)*, Genoa, Italy, 2006.

[VOG 96] VOGEL S., NEY H., TILLMANN C., "HMM-based word alignment in statistical translation", *Proceedings of the 16th Conference on Computational Linguistics*, Morristown, NJ, USA, p. 836–841, 1996.

[VOG 05] VOGEL S., "PESA:phrase pair extraction as sentence splitting", *Proceedings of the Tenth Machine Translation Summit*, Phuket, Thailand, 2005.

[WAG 74] WAGNER R. A., FISCHER M. J., "The string-to-string correction problem", *Journal of the ACM (JACM)*, vol. 21, num. 1, p. 168–173, ACM Press, 1974.

[WEL 06] WELLINGTON B., WAXMONSKY S., MELAMED I. D., "Empirical lower bounds on the complexity of translational equivalence", *Proceedings of the 21st International Conference on Computational Linguistics and 44th Annual Meeting of the Association for Computational Linguistics*, Sydney, Australia, Association for Computational Linguistics, p. 977–984, July 2006.

[WU 97] WU D., "Stochastic inversion transduction grammar and bilingual parsing of parallel corpora", *Computational Linguistics*, vol. 23, num. 3, p. 377–404, 1997.

[XIA 04] XIA F., MCCORD M., "Improving a statistical MT system with automatically learned rewrite patterns", *Proceedings of the 20th International Conference on Computational Linguistics (COLING)*, Geneva, Switzerland, p. 508–514, 2004.

[XIO 06] XIONG D., LIU Q., LIN S., "Maximum entropy based phrase reordering model for statistical machine translation", *Proceedings of the 21st International Conference on Computational Linguistics and the 44th Annual Meeting of the Association for Computational Linguistics*, Morristown, NJ, USA, p. 521–528, 2006.

[YAM 01] YAMADA K., KNIGHT K., "A syntax-based statistical translation model", *Proceedings of 39th Annual Meeting of the Association for Computational Linguistics*, Toulouse, France, p. 523–530, 2001.

[YOU 67] YOUNGER D. H., "Recognition and Parsing of context-free languages in time n^3", *Information and Control*, vol. 10, num. 2, p. 189–208, 1967.

[ZAI 09] ZAIDAN O. F., "Z-MERT: a fully configurable open source tool for minimum error rate training of machine translation systems", *The Prague Bulletin of Mathematical Linguistics*, vol. 91, p. 79–88, 2009.

[ZAS 09] ZASLAVSKIY M., DYMETMAN M., CANCEDDA N., "Phrase-based statistical machine translation as a traveling salesman problem", *Proceedings of the Joint Conference of the 47th Annual Meeting of the ACL and the 4th International Joint Conference on Natural Language Processing of the AFNLP*, Suntec, Singapore, p. 333–341, 2009.

[ZEN 02] ZENS R., OCH F. J., NEY H., "Phrase-based statistical machine translation", JARKE M., KOEHLER J., LAKEMEYER G. (eds), *KI-2002: Advances in Artificial Intelligence*, vol. 2479 of *LNAI*, Springer Verlag, p. 18-32, 2002.

[ZEN 03] ZENS R., NEY H., "A comparative study on reordering constraints in statistical machine translation", *Proceedings of the 41st Annual Meeting of the Association for Computational Linguistics*, Sapporo, Japan, p. 144–151, 2003.

[ZEN 06] ZENS R., NEY H., "Discriminative reordering models for statistical machine translation", *HLT-NAACL: Proc. of the Workshop on Statistical Machine Translation*, New York, NY, p. 55–63, 2006.

[ZHA 03] ZHANG Y., VOGEL S., WAIBEL A., "Integrated phrase segmentation and alignment algorithm for statistical machine translation", *Proceedings of International Conference on Natural Language Processing and Knowledge Engineering (NLP-KE'03)*, Beijing, China, October 2003.

[ZHA 04] ZHANG H., GILDEA D., "Syntax-based alignment: supervised or unsupervised?", *Proceedings of Coling 2004*, Geneva, Switzerland, p. 418–424, 2004.

[ZHA 06] ZHANG H., GILDEA D., "Efficient search for inversion transduction grammar", *Proceedings of the 2006 Conference on Empirical Methods in Natural Language Processing*, Sydney, Australia, Association for Computational Linguistics, p. 224–231, July 2006.

[ZOL 06] ZOLLMANN A., VENUGOPAL A., "Syntax augmented machine translation via chart parsing", *Proceedings on the Workshop on Statistical Machine Translation*, New York City, p. 138–141, 2006.

PART 4

Emerging Applications

Chapter 8

Information Mining: Methods and Interfaces for Accessing Complex Information

8.1. Introduction

Access to information can take various forms depending on the type of data processed, the systems which handle the data and user's expectations. Various research disciplines have consequently shown an interest in providing access to electronic information. A common functionality of these systems is the ability to restore part of the stored information to a user in accordance with the user's particular requirements. In the field of databases, database management systems (DBMS) ensure the management of structured information, and set-based languages such as SQL and OQL enable non-ambiguous queries to be written, hence ensuring selected data that correspond to the user's requirements. The response of a DBMS corresponds to a subset of stored data. These data are supplied in their original formats, in other words, without (post-) processing after selection, or in an aggregated format. In information retrieval (IR), the objectives are identical, but the type of information handled is different; it consists of information granules which can be termed as document units. Each document unit contains diverse information, and an additional problem in relation to the management of data is the encoding of this diverse information. As a document unit can be in different formats (text, graphical, audio, video, multimedia), these formats require a greater or lesser degree of complex processing in order to extract its representation. In the case of text documents, a representation can constitute one of the following in particular:

Chapter written by Josiane MOTHE, Kurt ENGLMEIER, and Fionn MURTAGH.

– indexing content (associating a set of representative terms from the content in each documentation unit);

– indexing using metadata;

– semantically tagging certain information (in order to extract certain predefined information from the content);

– structural tagging in XML (to identify how documentation units may be assembled).

The queries that reflect a user's requirements also need a particular type of encoding, one which is compatible with document encoding and which is relevant in the re-transcription of the user's requirements. The aim of this non-unique encoding for documents and queries is to support the search mechanisms used by an IR system (IRS) to locate information. The retrieved information is in a raw format. In other words, the part of the document which has been selected and which is readable by the user remains in an initial format (text, video, etc.). Hence, when using an IRS, the user consults raw information which has been retrieved; in other words, information as it has been stored and written by the original authors. The transformation of this information into knowledge is left to the user. Knowledge discovery systems aim to assist the user in this task by supplying him or her with detailed information drawn automatically from raw information. Access to information no longer consists of supplying the user with a selection of stored information, but of applying post-processing on a selection of information for the purposes of extracting synthetic results. With reference to databases, knowledge discovery has been defined as the extraction of implicit information which is not known but which is useful, from a set of data. The knowledge takes a variety of forms and generally serves as a support for decision-making. It can, for example, relate to the extraction of trends in purchasing behavior, the assessment of risk in the banking sector and so on. With reference to text information, the type of knowledge for extraction can also be varied: detection of the emergence of a domain, the geographical map of a domain, evolving terminology or the incorporation of terminology from a domain, the thematic map of an organization, collaborative networks and so on. When it is not the documents themselves that are being analyzed, but the behavior associated with IRS, an exploratory analysis can lead to the extraction of models that enable us, for example, to exploit the typologies of the queries, the variability of system responses or the performances of these systems.

In this chapter we therefore examine models that relate to visualization and exploratory analysis in IR. The chapter highlights diverse applications of data analysis and the visualization of information in IR. The first two sections consider access to information in the wider sense. In section 8.2 we will present different approaches which ensure a multidimensional visualization of information. On the one hand, the focus will be on models which aim to structure the language of indexing and research, and on the other hand the focus will be on models which derive from OLAP technology in order to provide overall visualizations of information. In section 8.3 the analysis methods used for the exploration of texts will be addressed and the consequent two sections will be devoted to the analysis of results obtained by IRS using data analysis methods. In section 8.4 both the variability and complementarity of system responses to the same requirements for information will be discussed. In section 8.5 we will show how evaluation methods in IR are either redundant or complementary. Section 8.6 concludes this chapter by highlighting several possibilities for research in the domain and acknowledges the significant contributions of others to the research.

8.2. The multidimensional visualization of information

Irrespective of the search system, users may face difficulties in making a query that is adapted to a targeted collection. In general, when a user is familiar with a collection in terms of what it contains, how it is structured, and when this user knows what he or she is looking for and how to describe it, there should be no particular problems in locating the information which corresponds to his or her requirements. If however, one of the above elements is missing, then the search can be difficult. A solution to this is to help the user by structuring the information space and informing him or her as to the content of the collection. Indexing documents, which associates descriptors with each set of contents, is a preliminary method for structuring and organizing a collection. The descriptors are used as input keys during a search. The descriptors can in turn be organized in such a way as to account for their dependence (hierarchical, ontological). Another method for structuring a collection is to take the metadata associated with each document into consideration. This method employs data that can be associated with the documents unambiguously such as the name(s) of the author(s), publication date, etc. Some of these elements can also be organized according to a hierarchical structure or ontology. Hence, the descriptor can be thought of as a particular aspect of meta-information. All these descriptive elements can therefore be combined during the search phase. They can also be used in classification processes or in the overall visualizations of documents

8.2.1. *Accessing information based on the knowledge of the structured domain*

In general, the descriptors chosen during automatic indexing are extracted from the contents of the document and considered to be independent from one another. This is known as 'bag of words' indexing [ZEL 54]. On the contrary, manual indexing relies on the use of a controlled vocabulary organized in the form of a thesaurus (standardized by ISO 2788 and ANSI Z39) and on indexing rules, in particular, those set out by the BNF (*Bibliothèque Nationale de France: National Library of France*). Different studies look at how descriptors extracted from the document contents during indexing are structured; this relates to constructing or helping to construct thesauruses or ontologies which act as a basis for indexing documents. The use of a structured vocabulary (thesaurus, ontology) during the search phase has given rise to interrogation modes and different types of interface.

In [EGR 02], the documents are associated with several concept hierarchies, each corresponding to either the various relative aspects of the content or to a type of meta-information. Figure 8.1 shows the suggested interrogation interface: the user can navigate in three hierarchies associated with the documents in the domain of astronomy and can select the concepts which interest him or her. Here, the three hierarchies correspond to authors (and at higher levels to the affiliated laboratories and countries), publication dates, and keywords from the thesaurus used by the main editors in the domain.

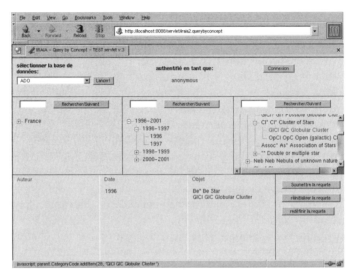

Figure 8.1. *Articulation of a query via navigation in concept hierarchies [EGR 02]*

On this interface, when a found document is visualized, the user visualizes complementary information on its indexing. On the right hand side of Figure 8.2, all the concepts indexing the document are displayed; this depends on which hierarchy the concepts belong to.

In [ENG 03], the obtained results are organized according to the concepts that are common to the query (see Figure 8.3): the clustering of documents is based on the correspondence between the terms that index the documents and those used in the query.

This is an example of a semantic search as regards both the interrogation method (via the concept hierarchies) and the consultation of the results (via the clustering of obtained documents). The advances in the Semantic Web domain have brought about the integration of ontologies into IR tools. Hence, for example, the OntoIR tool [GAR 03] allows access to resources by being ontology based. Navigation in the

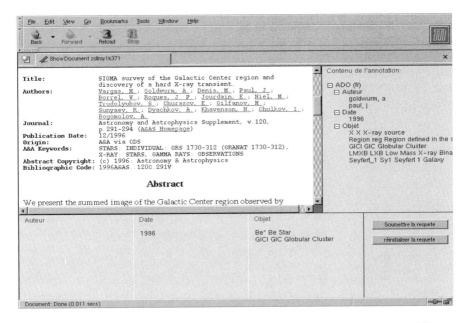

Figure 8.2. *Visualization of a specific document and query reformulation [EGR 02]*

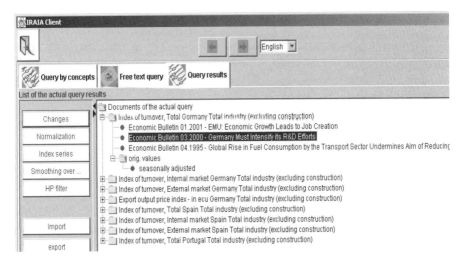

Figure 8.3. *Clustering of the documents found in relation to the concepts in common with the query [ENG 03]*

ontology which represents a domain allows the user to fine-tune his or her query (see Figure 8.4).

Fig. 1. Overall appearance of the OntoIR tool

Figure 8.4. *OntoIR interface [GAR 03]*

Similarly, Hernandez *et al.* [HER 07] present a model based on two ontologies: a domain ontology organizes the vocabulary, hence enabling the representation of the document contents, whereas a further ontology represents the metadata and their relations. Figure 8.5 shows the metadata linked to scientific publications (left) and the ontology of the astronomy domain (right). According to this interface, when an object is

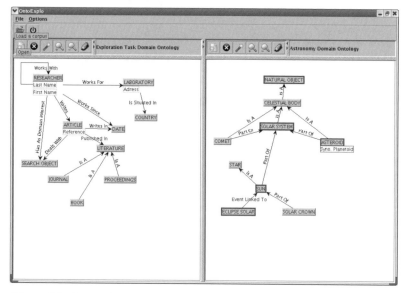

Figure 8.5. *OntoExplo: visualization of the task and domain ontologies [HER 07]*

selected, for example, the author *Cecchini* (in this case via the *Researcher/Last_Name* object), a contextual representation of the content of a collection of documents is displayed (Figure 8.6). On the left, the elements linked to the chosen author *Cecchini* can be seen (date of first publication in the system, the list of references from these publications, co-authors, affiliation) and on the right, the domain concepts that he discusses in his publications as well as their related information.

8.2.2. *Visualization of a set of documents via their content*

When using a traditional IRS, the user interrogates the system by formulating a query in "free" language. The system retrieves a list of those documents to the user which are likely to respond to his or her requirements, not forgetting the terms that are common to the query and to the content of the document. The user must therefore decide which documents he or she actually wishes to consult, or after having navigated the list of documents, may decide to reformulate the articulation of his or her requirements. Interfaces have been developed to help the user in the task of selecting the found documents. These same interfaces can also be considered as aids in the formulation of information requirements via an overall visualization of the available contents.

The study presented in [LEB 98] shows, for example, how to analyze the responses to open questions in an opinion survey. The text responses are analyzed with respect to the extracted semantic elements and with respect to the social-demographic categories

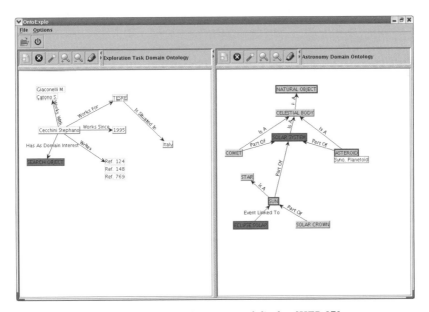

Figure 8.6. *OntoExplo: contextual display [HER 07]*

of the participants (combination of age and level of education). A correspondence analysis is applied after a syntactic and semantic level pre-processing of the responses.

In [POI 00], the set of documents is visualized by way of a Kohonen self-organizing map. Documents that are close in terms of their content (representative terms) are also close when represented graphically. On this interface (see Figure 8.7) the authors include a representation of the significant terms from the clustered documents.

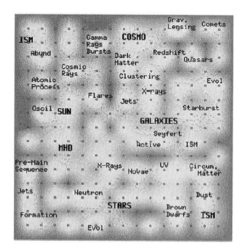

Figure 8.7. *Use of Kohonen self-organization maps to visualize a set of documents [POI 00]*

Murtagh *et al* [POI 00] visualize the semantics of filmscripts, and beyond filmscripts any other partially structured, time-ordered, sequence of text segments. The work is based on the notion of word pertinence that goes beyond just word frequency and instead takes a word in a mathematical sense as located at the average of all of its pairwise relationships. They capture semantics through context, taken as all pairwise relationships. Figure 8.8 displays a Correspondence Analysis principal factor plane of projections of 50 scenes (each represented with an x), and 1, 679 characterizing words (each represented with a dot). In this planar view of the two clouds, we see the cloud of scenes and the cloud of words.

Figure 8.9 shows a scriptcloud based on frequent words retained following application of a stoplist. Produced by an earlier version of Contentcloud, (www. contentclouds.com), using television program CSI 101.

In Easy-Dor [CHE 00], the user query and the system responses are represented in the form of a cone in which the axes correspond to the terms of the query or to a combination of these terms (see Figure 8.10).

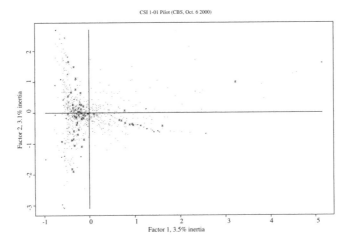

Figure 8.8. *Correspondance analysis considering filmscripts and terms [POI 00]*

CSI 1-01 Pilot

arms ass bathroom checks clippings crime deceased discoloration doll doorway
drives dusting examines fires flashback follicles forehead glances god gonna
grabs gurneys hallway homicide jar kit kneels lab latex leans love nail nods okay

opens picks prints pulls recorder robbery screams

shadowing shake sheets shuts sighs sir sits smiles spray stares stops straightens

suicide swabs toe toenail toilet trick underwear victim walks wallet yeah

Figure 8.9. *Scriptcloud based on most frequent terms [POI 00]*

The same approach is used for the WebSearchViz interface [NGU 07]; points of view are defined on this interface. These points of view correspond either to query components or to other points of interest (see Figure 8.11).

Other visualization interfaces for accessing information are presented in [BON 08]. A distinction can be made between interfaces that are aimed at navigation and interfaces that are aimed at the modalities of interrogation. With these interfaces, only the dimensions relating to the document content are considered. Other approaches take

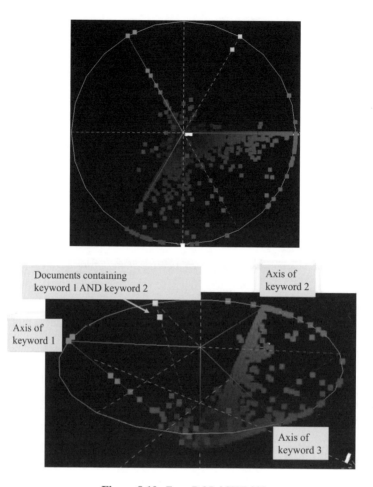

Figure 8.10. *Easy-DOR [CHE 00]*

several dimensions into account. For the interfaces described below, the dimensions are viewed as hierarchies displaying different levels of detail, thereby adhering to OLAP (OnLine Analytical Process) principles.

8.2.3. *OLAP principles applied to document sets*

DocCube [ALA 03] aims to help the user manage each of the two difficult tasks i.e. articulating his or her requirements and deciding to consult or navigate in an information space. One of the basic components of DocCube and also one of its originalities is in relation to the notion of the concept hierarchies which structure an information space. In fact these hierarchies correspond to various aspects which constitute each domain.

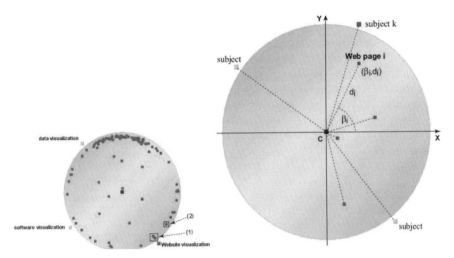

Figure 8.11. *WebSearchViz [NGU 07]*

Documents are attached to hierarchical nodes so that they can be accessed, as is the case in classification systems. In DocCube, this hierarchy-driven structuring of information is used to provide the user with overall visualizations of information, thus helping his or her search and his or her mining of the masses of available information. These overall visualizations are based on multidimensional modeling. In other words, this information is represented and organized according to different dimensions and the facts can be analyzed in an interactive fashion. In DocCube, the dimensions describe the knowledge associated with the studied domain(s). These dimensions are hierarchical; the hierarchy is represented by a "is a" or "is more specific than" link. The dimensions depend on the domain. Each of these dimensions is hierarchical, but the depth of the hierarchies varies. The measure (fact) that the user can analyze corresponds to the number of documents associated with the hierarchical values. As in OLAP systems, the value of this measure is recalculated according to the level of aggregation (i.e. granularity) the user is interested in. In addition, contrary to OLAP systems, the link to the raw information, in other words, to the document or Web page, is maintained. This may enable a return to the content when the synthetic representations of the content are not sufficient. The "warehouse" model on which DocCube relies contains one table per dimension, in other words, per domain concept hierarchy (see Figure 8.12). This respects the "star" model where a dimension is described in a single table. The "facts" table, which contains the measures that need to be analyzed while preserving the link to the dimensions, is also present in the model. The table of facts contains, in addition to the link to the dimension hierarchies, a reference to the document contents that corresponds to the document URL, and the strength of the link between the represented node and the document. The manner in which documents are linked to hierarchies is described in [ALA 03].

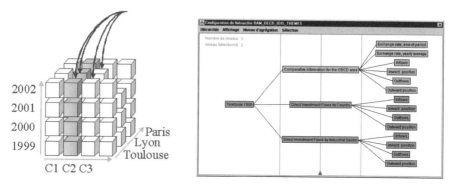

Figure 8.12. *DocCube: information cube and example of a hierarchy [ALA 03]*

DocCube provides overall visualizations of information relative to the collection of documents covering the domain chosen by the user. The axes of the cube correspond to dimensions, in other words, concept hierarchies (see Figure 8.13). The intersection of the axes corresponds to the number of documents associated with this axis. This information is represented in the form of a sphere whose size is proportional to the number of documents. This number is dynamically recalculated when the user changes the level of aggregation.

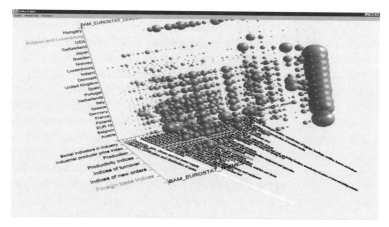

Figure 8.13. *3D representation of the DocCube [ALA 03]*

A slice function is utilized when the user wants to set the value of one of the dimensions and hence obtain a 2D view of the measures. In DocCube, the slice leads to an interaction via the cursor. The result of a slice is represented in Figure 8.14. The number of documents that come under the chosen criteria is displayed in the form of circles where the scale can be modified in an interactive way. This should help maintain the focus on only the predominant elements. It is also possible to ignore certain elements in the visualization (corresponding to a number that is too low or too high). This functionality also exists in a 3D visualization.

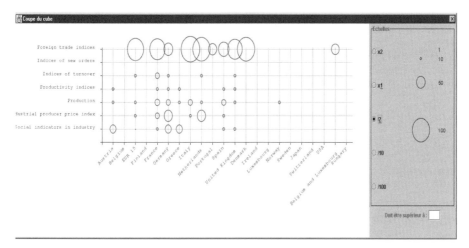

Figure 8.14. *The slice in the DocCube [ALA 03]*

An information requirement can be formulated directly by selecting one or more nodes in the 3D cube. After this operation, the list of references from the corresponding documents is displayed. This list is ranked according to assumed relevance. The keywords relating to the query are shown in the cube and also included in the resulting window. The score obtained by the documents depends on the weight associated with each document and to what extent the document is attached to the various hierarchies. In [RAV 07], the same type of approach creates more specific views of document collections. For example, Figure 8.15, rather than representing the number of times a "row" modality is in co-occurrence with a "column" modality, this co-occurrence is brought about by the representative keywords.

Figure 8.15. *Multidimensional representation of documents [RAV 07]*

[GHA 09] considers the specific case of the economic intelligence process which encompasses strategic analysis and information gathering. This process exploits information through the analysis of interactions in order to understand the behavior of an environment. The authors propose a multidimensional analysis model which includes both the specification of the requirement and a multidimensional representation of the information extracted from the documents in the form of 3D numerical matrices, thereby enabling the representation of relational information (two linked dimensions) and its development (third dimension).

This section has presented the work conducted on accessing information where the focus has been on the semantic aspects derived from metadata, or the terms/concepts extracted from the contents. Section 8.3 relates more specifically to the use of applied data mining techniques on textual information, and in particular, the example of domain mapping.

8.3. Domain mapping via social networks

Scientific and technological information watch activities are essential in today's world, whether it is for economic, administrative, or information retrieval activities. Companies and laboratories have to monitor the activities of their competitors, and identify information, technologies and government action that relate to their own sphere of activity. These "information gathering" activities are necessary in order to define alliance strategies, innovation and strategies adapted to requirements. Large-scale analysis becomes possible due to the availability of extensive sources of publications, patents, scientific literature and other data in electronic form. Tools should be used to extract and analyze practical elements in a relevant manner.

In information science, the analysis of citations and co-citations has been used as a means of overseeing scientific activities [WHI 98, WHI 03]; more recently it has become a means of evaluating scientific research [COU 08]. Citation analysis is utilized to identify core groups of publications, authors, and journals. For example, the ISI Knowledge SM website employs citation analysis to determine the history of the citations of a journal or authors. Similarly, in the context of web pages, hypertext references are extracted to determine the authority of a page and therefore reorder the found pages following a query [KLE 99]. Co-citation analysis is also used to detect author networks or to extract author maps or journal maps [ZIT 94, WHI 03]. As an example, CiteSeer gives a reference to the documents relating to a co-citation. Other digital libraries also provide a link to cited or citatory documents. DBLP (Digital Bibliography and Library Project) provide an index of the co-authors, thereby giving access to their publications in the same way as an ACM portal.

Digital libraries normally provide results in the form of a list of related items (list of related publications or authors), even though the benefit for the users of graphics-based interfaces in the analysis of results has been shown [CHE 02]. In this context, graphics and networks are powerful visualization techniques, essentially due to the fact that a fundamental principle of information mining is linking either concepts or objects. Such a tool can be easily understood by the user, even if the user is a non-specialist.

White *et al.* [WHI 04], for example, present an approach that distinguishes macrostructures inside a network in terms of dense subsets and their overlaps. Hence, Figure 8.16 shows a bipartisan graph (event-actors) for which the dense sub-graphs are surrounded by solid lines.

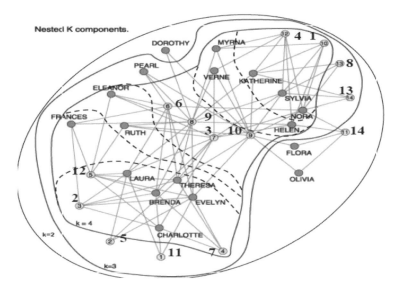

Figure 8.16. *Bipartisan network and sub-structures [WHI 04]*

Chrisment *et al.* [CHR 06] propose the use of networks to represent alliances during publications, for example, Figure 8.17 shows a *country affiliation of author - author* bipartisan graph. On this interface, the size of the points representing each element depends on their frequency of occurrence in the collection. The thickness of the lines is also representative of the strength of the link, for example, the strong collaborations between Israel and the USA are visualized.

Similarly, the thematic specificity of the countries via the terms used in the publications is represented in Figure 8.18. The rows of the matrix under analysis correspond to keywords and the columns correspond to countries. Some of the interesting sub-networks have been circled on the diagram; for example, Canada and Turkey are linked by topics of common interest and this link is not due to the publications which have been written by an author in Canada and another in Turkey, since in Figure 8.17 these two countries are not linked. Guenec *et al.* [GUE 08] show that this type of method enables us to map a domain, even in the case where the original documents are in a language that the user does not know.

Dousset and Loubier [DOU 08] present the use of graphs to analyze the dynamics of relational links. Analysis of the development of social networks is a direct application

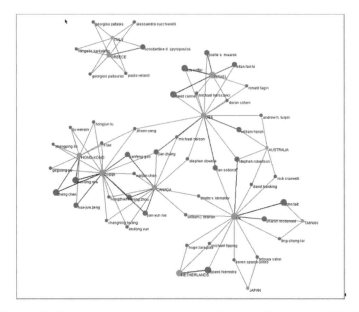

Figure 8.17. *Link between countries via co-writing scientific articles [CHR 06]*

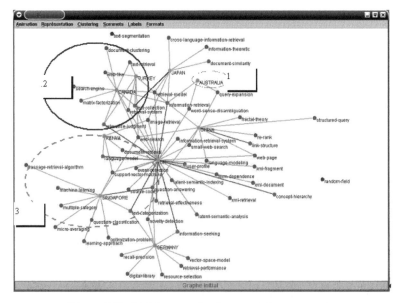

Figure 8.18. *Link between the theme and the country via
the analysis of scientific articles [CHR 06]*

of this work. According to the approach developed, the initial data represented by the relationships between objects are distributed according to a temporal dimension. Each node on the graph is no longer a simple point but a histogram that indicates the involvement of the object in the network as a function of time. It is then possible to extract time sub-structures, in particular when the structure is entirely situated in one time period as illustrated in Figure 8.19. The sub-network in the top right quadrant of the diagram is specific to the period 2003. In the center of the diagram, the network corresponds to the elements that relate to all the periods studied.

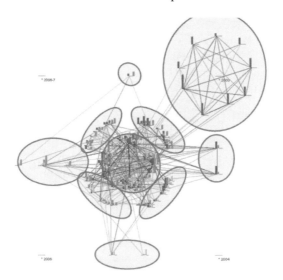

Figure 8.19. *Analysis of dynamic social networks [DOU 08]*

Consequently, methods of data mining can be applied to text sources in order to extract an internal structure from these sources. The principles are widely used in bibliometrics and technological information gathering. The previously mentioned methods can also be used for other purposes relative to IR and are presented in the following two sections.

8.4. Analyzing the variability of searches and data merging

8.4.1. *Analysis of IR engine results*

Studies have shown that the performances of a system can vary considerably (the system works well for one query but not for another). Burkley and Voorhees [BUR 04] consider that understanding the variability is complex owing to the parameters: the formulation of the query, the relationship between the query and the documents, and the characteristics of the system. This variability has been studied using detailed results from the systems. In [BAN 99], six methods were applied to better understand the performances of the participatory systems in a TREC Text Retrieval Conference. The results were analyzed, in particular from a matrix representing the average precision in relation to the systems on the one hand and the need for information on the other. They then used a hierarchical classification to try to extract groups of systems or groups of information requirements or topics. The chosen classification clustered those classes which minimized the distance between the closest objects (simple linking classification). In this study, the authors were unable to extract structures that could be deemed interesting. This can be explained by the classification method used (simple linking rather than a method which favors inertia minimization), by the absence of a return to the raw data (why are the objects clustered in terms of IR?) and ultimately, by the choice of a graphical representation which hid the distance between the groups found and therefore the true structure (see Figure 8.20).

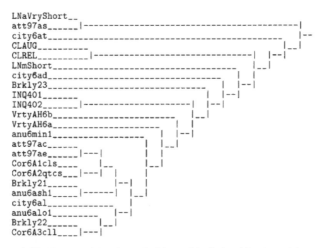

Figure 8.20. *Tree resulting from the hierarchical classification of the system by simple linking, Mean Average Precision - TREC6 Adhoc [BAN 99]*

Another type of analysis was performed in [MIZ 07]. One objective of their work was to identify a small set of topics which would be useful in distinguishing the effective systems from the non-effective systems. As in the previous study, the starting point was the matrix that represented the average precision for two dimensions: systems and topics. The data were first normalized and the data structure was extracted by applying a variation of the HITS (Hyperlink-Induced Topic Search) algorithm [KLE 99], used in particular for the detection of social networks or links between web pages. The authors reached the conclusion that the tests demonstrated the manner in which certain systems distinguish simple requirements for information from difficult topics and that a system could be considered as bad in relation to a set of topics, whereas a good system is one which may have difficulties in relation to certain requirements for information. They finally concluded that the simplest topics to process made it possible to better distinguish the effectiveness of a system. However, the authors did not explain how to exploit these results.

In reality, the analysis presented in [BAN 99] was undoubtedly not thorough enough to extract interesting elements. Hence, Figure 8.21 shows the classification of systems based on the same types of data (average precision from the ad hoc TREC results). The Ward hierarchical classification has been used here; at each stage it minimizes the inertia associated with the clustering of two classes.

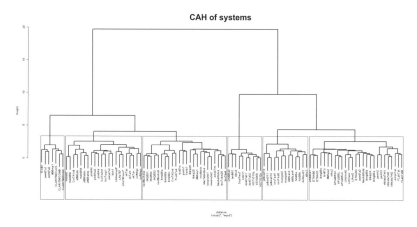

Figure 8.21. *Dendrogram of the hierarchical classification of systems –*
Mean Average Precision – TREC7 Ad hoc [BIG 11]

Six system classes have been formed; this number corresponds to the stabilization of the distances between two clusters when the number of classes is more than six. By analyzing the content of the classes and by returning to the initial matrix, it is apparent that the best systems have been clustered and that the worst systems have likewise been clustered. In [BIG 11], the same type of analysis shows that the topics are clustered in the same manner: the very difficult topics are clustered and the simple topics belong to the same class. The classification results also show that variants from the same system tend to be clustered. An example of how these results can be used will be provided in section 8.4.2.

8.4.2. *Use of data unification*

In the field of data fusion [FOX 94], the variability of the responses from a system is used: the lists of documents found by two or more systems are merged in order to create the final list of documents which will be provided to the user. [CRO 00, WU 06] have shown that merging is more effective if it brings in independent systems. This independence is generally based on an analysis of both common and different documents in the mergeable lists located by the systems. [LEE 97] shows, for example, that merging is more effective when the overlap between the relevant documents is larger than the overlap between the non-relevant documents. Beitzel *et al.* [BEI 03] suggested that the improvements in results through the use of merging is linked to relevant documents which can only be located in one of the lists of found documents. The complementarity or independence of systems can also be based on analyzing their effectiveness on a sample of documents. Hence, Figure 8.21 represents the dendrogram obtained after hierarchical classification (Ward method) has been applied to the matrix collecting the value of the MAP (Mean Average Precision) measure for each participating system (rows) and each information requirement (columns) after normalization (centering, data reduction). The outcome of the classification shows that the best systems tend to be clustered: the best systems are indeed better because of the similar results obtained for the same information requirements. Similarly, the systems which are less effective show the same behavior with respect to information requirements.

Using a factorial method in the analysis completes the observations. Figure 8.22 shows a graphical representation of the first two factorial axes after a factorial analysis has been conducted on the matrix. Slightly more than 30% of the information is represented here.

On axis 1, for example, the systems whose names begin with CLARIT (right hand side) contrast the systems whose names begin with KDxx (left hand side). A return to the raw data shows that the former indicate effective systems, whereas the latter indicate less effective systems. Similarly on axis 2, the systems situated in the bottom quadrant (negative coordinates) are the least effective systems; those with positive coordinates are the most effective systems. The complementarity that appears between the effective systems that contribute to axis 1 and those that contribute to axis 2 have been used to create a new method of merging. This method relies on a learning phase: a sub-collection of documents is used to discover which system should be associated with each information requirement (the system which is most effective for the document sub-set). The test phase relies on this learning to decide which system will process the information requirement for the rest of the collection. In the learning phase, the increase in the MAP is approximately 44% for the ad hoc TREC-7 collection. In the test phase, the improvement is 21% for the same collection. This improvement is reduced to 15% when a representative system of a class of systems is associated with each information requirement (rather than an individual system).

In section 8.5, a final application of IR data mining methods will be presented. It involves the study of the redundancy of performance measures used in IR.

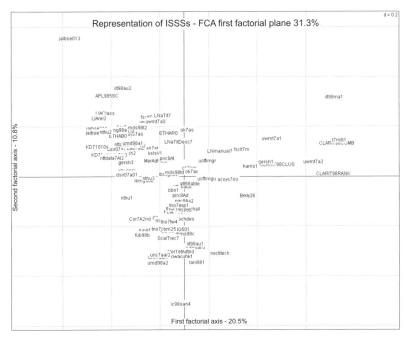

Figure 8.22. *The first two factorial axes – MAP – TREC7 Adhoc – systems [BIG 11]*

8.5. The seven types of evaluation measures used in IR

The evaluation of IRS is a key issue within the discipline. The evaluation model generally used today is based on the one developed in the Cranfield project [CLE 66]. It comprises a collection of documents on which the search is conducted, a set of test queries, and the list of relevant documents from the collection for each of the queries. This model also includes performance measures that are associated with recall and precision. It controls the impact of the search and of the modification of certain system parameters on the effectiveness; the cost is reasonable in relation to an evaluation that brings in users at each stage [ROB 81, VOO 02]. Even if certain evaluation frameworks have been proposed in order to better take into account the user and the acquisition of information [HER 94, JAR 00], the fact remains that the Cranfield model constitutes the dominant approach when evaluating IRS [BOR 03]. A second aspect concerns the number of evaluation methods used. The trec_eval evaluation program, mainly used by the TREC program (Text REtrieval Conference: trec.nist.gov), calculates a set of 135 measures. Some are more commonly used when the focus is on choosing comparison measures for several IR systems. MAP is one of the measures that can be cited (introduced in TREC2). This measure aggregates the precision-recall curves (they combine different points of measure). It is used for overall comparisons [VOO 07]. The high precision measurements (precision when 5, 10, etc. documents are retrieved) are more dependent on the effective number of relevant documents. Certain measures have been introduced more recently, for example, bpref [BUR 04], which objective is to limit the bias linked to the fact that the relevance of the documents is only known for a limited number of documents [SAK 08] and to limit the normalized average precision [MIZ 07]. Even if each measure is introduced to measure a precise phenomenon in IR, certain studies have focused on measuring their interrelation. Tague-Sutcliffe and Blustein [TAG 95] showed that the R-precision (precision when R documents are recovered, R being the number of relevant documents) and the average precision are strongly correlated on an ad hoc TREC-3. Aslam *et al.* [ASL 05] completed the analysis of these two measures using ad hoc TREC-8 data; the authors demonstrated a strong correlation which is possibly linked to the fact that these two measures are geometric approximations of the surface which is situated below the recall-precision curve (see Figure 8.23).

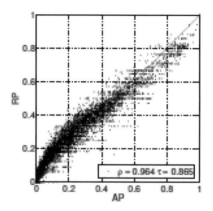

Figure 8.23. *Average precision versus R-precision for each execution in TREC-8 [ASL 05]*

[BUC 05] measured the correlation between seven measures on TREC-7 using the Kendall coefficient. They showed that the correlation between each pair of measures is always above 0.6 and that the strongest correlation is between R-precision and MAP. [ISH 03] analyzed the relationship between the F measure (which measures how the precision is reduced when the recall increases), the point when recall and precision are equal, and the 11 points of recall. The authors considered the coefficient ϕ on the 2×2 contingency table i.e. the cross classification table indicating the relevant/non-relevant documents in the rows and the found/unfound documents in the columns. The authors showed that the F measure and the coefficient ϕ had similar properties, and that the recall point was approximately equivalent to ϕ. [EGG 08] studied the correlation between the precision, the recall, and the F measure. The authors demonstrated that the precision function in relation to recall is a decreasing concave function, whereas that of recall in relation to fallout (percentage of non-relevant documents found) is increasing and concave (fallout + precision =1). [SAK 07] compared the measures based on a

Boolean relevance of the documents with measures based on a graduated relevance; it concluded that the recall based on graduated relevance is strongly correlated with the average precision. These studies concentrated on a reduced set of measures and in general on results obtained from a collection. It is equally important to consider the set of measures used and a set of different evaluation campaigns.

The overall analysis of the results obtained in the ad hoc TREC task after using the set of 130 measures proposed by the trec_eval software for the evaluation of an individual query (5 measures are in fact dedicated to the evaluation of a set of queries) shows that these measures can be mathematically clustered into seven homogeneous classes. The initial matrix which is analyzed in order to achieve this result includes the evaluation methods in the columns and the observations (results obtained for an information requirement, from a system, from a given year of TREC) in the rows; this matrix is composed of $23, 518$ rows and 130 columns. The matrix of linear correlations of performance measurements, which has been calculated using the Bravais-Pearson coefficient, is represented in the form of an image; the numerical values between -1 and $+1$ are coded according to a range of colors/the quantity of gray (see Figure 8.24). In fact, the correlation coefficient has to be between -1 and $+1$; its sign indicates the correlation direction and the absolute value corresponds to the importance of this correlation. Seventy-five percent of the $8, 385$ correlations are above 0.45: this therefore shows a strong correlation between the evaluation measures.

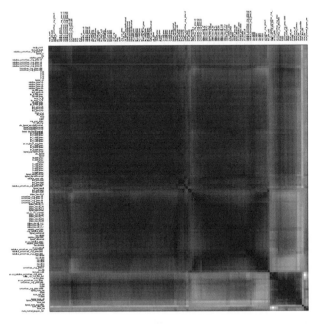

Figure 8.24. *Correlation matrix of the evaluation measures visualized in relation to the quantity of gray [BAC 12]*

A more fine-tuned analysis allows the measures to be clustered into large families. Hence, the original matrix can be used to classify the measures. In order to ensure data homogeneity, the matrix is normalized beforehand (centered, reduced). A hierarchical classification based on the Ward method obtains the dendrogram presented in Figure 8.25.

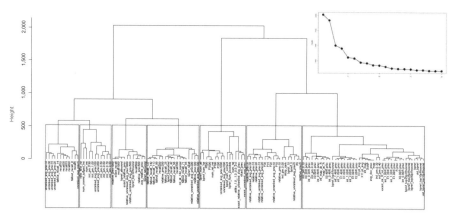

Figure 8.25. *Dendrogram representing the hierarchical classification of evaluation measures. Seven classes have been retained based on the decrease in the distances between the classes presented in the top right quadrant of the figure [BAC 12]*

One of the groups obtained is linked to a high level of precision ($P5$ to $P30$, interpolated recall ircl_prn. 0.00 and 0.10, bpref_5 and 10, high relative_prec, recip_rank, relative_prec5–30, map_at_R, and high relative_unranked_avg_prec). The high precision is particularly significant for Web-based engines, where the user is interested in the initial responses. The MAP measure is found in a different group with the ircl_prn.x measures (for $x = 0, 20$ to $0, 8$), bpref and old_bpref; we recall that MAP aggregates the recall-precision curves. A class regroups the measures in relation to the precision of large sets of found documents (exact_recall, recall500, recall1000). Fallout_recall, recall100, recall200, and relative_prec100 and 200 are also regrouped; these measures are not widely used in the literature. One class clusters the ircl_prn.0.90 and .1.00 interpolated recall as well as the recall at lower slice levels (recall 5–recall 30). Ircl_prn.90 measures the capacity of the system to obtain a good level of precision when numerous documents are found; this measure tends toward 0 ($19, 291$ values from $23, 518$ are zero for Ircl_prn.90). Similarly, Recall30, which is part of the same group, has a tendency to have specific values close to zero owing to the large number of relevant documents. It is mathematically logical for them to be clustered. Finally, the last group brings together particular measures which do not evaluate effectiveness (e.g. the number of relevant documents).

Thus, this analysis shows that the measures calculated by evaluation programs are redundant even if they do not evaluate the same thing. This implies that it is sufficient to choose a representative measure for each group in order to ensure a complete analysis of the effectiveness. This type of analysis can also be used before the introduction of a new measure in order to ensure its non-redundancy in relation to an existing measure.

8.6. Conclusion

In this chapter we decided not to present data analysis methods which have already mostly been well described, for example in [SEB 84, JOL 02, LEB 06, SAP 06]. Instead, we discuss various applications of these methods and associated visualizations in relation to IR and accessing gathered information. The use of varied mathematical methods in IR, in the wider sense, seems to be experiencing a stage of new development. The use of statistical methods emerged at the start of IR automation in the 1970s, in particular, with the analysis of the frequency of terms that led to methods for choosing indexing terms and their weighting [ROB 76]. The classification and categorization methods have largely contributed to the development of document clustering mechanisms [LEW 95, SEB 05], and then to the clustering of queries [WEN 01]. More recently, *learning to rank* principles (see Chapter 2 of this book) can be cited as an example of using mining functions [CAO 07]. In this task, a scheduling function is used to establish which documents should be restored from a list of documents. More specifically, in IR a score is associated with each document and scheduling is carried out according to the descending order of this score. In a learning phase, the examples to learn correspond to scheduled lists of relevant documents in relation to information requirements. The scheduling function is triggered by these examples. In the testing phase, other information requirements are used, but the scheduling function stays the same.

It is envisaged that different paths will be developed in the future. D. Harman indicated the importance of *Failure Analysis* during the RIAO conference of 2004. The analysis of failures and successes with a finite scale can ensure that all queries are not processed in the same manner, no matter what they are. In view of the Question/Answering systems which adapt the processing to the types of queries, the new IR systems would better adapt their processing capabilities if they were able to capture the search contexts related to the queries. The context makes reference to implicit or explicit knowledge concerning the intentions of the user, the user's environment and the system itself. As underlined in [ALL 03], despite recent interest in these problems, little progress has been made due to the difficulty of extracting and representing the knowledge pertaining to the users, the context, and the tasks. Future systems will be able to use the context and characteristics of the queries to infer the characteristics of information requirements, such as the type of query, the type of response, and the response level, and then use these characteristics in the search models. We share this viewpoint. We increasingly think that knowledge discovery systems and information retrieval systems follow the same goal, i.e. restoring information to the user. The distinction between raw information which the IR systems send and a gathered piece of information – still under discussion – should disappear to leave more space for information usage The process used by the tools can become transparent; the key element is hence the response of the system to the requirement of the user, no matter the type of requirement. A drawback to this development concerns the evaluation of responses of such an integrated system. Satisfying the user is not enough; the potential of the collections used to find the information should also be taken into account.

8.7. Acknowledgments

This chapter reports on work carried out in collaboration with colleagues, whom we want to thank profusely: Joël Alaux, Alain Baccini, Anthony Bigot, Claude Chrisment, Taoufiq Dkaki, Sébastien Dejean, Bernard Dousset, Daniel Egret, Gilles Hubert, Saïd Karouach, Laetitia Lafage.

8.8. Bibliography

[ALA 03] ALAUX J., CHRISMENT C., DOUSSET B., MOTHE J., "DocCube: multi-dimensional visualisation and exploration of large document sets", *Journal of the American Society for Information Science and Technology, JASIST, Special Topic Section: Web Retrieval and Mining*, vol. 54, no. 7, p. 650-659, 2003.

[ALL 03] ALLAN J., "Challenges in information retrieval and language modeling: report of a workshop held at the center for intelligent information retrieval", *ACM SIGIR Forum*, vol. 37, no. 1, p. 31-47, 2003.

[ASL 05] ASLAM J.A., YILMAZ E., PAVLU V., "A geometric interpretation of r-precision and its correlation with average precision", in *Proceedings of the International ACM SIGIR Conference on Research and Development in Information Retrieval*, Salvador, Brazil, p. 573-574, August 2005.

[BAC 12] BACCINI A., DEJEAN S., KOMPAORÉ D., MOTHE J., "How many performance measures to evaluate information retrieval systems", *Knowledge and Information Systems*, vol. 30, no. 3, p. 693-713, 2012.

[BAN 99] BANKS D., OVER P., ZHANG N.-F., "Blind men and elephants: six approaches to TREC data", *Information Retrieval*, vol. 1, no. 1/2, p. 7-34, 1999.

[BEI 03] BEITZEL S.M., FRIEDER O., JENSEN E.C., GROSSMAN D., CHOWDHURY A., GOHARIAN N., "Disproving the fusion hypothesis: an analysis of data fusion via effective information retrieval strategies", in *ACM Symposium on Applied Computing SAC*, Melbourne, Florida, USA, p. 823-827, July 2003.

[BIG 11] BIGOT A., CHRISMENT C., DKAKI T., HUBERT G., MOTHE J., "Fusing different systems according to query-topics", *Information Retrieval Journal*, Springer, vol. 14, no. 6, p. 617-648, 2011.

[BON 08] BONNEL N., CHEVALIER M., DOUSSET B., "Métaphores de visualisation des résultats de recherche d'information sur le Web", in BOUGHANEM M., SAVOY J., *Recherche d'information, état des lieux et perspectives*, Hermes, Lavoisier, p. 295-339, 2008.

[BOR 03] BORLUND P., "The IIR evaluation model: a framework for evaluation of interactive information retrieval systems", *Information Research*, vol. 8, no. 3, p. 152, 2003, available at informationr.net/ir/8-3.

[BUC 05] BUCKLEY C., VOORHEES E., "Retrieval system evaluation", in VOORHEES E.M., HARMAN D.K. (eds), *TREC: Experiment and Evaluation in Information Retrieval*, MIT Press, Cambridge, Massachusetts, p. 53-75, November 2005.

[BUR 04] BURKLEY C., VOORHEES E.M., "Retrieval evaluation with incomplete information", in *Proceedings of the International ACM SIGIR Conference on Research and Development in Information Retrieval*, Sheffield, UK, p. 25-32, July 2004.

[CAO 07] CAO Z., QIN T., LIU T.-Y., TSAI M.-F., LI H., "Learning to rank: from pairwise approach to listwise approach", in *International Conference on Machine Learning*, p. 129-136, 2007.

[CHE 00] CHEVALIER M., VERLHAC M., "ISIDOR: a visualisation interface for advanced information retrieval", in *International Conference on Enterprise Information Systems (ICEIS)*, Stafford, 04/07/2000-07/07/2000, Staffordshire University, p. 414-418, July 2000, http://www.staffs.ac.uk.

[CHE 02] CHEN C., "Visualisation of knowledge structures", in CHANG S.K. (ed.), *Handbook of Software Engineering and Knowledge Engineering*, vol. 2, p. 700, World Scientific Publishing Co., River Edge, NJ, 2002.

[CHR 06] CHRISMENT C., DKAKI T., DOUSSET B., KAROUACH S., MOTHE J., "Combining mining and visualization tools to discover the geographic structure of a domain", *Computers, Environment and Urban Systems*, Elsevier, vol. 30, no. 4, p. 460-484, 2006.

[CLE 66] CLEVERDON C.W., MILLS J., KEEN E.M., *Factors Determining the Performance of Indexing System*, Cranfield, vol. 1: *Design*; vol. 2: *Results*, Aslib Cranfield Research Project, College of Aeronautics, UK, 1966.

[COU 08] COUTROT L., "Sur l'usage récent des indicateurs bibliométriques comme outil d'évaluation de la recherche scientifique", *Bulletin de méthodologie sociologique*, vol. 100, p. 45-50, 2008.

[CRO 00] CROFT W., "Combining approaches to information retrieval", in *Advances in Information Retrieval: Recent Research from the Center for Intelligent Information Retrieval*, Chapter 1, Kluwer Academic Publishers, p. 1-36, 2000.

[DOU 08] DOUSSET B., LOUBIER E., "Temporal and relational data representation by graph morphing", in *Safety and Reliability for Managing Risk (ESREL 2008)*, support electronic, 2008.

[EGG 08] EGGHE L., "The measures precision, recall, fallout and miss as a function of the number of retrieved documents and their mutual interrelations", *Information Processing and Management*, vol. 44, no. 2, p. 856-876, 2008.

[EGR 02] EGRET D., MOTHE J., "Exploring bibliographic collections using concept hierarchies", in *Library and Information Services in Astronomy IV*, p. 233-241, 2002.

[ENG 03] ENGLMEIER K., MOTHE J., "IRAIA: a portal technology with a semantic layer coordinating multimedia retrieval and cross-owner content building", in *International Conference on Cross Media Service Delivery*, p. 181-192, May 2003.

[FOX 94] FOX E., SHAW J., "Combination of multiple searches", in *2nd Text Retrieval Conference (TREC-2), NIST Special Publication 500-215*, p. 243-252, 1994.

[GAR 03] GARCIA E., SICILIA M.-A., "User interface tactics in ontology-based information seeking", *Psychology Journal*, vol. 1, no. 3, p. 242-255, 2003.

[GHA 09] GHALAMALLAH I., DOUSSET B., "Modèle d'analyse multidimensionnelle dédié à l'intelligence économique.", in *Colloque Veille Stratégique Scientifique et Technologique (VSST 2009)*, support electronic, 2009.

[GUE 08] GUENEC N., LOUBIER E., GHALAMALLAH I., DOUSSET B., "Management and analysis of Chinese database extracted knowledge", in *BCS IRSG Symposium: Future Directions in Information Access*, electronic, September 2008.

[HER 07] HERNANDEZ N., MOTHE J., CHRISMENT C., EGRET D., "Modeling context through domain ontologies", *Journal of Information Retrieval, Special Issue Contextual Information Retrieval*, vol. 10, no. 2, p. 143-172, 2007.

[HER 94] HERSH W., ELLIOT D., HICKAM D., WOLF S., MOLNAR A., LEICHTENSTIEN C., "Towards new measures of information retrieval evaluation", in *Annual Symposium on Computer Application in Medical Care*, p. 895-899, 1994.

[ISH 03] ISHIOKA T., "Evaluation of criteria for information retrieval", in *IEEE/WIC International Conference*, p. 425-431, 2003.

[JAR 00] JARVELIN K., KEKALAINEN J., "IR evaluation methods for retrieving highly relevant documents", in *Conference on Research and Development of Information Retrieval*, p. 41-48, 2000.

[JOL 02] JOLLIFFE I., *Principal Component Analysis*, second edition, Springer, 2002.

[KLE 99] KLEINBERG J., "Authoritative sources in a hyperlinked environment", *Journal of the Association for Computing Machinery*, vol. 46, no. 5, p. 604-632, 1999.

[LEB 98] LEBART L., MORINEAU A., PIRON M., *Statistique Exploratoire Multidimensionnelle*, Dunod, Paris, 1998.

[LEB 06] LEBART L., PIRON M., MORINEAU A., *Statistique Exploratoire Multidimensionnelle-Visualisation et Inférence en Fouille de Données*, 4th edition, recast, Dunod, Paris, 2006.

[LEE 97] LEE J., "Analysis of multiple evidence combination", in *22nd International ACM SIGIR Conference on Research and Development in Information Retrieval*, p. 267-276, 1997.

[LEW 95] LEWIS D., "Evaluating and optimizing autonomous text classification systems", in *International ACM SIGIR Conference on Research and Development in Information Retrieval*, p. 246-254, 1995.

[MIZ 07] MIZZARO S., ROBERTSON S., "Hits hits TREC: exploring IR evaluation results with network analysis", in *30th International ACM SIGIR Conference on Research and Development in Information Retrieval*, p. 479-486, 2007.

[NGU 07] NGUYEN T., ZHANG J., "A novel visualization model for web search results", *IEEE Transactions on Visualization and Computer Graphics*, vol. 12, no. 5, p. 981-988, 2007.

[POI 00] POINÇOT P., LESTEVEN S., MURTAGH F., "Maps of information spaces: assessments from astronomy", *Journal of the American Society for Information Science*, vol. 51, no. 12, p. 1081-1089, 2000.

[RAV 07] RAVAT F., TESTE O., TOURNIER R., ZURFLUH G., "A conceptual model for multidimensional analysis of documents", in PARENT C., SCHEWE K.-D., STOREY V.C., THALHEIM B. (eds), *26th International Conference on Conceptual Modeling (ER '07)*, Springer-Verlag, LNCS 4801, p. 550-565, 2007.

[ROB 76] ROBERTSON S.E., SPARCK JONES K., "Relevance weighting of search terms", *Journal of the American Society for Information Science*, vol. 27, p. 129-146, 1976.

[ROB 81] ROBERTSON S., "The methodology of information retrieval experiment", in SPARCK JONES K. (ed.), *Information Retrieval Experiments*, Butterworths, London, p. 9-31, 1981.

[SAK 07] SAKAI T., "On the reliability of information retrieval metrics based on graded relevance", *Information Processing and Management*, vol. 43, no. 2, p. 531-548, 2007.

[SAK 08] SAKAI T., KANDO N., "On information retrieval metrics designed for evaluation with incomplete relevance assessments", *Information Retrieval Journal*, vol. 11, p. 447-470, 2008.

[SAP 06] SAPORTA G., *Probabilité, analyse des données et statistique*, 2nd edition, Technip, 2006.

[SEB 05] SEBASTIANI F., "Text categorization", in *Encyclopedia of Database Technologies and Applications*, p. 683-687, 2005.

[SEB 84] SEBER G., *Multivariate Observations*, Wiley, 1984.

[TAG 95] TAGUE-SUTCLIFFE J., BLUSTEIN J., "A statistical analysis of the TREC-3 data", in *In Proceedings of the Third Text Retrieval Conference (TREC-3)*, p. 385-398, September 1995.

[VOO 02] VOORHEES E.M., *The Philosophy of Information Retrieval Evaluation, Lecture Notes in Computer Science*, vol. 2406/2002, Springer, Berlin/Heidelberg, 2002.

[VOO 07] VOORHEES E., "Overview of the TREC 2006", in *The Fifteenth Text Retrieval Conference (TREC 2006). Proceedings, NIST Special Publication: SP 500-272*, p. 1-16, 2007

[WEN 01] WEN J.-R., NIE J.-Y., ZHANG H.-J., "Query clustering using content words and user feedback", in *24th International ACM SIGIR Conference on Research and Development in Information Retrieval*, p. 442-443, 2001.

[WHI 98] WHITE H., MCCAIN K., "Visualizing a discipline: an author co-citation analysis of information science 1972-1995", *Journal of the American Society for Information Science*, vol. 49, no. 4, p. 327-355, 1998.

[WHI 03] WHITE H., "Pathfinder networks and author co-citation analysis: a remapping of paradigmatic information scientists", *Journal of the American Society for Information Science*, vol. 54, no. 5, p. 423-434, 2003.

[WHI 04] WHITE D.R., OWEN-SMITH J., MOODY J., POWELL W.W., "Networks, fields and organizations: micro-dynamics, scale and cohesive embeddings", *Computational and Mathematical Organization Theory*, vol. 10, no. 1, p. 95-117, 2004.

[WU 06] WU S., MCCLEAN S., "Improving high accuracy retrieval by eliminating the uneven correlation effect in data fusion", *Journal of the American Society for Information Science and Technology*, vol. 57, no. 10, p. 1962-1973, 2006.

[ZEL 54] ZELLIG H., "Distributional structure", *Word*, vol. 10, no. 2/3, p. 146-162, 1954.

[ZIT 94] ZITT M., BASSECOULARD E., "Development of a method for detection and trend analysis of research fronts built by lexical or co-citation analysis", *Scientometrics*, vol. 30, p. 333-351, 1994.

Chapter 9

Opinion Detection as a Topic Classification Problem

9.1. Introduction

In recent years, the *classification of documents according to their opinion*[1] considered as a sub-task of document classification, has attracted a steadily growing interest from the Natural Language Processing (NLP) community. Various problems are resolved in document classification, including those which consist in determining the thematic of a document among a finite set of possible thematics. For example, in a corpus of journalistic documents, the task consists in classifying the thematics of texts as *politics, society, sports, arts*, and so on. The objective of opinion detection is to find out, for example, whether a positive or negative opinion is expressed in a text on a certain subject. From this perspective, positive and negative opinions can be considered as two classes which have to be attributed in the framework of the classical classification task. *A priori*, detection and classification of opinions might appear to be a simple task. For numerous reasons, the problem turns out to be rather complex and difficult to solve. An aggravating factor is that often only corpora of limited size and with an asymmetrical distribution of their classes are available.

However, the highly subjective nature of the documents (which may be, among other things, texts associated with products, music criticisms, cinema, political interventions, blogs, or discussion forums) adds to the difficulty of the task. This

---

Chapter written by Juan-Manuel Torres-Moreno, Marc El-Bèze, Patrice Bellot, and Fréderic Béchet.
1 Also known as sentiment classification, sentiment analysis, or opinion mining.

particular feature calls for solutions other than those currently used in a classical classification task [PAN 02].

In a classification based on opinion, complex language phenomena come into play. They can be found at all levels: lexical, syntactic and semantic. But they are also pragmatic when real-world knowledge is required. For example, to determine the polarity of the phrase: *The author offers, in this book, another of the gems which people have got used to*, it is essential to know the author. What other books has he written? Or even: are his books any good? With this previous knowledge (which may or may not be present in the same document in which the opinion is expressed) the extent of the underlying semantic field should be expanded, so that we can increase the chance of determining whether the opinion expressed is positive or if a lot of irony masks a negative opinion.

Studies on opinion classification in scientific literature deal mostly with English corpora. We will also discuss studies based on French corpora realized by [TOR 07, TOR 09]. These corpora concern films, books, video game reviews, political debates, and scientific articles. For obvious reasons, we will focus here on approaches attempting to remain language-independent as far as possible.

Classifying a corpus to a predetermined set of classes and its corollary, profiling texts, is a significant problem in the domain of text search. The aim of classification is to automatically assign a class to a given text object as a function of a profile which will or will not be defined depending on the classification method. A wide range of applications exists. They go from the filtering of large corpora (in order to facilitate information retrieval or scientific and economic monitoring) to the classification by the genre of the text to adapt the linguistic processes to the feature of the corpus. The assignment of a class to a text also involves the assignment of a value which can serve as a criterion in a decision process. The classification of a text according to the opinion expressed is a relevant practical problem, notably in market studies. Nowadays there is a strong demand by some companies for the capability to automatically assess whether the company image in a press article is positive or negative. Hundreds of products are evaluated on the Internet by professional or non-professional users on dedicated sites: what conclusive judgment can we derive from this collection of information provided by the consumer or the company which makes this product? Besides marketing another possible application concerns the articles of a collaborative encyclopedia on the Internet such as Wikipedia: does an article convey a favorable or an unfavorable judgement or is it rather neutral, in line with a fundamental principle of this free encyclopedia?

The core concepts that will be used are based on the adequate representation of the document and the numerical and probabilistic methods for their classification. The semantic orientation of an opinion (expressed as a word or a set of words, generally known as a term) willbe approached by numerical values: either by using the n-grams occurrences, or by conditional probabilities, or a combination of the two. A value exceeding an empiric threshold can be considered as an indication that it belongs to a positive class, or a negative one otherwise. Intermediate values indicate the degree of these implications.

The first attempts to automatically classify adjectives according to their semantic content were realized by [HAT 97] using conjunctions between adjectives. [MAA 04] have used the semantic distance of WordNet [FEL 98] between a word to classify the *good* and *bad* terms. [TUR 03] describe an unsupervised classifier based on the content of an opinion. The classifier decides whether the type of a document is positive or negative based on the semantic orientation of the terms the document contains. This orientation is calculated by estimating the *Pointwise Mutual Information* between a term in question and a pair of primer words that are unambiguous representations of the positive or negative orientations, through a search on Web pages in order to estimate their values. This system correctly ranks 84% of the documents of a small corpus related to cars. The same method when applied to a test corpus of cinema reviews obtains a precision of 65%, which is a particularly difficult task.

In [TOR 07] the authors describe a study that relies on corpora which contain not just two polarities but three: positive, negative, and neutral. This complicates the task in two ways. Firstly, the distribution of class sizes is highly skewed. Secondly, the typical size of the corpus available is rather limited and the characteristics of the polarities are not evident. In an original manner, [TAK 05] have employed the spin *up/down* models to characterize the polarity of the words. They use up/down systems to find the semantic orientations of words: either positive or negative (desirable or undesirable) according to the primer words. The output is a list of words indicating their orientation estimated according to the average field approximation. The authors point out that their approach is equivalent to that of entropy maximization. Even though these results are average in quality, we cite them to show the diversity of methods which can be applied in order to resolve this difficult problem.

9.2. The TREC and TAC evaluation campaigns

The NIST[2] is at the origin of several evaluation campaigns of natural language processing systems working on opinions. From 2008, the DUC conferences (*Document Understanding Conference*) were continued as evaluation tracks TAC (*Text Analysis Conference*)[3] of NIST, i.e. machine research of texts relying on (TREC) opinions, precise questions (TAC, QA), opinion summaries (TAC *Summarization*). These evaluations are performed on the Blog06 corpus [MAC 06] composed of 3 million texts issued from 1,000,000 blogs. Expressed in the form of a set of questions

---

2 National institute of standards and technology, http://www.nist.gov
3 Text analysis conference, http://www.nist.gov/tac/

relating to people, organizations, varied topics or objects, the goal is to detect all the opinions expressed in the blogs and provide the user with the most exhaustive view possible.

9.2.1. *Opinion detection by question–answering*

The objective of the *opinion QA track* of TAC is to precisely respond to questions that relate to an opinion expressed in the documents. For example, *"Who likes Trader Joe's?"* or *"Why do people like Trader Joe's?"* are two questions referring to the grocery shop chain *"Trader Joe's"* and aim at well-defined named entities (*rigid list*) as resonse or at difficult explicative responses (*squishy list*). In the latter case, the responses must contain the *nuggets* of information. Those are subdivided into essential information (*vital*) and exact but not essential information. The chains of responses generated by the systems can be in the following form: *"Trader Joes is your destination if you prefer Industrial wines (unlike Whole Foods)"*; *"Sure, we have our natural food stores, but they are expensive and don't have the variety that Trader Joe's has"*.

In 2008, nine teams have participated in the TAC evaluation campaign. For the 90 series of *rigid* questions, the best system has obtained an average F-score of 0.156, where the F-score is a combination of ($\beta = 1$) precision (number of correct responses divided by the number of responses supplied) and recall (number of correct responses divided by the number of known correct responses). In comparison, the manual reference score was above 0.559. The scores of the other eight teams in 2008 ranged between 0.131 and 0.011.

For the series of *squishy list* questions, the evaluation uses the pyramidal method [NEN 04]. It starts from a list of *nuggets* defined by a first assessor and later enriched by nine other judges from the responses provided by the participants. If, for instance, the average F-score ($\beta = 3$) of the assessors is in the order of 0.5, then those from the systems in 2008 should be 0.17.

The best scores were obtained by the University of THU Tsinghua (China) [LI 08] and IIIT Hyderabad (India) [VAR 08]. The first, THU QUANTA is based on the QUANTA questions–responses system enriched by the use of a lexicon expressing *sentiments*. The authors have tried several lexica, such as Hownet, Wordnet, or Mpqa but without much success as these do not establish the polarity of a word in context (e.g. the adjective *big* can be positive or negative). They have preferred to use their own lexicon, with a more limited size but without having the same inconvenience. The rigid questions are subdivided into two classes, each adopting a specific strategy for their resolution. Firstly, there are the questions asking for the names of blogs or the authors of messages and secondly there are the more classical (factual) questions requiring the precise named entities to be found. The questions are additionally labelled with the sentiment they express (positive or negative). A similar labeling is applied to the documents found in the documentary research phase using the

Lucene engine[4]. Lucene has two independent sets to process, i.e. the set of positive and the set of negative documents.

To extract the nuggets (*squishy* question) only documents that have a polarity similar to those of the questions are considered [LI 08]. The question analysis phase uses different NLP modules which perform morpho-syntactic and syntactic analyses, the resolution of anaphora, and the recognition of named entities. Opinion detection is executed by a labeler based on the resource of relationships PropBank[5]. PropBank together with the use of predefined patterns (e.g. *"reason for XXX"* or *"opinion about XXX"*) associates the detected predictive forms with an opinion verb, opinion carrier, and opinion object. Labeling with a positive or negative sentiment is in turn realized by using an ad-hoc lexicon of positive or negative "opinion words". Depending on the type of question, responses are extracted as a function of analyses based, among other things, on the occurrence frequency of words from the query in the selected phrases and in the document title as well as the number of carrier words of an opinion either by using a BM25 similarity associated with a density measure of the words of the question in the passages of the candidate phrases (traditional approach in question–responses). The extraction of nuggets is in turn realized by combining a pattern-based approach (for the *why* questions, for example) or external knowledge (list of actors and films extracted from the IMDB[6], for example).

The second system that obtained the best performance in 2008 essentially employs numeric approaches [VAR 08]. The architecture of the question–response system remains classical: question categorization, document and passage search (from Lucene and a Bayesian ranker), extraction of candidate responses, and possible candidates ranking. The categorization of questions enables us to determine the type of response, so that we can look for the polarity of the question. Support vector machines (SVM) and Bayesian rankers are used to this effect. The documents found by Lucene are classified into two categories based on their polarity and matched corresponding to that of the question. Responses to *rigid* questions are extracted following a recognition of Named Entities by the SNER software (*Stanford Named Entity Recognition*).

To extract *squishy* answers, the authors have chosen approaches close to those which were previously used for the DUC evaluation of 2007: selection of the more informative phrase according to a combination of divergence scores between the phrases (Kullback-Leibler distance) and similarity to the question. In order to determine the polarity of the questions, the authors have used lists of positive and negative words and have

---

4 Lucene is available at http://lucene.apache.org/.
5 http://verbs.colorado.edu/~mpalmer/projects/ace.html of the predicate-argument type. PropBank can be downloaded here (January 2012): http://verbs.colorado.edu/verb-index/pb/propbank-1.7.tar.gz.
6 Internet movie database.

established classification rules. In order to calculate the document polarity, they have decided to create two Bayesian rankers: the first to distinguish the opinion carrier phrases (no matter the polarity of opinions) and the second is for differentiating positive or negative opinions.

9.2.2. Automatic summarization of opinions

As a continuation of the task described in the previous section, NIST introduced a pilot evaluation titled *Opinion Summarization* in the domain of automatic summarization of TAC evaluation campaigns in 2008. The objective is to generate texts with a maximum length of 7,000 or 14,000 characters. They should summarize the opinions about certain precise topics found in the blogs. The topics are expressed in the form of a set of questions in natural language. For example, on the *Gregory Peck* topic, the questions in 2008 were as follows:

– *What reasons did people give for liking Gregory Peck's movies?*

– *What reasons did people give for not liking Gregory Peck's movies?*

Some of the extracts from the blogs which carry the opinions responding to questions asked are as follows:

– *I've always been a big Peck fan since I saw him in* To Kill a Mockingbird. A Charmed Life *is a fine biography of one my favorite actors.*

– *Gregory Peck can be seen playing his first character without absolutely any redeeming quality in this thriller* (Boys from Brazil).

– *After half an hour of the slow-paced antics of* Roman Holiday, *I voted to stop watching it, so I yoinked it from the DVD player, sealed up the disc in its return envelope.*

22 sets of questions (*topics*) are evaluated as a function of the readability of the summaries[7] (grammar, non-redundancy, structure, and coherence) as well as their informative richness by using the pyramidal method[8].

19 teams participated in this evaluation campaign in 2008. Among all systems, our systems [BOU 08] have pursued an automatic summarization approach by extraction, for certain ones, with a compression phase of phrases and post-processing to improve the readability of the final summary [DAN 08]. Some of the teams have used external resources such as WordNet[9] or Wikipedia[10]. As is often the case, numerical approaches

---

7 The nature of the corpus, text coming from blogs, has naturally increased the difficulty of obtaining highly readable texts.
8 See http://www1.cs.columbia.edu/~becky/DUC2006/2006-pyramid-guidelines.html.
9 http://wordnet.princeton.edu.
10 http://www.wikipedia.org.

were combined with symbolic approaches. [GEN 08] describes the system that has obtained the best score with respect to several criteria by employing deep syntactic analysis. The IIIT, Hyderabad [VAR 08] system applies methods similar to those described in the previous section for the *opinion QA track*. The main differences are at the ranking level so that we can determine the polarity of the phrases (SVM rather than Bayesian), and in the new usage of the SentiWordNet lexicon[11] which assigns a polarity to each *synset* of WordNet (positive, negative, or neutral).

9.2.3. *The text mining challenge of opinion classification (DEFT (DÉfi Fouille de Textes))*

In July 2007, the third edition of the text mining challenge DEFT (DÉfi Fouille de Textes) was organized [AZÉ 05, AZÉ 06]. The text mining challenge in 2007[12] was motivated by the need to put in place text searching techniques enabling us to classify texts according to the opinions they express. Specifically, it consisted of classifying the texts of four corpora in French language according to the opinions formulated. The task proposed by DEFT'07 falls into the application domain of decision making. The data made available to the participants of the challenge consisted of four heterogeneous corpora:

to see/read: 3,460 film reviews, books, shows and comic books, and associated grades. The latter is due to the fact that many film or book review organizations[13] in addition to the commentary assign a grade in the form of an icon. A three level grading system was employed which resulted in three distinct classes: 0 (bad), 1 (medium), and 2 (good);

video games: 4,231 video game reviews with an analysis of different aspects of the game (graphics, playability, length, sound, scenario, etc.) and an overall summary of the game. As in the previous corpus, a three level grading system with the classes 0 (bad), 1 (medium), and 2 (good);

proofreading: reiews of 1,484 scientific articles which aid the decision making of the program committees of scientific conferences and give advice and make recommendations to the authors. Again a three level grading system is applied. Class 0 is assigned to proofreadings that recommend rejection of the article. Class 1 contains the proofreadings that recommend acceptance either demanding major modifications or the referral of the paper to a poster session. Class 2 comprises all articles accepted without or with minor modifications. In

---

11 http://sentiwordnet.isti.cnr.it.

12 http://deft07.limsi.fr/.

13 For example see site http://www.avoir-alire.com.

this corpus (like the following one) the names of persons have already been anonymized;

debates: 28,832 statements of Members of Parliament on law projects discussed in the national assembly. Each statement is accompanied by the Members' vote: 0 (in favor) or 1 (against).

The organizers have split the corpora into two parts: one part (approximately 60%) of the data has been given to the participants as learning data in order to develop their methods, the other part (approximately 40%) has been reserved for the test phase. The use of any data beyond those provided by the organizing committee was forbidden. This specifically excluded access to Websites or whatever other source of information.

The challenge aims at classifying each text according to the opinion expressed, i.e. positive, negative, or neutral in the case of three classes, and for or against in the binary case (parliamentary debates corpus). To test our methods and fine tune their parameters, the learning set of each corpus has been split into five subsets of approximatively the same size (number of texts to process).

9.2.3.1. *Integration of systems*

Nine decision systems (to be presented later) using classifiers with different text representations (n-grams, n-lemmas, *seeds*, and terms) have been combined with the objective to obtain *different recommendations* on the label of a text. Furthermore, the goal is not to optimize the stand-alone results of each classifier but to use them as tools in their default setting and to approach the optimum by the combination of their results.

1) LIA_SCT [BÉC 00] is a classifier based on semantic decision trees *SCT-Semantic Classifin Tree* [KUH 95]). The texts are represented as lemmas. BoosTexter [SCH 00] is a wide margin classifier based on the *boosting Adaboost* algorithm [FRE 96]. Four of our systems use the *BoosTexter* classifier:

2) LIA_BOOST_BASELINE: a document is representated by word trigrams;

3) LIA_BOOST_BASESEED: each document is represented by *seeds* weighted by the number of its occurrences, in uni-gram mode;

4) LIA_BOOST_SEED: each document is represented by the words and also by *seeds*;

5) LIA_BOOST_CHUNK: The *LIA-TAGG* tools cuts the document into a set of lemmatized syntagms. Each syntagm contains a *seed* and the previous and following syntagms are also chosen as the representation. The other syntagms are not part of the representation of the document. *BoosTexter* is applied in the trigram mode on this representation.

6) SVMTorch [COL 02] is a classifier based on the Support Vector Machines (SVM) [VAP 82, VAP 95]. The LIA_NATH_TORCH system is obtained with *SVMTorch* and the input vector is represented by the *seeds* lexicon.

7) Timble [DAE 04] is a classifier that implements several *Memory-Based Learning* (MBL) techniques. The LIA_TIMBLE system applies the *TiMBL* tool to the *seeds*.

8) Probabilistic modeling of a uni-lemma and family of words. The texts have been slightly filtered (in order to keep little intonations such as a passive voice, interrogation, or exclamation forms), an aggregation process of composed words, and regrouped in the words of the same family (by using a dictionary with approximately 3,00,000 forms). Each document has been transformed into a bag of uni-lemmas. Then, the class to which document t belongs is calculated as:

$$P_t(w) \approx \prod_i \lambda_1 P_t(w_i) + \lambda_0 U_0 \qquad [9.1]$$

where $P(w)$ is the probability of belonging to word w, U_0 is a constant ...

9) Modeling according information theory. Here, we envisage going back to a classical information theory model, all the while looking to integrate some of the specificities of the problem. The formulation initially chosen is close to those employed during a previous DEFT [ELB 05]:

$$\widetilde{t} = \arg\max_t P(t) \times P(w|t) = \arg\max_t P(t) \times P_t(w) \qquad [9.2]$$

The labeling t can be based on values from a reduced cardinal set of two or three elements [0-1] or [0-2], *a priori* the problem seems to be simple, and the quantity of the data supplied is sufficient to learn the models well. Even if the specific vocabularies of different corpora are not large (between 9,000 different words for the smallest corpus and 50,000 for the largest), it remains that certain entries are under-represented. Also in line with what is normally done to calculate the value of the second term of equation [9.2] an n-lemma smoothing model has been opted for (n starting from 0 to 3):

$$P_t(w) \approx \prod_i \lambda_3 P_t(w_i|w_{i-2}w_{i-1}) + \lambda_2 P_t(w_i|w_{i-1}) + \lambda_1 P_t(w_i) + \lambda_0 U_0 \qquad [9.3]$$

The originality of the modeling used in DEFT'07 lies essentially in the discriminant aspects of the model. In the learning phase, the n-lemma counts are rescheduled in proportion with the discriminating power. This is estimated according to a point of view which complements the Gini impurity criteria:

$$G(w, h) \approx \sum_t P_t^2(t|w, h) \qquad [9.4]$$

This formula is employed to give more importance to the (w, h) events which appear only in one class ($G(w, h) = 1$) as compared to the other distributions. In the worst case, scenario $G(w, h)$ is $1/|T|$, if T is the class set.

9.2.3.2. *First results using integration*

Figure 9.1 illustrates the *F*-score performances of an incremental integration of the methods used. However, the order displayed has no impact on the final integration: it was only chosen to better illustrate the results. It can be seen that these results are above the average of results of the teams having participated in the DEFT '07 challenge, with all corpora combined.

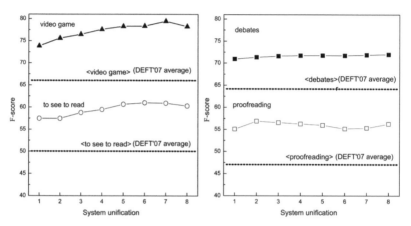

Figure 9.1. *F-score of unification following the 9 methods added. 1: BOOST_BASELINE; 2: 1 ∪ BOOST_BASESEED ∪ BOOST_SEED; 3: 2 ∪ Information theory; 4: 3 ∪ 1-gram; 5: 4 ∪ NATH_TORCH; 6: 5 ∪ TIMBLE; 7: 6 ∪ BOOST_CHUNK; 8: 7 ∪ SCT*

In Figure 9.2, an *F*-score of the validation set (V) vs. the test set (T), on the four corpora is shown. A remarkable coincidence between the two is observed, which signifies the learning and validation strategies in the five subsets and the integration of several rankers worked well.

The following section is dedicated to a variation of the 8th model described in section 9.2.3.1. This variation has been implemented since 2007 in one of the systems developed by the LIA, and most often yields the best results.

9.3. Cosine weights – a second glance

The index most often employed in information retrieval to quantify the similarity of two documents, or a document and a query is the cosine similarity measure. Equation [9.5] is given as a reminder. This index is also used in text classification to estimate the similarity of document *d* and class *c*. The problems linked to the disproportion of the size of the document and the class will not be discussed here due

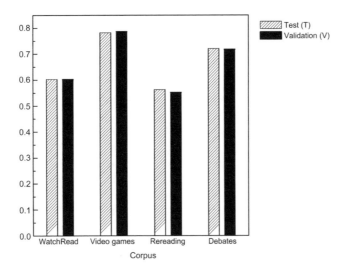

Figure 9.2. *Comparison of the F-score of the validation set (V) vs. the test set (T) for each of the corpora, obtained by the integrated system*

to lack of space:

$$\cos(d, c) = \frac{\sum_{i \in d \cap c} w_{i,d} \times w_{i,c}}{\sqrt{\sum_{i \in d} w_{i,d}^2 \times \sum_{i \in c} w_{i,c}^2}} \qquad [9.5]$$

with:

$$w_{i,x} = T_{i,x} \times \log \frac{N}{F_i} \qquad [9.6]$$

As shown in equation [9.6], the weights $w_{i,x}$ are generally obtained by calculating the product of two terms: the number of times (TF is written $T_{i,x}$ here), where the term i appears in the segment or the class x ($x = d$ or $x = c$), and an inverse function (IDF) of the number of (F_i) segments (among the set of N segments), where the term i appears at least once. We propose to enrich the weight calculation formula by adding a discriminant factor D and by allowing for a more or less larger elasticity of each of the three factors by an increase to a variable power (α, β, γ):

$$w_{i,d} = T_{i,d}^{\alpha} \times D_i^{\beta} \times \log^{\gamma} \frac{N}{F_i} \qquad [9.7]$$

$$D_i = G_i = 1 - I_i = \sum_{i=1}^{k} P^2(j|i) \qquad [9.8]$$

The three exponents found in equation [9.7] are also parameters. Their values are conveniently estimated on a development corpus. In the case where the data will lead to a β value of zero and if it also happens that $\alpha = \gamma = 1$, the classical TF.IDF which corresponds to equation [9.6] will be returned. This proposition therefore integrates, like in a particular case, the weight calculation generally employed in information retrieval.

During DEFT'07 [TOR 07], it has been proposed to retain as an estimation of the discrimination power associated with term i, the Gini purity factor which is easily derived, as demonstrated in equation [9.8], from the Gini impurity factor I_i by taking its complement to 1. When the cardinality k of the set of classes is greater than 2, it is often observed that among them there is a subset containing the classes presenting a strong collection among themselves, whereas they are distinctly different from the others. It can be easily identified that terms belonging to the two classes are connected to one another but not to others. If they do not completely identify a class, it is useful to measure at which point they reject one or even several. Their refuting power can be evaluated due to a relaxation of the Gini factor G_i' (see equation [9.9]). For this, research is conducted on the distribution P_r obtained by combining two classes. Among which the provided $(k-1)k/2$ possibilities gives the best Gini index:

$$G_i' = \max_r G_i(r) = \max_r \sum_{j=1}^{k-1} P_r^2(j|i) \qquad [9.9]$$

In order to play with the two tables, namely the determination and refuting tables, it is evident that it is only interesting when we combine the two criteria. (see equation [9.10]).

$$D_i = \lambda \times G_i + (1 - \lambda) \times G'i \qquad [9.10]$$

We note that the addition of a third term in equation [9.7] can be understood as a way to modulate each apparition of a term i in the document d up to a fraction of the unit proportional to discrimination power D_i. It remains to be defined what we will call a term and more specifically which are the lexical units meriting to be retained.

9.4. Which components for a opinion vectors?

Whenever possible, it is preferable to integrate components corresponding to lexical units formed from clustered terms into the opinion vectors rather than isolated words. This choice comes from an analysis of the difficulty of the problem.

Among the focus points researched to make a correct decision during the categorization process, it is possible to envisage the size of the text, length of the phrases, percentage of the root word, and adjectives or all other grammatical categories. However, it is natural to think that the most appropriate focus points are in fact the terms which compose the text, and, through their intermediary, the concepts to which they refer. However, these terms are mostly polysemic and ambivalent (this is the case for words such as *terrible, amateur, price, costly, rent, double, simple, first, last*, and so on).

Since there is no system that is performant enough to make a semantic disambiguation viable, it is easy to go back to an automatic process which through these discussion choices introduces noise in the data. This can possibly be done by maintaining all the viable sense assumptions associated with a probabilistic value. Another path has been proposed based on the following observation: it is most often in a close context where these ambiguities may be resolved. From this, encompassing an ambiguous word in a sequence sticking it to its close environment better identifies its use, and especially serves as a more precise indicator of the polarity.

9.4.1. *How to pass from words to terms?*

A preliminary stage, named pre-processing, enables us to pass from words to terms. Essentially, during this phase, it consists of splitting the text into lexical units, where a larger point of view is normally taken. Since instead of being content with segmenting it into constituent parts, the concatenation of contiguous words is performed to obtain types of *molecules* increasing the power to influence the decision toward one or the other opinions which are to be determined. While passing, misspelled words can be corrected, the inflected forms can be brought back to their roots, lemma, or stem. In order to produce so-called *discriminant clusterings*, or more briefly *clusterings*, it is recommended that these reductions should not be practiced systematically, but only if justified according to the discrimination power defined in [9.10]). These rules serve to overhaul the texts which will be automatically inferred from the corpus itself and are never written by a human.

The recommended method comes back to automatically inferring each rule according to the annotated learning corpus under the constraint that the result of its application leads to a better identification of the class supplied in the annotation. Owing to a set of experiments made on a given corpus (IMDB in this case[14]), in the rest of this chapter, the large comparative studies on the behavior of three possible methods among others to compose the words in terms will be presented:

1) *Classical collocations*: classically, different tests can be employed to calculate the collocations on a corpus (whether it is annotated or not): χ^2, the mutual information or the test of the likelihood relationship. This last criteria is employed by following the indications given by ([MAN 00]). We note that the calculation can be done on the

---

14 See section 9.5 "Experiments".

learning, development, and test corpus, without introducing a bias, since the annotations are not used, contrary to the three following methods;

2) *Collocations by class*: the same criteria as those retained for the calculation of collocations is used to calculate, class-by-class, a set of collocations (in this case named **coloclasses** in the following) specific to each class. We note that the different sets are united in the following. In this case, as in the previous and the following two, the procedure employed is iterative. From this, it is apparent that this is not optimal. It would be if we sought to determine in one pass the collocations no matter the number of their components;

3) *Discriminant clusterings*: the same procedure as in method 2, with a slight difference: the coloclasses are only the product of intra-class characteristics, but they are not determined by the inter-class characteristics. The Gini criteria[15] fills this gap. It should also be noted that here the clusterings are calculated class-by-class on the learning corpus, and rendered in an overall set at the end of the first phase.

REMARKS 9.1.– By briefly explaining where the idea of producing clusterings has come from, certain steps are taken toward the potential refinement of the model. Some of these paths are specifically discussed in the examples given in the following section.

To model the production of acoustic vectors in the initial speech recognition systems, just as in the 1980s, the Bakis machines such as those represented in Figure 9.3 A, have been used. The fact that the machine must be trained by the word does not give access to very large vocabularies. The passage with a phonetic representation relieves this problem. At each automatically phonetiscized word, it can correspond to a concatenation of the phonetic machines as illustrated in Figure 9.3 B, with more or less states, a certain number of full or empty transitions (discontinuous lines corresponding to the elided part of the phenomena) as well as the two paths differentiating fast flow and slow flow (presence of loops). In an attempt to get past this manner of proceeding which presumes, despite certain latitudes, a standardized pronunciation of the words, it has been envisaged, among other things, from real observations on the pre-learning corpora for each word or syllable automatically constructing a *fenonic baseform* machine dedicated to this base unit, and obtained by concatenating one or the other of the base cell chosen in a finite set of atoms as in Figure 9.3 C.

There is no question of confirming that there is a perfect transposition of the inference of acoustic machines to the acquisitions of clusterings from the annotated texts, but the analogy that can be established between the two domains can provide a

---

15 The terms w_1 and w_2 are clustered if, and only if, w_1 and w_2 have been contiguously observed at least once in a sufficient number of examples and if $G(w_1, w_2)$ is larger than an empirically determined threshold.

A: Bakis Machine

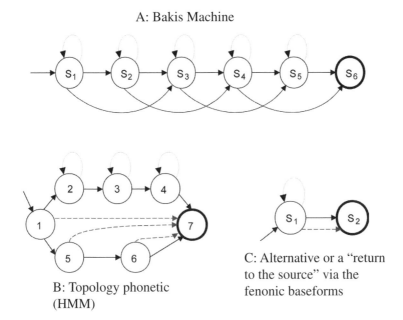

B: Topology phonetic
(HMM)

C: Alternative or a "return
to the source" via the
fenonic baseforms

Figure 9.3. *Markov machines*

glimpse of the improvements to come. First of all, we can note that a clustering is a concatenation in contiguous terms, which (in the sense D_i) is more discriminating than each of the terms composed of it. The empty transition model enabling jumping a state has not been incorporated in that which enables the modeling of ellipses. The presence of several possible paths to produce a sound on the graphic B, for example, leads to thinking that it would be just as appropriate to predict the development of alternative possibilities rather than, as done now, rewriting a word in another.

The reader is invited to imagine all the other perspectives that can be traced from this parallel established between the two domains. A non-negligible point is insisted on to illustrate what is lost by applying the substitution and composition rules (it is coloclasses or clusterings) to produce a unique version of the text from which the categorization is done.

In note 42 in which Perreau has inserted some of the commentaries published in the satire Persius16 VI[16], the translator explains that three different senses can be attributed to the phrase *"Non adeo inquis exossatus ager juxta est"* according to the assumptions made on the punctuation and such that *adeo* is taken for an adverb or for a verb. Only

16 *Persian Satires* translated and commented by A. Perreau, Paris: C.-L.-F. Panckoucke, 1832.

two are retained. If it is read: *"Non adeo, inquis, exossatus ager; juxta est"*, the meaning would be *"the heritage is not already in such a good state; as you wish"*; whereas if the reading is: *"Non adeo, inquis; exossatus ager juxta est"*, the passage can be interpreted as follows: *"I don't want, you say, any succession; Nearby, I have a well-cultivated field"*.

Even if it is not probable that these systems aim to process texts in Latin, this seems to be a good opportunity to choose an example in the language which no longer comprises some insiders in order to give others the image what these machines are up against. Not only the texts that are submitted to them which are written in a language which is, for them, far from being alive, but also they would still have to make the distinction between two possible meanings of the same phrase. To come back to the problem, it is interesting to make the decision of ranking a text in class X because by linking it according to the rule (or automatons) of the class X with the discriminating parameters learned from this class, a better cosine was obtained than class Y by linking the text according to the rules of the other class Y.

9.5. Experiments

The experiments presented here have led to the IMDB[17]. These data are described in a detailed manner in two publications [PAN 04, PAN 08]. This corpus is particularly well balanced in the sense that it contains 1,000 negative criticisms and 1,000 positive criticisms on cultural products (mostly films). They have been split into 1,400 for learning (700+ and 700−) and 600 for test (300+ and 300−). The development corresponds to a cross-validation performed seven times on a seventh learning (of 200 criticisms).

The discriminant terms (Table 9.2) obtained from the two iterations are mostly "more speaking" than the discriminant words (Table 9.1).

In Figure 9.4, it is possible to see how the number of composition rules of the terms evolve as a function of the number of iterations for each of the four assumptions discussed in section 9.4.1. As previously mentioned, this is done through the bias of rules of rewriting automatically inferred from the corpus. By playing on the thresholds discussed in note 15, a particular emphasis can be put on the rules of clustering incorporating a negation (some examples are given in Table 9.3).

Normalization and generalization of terms

Provided that the discriminant power of a term does not reduce, the coverage can be increased by replacing one (even many) of its components with another. These

---

17 Corpus available at: http://www.cs.cornell.edu/People/pabo/movie-review-data/.

POSITIVE CLASS			NEGATIVE CLASS		
22	1.0	magnificent	13	1.0	sucks
13	1.0	darker	12	1.0	vomit, justin
12	1.0	en	12	1.0	insulting, incoherence
11	1.0	seamles, ourselves	12	1.0	atrocious, 3,000
11	1.0	organized, lovingly	11	1.0	jolie
10	1.0	thematic, melancholy	10	1.0	uh, dud, degenerate
10	1.0	gattaca, gaining	9	1.0	shoddy, angelina
9	1.0	sullivan, steady	9	1.0	overwrougth
9	1.0	ideals, comforts	8	1.0	silverstone, missfire,liu
8	1.0	revolutionnary	8	1.0	shuttle, nutty
8	1.0	widescreen, perceive	8	1.0	horrid, haunted, coyote
8	1.0	juges, glorify	8	1.0	conceived, brukheimer
46	0.9	outstanding			...
		...	18	0.9	uninvolving
		...	29	0.9	ludicrous

Table 9.1. *Example of discriminating words*

POSITIVE CLASS		NEGATIVE CLASS	
22	is-excellent	13	is-poor
13	well-worth	12	is-terrible
12	right-time, is-rare	12	stupidity-of
11	characters-this	12	one-of-worst, 's-as-if
11	son-'s, very-effective, terrific-as	11	worst-movie, this-mess
10	other-film, disney-animated	10	to-waste
10	only-problem-with, ed-harris	9	up-a, amounts-to, SSTAR-i
9	world-that, see-by	9	this-turkey, in-bad
9	reality-of, out-of-life	8	case-i, aren't-good
8	of-pace, of-finest	8	not-enough-to, mission-to-mars
8	mood-of	8	mess-that, (-scott, can't-save)
8	is-fantastic, great-thing	8	is-not-good, bad-dialog
46	i'm-not-say, characters-with		...

Table 9.2. *Examples of discriminant terms*

rewritings can be justified by suppression of the repetition or tripling of letters, the final suppression of certain words, or even the substitution of letter sequences. For these three cases, examples of rules obtained automatically from the IMDB corpus while maintaining the discrimination power from *D* to 1 are represented in (Table 9.4). The numbers which precede each rule are the apparition frequencies in the learning corpus after unification.

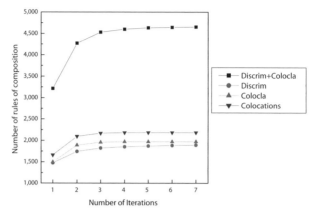

Figure 9.4. *Number of clustering rules automatically obtained from N iterations on the IMDB corpus*

doesn't-even	work
doesn't-go	anywhere
doesn't-have	clue
doesn't-help	either
doesn't-know	how
doesn't-really	matter

Table 9.3. *Example of IMDB clustering rules incorporating a negation*

Some of the rules can be discussed and a certain noise can be introduced but it is the price we have to pay to escape supervision of the process (which is translated by writing, rereading, and correction of rules).

9.5.1. *Performance, analysis, and visualization of the results on the IMDB corpus*

Since there are only two balanced classes in each of the sub-corpus of the IMDB set and since the system never abstains from answering, here the precision is equivalent to recall and to the F-score.

9.5.1.1. *IMDB performance*

The results obtained are equivalent in the test and development, and are the best of the cases at the same level as those published in [PAN 04]. As expected, the collocations calculated in a general manner give poorer results. The coloclasses and clusterings give equivalent results, but it is the union of the two sets which achieves better performance. The first iteration enables a leap of the results. After that, at best stagnation is observed,

Repetition of letters		Suppression of finals		Substitutions of letters	
21 uhh	uh	15 insultingly	insulting	9 atheism	atheist
15 moll	mol	14 atrociously	atrocious	8 unnerve	unnerving
13 lasser	laser	10 sullivans	sullivan	8 deliberation	deliberate
11 ooooh oooh	ooh	10 departments	depart	7 perrier	perry
8 unerving	unnerving	9 wilderness	wilder	6 ideologies	ideology
7 traveller	traveler	9 perceived	perceive	6 ideological	ideology
7 tatoo	tattoo	8 ineffectuality	ineffectual	6 homophobic	homophobe
7 surveilance	surveillance	8 divinely	divine	5 intolerant	intolerance
7 kauffman	kaufman	7 enchantment	enchant	5 homophobia	homophobe
7 cassanova	casanova	7 barreness	barren		

Table 9.4. *Example of repetition, suppression of finals and substitution of letters*

excellent-acting	excellent-performance
excellent-movie	excellent-film
lack-of-chuckle	few-chuckle
save-private-ryan-is	save-private-ryan
unstructured	poorly-construct

Table 9.5. *Examples of IMDB rewriting rules*

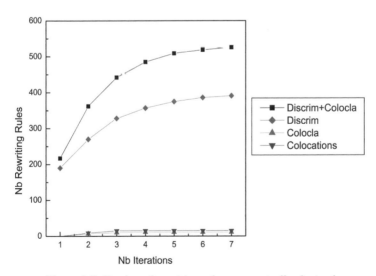

Figure 9.5. *Number of rewriting rules automatically obtained from N iterations on the IMDB corpus*

at worst oscillation or decrease. Finally, the comparison between the scores observed at the first iteration and the following demonstrate the gain due to the composition and rewriting rules.

Figure 9.6 shows that performance does not improve after the sixth iteration due to the good reason that there are no composition or rewriting rules which add to one or the other of the four assumptions retained (see Figures 9.4 and 9.5).

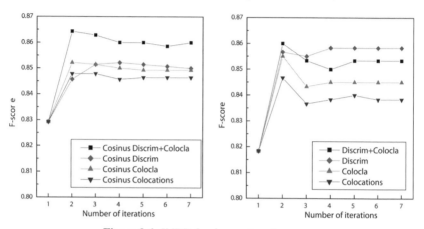

Figure 9.6. *IMDB development performances*

9.5.1.2. *Presentation and analysis of a 857_17527 IMDB example*

```
<DOCUMENT id="857_17527">
<NOTE valeur="neg"/>
<TEXT>
Claire Danes, Giovanni Iibisi, and, Omar Epps make a
likable trio of protagonists, but they're just about the
only palatable elements of the mod squad, a lame-brained
big-screen version of the 70s TV show. the story has
all the originality of a block of wood (well, it would
if you could decipher it), the characters are all
blank slates, and Scott Silver's perfunctory action
sequences are as cliched as they come. by sheer force
of talent, the three actors wring marginal enjoyment
from the proceedings whenever they're on screen, but the
mod squad is just a second-rate action picture with a
first-rate cast.
</TEXT>
<LIA_TAGG>
```

```
<s> ZTRM <s>
claire NNP claire
danes NNPS danes
, YPFAI ,
giovanni <UNK> giovanni
...
```

Example 857_17527 after 7 iterations:

```
HYP = NEG 0.52002 HYP = POS 0.47998 REF = NEG
```

```
DEB Claire Danes, Giovanni Ribisi, Omar Epps make
likable trio of protagonist but 're just about-only
palatable element of mod squad lame brain big-screen
version-of 70 tv-show story have-to-do-with all
originality of block of wood (well it-would if-you
could decipher it) characters-be blank slate scott
silver 's perfunctory action-sequences be as cliched
as come-by sheer force of talent three actors wring
marginal enjoyment from proceedings whenever 're-on
screen but mod squad is-just second rate action picture
with first-rate cast FIN.
```

It is always helpful to explain to the user the reasons that have driven the system toward making such and such a decision. This is classically done by framing, in a more or less subtle manner, each term with a color describing the class to which it contributes the most. However, this can also be done by creating an analogous table to Table 9.6 for recapitulating the 10 or 20 terms of the text contributing the most to the choice of each class.

TOP TEN NEGATIVE			TOP TEN POSITIVE		
marginal	0.0290	0.0290	come-by	0.0289	0.0289
about-only	0.0157	0.0446	picture	0.021	0.0499
action-sequences	0.0143	0.0589	version	0.0107	0.0606
perfunctory	0.0143	0.0732	first-rate	0.0058	0.0664
proceedings	0.0104	0.0836	likable	0.0054	0.0719
characters-be	0.0093	0.0929	enjoyment	0.0051	0.077
originality	0.0086	0.1015	palatable	0.0045	0.0815
characters	0.008	0.1095	element	0.0033	0.0848
is-just	0.0061	0.1156	version-of	0.0031	0.0879
sequences	0.0052	0.1208	it-would	0.0021	0.0900

Table 9.6. *Terms (under column 1) having the highest contribution (under column 2) to orient the decision toward one or the other two classes, below column 3 is the sum of contributions*

9.6. Extracting opinions from speech: automatic analysis of phone polls

Initial sections of this chapter have processed the expression of opinions in written texts. In this section, the problem of extracting opinions from oral messages will be presented, particularly the automatic analysis of opinion polls. The main difficulty of this type of corpus is the processing of spontaneous speech, typical for oral expression of opinions, for which Automatic Speech Recognition (ASR) nowadays are still imperfect.

Several studies have been carried out to identify positive or negative emotions in vocal messages collected in dialog situations. Acoustic parameters such as the fundamental frequency, energy of the signal, or even the values of the formatives have been used in conjunction with linguistic parameters [LEE 05]. A unification of linguistic parameters and acoustic parameters is also proposed [LIT 06] to predict the emotions attached to a vocal message. The selection of an optimal set of acoustic parameters linked to emotions is discussed in [NEI 06].

The application described in this section differs from the previous studies in that it focusses on detecting opinions that have not necessarily been expressed by emotional speech. It is for this reason we restrict our study to linguistic parameters. After describing the corpus used, two opinion detection methods will be used, one based on labeling methods performed on the ASR transcription modules; the other method consists of directly integrating this detection stage in the ASR process in order to increase the sturdiness of the detection.

9.6.1. *France Télécom opinion investigation corpus*

People are invited by a short message to call a free number to express their satisfaction of the customer service that they recently telephoned. By entering this number, the vocal message invites them to leave a message:

"*[...] You have recently contacted our customer service. We wish to ensure that you are satisfied with the help received during your phone call. You can leave your answer after the beep. Do not hesitate to share all your comments and suggestions for our service, since this will help us to improve it. We wish to thank you for your help and are always available to you. Leave your message after the beep*".

Since the messages were originally recorded by an automatic operator, no natural feature has facilitated automatic processing: no recommendation on the mode of elocution, open question, and even an incitation to leave comments. Thus, the collected messages are *realistic* and have varying length (from tens of words to hundreds of words). For this study, 1,779 messages collected over a period of 3 months, have been manually transcribed at the level of words, opinions, and markers (disfluency indications and discursive markers).

The corpus was divided into three sub-corpora. Around 50% of the phrases make up the learning corpus, 33% account for the development corpus, and 17% the test corpus. The application's lexicon comprises about 4,500 words.

Analysis of user satisfaction is performed by the poll analysis team according to 3 dimensions: the quality of the reception (denoted as *reception*), the waiting time to access the service (denoted as *wait*), and the efficiency of the service (denoted as *efficiency*). This last dimension is most represented in the corpus. It concerns both the evaluation of the responses with respect to the expectation of the user (in other words, has the problem been solved?). But it also refers to the quality of the information provided. Each subjective expression can receive two polarities: *positive* and *negative*. There are thus a total of six labels to characterize the subjective expression of the corpus.

In manual transcription, in each message, these expressions are indicated by a label. The corpus is in segments, each with one or more specific opinion. The aim of the automatic comprehension module is to find these segments and label them with one of the six labels. An example of a message with reference labels is given in Table 9.7.

"yes Mr SURNAME NAME I phoned the customer service yeah <seg label=reception,pos> I was very well received</seg> some <seg label=efficiency,pos> good information </seg> except that <seg label=efficiency,neg> it still does not work </seg> therefore I don't know if I made a bad correction or there is a problem otherwise <seg label=efficiency,pos label=reception,pos> the reception and advice was very appropriate </seg> even though <seg label=efficiency,neg> no positive result was obtained </seg> thank you goodbye"

Table 9.7. *Message example of the France Télécom opinion corpus with several opinions with the segment markers*

Nb concept by message	Distribution (% corpus)	Average size (nb words)
0	19.2	61.0
1	51.3	40.3
2 and more	29.5	60.8

Table 9.8. *Distribution of the messages in the France Télécom opinion corpus as a function of the number of concepts expressed*

Table 9.8 shows that the average size of a message does not increase as a function of the number of concepts that are expressed. It is interesting to note that more words are required to express none of the concepts researched than the number of words to express one. This is explained, by the fact that the speaker can express himself *off topic* just as much as on the cause of the problem or on his personal situation as on his feelings on the customer service and also, by the fact that a same segment of the message can support several criteria.

Concerning the average number of words necessary to express a concept, the concepts describing a negative polarity often require more words than the concepts describing a positive polarity. Thus: *"very good reception super very good thank you"* will be labeled *satSerAcc satisfied by the reception service* whereas *"I asked to remove the option but since I have still received numerous call I would like you to cancel them"* would be labeled *insatSerEff* for *unsatisfied by the service efficiency*.

One of the problems that these messages point out is that an identical concept can be seen several times in a message with opposite opinions. This is the case when the person is not entirely satisfied (e.g. satisfied by the customer service but not by the results) or that a temporal notion enters its discourse. An example of this type of message is given in Table 9.7.

9.6.2. *Automatic recognition of spontaneous speech in opinion corpora*

The transcription of spontaneous speech remains one of the challenges with which the ASR methods struggle even now. At the acoustic level, this speech will be characterized by hesitation, pauses, in the interior of words or even truncated words; at the linguistic level, the statements will often be truncated, glazed with auto correction and discursive markers difficult to predict by the statistical language models employed. Table 9.9 presents the transcription of a verbal message issued from this corpus which, without being part of the most difficult messages to process, illustrates well the type of difficulty shown.

This message is an example of spontaneous speech or *unprepared speech*. The numerous retakes and continuous correction in it illustrate the definition, and give rise to enormous transcription difficulties for the ASR systems. Even by assuming that the ASR models are sufficiently sturdy to transcript these messages into words, this type of output is not necessarily usable through the systems used for comprehension. In fact, in a spontaneous statement, the transcription of words represents only 1D of the message. It misses information linked to the signal of the speech itself: prosody, expressivity, and quality of the voice. Without this information, the message becomes difficult to understand, and it is not adapted to an in depth technical analysis, irrespective of the syntax or semantic.

In the absence of a viable representation of information linked to signal, the default analysis consists of looking into the statement for *nuggets* of information which characterize and respond to the task aimed for. For example, in the message of Table 9.9, the *nuggets* linked to the detection task are as follows:

> *"oh hello so its XX i don't know if you know who i am so in relation to the satisfaction of my personal satisfaction in relation to your service i would say that overall you have a very good customer service which knows how to listen not that i have much to it is a very very good if not in relation to what you have just put in place is a very good idea since there is a good response rate it's true that i'm obliged to recall several times and still someone takes the time to respond because when i'm told to give ideas I had nothing in my mind so i was forced to hang up and think about what i was going to say to you i think that that is the collective point or it is the negative point otherwise i am very satisfied overall otherwise there is one thing that i noted i have two accounts with you i find this a little inconvenient to not be able to access both at the same time when i call customer service so i find that a little disappointing that i am forced to spend more because its not the same person that deals with my folder it would have been good to regroup both folders so when i call i can accesses both folders separately otherwise i am grateful for the pleasantness and amiability of your customer team they are very nice and listen well and i wold like to thank you goodbye good day good evening"*

Table 9.9. *Message example of the France Télécom opinion corpus*

- "overall i am quite satisfied";
- "a very good customer service who knows how to listen";
- "it is very very good";
- "it is the negative point";
- "overall i'm very satisfied";
- "I find that a little inconvenient";
- "I find that a little disappointing";
- "I thank you for your pleasantness and amiability";
- "your customer service providers are very very nice and they listen well";
- "I thank you".

It is from these elements that a characterization of the message can be made, for example through automatic classification methods using the segments initially detected. If these segments can be relatively well modeled as being in number in the messages of learning corpus, it is not the same with other parts of the message, characterized by a large variation, and badly accounted by the statistic models due to this variation.

In fact, from the degree of freedom left to the user in the statement of their message, there is a large dispersion observed in the distribution of the word frequencies. This is even more the case in the message portions where the users share the origin of their problem which can in itself be quite varied. Once the proper nouns are filtered, the learning corpus in its set contains 2,981 different words for a total of 51,056 occurrences. Nearly half of the words appear only once in the learning corpus and the lexical restriction to words whose occurrence frequency is larger than or equal to 2, leads to a lexicon of 1,564 words for rate of words outside the vocabulary equal to 2.8%.

One of the first bigram language models was led on a learning corpus. The error rate on the words obtained on the test corpus is very significant, mainly due to digression and commentaries present in the messages. This is illustrated in Table 9.10. As can be seen the results deteriorate strongly when the size of the messages increases.

% word-error		> 20 ≤ 30	> 30 ≤ 40	> 40 ≤ 50	> 50 ≤ 60	> 60
	≤ 20					
average number of words	8.8	16.7	32.9	38.6	53.9	54.6

Table 9.10. *Correlation between the error rate on the words and the length of the messages (expressed in words)*

9.6.2.1. *Segmentation of the opinion support messages*

The two strategies were developed to extract and classify the subjective expression of vocal messages: one relies on the manual or automatic transcription of the messages; the other is integrated in the speech decoding process. These two strategies allow for the dissociation of the errors due to a bad word transcription of the opinion detection errors.

9.6.2.2. *Segmentation of messages with conditional random fields*

For the processing of transcriptions, a segmenter based on Conditional Random Fields (CRF) has been developed. CRF's have been used successfully in numerous labeling tasks such as morphosyntactic labeling or the detection of named entities. The main advantage of CRF's in relation to generative models such as the Hidden Markov Model (HMM) is the possibility of using a set of observations of a sequence to predict a label. It is thus not the only issue which constrains the attribution of a label to an observation but potentially all the previous and following observations. In this case, the learning corpus is formatted in a manner to associate a label to each word indicating if it is part of the opinion expression or if it belongs to an empty segment. During the analysis of a new message, the labels are asked by the CRF serve to find the segment boundaries. The labeler developed is based on the *CRF++* tool[18].

9.6.2.3. *Language models specific to opinion expressions*

In [CAM 06], a thematic language model was introduced to solve the problem of poor modeling of off-subject messages in relation to the task. The idea is to explicitly

---

18 Toolkit CRF++: http://www/chasen.org/ taku/software/CRF++/

model only the opinion carrying messages. For this, a sub-corpus was extracted for each label which regroups the set of segments associated with each label in the initial learning corpus. A language sub-model is then estimated for each label according to the associated sub-label. Furthermore, a bigram type encompassing model on the labels has been estimated to model the sequences between the different opinion segments. The portions which correspond to none of the opinion expressions are themselves modeled by a context loop phenomena, without *a priori* constraints on the sequence phenomena. Finally, a supplementary sub-model was estimated for the segments which correspond to politeness formulas, often found at the start and end of the message. In fact, these segments show a strong regularity and their modeling avoids larger deviation of the decoding in the loop phenomena model. The set is compiled of a unique model presented in Figure 9.8.

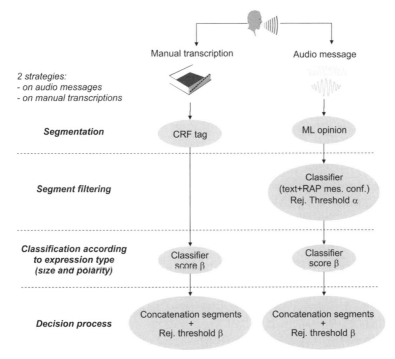

Figure 9.7. *Subjective expression detection and classification strategies for manual transcription and audio messages*

9.6.2.4. *Classification opinion*

To assign an opinion label to a segment containing a subjective expression, a classification method named *AdaBoost* [SCH 00] is used for each dimension, the segments labeled manually from the learning corpus. The simple rankers correspond

manually anotated message

> oh [markDis] well [:markDis] all was well [:satSerAutr] I didn't have much to ask either
> it was just to get [falseDep:] my mobile [falseDep:] um [retake:] telephone [:retake] since
> I lost it but the shop found it [markDis:] so there it is[:markDis] no [repeat:] no [:repeat]
> [satSerAcc:][retake:] the reception[:retake] was very good [:satSerAcc][Polform:] thank
> you good day [:Polform]

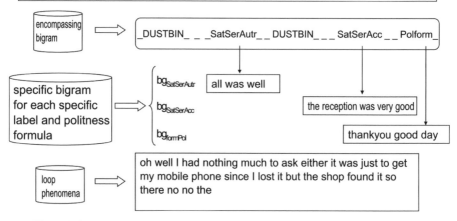

Figure 9.8. *Example of decoding with three types of thematic language models used*

to regular expressions automatically constructed on the corpus words. The complete method is presented in [CAM 09]. The ranker also gives a confidence score, and this score is used in the strategy presented in Figure 9.7 (β threshold).

9.6.3. *Evaluation*

The two message segmentation strategies have been evaluated in terms of precision and recall on the opinion detection task on the vocal statement corpus. Four lines are compared in Figure 9.9:

- manual transcription + manual segmentation;
- manual transcription + CRF segmentation;
- auto transcription + CRF segmentation;
- integrated method: transcription + segmentation (opinion language model).

As we can see, the results are strongly deteriorated when going from manual transcription to automatic transcriptions. If the CRF's give comparative results to manual transcriptions, they are strongly deteriorated by the high error rate of the transcriptions which is inevitable on this type of corpus. The detection method of the

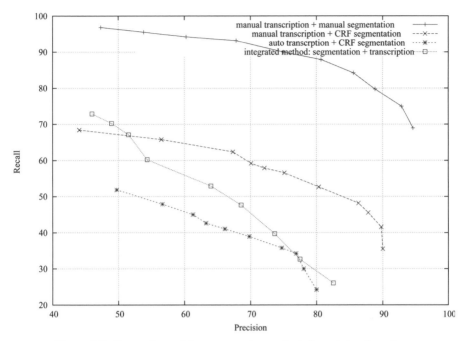

Figure 9.9. *Comparison of the segmentation methods for opinion detections*

opinion integrated in the ASR process due to the opinion language models reinforces the sturdiness of the detection system.

9.7. Conclusion

In this chapter, it has been shown how it is possible to consider the detection of opinions as a thematic classification problem. Employing identical methods in both cases, should facilitate the conjoined processing of the two tasks.

After having skimmed over different evaluation campaigns, we have focused our discussions on the methods and strategies employed by the LIA during its participation in DEFT 2007. After having discussed a unification strategy, the method specifically focused on the introduction of discriminant criteria on a similarity index, and the choice of the components in a vectorial representation of the documents was discussed.

For each of these approaches, experiments have been reported in order to show that the performance of these systems are situated at the best level and enable the user to understand why such types of decision were taken.

Finally, the specificities related to orally expressed opinions during investigations performed by France Télécom with respect to their clients were studied.

9.8. Bibliography

[AZÉ 05] AZÉ J., ROCHE M., "Présentation de l'atelier DEFT '05", in *Proceedings of TALN 2005 - Atelier DEFT '05*, vol. 2, p. 99-111, 2005.

[AZÉ 06] AZÉ J., HEITZ T., MELA A., MEZAOUR A.-D., PEINL P., ROCHE M., "Préparation de DEFT '06 (DÉfi fouille de textes)", in *Proceedings of Atelier DEFT '06*, vol. 2, 2006.

[BÉC 00] BÉCHET F., NASR A., GENET F., "Tagging unknown proper names using decision trees", in *38th Annual Meeting of the Association for Computational Linguistics, Hong Kong, China*, p. 77-84, 2000.

[BOU 08] BOUDIN F., EL-BÈZE M., TORRES-MORENO J.-M., "The LIA update summarization systems at TAC-2008", in *Proceedings of the Text Analysis Conference 2008*, Gaithersburg, USA, 2008.

[CAM 06] CAMELIN N., DAMNATI G., BECHET F., MORI R.D., "Opinion mining in a telephone survey corpus", in *Proceedings of the International Conference on Spoken Language Processing (ICSLP)*, Pittsburgh, USA, p. 1041-1044, 2006.

[CAM 09] CAMELIN N., BÉCHET F., DAMNATI G., MORI R.D., "Opinion analysis of spoken surveys", 2009.

[COL 02] COLLOBERT R., BENGIO S., MARIÉTHOZ J., Torch: a modular machine learning software library, in Technical Report IDIAP-RR02-46, IDIAP, 2002.

[DAE 04] DAELEMANS W., ZAVREL J., VAN DER SLOOT K., VAN DEN BOSCH A., TiMBL: Tilburg Memory Based Learner, Version 5.1, Reference Guide, Report, ILK Research Group Technical Report Series, 2004.

[DAN 08] DANG H., OWCZARZAK K., "Overview of the TAC 2008 update summarization task", in *Proceedings of the Text Analysis Conference (TAC)*, 2008.

[ELB 05] EL-BÈZE M., TORRES-MORENO J.-M., BÉCHET F., "Peut-on rendre automatiquement à César ce qui lui appartient? Application au jeu du Chirand-Mitterrac", in *TALN 2005 – Atelier DEFT '05*, vol. 2, p. 125-134, 6-10 June 2005.

[FEL 98] FELLBAUM C. (ed.), *WordNet: An Electronic Lexical Database*, MIT Press, 1998.

[FRE 96] FREUND Y., SCHAPIRE R.E., "Experiments with a new boosting algorithm", in *Thirteenth International Conference on Machine Learning*, p. 148-156, 1996.

[GEN 08] GENEST P., LAPALME G., NERIMA L., WEHRLI E., "A symbolic summarizer for the update task of TAC 2008", in *Proceedings of the First Text Analysis Conference*, Gaithersburg, Maryland, USA, 2008.

[HAT 97] HATZIVASSILOGLOU V., MCKEOWN K.R., "Predicting the semantic orientation of adjectives", in *Proceedings of the Eighth Conference on European Chapter of the Association for Computational Linguistics*, Morristown, NJ, USA, Association for Computational Linguistics, p. 174-181, 1997.

[KUH 95] KUHN R., DE MORI R., "The application of semantic classification trees to natural language understanding", *IEEE Transactions on Pattern Analysis and Machine Intelligence*, vol. 17, no. 5, p. 449-460, 1995.

[LAF 01] LAFFERTY J., MCCALLUM A., PEREIRA F., "Conditional random fields: probabilistic models for segmenting and labeling sequence data", in *Proceedings of 18th International Conference on Machine Learning*, Morgan Kaufmann, San Francisco, CA, p. 282-289, 2001.

[LEE 05] LEE C., NARAYANAN S., "Toward detecting emotions in spoken dialogs", *IEEE Transactions on Speech and Audio Processing*, vol. 13, no. 2, p. 293-303, 2005.

[LI 08] LI F., ZHENG Z., YANG T., BU F., GE R., ZHU X., ZHANG X., HUANG M., "THU QUANTA at TAC 2008 QA and RTE track", in *Proceedings of Human Language Technologies Conference/Conference on Empirical Methods in Natural Language Processing (HLT/EMNLP)*, Vancouver, BC, Canada, 2008.

[LIT 06] LITMAN D., ROSÉ C., FORBES-RILEY K., VANLEHN K., BHEMBE D., SILLIMAN S., "Spoken versus typed human and computer dialog tutoring", *International Journal of Artificial Intelligence in Education*, vol. 16, no. 2, p. 145-170, IOS Press, 2006.

[MAA 04] MAARTEN J.K., MARX M., MOKKEN R.J., RIJKE M.D., "Using Wordnet to measure semantic orientations of adjectives", in *National Institute for*, p. 1115-1118, 2004.

[MAC 06] MACDONALD C., OUNIS I., The TREC Blogs06 Collection: Creating and Analysing a Blog Test Collection, Report, Department of Computer Science, University of Glasgow Tech Report TR-2006-224, Glasgow, 2006.

[MAN 00] MANNING C.D., SCHÜTZE H., *Foundations of Statistical Natural Language Processing*, The MIT Press, 2000.

[NEI 06] NEIBERG D., ELENIUS K., LASKOWSKI K., "Emotion recognition in spontaneous speech using GMMs", in *Ninth International Conference on Spoken Language Processing*, ISCA, p. 809-812, 2006.

[NEN 04] NENKOVA A., PASSONNEAU R., "Evaluating content selection in summarization: the pyramid method", in *Proceedings of HLT-NAACL*, vol. 2004, 2004.

[PAN 02] PANG B., LEE L. VAITHYANATHAN S., "Thumbs up? sentiment classification using machine learning techniques", in *Empirical Methods in Natural Language Processing*, p. 79-86, 2002.

[PAN 04] PANG B., LEE L., "A sentimental education: sentiment analysis using subjectivity summarization based on minimum cuts", in *Proceedings of the 42nd ACL*, p. 271-278, 2004.

[PAN 08] PANG B., LEE L., "Opinion mining and sentiment analysis", in *Foundations and Trends in Information Retrieval 2(1-2)*, p. 1-135, 2008.

[SCH 00] SCHAPIRE R.E., SINGER Y., "BoosTexter: a boosting-based system for text categorization", *Machine Learning*, vol. 39, p. 135-168, 2000.

[TAK 05] TAKAMURA H., INUI T., MANABU O., "Extracting semantic orientations of words using spin model", in *ACL '05*, p. 133-140, 2005.

[TOR 07] TORRES-MORENO J.-M., EL-BÈZE M., BÉCHET F., CAMELIN N., "Comment faire pour que l'opinion forgée à la sortie des urnes soit la bonne? Application au défi DEFT 2007", in *AFIA/DEFT '07*, p. 119-133, 4-6 July 2007.

[TOR 09] TORRES-MORENO J.-M., EL-BÈZE M., BÉCHET F., CAMELIN N., "Fusion probabiliste pour la classification d'opinions", in *DEFT '09*, p. 10-25, 22 June 2009.

[TUR 03] TURNEY P., LITTMAN M., "Measuring praise and criticism: inference of semantic orientation from association", *ACM Transactions on Information Systems*, vol. 21, p. 315-346, 2003.

[VAP 82] VAPNIK V.N., *Estimation of Dependences Based on Empirical Data*, Springer-Verlag Inc., New York, USA, 1982.

[VAP 95] VAPNIK V.N., *The Nature of Statistical Learning Theory*, Springer-Verlag Inc., New York, USA, 1995.

[VAR 08] VARMA V., KRISHNA S., GARAPATI H., REDDY K., PINGALI P., GANESH S., GOPISETTY H., BYSANI P., SARVABHOTLA K., REDDY V. *et al.*, "Iiit hyderabad at TAC 2008", in *Text Analysis Conference*, USA, 2008.

Appendix A

Probabilistic Models: An Introduction

A.1. Introduction

Although situated at the end, this last chapter is meant as an introduction to the models presented in the rest of the book. It introduces, with all the necessary details, the simplest probabilistic models used in the statistical processing of text collections. A good comprehension of these models will be required to follow the developments and more advanced issues presented in this book. It has therefore been thought useful to cover this more basic material in this Appendix, so as to make this book entirely self-contained. Alternatively, the reader may refer to some excellent textbooks covering similar topics, such as [CHA 93, MAN 99, JUR 00]. This chapter is also an opportunity to lay down some notations and to formulate some of the questions that appear throughout the entire book: How to define a probability distribution over a set of documents? Over a set of sentences? and so on.

This chapter is organized in five sections: in the first (section A.2), several instantiations of the simplest supervised categorization model[1], the so-called *naive Bayes* model, are presented. For a good comprehension of these models it is useful to read Chapter 1, which cover related models, in the context of information retrieval applications. Chapters 3 and 4 are devoted to more sophisticated (and often more accurate) models for categorization tasks. Section A.3 then introduces *unsupervised learning* problems, through the study of *latent* (or *hidden*) *variable* models: these

---

Appendix written by François YVON.

1 The term classification is also found in the literature, but categorization seems to be less ambiguous, and therefore preferable. However, the terms class and category will be used interchangeably.

techniques are used to automatically partition document collections into thematically homogeneous subsets. Such problems are also developed in Chapter 5.

We then study the modeling of *sequences* and consider Markov models in section A.4. These models play a critical role in numerous applications involving the processing of text data. Among the applications discussed in this book, machine translation (Chapter 7) can be specifically noted; these models are also widely used for automatic speech recognition or for spelling correction applications.

These models are generalized to the case of pairs of sequences having the same length. The most common situation is when an output sequence must be inferred given the corresponding input: such tasks are known as *sequence labeling*. Hidden Markov models, discussed in detail in section A.5, are suitable for this type of problem. Sequence labeling problems are discussed at length in Chapter 6, and are also discussed in the chapter dedicated to statistical machine translation (Chapter 7).

Again, for the sake of completeness, we close this Appendix with a few reminders on probability theory, so that the development of different topics can be followed without referring to external sources. There are many good textbooks, such as [HAM 93, RES 99] to which the reader is referred for a more in-depth introduction to probability theory.

A.2. Supervised categorization

This section is a step-by-step introduction to probabilistic modeling, instantiated here in the framework of a simple document filtering application. It uses the basic concepts of probability theory presented in section A.7. A more up-to-date presentation of state-of-the-art statistical tools for text categorization tasks is given in Chapters 3 and 4.

A.2.1. *Filtering documents*

The task considered here is a document filtering task, which consists of labeling text documents with a Boolean variable which conventionally takes the values of 0 (reject the document) or 1 (accept the document). Such decisions must be for instance taken by spam filtering systems that are now commonly integrated within e-mail management software. We first need to specify a (probabilistic) model of the various entities involved in this task. We thus introduce:

– a random variable X, taking its values in the set $\mathcal{X}$ of all the possible documents. Each document will thus be considered as a particular realization x of this random variable;

– a random variable Y, taking its values in $\mathcal{Y} = \{0, 1\}$, which represent the class or category of the document.

Let us now assume that we can compute, for each possible realization (x, y) of the pair (X, Y), the joint probability $P(X = x, Y = y)$. If x is a document whose class y is unknown, it is then possible to compute, for each category y in $\{0, 1\}$, the conditional probability of y given x. Using Bayes rule, we have:

$$P(Y = y | X = x) = \frac{P(X = x, Y = y)}{P(X = x, Y = 0) + P(X = x, Y = 1)} \qquad [A.1]$$

This quantity is often referred to as the *posterior probability*. When nothing is known about X, the possible realizations of Y are specified through the *prior probability*, denoted by $P(Y = y)$, of observing the outcome y. The posterior probability thus formalizes the information provided by the knowledge of x about the possible realizations of Y. The best decision rule is then to assign x to the category y^* that maximizes this term:

$$y^* = \underset{y \in \{0,1\}}{\operatorname{argmax}} P(Y = y | X = x) \qquad [A.2]$$

It can be shown that this rule minimizes the expectation of the error rate. Note that the denominator of $P(Y = y | X = x)$ is the same for the two values of y; the program defined by [A.2] is thus equivalent to:

$$y^* = \underset{y \in \{0,1\}}{\operatorname{argmax}} P(X = x, Y = y) \qquad [A.3]$$

This maximization step, which implies the computation of the *posterior* probabilities for the unobserved variable, is the *inference step*.

At this stage, the only problem that remains is to define terms such as $P(X = x, Y = y)$, that is to model the *joint distribution* of these two random variables. The standard approach consists of breaking down this term according to: $P(X = x, Y = y) = P(Y = y) P(X = x | Y = y)$. An interpretation of this decomposition is that it corresponds to a hypothetical *generation model* that produces pairs (category, document) as a two step process:

1) a category y is first chosen with prior probability $P(Y = y)$;

2) the document x is then produced using the distribution $P(X = x | Y = y)$, which depends on the value y obtained during the first step. The differences between the two classes of documents are thus reflected by different conditional distributions.

Step 1 calls for no further comments; its implementation only requires knowledge of the prior probabilities of the two classes. In the following, these two values will be denoted p_0 (for category 0) and $p_1 = (1 - p_0)$ (for category 1). Step 2 is more delicate, since it requires the specification of two probability distributions over the set of all the possible documents. In the following sections, we present two possible definitions (among many) of these distributions along with the associated estimation procedures. In the first approach, termed the *Bernoulli* model, each document is characterized by the simple presence/absence of words from a predefined vocabulary; in the second, we use the *multinomial* model, which additionally takes into account the number of occurrences of words in the documents.

A.2.2. The Bernoulli model

A.2.2.1. *Representing documents*

The set of all possible text documents is quite difficult to grasp; the Bernoulli model therefore makes the simplification that documents are characterized by a very basic information regarding the presence/absence of certain words[2].

This representation, where each document is viewed as a mere set of occurrences, is known as the "bag-of-words" representation. It is common to use simple preprocessing tools to derive such representations from texts, such as filtering the most frequent words, which are often *function words*. A second very useful preprocessing, in particular for morphologically complex languages, uses *normalized* representations of graphical words. This normalization can take the form of a *lemmatization*, which consists of grouping together the different inflected forms of the same lemma. For instance, in French, the conjugated forms of the same verb would be replaced by the corresponding infinitive form, and so on. A more drastic normalization consists of grouping all the lemmas belonging to the same morphological family under a single indexation term: for instance, "judge", "judgment" and "judgmental" would all be mapped onto their common root "judg-". This process is known as *racinization*. In other circumstances, complex units can also be introduced into these representations, such as compound words, or in a simplified version, word *n*-grams. Note that the linguistic processes involved in these normalization operations are often complex, and in practice, only rough approximations are ever obtained.

From now on, we will assume that the vocabulary V is fixed and that it contains n_W terms. In this bag-of-words representation, a document d is represented by a binary vector x in $\{0, 1\}^{n_W}$ such that component x_w is 1 if the term w occurs at least once in d and 0 otherwise.

---

2 This representation assumes that the notion of an orthographic word form has been established, which is not without its difficulties. In the remainder of this chapter, the neutral word "term" will be used to define the units making up the vocabulary.

As an illustration, consider the following 10 word vocabulary: $V = \{$of, the, to, a, in, is, it, and, on, be$\}$[3] Using a bag-of-words representation, the previous paragraph would then correspond to the following vector:

$$
\boldsymbol{x}^T = \begin{bmatrix} \text{of} & \text{the} & \text{to} & \text{a} & \text{in} & \text{is} & \text{it} & \text{and} & \text{on} & \text{be} \\ 0 & 1 & 0 & 1 & 1 & 1 & 1 & 1 & 1 & 0 \end{bmatrix}
$$

The set of all possible documents (the possible values of variable X) is thus reduced to the set $\mathcal{X}$ of all the n_W dimensional Boolean vectors.

A.2.2.2. The Bernoulli model

To model these Boolean vectors, the simplest approach assumes that each component of the random variable X is independent from the others and that the random variable X_w associated with the term w is a Bernoulli variable parameterized by b_w. This simply means that X_w is 1 with probability b_w and 0 with probability $1 - b_w$. Given the crudeness of this independence assumption, this model (as well as the one presented in section A.2.3) is often referred to as the *naive Bayes model*. Under these hypotheses, the probability of a document-vector $\boldsymbol{x}$ is simply written as a product of factors b_w for each word w occurring in the document, and of factors $(1 - b_w)$ for each word absent from the document. The probability of $\boldsymbol{x}$ is then expressed as a product over the vocabulary[4]:

$$
P(X = \boldsymbol{x}; \boldsymbol{b}) = \prod_{w=1}^{n_W} b_w^{\,x_w} (1 - b_w)^{(1 - x_w)} \tag{A.4}
$$

The filtering model rests on the hypothesis that the documents in class 0 and in class 1 are generated according to probability distributions whose parameters are different. This model is therefore fully parameterized, on the one hand by the prior probabilities (p_0 and $p_1 = 1 - p_0$); and on the other hand by two vectors $\boldsymbol{b}_0$ for class 0 and $\boldsymbol{b}_1$ for class 1. Assuming these parameters are known, it is possible to compute the values involved in the decision rule [A.3]. For instance, for class $Y = 0$:

$$
P(Y = 0, X = \boldsymbol{x}; p_0, \boldsymbol{b}_0) = p_0 \prod_{w=1}^{n_W} b_{0,w}^{\,x_w} (1 - b_{0,w})^{(1 - x_w)} \tag{A.5}
$$

---

3 For applications aiming to model the "content" of a document, considering such a vocabulary would be particularly limiting and in practice, it is common to discard the most frequent words, which are often the least informative ones. However, when focusing on the style of a document, focusing on function words is a perfectly legitimate approach.

4 The notation $P(X = \boldsymbol{x}; \boldsymbol{b})$ makes explicit the role of the parameter vector $\boldsymbol{b}$. Notations such as $P_{\boldsymbol{b}}(X = \boldsymbol{x})$ are also found in the literature; in fact, in a strictly Bayesian approach, where parameters are random variables, the correct notation would be $P(X = \boldsymbol{x}|\boldsymbol{b})$.

We now have all the necessary elements to compute the optimal class of any document in this model. It is a simple matter of evaluating terms [A.5] for $Y = 0$ and for $Y = 1$, and to select the class for which this term is maximum.

The last question that needs to be addressed concerns the setting of parameter values p_0, b_0 and b_1. These calculations correspond to the *model estimation* (or *model training*) stage, whose main principles are outlined in the next section.

A.2.2.3. *Parameter estimation*

To estimate the parameters, supplementary information must be available, in the form of exemplar realizations of the random variables that need to be modeled. In the context of document filtering, we thus assume that we have access to a set of examples of pairs of document vectors x together with the associated class label. An additional hypothesis is that these examples are statistically independent of one another. The training corpus is thus a set of n_D elements $\mathcal{C} = \{(x^{(n)}, y^{(n)}), n = 1 \ldots n_D\}$.

The *likelihood* of the corpus is a function of the parameters p_0, b_0 and b_1, which takes the simple form of a product of the probabilities of the documents in the corpus[5]:

$$\mathcal{L}(p_0, b_0, b_1) = P(\mathcal{C}; p_0, b_0, b_1) = \prod_{n=1}^{n_D} P(X = x^{(n)}, Y = y^{(n)}; \theta), \qquad [\text{A.6}]$$

where θ represents the set of all the model parameters.

The general principle that will be adopted consists of choosing the parameters that maximize this quantity. The intuition is that if the data were effectively generated as specified by the model, then these parameter values would maximize the probability of the (observed) training corpus. This principle is the *maximum likelihood* principle.

We thus need to maximize a multidimensional function in p_0, b_0, and b_1. To solve this optimization program, it is easier to consider the logarithm of this function (*the log-likelihood*), which contains a summation instead of a product. Grouping documents according to their class value yields the following expression for the log-likelihood:

$$\ell(\theta) = \sum_{n,\, y^{(n)}=0} \log P(Y = 0, X = x^{(n)}; \theta) + \sum_{n,\, y^{(n)}=1} \log P(Y = 1, X = x^{(n)}; \theta) \qquad [\text{A.7}]$$

---

5 Through the assumption that documents are statistically independent.

Replacing terms $P(Y = y, X = x^{(n)}; \boldsymbol{\theta})$ by their definition (see [A.5]) yields:

$$\ell(p_0, \boldsymbol{b_0}, \boldsymbol{b_1}) = \sum_{n,\, y^{(n)}=0} \left(\log(p_0) + \sum_{w=1}^{n_W} x_w^{(n)} \log(b_{0,w}) + (1 - x_w^{(n)}) \log(1 - b_{0,w}) \right)$$

$$+ \sum_{n,\, y^{(n)}=1} \left(\log(1 - p_0) + \sum_{w=1}^{n_W} x_w^{(n)} \log(b_{1,w}) + (1 - x_w^{(n)}) \log(1 - b_{1,w}) \right) \quad \text{[A.8]}$$

Maximizing this function implies to compute and cancel the partial derivatives with respect to each of the parameters, thereby leading to the following equations (recall that $\mathbb{I}(x)$ is the indicator function whose value is 1 if x is true, and 0 otherwise):

$$\frac{\partial \ell(p_0, \boldsymbol{b_0}, \boldsymbol{b_1})}{\partial p_0} = \frac{\sum_n \mathbb{I}(y^{(n)} = 0)}{p_0} - \frac{\sum_n \mathbb{I}(y^{(n)} = 1)}{1 - p_0} = 0$$

$$\forall y \in \{0, 1\}, w \in [1:n_W], \quad \frac{\partial \ell(p_0, \boldsymbol{b_0}, \boldsymbol{b_1})}{\partial b_{y,w}} = \sum_{n, y^{(n)} = y} \frac{x_w^{(n)}}{b_{y,w}} - \frac{1 - x_w^{(n)}}{1 - b_{y,w}} = 0$$

By solving these equations, we obtain the following estimators (we denote $F(y)$ the number of documents in class y, and $F(y, w)$ is the number of documents containing the term w in class y):

$$\widehat{p_0} = \frac{F(0)}{F(0) + F(1)} \qquad\qquad \text{[A.9]}$$

$$\widehat{b}_{y,w} = \frac{F(y, w)}{F(y)}, \forall y \in \{0, 1\}, w \in [1:n_W] \qquad\qquad \text{[A.10]}$$

In practice, we use for $\widehat{b}_{y,w}$ an estimator of the form:

$$\widehat{b}_{y,w} = \frac{F(y, w) + \epsilon}{F(y) + 2\epsilon}, \text{ with } \epsilon > 0 \qquad\qquad \text{[A.11]}$$

This prevents setting $\widehat{b}_{y,w} = 0$ when $F(y, w) = 0$, i.e. when term w does not appear in any document of the class y, and likewise for $\widehat{b}_{y,w} = 1$. Failing to make this adjustment, any document containing a term unseen in the training documents of class y would have a zero probability of belonging to that class. This adjustment is referred to as *parameter smoothing*[6].

A.2.2.4. *Summary*

The development of a filtering model relying on Boolean representations of documents therefore includes the two following stages:

– estimation of the model parameters from a set of learning documents, delivering estimators $\widehat{p_0}, \widehat{\boldsymbol{b}_0}$, and $\widehat{\boldsymbol{b}_1}$ for $p_0, \boldsymbol{b}_0$, and $\boldsymbol{b}_1$, respectively. As will often be the case in this book, estimation boils down here to optimizing a certain function of the parameters, known as the *loss function*: in the framework considered here, the loss function is simply the log-likelihood function;

– once the estimation has been performed, the label of new documents is only based on the evaluation of terms given in equation [A.5] where we replace the "true" (unknown) parameter values with the values estimated during learning.

During the first stage, knowledge of classes of the training documents is used to estimate the model parameters; during the second stage, knowledge of the parameters is used to infer the unknown class of a new document. This is a *supervised* learning framework, which assumes the availability of a corpus of labeled examples. In section A.3, we will show, by studying a simple case, how to carry out learning even in the absence of supervision data: this is known as *unsupervised learning*. Chapter 5 presents a very thorough panorama of unsupervised learning in a probabilistic framework.

A.2.3. *The multinomial model*

The representation of documents used in the previous section is over-simplistic, as it does not take into account the order of the words in the document nor their number of occurrences. The *multinomial model*, presented in this section, is one possible way to take term frequencies into account. The Bernoulli and multinomial models are compared empirically in [MCC 98], which concludes that the multinomial model is better.

A document is now represented by an n_W dimensional integer vector x; each component x_w corresponds to the number of occurrences of term w in the document. We denote $T = \sum_w x_w$ the total number of occurrences in the document (i.e. its length).

---

6 The smoothing method used here is known as *Laplace smoothing* (when $\epsilon = 1$) or, more generally, as *Lidstone smoothing*. In section A.2.5, we will have the opportunity to derive a theoretical justification for this formula.

To model these vectors, we use the multinomial distribution, yielding the following expression for the probability of a document[7]:

$$P(x; T, b) = \frac{T!}{\prod_{w=1}^{n_W} x_w!} \prod_{w=1}^{n_W} b_w^{x_w} \qquad [A.12]$$

The length T and the n_W dimensional vector b in equation [A.12] are the parameters of the multinomial distribution; b satisfies the two following properties: $\forall w, b_w \geq 0$ and $\sum_{w=1}^{n_W} b_w = 1$. The filtering model is thus completely specified by the knowledge of p_0, which determines the prior probability of class 0, and of the vectors b_0 and b_1, which model the probability of the documents in classes 0 and 1, respectively. Given these parameters and a count vector x, it is possible to compute the terms involved in equation [A.3]: the class conditional probabilities are obtained using equation [A.12] with the two values b_0 and b_1; the prior terms are simply p_0 for class 0 and $(1 - p_0)$ for class 1. This simple calculation determines the most likely class for any document x.

A.2.3.1. *Parameter estimation*

Parameter estimation for this model relies on the same general principle as before, namely the maximization of the likelihood function. Assuming again that we have a set of annotated examples $\mathcal{C} = \{(x^{(n)}, y^{(n)}); n = 1 \ldots n_D\}$, the log-likelihood is given by:

$$\begin{aligned}
\ell(p_0, b_0, b_1) = &\sum_{n, y^{(n)}=0} \log P(Y = 0, X = x^{(n)}; p_0, b_0) \\
&+ \sum_{n, y^{(n)}=1} \log P(Y = 1, X = x^{(n)}; p_1, b_1)
\end{aligned} \qquad [A.13]$$

Decomposing $P(Y = 0, X = x^{(n)})$ as $P(Y = 0) P(X = x^{(n)} | Y = 0)$ and plugging in [A.12], the log-likelihood is re-written as:

---

7 In equation [A.12], the probability of a document *depends on its length* T: this is because one parameter of the multinomial distribution corresponds to the total number of draws, that is to the length of the document. As long as this model is not used to compare the probability of two documents, it is possible to assume that T is known and does not need to be modeled: this point of view will be adopted from now on. It remains that equation [A.12] defines a distribution over all the documents of length T and that, to obtain a distribution on all possible documents, the length would have to be modeled, by assuming, for instance, that T follows a Poisson distribution.

$$\ell(p_0, \boldsymbol{b_0}, \boldsymbol{b_1}) = \sum_{n,\, y^{(n)}=0} \left(\log(p_0) + \sum_{w=1}^{n_W} x_w^{(n)} \log(b_{0,w}) \right)$$

[A.14]

$$+ \sum_{n,\, y^{(n)}=1} \left(\log(1 - p_0) + \sum_{w=1}^{n_W} x_w^{(n)} \log(b_{1,w}) \right) (+ \text{ a constant term})$$

In this model, the maximization of the log-likelihood gives rise to a constrained optimization program, as the solutions $\boldsymbol{b_1}$ and $\boldsymbol{b_2}$ must satisfy the above conditions $\left(\sum_w b_{0,w} = \sum_w b_{1,w} = 1 \right)$. The Lagrangian associated with this program must thus be formed, by introducing Lagrange multipliers λ_0 and λ_1, associated with the two previous equality constraints. The optimality conditions (Karush-Kuhn-Tucker conditions) thus lead to the following system of equations:

$$\begin{cases} \dfrac{\partial \ell(p_0, \boldsymbol{b_0}, \boldsymbol{b_1})}{\partial p_0} = \dfrac{\sum_n \mathbb{I}(y^{(n)}=0)}{p_0} - \dfrac{\sum_n \mathbb{I}(y^{(n)}=1)}{1-p_0} = 0 \\ \forall y, w,\ \dfrac{\partial \ell(p_0, \boldsymbol{b_0}, \boldsymbol{b_1})}{\partial b_{y,w}} = \sum_{x^{(n)},\, y^{(n)}=y} \dfrac{x_w^{(n)}}{b_{y,w}} - \lambda_y = 0 \\ \forall y,\ \sum_{w=1}^{n_W} b_{y,w} = 1 \end{cases}$$

By solving this system, the following estimators are obtained (as previously, $F(y)$ is the number of documents in class y):

$$\widehat{p_0} = \frac{F(0)}{F(0) + F(1)}$$

[A.15]

$$\widehat{b}_{y,w} = \frac{\sum_{n,\, y^{(n)}=y} x^{(n)}}{\sum_{w=1}^{n_W} \sum_{n,\, y^{(n)}=y} x_w^{(n)}}, \forall y \in \{0,1\},\ w \in [1\!:\!n_W]$$

[A.16]

As was already the case for the Bernoulli model, the maximum likelihood estimators are defined ratios with a very simple interpretation. For instance, $\widehat{b}_{y,w}$ is the ratio between the total number of occurrences of the word w in all the documents in class y and the total number of words contained in all the documents of this class. This quantity can be interpreted as the probability that a randomly chosen occurrence in a document of this class corresponds to the word w. Once again, it is often necessary to implement parameter smoothing techniques, in order to guarantee that $\widehat{b}_{y,w} > 0$ for all values of y and w. A simple way of doing so is to add a small positive factor to the term $\sum_{n,\, y^{(n)}=y} x_w^{(n)}$, by correcting the denominator, so that all the $\widehat{b}_{y,w}$ remain correctly normalized (i.e. sum to 1).

Once the parameters are estimated, it is finally possible to decide the optimal class of any new document. This is performed using the rule represented by equation [A.3], whose terms we now know how to compute.

A.2.4. *Evaluating categorization systems*

The development of probabilistic models, as with any software development activity, must include an evaluation stage, during which the quality of the resulting system is assessed. Setting aside issues such as the execution speed or the quality of the user interface, the main evaluation criteria of an automated categorization model should be the correctness of its predictions.

The standard evaluation protocol thus requires the availability of a set of test instances, drawn independently and disjoint from the learning corpus, and for which the correct class label is known. By comparing the correct label with the prediction of the classifier, it is possible to get a numerical estimate of its performance. More precisely, let $\mathcal{C} = \{(x^{(n)}, y^{(n)}), n = 1 \ldots n_D\}$ represent such a test set, and let $\{\widehat{y}^{(n)}, n = 1 \ldots n_D\}$ represent the set of labels predicted by the system. A first measure of interest is the *empirical error rate*, also known as the *correction*:

$$\widehat{e} = \frac{1}{n_D} \sum_{n=1}^{n_D} \mathbb{I}(y^{(n)} \neq \widehat{y}^{(n)}) \tag{A.17}$$

This quantity is an estimator of the expectation of the error rate, and is simple to compute and to interpret. In many situations, this metric needs to be refined to account for the asymmetry between classes. Consider, for instance, a spam filtering system: it is probably more harmful to reject a valid message than to accept a message that should have been filtered. Generalized evaluation metrics are based on the statistics given in Table A.1.

	$y = 0$	$y = 1$
$\widehat{y} = 0$	$n_1 = \sum_n \mathbb{I}(y^{(n)} = 0 \wedge \widehat{y}^{(n)} = 0)$	$n_2 = \sum_n \mathbb{I}(y^{(n)} = 1 \wedge \widehat{y}^{(n)} = 0)$
$\widehat{y} - 1$	$n_3 - \sum_n \mathbb{I}(y^{(n)} = 0 \wedge \widehat{y}^{(n)} = 1)$	$n_4 = \sum_n \mathbb{I}(y^{(n)} = 1 \wedge \widehat{y}^{(n)} = 1)$

Table A.1. *Quantities used in error measures*

The empirical error is directly obtained as $\frac{n_2+n_3}{n_D}$, but other interesting quantities are also derived from this table. For example, the error rate can be computed separately for each class: for instance, the error rate for class 0 is $\frac{n_2}{n_1+n_2}$. By assuming that class 0 corresponds to the documents that must be filtered, the *recall* for this class is defined as the ratio between the number of documents correctly filtered (n_1) and those that should have been filtered ($n_1 + n_3$). Similarly, the *precision* corresponds to the ratio between the number of documents correctly filtered and the total number of documents filtered ($n_1 + n_2$). A good system must simultaneously have good precision and good recall. These two quantities are summarized by the F-measure, defined below:

$$\text{Recall } R = \frac{n_1}{n_1 + n_3}$$

$$\text{Precision } P = \frac{n_1}{n_1 + n_2}$$

$$\text{F-measure } F = \frac{2PR}{P + R}$$

Finally, it is possible to distinguish the two error types, i.e. to distinguish those made by erroneously rejecting a positive sample (*false negative*) from those made by assigning a class label of 1 to a negative instance (*false positive*).

The evaluation measures presented in this section are always defined with respect to a particular test set: their value is thus subject to statistical variations depending on the test set used. In order to obtain better estimates of the actual performance, it is possible to compute error rates on several test sets and to average the resulting values. A standard evaluation protocol, known as *cross validation*, consists of randomly partitioning an annotated corpus into k sub-corpora. Each of these sub-corpora is successively used to evaluate the performance of a model trained using the remaining $k - 1$ sub-corpora. The final performance estimate is computed as the average of the k error rates thus obtained.

A.2.5. *Extensions*

The estimation strategy developed in the previous sections, which consists of finding the parameters maximizing the likelihood function, is conceptually simple and relies on solid foundations. This approach involves the specification of a probabilistic generation model expressing the *joint* probability of the observation and its label: such models are often referred to as *generative* models. Other approaches are possible, which are based on different principles. For example, rather than trying to maximize the likelihood function, we could try to minimize quantities more directly related to the error rate, or to its expectation. This idea is comprehensively explored in Chapters 3 and 4, in which various ways to develop alternative training criteria in a *discriminative* learning framework are presented.

In the following paragraphs, we will discuss another estimation strategy, which implements a different point of view, often referred to as *Bayesian*, on the modeling activity. In a nutshell, the Bayesian perspective makes no principled distinction between the random variables that are modeled, and the model parameters associated with them. By viewing parameters as random variables, it becomes possible to develop a unified framework within which estimation and inference are no longer truly distinguished.

In this approach, the learning procedure aims to use a set of data samples, denoted here by $\mathcal{C}$, to refine prior knowledge regarding the distribution of the parameter values.

The underlying principle is no different from decision rule [A.3]: observing $\mathcal{C}$, the "best" value θ^* of the parameter is thus:

$$\theta^* = \underset{\theta}{\operatorname{argmax}} \, P(\theta|\mathcal{C}) \qquad\qquad\qquad [A.18]$$

where $P(\theta|\mathcal{C})$ is the posterior distribution of the parameters given the observations in $\mathcal{C}$. According to Bayes's rule, $P(\theta|\mathcal{C})$ is proportional to the product $P(\mathcal{C}|\theta)\,P(\theta)$[8]:

– $P(\mathcal{C}|\theta)$ is already familiar and corresponds to the likelihood function;

– $P(\theta)$ is a prior term, which reflects prior knowledge regarding the distribution of θ.

In the absence of prior knowledge, a non-informative (for instance, uniform) distribution can be chosen to reflect our uncertainty regarding θ. The optimization program [A.18], which corresponds to the computation of the *maximum a posteriori*, often abbreviated as MAP, now involves maximizing the product of the likelihood *and* of the prior term.

Let us illustrate this approach for the multinomial model, in which $\theta = \{p_0, b_0, b_1\}$. To make the computation of [A.18] easier, we will choose a *Dirichlet distribution* as prior distribution over the parameters b,[9]. The Dirichlet distribution is parameterized by a n_W-dimensional parameter vector α. To simplify the following discussion, we assume for the rest of this section that p_0 is known and does not need to be estimated[10].

The prior probability of b_0 and b_1 is thus written as:

$$\forall y \in \{0,1\}, P(b_y) = \frac{\Gamma(\sum_{w=1}^{n_W} w)}{\prod_{w=1}^{n_W} \Gamma(\alpha_w)} \prod_{w=1}^{n_W} b_{y,w}{}^{\alpha_w - 1}$$

where Γ denotes the Euler Gamma function.

The resolution of program [A.18] is facilitated by the observation of the similarity between the likelihood function, which is essentially a product of terms of the form $b_{y,w}{}^{\sum_n x_w^{(n)}}$ (see equations [A.12] and [A.14] on pages 377 and 378) and the prior term, which is mainly a product of terms of the form $b_{y,w}{}^{\alpha_w - 1}$. The posterior distribution,

---

8 The denominator is ignored, as it does not depend on θ and plays no role in the program defined by equation [A.18].

9 This choice, which significantly simplifies the mathematical derivations, is justified by the fact that the Dirichlet distribution is *conjugate* to the multinomial distribution. This implies, as we will see, that the posterior distribution of b is also a Dirichlet distribution.

10 If needed, then we could use as prior distribution for p_0 a Beta distribution, which is the conjugate to the Bernoulli distribution.

which combines these two terms, is thus, up to a normalization term, a product of factors $b_{y,w}$, whose exponent is simply the value of the total count of w in the documents of class i, augmented by $\alpha_w - 1$. The *posterior* probability thus takes the following form (the normalization factor is omitted):

$$P(\boldsymbol{\theta}|\mathcal{C}) \propto \prod_{y=0,1} \prod_{w=1}^{n_W} b_{y,w}^{\alpha_w - 1 + \sum_{n, y^{(n)}=y} x_w^{(n)}}$$

The posterior distribution of the parameters therefore also follows a Dirichlet distribution and the solution of program [A.18] corresponds to the *mode* of distribution. When choosing a *non-informative* prior, in which all the components of the meta-parameter $\boldsymbol{\alpha}$ are equal to α, the solution of program [A.18] is directly given by:

$$\widehat{b}_{y,w} = \frac{\alpha - 1 + \sum_{n, y^{(n)}=y} x_w^{(n)}}{\sum_{w=1}^{n_W}(\alpha - 1 + \sum_{n, y^{(n)}=y} x_w^{(n)})}, \forall y \in \{0, 1\}, w \in [1:n_W] \qquad [A.19]$$

Let us point out the similarity between [A.19] and [A.16], which ultimately differ only by the presence of the term $\alpha - 1$ which corrects ("smoothes") the observed counts. In this particular case (as in many others), the use of priors over the parameters yields smoothed estimators that are derived from general and theoretically justified principles rather than from heuristic rules. Another interpretation of this approach is to view it as a remedy against *overfitting*. *Overfitting* corresponds to a situation where the training instances have been learned "too well", which is detrimental to the ability to generalize to new data. In our context, overfitting occurs when (unreliable) probability estimates are derived for unfrequent words, for which little statistical information can be collected in the data; for these words, the prior term $\alpha - 1$ in [A.19] significantly contributes to keep the corresponding parameter value close to its default value. As more occurrences are collected, the term $\sum_{n, y^{(n)}=y} x_w^{(m)}$ overwhelms the prior, and as n tends to infinity, $\widehat{b}_{y,w}$ tends to the maximum likelihood estimate. The additional prior term in the new objective function thus acts as a regularizer and improves the resulting estimates.

Maximum a posteriori estimation, which implies the manipulation of distributions over parameter values, is only a first step towards the implementation of the Bayesian "program". This is because its outcome is a point estimate, which singles out one particular value of $\widehat{\boldsymbol{\theta}}$, namely the (maximum) mode of the posterior distribution. This value is then plugged in the decision rule [A.3]. A more orthodox approach would be to dispense with point estimates and to design a decision rule that takes into account the whole posterior distribution, rather than just one value. This is achieved by reformulating the decision rule [A.2] by *integrating out* the parameter values. We have initially postulated that the best prediction y^* associated with x is defined by:

$$y^* = \underset{y \in \{0,1\}}{\operatorname{argmax}} P(Y = y|X = x)$$

or more precisely, by making explicit the role of the parameter vector $\boldsymbol{\theta}$:

$$y^* = \underset{y \in \{0,1\}}{\operatorname{argmax}} P(Y = y | X = x; \boldsymbol{\theta})$$

$\boldsymbol{\theta}$ is of course unknown and the only knowledge used for inference is extracted from the training corpus $\mathcal{C}$. A proper formulation of the decision rule is thus:

$$y^* = \underset{y \in \{0,1\}}{\operatorname{argmax}} P(Y = y | X = x | \mathcal{C})$$

$$= \underset{y \in \{0,1\}}{\operatorname{argmax}} P(Y = y, X = x | \mathcal{C})$$

To use this rule, we must compute $P(Y = y, X = x, \mathcal{C})$, by integrating out $\boldsymbol{\theta}$, using:

$$P(Y = y, X = x, \mathcal{C}, \boldsymbol{b_0}, \boldsymbol{b_1}) \propto \prod_{y'=0,1} \prod_{w=1}^{nw} b_{y',w}^{\sum_{n,y^{(n)}=y'} x_w^{(n)} + \alpha_w - 1} \prod_{w=1}^{nw} b_{y,w}^{x_w},$$

then by marginalization (integration) over parameter values:

$$P(Y = y, X = x, \mathcal{C}) = \int_{\boldsymbol{\theta} \in \mathbb{R}^+} P(Y = y, X = x, \mathcal{C}, \boldsymbol{b_0}, \boldsymbol{b_1}) d\boldsymbol{\theta}$$

This integral has the same form as the normalization constant of the Dirichlet distribution and can be computed analytically. As a result (a similar term is calculated for $Y = 1$):

$$P(Y = 0, X = x | \mathcal{C}) \propto$$

$$\frac{\prod_{w=1}^{nw} \Gamma(\alpha_w + x_w + \sum_{n, y^{(n)}=0} x_w^{(n)})}{\prod_{w=1}^{nw} \Gamma(\alpha_w + \sum_{n, y^{(n)}=0} x_w^{(n)})} \frac{\Gamma(\sum_{w=1}^{nw} \alpha_w + \sum_{n, y^{(n)}=0} x_w^{(n)})}{\Gamma(\sum_{w=1}^{nw} \alpha_w + x_w + \sum_{n, y^{(n)}=0} x_w^{(n)})}$$

The optimal decision y^* is obtained by comparing $P(Y = y, X = x | \mathcal{C})$ for the two possible values of y and by choosing the maximally likely class. Experiments described in [RIG 06] suggest that this approach does not necessarily lead to better performances. However, it seems to yield more reliable values for the posterior probabilities $P(Y = y | X = x)$ than the use of maximum likelihood estimates.

A.2.6. A first summary

In the first part of this section, two simple models have been presented to estimate and use a probabilistic classification system. Based on this simple canvas, multiple variations are possible, which consist, in particular, of using other count models. The two models used here are based on the naive hypothesis that the term occurrences are independent[11]. This hypothesis is very questionable, and has been invalidated on

---

11 Technically, they are conditionally independent given the class.

many corpora. In particular, we can empirically observe that the most typical words in a document are used repeatedly and tend to occur much more frequently than would be predicted under the multinomial model (see e.g. [CHU 95, KAT 96]). These observations have led to the development of other count models, based for example on the Poisson distribution [CHU 95], negative binomial-distribution [JAN 03], Dirichlet-Multinomial distribution [MAD 05], and so on[12]. As an exercise, readers are invited to reproduce the derivations developed in this section using, for instance, a Poisson distribution to model the number of occurrences of each term, and to derive the equations for the categorization case with n_K (> 2) classes.

A.3. Unsupervised learning: the multinomial mixture model

In previous sections, we have presented the general framework of supervised classification, or, more precisely, of supervised estimation of a classification model. We have seen how supervision information, available in the form of a corpus of labeled documents, is used to compute estimates [A.15] and [A.16] for the parameters of a multinomial model. In a more subtle manner, supervision information is also used to *select the model*: only the categories observed in the training corpus have a non-zero probability in the model; only the words seen in the training corpus are associated with parameters $b_{c,w}$.

In this section, it will be shown that, once the model type has been selected, it is actually possible to estimate the parameters *without any supervision information*, and in particular without knowing the "true" class of documents. This approach results in a *non-deterministic clustering* of collections, which can be useful for exploratory text data analysis: when documents are clustered based on their thematic content, this family of models is known as *topic models*. Probabilistic topic models constitute the main subject of Chapter 5, which contains a very complete presentation of these models.

A.3.1. *Mixture models*

Let us first reconsider the generative model presented in the previous section, by assuming that the number of categories[13] n_K is now arbitrary. The prior probabilities associated with these categories are denoted $c_1 \ldots c_{n_K}$. This model specifies the form of the joint probabilities for pairs (class, document); it is also possible to express the probability of a document x by summing over all possible classes according to:

---

12 Readers can refer to section A.7.4 for a presentation of some usual probability distributions.
13 In this section, the term "topic" will also be used and the models studied in this section are called topic models.

$$P(X = x; \theta) = \sum_{y=1}^{n_K} P(Y = y, X = x; \theta)$$

$$= \sum_{y=1}^{n_K} P(X = x | Y = y; \theta) P(Y = y; \theta)$$

[A.20]

By modeling each class conditional probability $P(X = x | Y = y)$ by a multinomial distribution and $P(Y = y)$ by a discrete distribution, the probability of a document is thus expressed as a function of the parameters b and c.

Let $\mathcal{C} = \{(x^{(n)}), n = 1 \dots n_D\}$ denote as previously a corpus of documents, and further assume that (i) $\mathcal{C}$ is subdivided into n_K classes and (ii) the indexing vocabulary is fixed and contains n_W terms. It is thus possible to express the log-likelihood of $\mathcal{C}$ as follows:

$$\ell(\theta) = \sum_{n=1}^{n_D} \log(P(X^{(n)} = x^{(n)}; \theta))$$

$$= \sum_{n=1}^{n_D} \log \left(\sum_{y=1}^{n_K} P(X^{(n)} = x^{(n)} | Y^{(n)} = y; \theta) P(Y^{(n)} = y; \theta) \right)$$

[A.21]

As previously, we can estimate the parameters by maximizing equation [A.21] with respect to b and c, under the appropriate normalization constraints ($\sum_y c_y = 1$, etc.). This optimization problem is, however, more complicated than the problems considered in the supervised setting, for two reasons. First of all, the objective function is no longer log-concave, which reduces the hope of finding a global maximum; furthermore, canceling the partial derivatives of the objective leads to equations that cannot be solved analytically.

It is however possible to *numerically* solve this optimization problem. The intuition of the approach that we will develop here relies on the following observation. We have seen, that if the document classes are known (supervised case), then the optimization of [A.21] is easy and leads to the estimators presented in equations [A.15] and [A.16]. Conversely, when the parameters are known, computing the category of documents is easy, thanks to equation [A.3], which determines the most probable class. This suggests using an iterative algorithm which consists of alternatively assigning documents to the most likely class, and then updating the parameters based on the category thus obtained. In essence, the algorithm presented in the following sections justifies and extends this very simple idea.

A.3.2. *Parameter estimation*

A.3.2.1. *A generic approach: the EM algorithm*

The standard way to solve the optimization problem [A.21] is to address it indirectly, by optimizing an *auxiliary* function. This function should be easy to manipulate and such that its optimization should improve the likelihood. This auxiliary function is parameterized by the vector θ', which has the same components as θ: c' for the prior class probabilities and b'_y for the parameters of the distribution associated with the class y.

We denote in the following $\gamma^{(n)}(y, \theta') = P(Y = y|x^{(n)}; \theta')$ the posterior probability that document $x^{(n)}$ belongs to class y when the value of the parameter vector is θ'. $\gamma^{(n)}(y, \theta')$ therefore defines a vector of dimension n_K whose components add up to 1 and is computed directly according to [A.1]. We also denote $\ell^{(n)}(y, \theta)$ the function of θ and y defined by $\ell^{(n)}(y, \theta) = \log P(X^{(n)} = x^{(n)}, Y^{(n)} = y; \theta)$. $\ell^{(n)}(y, \theta)$ is the *complete* log-likelihood associated with the observation $x^{(n)}$ under the hypothesis that the corresponding class is y. Using this new notation, the auxiliary function is defined as:

$$Q_{\theta'}(\theta) = \sum_{n=1}^{n_D} \sum_{y=1}^{n_K} P(Y = y|x^{(n)}; \theta')\ell^{(n)}(y, \theta) \qquad [A.22]$$

$Q_{\theta'}(\theta)$ is therefore the expectation of the log-likelihood of the complete data, under a conditional probability distribution whose parameters are defined by θ'. Why should we be interested in $Q_{\theta'}$? The answer is given in the following derivation[14], in which we show that, for any value of θ', the value of θ that optimizes the auxiliary function also improves the likelihood.

For any values of y and θ, the joint distribution can be decomposed as:

$$P(x^{(n)}, y; \theta) = P(y|x^{(n)}; \theta)\, P(x^{(n)}; \theta)$$

Taking the logarithm and reordering the terms yields:

$$\log(P(x^{(n)}; \theta)) = \ell^{(n)}(y, \theta) - \log(P(y|x^{(n)}; \theta))$$

By taking the expectation with respect to any probability distribution q over the set of classes:

$$\sum_{y=1}^{n_K} q(y) \log(P(x^{(n)}; \theta)) = \sum_{y=1}^{n_K} q(y)\ell^{(n)}(y, \theta) - \sum_{y=1}^{n_K} q(y) \log(P(y|x^{(n)}; \theta)) \quad [A.23]$$

---

14 This derivation can be skipped without loss of continuity.

As $\log(P(x^{(n)}; \theta))$ does not depend on y, it can be extracted from the sum and the term on the left is simply $\log(P(x^{(n)}; \theta))$. The first term on the right is the auxiliary $Q_{\theta'}$ when choosing for q the conditional distribution defined by $q(y) = \gamma^{(n)}(y, \theta')$. To analyze the second term on the right, let us recall that the Kullback–Leibler (KL) divergence[15] between the two distributions q and q' over a set A is defined by :

$$D(q||q') = \sum_{y \in A} q(y) \log(q(y)) - \sum_{y \in A} q(y) \log(q'(y))$$

The KL divergence corresponds to the opposite of the difference between the entropy of distribution q and the cross-entropy between the distributions q and q'. When choosing for q the conditional distribution $q(y) = \gamma^{(n)}(y; \theta')$, the second term of the equation [A.23] is then interpreted as the cross entropy between the posterior distribution induced by θ and that induced by θ'. Let us then denote $H_{\theta'}(\theta)$ the sum of these terms over all the documents: $H_{\theta'}(\theta) = \sum_{n=1}^{n_D} \sum_y \gamma^{(n)}(y, \theta') \log(P(y|x^{(n)}; \theta))$. For any value of θ, the following is obtained by summing [A.23] over all documents:

$$\ell(\theta) = Q_{\theta'}(\theta) - H_{\theta'}(\theta)$$

Let us assume that the parameters of the model are fixed and equal to θ', and let θ^* be the value maximizing $Q_{\theta'}(\theta)$. By virtue of the previous equation, we have:

$$\ell(\theta') = Q_{\theta'}(\theta') - H_{\theta'}(\theta')$$
$$\ell(\theta^*) = Q_{\theta'}(\theta^*) - H_{\theta'}(\theta^*)$$

Taking the difference yields:

$$\ell(\theta^*) - \ell(\theta') = (Q_{\theta'}(\theta^*) - Q_{\theta'}(\theta')) + (H_{\theta'}(\theta') - H_{\theta'}(\theta^*))$$

The first term of the part on the right is positive, since θ^* maximizes $Q_{\theta'}(\theta)$; the second term is also positive, since it is the sum, over all documents, of Kullback–Leibler divergences between the posterior distributions induced respectively by θ' and θ^*. We can deduce that $\ell(\theta^*) - \ell(\theta') \geq 0$: at a fixed θ', optimizing $Q_{\theta'}(\theta)$ leads to parameter values that also improve the log-likelihood of the data. This result explains why it is interesting to optimize $Q_{\theta'}(\theta)$ instead of $\ell(\theta)$, as we know that any improvement in the auxiliary function will also improve the log-likelihood.

We are now in a position to give a first outline of the EM algorithm: this iterative procedure simply consists of constructing a sequence of values $\theta_0 \dots \theta_k$, so that each parameter θ_k is obtained by maximizing $Q_{\theta_{k-1}}(\theta)$. It can be proven that this approach converges toward a saddle point of the likelihood function.

---

15 See section A.7.3.2.

A.3.2.1.1. Optimizing the auxiliary function

We now turn to the problem of optimizing the auxiliary function. For the multinomial mixture model, this function takes the following form:

$$Q_{\theta'}(\theta) = \sum_{n=1}^{n_D} \sum_{y=1}^{n_K} \gamma^{(n)}(y, \theta') \log(P(x^{(n)}, y; \theta))$$

$$= \sum_{n=1}^{n_D} \sum_{y=1}^{n_K} \gamma^{(n)}(y, \theta') \log(P(y; \theta) \, P(x^{(n)}|y; \theta))$$

$$= \sum_{n=1}^{n_D} \sum_{y=1}^{n_K} \gamma^{(n)}(y, \theta') \left(\log(c_y) + \sum_{w=1}^{n_W} x_w^{(n)} \log(b_{y,w}) \right) + C^{\text{st}}$$

Contrary to $\ell(\theta)$, this function is easy to optimize. For instance, maximizing $Q_{\theta'}(\theta)$ with respect to c under the normalization constraints requires us to compute the gradient of the Lagrangian $L_{\theta'}(\theta)$. Denoting ν the Lagrange multiplier associated with the constraint $\sum_y c_y = 1$, the partial derivative with respect to component c_y is:

$$\frac{\partial L_{\theta'}}{\partial c_y} = \frac{1}{c_y} \sum_{n=1}^{n_D} \gamma^{(n)}(y, \theta') - \nu$$

By canceling out the gradient, the expression for the optimal value of c is obtained. Using a similar reasoning for the parameters $b_{c,w}$, the following equations are finally obtained, which specify the update rule for parameters c and b according to the current parameters c' and b':

$$\gamma^{(n)}(y, \theta') = \frac{c'_y \prod_{w=1}^{n_W} b'^{x_w^{(n)}}_{y,w}}{\sum_z c'_z \prod_{w=1}^{n_W} b'^{x_w^{(n)}}_{y,w}} \qquad [A.24]$$

$$\widehat{c}_y = \frac{\sum_{n=1}^{n_D} \gamma^{(n)}(y, \theta')}{\sum_z \sum_{n=1}^{n_D} \gamma^{(n)}(z, \theta')} \qquad [A.25]$$

$$\widehat{b}_{y,w} = \frac{\sum_{n=1}^{n_D} \gamma^{(n)}(y, \theta') x_w^{(n)}}{\sum_z \sum_{n=1}^{n_D} \gamma^{(n)}(z, \theta') x_w^{(n)}} \qquad [A.26]$$

It is interesting to compare equation [A.26] and the estimator obtained in the supervised case (see equation [A.16]): as in the supervised case, the estimators obtained here are basically ratios of counts. However, since the class assignments are unknown, each document $x^{(n)}$ contributes to the estimates for class y in proportion of the posterior probability of that class. This probability is given by $\gamma^{(n)}(y, \boldsymbol{\theta}')$. It is finally possible, and often useful, to slightly modify equations [A.25] and [A.26] and to include a smoothing factor[16], in order to avoid null values for the estimates of the parameters $b_{y,w}$.

A.3.2.2. *The EM algorithm: complements*

In summary, we have shown in this section how it is possible to estimate the parameters of a probabilistic model such as those presented in section A.2 *without any supervision data*. In the case of the multinomial model, this approach relies on an iterative algorithm involving three equations (see Algorithm A.1), which correspond to the two main stages of the algorithm. In the **E**-step (expectation), the posterior probability of each class is computed according to [A.24], as these values are used in the expression of the auxiliary function. In the **M**-step (maximization), the auxiliary function is maximized and new parameter values are computed. This algorithm is iterated up to the stabilization of the objective function. Upon convergence, we have an estimated value $\widehat{\boldsymbol{\theta}}$ for the parameters, as well as, for each observation $\boldsymbol{x}^{(n)}$ and for each class y, the posterior probability of the class given the observation $\gamma^{(n)}(y; \widehat{\boldsymbol{\theta}})$. Let us finally note that this algorithm is very general and applies to other distributions and to other models: see, for instance, section A.5 in this chapter, the PLSA model detailed in Chapter 5, and the alignment models used in machine translation in Chapter 7.

Algorithm A.1. EM algorithm for the multinomial mixture model

---

Inputs: $\mathcal{C} = \{\boldsymbol{x}^{(n)}, n = 1 \ldots n_D\}, \epsilon, n_K$
$\boldsymbol{\theta}_0 \leftarrow$ InitTheta();
$t \leftarrow 0$;
while $(t = 0 \ \ or \ \ \|\boldsymbol{\theta}_t - \boldsymbol{\theta}_{t-1}\|_2 > \epsilon)$ **do**
    // **E**-step
    for $n \in [1{:}n_D]$ **do**
        for $y \in [1{:}n_K]$ **do**
          | Compute $\gamma^{(n)}(y, \boldsymbol{\theta}_t)$ according to [A.24]
        end
    end
    // **M**-step
    Update $\boldsymbol{\theta}_{t+1}$ according to [A.25] and [A.26];
    $t \leftarrow t + 1$;
end
return $\boldsymbol{\theta}_t; \{\gamma^{(n)}(y, \boldsymbol{\theta}_t), n \in [1{:}n_D], y \in [1{:}n_K]\}$

---

16 Once again, smoothing can be justified theoretically by adding a prior distribution on the parameters, see the discussion in section A.2.5.

When the likelihood function is not convex (as is the case for the multinomial model), the EM algorithm only computes locally optimal values. When implementing Algorithm (A.1) in high dimensions, the values reached at convergence will strongly depend on the initial values; the initialization stage thus plays an essential role in the behavior of the algorithm. There are many ways to implement this initialization, such as randomly assigning documents to classes and running one iteration of the M-step (see [RIG 06, Chapter 4]).

To complete this section, it should be stressed that there are numerous variations of this algorithm: readers can refer to [NEA 98] for a very enlightening analysis and a discussion of some possible extensions.

A.3.3. *Applications*

A.3.3.1. *Exploratory analysis of the document collections*

The unsupervised estimation of a mixture model for a collection of documents yields a probability distribution for each document, denoted $\{\gamma^{(n)}(y;\theta), y \in [1:n_K]\}$, which corresponds to the posterior probability of each class given the document and which expresses the strength of the association between a document and a class. From this point of view, this model performs a non-deterministic clustering of the document corpus. It is also possible to compute a *deterministic clustering*, by assigning each document to the most likely class. This amounts to turning $\gamma^{(n)}(y;\theta)$ into a Boolean vector, which will have one component equal to 1 (for the most probable value of y) and all the others equal to 0. The resulting classes of documents can be used, for instance, to perform exploratory analyses.

The information output by the EM algorithm is, however, *richer* than the one obtained using conventional deterministic partitioning algorithm (such as the k-means algorithm) and it is possible to use it in multiple ways:

– by using the distributions $\gamma^{(n)}(y, \theta)$ to identify the classes that are most strongly associated with observation; the corresponding observations are, in a certain sense, the best representatives of the class;

– by viewing the vectors $\{\gamma^{(n)}(y, \theta), y \in [1:n_K]\}$ as *projections* of the observation $x^{(n)}$ into a smaller subspace. Let us recall that, in the bag-of-words model, each document is a point in a n_W dimensional space; the vector of posterior probabilities maps $x^{(n)}$ into a much smaller subspace: the simplex[17] in dimension n_K. Using this new representation, it remains possible to compare points, to compute distances and similarities, and so on.

In practice, however, the projections induced by vectors $\gamma^{(n)}(y, \theta)$ are such that documents are often positioned in the "corners" of the simplex. This means that the

---

17 The simplex in dimension d contains all the points where the coordinates are positive and are adding to 1.

vectors $\gamma^{(n)}(y, \boldsymbol{\theta})$ usually contain only one component close to 1, whereas all the others are very close to 0. To obtain more useful representations of documents in small subspaces, the methods presented in Chapter 5 are often preferable.

A.3.3.2. *Conclusions and additional remarks*

In this section, we have presented a method for computing document clusters in an unsupervised manner. This method relies on the same probabilistic models of documents as the ones used for supervised classification. It uses an iterative algorithm enabling the numerical optimization of the log-likelihood of the observations, the EM algorithm, the implementation of which has been detailed and justified.

These techniques have been extended in the literature in multiple directions: first of all, by considering other count models than the multinomial model; but also by considering other learning regimes. It is, for example, easy to simultaneously integrate labeled and unlabeled data [NIG 00]. One way to do so is to use the labeled data to compute a parameter vector $\boldsymbol{\theta}_0$; this vector can then be used as an initial value when running the EM algorithm on the unlabeled data. The EM algorithm can also be modified to simultaneously handle labeled and unlabeled data: it suffices to replace the vector $\gamma^{(n)}(y; \boldsymbol{\theta})$ for labeled data with a Boolean vector representing the class assignment. Another learning protocol which generalizes the framework presented here consists in presenting and processing the learning data sequentially, rather than as a batch. This means that a new clustering must be produced each time a new data sample is collected. Here again, extensions of the EM algorithm have be proposed, enabling us to effectively perform learning in an *on line* manner [CAP 09].

A.4. Markov models: statistical models for sequences

In this section, another family of probabilistic models, which take the sequentiality of texts and sentences into account is presented: these models are known as *sequence models*. We only review here the most elementary models, Markov models, which rely on the hypothesis of bounded conditional dependencies between occurrences of elements in the sequence. The main difference with the bag-of-words approach, is that the occurrences within a text are no longer deemed independent from one another. However, the probability of each token in the sequence is only influenced by a few preceding words, the most simple case being that of a first order dependencies. The model is first introduced; we then discuss estimation issues and present some practical applications.

A.4.1. *Modeling sequences*

A literary presentation of Markov models is given in the following quote from the French writer and mathematician Raymond Queneau, cited in [BEN 05]:

"This is it. If letters are drawn at random from the alphabet, an incomprehensible text is produced, where only purely random sequences appear. Let us call this the *jargon number 0*. A *jargon number 1* can then be conceived, where letters are distributed according to their probability of occurrence (or their frequency) in the given language. In the *jargon number 2*, the probability that a letter will follow another letter is computed, again for the given language. The resulting text will resemble a known language. Going on like this, upon reaching *jargon number 4* (also known as *trigram*)[18], sentences are obtained such as: *Sorry and there was of its wing the bodies of bag.* These works by Markov date back from 1910".

In this definition, Queneau describes Markov models as probabilistic models, which are used to *generate* sequences (letter sequences here[19]). In the "jargon number 0" model (a uniform model) or in the "jargon number 1" (*unigram* model), each token is independent of the previous one. However, in "jargon number 2" (*bigram* model), each letter is conditioned by the previously generated letter and *only by that letter*; previously generated letters do not influence the current outcome. This characteristic defines what is known in modern terms as *a first order Markov chain*.

Formally, a Markov chain is a sequence of random variables $X_{[1:T]} = X_1, X_2, \ldots X_T$ such that, for any value of t, the "future" value of X_{t+1} only depends on the current value of X_t, and not on the preceding values[20]. This implies that:

$$P(X_{t+1} = x | X_{[1:t]} = x_{[1:t]}) = P(X_{t+1} = x | X_t = x_t) \qquad [A.27]$$

When this property is satisfied, the joint probability of a sequence $X_{[1:T]}$ is decomposed as:

$$P(X_{[1:T]} = x_{[1:T]}) = P(X_1 = x_1) P(X_2 = x_2 | X_1 = x_1)$$

$$\ldots P(X_T = x_T | X_{[1:t-1]} = x_{[1:t-1]})$$

$$= P(X_1 = x_1) \prod_{t=2}^{T} P(X_t = x_t | X_{t-1} = x_{t-1}) \qquad [A.28]$$

This factorization reflects the generation process described by Queneau: a letter is first generated, corresponding to the random variable X_1; the second letter is then generated conditionally to the first one, and so on till the end.

---

18 Queneau is wrong here: in modern terms, this would be a quadrigram.

19 Or rather character sequences, since the generated sequences include the space character.

20 More precisely: given X_t, x_{t+1} it is independent from $X_{t'}$ for all $t' < t$.

This definition can be generalized to higher orders: a second order chain is such that the future value only depends on the two previous values, and so on. In the following, we will only consider Markov chains in which each variable X_t takes its values from a finite set $\mathcal{X}$. Possible values for X_t are thus integers in $[1:N]$.

A *stationary* (or time-homogeneous) Markov chain is such that the terms in equation [A.27] do not depend on the time t at which the chain is considered, i.e.:

$$\forall i, j, t, P(X_{t+1} = j | X_t = i) = P(X_t = j | X_{t-1} = i) = a_{ij}$$

For each value i in $[1:N]$, $\sum_{j=1}^{N} a_{ij} = 1$ must hold: the matrix $A = \{a_{ij}, i = 1..N, j = 1...N\}$ is therefore a *stochastic* matrix. A stationary Markov chain can also be represented in the form of a state graph with one state for each possible value of X_t and one arc weighted by a_{ij} between states i and j. To completely describe the behavior of a stationary chain, we just need to know A, which describes the state transition probabilities, as well as the initial state of the model, described by an initial probability vector c: c_i represents the probability of starting the computation in state i. As in previous sections, θ will denote the set of all model parameters.

Let us consider, for instance, the Markov model displayed in Figure A.1, assuming that the initial probability vector is defined as $c = (0.5; 0.3; 0.2)$.

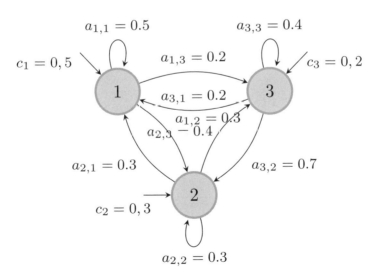

Figure A.1. *Three-state Markov model*

For the model represented in Figure A.1, the probability of the sequence $X_1 = 1$, $X_2 = 1, X_3 = 3, X_4 = 2$ is computed as $0.5 \times 0.5 \times 0.2 \times 0.7$. As this example shows, this model defines a probability distribution *over sets of sequences having the same length*. For instance, for this model, three sequences of length 1 are possible, and the sum of the probabilities of these sequences is equal to 1: $X_1 = 1$ (probability 0.5), $X_1 = 2$ (probability 0.3), and $X_1 = 3$ (probability 0.2). More generally, it can be shown that:

$$\forall T, \quad \sum_{x_{[1:T]} \in [1:N]^T} P(X_{[1:T]} = x_{[1:T]}; \boldsymbol{\theta}) = 1 \qquad [A.29]$$

If N is the number of states of the model, the number of parameters of a first order Markov model is $N - 1$ for the initial probabilities, to which the transition $N(N-1)$ probabilities are added. More generally, the number of parameters increases exponentially with the order of the model, which explains why only models with a low order are usually considered in practice.

A.4.2. *Estimating a Markov model*

Estimating the parameters of a Markov chain can be performed using a sample of sequences $\{x_{[1:T^{(n)}]}^{(n)}, n = 1 \dots N\}$ assumed to be generated independently by the Markov chain. Here again, it is possible to resort to the maximum likelihood principle. The likelihood is written as:

$$\mathcal{L}(A, c) = \prod_{n=1}^{N} P(x_1^{(n)} \dots x_{T^{(n)}}^{(n)}; \boldsymbol{\theta})$$

$$= \prod_{n=1}^{N} c_{x_1^{(n)}} \prod_{t=2}^{T^{(n)}} P(x_t^{(n)} | x_{t-1}^{(n)}; A)$$

$$\qquad [A.30]$$

$$= \prod_{n=1}^{N} c_{x_1^{(n)}} \prod_{t=2}^{T^{(n)}} a_{x_{t-1}^{(n)}, x_t^{(n)}}$$

$$= \prod_{i=1}^{n_K} c_i^{F(i)} \prod_{i,j} a_{i,j}^{F(i,j)}$$

In this last equation, $F(i)$ is the number of sequences starting in state i and $F(i,j)$ denotes the number of occurrences, aggregated over all sequences, of the succession of states i and j. From this, optimal values for $a_{i,j}$ and c_i are easily derived. These values maximize equation [A.30], subject to the stochastic constraints: $\sum_i c_i = 1$ and $\forall i, \sum_j a_{i,j} = 1$. This optimization problem is very similar to the one defined by equation [A.13]. It can be solved in the same way (by canceling the partial derivatives of the Lagrangian) and results in the following solutions:

$$\widehat{c}_i = \frac{F(i)}{\sum_k F(k)} \qquad\qquad\qquad\qquad \text{[A.31]}$$

$$\widehat{a}_{i,j} = \frac{F(i,j)}{\sum_k F(i,k)} \qquad\qquad\qquad\qquad \text{[A.32]}$$

Here again, the maximum likelihood can be solved analytically and yields very simple estimators, which are calculated as a mere ratio of number of occurrences.

A.4.3. *Language models*

Markov models or *n-gram models* are ubiquitous in probabilistic natural language processing and are used, under the name of *language models* in numerous applications. Readers can specifically refer to [JEL 90] for an introduction to these models in the context of automatic speech recognition applications, as well as to [ROS 00, GOO 01] for more recent reviews of the state of the art. The application to sequences taking values in very large label sets, on the one hand; the estimation of parameters from actual corpora, on the other hand, raise a certain number of practical issues, which are discussed in the next paragraphs.

A.4.3.1. *Estimating language models*

Given the sequential nature of linguistic utterances, it is natural to consider, as Markov did, sequence models to define distributions over sets of words, sentences or documents. As discussed above, estimating such models is a simple matter of counting the number of occurrences of short subsequences (typically comprising between 2 to 8 symbols). Given a finite vocabulary V of size n_W, assume that we intend to model word sequences with a first order model. Observations will therefore be types in a very large set (depending on the languages and applications, the size n_W of the vocabulary ranges from a few thousand to a few hundred thousands).

The corresponding model will therefore include one state for each vocabulary entry and the size of transition matrix A grows with the square of n_W. If, for instance, V is in the order of 10^5 words, 10^{10} parameters $a_{i,j}$ will need to be estimated, each expressing the probability that word j follows word i. As each parameter value is estimated based on counts (see [A.32] and [A.31]) we would then have to consider corpora containing at least several billion occurrences to observe all the possible words bigram and to ensure that each parameter gets a strictly positive value. In reality, word occurrences are very unevenly distributed and most of the occurrences are concentrated on a small number of types, while most vocabulary entries are very rarely observed. This implies that even when processing very large corpora, the vast majority of bigrams (i,j) are never observed, resulting in null values for the corresponding parameter $\widehat{a}_{i,j}$. This is obviously not acceptable, as the corresponding model would assign a zero probability to any sequence containing an unobserved bigram. The problem is identical to the one encountered earlier when discussing estimation problems for the Bernoulli and multinomial models, and only gets worse for higher order models. It is no wonder then that smoothing techniques for Markov models have given rise to a vast literature. Readers can refer to [CHE 96] for an empirical study of smoothing techniques, and to [MAC 94, TEH 06] for a Bayesian account.

A second practical problem raised by these models is that they define probability distributions over sets of fixed size sequences: consequently, the probabilities of two sequences differing in length are not directly comparable. To solve this problem, the model must include a probability of stopping the generation process, yielding a probabilistic model that is formally equivalent to stochastic automata (see [DUP 05]). Another way of obtaining this same result is to add an additional end symbol (or, equivalently, an additional state) to materialize the end of the generation process. By definition, this new state will not have any outgoing transition.

A.4.3.2. *Some applications of language models*

A.4.3.2.1. Language identification

A first application of language models is document classification, already discussed in section A.2. Markov models use document representations that go beyond the "bag-of-words" model, and in which, in particular, the sequentiality of the symbols that compose the document is preserved. In the simplest scenario, the document could be represented as a sequence of alphabetic symbols, but it could also, depending on the applications, be viewed as a sequence of forms, of lemmas, etc. Let us simply assume that document d is represented by a sequence $x_{[1:T]}$.

The joint probability of a document and a class is now a function of class specific Markov model parameters (denoted here respectively as $c_{y,i}$ for the initial probability of state i in class y and $a_{y,i,j}$ for the transition probability between i and j for class y). Finally, p_y denotes the prior probability of class y:

$$P(Y = y, X_{[1:T]} = x_{[1:T]}; \boldsymbol{\theta}) = P(Y = y; \boldsymbol{\theta}) P(X_{[1:T]} = x_{[1:T]}|Y = y; \boldsymbol{\theta})$$

$$= p_y c_{y,x_1} \prod_{t=2}^{T} a_{y,x_{t-1}^{(n)},x_t^{(n)}} \tag{A.33}$$

Such a model could for instance be useful in a language identification scenario, where the goal is to recognize the language in which a text is written. Using Markov models of letters, all that is required is to implement the following stages:

– from a training sample of labelled documents, i.e. documents whose language are known, estimate the model parameters associated with each language according to equation [A.33]. If the order of the model is $n - 1$, this step boils down to computing the counts of all letter n-grams;

– for a test document, decide the optimal language assignment according to equation [A.3], in which the term $P(x_{[1:T]}, y)$ is computed by [A.33].

This type of modeling has been used to recognize the language of entire documents as well as isolated words, to identify the author of a text, or even to automatically segment emails so as to identify sections such as header, body, signature, and so on.

A.4.3.2.2. Assessing grammaticality

In Natural Language Processing applications, the most common use of Markov models corresponds to situations where various hypotheses, taking the form of sequences of symbols, have to be compared. This is the case, for instance, in automatic speech recognition (see for example [JEL 97]): expressed as a probabilistic decision problem, the automatic transcription of speech consists of finding the maximally likely word sequence given the observed speech signal. A similar problem arises in grammar correction, where we seek the most likely correct word sequence given the possibly noisy input, or in statistical machine translation (see Chapter 7).

These applications are quite different from previous ones: here, the input is given (and takes the form of a speech signal or a sentence in source language), and is modeled by a random variable Y. We then need to find the sequence (the transcription of the signal or the translation of the source) X maximizing $P(X|Y)$. According to Bayes rule, we know that this problem is equivalent to looking for the sequence maximizing $P(X) P(Y|X)$, where the first term provides a rough assessment of the grammaticality of X and can be computed by a Markov model. Markov models are used here to compare the probabilities of different sequences X, in particular sequences *of different length*. As previously mentioned, such a comparison would only be meaningful if $P()$ would define a distribution over the set of all possible sequences. This is generally not sufficient, as the probability of a sequence of length T involves the product of T terms between 0 and 1 and is generally smaller than the probability of a sequence of length $T - 1$, all the more so of a sequence of length $T - 2$. It is, therefore, necessary to add penalization terms (known in the speech recognition jargon as *word insertion bonus*) to make up for these length differences.

A.5. Hidden Markov models

In this section, we introduce hidden Markov models, which are widely used in the statistical processing of language data (see, for instance, [CHA 93, MAN 99] for natural language processing applications and [RAB 93], which focuses on applications in speech recognition).

A.5.1. *The model*

A hidden Markov model (HMM) is a generation model for pairs of random variables representing sequences $(X_{[1:T]}, Y_{[1:T]})$ having the same length. We assume here that each sequence contains symbols from a finite alphabet: $[1: n_K]$ for the values of Y_t and $[1: n_W]$ for the values of X_t. Conventionally, the elements in $Y_{[1:T]}$ correspond to states and those in $X_{[1:T]}$ will be referred to as observations, as these models are typically used to infer the best sequence $y^*_{[1:T]}$ of states given the observation $x_{[1:T]}$. In this setting, the states are *hidden* and correspond to unobserved variables.

The generation of sequence pairs generalizes the generation process of a Markov chains presented in previous section. In fact, in a first order HMM, $Y_{[1:T]}$ is a first order Markov chain, the parameters of which are denoted, as previously, by a vector c and by a stochastic matrix A. The novelty is a mechanism for generating observations: at each "instant" t, when the system is in state Y_t, the current observation X_t is chosen by drawing according to a distribution *which only depends on the current state*; the following state Y_{t+1} is then chosen as prescribed by the transition probabilities in A. As we consider here situations in which the observations take discrete values, it is natural to associate a discrete distribution with each possible value i of Y_t, the parameters of which are defined by a vector b_i. Each component $b_{i,j}$ corresponds to the probability of choosing observation j when in state i. In the discrete case, the parameters are thus defined by a set θ of parameters comprising the vector c, the $(n_K \times n_K)$ transition matrix A and the $(n_K \times n_W)$ matrix B. Other kinds of observations would require other types of probabilistic models. For instance, in speech processing, observations are vectors in $\mathbb{R}^d$ and the distributions associated with the states are (mixtures of) multidimensional Gaussian distributions; when observations are documents rather than words, it is natural to associate a multidimensional binomial distribution or a multinomial distribution with each state, etc.

Figure A.2 represents a three-state hidden Markov model ($n_K = 3$); each state is associated with a discrete distribution on a set of $n_W = 3$ "terms".

Hidden Markov models can be thought of as generalizing the two models studied in the previous sections. As in classification models, observations are generated in a two step process: first choose the category (class) Y, then, conditioned on the value of Y, generate X. As in Markov models, Y is observed over time; the values of Y_t depend on the value of Y_{t-1}. To infer the class associated with an observation, both aspects of the model will have to be considered simultaneously.

The joint probability of a pair of sequences is therefore written as in a Markov model for the sequence $Y_{[1:T]}$; the probability of sequence $X_{[1:T]}$ is a product of the probabilities of emitting X_t in state Y_t. Combining both terms yields:

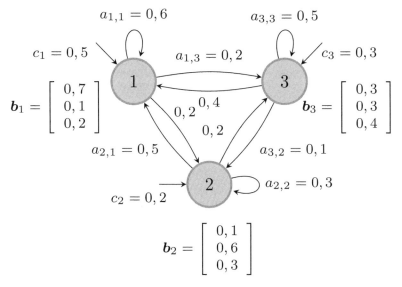

Figure A.2. *A three-state hidden Markov model*

$$P(X_{[1:T]} = x_{[1:T]}, Y_{[1:T]} = y_{[1:T]}; \boldsymbol{\theta}) = c_{y_1} \prod_{t=2}^{T} a_{y_{t-1}, y_t} \prod_{t=1}^{T} b_{y_t, x_t} \qquad [\text{A.34}]$$

For the model presented in Figure A.2, the probability of the pair $(X_{[1:T]} = 1211, Y_{[1:T]} = 2312)$ is computed as:

$$P(X_{[1:T]} = 1211, Y_{[1:T]} = 2312) = 0.2 \times 0.2 \times 0.4 \times 0.2 \times 0.1 \times 0.3 \times 0.7 \times 0.1$$

A.5.2. *Algorithms for hidden Markov models*

In the HMM literature, it is usual to study, following [RAB 93], the *three problems* of hidden Markov models. These problems correspond respectively to the computation of the probability of an observation sequence; the computation of the optimal state sequence given the observation sequence (*optimal decoding problem*); and finally, the problem of unsupervised parameter estimation, giving rise to three algorithms known as *forward algorithm*, *Viterbi algorithm* and *forward-backward algorithm*, respectively. The latter is used to derive the HMM specific version of the expectation-maximization (EM) algorithm, already presented in section A.3.2 in the context of mixtures of multinomial models. In this section, these problems and their solutions are presented. We also discuss two additional and less often studied problems: the questions of *optimally local decoding* and of fully supervised estimation.

A.5.2.1. *Marginal probability of an observation sequence*

The first question we address is the computation of the probability of an observation sequence $P(x_{[1:T]}; \boldsymbol{\theta})$. By virtue of the marginalization rule [A.49], this term is written as:

$$P(x_{[1:T]}; \boldsymbol{\theta}) = \sum_{y_{[1:T]}} P(x_{[1:T]}, y_{[1:T]}; \boldsymbol{\theta}) \qquad [A.35]$$

This computation only involves well known terms defined in [A.34]; it is, however, difficult to perform as the summation runs over all the sequences of T states, the number of which increases exponentially with T. For instance, in the previous example, $P(X_{[1:T]} = 1211)$ is the sum over $n_K{}^4$ possible state sequences, as this sequence can be emitted along the path $Y_{[1:T]} = 1111$, or along the path $Y_{[1:T]} = 1112$, etc.

A.5.2.1.1. Forward recursions

This computation can still be performed efficiently using a well known algorithm known as the *forward algorithm*. The general idea is to recursively compute, for each value of t, a vector $\boldsymbol{\alpha}_t$, the components $\alpha_{t,i}$ of which correspond to $P(X_{[1:t]} = x_{[1:t]}, Y_t = i; \boldsymbol{\theta})$.

To start, let us note that the total probability $P(X_{[1:T]} = x_{[1:T]}; \boldsymbol{\theta})$ is obtained by summing, over all the n_K states, terms $\alpha_{T,i} = P(X_{[1:T]} = x_{[1:T]}, Y_T = i; \boldsymbol{\theta})$. The computation of the vectors $\boldsymbol{\alpha}_t$ can be performed in an efficient manner, since:

$$\begin{aligned}
\alpha_{t,i} &= P(X_{[1:t]} = x_{[1:t]}, Y_t = i; \boldsymbol{\theta}) \\
&= P(X_t = x_t | X_{[1:t-1]} = x_{[1:t-1]}, Y_t = i; \boldsymbol{\theta}) P(X_{[1:t-1]} = x_{[1:t-1]}, Y_t = i; \boldsymbol{\theta}) \\
&= P(X_t = x_t | Y_t = i; \boldsymbol{\theta}) P(X_{[1:t-1]} = x_{[1:t-1]}, Y_t = i; \boldsymbol{\theta}) \\
&= b_{i,x_t} \sum_{j=1}^{n_K} P(X_{[1:t-1]} = x_{[1:t-1]}, Y_t = i, Y_{t-1} = j; \boldsymbol{\theta}) \\
&= b_{i,x_t} \sum_{j=1}^{n_K} P(Y_t = i | Y_{t-1} = j; \boldsymbol{\theta}) P(X_{[1:t-1]} = x_{[1:t-1]}, Y_{t-1} = j; \boldsymbol{\theta}) \\
&= b_{i,x_t} \sum_{j=1}^{n_K} a_{j,i} \alpha_{t-1,j}
\end{aligned}$$

We thus derive a simple recursive expression for $\boldsymbol{\alpha}_t$, which depends on $\boldsymbol{\alpha}_{t-1}$ and on the various model parameters. Initializing $\boldsymbol{\alpha}_1$ according to $\alpha_{1,i} = c_i b_{i,x_1}$ completes our presentation of the *forward* algorithm, which is formalized by Algorithm A.2. This algorithm is quadratic in n_K, as the computation of each of the n_K components $\alpha_{t,i}$ requires a sum over n_K terms. It is linear in the length T of the sequences.

Algorithm A.2. Forward algorithm

Inputs: $x_{[1:T]}$
Data: θ
for $i \in [1:n_K]$ **do**
$\quad | \quad \alpha_{1,i} = c_i b_{i,x_1};$
end
for $t \in [2:T]$ **do**
$\quad$ **for** $i \in [1:n_K]$ **do**
$\quad\quad | \quad \alpha_{t,i} = b_{i,x_t} \sum_{j=1}^{n_K} \alpha_{t-1,j} a_{j,i}$
$\quad$ **end**
end
return $P(x_{[1:T]}) = \sum_{j=1}^{n_K} \alpha_{T,j}$

A.5.2.1.2. Backward recursions

The computation of the marginal probability of a sequence $x_{[1:T]}$ is not directional: it can be performed, as shown above, from left to right. It can also be performed from right to left, which corresponds to another factorization of the sum of products in equation [A.35]. These "backward" recursions imply the definition of another set of vectors, denoted here β_t, where each component $\beta_{t,i}$ corresponds to $P(x_{[t+1:T]}|Y_t = i; \theta)$, which is the probability of generating the end of the observation sequence $x_{[t+1:T]}$, when the model is in state i at time t. Elementary manipulations yield a recursive expression for this quantity, giving rise to another algorithm, the *backward algorithm*, for computing the marginal probability of an observation sequence (see Algorithm A.3).

Algorithm A.3. Backward algorithm

Inputs: $x_{[1:T]}$
Data: θ
for $i \in [1:n_K]$ **do**
$\quad | \quad \beta_{T,i} = 1;$
end
for $t \in [T-1:1]$ **do**
$\quad$ **for** $i \in [1:n_K]$ **do**
$\quad\quad | \quad \beta_{t,i} = \sum_{j=1}^{n_K} a_{i,j} b_{j,x_{t+1}} \beta_{t+1,j}$
$\quad$ **end**
end
return $P(x_{[1:T]}) = \sum_{i=1}^{n_K} b_{i,x_1} c_i \beta_{1,i}$

It should finally be noted that for all values of t, the quantity $\alpha_{t,i}\beta_{t,i}$ corresponds to the cumulated probability of all the paths passing through state i at instant t. This implies that *at each time* t, the knowledge of α_t and β_t is sufficient to compute the marginal probability of $x_{[1:T]}$ by summing over all the possible states according to:

$$P(x_{[1:T]}; \boldsymbol{\theta}) = \sum_{j=1}^{n_K} \alpha_{t,j}\beta_{t,j}$$

A.5.2.2. *Optimal decoding*

A.5.2.2.1. The Viterbi algorithm

The problem of optimal decoding is the computation of the most likely state sequence $y^*_{[1:T]}$ given the observation sequence. It is simply defined as:

$$y^*_{[1:T]} = \operatorname*{argmax}_{y_{[1:T]}} P(Y_{[1:T]} = y_{[1:T]} | X_{[1:T]} = x_{[1:T]}; \boldsymbol{\theta})$$

$$= \operatorname*{argmax}_{y_{[1:T]}} P(X_{[1:T]} = x_{[1:T]}, Y_{[1:T]} = y_{[1:T]}; \boldsymbol{\theta})$$

[A.36]

The equivalence between these two formulations of the problem is again a consequence of Bayes' rule (see the equivalence between [A.2] and [A.3]).

Computing this maximum requires again to solve a combinatorial problem, since all the possible sequences of states must be compared. The solution is, here again, provided by dynamic programming techniques. Let us introduce the vector δ_t, whose i^{th} component is defined by: $\delta_{t,i} = \max_{y_{[1:t]}, y_t=i} P(X_{[1:t]} = x_{[1:t]}, Y_{[1:t]} = y_{[1:t]}; \boldsymbol{\theta})$. In words, $\delta_{t,i}$ is the maximum joint probability of a pair of prefixes $(x_{[1:t]}, y_{[1:t]})$ reaching state i at time t.

It is clear that the state j preceding i on this optimal path is itself on an optimal path reaching state j at time $t-1$. If this were not the case, there would be a better path reaching i at time t. From this optimal sub-path property, a recursive expression is readily deduced for δ_t enabling to solve the optimal decoding problem thanks to dynamic programming algorithm, (see Algorithm A.4, known as the Viterbi algorithm [VIT 67]). As is the case with shortest paths algorithms, it is also necessary to define back-pointers $\phi_{t,i}$ in order to store the predecessor state of i along the best path reaching i at time t. As for the forward algorithm, the complexity of this algorithm is $O(Tn_K^2)$.

Algorithm A.4. Viterbi algorithm

Input: $x_{[1:T]}$
Data: θ
for $i \in [1:n_K]$ **do**
  $\delta_{1,i} = c_i b_{i,x_1}$;
  $\phi_{1,i} = 0$;
end
for $t \in [1:T]$ **do**
  for $i \in [1:n_K]$ **do**
    $\delta_{t,i} = \max_{1 \leq j \leq n_K} \delta_{t-1,j} a_{j,i} b_{i,x_t}$;
    $\phi_{t,i} = \text{argmax}_{1 \leq j \leq n_K} \delta_{t-1,j} a_{j,i} b_{i,x_t}$;
  end
end
$y_T^* = \text{argmax}_{1 \leq j \leq n_K} \delta_{T,i}$;
for $t \in [T-1:1]$ **do**
  $y_t^* = \phi_{t+1, y_{t+1}^*}$
end
return $(y_{[1:T]}^*, P(y_{[1:T]}^*))$

A.5.2.2.2. Locally optimal decoding

In most practical sequence labeling applications, the performance is not evaluated based on the number of sequences correctly labeled, but on the number of individual symbols correctly inferred. For instance, the quality of part-of-speech taggers is typically assessed by the number of words receiving the correct tag, rather than by the number of entirely correct sentences. In this context, the rule defined by [A.36] is no longer optimal and it is preferable to infer a sequence $y_{[1:T]}^*$ by minimizing the probability of an error at each of the position of the sequence, yielding the following decision rule:

$$\forall t, y_t^* = \underset{1 \leq i \leq n_K}{\text{argmax}} \, P(Y_t = i | X_{[1:T]} = x_{[1:T]}; \theta)$$

$$= \underset{1 \leq i \leq n_K}{\text{argmax}} \, P(X_{[1:T]} = x_{[1:T]}, Y_t = i; \theta) \qquad \text{[A.37]}$$

As previously noted, $\epsilon_{t,i} = P(X_{[1:T]} = x_{[1:T]}, Y_t = i)$ can be computed exactly using the fact that:

$$\epsilon_{t,i} = P(X_{[1:t]} = x_{[1:t]}, Y_t = i) \, P(X_{[t+1:T]} = x_{[t+1:T]} | X_{[1:t]} = x_{[1:t]}, Y_t = i)$$

$$= P(x_{[1:t]}, Y_t = i) \, P(x_{[t+1:T]} | Y_t = i) \qquad \text{[A.38]}$$

$$= \alpha_{t,i} \beta_{t,i}$$

This derivation is a direct consequence of conditional independence assumptions: conditionally to the current state Y_t, the "future" $X_{[t+1:T]}$ does not depend on the "past" $X_{[1:t]}$. Quantities used in [A.37] can then be deduced through normalization:

$$P(Y_t = i|X_{[1:T]} = x_{[1:T]}; \boldsymbol{\theta}) = \frac{\alpha_{t,i}\beta_{t,i}}{\sum_k \alpha_{t,k}\beta_{t,k}} \qquad [A.39]$$

In summary, there exists a second algorithm for recovering an optimal state sequence, which consists of computing vectors $\boldsymbol{\alpha}_t$ and $\boldsymbol{\beta}_t$, and then choosing at each time t the optimal state based on [A.37]. When error rates are computed on a per token basis, this technique can provide slightly better performance than those obtained delivered by Viterbi decoding [MÉR 94].

A.5.2.3. *Supervised parameter estimation*

In many applications, such as those presented in Chapter 6 (part-of-speech tagging, named entities recognition), supervision data is available to estimate the HMM parameters in the form of a set of pairs of sequences $\{x^{(n)}_{[1:T^{(n)}]}, y^{(n)}_{[1:T^{(n)}]}, n = 1 \ldots N\}$.

As for the previous models, parameter estimation can be performed using the maximum likelihood principle, which prescribes to maximize the likelihood function with respect to $\boldsymbol{\theta} = (\boldsymbol{c}, \boldsymbol{A}, \boldsymbol{B})$:

$$\mathcal{L}(\boldsymbol{\theta}) = \prod_{n=1}^{N} P(x^{(n)}_{[1:T^{(n)}]}, y^{(n)}_{[1:T^{(n)}]}; \boldsymbol{\theta}) \qquad [A.40]$$

The constraints considered here are the following: $\sum_i c_i = 1$; $\forall i, \sum_j a_{i,j} = 1$; $\forall i, \sum_j b_{i,j} = 1$. Note that the first two constraints were already present in the maximum likelihood program for the Markov chains presented in section A.4.2.

A closer look at the joint distribution of $(X_{[1:T]}, Y_{[1:T]})$ (given in equation [A.34] and recalled below) shows that it is a factor of three terms:

$$P(x_{[1:T]}, y_{[1:T]}) = c_{y_1} \times \prod_{t=2}^{T} a_{y_{t-1},y_t} \times \prod_{t=1}^{T} b_{y_t,x_t}$$

The log-likelihood $\ell(\boldsymbol{c}, \boldsymbol{A}, \boldsymbol{B}) = \log(\mathcal{L}(\boldsymbol{c}, \boldsymbol{A}, \boldsymbol{B}))$ thus decomposes into three sums. The first one only depends on the vector $\boldsymbol{c}$; the second (and the third, respectively) only involve coefficients of $\boldsymbol{A}$ (of $\boldsymbol{B}$, respectively). The optimization of $\ell(\boldsymbol{c}, \boldsymbol{A}, \boldsymbol{B})$ can thus be performed separately for each group of parameters. For the first two groups, which parameterize the Markov chain modeling the behavior of $Y_{[1:T]}$, the same estimators as those given in equations [A.31] and [A.32] are obtained. For the coefficients of $\boldsymbol{B}$, the same estimators as for the multinomial model are found. In summary:

$$\forall i, \widehat{c}_i = \frac{\sum_{n=1}^{N} \mathbb{I}(y_1^{(n)} = i)}{\sum_k \sum_n \mathbb{I}(y_1^{(n)} = k)} = \frac{F(i)}{\sum_k F(k)} \tag{A.41}$$

$$\forall i, j, \widehat{a}_{i,j} = \frac{\sum_{n=1}^{N} \sum_{t=1}^{T-1} \mathbb{I}(y_t^{(n)} = i, y_{t+1}^{(n)} = j)}{\sum_k \sum_n \sum_{t=1}^{T-1} \mathbb{I}(y_t^{(n)} = i, y_{t+1}^{(n)} = k)} = \frac{F_t(i,j)}{\sum_k F_t(i,k)} \tag{A.42}$$

$$\forall i, j, \widehat{b}_{i,j} = \frac{\sum_{n=1}^{N} \sum_{t=1}^{T-1} \mathbb{I}(y_t^{(n)} = i, x_t^{(n)} = j)}{\sum_k \sum_n \sum_{t=1}^{T-1} \mathbb{I}(y_t^{(n)} = i, x_t^{(n)} = k)} = \frac{F_o(i,j)}{\sum_k F_o(i,k)}, \tag{A.43}$$

where $F_t(i,j)$ counts the number of times state j follows state i, and $F_o(i,j)$ counts the number of times observation j is generated in state i. Here again, the relative sparsity of data, in comparison to the number of parameters, in particular the data required to estimate $\boldsymbol{B}$, justifies the use of the same smoothing techniques as those previously mentioned.

A.5.2.4. *Unsupervised parameter estimation*

A.5.2.4.1. An iterative method, again

It is possible to estimate hidden Markov model even when the supervision information is more scarce. It may, for instance, happen that the state sequence is entirely hidden and that only observation sequences $\{x_{[1:T^{(n)}]}^{(n)}, n = 1 \ldots N\}$ are available for training. Two other situations are commonly encountered in practice. First, the situation in which $y_{[1:T]}$ is partially known: at each time t, y_t takes its values in z_t with z_t a small sub-set of states. This happens, for instance, when training a part-of-speech tagger with the help of a dictionary which restricts, for each type, the set of possible labels (morphosyntactic categories). Another situation of partial supervision is when the training data $Y_{[1:T]}$ lacks "duration" information: each time the chain $Y_{[1:T]}$ enters a state i ($\forall t \in [t_1:t_2], y_t = i$), the supervision data only records the passing in state i, without recording the length of the corresponding time interval. In this situation, the sequences of states and observations do not have the same length and *segmentation* or *alignment* problems arise. The reader can refer to Chapter 7 for a discussion of alignment problems in the context of machine translation.

As before, one possible way to estimate the parameters is to maximize the likelihood function. If only $X_{[1:T]}$ is observed, the likelihood is written as:

$$\mathcal{L}(A, B, c) = \prod_{n=1}^{N} P(x_{[1:T^{(n)}]}^{(n)}; \boldsymbol{\theta}) = \prod_{n=1}^{N} \sum_{y_{[1:T^{(n)}]}^{(n)}} P(x_{[1:T^{(n)}]}^{(n)}, y_{[1:T^{(n)}]}^{(n)}; \boldsymbol{\theta}) \tag{A.44}$$

[A.44] must then be maximized, under the same constraints as before: $\sum_i c_i = 1; \forall i, \sum_j a_{i,j} = 1; \forall i, \sum_j b_{i,j} = 1.$

The logarithm of [A.44] is a sum of terms such as $\log(\sum P(x^{(n)}_{[1:T^{(n)}]}, y^{(n)}_{[1:T^{(n)}]}; \theta))$, which make the analytical resolution of this program impossible. Furthermore, the objective function is no longer log-concave, which implies that the optimum is no longer unique. As before, it is still possible to implement iterative optimization methods as follows. Recall that when labeled data is available, it is easy to estimate the parameters (by [A.41]–[A.43]); conversely, when the parameters are known, it is possible to infer (using the Viterbi algorithm) the optimal state sequence $\tilde{y}^{(n)}_{[1:T^{(n)}]}$ given $x^{(n)}_{[1:T^{(n)}]}$. This observation suggests an iterative strategy developed in Algorithm A.5, which alternates between inference of the optimal state sequence (Viterbi function) and parameter update steps according to [A.41]–[A.43] (Update function).

Algorithm A.5. An iterative algorithm for the unsupervised estimation of Markov models

Input: $\{x^{(n)}_{[1:T^{(n)}]}, n = 1, N\}$
$k \leftarrow 0;$
$\theta_0 \leftarrow$ Initialize();
while $(\|\theta_k - \theta_{k-1}\|_2 > \epsilon)$ **do**
    for $n \in [1:N]$ **do**
        $\tilde{y}^{(n)}_{[1:T^{(n)}]} \leftarrow$ Viterbi($x^{(n)}_{[1:T^{(n)}]}, \theta_k$);
    end
    $\theta_{k+1} \leftarrow$ Update($\{(x^{(n)}_{[1:T^{(n)}]}, \tilde{y}^{(n)}_{[1:T^{(n)}]}), n = 1, N\}$);
    $k \leftarrow k + 1$
end
return θ_k

This approach has been shown to be a pragmatic answer to the likelihood optimization problem (see, for example, [MÉR 94]); however, convergence of the algorithm is not guaranteed and its efficiency varies depending on the context.

A.5.2.4.2. The auxiliary function and its optimization

A theoretically sounder approach consists of instantiating, for the hidden Markov models, the *Expectation-Maximization* (EM) algorithm, already presented in section A.3.2. As previously mentioned, the implementation of this algorithm requires the introduction of a new function of θ, known as the auxiliary function of the EM algorithm, and denoted $Q_{\theta'}(\theta)$. This function is defined as:

$$Q_{\theta'}(\theta) = E(\ell(X, Y; \theta)|X, \theta') \tag{A.45}$$

The auxiliary function is the expectation, for a conditional probability distribution parameterized by θ', of the log-likelihood of the complete data. Using the same arguments as in section A.3.2, it can be shown that any value θ^* maximizing $Q_{\theta'}(\theta)$ will yield a better value of the likelihood function than θ'.

We now turn to the problem of optimizing the auxiliary function. We denote $\gamma^{(n)}(y_{[1:T^{(n)}]}, \theta') = P(y_{[1:T^{(n)}]}|x^{(n)}_{[1:T^{(n)}]}; \theta')$, where θ' is a set of parameters comprising c' for the initial probabilities, A' for the transition probabilities and B' for the state-specific distributions modeling the observations. Using these notations, the auxiliary function is written as:

$$Q_{\theta'}(\theta) = \sum_{n=1}^{N} \sum_{y_{[1:T^{(n)}]}} \log(P(x^{(n)}_{[1:T^{(n)}]}, y_{[1:T^{(n)}]}; \theta))\gamma^{(n)}(y_{[1:T^{(n)}]}, \theta')$$

$$= \sum_{n=1}^{N} \sum_{y_{[1:T^{(n)}]}} \log(P(y_1) \prod_{t=1}^{T^{(n)}} P(x^{(n)}_t|y_t) \prod_{t=2}^{T^{(n)}} P(y_t|y_{t-1}))\gamma^{(n)}(y_{[1:T^{(n)}]}, \theta')$$

$$= \sum_{n=1}^{N} \sum_{y_{[1:T^{(n)}]}} \left(\log(c_{y_1}) + \sum_{i,k} F(i,k) \log(b_{i,j}) \right.$$

$$\left. + \sum_{i,j} F(i,j) \log(a_{i,j}) \right) \gamma^{(n)}(y_{[1:T^{(n)}]}, \theta')$$

Contrary to $\ell(\theta)$, this function is (relatively) easy to maximize. For example, maximizing $Q_{\theta'}(\theta)$ with respect to c yields the following optimality conditions, where the Lagrange multiplier ν corresponds to the constraint $\sum_i c_i = 1$:

$$\frac{\partial Q_{\theta'}}{\partial c_i} = \frac{1}{c_i} \sum_{n=1}^{N} \sum_{y_{[1:T^{(n)}]}} \mathbb{I}(y_1 = i)\gamma^{(n)}(y_{[1:T^{(n)}]}, \theta') - \nu$$

$$= \frac{1}{c_i} \sum_{n=1}^{N} P(Y^{(n)}_1 = i|x^{(n)}_{[1:T^{(n)}]}; \theta') - \nu$$

By canceling the gradient, the optimal value of c is computed as follows, using the fact that the denominator is simply equal to N, whereas the numerator is given by [A.39]:

$$\widehat{c}_i = \frac{\sum_{n=1}^{N} P(Y_1^{(n)} = i | x_{[1:T^{(n)}]}^{(n)}; \boldsymbol{\theta}')}{\sum_k \sum_{n=1}^{N} P(Y_1^{(n)} = k | x_{[1:T^{(n)}]}^{(n)}; \boldsymbol{\theta}')}$$

$$= \frac{1}{N} \sum_{n=1}^{N} \frac{\alpha_{1,i}^{(n)} \beta_{1,i}^{(n)}}{\sum_k \alpha_{1,k}^{(n)} \beta_{1,k}^{(n)}}$$

[A.46]

This formula is reminiscent of equation [A.41] which gives the optimal value of c in the fully supervised case. The only difference is that, in the unsupervised case, the initial states are unknown: each possible initial state is thus weighted by the probability that it is the initial state for the observation sequence $x_{[1:T^{(n)}]}^{(n)}$ and current set of parameters $\boldsymbol{\theta}'$.

Deriving optimality conditions with respect to transition probabilities $a_{i,j}$ is similar and introduces one Lagrange multiplier μ_i for each constraint $\sum_j a_{i,j} = 1$:

$$\frac{\partial Q_{\boldsymbol{\theta}'}}{\partial a_{i,j}} = \frac{1}{a_{i,j}} \sum_{n=1}^{N} \sum_{y_{[1:T^{(n)}]}} \sum_{t=1}^{T^{(n)}} \mathbb{I}(\{Y_t = i, Y_{t+1} = j\}) P(y_{[1:T^{(n)}]} | x_{[1:T^{(n)}]}^{(n)}; \boldsymbol{\theta}') - \mu_i$$

$$= \frac{1}{a_{i,j}} \sum_{n=1}^{N} \sum_{t=1}^{T^{(n)}} P(Y_t = i, Y_{t+1} = j | x_{[1:T^{(n)}]}^{(n)}; \boldsymbol{\theta}') - \mu_i$$

$$= \frac{1}{a_{i,j}} \sum_{n=1}^{N} \sum_{t=1}^{T^{(n)}} \frac{P(Y_t = i, x_{[1:t]}^{(n)}; \boldsymbol{\theta}') a_{i,j}' b_{j,x_{t+1}^{(n)}}' P(x_{[t+2:T^{(n)}]} | Y_{t+1} = j; \boldsymbol{\theta}')}{P(x_{[1:T^{(n)}]}^{(n)}; \boldsymbol{\theta}')} - \mu_i$$

The latter term contains two familiar quantities, namely $\alpha_{t,i}^{(n)} = P(Y_t = i, x_{[1:t]}^{(n)}; \boldsymbol{\theta}')$ and $\beta_{t+1,j}^{(n)} = P(x_{[t+2:T^{(n)}]} | Y_{t+1} = j; \boldsymbol{\theta}')$. After renormalization, the following estimates are obtained:

$$\widehat{a}_{i,j} = \frac{\sum_{n=1}^{N} \sum_{t=1}^{T^{(n)}} \alpha_{t,i}^{(n)} a_{i,j}' b_{j,x_{t+1}^{(n)}}' \beta_{t+1,j}^{(n)}}{\sum_k \sum_{n=1}^{N} \sum_{t=1}^{T^{(n)}} \alpha_{t,i}^{(n)} a_{i,k}' b_{k,x_{t+1}^{(n)}}' \beta_{t+1,k}^{(n)}}$$

[A.47]

As in the supervised case, parameter estimates take the form of ratios of counts; the main difference is that the sequences of states being unobserved, each possible state sequence must be taken into account in proportion of its posterior probability. Finally, the maximization of the auxiliary function with respect to $b_{i,j}$ gives rise to the following solution:

$$\widehat{b}_{i,j} = \frac{\sum_{n=1}^{N} \sum_{t,x_t^{(n)}=j} P(Y_t = i | x_{[1:T^{(n)}]}^{(n)}; \boldsymbol{\theta}')}{\sum_k \sum_{t,x_t^{(n)}=j} P(Y_t = i | x_{[1:T^{(n)}]}^{(n)}; \boldsymbol{\theta}')}$$

[A.48]

In [A.48], terms such as $P(Y_t = i | x_{[1:T^{(n)}]}^{(n)}; \boldsymbol{\theta}')$ are again computed using equation [A.39]. To summarize, the unsupervised estimation procedure of hidden Markov models using the EM algorithm is given in Algorithm A.6, whose resemblance with Algorithm A.5 should be noted. This algorithm is also known as the Baum-Welsh algorithm, or the forward-backward algorithm.

Algorithm A.6. The EM algorithm for hidden Markov models

Input: $\{x_{[1:T^{(n)}]}^{(n)}, n = 1, N\}$
$k \leftarrow 0$;
$\boldsymbol{\theta}_0 \leftarrow \texttt{Initialize}()$;
while $(\|\boldsymbol{\theta}_k - \boldsymbol{\theta}_{k-1}\|_2 > \epsilon)$ **do**
    for $n \in [1:N]$ **do**
        $\boldsymbol{\alpha}^{(n)} \leftarrow \texttt{Forward}(x_{[1:T^{(n)}]}^{(n)}, \boldsymbol{\theta}_k)$;
        $\boldsymbol{\beta}^{(n)} \leftarrow \texttt{Backward}(x_{[1:T^{(n)}]}^{(n)}, \boldsymbol{\theta}_k)$;
    end
    $\boldsymbol{\theta}_{k+1} \leftarrow \texttt{Update}(\{(x_{[1:T^{(n)}]}^{(n)}, \boldsymbol{\alpha}^{(n)}, \boldsymbol{\beta}^{(n)}), n = 1 \ldots N\})$;
    $k \leftarrow k + 1$;
end
return $\boldsymbol{\theta}_k$

In the first part of this algorithm, the vectors $\boldsymbol{\alpha}^{(n)}$ and $\boldsymbol{\beta}^{(n)}$, which are both required to evaluate the expectation of the hidden variables, are computed using the procedures presented above: this is the E(xpectation)-step of the algorithm. The second part simply applies the Update function using equations [A.46], [A.47], and [A.48]. As these equations correspond to the optimality conditions for the auxiliary function, this step is the M(aximization) step of the algorithm.

A.5.2.4.3. Complements

Irrespective of the approach (Algorithm A.5 or Algorithm A.6), the solution achieved by this iterative procedure strongly varies depending on the initialization strategy. A particularly favorable situation, in this context, is when small quantities of labeled data, as well as large quantities of supplementary unlabeled data are both available, which corresponds to the *semi-supervised learning* framework. In such a setting, the labeled data can be used to estimate appropriate initial values, which will yield better parameter estimates when the EM algorithm is applied to the unlabeled training set.

A.5.2.5. *An application: thematic segmentation of documents*

Hidden Markov models can be used to solve all the supervised sequence labeling problems, such as those discussed in Chapter 6. They are also useful to perform automatic word alignment of parallel sentences which are necessary in statistical machine translation, as detailed in Chapter 7. In the following, a third application, document segmentation, is briefly presented.

The application of information retrieval techniques to audio documents (or transcriptions of audio documents) such as Broadcast News, faces specific difficulties: some recordings are very long and intrinsically multi-thematic. This means that a user willing to retrieve a short passage will have to listen to many irrelevant parts. A typical post-treatment of automatic speech recognition is to segment the transcription into thematically homogeneous sequences, so as to facilitate their indexation, search, and consultation. Numerous audio or visual cues, such as jingles for radio data, can be used to facilitate this process. Taking the textual content of the document into account provides complementary information and usually improves performance.

One possible way to handle this task is to assume that each document is a sequence of utterances generated by a hidden Markov model, with one hidden state for each possible topic. Each utterance can then be represented as a bag-of-words and a multinomial distribution is associated with each state. Alternatively, more complex document representations (see Chapter 5) can be entertained.

Based on such a model, it is possible to estimate the various parameters using the algorithms introduced in the previous sections, adapted to the case of multinomial distributions. In the resulting model, the parameters of the multinomial distributions characterize the topics; the transition probabilities characterize the temporal organization of broadcasts.

In this approach, setting the "right" number of hidden states is important to achieve good segmentation performances. To facilitate learning, the number of relevant topics and the associated values of the multinomial parameters can be determined using an annotated corpus where a segmentation in coherent thematic fragments has been manually performed.

A.6. Conclusion

In this Appendix, a number of basic probabilistic models have been reviewed: the "naive Bayes" model for supervised categorization, the multinomial mixture model for topic analysis, Markov models and Markov models with hidden states for modeling sequences of random events. For each of these models, we have shown how to perform the two main steps required for their implementation: parameter *estimation*, using a set of learning examples and *inference*, consisting of computing the posterior distribution of random variables of interest. Along the way, a number of typical applications of these models have been presented, some of which are also reconsidered elsewhere in this book. This Appendix has finally been an opportunity to raise problems related to the *evaluation* of automatic text analysis tools and to introduce some of the most common metrics.

Beyond this exposition of elementary models, we have also tried to illustrate the principles and methods of probabilistic inference, which are at the core of most chapters in this book. A good understanding of these principles will also enable readers to get a better grasp of models involving more complex dependencies, in particular those that are used in many natural language processing applications such as probabilistic syntactic analysis, information extraction, or even machine translation. Taking into account the success and spread of these principles to all sub-domains of pattern recognition (automatic speech recognition, image analysis, etc.) and to related domains (information retrieval, bibliographic data analysis, collaborative filtering recommendation systems, etc.), it is hoped and expected that a good understanding of these methods will enable easy access to these new families of applications.

A.7. A primer of probability theory

In this appendix to the Appendix, we briefly recollect some fundamental concepts and results of probability theory that are used throughout this chapter, as well as in numerous other places in this book. The knowledge of these basic notions and results does not entirely replace the study of dedicated textbooks. The interested reader should, for instance, refer to [HAM 93, RES 99] for incomparably more detailed and thorough introductions to probability theory.

A.7.1. *Probability space, event*

Ω is a set, called the *event space*, containing the possible results of a random experiment; a subset E of Ω is called an *event* and an *elementary event* is a singleton in Ω. Two particular cases are $E = \emptyset$ (impossible event) and $E = \Omega$ (certain event).

DEFINITION A.1. – *Let Ω be an event space, T is a σ-algebra on Ω if T contains Ω, is closed by complementation and by infinite union. Formally, if $A_1 \ldots A_i \ldots$ belong to T, then $(\bigcup_{i \in \mathbb{N}} A_i)$ must also belong to T, and so does $\overline{A_i}$, the complement of A_i. When T is a σ-algebra over Ω, the pair (Ω, T) constitutes a* measurable space.

It can be noted that the closure property noted above imply, by application of the Morgan law[21], the closure over infinite intersections. In the following, the case where Ω is finite or countable is mainly considered. In this case, the set of all subsets of Ω (its powerset) is a σ-algebra.

---

21 If A and B are two sets, then $A \cap B = \overline{\overline{A} \cup \overline{B}}$.

DEFINITION A.2. – *A probability space is a triplet* (Ω, T, P) *where* (Ω, T) *is a measure space and* P() *is a probability, in other words a function from T into* $[0: 1]$ *such that:*

- *1)* $P(\Omega) = 1$;
- *2) if* $\forall m \neq n, A_n \cap A_m = \emptyset$, *then* $P(\bigcup_{i \in \mathbb{N}} A_n) = \sum_{i \in \mathbb{N}} P(A_i)$.

When Ω is a finite set, these conditions are equivalent to:

- 1) $\forall \omega \in \Omega, P(\omega) \geq 0$;
- 2) $\sum_{\omega \in \Omega} P(\omega) = 1$.

If Ω is countable, the second requirement is that the infinite sum $\sum_{\omega \in \Omega} P(\omega)$ should be convergent (i.e. should have a finite limit).

Let A and B be two events, the *joint probability* of A and B is defined as the probability of their intersection.

PROPOSITION A.1. – *Let* (Ω, T, P) *be a probability space and A and B any two events, then* $P(A \cup B) = P(A) + P(B) - P(A \cap B)$. *The following proposition follows.*

PROPOSITION A.2. – *Let* (Ω, T, P) *be a probability space and A and B two* incompatible *events, in other words, events such that* $A \cap B = \emptyset$, *then* $P(A \cup B) = P(A) + P(B)$.

PROPOSITION A.3. – *Let* (Ω, T, P) *be a probability space and A any event, then* $P(\overline{A}) = 1 - P(A)$.

A.7.2. *Conditional independence and probability*

DEFINITION A.3. – *Let* (Ω, T, P) *be a probability space and A and B two events with* $P(B) \neq 0$, *the conditional probability given B is the function* P_B *defined by*:

$$P_B(A) = \frac{P(A \cap B)}{P(B)}$$

It is routine to check that for all B, P_B defines a probability function, in particular that condition 2) of definition A.2 above is verified. In the following, the conditional probability of A given B is denoted as $P(A|B)$.

DEFINITION A.4. – *Two events A and B are* independent *if, and only if,* $P(B) = 0$ *or* $P(A|B) = P(A)$. *In the latter case, it is equivalent to write* $P(A \cap B) = P(A) P(B)$.

A.7.2.1. *Three fundamental formulas*

PROPOSITION A.4. – *Let* (Ω, T, P) *be a probability space and let A and B be two events such that* $P(B) \neq 0$, *then:*

$$P(A \cap B) = P(B) P(A|B)$$

This formula, which generalizes to the intersection of an arbitrary number of events, is a direct corollary of the definition of a conditional probability.

PROPOSITION A.5. – *Let* (Ω, T, P) *be a probability space,* $\{A_1 \ldots A_n\}$ *a set of non-zero probability and pairwise disjoint events, and B any event such that* $P(B) \neq 0$ *then:*

$$\forall i, P(A_i|B) = \frac{P(B|A_i) P(B)}{\sum_i P(B|A_i) P(A_i)}$$

This formula, which is also a direct corollary of the relationship between the conditional and joint probabilities, is known as the Bayes rule or Bayes law.

A third very useful formula is the marginalization rule, which relates joint and marginal distributions.

PROPOSITION A.6. – (Ω, T, P) *is a probability space,* $\{A_1 \ldots A_n\}$ *is a set of non-zero probability and pairwise disjoint and B is any event, then:*

$$P(B) = \sum_{i=1}^{n} P(A_i \cap B) = \sum_{i=1}^{n} P(B|A_i) P(A_i)$$

A.7.3. *Random variables, moments*

In practice, probability spaces are only indirectly manipulated, through functions from probability spaces into some appropriate co-domain (typically $\mathbb{R}$). This enables us to easily "import", into the probability domain, of standard operations on $\mathbb{R}$: sum, product, and more generally any function whose domain is $\mathbb{R}$. This generalization is operated by the the notion of *random variable*.

DEFINITION A.5. – *Let* (Ω, T, P) *be a probability space, a real* random variable *(on* Ω*) is a function X from* Ω *into* $\mathbb{R}$ *such that:* $\forall x \in \mathbb{R}, \{\omega \in \Omega$ *such that* $X(\omega) \leq x\}$ *is an event in T.*

This latter condition makes expressions such as $P(X \leq x)$ meaningful via $P(X \leq x) = P(\{\omega \in \Omega$ such that $X(\omega) \leq x\})$, as well as, using basic properties of a σ-algebra, to $P(X > x)$, to $P(x \geq X \geq y)$, and so on. Likewise, if X and Y are two random variables, their sum is a random variable $Z = X + Y$, as well as their product, etc.

In this book, we mainly focus on discrete random variables, which are defined as follows.

DEFINITION A.6. – *A real random variable is* discrete *if the image of* Ω *under X is a finite or countable set. If* $X(\Omega) = \mathcal{X} = \{x_1 \ldots x_n \ldots\}$, *then the distribution of X is the set of numbers* $\{p_i, i = 1 \ldots n\}$ *in* $[0:1]$ *defined by* $\forall i, p_i = P(\{\omega \in \Omega$ *such that* $X(\omega) = x_i\}) = P(X^{-1}(x_i))$. *We use the notation* $P(X)$ *to refer to the distribution and* $p_i = P(X = x_i)$, *or even* $P(x_i)$ *for the probability of a particular value.*

The above notions (independence, conditional probability) and the related formulas (Bayes rule, marginalization total probability) are straightforwardly adapted for random variables using inverse images. All that is needed, is the notion of joint random variable.

If X and Y are two random variables over the same probability space, then $Z: \Omega \rightarrow \mathbb{R} \times \mathbb{R}$ is a joint random variable which maps ω into the pair $(X(\omega)Y(\omega))$. If X and Y are discrete, the distribution of Z is $P(X = x, Y = y)$ defined by:

$$P(X = x, Y = y) = P(\{\omega \in \Omega \text{ such that } X(\omega) = x \text{ and } Y(\omega) = y\})$$

$$= P(\{\omega \in \Omega \text{ such that } X(\omega) = x\} \cap \{\omega \in \Omega \text{ such that } Y(\omega) = y\})$$

It follows that two variables X and Y defined on the same probability space are independent if, and only if, $\forall x \in \mathcal{X}, \forall y \in \mathcal{Y}, X^{-1}(x) = \{\omega \in \Omega \text{ such that } X(\omega) \leq x\}$ and $Y^{-1}(y)$ (identically defined) are two independent events, which can be rewritten as: $P((X = x, Y = y)) = P(\{\omega \in \Omega \text{ such that } X(\omega) = x \text{ and } Y(\omega) = y\}) = P(X = x) P(Y = y)$.

We also have, for any two discrete random variables[22], the two following results:

$$P(X = x) = \sum_{y \in \mathcal{Y}} P(X = x, Y = y)$$

$$= \sum_{y \in \mathcal{Y}} P(X = x | Y = y) P(Y = y)$$

[A.49]

and:

$$P(Y = y | X = x) = \frac{P(X = x, Y = y)}{\sum_{y' \in \mathcal{Y}} P(X = x, Y = y')}$$

$$= \frac{P(X = x | Y = y) P(Y = y)}{\sum_{y' \in \mathcal{Y}} P(X = x | Y = y') P(Y = y')}$$

[A.50]

A last useful generalization, also commonly used, is when X is a function of Ω into $\mathbb{R}^n$ and defines a *multidimensional random variable*. In the following, multidimensional variables (and their values) are distinguished from scalar variables by the use of boldface notations such as X for a variable and x for its value.

A.7.3.1. *Moments*

A random variable is characterized by its *moments*, the most elementary being the expectation and the variance, the definitions of which are recalled below.

---

22 These formulas can be generalized to arbitrary (non-discrete) variables.

DEFINITION A.7. – *The expectation of a discrete random variable X is defined by*:

$$\mathbb{E}(X) = \sum_{x \in \mathcal{X}} x \, P(X = x).$$ [A.51]

The expectation is a linear operator and we will use the fact that $\mathbb{E}(X + Y) = \mathbb{E}(X) + \mathbb{E}(Y)$. When X is a multidimensional variable, the expectation is computed according to [A.51] for each of the components X.

DEFINITION A.8. – *The variance of a discrete random variable X is defined by*:

$$\mathbb{V}(X) = \mathbb{E}((X - \mathbb{E}(X))^2) = \sum_{x \in \mathcal{X}} (x - \mathbb{E}(X))^2 \, P(X = x)$$ [A.52]

The behavior of a pair of random variables is characterized by their covariance, which is defined by:

DEFINITION A.9. – *The covariance of a pair of discrete random variables (X, Y) is defined by*:

$$\text{Cov}(X, Y) = \mathbb{E}((X - \mathbb{E}(X))(Y - \mathbb{E}(Y)))$$

$$= \sum_{x \in \mathcal{X}, y \in \mathcal{Y}} (x - \mathbb{E}(X))(y - \mathbb{E}(Y)) \, P(X = x, Y = y)$$ [A.53]

The covariance measures the strength of the association between the two variables. It can easily be shown that it is zero when the two variables are independent (using the fact that $\forall x, y, P(X = x, Y = y) = P(X = x) P(Y = y)$ and reorganizing the sum in [A.53]). The latter result is also useful to prove that the variance of a sum of independent random variables is the sum of their variances.

The concept of covariance is useful to generalize the notion of variance to the multidimensional case. When X is a multidimensional variable, its behavior is characterized by its *variance-covariance matrix*, whose general term $c_{i,j}$ is the covariance between components X_i and X_j (each diagonal term $c_{i,i}$ is then the variance of component X_i).

A.7.3.2. *Entropy and related notions*

There are other important quantities that characterize random variables, or even measure the association between two variables. Several useful quantities used in Information Theory [COV 91] are defined below.

DEFINITION A.10.– *Let X be a discrete random variable with distribution P, the following quantity is called the entropy of X entropy, denoted $H(X)$[23]:*

$$H(X) = -\mathbb{E}(\log(P(X))) = -\sum_{x \in \mathcal{X}} P(X = x)\log(P(X = x)) \qquad \text{[A.54]}$$

It is easy to see that $H(X)$ is a positive quantity. The entropy is interpreted as an ambiguity measure of the different alternatives under the distribution P and varies between the value 0, which corresponds to the case where the distribution P is deterministic (one outcome has a probability of 1, all the other outcomes are impossible) and the value $\log(N)$, which corresponds to a uniform distribution over the set of N possible outcomes and is the case of maximum ambiguity. The latter result can be derived from the following general property.

PROPERTY.– *When P and Q are two probability distributions on the same discrete set $\mathcal{X}$, then:*

$$-\sum_{x \in \mathcal{X}} P(X = x)\log(P(X = x)) \leq -\sum_{x \in \mathcal{X}} P(X = x)\log(Q(X = x))$$

or

$$H(X) \leq -\sum_{x \in \mathcal{X}} P(X = x)\log(Q(X = x))$$

or equivalently

$$0 \leq \sum_{x \in \mathcal{X}} P(X = x)\log\left(\frac{P(X = x)}{Q(X = x)}\right)$$

The proof relies on the concavity of the log function, which ensures that, for all discrete variables V, $\mathbb{E}(\log(V)) \leq \log(\mathbb{E}(V))$. By choosing $V = \log\left(\frac{Q(X)}{P(X)}\right)$, after elementary manipulations, the desired result is obtained. It suffices to take Q equal to the uniform distribution to obtain property $H(X) \leq \log(|\mathcal{X}|)$.

The quantity $\sum_{x \in \mathcal{X}} P(X = x)\log\left(\frac{P(X=x)}{Q(X=x)}\right)$, which appears in the expression of the previous property, is called the *Kullback-Leibler divergence* between distributions P and Q, and is often written as $D(P||Q)$. This quantity is positive and is equal to zero if and only if the two distributions are identical. For these two reasons, it can be used as a measure of comparison between the two distributions: the smaller the divergence, the

---

23 When the log in the following formula is taken in base two, the resulting quantity is expressed in bits.

closer the distributions. It is must be noted that this quantity does not define a distance between distributions, in particular since it is not symmetric.

The entropy and related quantities are also useful to measure the degree of association between two random variables.

DEFINITION A.11.– *Let X and Y be two discrete random variables, the joint entropy of X and Y is written as*:

$$H(X,Y) = -\sum_{x \in \mathcal{X}} \sum_{y \in \mathcal{Y}} P(X = x, Y = y) \log(P(X = x, Y = y))$$

When these variables are independent, the term $P(X = x, Y = y)$ breaks down into the simple product $P(X = x) P(Y = y)$. Simple algebraic manipulations immediately yield the following result:

PROPOSITION A.7.– *When X and Y are independent then*:

$$H(X,Y) = H(X) + H(Y)$$

This result establishes a link between the entropy of the joint distribution and that of the marginal distributions in the situation of independence. It is interesting to study these quantities to measure the degree of association between the random variables. This intuition is formalized by the notion of *mutual information*.

DEFINITION A.12.– *Let X and Y be two discrete random variables, the mutual information of X and Y is*:

$$I(X,Y) = \sum_{x,y} P(X = x, Y = y) \log \left(\frac{P(X = x, Y = y)}{P(X = x) P(Y = y)} \right) \qquad \text{[A.55]}$$

The mutual information corresponds to the Kullback-Leibler divergence between the joint distribution and the product of the marginal distributions, and therefore has all the properties of a mutual information. As a consequence, this quantity is null if, and only if, these two values are equal, in other words if X and Y are independent. Mutual information can also be interpreted by introducing conditional distributions as follows:

$$I(X,Y) = \sum_{x,y} P(X = x, Y = y) \log(\frac{P(X = x, Y = y)}{P(X = x) P(Y = y)})$$

$$= \sum_{x,y} P(X = x | Y = y) P(Y = y) \log(P(X = x | Y = y))$$

$$- \sum_{x,y} P(X = x, Y = y) \log(P(X = x))$$

$$= \sum_y P(Y = y) \left(\sum_x P(X = x|Y = y) \log(P(X = x|Y = y)) \right)$$

$$- \sum_x \log(P(X = x)) \sum_y P(X = x, Y = y)$$

$$= H(X) - \sum_y P(Y = y)H(X|Y = y)$$

The term $\sum_y P(Y = y)H(X|Y = y)$ is the expectation of the entropy of X, conditioned by the possible values of Y and corresponds to the (opposite of the) *conditional entropy* of X and Y, simply written as $H(X|Y)$. The following relationship is deduced (in which X and Y play symmetric roles):

$$I(X, Y) = H(X) - H(X|Y)$$

In this form, it appears that the mutual information between X and Y can be interpreted as the ambiguity of X which is not "resolved" by knowledge of Y. When Y enables to fully predict X, which happens in case of a deterministic association, $H(X|Y) = 0$ and $I(X, Y) = H(X)$. Conversely, if X and Y are independent, the knowledge of Y brings no information on X and $H(X|Y) = H(X)$, which implies that the mutual information is zero. The mutual information can thus be used to measure the association between the two variables.

It should finally be noted that the mutual information defined by [A.55] is a sum of terms in the form $P(X = x, Y = y) \log \left(\frac{P(X=x,Y=y)}{P(X=x)P(Y=y)} \right)$, where each term corresponds to the *pointwise mutual information* between values x and y.

A.7.4. *Some useful distributions*

In this last section, we briefly introduce some of the most common discrete laws, which should cover most of the application fields discussed in this book. We omit here the negative binomial and the hyper-geometric distributions, which are also used in many text mining and information retrieval applications. Their definition will be found in most probability textbooks.

A.7.4.1. *Bernoulli distribution*

The most basic discrete distribution is the Bernoulli distribution, which defines a probability on a set of binary events, such as the toss of a coin. The possible values of X are then $x \in \{0, 1\}$. This distribution is parameterized by a real number $p \in [0: 1]$ defined by $p = P(X = 1)$; it then follows that $P(X = 0) = 1 - p$.

The expectation of a Bernoulli distributed variable X is:

$$\mathbb{E}(X) = \sum_{x \in \{0,1\}} x\, P(X = x) = P(X = 1) = p$$

Its variance is also a simple function of p:

$$\mathbb{V}(X) = \sum_{x \in \{0,1\}} (x - p)^2\, P(X = x) = p^2(1 - p) + (1 - p)^2 p = p(1 - p)$$

A.7.4.2. *Binomial distribution*

The binomial distribution corresponds to the repetition of n independent draws from the same Bernoulli distribution parameterized by p. A binomial variable X is therefore the sum of n *independent* Bernoulli variables X_i, and its values are integers between 0 and N. The probability of observing the value k times is therefore:

$$P(X = k) = \begin{cases} \binom{n}{k} p^k (1 - p)^{n-k} & \text{if } 0 \geq k \geq n \\ 0 & \text{if not} \end{cases}$$

Being a sum of n independent Bernoulli variables, the expectation of a binomial variable is easily derived as:

$$\mathbb{E}(X) = \sum_{k=0}^{n} \mathbb{E}(X_i)$$

$$= np.$$

Using the independence assumptions of the X_is, the variance is obtained as:

$$\mathbb{V}(X) = np(1 - p)$$

A.7.4.3. *The Poisson distribution*

The Poisson distribution has a single real parameter $\lambda > 0$ and takes the following form:

$$P(X = n) = \frac{\lambda^n \exp(-\lambda)}{n!}$$

One peculiarity of this distribution is that its expectation is equal to its variance. If X is Poisson distributed with parameter λ:

$$\mathbb{E}(X) = \mathbb{V}(X) = \sum_{n \in \mathbb{N}} n \frac{\lambda^n \exp(-\lambda)}{n!} = \lambda$$

This distribution assigns a non-zero probability of occurrence to any positive integer. As the distance from the mean value increases, this probability become more and more negligible. In the context of the statistical modeling of text corpora, this distribution can be used to model frequencies of occurrences of terms, the length of texts, etc.

A.7.4.4. *Multinomial distribution*

The multinomial distribution generalizes the binomial distribution to the case where the number of possible outcome is greater than two. A typical example of multinomial distribution is obtained by placing balls colored with n_W colors into an urn, and drawing at random n balls (replacing them after each draw). Each of the n draws therefore is a color in $\{1 \ldots n_W\}$; the final result is a realization of a multinomial variable corresponding to the n_W-dimensional vectors x, where the ith component x_i corresponds to the number of draws of color i (this implies that $\sum_i x_i = n$). For instance, if we perform 10 draws from a box containing balls colored using 5 colors, the result is a vector $x^T = (x_1, \ldots, x_{10})$, where x_1 is the number of times a draw for color 1 has been drawn, etc. The multinomial distribution is parameterized by a n_W-dimensional vector β such that $\sum_i \beta_i = 1$ on the one hand and by the number of draws n, on the other hand. The probability of a particular outcome is defined as:

$$P(X = x = (x_1 \ldots x_{n_W})^T) = \frac{n!}{\prod_i x_i!} \prod_i \beta_i^{x_i}$$

To calculate the expectation (a vector) and the covariance matrix, it is necessary to perform a summation over all n_W-dimensional vectors whose components sum to n. The following results are obtained:

$$E(X_i) = n\beta_i$$

and:

$$V_{i,j} = \begin{cases} n\beta_i(1 - \beta_i) \text{ if } i = j \\ -n\beta_i\beta_j \text{ otherwise} \end{cases}$$

A.8. Bibliography

[BEN 05] BENS J., *Genèse de l'Oulipo: 1960-1963*, Le castor astral, Paris, France, 2005.

[CAP 09] CAPPÉ O., MOULINES E., "On-line expectation-maximization algorithm for latent data models", *Journal Royal Statistical Society B*, vol. 71, no. 3, p. 593–613, 2009.

[CHA 93] CHARNIAK E., *Statistical Language Learning*, MIT Press, Cambridge, MA, USA, 1993.

[CHE 96] CHEN S. F., GOODMAN J. T., "An empirical study of smoothing techniques for language modeling", *Proceedings of the 34th Annual Meeting of the Association for Computational Linguistics (ACL)*, Santa Cruz, NM, p. 310–318, 1996.

[CHU 95] CHURCH K. W., GALE W. A., "Poisson Mixtures", *Natural Language Engineering*, vol. 1, no. 2, p. 163–190, 1995.

[COV 91] COVER T. M., THOMAS J. A., *Elements of Information Theory*, Wiley, New York, USA, 1991.

[DUP 05] DUPONT P., DENIS F., ESPOSITO Y., "Links between probabilistic automata and hidden Markov models: probability distributions, learning models and induction algorithms", *Pattern Recognition: Special Issue on Grammatical Inference Techniques & Applications*, vol. 38, no. 9, p. 1349–1371, 2005.

[GOO 01] GOODMAN J. T., "A bit of progress in language modeling", *Computer, Speech and Language*, vol. 15, no. 4, p. 403–434, 2001.

[HAM 93] HAMMING R. W., *The Art of Probability for Scientists and Engineers*, Addison Wesley, 1993.

[JAN 03] JANSCHE M., "Parametric models of linguistic count data", *Proceedings of the 41st Annual Meeting on Association for Computational Linguistics - Volume 1*, ACL '03, Stroudsburg, PA, USA, Association for Computational Linguistics, p. 288–295, 2003.

[JEL 90] JELINEK F., "Self-organized language modeling for speech recognition", *Readings in Speech Recognition*, San Mateo, CA, USA, Morgan-Kaufman, p. 450–506, 1990.

[JEL 97] JELINEK F., *Statistical Methods for Speech Recognition*, The MIT Press, Cambridge, MA, USA, 1997.

[JUR 00] JURAFSKY D., MARTIN J. H., *Speech and Language Processing: An Introduction to Natural Language Processing, Computational Linguistics and Speech Recognition*, Prentice Hall, 2000.

[KAT 96] KATZ S. M., "Distribution of content words and phrases in text and language modelling", *Natural Language Engineering*, vol. 2, no. 1, p. 15–59, 1996.

[MAC 94] MACKAY D. J., PETO L., "A hierarchical Dirichlet language model", *Journal of Natural Language Engineering*, vol. 1, no. 3, p. 1–19, 1994.

[MAD 05] MADSEN R. E., KAUCHAK D., ELKAN C., "Modeling word burstiness using the Dirichlet distribution", *Proceedings of the 22nd International Conference on Machine Learning (ICML)*, p. 489–498, 2005.

[MAN 99] MANNING C. D., SCHÜTZE H., *Foundations of Statistical Natural Language Processing*, The MIT Press, Cambridge, MA, USA, 1999.

[MCC 98] MCCALLUM A. K., NIGAM K., "A comparison of event models for Naive Bayes text classification", *AAAI-98 Workshop on Learning for Text Categorization*, p. 41–48, 1998.

[MÉR 94] MÉRIALDO B., "Tagging english text with a probabilistic grammar", *Computational Linguistics*, vol. 20, no. 2, p. 155–172, 1994.

[NEA 98] NEAL R. M., HINTON G. E., "A view of the EM algorithm that justifies incremental, sparse, and other variants", *Proceedings of the NATO Advanced Study Institute on Learning in graphical models*, Norwell, MA, USA, Kluwer Academic Publishers, p. 355–368, 1998.

[NIG 00] NIGAM K., MCCALLUM A. K., THRUN S., MITCHELL T. M., "Text classification from labeled and unlabeled documents using EM", *Machine Learning*, vol. 39, no. 2/3, p. 103–134, 2000.

[RAB 93] RABINER L., JUANG B., *Fundamentals of Speech Recognition*, PTR Prentice Hall, Englewoods Cliff, NJ, 1993.

[RES 99] RESNIK S. I., *A Probability Path*, Birkhaüser, Boston, 1999.

[RIG 06] RIGOUSTE L., Méthodes probabilistes pour l'analyse exploratoire de données textuelles, PhD thesis, École Nationale Supérieure des Télécommunications, 2006.

[ROS 00] ROSENFELD R., "Two decades of statistical language modeling: Where do we go from here?", *Proceedings of the IEEE*, vol. 88, no. 8, p. 1270–1278, 2000.

[TEH 06] TEH Y. W., "A hierarchical Bayesian language model based on Pitman-Yor processes", *Proceedings of the 21st International Conference on Computational Linguistics and 44th Annual Meeting of the Association for Computational Linguistics*, Genova, Switzerland, p. 985-992, 2006.

[VIT 67] VITERBI A. J., "Error bounds for convolutional codes and an asymptotically optimal decoding algorithm", *IEEE Transactions on Information Theory*, vol. 13, p. 260–269, 1967.

List of Authors

Alexandre ALLAUZEN
LIMSI-CNRS
University of Paris Sud
Orsay
France

Massih-Réza AMINI
LIP6
University of Paris 6
France

Anestis ANTONIADIS
LJK
University of Grenoble 1
France

Sujeevan ASEERVATHAM
LIG
University of Grenoble 1
France

Fréderic BÉCHET
LIF
University of Aix-Marseille
France

Patrice BELLOT
LSIS
University of Aix-Marseille
France

David BUFFONI
LIP6
University of Paris 6
France

Michel BURLET
G-SCOP
University of Grenoble 1
France

Jean-Cédric CHAPPELIER
School of Computer and Communication
Sciences (IC)
Ecole Polytechnique de Lausanne (EPFL)
Switzerland

Stéphane CLINCHANT
LIG
Xerox Research Centre Europe
University of Grenoble 1
France

Yves DENNEULIN
LIG
Grenoble INP
France

Marc EL-BÉZE
LIA
University of Avignon
and the Vaucluse
France

Kwa ENGLMEIER

Patrick GALLINARI
LIP6
University of Paris 6
France

Eric GAUSSIER
LIG
University of Grenoble 1
France

Josiane MOTHE
Institut de Recherche
en Informatique
de Toulouse IUFM
University of Toulouse
France

Fionn MURTAGH

Jean-Michel RENDERS
Xerox Research Centre Europe
Grenoble
France

Isabelle TELLIER
LaTTiCe
University of Paris 3
Sorbonne Nouvelle France
France

Marc TOMMASI
University of Lille
INRIA Lille Nord Europe
France

Juan-Manuel TORRES-MORENO
LIA
University of Avignon and
the Vaucluse
France

Tuong Vinh TRUONG
LIP6
University of Paris 6
France

Nicolas USUNIER
LIP6
University of Paris 6
France

François YVON
LIMSI-CNRS
University of Paris Sud
Orsay
France

Index